Reared in a Greenhouse

The Stories—and Story—of Dorothy Winthrop Bradford

Reared in a Greenhouse

The Stories—and Story—of Dorothy Winthrop Bradford

Dorothy B. Wexler

GARLAND PUBLISHING
A member of the Taylor & Francis Group
NEW YORK & LONDON
1998

Library of Congress Cataloging-in-Publication Data

Wexler, Dorothy B., 1932–

Reared in a Greenhouse: The Stories–and Story–of Dorothy Winthrop Bradford / Dorothy B. Wexler.

p.   cm.

ISBN 0-8153-3208-4 (hardcover)

ISBN 0-8153-3254-8 (paperback)

1. Bradford Dorothy Winthrop, 1905–1987. 2. Winthrop family.

3. Bradford family. 4. New England—Biography. I. Title.

CT275.B59313W48   1998

974'.04'0922—dc21

[B]   98-17584

        CIP

FIRST EDITION

Published by Garland Publishing, NYC

Designed by Vertigo Design, NYC

Printed on acid-free paper

TO MY MOTHER
Whose own life was her finest story

Contents

Praise & encouragement have produced far greater results in this world than fault finding + belittlement — especially with tender flowers who have been reared in greenhouses like me.

Excerpt from a letter my mother wrote me, February 28, 1958

Prologue

Susie Winthrop had the idea. She had listened to many a tale told by Dorothy Winthrop Bradford—her aunt-by-marriage and my mother—of the sprawling Winthrop clan into which she'd married when she became the wife of Freddy, Jr., in 1968. She realized that stories like these couldn't be told about every family and that information like her aunt's, which went all the way back to Civil War days, was rare. Dorothy W. Bradford had a prodigious memory and knew all the proper Bostonians, not only of her own generation, but also of the more colorful generations of her parents and grandparents. When I would read her an obituary of a Higginson or a Beale, of a Dabney or a Wigglesworth, she would spill out the story of their lives, and those of their uncles and aunts and their children. Branching, top-heavy family trees, who begat whom and who was begotten by whom, were as clear to her as they are murky to most of us today.

Susie knew that as long as her aunt told stories about them, all the uncles and aunts and cousins would not be forgotten. But when she went, most of the stories would die with her. So Susie took it upon herself to tape record her aunt's family memoirs.

Dorothy Bradford was nearing eighty when the project started. By then the family had grown to 168 Winthrop descendants of the family founders, as we thought of them: my mother's grandfather and grandmother, Robert and Kate Winthrop. In the immediate family, that of my mother and her four siblings, there were sixty-seven: four of us (me and my three siblings) and twenty-three children of her brothers and sisters (her nieces and nephews), followed by forty great-nieces and -nephews and four great-great-nieces and -nephews. In addition, there were the 101 progeny of my mother's Winthrop uncles and aunts: twenty-one Keans, van Roijens, Morses in our generation; fifty-six with all kinds of new names in our children's generation; and another twenty-four with yet other names in the generation after that.[1]

As my mother began recounting, her memory was still sharp but her strength was ebbing. She would sit with Susie in her soft-green chair in the corner of the large dining room, winter sun flooding in, and talk on and on. During the following summer I transcribed the tapes—my mother still in her little corner as I typed, chortling over the stories as she listened to her own voice telling them.

No one knew this at the time, but nearly a decade earlier, my mother had made a stab at writing her family memoirs. She didn't get very far, why we don't know. She was entering her seventies and soon she would be slowed down by heart trouble. But among her papers, after she died, was found this little scrap, written on a piece of Raggedy Ann note paper:

Some of the younger generation have from time to time suggested that I write down my recollections.

This idea must have started, I think, long ago when I used to regale some of the nieces, nephews and offspring with tales of how badly behaved my brothers and I were as children. Our exploits were listened to with delight by the young and with consternation by Nanny [the Scottish nanny who had helped raise the Fred Winthrop seven], who was trying so hard to bring up her charges in the way that they should go.

My 70th birthday seemed a good time to start recollecting. I remember so well when my Grandma Amory was 70 years old and to me how old she seemed! Night after night I prayed my first real prayer that Grandma would live to be 72, for naturally, to a childish mind, two years is an eternity.

So I hope my grandchildren will also pray for me with similar effectiveness. My Grandma lived to be 86.

Dorothy W. Bradford lived to be eighty-two. After her death, the fifty-odd pages of typed notes yielded from the recording sessions seemed fragmentary and somewhat pointless. They needed her laugh to bring them alive, her embellishments to give them shape. It seemed a pity not to do something with them, but they couldn't stand alone. I poked about her papers and possessions to discover additional information. There were two plastic envelopes full of old family papers, letters, and genealogies, as well as a scrapbook made by her maternal grandmother, Grandma Amory, and passed on down to her. There was a compendium of Boston's richest families, dated 1851. There were all the dusty books on the bottom shelf in the library—various volumes about Winthrops and Gardners—and the scrapbooks of letters received by my mother's father when his wife, my mother's mother, had died. We all knew about these long-untouched tomes. But none of it added up to the family story that I somehow felt compelled to weave out of the family stories.

The following summer, in late August, the whole family reassembled at Black Brook Farm, the family place in Hamilton. We had promised the grandchildren that each could choose some memento of their grandmother to keep for themselves. So the eight went roaming through the house. The best hunting ground was their grandma's huge closet, an incredible treasure trove with its cupboards and drawers, its closets within closets, housing everything from Christmas presents to vital papers, from coffee pots and crackers to hammers and screwdrivers, from family jewels to 1930s shoes, tidy house dresses, and comfortable slippers. Combs they found, and red flannel underwear, jackets and little books—and then Amanda, twelve, appeared where we were waiting and asked, "Can I have Grandma's diaries?"

We were nonplussed. Her diaries? What diaries? We dashed upstairs and there, hidden way at the back of one of the inner closets, were several black metal boxes trimmed with gold. Inside one was a neatly arranged set of notebooks, and on top, written in a teenager's hand, the following bold warning:

> I trust you on your honour <u>not</u> to examine, look at, or read anything in this box. Sooner burn everything.
> dw
> 11-11-20

Beneath, in faded pencil but a more mature hand:

> I have herein said some horrid things about people. I don't deny their truth, but I regret having thought and written them.

Other boxes contained letters, all neatly tied in bunches, many in the handwriting of her mother and father, her grandmothers, and the uncles and aunts she had told us about. All had been carefully labeled and laid away. There must have been hundreds.

It never occurred to us to burn this treasure. We started sampling the diaries, our eyes growing wider by the minute. Here was my mother's stepmother, and they were fighting about the car! Here was her adored Grandma Amory, rescuing her from a fainting fit at the Boston armory. Here were her father, her brothers Robert and Freddy, her half-siblings Nat and Katharine, her outrageous Uncle George, a mysterious friend called Goaty. Here were Uncle Gren and Uncle Beek and Aunt Kitty. Here was our own father, of whom she'd written with all her accustomed reserve stripped away: "There is something precious and old-fashioned about him which I love, something chivalrous, seldom met with now." And here, with a pain we'd never imagined, her anguished words of longing for her mother, the mother she had barely known, the beautiful mother who had died when she was only two.

These boxes contained the stuff that her memories were made of—the first telling of the stories, the stories in their original form. Maybe this was the reason my mother hadn't gotten around to writing her family stories: she had already recorded them.

The diaries and letters contained much more than the family tales. They offered historical context, an intimate view of a way of life long gone—of a period when leisure time was plentiful and cars were few, when Hamilton was open country and Boston a closed society, when trying to be good was more important than trying to have fun. They provided an intimate view of the vanished lifestyle of the upper classes between the two world wars—and proof that the serenity of country life doesn't necessarily bestow peace of mind, that the security of social position doesn't always mean wishing to take one's place in society. More compelling, they revealed a person we had rarely glimpsed: someone who throughout her teenage years and early twenties was often tortured with self-doubt, who suffered greatly, someone seemingly radically different from the confident, cheerful person who had brought us up, who was described in her obituary as "the most loved person in town."

If these boxes revealed not just my mother's stories but also her own story, so too the dusty old volumes around the house and the letters and scrapbooks carefully stored away began to yield a larger story, dating back to the Civil War. Reconstructing this story took me to the Massachusetts Historical Society and the New-York Historical Society; to correspondence with Green-Wood Cemetery in Brooklyn; to the Fogg Museum at Harvard; to old diaries kept by my mother's Grandmother Winthrop and letters and memorabilia from a Winthrop Civil War general; to social histories of the period; to books about Edith Wharton and J. Pierpont Morgan and Teddy Roosevelt; and into many other nooks and crannies. Nonetheless, the impetus for these forays, the heart of the tale, remained the old letters and scrapbooks, the pamphlets and booklets that my mother had carefully saved. The result is much further reaching than what my mother had in mind. But the huge mound of undigested family papers of which she was custodian, together with her own oral history, acted as a spur.

Inevitably, like the archeologist patching together a vase, I ended up with jagged little gaps here and there. The family founder, for example, Robert Winthrop, my mother's paternal grandfather, remains a shadowy figure; he died more than a decade before my mother's birth and, unlike her maternal grandfather, Charles Walter Amory, left no letters that I know of. Her uncle Dudley Winthrop, the sportsman who died when she was a girl, was harder to reconstruct than her uncle Grenville Winthrop, who lived till she grew up, who had daughters she knew, and whose art collecting has been covered by other writers. Those who received mention in her diaries, those who wrote letters, were easier to realize than those who didn't. Though some of these individuals made only cameo appearances, I chose to include whatever I could find about any member of the extended family she talked about, even if the portrait that resulted was sketchy.

Ironically, though the spark for the project was the Winthrops, and though many of my mother's stories were about the Winthrop men, the story as a whole turned out to have a different slant. Its core was the other side of the family, her mother's. And the central characters, other than her father, were all women: my mother's Grandmother Amory, her mother, and herself. In part this arose from the richness of materials about them, but even more, from their own richness of heart.

Just as I thought I was on the homestretch with the text, we made a final discovery. I knew we had a lot of old pictures that I had hoped to include in the book, but I was nervous about the quality. Most of those in the scrapbooks were faded and yellowed with age. When my daughter Dodi had asked if she could have some of "Grandma's negatives," I had casually agreed. A Christmas present she gave me in 1996, several oversize contact sheets made from the negatives, showed me how wrong I had been. Here were 1920s pictures pasted in my mother's scrapbooks, but as fresh as the day they were taken. A couple of months later, when my sister Libby and I were checking through my mother's scrapbooks and loose photos, we came across an even more exciting find: negatives from her parents' family photos that dated back nearly a century when she and her brothers were babies. Age hadn't hurt them at all. The pictures would be as clear as day. Yet another surprise greeted me when I took the photos from my Grandma Amory's day, Civil War times, into a photo studio to be reproduced. The experts there were amazed, telling me that this family collection, so carefully preserved in my mother's closet, amounted to a valuable history of photography. They marveled not only at the period look of the individuals but at the high-grade paper and slow careful processing that made the images clearer and richer than most photos taken today.

Looking back, I wish I'd paid more attention while my mother was alive, asked her more questions, remembered more tales. If only I could ask her, I often think. But I also like to imagine that my mother would enjoy these efforts—that she would sit in her chair as she used to and chuckle as she relived those days and revisited the people who dwelled so clearly in the recesses of her memory.

part ONE

The Ancestors of
Dorothy Winthrop Bradford

Beginnings
chapter ONE

Left: *Elizabeth Gardner Amory*
Right: *Frederic Winthrop*

*F*or *one who* would inherit the mantle of family historian, my mother had two strikingly different mentors. Her father and her Grandmother Amory didn't agree on how to record family history. Nor did they see eye to eye on which families were important—or indeed why.

Her father, Frederic Winthrop, was a member of the ninth generation in an unbroken line of Winthrop males in America, a direct descendant of two revered colonial governors, John Winthrop of Massachusetts Bay Colony and his son, John Winthrop, Jr., of Connecticut. My mother thought of him as a historian, a man who nearly every day would dutifully set off to the august Massachusetts Historical Society and delve into some obscure cranny of Winthrop family lore. His focus was very one-sided, however. As my mother would say, "He didn't talk very much about the Winthrop women, but the Winthrop men were very important." On the other side, she listened to the bubble-pricking voice of Grandma Amory—Elizabeth "Libby" Gardner Amory—whose ancestor Thomas Gardner had arrived in Massachusetts in 1624, six years before any Winthrop had set foot on these shores. Grandma Amory was down-to-earth and impressed by no one. As she would say to my mother, "I don't see why the Winthrop men are so important. They haven't done anything for generations. Look at the Adams family. Of course, the Adamses write books … even if they don't amount to much this minute, but they did down through the ages. They've always been scholars or students or teachers, or authors or something … or in politics."

Superficially, my mother's father and grandmother seemed peas from the same pod. Her father, though born and raised in a wealthy and respected New York family, had clung to his historic New England roots and returned to the Boston area to marry and raise a family. Her grandmother was vintage Boston, less wealthy but equally respectable, a Gardner by birth and an Amory by marriage. But Fred Winthrop was uncompromisingly proud of his clan. This attitude stretched all the way back to his original American forebear, Governor John Winthrop, who believed that he and his fellow governing Puritans were "God's elect … chosen to rule as ministers and magistrates over the whole community."[1] It lived on in revolutionary times, when Winthrops "were notorious for their condescending attitude toward social inferiors,"[2] and remained ingrained in the Winthrop consciousness of Fred's day.

Grandma Amory questioned the very root of this faith. In her view, history should have anointed her ancestor Thomas Gardner as first governor of Massachusetts Bay Colony, not John Winthrop. Gardner had come to Cape Ann dirt poor, leader of a small company that was supposed to establish a farming community in Gloucester. Finding nothing but rocky soil, a "few stout hearts" from the band had moved to what would become Salem, where—as Grandma Amory wrote in a mini–family history—they had "staid at the hazard of their lives.… It was a small settlement, but industrious and hard-working. They had wives and children." In her mind, this was proof enough. As she wrote, "There can be no doubt of the fact that Thomas Gardner, as Overseer of the Plantation at Cape Ann, was the first man in authority on the soil of what developed into the Massachusetts Bay Colony."[3]

History, of course, placed the governor's mantle on John Winthrop, and credits him as well for his courage, generosity, and wisdom while excusing his stiff-necked piety in light of the stresses of survival in the New World. It looks more kindly yet on John, Jr., who was as able as his father but easier by nature and gifted with a restless curiosity.[4] Even granting the first two Winthrops their primacy, however, Grandma Amory was on to something when she observed that the Winthrop aura had faded, that the Winthrops of her time were resting on their historical laurels. According to the authoritative *Dictionary of American Biography*, only two of the seven Winthrops selected as "important Americans" were "modern" figures (mid- to late nineteenth century).[5] One of these was Civil War writer Theodore Winthrop (1828–61), whose career, like a Roman candle, had flamed briefly (ignited primarily by his early death on the battlefield), then died. The other was Robert C. Winthrop (1809–94), a Bostonian whose first wife had grown up under the same roof as Grandma Amory's

Governor John Winthrop of Massachusetts Bay Colony, 1588-1649 (courtesy Harvard University Portrait Collection, gift of Robert Winthrop, representing the Winthrop family, to Harvard University, 1964)

father and whom she would refer to as "Uncle Winthrope" (refer to Chart 1). Robert C. Winthrop was a living embodiment of the family tradition of pride, once bragging of his own "remarkable record [of having known]... every one of our twenty-three Presidents except Washington, who died nine years before I was born."[6] Granted, his long list of accomplishments spanned the century: speaker of the state legislature, congressman, speaker of the House of Representatives, senator from Massachusetts, philanthropist, orator, and for thirty years president of the Massachusetts Historical Society. But many found him pompous, vain, and long-winded—Robert "Chloroform" Winthrop, the abolitionists, who were not happy when he led the opposition to President Lincoln's second term, called him.[7] Moreover, neither of his sons—Grandma Amory's contemporaries—was terribly distinguished. One son, Robert C., Jr., had followed his father as president of the Massachusetts Historical Society, but he quit in a fit of pique, explaining by letter that it didn't suit him to remain a member after the organization had moved from Tremont to Boylston Street because the new location was too "remote" from his house.[8] The other son, John, had left Boston to become a gentleman farmer in Stockbridge, where he earned a name for himself as a diligent member of the highbrow Lenox Club but also a bit of a rapscallion, "always in debt" and "constantly tight."[9]

As an explorer of Winthrop family lore, Fred Winthrop was one of those gentlemen of good family who are "genealogists and antiquarians rather than historians."[10] As he explained to my mother, he wrote nothing because "he couldn't express himself well." His activity consisted rather of attending to the artifacts—the family papers, coat of arms, land holdings, portraits—that proved, for one brief shining moment, that the Winthrops were America's first family. Most notable of these was the huge collection of the Winthrop family papers—today contained on fifty-three microfilm reels—at the Massachusetts Historical Society, the bulk of which had been donated by Robert C. Winthrop, Jr., just before Fred Winthrop joined in 1908. The crowning glory of the collection had arrived a century earlier, in 1803: Governor John Winthrop's journals, two small, weathered booklets containing—in his indecipherable and faded scribble—the story of the first difficult years of New England's early settlers.[11] The rest of the family papers trickled in during the second half of the nineteenth century.[12] When Fred joined, all that was missing was the portion that had been bequeathed to his grandfather, Thomas Charles Winthrop—lost to this day.

Another of Fred Winthrop's absorbing projects was confirming that the family had a bona fide coat of arms. Since the days of William the Conqueror, the Winthrop name had been floating around in the mists of medieval England, variously spelled Wynthropp, Winethorpe, Wymthorpe, Wimpthorpe, and Wymundthorpe.[13] But it wasn't until Governor John Winthrop's grandfather, Adam (1498–1562), had risen in the ranks of a clothworker company and been granted the right to bear arms by King Edward VI in 1548 that there was any family history to speak of. The right to their crest—a hare on a green mound, ears back, ready to spring, and beneath, a lion rampant—had come to America with Governor John Winthrop in 1630. The Winthrops knew this, but America was bursting with "wannabes," others who were claiming coats of arms. In 1916, when the New England Historic Genealogical Society's Committee on Heraldry began to compile its *Roll of Arms*, Fred Winthrop leapt quick as the family hare to ensure the Winthrops a place among the elect. As a result of his swift move, the family is now listed seventh among more than six hundred names whose claim to a coat of arms has been "listed and proved" by the Society.[14]

Land holdings were another vestige of Winthrop preeminence. In colonial days, Winthrop holdings seemed to be everywhere, islands here, farms there, a lead mine (Tantiusques) near Sturbridge, Massachusetts, and various huge and undefined tracts in the "wild" interior. Fisher's Island off New London was the star attraction, with three thousand acres of woods, rolling hills, pastures, ponds, and shoreline. But members of the family also held Governor's Island in Boston Harbor; the Elizabeth Islands;[15] and Swan Island in the Kennebec River in Maine. In addition, Winthrops owned, but usually leased out, large farms, including Governor John Winthrop's Tenhills Farm near Boston, the seven-hundred-acre Poquonock Farm in Groton, Massachusetts, the thousand-acre Pond Farm near Lynnfield and Peabody, Massachusetts, and a great ten-square-mile stretch called the Manor and Royalty of Groton Hall on the South Shore of Long Island. More urban than rural, Winthrops had also founded a number of New England towns and cities. Of course, Governor John Winthrop had founded Boston, the "citty on a hill."[16] His son John, Jr., founded New London and Saybrook, Connecticut, as well as Ipswich, Massachusetts;[17] another son, Deane, founded Groton, Massachusetts; and one of Governor John Winthrop, Sr.'s great-grandsons, Adam, founded Worcester, Massachusetts.[18]

By Fred Winthrop's generation, however, the lands were gone and all that remained were the stray landmarks. Fred clipped stories on efforts to save various ones—the Royall House in Medford, which had been the country seat of the first Governor Winthrop, and the three-hundred-year-old Deane Winthrop House in the same locale. He also clipped Winthrop-related stories, for instance, a newspaper account of the unveiling of marble tablets at the First Church (Unitarian) in Boston to commemorate founders John Winthrop, Thomas Dudley, Isaac Johnson, and John Wilson. And he volunteered his and his brothers' financial help in refurbishing Boston's Copley Square if only the mayor, John F. Fitzgerald ("Honey-Fitz"), would agree to change the name to Winthrop Square.

The Winthrop family crest, among the first coats of arms in America to be "listed and proved" by the New England Historic Genealogical Society's Committee on Heraldry

Finally, the Winthrops could boast of a long string of family portraits, a collection dating back to Adam Winthrop in England and representing an unbroken line of mostly sons of sons through Fred's own generation. Even in the mid-nineteenth century, people were impressed. One journalist noted, in a listing of New York's richest men, "The Winthrops have their family portraits for eight generations, as far back as the 15th century, when they left their rich possessions in England to found the city of Boston."[19] To my mother's father and his siblings, who grew up with their overbearing gaze dominating the Winthrop family dining room in New York, they must have stood as somber and undeniable proof of the permanence of the Winthrop pedigree. But dining rooms and reverence for family elders have since shrunk, and my mother's brother Robert, who inherited the collection from his father's brother Grenville, decided it would be best to rid the family of the whole lot. His solution was to give all fourteen portraits to Harvard, which received them with great fanfare, noting that family dynasties such as the Winthrops contribute to the country's "social stability. [They] ... tend to be conservative in politics and in social outlook, but their conservatism is usually accompanied by force of character and a courage to stand behind principle."[20] Today, the Winthrop ancestors gaze down from the walls of the library in Harvard's Winthrop House, where students may well be oblivious of the venerable company observing them coldly from above.[21]

The unquestioned social position of the Winthrops must also have given Fred Winthrop confidence about the family's importance. Of the three major Winthrop branches in New York, his own, in fact, was the least splashy. The other two had been tapped as members of the Four Hundred, the *crème de la crème* of New York society, whose number had been fixed in 1892 by Ward McAllister, based on the number of people who would fit into Mrs. William Backhouse Astor's ballroom. Representing the elder branch (those descended from Fred's great-grandfather Francis Bayard Winthrop through his son John Still) were Mr. and Mrs. Buchanan Winthrop and a "Miss Winthrop" (presumably Buchanan's daughter Marie, nineteen).[22] Representing the younger branch (those descended from Francis Bayard's younger brother, Benjamin) were Egerton Winthrop, Sr., and his son Bronson. This younger branch was so elegant that their fame would carry beyond the press accounts of the day. Egerton, Sr., was summed up in Edith Wharton's memoirs as one of those late nineteenth-century American gentlemen, cosmopolitan, cultured, with "princely wealth,"[23] who chose to live lives of "dilettantish leisure."[24] And Bronson, who cofounded the eminent New York law firm of Winthrop, Stimson, was said, in a firm history, to be thought of by his colleagues as "the exquisite," whose "courtly home was attended by servants in livery and furnished in the tradition of refined, history-conscious families—with 'the silver of four generations on the sideboard.' "[25] (Refer to Chart 2.)

New York was so awash with Winthrops when Fred was growing up that people were always mixing them up. Fred's newspaper clippings often identify brothers as cousins and cousins as brothers.[26] At Harvard, no one knew who had gotten which grade in ancient art, Fred's brother Grenville or Bronson's brother Egerton, who was a year ahead.[27] To outsiders, it seemed that the Winthrop family tree spread so wide that "the sun never sets on the Winthrops."[28] Fred knew, however, that you couldn't count on Winthrops always being around. The secret of continuity lay in the male of the species, for men and men only could carry on the all-important family name.

Over the generations, Winthrops had been remarkably lucky in keeping their name alive. They had exercised "first family leadership" for over two hundred years, surviving longer than any other prominent Boston family.[29] Until 1800, however, they had hung on by only a few male strands. Then, the branches had sprouted wide and fruitful—more than two dozen male Winthrops born per generation during the early to mid-nineteenth century. By Frederic's own generation, alas, the number was dwindling again, with only nine male Winthrops living in Boston or New York and personally known to him. And these nine had eked out a mere five sons among them.[30] The Winthrop male was again beginning to look like an endangered species. The future, the family name, might rest with Fred Winthrop's three sons alone. No wonder he thought Winthrop men—and especially his own sons—so important. As he would say to my mother, dismissing his own sisters, "They were only girls. You can't carry on a family that way." (Refer to Charts 2 and 3.)

Succeeding generations claim that Fred Winthrop and his brothers believed so strongly in the importance of being Winthrop that they called themselves the Holy Family.[31] This precise term was not found in any of the letters or diaries my mother saved. What was found, however, was a reference to a "Saturday night holy society." It was used by Fred Winthrop's younger brother Beekman in a letter he wrote my mother dated January 7, 1940, to describe his dinner that evening with Grenville, his only remaining brother. "Tonight," he wrote, "the Saturday evening holy society consisted only of two old grey bearded gentlemen."[32]

— • —

If Fred Winthrop saw family history as a quasi-public interest to be probed and preserved by the Massachusetts Historical Society, Grandma Amory regarded it as a homespun matter, a labor of love involving bits of family lore, genealogies, scrapbooks, and stories. For Fred Winthrop, family history was written for future generations, both family and outsiders. For Grandma Amory, family tales were for her immediate family, her own children and grandchildren. For Fred, family history served largely to extol deeds; for Grandma Amory, the only interesting point was personalities. For Fred, history rode on the lives of the men; for Grandma Amory, women were equally important. For him, family history was a serious business; for her, it was fun.

Her own pedigree was a stew of well-aged family names, redolent with Gardners, Putnams and Pickerings, Russells and Lowells. Moreover, unlike the most famous Winthrops, these were not dusty colonial fossils.[33] Nineteenth-century

Boston and vicinity were swarming with the famous and brilliant Lowells: author James Russell Lowell, poet Amy Lowell, president of Harvard College Abbott Lawrence Lowell, astronomer Percival Lowell, and architect Guy Lowell were all cousins of Grandma Amory. In Boston, as it was said, "the Lowells talk to the Cabots and Cabots talk only to God."[34] Anyone with connections like this might well wonder why Winthrops thought they were so important.

Her immediate family, the Gardners, had their papers, though these were but a few stray stalks compared with the voluminous Winthrop sheaves. Grandma Amory gathered what she had on hand (mostly old letters and a genealogy kept by her grandfather Samuel Pickering Gardner) in the slim, typewritten volume she called *The Gardner Family of Salem and Boston*. On the first page, she pasted a newspaper picture of a prehistoric man, captioned "The gentleman from Piltdown." Beneath this she wrote, "2,000,000 years ago. Our first ancestor!" She also included pictures of old family houses. "How uncomfortable!" she noted beside a picture postcard of the so-called Coffin House on Nantucket. In the preface, she commented that she had produced the volume "solely" for her children in hopes that they too would take an interest in family history.

Grandma Amory's view of colonial history turned conventional wisdom upside down. Not only did she claim Massachusetts' first governorship for her ancestor Thomas Gardner, but she also challenged comments being spread by the Endicotts about her Gardner forebears. The Endicotts were saying that Tom Gardner and his group were "a mere handful [of] squatters, having no right to the place [Salem]." Grandma Amory countered this in her own historical sketch: when John Endicott led an advance party for John Winthrop in 1629, "appear[ing] from England with a large company and a charter from Charles I to settle and form a town, [it was] much to the disgust of the few farmers there who complained and told them so, but could not of course drive them out." Having no other choice, Gardner and his small settlement had been absorbed by the larger contingent. Was it right for the Endicotts to claim that their forebears were the first legitimate settlers? "As far as right is the question," Grandma Amory wrote in a typed addendum to *The Gardner Family*, "what right had Charles I to the land? He did not get it by fighting, nor did he buy it from the Indians. Why was not he a squatter?"

History played odd tricks, she thought. In society, family positions come and go, and the quirks of fate have a lot to do with who is up and who is down. When a son of "squatting" Tom Gardner had married a niece of John Winthrop, she mused in her typed addendum, the Winthrops were "far above them in rank." But in less than two centuries the Winthrops and Gardners had become social equals. In 1832 no one questioned Robert C. Winthrop's choice when he took as his wife another Gardner—Eliza Cabot Blanchard. Eliza, Grandma Amory's second cousin, had been brought up with Grandma Amory's father and uncle after she was orphaned as a small child. (Refer to Chart 11.) It all went to show, Grandma Amory wrote, that "three hundred years and much less, makes nice respectable folks on a level. I feel as good as any Endicott or Winthrop. Strange to say!"[35]

In her old age, Grandma Amory decided to go to a reception at the old burying ground in Salem to see what she could learn about her Gardner heritage. Six hundred people had been invited, she wrote in a letter to a friend, but only three dozen came—"frumps from Salem, and so very plain!" She searched for Gardner headstones in vain. And when she asked the head usher about the Gardners, he said he'd never heard of them. "Is it possible," she wrote in a letter to her daughter-in-law May Amory, "that we were not in Society, and we thought we were as good as anybody there! The Peabodys and the Crowninshields were swell, and very rich—but made their money by bringing slaves from Africa! *We* didn't do that, and were not very rich, but must have been buried somewhere."

Grandma Amory certainly believed the importance of being a Gardner matched the importance of being anyone, and she toiled long and hard over her family trees. She traced the lineages of four of the early settler families with which she was linked (Russells, Lowells, Gardners, and Winthrops) and annotated a fifth, an already existing genealogy of the Amory family.[36] On the other hand, she was more interested in family eccentricities than in family excellence, noting with fascination the quirks of both the Amorys and the Gardners. On the Amory family tree, for example, she wrote "ugly" beside Thomas C. Amory and his sister Isabella and "frightfully ugly, but elegant" next to James S. Amory. Beside Hetty S. Meredith she wrote "crazy," beside Susan C. Lowell, "insane once," and next to W. Amory Prescott, "softening of the brain." She wrote that Jonathan Amory was "surnamed wicked Jonathan," that the three children of Thomas C. Amory and his second wife ("nurse or housekeeper") had "no social position," and that Thomas Garner [sic] who married Harriet Amory had "drowned in his yacht."[37] And she passed down to my mother, with none of the gravity it warranted, the tale of the "sad accident" of Thomas, Boston's first Amory, who drowned in a vat of liquor in 1728.[38] She was no less merciful when it came to the Gardners. Two out of twenty-one Gardner first cousins, two out of her six nieces and nephews, and a few more distant cousins were tarred as being "insane," or for drinking or committing suicide.

To Grandma Amory, seeking out ancestral connections was more a parlor game than a scholarly pursuit, and personal recollections were better indicators of historic truth than any genealogy or history. As she wrote elsewhere, "It is so stupid reading about our ancestors, died, born, married, and so repeated along a long list. I mean to write a few words of description about the ones I knew."

The "few words of description" were separate from customized Gardner family history. They were typed on loose sheets of paper and sounded as if she were talking to you. Of her husband, Charles Walter Amory: "handsome, clear brain, sweet nature, easy and a firm character. He made friends and gained the confidence of all. Generous and liberal." But of his older brother William and his three wives, she was withering. "I have just seen Louise Amory [the third wife], she looks very nervous and ill. She came to Boston to see her doctors, and they suggest pulling out her teeth and going to Switzerland to take sun baths from violet rays....The first [Ellen Brewer] was amiable and fashionable and cared for swell things, but was not inter-

· 11 ·

BEGINNINGS

esting. Number two [J. Philomena Guischard] was a dragon, tremendous will, she dominated William and the girls.... As to William, I found him a great bore ... most uninteresting, small, harmless."

Like Fred Winthrop, Grandma Amory was also interested in preserving family relics. She cared nothing for such showy fare as a family coat of arms, poking fun at her grandfather Samuel P. Gardner for pasting a bookmark bearing a family crest into all his books when in fact he "did not inherit any such swell thing."[39] She did, however, keep the outfit her grandfather had worn for his marriage in 1797 to Rebecca Russell Lowell. This lady with the melodic name was the daughter of Judge John Lowell (1743–1802) and granddaughter of the Honorable James Russell.[40] The bridegroom's wedding coat was of "blue silk brocade ... with wide lapels, embroidered in blue, wide cuffs, embroidered in blue," and across his chest, he wore "a bright yellow satin ribbon." The wedding coat and sash became a family heirloom, ending up with my mother, who turned them over to the Wenham Historical Society in 1977—nearly two hundred years after Sam Gardner's wedding day.[41]

In Grandma Amory's mother's generation, a series of family portraits was begun, which by my mother's day had grown to four. Unlike the Winthrop male collection,[42] these were daughters of daughters, or the "distaffs," as my mother would call them. As she wrote me in the late 1950s, "We have moved the distaffs to the dining room over the mantel, and have hung a lot of hunting prints in the library." Of course, the distaffs did not represent as imposing an array in our dining room as had the somber collection of Winthrops in Grandma Winthrop's. They were modest, dainty miniatures, ovals in small gold frames. First to be painted had been Grandma Amory's mother, Helen Read Gardner, at age forty-one, in 1860 in Lenox, a likeness which was, in her daughter's opinion, "very poor. She was beautiful." The artist, identified on the back of the portrait as a Mr. Stone (almost certainly New York portrait painter William Oliver Stone), painted Grandma Amory that same summer, when she was still a young woman of barely seventeen. Years went by and then Grandma Amory's daughter Dorothy, my mother's mother, was added, painted by the excellent Austrian portraitist Herman Hanatscheck. He wrote to my mother that this portrait was one that even his visitors found arresting "because of her marvelous beauty." When he subsequently painted my mother, a work completed in 1936, he wrote that he had hoped to "use some of the expression of the Bachrach picture [most likely from her wedding], by far the best Bachrach picture which I ever saw. At least I will try to get something of the happy mood." It's unlikely that such poetic thoughts ever crossed the minds of the painters who immortalized Adam or John, or even Robert C. Winthrop.

Grandma Amory would have enjoyed watching the portrait series grow, for she believed women had just as much reason to be memorialized as men. Women, she wrote, quoting historian Francis Parkman, had the "function of the civilizing agent" of society. Men might be charged with rearing the "political superstructure," but they were "belittled and cramped by the competition of business." Spared such pressures, women had better opportunities for "moral and mental growth" and were thus better able to "lay [the] foundation" of society.[43]

Helen Maria Gardner, 1819-88

Elizabeth Gardner Amory, 1843-1930

Dorothy Amory Winthrop, 1878-1907

Dorothy Winthrop Bradford, 1905-87

Grandma Amory also kept a scrapbook in which she created a record of five generations of her immediate family. Filled with photos and little comments, it is worlds apart from the scrapbook kept by Fred Winthrop. His was a collection of newspaper clippings with the only personal touches being corrections about Winthrops he made in pen. Hers bears a woman's imprint—homey, motherly, and personal.

On the cover of her scrapbook Grandma Amory pasted a label: "E. G. Amory: for Dorothy to keep up." No doubt my mother remembered this charge as she told us the tales of her two families. She got a great kick out of the differences they represented. Both were top drawer, but Grandma Amory's Boston side was filled with old socks and warm underwear, the New York Winthrop side with pearls and silk stockings. My mother—a Bostonian—was cut from the same cloth as the old socks and underwear. She respected the Winthrops, but Grandma Amory, with her irony and her humor, was the one to whom she felt closer.

An Amory and Gardner Union

chapter TWO

Libby Gardner Amory, charcoal drawing, undated and unattributed.
This reproduction is from a glass negative, kept by my mother and
labeled "Print on glass of Grandma's portrait."

"*C.W.A. May 1862* first came into my life (and remained there)," she wrote under the picture of the clear-eyed young man in his sports coat and bow tie. She was Elizabeth Gardner, then almost nineteen and eventually to become my mother's grandmother, and he was Charles Walter Amory, then a junior at Harvard and later to become my mother's grandfather. But he was called Ned and she was called Libby, from the first until the last.

Ned Amory, about 1861

They had grown up as neighbors, for when Ned was a toddler of two and Libby a baby of one, Libby's family, the George Gardners, had bought a house at 67 Beacon Street, just a few houses down Beacon Hill from where Ned and his family dwelt.[1] Social historians would describe Beacon Hill as that steep incline where Boston's finest families built elegant homes bespeaking exclusivity and permanence. But years later, when Libby typed out her memories of growing up on Beacon Street, she made it sound much simpler:

> I remember so well coming down Beacon Street in the year 1855, a child [of twelve], and looking with pleasure at the lovely view before me. The English elms were large and healthy with large branches spread over the sidewalk and half way over the street. At the bottom of the hill was water. There was no Arlington Street and the water began at the Garden which was a third smaller then. Across the stretch of blue water was a hilly country. Green and as far as I could see unbuilt upon. I thought how lovely Boston was.

She and Ned must both have played in Boston Common, that tree-filled, grassy fifty-acre park in the heart of Boston which had been set aside in 1640 as "open ground or common field" for Bostonians to enjoy and where cows had grazed until just a few years before Libby and Ned were born.[2] The Common was directly across the street from their houses and the Boston Garden, in the flat land below.

> Ladies and often gentlemen walked in the shady malls, for we never left the city till after the glorious Fourth, with its noise and many accidents. The Garden was a large field guiltless of the mower or hay or any care but enchanting to us children for there was a small greenhouse, with John Gormly as gardener. He was kind to us and let us play with the cat and many kittens, occasionally giving us one. The circus came in warm weather and pitched its tent on the Common and we were taken to see the wonders displayed in its one ring.

Libby also wrote of how, on steamy summer days, children would repair to the Braman's Baths.

> Then when hot weather began we were sent into Braman's Baths. These were in the river about where Back St. and Brimmer now meet. A large tank in the center with ropes around the edge to cling to, one end consisted of a flight of slimy steps with the water coming through, occasionally a cabbage leaf and other unpleasant suggestions of a dump heap came floating through. However, the bath was a great delight to us. Friends of all ages in the tank together.

If summer brought heat, it also brought flies, swarms of them:

> But the flies in our house! There were stables in Charles St. and I suppose that made the nuisance worse for houses near. For in those days we never had or heard of mosquito nets for the windows and the rooms were full of flies and mosquitoes. I so well remember my mother shutting the shutters with the exception of a stream of light and rounding up all the flies with a towel toward that open light and in that way getting rid of armies of them. Still, at table we always had wire cages with a handle on the top, over all the food. We helped ourselves to bread and butter or cake and before replacing it, shook it all around so as to get rid of the flies.[3]

Ned Amory lived up the hill from Libby; his family was also a notch up the social scale from hers and his lifestyle, several above. He would grow up under a roof supplied by his grandfather, the fabled Boston millionaire David Sears (1787–1871), businessman and land developer, state senator and U.S. congressman, Harvard

Libby Gardner,
February 1861

"David Sears when very old"
(caption from Libby
Amory's scrapbook)

The Sears house, 42 Beacon Street, after 1872 when "the Somerset Club bought it and carried along the stone wall, put a door in it, and planted vines" (caption in Libby Amory's scrapbook)

Photo of portrait of William Amory, Ned Amory's father, by Daniel Huntington. Portrait itself belongs to Dr. Catherine Lastavica.

overseer and philanthropist. The two-story granite house at 42 Beacon Street had been designed by a Paris architect, and in 1821 the Sears family moved in. In 1831, when David Sears doubled its size, adding a third story and an extension on the downhill side, Bostonians knew to it as the city's costliest mansion.[4] Today, it houses the Somerset Club, long the retreat of choice of Boston clubmen.

David Sears could well afford such a house, for with a fortune of $1.5 million in 1855 he was reputed to be one of only ten pre–Civil War millionaires in Massachusetts.[5] Sears had come by his wealth in part through inheritance, thanks to his father, merchant David Sears, Sr. (1752–1816), who had left him $800,000, the largest amount ever to have been inherited in New England by a single individual. And he added to his prospects by marrying the wealthy Miriam Clarke Mason, daughter of U.S. senator Jonathan Mason.

David and Miriam Sears would expand their Beacon Hill domain as their eight children grew up and got married. Their oldest was Anna, and when she married William Amory in 1833, David Sears arranged that they should live in an extension of their house, at 43 Beacon. It was here that Ned Amory was born about nine years later and here that the William Amory family remained for another eleven years, until they moved two doors up, to 41 Beacon, in yet another extension built by David Sears, this originally for his daughter Harriet and her new husband, Salem-born George Crowninshield.[6]

If not as wealthy as the Sears, the Amorys nonetheless boasted connections by marriage to many other venerable Boston names—Lawrences and Lees, Lowells and Lorings, Putnams and Paynes. And the Amory name was acceptably weathered, for Boston family founder Thomas Amory had arrived from South Carolina in 1720. William Amory, who in his position as treasurer of the Amoskeag mills held "one of the great treasuryships" of New England,[7] was also rich enough, with just sufficient wealth ($100,000) to be ranked among the richest men of Massachusetts.[8]

Ned Amory took after his father William, who was, Libby wrote, "the sweetest tempered and eas[iest]-going man ... intellectual, reading all the time, and a wonderful memory ... very handsome ... [with] the most beautiful teeth one ever sees, pearly white and regular." Ned's mother was not so easy-going. By age thirty, Anna Sears Amory was deaf, a tribulation of which she was constantly reminding her children. She once wrote Ned, "Of late years, you have all cast me off, and no one thinks of speaking to me, except when I can do something for them. Perhaps it can't be helped—but God grant you may never any of you know the *Purgatory* I have lived." Libby was not being unkind when she wrote that although Anna Sears Amory "had an air of great elegance and refinement ... [she was] morbid and quite melancholy in temperament." (Refer to Chart 6.)

REARED *in a* GREENHOUSE

Libby Gardner had no David Sears in her pedigree, but she thought it just as good to have come up the hard way, as her maternal grandfather, James Read, had done. Born November 19, 1789, James Read was one of ten children, a son of the Cambridge postmaster. James gave up school at fourteen and, as Libby would write later, "went into the city as a clerk somewhere. To save the expense of the omnibus hourly, I suppose he walked, and passed only a very few houses until he arrived in town." In time he entered the dry goods business, soon operating under the firm name of James Read and Company and offering "broadcloths, of superfine and middling quality."[9] By the age of twenty-six, he was well enough established to consider marriage. His choice was Hannah Palmer, daughter of a Boston boardinghouse keeper, "very tall and straight, most vivacious, full of spirits, red hair or very sandy colored, blue eyes."[10] They boarded with her mother, Jerusha Johnson Palmer, for seven years. But as daughters kept being born (there were four in all), and money being made, the Reads moved out of town to a home of their own in West Roxbury.[11]

Anna Sears Amory, Ned Amory's mother. "Photograph of Anna, Mrs. Amory, very poor, not giving her air of distinction" (caption in Libby Amory's scrapbook)

James Read, Libby Gardner's maternal grandfather

In the wake of the Panic of 1837 commercial houses throughout the country were toppling, among them James Read and Company, which collapsed in 1842. But his was no ordinary bankruptcy: "We probably have never had a failure that created such sympathy and threw such a gloom over the community," wrote Libby's father, George Gardner, to his brother John Lowell Gardner, in 1842. By then, George Gardner had been married for four years to Helen Maria, one of James Read's four daughters. His letter went on to say that "not one of his [Read's] creditors … but has expressed his deep sorrow at the event … and have professed their own losses as of no importance in comparison."[12] In a sequel that became legend throughout Boston, Read made a vow to repay every cent he owed, the colossal sum for the day of $850,000.[13,14] Liquidating company assets brought $800,000, and Read earned the balance of $50,000 over the next two and a half years, turning it all over to his creditors.[15] For James Read, however, this was a pattern long established: as a teenager, he'd won $2,000 in a lottery and used the entire sum to pay off his father's debts.[16]

Libby would remember her grandfather Read as "fine, honest, good, kind, public-spirited, generous, a genial nature," though her grandmother Read struck her as "shy, a touch morbid at times, perhaps because she had a trying life but had strong character." The "trying" times may have had less to do with her own humble bloodlines and her husband's financial reverses than with the unhappy lives of her daughters. Except for Helen, it was a sorry spectacle of marital separation, children's deaths, suicide, and spinsterhood.[17] None of the reverses, however, shook Libby's view of the place her grandfather had earned in society: "And here am I, one of the best families of Boston thinking no one is too good for my family."[18]

Helen Maria Read Gardner, Libby Gardner's mother

To be sure, the Gardners—Libby's father's side of the family—had been established somewhat longer in Boston society than the Reads. Like so many Massachusetts families, they had come of financial age in the days of the clipper ships and the Indies trade. Theirs was a tale of families being swept from Salem to Boston, gathering wealth as they went, until the shipping business began to run out of steam after the Civil War. Libby had three such salty generations in her family. Her great-grandfather John Gardner (1731–1805), born in Salem, was a shipmaster who engaged in the West Indian trade in his early years. By the time he was thirty-three, however, he'd retired, first buying himself a "mansion" in Salem but then settling for nearly thirty years on a large farm in Wenham.[19] John's son, Samuel Pickering Gardner, would bow to the dictates of the new larger-keeled boats, abandoning the shallow waters of Salem harbor for the better anchorage of Boston where he set up as a wealthy merchant. His son and Libby's uncle, John Lowell Gardner, was more prosperous still, with his large fleet amassing a fortune estimated at $5 million at his death,[20] and earning a place in history as the "last of the East India merchants."[21]

Libby had been born into the other—the lesser—branch of the family. Like John Lowell, her father, George, was a merchant, but he suffered at every turn in comparison with his older brother. John was the owner of thirty ships; George owned four.[22] John married the wealthy Catherine E. Peabody, whose inheritance included Roque Island off the coast of Maine and various small islands nearby; George married Helen Maria Read, "a beautiful girl"[23] but barely second-generation Boston society. John bought himself a twenty-acre estate in Brookline, and built a rambling summer home; George's outlying properties were in more distant and less fashionable Beverly, and included part of an old schoolhouse lot.[24] John had three married sons who could carry on the family name—and a daughter-in-law, Isabella Stewart Gardner, who would make it famous;[25] George's only son died young. John was formal in manner, but behind his businesslike mien was a merry twinkle;[26] George, according to his granddaughter Mary Curtis, was said to have been as "dull as dishwater." (Refer to Chart 7.)

George and John had been carefully brought up by their father Samuel Pickering Gardner. In a long and sober treatise entitled "Advice to my Sons," he had prescribed how his boys, then three and eight, should behave. "In order to fill your mind with *useful* knowledge, I would advise you to waste no time on works of little minds; under this head I include nearly all modern novels; most of the poetry that has been written within the last seventy-five years; and many of the periodical publications." Though he would allow them to read *The Arabian Nights Entertainment*, *Robinson Crusoe*, and *Gulliver's Travels*, his advice was to "confine yourselves almost entirely to works of acknowledged merit," among which he listed first of all the writings of such Greek worthies as Herodotus, Thucidides, Xenophon, Caesar, Livy, and Tacitus. Read the classics, he went on, but don't collect rare books: "Such things discover a mind more devoted to parade than to the true use of knowledge. Books that are rare, are generally so, because they are of but little value." He warned the boys against laziness: "Do not suffer your time to pass unemploy'd … be particularly careful that hours and half hours do not slip away in sauntering about or in trifling employments." Overall, he expected the highest standards of behavior: "to acquire … self-respect, you must abstain from all acts that forfeit it, such as lying, prevaricating, undue selfishness, meanness, swearing, idleness, every species of Buffoonery, or mimicry, censoriousness, a petulant temper, boasting and the like." Even their speech mattered: "Take great pains to acquire a distinct and graceful utterance, the first and most important step towards attaining of which is to speak deliberately." They must not switch jobs: "Adopt some regular course of business, and if you are industrious, economical, and (what I have no doubt you will be) honest, you will be rich and respectable."[27]

When they grew up, both brothers worked hard but it was John who shone. John graduated from Harvard in the class of 1821 whereas George ducked out after a year to go to work in a counting house. The brothers worked together for the next twenty years.[28] One imagines George's fingers smudged with accountant's ink and his brow furrowed with a trader's worries, John enjoying the fruits of their joint endeavors. In 1831, for example, George was in Boston rectifying the monthly accounts late into the evening while John was in Paris shipping home beautiful furniture.[29] When George went to Europe two years later, his was a trip aboard the brig *Pioneer* to learn the import-export business from the hold up, so to speak: "Sailed … for Cuba, there loaded her with sugar and coffee, proceeded to Genoa, sold the cargo, went in ballast to Palermo, put aboard in Sicily cargo, sent the vessel home, and remained in Europe to travel."[30] In 1836 John was back in Europe and George was writing that he was working late again, this time paying off about $80,000 in debts that John had left behind. George never seemed to mind: "I have to work hard," he wrote John in 1836, "to keep this ship afloat. Not that she leaks, but to make her sail well."[31] His letters were barely legible streams of particulars on prices, demand, and availability of brimstone, saltpeter, indigo, blue vitriol, copper, sugar, bourbon, lemons, oranges, and silks. He signed off in one: "Your children are both well. Give my love to Caty and Mrs. Endicott. Money at $1/2$ per month. G.G."

George did have a barely discernible touch of humor. He wrote John during his 1931 sojourn in Europe that "someone gave me two letters of introduction in Geneva to two gentlemen that have been dead for a number of years."[32] When John was abroad in 1836, George wrote him to disregard all rumors insinuating that he was a gay blade about town: "I have been contributing my house toward the amusement of the town of late, everyone says I

George Gardner, Libby Gardner's father

The two younger Gardner sisters, Clara, 6, and Libby, 8, in 1851

am engaged or likely to be. The first is not true and there is not the most distant prospect of the second." (In fact, George Gardner and Helen Maria Read were wed less than three years later.) But even to his daughter Libby, her father came off as less appealing than her uncle John. George Gardner, she wrote, was "not handsome, careful and sagacious, nervous and uncontrolled." John Lowell Gardner, by contrast, struck her as "lively in talk and witty, smart in business." At the end of the day, however, George Gardner was professionally well established. His appointments eventually included bank director, insurance company director, and president of several manufacturing companies,[33] and he was able to provide his family with a comfortable home and summers away.

By the late 1850s, George and Helen Gardner had produced a promising brood of four—Helen, Frank, Elizabeth, and Clara. (Refer to Chart 8.) We catch a glimpse of their daily lives from a journal Libby kept in her fourteenth year. Libby's delight in those years was playing tricks with—or on—her younger sister, Clara. Clara, for example, had thought some tooth wash that Libby had been given by the dentist was red ink and tried to write with it. Without a word Libby put some in her mouth, terrifying her younger sister, who thought it was laudanum. "Afterwards I told her," wrote Libby contritely. More typically, however, the girls were partners in crime, as on the occasion when they threw empty thread spools out the window, aiming at passersby below. It ended abruptly when, in Libby's account, "Clara's hit a very corpulent gentleman … [who] looked round and we poped in."

They were innocent days for the two girls, and full of laughter. A certain dreaded Aunt Johnson was one cause. This caretaker insisted on "scrubbing" them down in front of the fire after their baths. Clara was the first victim, and Libby couldn't help laughing, her sister looked so "woebegon." Libby insisted she wouldn't be subjected to the same treatment. She was wrong. After her bath, "Aunt Johnson rushed up to me with a coarse towel that she had been warming [and began rubbing] so—so hard that I thought she was going to scrub the skin off, and there was Clara all the time laughing away in bed."

Libby loved to doodle, illustrating the wry comments in her journal with vigorous stick figures. There is a picture of Aunt Johnson marching into a party, with a "horrid little old worm-eaten plaid shawl, the very worst one she could find in our drawers. I never felt so mortified in all my life." We see the substitute minister madly gesticulating at his congregation, a "thin … stupid" man "rolling round his

A passage from Libby Gardner's 1857-58 diary

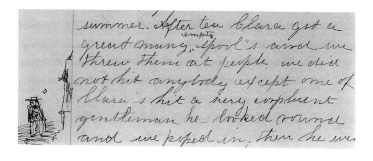

REARED *in a* GREENHOUSE

arms so funny sometimes he looked grave [sometimes] quite the reverse." And the "corpulent" passerby so nicely nailed with a thread spool.

Libby Gardner was a guileless teenager, still playing with dolls, raising bunnies, feeding nuts to the "cunning little squirells," and bending to adult rules. When she was warned not "to wade in the brook," she didn't. She was up with the sun, had usually walked around the Common with her friend Kitty before six o'clock breakfast, and was in bed before nine. The closest she came to losing her temper was when a corset sales-woman refused to measure her, sending her home for a second time with a corset that was still "too loose." "I felt as if I could bite her," Libby fumed.

In 1861, Libby's eighteenth year, catastrophe struck the fam-ily—her only brother, Frank (Francis Lowell), suddenly took ill with diphtheria and died. Libby was not as close to Frank as she was to Clara. When younger, Frank could be "grumpy," a tease (he read Clara's journal), and intimidating (he scolded Clara for getting ready for bed too slowly). But in 1861 he was a junior at Harvard, respected and well liked, and with a certain dreaminess about him: "sometimes, he just sat for half an hour and gazed at the trees," wrote one of his friends.[34] On February 5, he left home in perfect health for a house party at Cotuit on Cape Cod. Though shortly after his arrival he complained of a sore throat, no one thought anything of it. A diphthe-ria epidemic was raging, however, and suddenly, on the fifth day of his visit, February 10, the symptoms had become "alarming." Within a few hours, he was dead. His family hadn't even known he was ill.[35] It was unspeakably sad for them. The only son, Frank had been brought up with a "tender solicitude" that made him unusually "refined and thoughtful," wrote one of his friends. Oliver Wendell Holmes, the future Supreme Court justice who was a year ahead of him at Harvard, thought that Frank Gardner promised to be "among [society's] brightest acquisi-tions." The more one knew him, Holmes wrote, "the more everyone appreciated his consideration for others and tender, yet manly spirit."[36]

The Gardners spent the two summers after Frank's death in Lenox. This was still a simple, picturesque village, one that was attracting the flower of New England's intellectual life—Henry Wadsworth Longfellow, Herman Melville, Nathaniel Hawthorne, Henry Thoreau. In time, a wave of wealth would sweep over the Berkshires, replacing poetic thoughts with stately palaces. Looking back years later, Libby found the old days more to her taste.

"Francis Lowell Gardner, 19 years 8 months" (caption in Libby Amory's scrapbook under this picture of her brother)

> We boarded at Mrs. Flints.… The Curtis Hotel [later to become large and grand] was round the corner and a very small place. This was before rich people came and built swell mansions all over the place and had parties and receptions. Life was homelike and very quiet, driving in the afternoon was our gaiety and we made a few pleasant friends from New York who were boarding in the same cheap way. I should not like

the place now. In the mornings we would take our bath or work and walk up to the ledge on the Aspinwall place. It was very beautiful. I think now there is a large hotel there. We were steeped in the beauties of nature and life was happy.

It was just before the start of their second summer in Lenox that Ned Amory had caught Libby's eye. She had finished Miss Ware's School and a two-year course at Professor Agassiz's School, a secondary school for girls, and thought of herself as "grown up." Ned did not come to visit her in Lenox, so she was looking forward to the autumn and her coming-out.

Coming-out parties in those years were not the glitzy affairs that they were to become in the next century. Dancing itself had only recently become an accepted social activity, thanks to an Italian count, Lorenzo Papanti, who arrived in Boston in 1827 and initiated Boston's first families into the polka and the quadrille, and later the waltz. Among the few Bostonians who had befriended this Italian immigrant were Libby's Read grandparents; they would invite him and his young bride for supper in West Roxbury, and when Signora Papanti entertained them afterward with Italian songs, Mrs. Read would close the windows and shutters to prevent some passerby from overhearing songs that "were thought to be shocking." By the time of the Civil War, Papanti's Hall, with its floor on springs and its $1,200 chandelier, had become the preferred site of the Boston ball. Papanti never forgot his early patron. When James Read died in 1870, his grandson James Chadwick remembered the dancing master "with his curly brown wig askew and tears running down his aged, furrowed cheeks, [telling him] that Mr. Read had been the best friend he had had in this country."[37]

Ned Amory observed all the social niceties decreed by Papanti: "My Dear Miss Gardner," he wrote to her in 1863, "Will you give me the german [an intricate dance, marked by frequent changes of partners] at the last of the six dancing classes? Hoping to be fortunate in finding you disengaged. I am, Very Truly Yrs. C. W. Amory." Libby kept the treasured invitation, tucking it into an envelope and affixing a picture of her handsome young Harvard senior on the page opposite. Above his note she wrote, "This was most thrilling to me!"

She had a delightful time during her coming-out year (the winter of 1862–63), for Ned was at all the dances. These took place once a week in Papanti's Hall, and, as Libby recollected, they dressed in "cheap and simple clothes and danced the german not quite stretching round the hall. It was a pretty sight and we had so much dancing of the waltz that girls and boys danced it well and lightly. It was great fun."[38]

— • —

The Civil War had been raging for a year by the time the 1862–63 season was under way; its repercussions must have curbed the style of the debutante parties. It was a "cruel war," Libby wrote, but the cause was noble. People thought "the war could not last long," and "the young men [were] all volunteering and the women cheering them on."[39] For her part, Libby "despised" the few who stayed out. She listed three she particularly scorned: Theodore Chase, Charley Gibson, and Robert Winthrop. Perhaps her later skepticism regarding Winthrop men sprang in part from her memories of this same Robert C. Winthrop, Jr., the son of her "Uncle Winthrope," as she referred to him in her teenage diary. (Refer to Chart 11.) A Harvard College and Law School graduate, Robert had chosen to wait out the war visiting European watering spots. His excuse, he wrote later, was his "liability to water on the knee." Even had this not been the case, the service would have been "distasteful" to him because he had friends and relatives in the South and, furthermore, he thought that the war was the Republicans' fault.[40]

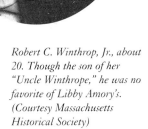

Robert C. Winthrop, Jr., about 20. Though the son of her "Uncle Winthrope," he was no favorite of Libby Amory's. (Courtesy Massachusetts Historical Society)

The war was also putting a damper on life at Harvard, from which Ned was slated to graduate in the spring of 1863. In those years the "sole great college event of the year" was the annual Harvard-Yale boat races, and Ned, who had grown up rowing on the Charles River, had helped expand the race to the class level. Once the war began, however, he called a halt to the competition.[41]

By the time Ned graduated, the war was into its third year and Harvard boys were no longer joining up. How much more noble, Libby thought, to go to war at that time rather than earlier when everyone thought it would be a quick, easy fight.[42] Pulling strings was generally how a young man stayed out. But not Ned Amory. He wrote his first cousin, Lieutenant Colonel Caspar Crowninshield, regiment commander of the Second Massachusetts Cavalry, asking his intercession to get him in. Reluctantly, Crowninshield agreed to request the governor to give his cousin a commission. But in his opinion, as he wrote Ned's mother, Ned would do better to "travel in Europe for a year or so, and see a little of the world, then come home, go into some kind of business, marry and become one of the 'solid men of Boston.' "

"Harvard freshman crew 1860. Beat Yale badly — it was the first time the freshman rowed against Yale — Ned Amory far right" (caption in Libby Amory's scrapbook)

Ned Amory's commission as second lieutenant in the Second Massachusetts Cavalry was granted on April 9, 1864, less than a year after he graduated. Later that month, on the 24th, he reported for duty. "He went to the war," wrote Libby later. "I liked him all the more—but suffered much." She had reason to worry. More than one out of every ten Harvard students who entered the military would die in the Civil War.[43] Moreover, Ned had begun his service on the eve of the bloodiest fighting. During the six weeks between May 4 and June 18, 1864, the North would lose 65,000 men—dead, wounded, or missing—as General Grant forced General Lee south, trying again and again to push around the Confederate army's right flank to capture Richmond and end the war.[44] Luckily, Ned Amory and his regiment were north of the main field of

battle, stationed near Falls Church, Virginia, with the mission of guarding Washington, D.C., about fifteen miles to the east. Ned had seen combat twice, at Rectortown on April 30 and at Difficult Run on May 24. In June, he fell ill with "malarial infection of the bowels."[45]

Bed-ridden for a month, he was released from the hospital just in time for the Fourth of July, 1864. His unit spent the day playing sports and racing their horses. But that afternoon an alert came: an enemy attack was feared through the Blue Ridge Mountains. Major William Hathaway Forbes, Amory's immediate commander, headed west with 150 men to scout the enemy's whereabouts.

The Yankees rode into an area crawling with the feared guerrillas of the infamous Colonel John Singleton Mosby. Mosby's Partisan Raiders had been attacking Union parties, many of them small and defenseless, so ferociously and successfully that whole counties in northern Virginia had become known as Mosby's Confederacy.[46] On July 6, in another lopsided attack, the raiders struck again. Forbes' small party was in an open field close to where Dulles Airport stands today when Mosby's larger forces swept down. Wrote one of the Mosby troops: "We wheeled and sent up a blood-curdling yell which was so much a part of our tactics…. We swept into their line like a hurricane, each man with a drawn six-shooter." Forbes' men "could not stand the rain of pistol-balls," and half were soon "a mass of struggling, cursing maniacs, each striving to slay his antagonist." Major Forbes made a heroic figure: he "occupied the centre of the action, standing in his stirrups, with sabre drawn fighting desperately…. A bullet ripped into Forbes' horse and he went down under the dying animal, pinned helplessly, and had to surrender." Less majestic was the fall of Ned Amory, who had turned to face the foe. "His horse became unmanageable and dashed against the branches of a tree knocking off his glasses and then he could not distinguish friend from foe and was captured."[47]

Thanks to the telegraph—by 1861, Samuel Morse's invention had swept the country—Ned Amory's family knew of his capture less than forty-eight hours after it happened. On July 7, Forbes sent a note of his and Ned's captivity to Caspar Crowninshield, and on the eighth, Crowninshield telegrammed Ned's father about his son (apparently, family channels were still more efficient than official ones). Colonel Crowninshield followed up with a letter seeking to reassure the father that his son would be all right:

> Ned was taken prisoner and was not wounded…. [He] will be treated well by Mosby…. Major Forbes will be with him and they will be a comfort and assistance to each other. I shall send John, Ned's servant, home on Monday, and his trunk and things by express to 41 Beacon.

This news was cold comfort to the Amorys, who had heard many accounts of the starvation, filth, and exposure Northerners suffered in Southern prisons. Prisoner exchanges had ended a year earlier, in mid-1863, and from then on the makeshift encampments began filling with Union captives. Word was soon trickling north of the appalling conditions. By December 1863 many Northern papers were publishing accounts of the "skeletons ... who had once worn the Federal Uniform."[48]

The story of Amory's ordeal was told in an account written by his unit's chaplain, Reverend Charles A. Humphrey. Ned later annotated the narrative with a dismissive "This all seems much exaggerated to me." Libby annotated his comment with one of her own: "Ned *always* thinks things are exaggerated."

Overblown or not, the story would become the central fact of her husband's life. "He was very ill all the hot weeks in Charleston prison—and *never* well afterwards—Chronic diarrhea wasted his health—but he did all he could, showing great energy—wonderful courage, and patience," she wrote below Crowninshield's reassuring letter. With her daughter Dorothy, Libby painstakingly copied in seventy-five longhand pages the entirety of Humphrey's narrative. At age seventy-eight she turned the document over to her granddaughter Dorothy, my mother, who took measures to preserve it further, arranging for copies to be typed up for me and my siblings. And so we have today the complete story of Ned Amory's captivity.

Humphrey recounts that from July 9 to 12, Ned's unit endured a march south to the Orange Court House, followed by a trip by boxcar to Lynchburg, Virginia.

> We started without breakfast at half past three and got nothing to eat till we reached Orange Court House at noon.... [where] we were fed on cold corn cake and uncooked pork, and then put into box cars and transported to Gordonsville. These cars had been used for carrying cattle and had not been cleaned, nor would the guards let us clean them; and at night we were herded to-gether in a cattle yard, and had to sleep upon the ground noisome with filth.

From July 12 to 17 they were in Lynchburg. Humphrey made special note of the plight of Lieutenant Amory, writing that he had begun "to show signs of failing strength." "His trouble was aggravated by the coarse and unpalatable food," wrote Humphrey. "Our daily ration was one corn cake baked as hard as a stone and weighing about half a pound, with this was frequently served one third of a pound of pork, which I could never eat, for it was always rusty and usually rotten." The chaplain thought that Amory needed white bread rather than the "irritating" corn meal, and to pay for it he traded his $9 boots for $250, enough—even in the inflated Confederacy currency of the day—to enable Ned to eat safely for a while, at least.

Conditions in Lynchburg got worse. The prisoners were put in the low-ceilinged attic of a small building. There was

> a tub of filth at the other end of the room. We begged to be allowed to remove this nuisance, but the guard was under order not to permit it.... The next day ... forty tattered and dirty deserters from the rebel army, and a score of felons condemned and awaiting sentence, were crowded in with us.... Headache and lassitude and prisoners' scourge—diarrhoea—so reduced our vitality that all appetite was gone and the stomach revolted from food. The second night—with the added number of prisoners—there was not room for all of us to stretch upon the floor to sleep.

Then it was on to Macon, Georgia, an eight-day journey.

> We were packed in box cars, fifty or more in each, and each man given a ration of three pieces of hard bread.... We were so crowded that we could not all lie down at once....
>   In Danville, the ... cow beans fed to us in half cooked soup were even more to be dreaded than the starvation rations of corn meal.... The beans ... being tough and indigestible made us all sick.... [The guards started randomly shooting prisoners.]
>   [In Augusta] we encamped in an open field for ten hours. Here some of us clubbed to-gether and invested in a watermelon, but we were so weak and exhausted that it made us all sick.

In August, after a short stay at the Macon stockade, the unit's officers were transferred to Camp Oglethorpe, also in Macon.

> We were herded in a large pen with about 1,600 other officers surrounded by a strong stockade fifteen feet high.... The only water for washing and drinking was furnished by a small and rather stagnant brook running through the enclosure, and of course it received all the drainage from the prison pen.... [We were] exposed each day to the festering rays of the sun.... In this exhausting life men soon became living skeletons and the monotony of frequent death was never relieved.

Ned's condition continued to deteriorate. Humphrey did what little he could to ease his comrade's discomfort. On July 29, "I washed two handkerchiefs, two pairs of drawers and one shirt for Major Forbes and Lieutenant Amory." On August 1, "Lieutenant Amory is much reduced by chronic diarrhea, and Forbes and I have to cook for him and nurse him."

By mid-August the group had been moved again, this time to Charleston, under the fire of Union guns. Humphrey continued to worry about his sick companion. On August 16 he wrote, "Mr. Amory is worse today, and the guards charge fifty cents a quart to bring water to us from a pump just outside."

Humphrey's account of his own captivity ends as of September 2, when he was released. Among his first acts as a free man was to try to arrange with the commissioner of exchange for Ned's release. His intercession was successful: Amory left prison on October 1, 1864. It was "in time to save his life," wrote Humphrey, "though with a broken constitution that can never be made whole." "Too true!" wrote Libby beside this passage, as she came to the end of the long job of copying the narrative.

— • —

Ned Amory came home to Boston by train. His father and sister were at the station to meet him. Although his father had done what he could to send notes, money, and a box containing a few "necessaries" in the way of food and clothing,[49] there had been very little communication between Ned and his family during his three months in captivity. Ned had answered his mother's few anguished notes—"you are never absent from your poor Mother's heart"—cheerfully, with no mention of his health. Even though the family had been warned, they didn't recognize the gaunt figure who emerged from the train. He looked like "someone in the last stages of consumption, having a weak hacking cough and almost skeleton-like emaciation."[50]

By December, though he had gained weight, Ned was still weak and his friends and family were urging him to stay home, to let victory come without him. But Ned wanted to be there for the finish; no doubt a note from Caspar Crowninshield, who had just been over to Loudon county "to see your friend Mosby," whetted his appetite for a return visit to the front. "He was not at home," wrote Crowninshield to Ned of his erstwhile captor. "But we saw some of his family and liked them so much that we brought them back with us. I was very sorry not to see Mosby. I should like to pay him what I owe him."

With his doctor's permission, Ned Amory returned to the war in January 1865. The glory days for the North were not long in coming. Victory was already inevitable, clinched by the Union's capture of Atlanta on August 31 and the destruction of General Early's army in the Shenandoah Valley in mid-October.[51] But as 1865 dawned, no one knew how long it would take, or who would be killed. War was a perilous business, and when Ned went back to his regiment Libby's fears returned. "Among the painful remembrances of those days," she wrote later, "is the ever-present weight of the heart. I went about with the half-choking sense of grief I dared not think of—like one who is dragging herself to the ordinary labors of life from some terrible and recent bereavement."

Ned had barely survived his first exposure to the front. His second assignment had its hazards as well, though Ned did his best to downplay them. He was posted in the cold and wintry snows of the Shenandoah Valley with General Philip Sheridan, the feisty cavalryman who was chafing that he and his two crack cavalry units were so far removed from the action. Ned made light of the tedium. He wrote humorously to his mother about hapless days spent building log huts. His own shack, he wrote, "has been a complete failure.... I have a good one now ... except that the chimney smokes so that I have to leave, whenever a fire is lighted. I shall tear only the chimney down this time." In another letter, he reassured her that "everything is lovely. I am well and getting so stout that I'm almost afraid to take my clothes off at night for fear that I should not be able to get into them in the morning."

When he wrote Libby, he transformed the homemade hut into his "spacious mansion of mud and logs." His letters to Libby centered not on his discomforts, but on their friends, on her, and on his ardent hopes for their future together. He had a charming way with words, a knack for making poetry out of the simple comings and goings of their friends. He had learned that a certain Frank Loring was leaving Boston. "How friends get scattered," he mused, "and little sets get broken up, like coffee cups, never to be repaired, for although the pieces come together again, they never join as they were before." His attachment to Libby, he hoped, should never be shattered like that.

Every thought of home ... is connected with thoughts of you.... I am willing to go through all that human nature can endure, if I may live to see that day [the day of victory], but even then you will control my happiness, you will have it in your power to say whether I shall be happy or miserable. I shall hope until I am forbidden to hope any longer.[52]

In late February, General Sheridan was ordered, at last, to head south and finish off what was left of General Early's once formidable army. The march from Winchester, Virginia, to the little town of White House, east of Richmond, took three weeks. "I will tell you of my pleasure trip with Phil Sheridan," Ned later wrote to Libby. "It is a short story. We marched and we marched. There were no exciting times." Historical accounts agree: the main excitement of the trek was the demolition of the pitiful remains of General Early's fighting force at Waynesboro. Otherwise, the ten thousand Union soldiers just marched: thirty-mile marches the first two days, then shorter marches and a short skirmish with Early, reaching their destination on March 19.[53]

The day after, Ned wrote his mother in droll vein. Assuming she probably knew more from the papers than he about their doings, he decided instead to report about himself: "To begin with, I am horrid dirty. I am very well and sunburned red as a beet. My boots have the legs burned off. Also a large hole burned in my pants and a tear in my coat, which I have neatly sewed up." His plans for the day: to cool off and clean up with a swim in the Pamunkey River.

Over the next weeks a series of events would unfold that, for sheer drama, have seldom been matched in American history. On March 23 President Lincoln would leave Washington and sail on the *River Queen* down to City Point, the base of the Army of the Potomac, where he would meet with Generals Grant and Sherman to lay plans for an attack that would at last end the terrible war. It came on April 1 and 2. The remains of Lee's straggling forces fled, first from Five Forks, then from Petersburg—the last rebel stronghold—and finally from the Union capital, Richmond.

Ned Amory was in City Point when Lincoln was there, in Petersburg when victory came. But though history was breaking all around, his letters were as nonchalant as ever, perhaps by natural inclination, perhaps because he remained on the fringes of the fray, perhaps because he didn't dare hope for the end. This is how he summed up events in a letter to his mother: "The other day, Grant, Sherman, Sheridan and A. Lincoln met together at City Point. Something ought to come of that. The next day, Grant went to the front. Sherman went somewhere, and Sheridan started off again. I don't know where A. Lincoln went, but that don't matter, so long as his son Robert Todd, Capt on Grant's staff, went to the front, I suppose to see that Richmond was properly taken."[54]

He found City Point "the stupidest of all stupid places." Half his regiment's horses had been "used up by the big raid" (presumably on Fort Stedman, March 24–25) and he had to hang around the supply depots with Sheridan's oxymoronic Dismounted Cavalry listening to the nearby fighting at Five Forks and Petersburg.

Sometimes, he wrote his mother, when the battling got "very heavy, we are all turned out and marched to some port to hold it in case of disaster, of course a humbug, for we have no more disasters, and if we did, I'm afraid dismounted cavalry couldn't stop it." Horses were eventually found for him and his fellow soldiers, but they were held in reserve with "nothing to do, but watch and listen to the fighting." It was not until the morning after "the rebs" evacuated Petersburg and Richmond that Ned and his remounted friends were allowed to march "triumphantly" into Petersburg. No sooner was he there than he was assigned to "a soft place," as General Wilcox's escort and bodyguard, with no duty other than to "ride around the country and see that nothing is coming."

With Lee's surrender, Ned abandoned his wry understatement. "I almost fear sometimes that I shall wake up and find that I've been dreaming, it is too good to be true," he wrote Libby. After the horrible news of Lincoln's assassination—"It was a diabolical act," he wrote his mother—Ned finally dared think of home. He wrote Libby, "I want to come home terribly. I grudge every day and feel as if I were being imposed upon, being kept here. Camp life is the slowest most monotonous life possible."

Another three months of service lay ahead of him. In April he was sent south with other troops to force diehard General Joseph E. Johnston to surrender. The ten-day trip was "like a picnic, a beautiful thickly wooded country, foliage all out, perfect weather, no hard marches." But he was shocked at the way Sheridan's cavalry had laid waste to the land: "The garden of Eden would become a desert if [such troops] should be sent there.… The suffering, caused by subsisting on the country, is terrible. The inhabitants are left to starve." With his usual luck, Ned discovered, upon his arrival, that General Johnston had just surrendered. In May, he was sent to Washington, where, Libby wrote later, he "got a pass to go into the city to get a bath" and where he marched in the immense review of the victorious armed forces.

Modest Ned even allowed himself a touch of personal pride. "I often congratulate myself," he wrote Libby, "that I did not follow the example and advice of most of my classmates and friends, and let this war come to a close, without taking some part, however small, in it. My part has been small, but still I can feel a sort of right to claim a share of the glory; the humblest soldier in the army has a right to feel proud now."

— • —

The way he came home was just like Ned. He had written his family not to expect him until August 1, but he was mustered out early, on July 7, and arrived unexpectedly and unannounced at the family home in Longwood a week later, on July 14. His mother wrote to his sister Harriet how surprised she was. "To think of our old Ned walking in so quietly, and looking through the window … without our having an idea of his coming."

Though his health had held up during the war, it now became frighteningly fragile. He lost twenty pounds in three weeks, and by August 1, Mrs. Amory wrote Harriet, he weighed no more than she did. Two weeks later she was even more worried: "I found Ned stretched on the sofa covered up in a cloak, with head and hands very feverish and hot—and he shivering.… A new change in the disease had taken place, and he now has intermittent chills and fevers." He was a pathetic figure. "Poor Ned seems no better, takes a book, wanders about, lies on the sofa, and in the afternoon, to change the scene, and get some air, has twice driven out, in the slow, lumbering carriage with me, utterly unable to drive himself."

The doctors recommended a long trip to Europe to restore his health, and so he left home—and Libby—for nearly a year, going from Naples to Norway and Sweden. When he returned, if not the picture of health, he was at least fit enough to resume his life, including his courtship of Libby Gardner. She accepted his hand at last, somewhat to the surprise of Ned's bachelor friend J. C. Warren. "Your first letter was so gloomy," he wrote Ned in March 1867 from Vienna, "that I hardly dared to hope that Fortune, or rather Miss Libby, would turn so soon in your favor."

The only record we have of Ned and Libby during their engagement is on a loose sheet of paper written by my mother and tucked into one of her diaries. Libby and Ned were in Nahant, visiting with the parents of senator-to-be Henry Cabot Lodge (then seventeen) when who should appear but novelist-to-be Henry James (he and Libby were both twenty-four). The budding writer took a great interest in the young couple, in part because of Ned's war service but more because of something Libby did. She was standing in the ocean when she heard a "piercing yell" from a French girl a little farther out. After reaching her with "a stroke or two," she helped the girl to shore. Libby, who had "thought nothing of it," was mortified when the girl brought her a basket of flowers and showered her with profuse thanks. Worse still, the "fuss" she so "hated" had taken place "in Henry James' hearing."

As for the wedding, which took place on October 23, 1867, "everyone says [it] went off finely," and the bride looked beautiful, Libby's father wrote her afterward. The only blemish was that some spoilsport thought "the host" should have gotten "tight"—something that "dull as dishwater" George Gardner apparently refrained from doing.

It is only through these outsiders that we know anything of the courtship and wedding of Libby Gardner and Ned Amory. What went on between them during those months will remain forever private. But it's not hard to divine. The two seemed so well suited to one another—they shared a wry sense of humor and modest tastes. He was a bit gentler, more poetic; she had the more ardent spirit and vigorous common sense. But unlike others of their set, who, as he wrote, had "scattered" like coffee cups and saucers "never to be repaired," the two of them had been brought closer by the travails of war. Ignited before its onset, their bond would in the end burn merry for forty-seven years of marriage.

A Winthrop and Taylor Union

chapter THREE

Kate Winthrop's house in New York City

On April 3, 1865—that anxiously awaited day when Richmond finally fell to the army of General Ulysses S. Grant—Robert Winthrop of New York City had much to be thankful for. He was thirty-two years old, had been married five years to Kate Wilson Taylor,[1] daughter of one of New York's most respected merchant-businessmen, Moses Taylor, and was the father of two little boys—Robert Dudley, almost four, and Grenville, an infant of two months. The family was settled at 118 Fifth Avenue, in a house owned by his father-in-law and only two doors away from 122 Fifth Avenue where the Taylors lived.[2] The Winthrop house was at the corner of 20th Street, a comfortable brick dwelling that was perfect for their family.

Starting their family had brought heartbreak twice. Two infant children had died—a daughter, Kate Taylor Winthrop, in 1860, and a son, Grenville M. Winthrop, named after Robert's younger brother, in 1863.[3] Now, however, the couple had two hale and hearty sons and no reason not to hope for more children.

Professionally, Robert Winthrop had made an equally promising start. He had gone to work young, with the New York branch of the distinguished Glasgow banking firm of J. & A. Dennistoun Wood, one of the principal financiers of the country's cotton and sugar trade during the first half of the century.[4] In 1859, the year of his marriage, he moved on to become a partner in the banking firm of Read, Drexel.[5] Robert's new partnership with Philadelphia banker Anthony J. Drexel signaled his entrance into the company of America's high-powered money men. In 1862, at twenty-eight, Robert Winthrop was admitted to the New York Stock Exchange. In 1863,

REARED *in a* GREENHOUSE

with the retirement of W. G. Read, he and Drexel remained the sole partners of Drexel, Winthrop, with Drexel the senior and Winthrop the junior partner.[6]

Drexel, Winthrop had its offices in the heart of Wall Street, the City Bank building where Robert Winthrop's father-in-law held sway as president of the bank and controller of a far-flung empire of business concerns. Right across the street was the Merchants Exchange, a domed-top granite mass where the New York Stock Exchange held its meetings and pulled the strings of the nation's business. If the South had been devastated during the four years of war, New York had suffered little. Balls and receptions had gone right on and business had never been better.[7]

On August 15, 1862, his brother Frederic, a captain with the Army of the Potomac, had written Robert, summing up his situation nicely.

> You must be settled very pleasantly by this time in your new home. You are a damned lucky dog to get such a woman as Kate is: and that enormous baby of yours [Dudley], how is it! It's evidently a big thing. Kiss them both for me and in particular remember me to Kate.

— • —

It's hard to know whether, by "such a woman," brother Frederic was referring to Kate or her purse. Kate Wilson Taylor was a fine-looking young woman—not pretty exactly, but with a solid mien. She and her brothers and sisters had had a worthy upbringing. Religion came first: both her parents, Catherine and Moses Taylor, were devout Presbyterians. Next to God came work. As Henry Clews, noted diarist of Wall Street, wrote of him later, Moses Taylor "had no social aspirations and no interest in anything but business. It was his idol. Few men have been harder workers from their early life up to their last days."[8] Third in the trinity of Taylor values was education: Moses Taylor made sure his children were better schooled than he—he had gone to work at fifteen—and arranged for his three daughters to have private tutors plus plenty of good reading material at home. It was a creed that left little room for foolishness or fun. (Refer to Chart 4.)

On the eve of her marriage Kate appeared to be not only sober, but also vulnerable, even fearful. In her "inspirational" notebook appears a "Catechism for the Engaged," dated six months before her wedding. In a worried plea, the young woman of the poem implores: "Before I trust my fate to thee or place my hand in thine ... [promise me that you have no] regret, [that nothing else] holds thy spirit yet.... [And if you have other interests], speak now, lest at some future day, my whole life wither and decay." Infidelity wasn't her only fear. She saved poems that portrayed husbands as uncontrolled louts and their wives as long-suffering victims. "A man may be ill-tempered ... or swear and behave like a brute/ but an ill-tempered quarrelsome woman is a

Kate W. Taylor, about the time of her marriage (Robert Winthrop Kean's Fourscore Years, *courtesy Hamilton Fish Kean II)*

nuisance on earth," went one. Another allowed as how a woman's only recourse was to stoically endure her husband's ugly ways: "If a man falls into a violent passion, and calls me all manner of names/ The first word shuts my ears and I hear no more."

It is highly unlikely that Kate had to endure either a playboy or a boor in her husband Robert. Everything points rather to his having been "a quiet, gentle soul."[9] The poems she clipped on the loss of a child, however, reflect a genuine sorrow. Children died frequently during the mid-nineteenth century; her own losses were the common burden of many a young bride, as this poem in her collection attests:

> *I think how sad my heart would be to put them out of sight*
> *For in a trunk upstairs, I've laid two socks of white and blue …*
> *If called to put those boots away*
> *Oh, God, what should I do?*
> *I mourn, that there are not tonight*
> *Three pairs instead of two.*

Above all, Kate clipped or copied pious bromides on how to avoid sin and attain salvation. "Into thy hands my God, I gladly fall/ Resigning there my life, my will, my *All*," pledges one. Kate Winthrop, like many women of her day, was constantly looking to God to help her mend her ways—though her way was already what seems to us today preternaturally straight and narrow.

For Robert, Kate's piety would not have seemed excessive. His mother, Georgiana Maria Winthrop, was at least as godly as her daughter-in-law Kate. When Robert's younger brother Grenville got married, she hastened to advise him as to his spiritual life: "I wish my darling child you would commence at once, if you have not already, to ask a blessing before and after every meal … and also dear Grenville, at night begin at first if only a few words to read in your Bible a prayer and so by degrees you will find it one of your chief comforts of life."

With regard to her purse, Kate's was already sizable at the time of her marriage. Family lore has it that she set Robert Winthrop up in business, and it may have been she who provided the $3,000 that enabled him to buy his seat on the Stock Exchange in 1862. The Taylors, however, hadn't always been so wealthy. Kate's great-grandfather, the first Moses Taylor, had emigrated from England to New York City in 1736 and had been a humble "Brass and Copper kettles" salesman on Maiden Lane.[10] His son, Jacob Bloom Taylor, had started out as a cabinet maker, but a lucky break that made him business agent for the legendary John Jacob Astor would transform his family's life. By the early 1830s, after his son Moses had married Catherine Wilson and wanted to strike out on his own, Jacob Taylor could lend him enough money—$35,000—to launch his own business career.[11]

It took only seven years for Moses Taylor to rise from a novice "commission agent" to one of New York's leading merchants. His trading company, Moses Taylor and Company, cornered a major chunk of the market for America's leading imported food staple, sugar, and between 1834 and 1838, Taylor had increased his net worth

REARED *in a* GREENHOUSE

from $86,000 to $200,000.[12] In 1837 he was enlisted as a director of City Bank. The bank was then small, with only 3.1 percent of the total assets shared among the city's twenty-three banks. But John Jacob Astor, by then New York's richest man and one of the bank's customers, helped keep it afloat during the 1837 financial panic. For years afterward, people believed that Taylor's connection with Astor had "brought gold into his coffers."[13] Astor may have helped. But more crucial was Moses Taylor's own acumen and vision.

As Kate grew up, Moses proved the value of sagacity and creativity. By 1859 he had assembled a personal empire of vibrant new enterprises—utilities, mining, communications, and most important, railroads. His desk at City Bank, of which he became president in 1856, became the command center: from here he ran his various concerns, monitoring their performance, reviewing their capital expenditure programs, and deciding how they would be financed.[14]

The Civil War confirmed Moses Taylor's stature as a pillar of New York's financial community. When the federal government needed a huge infusion of cash to arm, feed, and clothe the Union troops, Taylor became spokesman for the nation's bankers, agreeing to help market the whopping $150 million in government bonds that Washington had issued. In 1864 President Lincoln had offered Taylor the portfolio of sub-treasurer of the United States, second only to the secretary of the treasury in rank. Secretary of the Treasury William P. Fessenden had been so eager to bring this highly regarded and influential New York Democrat into the administration that he appointed Taylor without his consent. Taylor, however, declined, perhaps preferring the independence of his powerful position in the private sector.[15]

Fifteen years earlier, when Kate was a little girl, the Taylors had begun to acquire some of the social trappings to which their lofty financial station entitled them. They moved to stylish Fifth Avenue, where her father bought a lot and built a house. They sampled resort life at Newport, a far tonier vacation spot than the New Jersey shore, where they had summered up till then. They also left the Presbyterian church and bought a pew at the more fashionable St. George's Episcopal Church.

Though this all signaled they were now "in society," the Taylors remained aloof from it. The house at 122 Fifth Avenue was "comfortable and even fashionable [but] … in no way ostentatious."[16] In social Newport the women spent their time sitting on the porch, taking walks or carriage rides, sewing, and reading. Finally, the family returned to New Jersey, whose bucolic quiet they preferred. Kate's mother "never cared for society," as her obituary would put it, perhaps because her beginnings were extremely modest. She was a second-generation immigrant, the daughter of a Scot who had earned his living as a baker and a grocer.[17]

In October 1860 the Taylors made an exception to their worthy ways. Who could resist? The Prince of Wales—the future King Edward VII—was coming to New York. Moses had been asked to serve on the invitation committee and to sail out to meet the English celebrity. The Taylors would sit in an upstairs box to watch the gala ball at the Academy of Music. One hopes that is where they were seated when the evening reached its climax. As social chronicler and climber Ward McAllister

Moses Taylor as a young man (Robert Winthrop Kean's Fourscore Years, *courtesy Hamilton Fish Kean II)*

described it, there was such a press of dancers that, at the height of the festivities, the floor collapsed, "dropping the guests gently to the cellar below and leaving the Prince … on the edge of the precipice." The damage was soon repaired, but crowd control remained a problem. Everyone wanted a glimpse of the royal party supping in a private room at an enormous horseshoe table. John Jacob Astor and other prominent citizens were stationed at the doors to make sure the gawking crowd was admitted in small stages.[18]

— • —

The Taylors had beat the Winthrops to New York by some fifty years. But when the Winthrops finally arrived, just after the Revolution, they did so in force. By 1797 three Winthrop brothers were merchants on Wall Street: Francis Bayard, Robert's grandfather, at 29 Wall Street, Benjamin at 43, and William at 52. They had arrived just as New York was emerging from the effects of the Revolution. Eight years of occupation and the flight afterward of thousands of terrified Tories had left the place with only ten thousand residents, though it would spring right back, more than tripling to its prerevolutionary size by the end of the decade.[19] The Winthrop brothers found a small town of low wooden houses, businesses, and churches lined randomly along the waterfront—a charming spot, with rolling hills, meandering streams, and pleasant trees, cattle yards beyond, and then the country seats of the great New York families, charming farms or "bouweries."[20]

John Still Winthrop, 1720-76, progenitor of all modern-day Winthrops (courtesy Harvard University Portrait Collection, gift of Robert Winthrop, representing the Winthrop family, to Harvard University, 1964)

The Revolution changed the course of American history, not only politically but economically, for with it began the huge surge of wealth, business, and trade that would mark the nineteenth century. The Revolution also marked the turning point of Winthrop family history, as their priorities changed from rendering public service to replenishing private coffers. The first governor John, though he left England a prosperous man, had spent heavily to support his colonial responsibilities. By 1640 his private affairs badly neglected, he was practically bankrupt.[21] At his death his estate was smaller than the one he had inherited.[22] The governor's son, John, Jr., would spend much of his life in debt. One of his sons, Fitz-John, left debts unpaid, while the other, Wait Still, borrowed money much of his life and died intestate.[23] Wait Still's son John was so slow in arranging to pay off his father's debts that he was arrested and required to produce bail of £4,000 as protection for one of his guarantors.[24] He finally simply repaired to England, leaving his debts, his wife, and his children to fend for themselves. (Refer to Chart 1.)

One of those children, John Still (1720–76), did much to bring order to the family finances. His landholdings were impressive, including all of Fisher's Island off the Connecticut coast at the entrance of Long Island Sound,[25] over three thousand acres of land surrounding a mine in Sturbridge, Massachusetts,[26] and a seven-hundred-acre farm in Groton.[27] Land was a headache, and not as lucrative as it might be, but the income had been sufficient to enable John Still to build "the best [house]"[28] in New London, on a rise with a view of Winthrop's Cove, down the Thames River to Fisher's Island Sound.[29] But he had twelve children, and if his sons wanted to continue living in this agreeable style, they would have to strike out on their own.

It was his children, the enterprising sixth generation of Winthrops in America, and particularly the three in New York, who paved the way for a new type of Winthrop—still public-spirited but more business-minded, more interested in making money than their forefathers. All of John Still's sons left the backwater of New London to seek their fortunes elsewhere. While Francis Bayard, William, Benjamin, and John (who died young) headed for New York City, Joseph went to Charleston and Thomas Lindall returned to Boston.[30] (Refer to Chart 2.) Robert headed for England[31]—his departure for the motherland seemingly all there

Francis Bayard Winthrop, 1754-1817, Frederic Winthrop's great-grandfather (portrait by John Trumbull, courtesy Harvard University Portrait Collection, gift of Robert Winthrop, representing the Winthrop family, to Harvard University, 1964)

is to present-day rumblings that Winthrops had Loyalist sympathies during the Revolution.[32] Even the daughters, all but one, left New London, most profitably Ann, who like her brother Thomas Lindall went to Boston. There she married David Sears, one of the city's great merchants and Ned Amory's great-grandfather.

All did well and Francis Bayard "prospered exceedingly."[33] His was one of the names affixed to the 1792 Tontine Coffee House agreement,[34] the document that marked the birth of the New York Stock Exchange.[35] In 1797 he became a director of the New York branch of the nation's new federal banking system.[36] Sometime during this period, Francis Bayard also bought an out-of-town estate, Turtle Bay Farm, on the east side of Manhattan near what is today 46th Street.[37] This placed him squarely in the company of established old families like the Stuyvesants, Bayards, Beekmans, Roosevelts, de Lanceys, and de Peysters who owned retreats just outside the city limits.

None of Francis Bayard's four sons seems to have carved an equally prestigious spot for himself in the city's life. Two left town (Francis Bayard moving to quieter New Haven, William Henry returning to New London and the family property at Fisher's Island), while the others, John Still and Robert's father Thomas Charles, remained in New York as merchants.[38] But though the family had arrived in town with more substantial assets than the Taylors, by the 1840s they were left behind in the gold dust stirred up by young Moses.

Guessing how much people were worth had become a favorite New York pastime. *The Wealthiest Citizens of New York*[39] (doubtless the prototype for Boston's later *Catalogue of the Richest Men of Massachusetts*) listed everyone who had assets of $100,000 or more. While Taylor handily gained admission, only two Winthrops

A WINTHROP AND TAYLOR UNION

would be granted entrance, and these by the skin of their teeth and the purse strings of women. Henry Rogers Winthrop, Francis Bayard's grandson and John Still's son, made it in 1844 "in expectation of inheriting this amount by his marriage to Miss Hicks, a granddaughter of the late Thomas Buchanan."[40] Benjamin R. Winthrop, son of Francis Bayard's brother Benjamin, was admitted in 1854, this time thanks to the advantageous marriage of his father to Judith Stuyvesant.[41]

Left out entirely was Robert's father, Thomas Charles. He had married suitably enough, to Georgiana Maria Kane, from yet another prominent New York merchant family,[42] and in time he became "an established commission merchant." Otherwise, all that seems to be known of Thomas Charles was that he moved a lot (he had five business addresses and five home addresses[43]) and had a lot of children (six boys and two girls). Whatever fortune Thomas Charles might have accumulated would have faded fast as it was divided among his many progeny.

With his marriage to Kate Taylor, Robert was following in the footsteps of his great uncle Benjamin and his cousin Henry Rogers, who had also married money. But there was a difference. The first two had hitched their wagons to old names, whereas Robert Winthrop was hitching his to a rising star.

— • —

On April 3, 1865, Robert Winthrop's thoughts were surely far from family and home. The joy of the day would have filled his soul. "VICTORY," the *New York Times* proclaimed in large letters on its first page. "Glorious Results after 3 days of Continuous Fighting. Overwhelming Defeat of the Rebel Armies." All morning, the newsboys had been shouting "Extra" as news came in about the collapse of Richmond. The rebel capital, the home of the Confederate president, had fallen, ruined and in flames. School-children shut their books and rose to sing national anthems. The Stars and Stripes flew on Broadway. And across from Robert Winthrop's office, on the balcony of the Merchants Exchange, business leader Simeon Draper read the latest dispatches to the crowd assembled below. The air was filled with their cheers and the throng of hundreds rejoiced that at last the war was won.[44]

For the Winthrop family, the dispatches meant they could at last stop worrying about Frederic, by then a general who had been in the thick of the recent fighting. The *Times* had carried a communiqué dated April 1 indicating that though the loss among officers had been great, "no general officers" had been killed.[45] This would mean, they must have thought, that Frederic had survived the war.

Frederic had been the only one of Thomas Charles' six boys to don the blue Union uniform. Robert and his older brother Frank (Charles Francis) had been too old, twenty-eight and thirty-three, when war broke out, the two youngest underage: Eugene (Gene) seventeen, Clarence thirteen. Grenville had been twenty-four, but he was about to be married. So it was only Frederic who had gone to war. (Refer to Chart 3.)

He more than made up for the rest of them. He had enlisted for service on April 19, 1861, only five days after the humiliating fall of Fort Sumter. That evening, Frederic Winthrop—then twenty-one and already in his sixth year as an employee of a New York City banking house—had met Major Robert Anderson, the heroic commander at Fort Sumter, at a dinner given by William H. Aspinwall. The talk had all been of the departure of New York's Seventh Regiment. Instead of going straight home after the dinner, Frederic and several other young men present made their way to a recruiting station. Two days later, Frederic Winthrop set off to Washington, a private in the ranks of Company F of the Seventy-first Regiment New York state militia. The avalanche had begun. By the end of the war, more than fourteen percent of New York City's population would have been sent to the field.[46]

Civil War General Frederic Winthrop (courtesy Angela Winthrop, photographed by Philip Reeser)

Over four years, Fred Winthrop produced a record to make a family proud. He joined the Army of the Potomac in October 1861 and fought in all the great battles: Bull Run, Antietam, Fredericksburg, Gettysburg, the Wilderness. His gallantry and leadership sent him rising swiftly in the ranks. In October 1861 he was promoted to captain, in August 1864 to colonel, and on November 1, 1864, he was appointed brevet brigadier general, U.S. Volunteers. Few if any Union generals were so young. Officially, his promotion was dated August 1, 1864, two days shy of his birthday. He was still only twenty-four years of age.

But Frederic Winthrop's letters home had more to do with maidens than battlefield drama and were more humorous than heroic. He saved his most graphic observations for his brother Gren. In a letter dated January 5, 1863, he describes a scene found in a small rural town in the South.

> The occupants of the dwelling house, exclusive of ourselves, number 4 persons. An old woman some 80 years of age, two young men about 23 to 28 years of age and who I strongly believe to be guerrillas, and a young lady whom the old woman calls her *niece*, aged at least 45 with wonderfully flat breasts, a few stray teeth, and as luxuriant a growth of hair on her head as a youth of 16 might be supposed to have on his upper lip. I think it is needless for me to say that I do not contemplate seduction.

Not surprisingly, seduction, though not always feasible, was often on his mind. His thoughts even turned to his revered ancestor, Governor John Winthrop, and his four wives:[47] "The only conclusion I can come to is that he was a damned old lecherous son of a bitch."[48]

If there wasn't much whoring, there was plenty of death, which Frederic reported in a wry, detached manner. A captain in the Third Brigade "got drunk, fell off his horse in Cedar Run and was drowned." Death on the battlefield was equally droll, as reported in a letter to Robert: "One of our men brought down a son of a bitch from the top of a tree and they say he came tumbling ass over head just like a squirrel." His own death, if it came, would be as casual as any other: "In case I am sent to the dust in the coming fight, I have given directions to have my trunk sent home to you. The only valuable things I possess, however, are my sword and commission which I trust will go down to my posterity!"[49]

— • —

On the evening of April 3, the day New Yorkers spent in rejoicing, the day of the news that no Union generals had been killed, a telegram was received by Grenville Winthrop:

> Your brother Frederic was killed on the second inst. His body embalmed is at … Hospital City Point…. His baggage is with him. Yours with much sorrow. Joes R. Campbell, 1st Lieut.

Where, how? The family had no details, but they knew they must make immediate arrangements to bring Frederic's remains home. Grenville left immediately for Washington, but there was a terrible mix-up, and it took four days before his brother's body finally arrived there for shipment to New York.

Details of Frederic Winthrop's death would arrive well before his body. Newspapers in New York and Philadelphia were filled with the story, a heroic tale full of irony, a cruel end to a "crewel" (as it was sometimes written at the time) war. He had fallen at the battle of Five Forks, the last big battle of the war, one of the last generals—and certainly the youngest—to be killed before Richmond fell. His final moments were described in *The World: New-York* (April 5):[50]

> He was riding along the breastworks, and in the act as I am assured of saving a friend's life, was shot through the left lung. He fell at once, and his men who loved him, gathered around and took him tenderly to the rear, where he died before the stretcher on which he lay could be deposited before the meeting-house door. On the way from the field to the hospital he wandered in his mind at times, crying out, "Captain Weaver how is that line? Has the attack succeeded, etc." When he had been resuscitated for a pause, he said: "Doctor, am I done for?" His last words were: "Straighten the line." And he died peacefully.

Within a few weeks of the funeral, the family would find out what really happened as Frederic lay dying, a sadder and somewhat less epic tale than the news accounts they had read. The messenger was Captain Campbell, Frederic's aide-de-camp, who had hurried to his side as soon as he learned that he had fallen. In a letter to Grenville dated April 15, Campbell related what he knew of Winthrop's final hours.

> He was in great pain all the time. He would call out to me in his pain and ask if any cared for him now, and he seemed grateful to me for remaining with him. He would seize my hand, squeeze it, and press it to his lips…. [After about two hours] it was evident he was dying, and at half past 4 p.m. the 1st inst. he breathed his last. He died easily and as a soldier dies.

Certainly, with his forthright wit and swashbuckling bravery, Frederic Winthrop had earned a place in the Winthrop pantheon. Moreover, had he lived to marry and have children, he might have changed the course of Winthrop history. But Frederic didn't live, and so his brother Robert was left holding the patriarchal reins. Today, it seems, Robert Winthrop's progeny are the only direct descendants of Governor John Winthrop who will carry on the name of Winthrop into the future.[51] (Refer to Charts 2 and 3.)

— • —

During the postwar years Robert would move to the center stage of his extended family. Among his first acts—perhaps because Frederic had to be laid to rest initially in the de Peyster family vault in the Trinity Church courtyard at the corner of Wall Street and Broadway—Robert took steps to create a proper burial place for Winthrops. On April 23, eleven days after his brother's funeral, he purchased a large lot at Green-Wood Cemetery in Brooklyn, the burial ground of choice among New Yorkers of the day, and had a mausoleum built with ample room not only for Frederic, but for his parents, his sisters and brothers, and his children. Ten years after the Civil War, his father and four of his siblings were dead and he was the one remaining male head of family. But by then he had produced his own formidable brood—four sons: Dudley, Grenville, Frederic, and Beekman, and two daughters, Katharine and Albertina. (Refer to Chart 5.)

In 1871 Robert was thirty-eight and a comfortably established partner in Drexel, Winthrop & Co. when along came what could have been the opportunity of a lifetime. International banker Junius Morgan, casting about for a new partner for his brilliant and mercurial son J. Pierpont Morgan, thought that Winthrop's Philadelphia partner, the urbane and wealthy Anthony J. Drexel, would provide the right mix of prudence and financial power. Winthrop, for whatever reason, was left by the wayside as this financial behemoth took shape. One family story is that J. P. Morgan invited both Drexel and Robert Winthrop to join the new firm. The plan, however, was that Winthrop would go to Paris to set up a branch there—a move he didn't want to make.[52] Another version holds that he dropped out because he didn't want to get involved in the speculative European markets in which the Morgan money was heavily invested.[53] The Morgan side of the story, however, is that Drexel wasn't particularly interested in keeping Winthrop in the new partnership. According to this tale, Drexel had written Junius Morgan that Winthrop was an "excessively cautious" lender who had not lived up to his expectations. "A proud and wealthy man, with many outside interests," the account continues, Winthrop resigned to take care of his personal and family affairs and help out his sixty-five-year-old father-in-law, Moses Taylor.[54]

Whatever the impetus, 1871 saw the birth of Robert Winthrop and Company, "private" bankers and members of the New York Stock Exchange, with Robert Winthrop holding the bulk of the business and his brother Charles Francis, the remaining one-sixteenth share. It would grow into an "important" family banking enterprise through which Robert Winthrop "multiplied his family's fortune many times over."[55] Meanwhile, Drexel, Morgan would become the stand-alone J. P. Morgan, the formidable Morgan empire, one of the greatest financial and commercial powers in U.S. history.[56]

Moses Taylor would die a little more than a decade after Robert Winthrop struck out on his own, on May 24, 1882. City flags flew at half-mast, just as they had at the funeral of Robert's brother, Frederic. But unlike the young general's passing, Moses Taylor's was front-page news in all the major metropolitan dailies. "An Old Merchant's Death," headlined the *New York Times* of May 24, 1882—"The History of a Self-Made Man." Moses Taylor was reputed to be the equal of the greatest business titans of the day. He had been a "financial pillar," a title he had earned by helping to finance the Union in the Civil War. He was ranked with Cornelius Vanderbilt and Jay Gould as one of the giants of railroad financiers. And he had helped fund the laying of the Atlantic cable, standing tall with others who had invested in this extraordinary technological breakthrough—David Dudley and Cyrus Field, S. E. B. Morse and Peter Cooper among them.[57]

Her father's death made Kate Winthrop and her four siblings wealthy. Moses Taylor was reported to have left an estate valued at between $40 and $45 million—a sum that would translate into $8 million trusts for each of his five children.[58] The Winthrops, however, didn't choose to upgrade their lifestyle, remaining instead in the house at 118 Fifth Avenue that had so impressed Robert's brother Frederic, near Kate's widowed mother at 122. The neighborhood had been deteriorating for years. Just a few blocks away were thousands upon thousands of immigrant families packed into rat-infested tenements, victims of poverty, discrimination, and disease. As early as 1872 their neighbors, the senior Theodore Roosevelts, had gone uptown, leaving their house to be replaced by a sewing machine factory.[59] In 1888, when Kate and Robert's oldest daughter, Kitty, had her wedding reception at 118 Fifth Avenue, the house was dismissed by *Town Topics*[60] as an "old-fashioned brick house … probably the plainest residence today on Fifth Avenue." But neither the Taylors nor the Winthrops seemed to mind.

Sometime in 1892, however, the Winthrops finally left the area that had been their home for more than thirty years and resettled at 38 East 37th Street, at the corner of 37th and Park Avenue. The new house was in the Murray Hill section of New York, which extended from 33rd to 42nd Street and from Third to Sixth Avenue. Generally, this was where you went if you were from an old family and you wanted to be near everyone else. Kate Winthrop's sisters, Albertina (Mrs. Percy Pyne) and Mary (Mrs. George Lewis) lived there, as did Winthrop cousin Egerton Leigh Winthrop. So did the families into which two of the Robert Winthrop sons, Grenville and Beekman, would marry—the Trevors and the Woods. So did old families like the Laniers and the Appletons. And, here too, as my mother remembered, Kate Winthrop settled homes upon her own children as they got married. No shops, no apartment houses, few churches. Murray Hill was very quiet, very family. Not even the exteriors were pretentious. Most of Murray Hill was an unbroken sea of brownstones, so uniform in appearance that Mrs. Thomas (Fanny) Trollope, the novelist's mother (seemingly anticipating by a century and a half President Reagan's famous comment on trees), had been inspired to write: "When you have seen one [brownstone], you have seen [them] all."[61]

Sadly, Robert and Kate had little time to enjoy their new house together. He would die in November 1892, from heart trouble, at the age of fifty-nine. Kate was devastated by her husband's death. Seeking solace in her book of "inspirational" sayings, she imagined him at last in heaven:

> *One Less at Home ... the charmed circle broken*
> *A dear face missed day by day from its accustomed place.*
> *But cleansed and perfected by Grace.*

A clipping dated June 1, 1895, suggests that three years later the heartache was still there: "It is very difficult to be strong, when all the *meaning* is gone out of your life."

Though he had never hit the financial heights, Robert Winthrop left an exemplary legacy, and his obituary was modest but respectful. The clipping in his son Frederic's scrapbook describes him as "for many years a well-known banker," and notes his connections with "an old New England family," his trusteeship with New York Life Insurance and Trust Company, the Orthopaedic Hospital, and his membership in the Union, Knickerbocker, Riding, and Metropolitan clubs. It was the profile of a worthy gentleman, one who had brought new professional credibility to an old family and had done so in a modest and unassuming way.

Kate's mother, Catherine Wilson Taylor, died two months after Robert, on New Year's Eve. Her death was greeted in an even more

Robert Winthrop, 1833-92, president, Robert Winthrop and Company, 1871-92, official portrait now at Wood, Struthers and Winthrop (courtesy Wood, Struthers and Winthrop Collection)

A WINTHROP AND TAYLOR UNION

subdued fashion than his. She had lived a long life and, at eighty-three, as her obituary noted, she had become a woman of such a "retiring disposition that she had passed out of the minds of many of those who knew her husband and her children."

During Robert's lifetime, neither he nor Kate had sought the social spotlight. Both were "nobs," the term coined by society's self-appointed arbiter Ward McAllister to separate the conservative old families from the "swells," rich and often vulgar newcomers like the Vanderbilts, who had outdone everyone by building an entire block of mansions along Fifth Avenue shortly after the Civil War.[62] Nobs could dress shabbily, squirrel away their money, and look down on swells, but swells never looked down on nobs. Robert particularly, despite his lineage, had no sense of entitlement. He seemed determined to prove that he was worthy both of the name he had inherited and the wealth that his marriage had brought him. "There but for the grace of God go I," he would say, when he encountered a beggar or a drunk in the street.[63]

Kate, though she had a swell's credentials (plenty of new money), was more outspokenly nobbish than Robert. She filled her "inspirational" notebooks with poems poking fun at society figures. We meet "Mrs. Lofty," for example, whose carriages and jewels and gold could not compare to love of family. And we find "A Catechism on What is Society," which derides dinner parties as "Dining under difficulties" and states that the purpose of stepping out in society is to be called "awfully jolly."

Kate counted among her close friends two women who looked as grandly down upon social climbers as she did. Her grandson Robert Winthrop Kean remembered that the pair, Edith Wharton and Sara Delano Roosevelt, would often drop by at teatime.[64] No fool would have been gladly suffered at these "power" teas. The well-born Wharton—remembered by one contemporary as "slender, graceful, and icy cold, with an exceedingly aristocratic bearing"[65]—made her name primarily by drawing devastating word portraits of New York society. As for Sara Delano Roosevelt, mother of Franklin, biographer Blanche Wiesen Cook wrote: "A prominent member of society in New York, Boston, Paris, and London … she was rigid in her views, and opinionated on all matters. She hated, with considerable verve and in no particular order, ostentation, vulgarity, shabby politicians, the new resorts of the new rich, and virtually all races, nationalities, and families other than her own."[66] Kate Winthrop could be just as scathing as her two women friends. Her grandson remembered her grumbling about Mrs. E. H. Harriman's having been given the seat of honor at a dinner party one evening. Mrs. Harriman, she sniffed, had probably earned her place at the right hand of the host "just because her husband has made so much money."[67]

Unlike her husband, however, Mrs. Winthrop was lordly not only toward the common rich but also toward the common man. "Please be quiet. My children are trying to sleep," she reportedly once chided a noisy garbageman clattering outside her Fifth Avenue window. When the garbage collector shot back a rude comment, she promptly lodged a complaint with the Sanitation Department. "I am Mrs. Robert Winthrop," she is said to have announced, "and my garbage man is not a gentleman." "I'm sorry, Mrs. Winthrop," the official is claimed to have replied, "but it's very hard to get a gentleman to pick up your garbage."[68]

After the inheritance from her father, after the move to Murray Hill, and after her husband's death, Kate Winthrop began to shuck some of her modest ways and assume the proportions of a grand dowager. The interior of the Murray Hill house was, at least in my mother's recollections, quite awe-inspiring: "Everything was enormous and heavy … the dark brown woodwork, the furniture, the ornamentation. The rugs were so thick you couldn't hear a thing when people walked along. That was stylish—and very practical. It never got dirty.… In the dining room, somebody was standing behind each chair at the table … a first butler, a second butler, and a couple of maids flourishing around." *Town Topics*, when it covered the wedding reception of the younger Winthrop daughter, Tina, in 1904, would approve of the new Winthrop abode. It is "just the right sort … for a home wedding, for there is a great wide hall with big square rooms on each side, the library all in dark carved oak with its halls decorated by portraits of illustrious ancestors." Even the neighborhood was becoming more noble. Around 1888, J. P. Morgan had bought himself a brownstone at 36th Street and Madison Avenue, around the block from where the Robert Winthrops would move. Morgan had moved to Murray Hill to avoid the nouveaux riches and their "elephantine splendor" further uptown.[69] But in a little more than a decade, he had purchased all the property behind his house and hired famed New York architect Charles McKim to build a Italian Renaissance palace to house his ever-growing collections of art and rare books and manuscripts. By 1906 at the other end of 37th Street stood Kate Winthrop's architecturally resplendent new neighbor, the Pierpont Morgan Library.[70]

Kate Winthrop's house at 38 East 37th Street in New York City (Robert Winthrop Kean's Fourscore Years, *courtesy Hamilton Fish Kean II)*

Kate Winthrop entertained lavishly and often in her new house, preparing careful written instructions for the staff on each event, complete with a seating chart and menu. A nucleus of immediate family was always present. The inner circle would be amplified by marital connections (Kanes, Taylors, Bends), adorned by lady friends for her unmarried sons—May Bird for Dudley ("Mr. R. D. Winthrop"), Melza Wood for Beek ("Mr. B. Winthrop"), Dorothy Amory for Fred ("Mr. F. Winthrop"), and topped off by the occasional celebrity (the opera singer Miss Emma Eames appears on one list). Dinners were usually at eight and fare commonly included ten courses. On Tuesday, December 13, 1898, the hour was advanced to 7:15 p.m. for a pre-theater dinner held in honor of Miss Dorothy Amory of Boston. The number of courses, however, remained fixed: oysters on the half shell, soup, timbale of fish, spaghetti timbales, saddle of lamb with potatoes and green beans, quail with mayonnaise, celery and lettuce, Imperial pudding, fruit and bonbons, coffee and cordials—a cavalcade of calories washed down with sherry and claret and champagne.[71] One can only hope that the evening's theatrical fare—"On and Off"—was a light and airy confection after the weighty repast.

The Long Courtship

chapter FOUR

Left: *Dorothy Amory in January 1895, age 16*

Right: *Fred Winthrop, 1895*

The letter was postmarked October 28, 1895. Dorothy Amory of Boston had only recently turned seventeen, and she was writing to her brother Billy's one-time Harvard roommate, twenty-eight-year-old Frederic Winthrop of New York:

Dear Mr. Windthrop [*sic*], My candy is delicious! Chocolate is my favorite kind of candy, especially Maillard's.

He sent her a silver mirror for Christmas and roses for Valentine's Day, photographs of visits together and a paper cutter. In the summer of 1897 he visited Wareham, where her family summered, and they played chess all evening; kept a battledore and shuttlecock rally going 2,270 times without a miss; rode together; played tennis together. He went to her coming-out party, sent her more flowers.

On the afternoon of October 22, 1897, two years after the first box of Maillard's chocolates and six years after he had first seen her, Fred and Dorothy took a long walk in the country and he told her that he hoped someday she would be his wife. She gave him no encouragement. In February of 1898 he asked her again. In April, she finally began addressing him as Fred.

And so began the courtship of my mother's parents, which dragged on for seven long years as a dogged Fred pursued a merry and capricious Dorothy. It was the story of an old-family New Yorker attempting to win the heart of an old-family, but not so proper, Bostonian. It was the story of Fifth Avenue decorum wooing Beacon Street simplicity, of family dignity courting unaffected home warmth. It was the story of Frederic Winthrop, third son of New York banker Robert and his wife Kate, pursuing Dorothy Amory, the youngest daughter of Libby and Ned Amory. And, in the intertangled webs of family trees, it was the story of the love affair of cousins. Fred Winthrop's great-grandfather Francis Bayard Winthrop, founder of a New York branch of the Winthrop family, and Dorothy Amory's great-great-grandmother Ann Winthrop, who had married wealthy Bostonian David Sears (her father's great-grandfather), had been brother and sister. So Fred and Dorothy were third cousins once removed. (Refer to Chart 12.)

Dorothy, 13 or 14

Fred had had his first glimpse of Dorothy when she was only thirteen. He had just graduated from Harvard, class of 1891, and was visiting Billy at the Amory summer place in Wareham, located on the way to Cape Cod. There he spotted Dorothy, running across a field. To his eyes "she was the most beautiful child" he had ever seen. The moment would become a legend in the family history—the defining point for the rest of Frederic Winthrop's life. "I think," he wrote later, "I must have loved her from the time that I first knew her."

For four years after Harvard, Fred Winthrop experimented with different lifestyles. He put in a year at Harvard Law School, took trips big-game hunting in Wyoming and exotica-exploring in Japan.[1] He worked at Robert Winthrop and Company in New York. And he traveled to Boston to see Dorothy. There he would stay with the Amorys, ostensibly to see Billy, though by then he was thinking of Billy "more in the light of *her* brother, than as my friend." By 1895, when he began to write her, she was never out of his thoughts.

Of Dorothy's loveliness there was little doubt. On a hot day one summer, she was playing in her mother's room at Longwood and her mother took a picture. Years later, Libby Amory wrote on the back: "She looked so beautiful … her hair curled up and the lovely expression in her eyes.… I shall never forget the day. I could not take my eyes off her."[2] Her looks were elusive, defying the talents of portraitists. When the excellent crayon portrait draughtsman Samuel Worcester Rowse sketched her at the age of two, he admitted there was "something in this child's face that he could not get."[3] When Dorothy was twelve, one Joseph Lindon Smith attempted to paint her: "A *very* poor likeness," wrote her mother on the back of the portrait. Fred also disliked the picture, writing on the back, "Her hair was much lighter than appears in the portrait. Brown but shot with copper that shone when the sun was on it. The eyes were brown with gold."

Dorothy Amory, age 2, sketched by Samuel Worcester Rowse

Shortly after Frederic first saw her, the society press took note of the lovely young thirteen-year-old. Dorothy was her sister Clara's only attendant when Clara was married to the highly eligible T. Jefferson Coolidge, Jr., on the last day of September

*The Amory sons, Billy, 10, and George, 5, with Pompey —
"just a dog," perhaps — but a
matchless friend as well*

1891. The young bridesmaid might easily have been obscured by her older sister, the "daintily clad" bride, as she stepped from her carriage into the "mellow light … [of] the sun's rays" and tarried a moment at the portal of the Brookline Unitarian Church "for the last touches to her veil and train." But the press spotted her: "Miss Dorothy Amory was a quaint picture of girlish loveliness in white muslin, the red roses in her hand and the pink flush in her cheeks lending the only color."[4] At twenty, in New York and attending the first assembly ball of the 1898 season, she even captured the attention of a jaded New York society observer. "Boston has never been famed for the beauty of its women," the account matter-of-factly noted. Miss Amory, however, was judged an exception; she "possessed a freshness and a charm absolutely unsurpassed by any New Yorkers present."[5]

— • —

"Freshness and charm"—the words describe Dorothy's personality as well. Of the four Amory children, Dorothy was the youngest and the pet. Captioning a picture of her two sons, Billy, ten, and George, five, in her scrapbook, Libby Amory wrote only of the dog sitting between them: "You were just a dog, Pompey … but no friend ever stood with us so firmly or so unselfishly as you." A photo of daughters Clara and Dorothy, however, is lovingly inscribed "our two dear girls"; one of baby Dorothy, in hat and coat sitting in the snow, "Our darling Dorothy"; and of Dorothy with her father, "Dorothy, 6, and her dear chum, CWA." (Refer to Chart 9.)

Because of her husband's continuing ill health and her own predilections, Libby Amory sought always to provide a quiet home life for Ned and their four children. At first it was a little hard, for upon their marriage in 1867 the newlywed couple had to bow to convention and move in with the Amorys on Beacon Hill. It was all rather "trying," wrote Libby later, for Mrs. Amory wanted them to remain "forever." The

*"Our two dear girls," Libby
Amory wrote under this
photo of Clara, just 16, and
Dorothy, 9.*

anxious flutterings of her mother-in-law must only have aggravated the situation when Libby miscarried that winter. Mr. Amory heeded his daughter-in-law's wishes and soon bought the couple a house at 90 Charles Street, just down Beacon Hill from where the senior Amorys lived.[6]

The Ned Amorys spent six winters on Charles Street, but Libby "*longed* for the country." She would

REARED *in a* GREENHOUSE

sit at her window and sketch, capturing the dreariness of winter in the city, a dismal line of jagged roofs, leafless trees, and cold and huddled people trudging along below. Her teenage love for sketching had developed into a considerable artistic gift; she often amused herself by drawing, by sculpting small statuettes with a Greco-Roman cast, and by creating exquisite Persian-style pottery in bold turquoises and blacks. But her hobbies couldn't divert her from the domestic pall: "The children were puny, and Ned's health was wretched." Fortunately, the Amorys had a particularly appealing and convenient retreat—Longwood, a twenty-five-acre rural paradise in Brookline, just a couple of miles outside the Boston City limits. The property had come into the family through Ned's grandfather David Sears, who planned that all his children should have homes in the country and had accordingly bought up "a great tract [two hundred acres of choice real estate] two and one-half miles west of the State House,

Libby Amory's drawing of life on Charles Street in Boston in the early 1870s

stretching from the Charles River on the north to Muddy Brook and beyond on the South."[7] Ned had passed springs and autumns there during his youth, in a house built by David Sears for Ned's mother. It was a two-story wooden Victorian, with porches all about, gingerbread filigrees enlivening the gables and many little

Our darling Dorothy.

Far left: *From Libby Amory's scrapbook*

Left: *"Dorothy, 6, and her dear chum, CWA" (caption in Libby Amory's scrapbook)*

balconies—but fit only for summer living. "Delighted" to have one of her children occupy it, Mrs. Amory had the house winterized and the Ned Amorys moved in. It was the autumn of 1875 and here they would remain for sixteen happy years.

We were "comfortable" there, Libby wrote. "The climate proved much milder than in town, as we were very much sheltered from the winter winds, and floods of sunshine poured into the house." They loved watching the oaks change color each October to "every fascinating hue," and the children would skate on Hall's Pond each winter and coast on the deep hollows and slopes that bordered the driveway.[8] They gave sleighing parties often. In the spring, the girls would seesaw on a plank resting on an enormous log, no doubt cut from one of the oaks that studded the property.

Because of his poor health, Ned Amory's early career had proceeded in fits and starts. After a few months, he had to leave his first job, with the house of Haughton, Perkins and Company. In 1868, he formed a partnership with H. C. Wainwright under the name of Wainwright and Amory at 40 State Street but had to give up work entirely during the family's first two winters in Longwood. He probably enjoyed the enforced leisure in the country with Libby at his side: "We drove all the time, morning, and afternoon," she wrote; "he was very fond of skating and was a beautiful skater, loved horseback."

Summers were a particular trial, for Ned's health was worst in warm weather. He spent several on a "small yacht for his health." Later he bought a share in the Ristigouche Salmon Club in Canada, but after retreating to the primitive wilds he would return home, "keel over and take to his bed." While he was away, Libby

Libby Amory's sketch of the house at Longwood where she and Ned lived for 16 years. By the time the couple moved there in 1875, several of David Sears' children had sold the lots their father had divided among them in 1830. Ned's parents, however, David Sears' daughter Anna and husband William Amory, loved their land — a choice central piece of about 25 acres — and gladly turned it over to Ned and Libby when they could no longer use it. Today, busy Beacon Street takes people back and forth from Boston to Brookline along one side of the property. But the rest is a pleasant residential area, and names like Amory Playground, Amory Woods, and Amory Street recall the days when two generations of Amorys lived there.

Plum Cove Estate, the George Gardners' house in Beverly, Massachussetts, where Libby and Ned Amory often summered with her family

would take the children different places: sometimes Nahant with the Amory clan, more frequently to her parents' place in Beverly on Boston's North Shore. She thought of it as "beautiful Beverly," for Plum Cove Estate, which her parents bought in 1874, had an ocean-front view. The house itself, however, which was designed by her father, was a gloomy turreted mansion with dark staircases and overbearing wallpaper vying for attention with busy draperies, agitated upholstery, and dizzy oriental rugs.[9]

When Dorothy was born in Beverly Farms on July 17, 1878, the Amorys had been married nearly twelve years. Their way was still unclear: they were still living to some extent on their families' largesse, his in the winter and hers or his in the summer, and at thirty-six Ned had yet to hit his professional stride. Perhaps the arrival of "darling Dorothy" was a good omen, for in 1880 Ned was elected treasurer of Amory Manufacturing, the first of a string of important textile companies where he was to make his mark. In 1882 his firm merged with Langdon Manufacturing, and in 1898 Ned Amory became treasurer of New Hampshire's Amoskeag Manufacturing (succeeding T. Jefferson Coolidge, Sr.). In his prime, with directorships in most of Boston's leading businesses, Amory had gained a reputation as one of two or three of the highest business authorities on State Street. In 1905, when Amoskeag purchased the Manchester and the Amory Mills, becoming the largest cotton manufacturer in the country, if not the world, the directors turned to Amory to take charge. His health, however, did not permit, and instead he agreed to serve as president of the enlarged company.[10]

Below left: *Dorothy at 3 years, 9 months*

Below: *Libby Amory wrote on the back of this photo of Dorothy at 6, "On the way to Nahant ... I stopped at a cheap photographers, pinned two crimson roses on the front of the dress of this enchanting child — I thought it was poor, not good looking enough...."*

View from Mosquito Hut where the Amorys summered "in and on the water" for 18 happy years, August 1895

George G. Amory, just 12

The Amorys, of course, could have used Ned's professional perches to branch out socially. Both Ned and Libby, however, preferred nesting at home. No grandiose summer place for them, either. In 1885 the family decided to build their "first and only summer home." It was a simple shingled affair—a hut, Libby called it—located in Wareham, constructed in two months for six thousand dollars. She christened it Mosquito Hut and bought embossed stationery to match—a flying green insect placed tastefully above the name.

"The family lived in and on the water and led a quiet life and were happy for 18 years," Libby Amory wrote under a photo of their homey seaside cottage. And so it continued—all but once when son George had a house party. Years later my mother used to say, "Everyone wondered how Grandma Amory could have had a son like Uncle George." From an early age, he wasn't anything like the other three. By his mid-teens he had become so "unruly" (his mother's word) that he had to be dispatched to boarding school, from where he sent his mother wheedling letters. Libby pasted one in her scrapbook. "My dearest darling," it began, "this is the first time I am able to write you without my eyes filling with tears. I really think there is not any son in the world who loves their mam so much. I never realized how dear you all are to me till now, and I am beginning to appreciate Clara more." Then began the grievances. "I went out and tried for the 22 and hurt my arm a little. Palmer is a fearful dude with about 20 suits to my 3. He changes his clothes 3 times a day." And the beseeching: "Do come up and see me. We are not allowed to go home Thanksgiving."

The Mosquito Hut house party came a few years later. George was nineteen, about to begin his sophomore year at Harvard, and certainly old enough to know better. Libby was the adult-in-residence and she had "a horrid time." "I am almost dead!" she wrote his older brother, Billy. "I never saw such lively girls. They tear about and I am not only afraid they will drown but that they ought not to do the things they do, and I never know beforehand…. [They are] not in the least flirtatious or common in that way. They are always singing, 'Lizzie Borden with an axe/Chopped her mother 40 whacks….' "

If George was a trial, Clara was a treasure and her marriage to T. Jefferson Coolidge, Jr., doubled the family's pleasure. The families were old friends, Jeffie's father, T. Jefferson Coolidge, Sr., having been "on intimate terms for 30 years" with Clara's grandfather, William Amory, and having succeeded the elder Amory in the management of the Amoskeag Mills.[11] Jeffie found Clara enchanting, writing her father during the summer of 1891 that she was "all that any man could ask for and more than any deserve. She is just the most sensible, cheerful, loving woman in the world." The Amory family was just as pleased with the match. Libby Amory noted in her scrapbook over a photo of Jeffie and Clara chatting companionably, "Jeffie comes into our family and adds greatly to our happiness. He was the kindest of sons and ready to help us all."

Above: Clara Amory and Jeffie Coolidge, engaged, 1891

Above left: Clara Amory, at 2 or 3

The Coolidges were more than kind and helpful, they were historic and wealthy. Genealogically, the Coolidge lineage harked back to Thomas Jefferson, third U. S. president (Jeffie was his great-great-grandson). Financially, Jeffie's father, Thomas Jefferson Coolidge, Sr., had seen the need to move beyond his early nineteenth-century presidential fame by adding midcentury purchasing power, vowing, after grad-

A photo of the Amorys' new house in Boston, from Libby Amory's scrapbook

uation from Harvard to "devote myself to the acquisition of wealth."[12] His marriage to Mehitable Sullivan Appleton, daughter of one of the tycoons of the Merrimack Valley textile mills, hadn't hurt. By the time of his son's marriage to Clara, T. Jefferson Coolidge was among Boston's most prominent businessmen, with treasurer of the Amoskeag Mills and directorships at banks, insurance companies, and railroads in Boston and beyond among his credentials. Shortly after his son's wedding, T. J. Coolidge, Sr., topped off his résumé with his appointment as U.S. minister to France, a post his great-grandfather Thomas Jefferson had held a century before.[13]

The year of Clara's marriage, with George away at school, Billy completing Harvard, and Ned's career ever more demanding, the Amorys decided to move back into Boston. They chose a

"The Longwood Whist Club," with Ned Amory, center

Below: *Elizabeth Gardner Amory, probably in her thirties. Undated drawing by Samuel Worcester Rowse, with message in Libby Amory's handwriting on the back: "My portrait to my son-in-law Jeffie." Though clearly authentic, the picture captures a different look from that in other pictures of Libby Amory. (Courtesy, Dr. Catherine C. Lastavica, photographed by Philip Reeser)*

Below right: *A page from Dorothy Amory's 1892 diary. She was 13.*

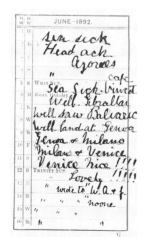

spot at 278 Beacon Street, in Back Bay, just a few blocks from where they had grown up. Though Back Bay and *crème de la crème* were later to become synonymous in the public mind, at the time it was still Beacon Hill that had the aura of social supremacy. Back Bay was a residential parvenu, having until recently been a swamp bordering the dammed-up Charles River.

Libby missed the open hills and fields of Longwood. "It was never like our country home," she wrote dolefully above a picture of their new Boston house. Her architect, she thought, "had little taste." The Amorys' place, however, looked just like all its neighbors, old-fashioned row houses filled with fellow old-time Bostonians: Mrs. Robert Hooper at 276 Beacon, F. L. Higginson at 274, and the John Shepards at 280. A short way away, at 296 Beacon, lived Oliver Wendell Holmes.[14]

Libby Amory had thought that, once they moved into town, they might be able to entertain more. But Ned, working downtown, wasn't up to it. So after a short time she decided "to decline all invitations" and found that thereafter "he was stronger for it." He would just come home, shedding "all thoughts of [business], like a coat, on entering the house." Once in a great while he would go to the club, but what he enjoyed most was playing whist once a week with four friends.

Dorothy didn't let her parents' tranquil lifestyle cloud her exuberant spirits. In what must be must be the world's tiniest diary (its pages measure one by three inches), she penciled in her daily doings for the first half of 1892. "Dancing. Fun!!!!" And again, "Dancing. Fun!!!!!!!!!!!!!!" And yet again, "Dancing. I love it more than anything!!!!!!!!!!!!!!!!!!!!!" She loved riding, too, and parties. In Switzerland, climbing a glacier, she slipped on a pile of rocks and turned her ankle. It didn't "in the least affect her spirits," her mother wrote Billy,

"which are always cheerful." The only part that bothered her, Dorothy herself wrote Billy, was being borne on a sort of chair. "I *hate* chaise," she explained, "because it is so hard on the men. They puff and pant under me!" On this trip she sketched as readily as her mother and took just as droll a view of life. In Venice she wrote, "We saw some tombs, I am glad I'm not dead." Of Rubens' fleshy men and women, she wrote, "They were beautifully painted but I thought there was too much skin about them."[15]

Above: Boating at Wareham: *Fred Winthrop and Dorothy Amory,* center

Above left: Tennis at Wareham, 1897. *The players are Fred Winthrop and Mary Curtis.*

— • —

Some six years later Dorothy wrote laughingly to Fred, "Of course, I shall live in town with my parents and be devoted to them as usual, except for six or seven days a week!" But her parents never expected Dorothy to stay at home and serve crackers and cheese for her father's whist evenings. "If you want to 'keep' your children," Libby Amory would tell my mother years later, "then let them go." By then Dorothy Amory was twenty, busy and in great demand. She rode, played tennis and golf, sailed and rowed. In the summer there were visits to Wareham and Magnolia with family and to Dark Harbor with friends; in the winter, house parties in Aiken, hunt balls, cotillions, dinners, and theater parties.

Prima ballerinas from the Vincent Club Show, 1900-1, from Mary Curtis's scrapbook

The men flocked about her, but her flirtations were harmless. In fact, Dorothy seemed happiest with family and female companions. Performing their annual antics at the Vincent Club show, she and her girlfriends understood each other's silly jokes. Anticipating an upcoming house party, she wrote Fred, "I do hope you won't come to see me there! There are always lots of girls around and I don't believe you would enjoy coming any more than I would enjoy having you." She often told her club-mates that she was tempted not to marry because it would sever her from the Vincent Club.

To Be Young Was Very Heaven was how Dorothy's friend Marian Lawrence (Peabody) thought about the pranks they shared. In her diaries, published under that sunny title years later, Mrs. Peabody described an all-girl dinner party she gave in 1898. For once, Dorothy Amory was voted only the second most beautiful. Maybe this was because the winner had come dressed as the Empress Eugenie, complete with a gorgeous aquamarine necklace that had belonged to the Marquise de Lafayette, while Dorothy had come as a nun. "The beautiful nun," however, was not to be outdone: "She danced a wonderful *pas seul* ballet. She kicked over her head and did splits and thoroughly electrified us until we discovered she had a third leg which she manipulated with her arm very skillfully amid much lace and lingerie."[16]

Fortunately, Fred, not the sort to kick up his heels, wasn't privy to these capers (the only man "allowed" was "old Mr. Hunnewell"). But he did continue his challenging chase, as dogged as ever. And the more he pursued, the farther out of reach Dorothy seemed to dart. Her letters grew colder.

> You are very kind to ask us to your Aunt's house, but we are none of us going on to New York.
>
> You are very kind to ask us to go to the Pudding Show, I am afraid we can not as we have already made our plans.
>
> Your violets were lovely and I thank you *very* much, but I wish you wouldn't send them so often....
>
> I shall be busy Tuesday morning....

REARED *in a* GREENHOUSE

The notes were often signed "in haste, Dorothy."

He still went to Boston, to visit the Amorys and other college friends, and in hopes of seeing Dorothy. His efforts were often futile. After three days at the Amorys', "saw Dorothy at breakfast for the first time." Another day: "I took a walk around the lake alone." And another: "Dorothy was at the Country Club to see the races, but she had several men with her all the time, so I did not see much of her." And in early 1899: "D. for some unknown reason was very chilly to me."

As the "courtship" neared its fourth anniversary, he turned to her mother for advice. Libby, though she found Fred agreeable,[17] was characteristically blunt. Fred described her reaction in his diary: "She thought that D. knew her own mind" and that it was "a pity for me to waste my time." Indeed, Dorothy did know her mind, and she expressed it in a letter dated October 13, 1899: "I do not care for you any more than I did, and I feel sure I never will, though of course you must know I like you. I would never take anyone I did not love. The fault lies in me, not in you."

— • —

Why did Dorothy keep Fred at arm's length? What did he see in her that she missed in him? She was puckish and merry, he was solemn and formal. ("Looking forward to shocking you," she signed one of her notes to him.) She preferred chatter and friendship, he preferred to be buried in books. Her family relationships were free and loving, his reserved and formal. Fred loved her for all the things she was and he wasn't. But it was harder for her to love him.

In addition to being solemn, Fred had one painfully obvious liability: a terrible stutter. This speech defect tortured him so that in 1888 he had considered dropping out of Harvard and going to Paris in search of a cure. Rather than discussing this openly with his father, he wrote:

> You will probably say at first that it would be very foolish to go to all this expense and trouble for so small a thing; but if you knew what a trial and misfortune it was to stutter, you would see that it was not such a small thing after all. Because if I am not cured, by the time I go into business, I will never be able to accomplish anything, and besides my life would be a great deal happier if I could behave as other people do.

He tried everything he could think of—reading aloud, abstaining from drink—but the problem seemed insoluble. "Appeared like a damn fool," was but one of his laments in his diary.[18] In part, it stemmed from shyness—a Winthrop trait. According to Edith Wharton, her friend Egerton Winthrop was "subject, with all but his intimates, to fits of shyness which made him appear either stiff or affected."[19] Egerton's son Bronson seemed similarly afflicted; he suffered so from "extreme shyness," according to his law firm history, that it became the only barrier between him and being "perfectly blessed."[20] All Fred's brothers were shy, each in his own way. Fred's oldest brother, Dudley, according to a nephew, covered his social awkwardness by "being gruff and talking in jerky, short sentences."[21] Grenville would prove

Fred Winthrop, undated: solemn, shy, and smitten with Dorothy

Beekman Winthrop in his sitting room at Harvard

completely inept with his motherless daughters. Only Beekman seemed comfortable with everyone, though his stilted if charming letters suggest a façade. The shyness lived on in my mother's generation of Winthrops. The Winthrop "embrace" has been described as an arm's-length handshake, stiffly proffered.[22]

Whatever the origin, Fred's shyness and stuttering fed on each other. The more he stammered, the more dispirited he became—and the less appealing he must have seemed to Dorothy. She couldn't have been very charmed by a letter he wrote July 1, 1898, shamelessly displaying his raw feelings. In an awkward left-handed script, he wrote that he had dreamed of her while recovering from a "rather bad case of blood poisoning in my wounded hand." She had appeared to him, he wrote, "dressed as a doctor's nurse; the costume was most becoming, but you treated me so cruelly in fixing my hand, that I woke up."

From the summer of 1895 on he kept a diary recording "every time I saw Dorothy from that time until our marriage." Its entries—"Took 12:30 train to Hamilton.... Called on Dorothy at 4. Was told the Lunch Club was still there and to come back later. So went back about 5:30 & stayed till 6:15"—have all the exuberance of a train schedule.[23] The entries also include dour tales of trips to Hamilton where Rodolphe L. Agassiz, grandson of the great Swiss naturalist Louis Agassiz, and his wife Marie would take him in, after Dorothy would spurn him. Dolph and Fred were great friends from Harvard: they ushered at their friends' weddings, dined together often at the Somerset and Union Clubs in Boston, and theatered together. But Fred must have seemed a sober companion even to Dolph. He rarely let down his guard, not even after the wedding in 1897 of fellow Harvard grad and Porcellian clubmate Hugh Whitney to Eleanor Shattuck. The ushers, Fred and Dolph among them, were seen by the press as "about as stunning a lot of fellows for style and good looks as have ever acted in that capacity in that or any other city." But after the reception, when the company repaired to Dolph's for a little more liquid uplift, Fred stood apart, grumbling later in his diary that his male friends were so "impossibly tight" that "Marie wouldn't come down to dinner."

Owing probably to his social unease, Fred seemed to prefer the quiet dinner and theater with one or two of his male friends. He also often escaped into books. Though not too scholarly (that was frowned upon), he read continuously, a book a week by his 1901 count.

Shy as he was, and given the nobbish tendencies of his family, Fred must have felt ill-fitted for the dazzle of the Gilded Age. His first taste came when, at eighteen, he was inducted into the charmed circle of Harvard undergraduate life and from there into a fashionable social circle. Every generation of Winthrops had had at least one underclassman at Harvard.[24] But up until the 1880s, it was the Boston Winthrops who had sent their sons to Harvard.[25] Few of the New York Winthrops had even gone to college, and those who had generally went to Yale. The Robert Winthrops decided to break with this tradition and send their sons off to Cambridge. Perhaps

Robert Winthrop was attempting to rekindle in his sons an enthusiasm for their New England heritage. Or perhaps he saw the Boston branches dwindling and wanted to reestablish the Winthrop presence in the land of his ancestors.

Whatever the explanation, they all went: Dudley, class of 1883; Grenville, 1886; Fred, 1891; and Beekman, 1897. The atmosphere at Harvard was highly rarefied. College was still a privilege, an opportunity afforded to only one in every five thousand Americans. And the sons of Boston's elite—together with the stray upper-crust Philadelphian or New Yorker—represented only about one-tenth of any class, a self-satisfied few who were known to affect gold-headed walking sticks, three-piece suits, and anglicisms. Even New Yorker Teddy Roosevelt, three classes ahead of Dudley, was so taken by the exclusive Harvard scene that shortly into his freshman year he was saying "by Jove" and "dear old boy."[26] The pinnacle, of course, was induction into the Porcellian Club, where one could dine on partridge and fine wines, served by a liveried black servant. Grenville, Fred, and Beekman were all members.[27]

"Breakfast room in Porcellian Club — Lewis" (caption in Fred Winthrop's scrapbook)

If clubs opened many doors, wearing the crimson opened more. Fred, six feet tall and a muscular 175 pounds, was an excellent athlete. He made the varsity crew his junior year and was a champion boxer, winner in his junior year of both the middleweight and heavyweight classes. After graduating, he continued to work out at the New York Athletic Club, where he was a star. As one professional California boxer by the name of Joe Choynski discovered one day, after confidently asking to be pitted against the club's "best pupil," Winthrop also turned out to be a masterful opponent. Deflecting all Choynski's blows, he administered so mighty a thwack that the Californian had to see a doctor the next day. Winthrop, Choynski discovered, had broken his rib.[28] Some years later, on the train to Boston, Fred was accosted by a group of young toughs—they moved his bag, taunted him, and then sat on the arm of his seat. This was too much. Fred lit into the group, leaving them bruised and doubtless astonished. It was a startling contrast: beneath Fred's shy and stuttering surface lurked a man of steel.

Fred Winthrop, an athlete at Harvard

Also, deep inside, Fred remained as nobbish as his mother, clipping with approval an article from the Paris *Herald* which singled out the Winthrops for having withstood the onslaught of "the ostentation of the parvenus."[29] But after returning to New York from college, stutter or not, Fred accepted invitations to join in the fun with these parvenus. On June 6, 1895, for example, he was best man at the wedding of James Abercrombie Burden, a fellow Porcellian Club member, to Florence Adele Sloane, whose mother was a Vanderbilt. There were private trains to Lenox for the guests and frock coats, high hats, and gifts of small emerald and diamond scarfpins for the ushers. Fred was an observer at other Vanderbilt weddings, each with

THE LONG COURTSHIP

its delicious morsel of excess. When Emily Vanderbilt Sloane married John Henry Hammond, the wedding bell of roses and lilies over the altar crashed to the floor, just seconds before the ceremony, bringing forth a "ripple of dismay" from the crowd and a "heavy voice" murmuring "absit omen" (may this not be a bad omen).[30] When Adele and Emily's first cousin Alfred Gwynne Vanderbilt chose Newport to wed because they thought the wedding could be "more quietly celebrated" there in winter than in New York, the groom's father Cornelius Vanderbilt hired special trains and the two hundred wedding guests were housed in summer cottages opened specially for the occasion.

Newspaper clippings of these gaieties ended up in Fred's scrapbook, along with stories about the antics of his cousins.[31] The 1890 wedding of his third cousin Egerton Winthrop, Jr., to Emmeline Dore Heckscher had opened "Newport's season with a snap." Crowds had gawked as the groom and his best man, brother Bronson, arrived at the church "with a great flourish—horses, servants, and all decked out in huge wedding favours." On the Taylor side, Fred's first cousin Moses Taylor (son of his mother's brother Henry—refer to Chart 4), made a splash in the scrapbook when he was described as being engaged in "devotional exercises, with Miss Gertrude Vanderbilt as his shrine." This was the very same Gertrude Vanderbilt who the next year married Harry Payne Whitney in mind-boggling splendor in Newport. The press made much of the rivalry of these two rich young men, hot in pursuit of the heiress. Moses, twenty-five, was said to be a "well-known young man about town and the possessor of millions" and a "chum" of Gertrude's late brother W. H. Vanderbilt. But Harry Payne Whitney, also a friend of Gertrude's brother, was heir apparent to far more money. When he learned of Taylor's engagement to Gertrude, Whitney showed himself a man "of purpose and of action": he "made no moan," did not, as rumored, contemplate suicide, but instead, he "finished tying his tie," went forthwith to Newport, and undertook a "fair but untiring and finally vigorous rivalry with young Moses Taylor." If Harry had beaten Moses to Gertrude, Moses beat Harry to the altar by a week. He married Edith Bishop, the wedding was in Newport, and among the assemblage of notables were many Winthrops, including Fred, an usher, and his mother Kate. Mrs. F. W. Vanderbilt gave the couple a gold toilet set.

— • —

The small and unobtrusive notice appeared in a New York newspaper.

New York, March 31st, 1900

MR. Frederic Winthrop has this day
retired from our firm.

Robert Winthrop & Co.

As he would later explain in a letter to his children recounting the story of his love for their mother, Fred Winthrop had decided to move to Boston "so as to be near Dorothy." No doubt the Boston lifestyle, the open country, riding, and the conservative New England attitude toward life appealed to him.[32] But the real reason was that for the past four or five years, he had had no heart for his work; all he had wanted was to get away and see Dorothy.

"Do be awfully careful," Kate Winthrop warned her son. "They're all atheists up there, and most of them are crazy."[33] By atheists she was referring to what she considered the lost tribe of Unitarians, of which the Amorys were pew-owning members. A faithful Episcopalian and herself a pew-proprietor at fashionable Grace Church, Kate Winthrop had done her best to infuse her children with an equally strong faith, insisting they go to church two or three times on Sunday. Her zeal, not surprisingly, had the opposite effect, at least on Fred. "Never heard so much damn nonsense in all my life," he muttered to my mother, the only time she ever went to church with him.

Grandma Winthrop, about 1897 (Robert Winthrop Kean's Fourscore Years, *courtesy Hamilton Fish Kean II)*

Despite what appeared to my mother as Kate Winthrop's matriarchal, strait-laced ways, Fred was devoted to his mother. He felt guilty for staying away so much and then, when he was at home, for not being "very charming or cheerful." He wrote Dorothy, "She is certainly the dearest person in the world next to you, and the best mother a person could have."[34] His departure to Boston was hard on Kate. Four months after the official farewell, she pasted in her inspirational notebook the resigned question: "Why do we always hope that in new lands, new places, we will find better selves, happier selves? The superstition dies hard." A widow of eight years, a woman who had passed her sixtieth birthday, Kate Winthrop was perhaps also fearing the loneliness of old age: *"Oh les enfants—quelle torment et quelle joie!"* (Oh children, what torment, what joy), read another of the clippings in her notebook.

In fact, until Fred left home Mrs. Winthrop had been fortunate in having all her children nearby (refer to Chart 5). Elder daughter Kitty lived at 25 East 37th Street, just a few doors away, in a house that her mother had renovated for her and her family, husband Hamilton Fish Kean and their two sons, John and Robert Winthrop (or Winthrop as they called him) Kean. And during the summers, the Keans would migrate with Kate Winthrop to her place in Elberon, New Jersey, to enjoy the sea breezes and sit on the veranda looking at the ocean.[35] Tina was still living with her mother and, pushing thirty, appeared to be headed toward permanent residence there. Dudley, after some youthful gallivanting, was the elder Winthrop at Robert Winthrop and Company. Grenville, his wife Mary, and their two daughters lived across the street, at 10 East 37th Street, and Gren had recently joined the firm as well. Beekman was about to graduate from Harvard Law School. A fine

Three Winthrop "men," Dudley (front, far left), *Fred* (middle row, far left), *and Beekman* (back row, second to right), *with friends in Elberon, New Jersey, in 1882, perhaps at their parents', or perhaps at their Moses Taylor grandparents'. In 1879 the Taylors built a summer home there (though it had stained glass windows and an elevator, it was not considered ostentatious) and provided a lot next door for their daughter Kate and her family.*

THE LONG COURTSHIP

Hamilton Fish Kean, 1887

Kitty Winthrop Kean with son John, 1889

John Kean III, 18 months, May 1890

Robert Winthrop Kean, 16 months, January 1895

Tina Winthrop, about the time of her marriage (courtesy Tina van Roijen van Notten)

student, he would make an excellent addition to the company. It was unfortunate about Fred, but his shyness made it hard for him to operate in the business world, and five out of six children within reach was a satisfactory record.

Kate Winthrop was very close to her eldest daughter and must have been happy about the way Kitty's life was unfolding. Her marriage to Hamilton Fish Kean had been launched auspiciously. Held at Grace Church twelve years earlier, the wedding had been hailed by *Town Topics* as "a blue-blooded affair throughout … [attended by] everybody of any consequence in the social world … [all] of the Knickerbocker faith." Ham came from a fine family and had settled down in business. Had she known what the future held, Kate Winthrop would have been prouder yet of her new son-in-law and his family, for Ham's brother John had founded what would become a distinguished political dynasty. At the time of Ham and Kitty's wedding, John had served two terms in Congress (1882–84 and 1886–88) and would be elected senator from New Jersey from 1899 to 1911. Ham would follow in his footsteps, representing New Jersey in the U.S. Senate from 1929 and 1934. In the next generation, one of Ham and Kitty's two sons, Robert Winthrop Kean, would be elected to the U.S. House of Representatives and serve ten consecutive terms, from 1939 to 1958. In the third generation, Robert Winthrop Kean's fifth child, Thomas Howard Kean, would be a two-term New Jersey governor, from 1982 to 1989.

Had she known what the future held for her other daughter, Kate might have been proud as well. Poor Tina had had a difficult time growing up, as my mother used to tell us:

Aunt Tina was a very sweet, very lovely person, but her four older brothers didn't think so and they shut her up at every possible moment, stepped on her hard, and they began to call her dummy, so of course, the more they called her dummy, the dumber she got. She finally got engaged to a very nice young man who was very musical. Well, you don't marry a musical man, so all the brothers went to him and told him he

REARED *in a* GREENHOUSE

better bow out of the picture. He was not to marry their sister. And so he didn't. He retired from the picture. Eventually, he married a woman who looked exactly like my aunt.

Tina finally did get married, in 1904, but to a then obscure Dutch diplomat who would take her away forever. The press covering the wedding had unearthed little about the young Dutch groom, a Mr. Jan Herman van Roijen. "About" thirty-three, he was known to be the chargé d'affaires of the Dutch legation and a "favorite" in diplomatic and "residential" circles in Washington. His best man was the new minister of the Netherlands, Jonkheer de Marees van Swideren, but there were no ushers at the wedding. Nor were there any celebratory excesses to impress the press. It was a "simple" home ceremony to which only intimate friends were invited. And even though some three hundred people, representing "all of the older New York families," attended the reception, a great many of them were said to be from "the older set who seldom attend such functions."

The Jan Herman van Roijens, about 1911: Tina, Robert, about 3, Jan Herman, Jr., the future diplomat, about 5, and Jan Herman, Sr.

As in Kitty's case, a crystal ball would have revealed another distinguished dynasty in the making. Jan Herman van Roijen would become Dutch minister (today the post is ambassador) in Japan, Rome, and the United States; his son Jan Herman would follow in his footsteps, with a distinguished forty-year career in the Dutch foreign service, including a posting as Dutch ambassador to the United States from 1950 to 1964 and as ambassador to the Court of St. James's from 1964 to 1970, when he retired; in his turn, his son Jan Herman van Roijen would become an ambassador, his appointments including Israel, Canada, Indonesia, and the Court of St. James's. A representative of the fourth generation—the third Jan Herman's niece, Henriette Houben-van Notten—recently completed her first posting, as second secretary and diplomatic advisor to the Dutch ambassador in Washington, where her grandfather and great-grandfather headed the embassy before her.

Dudley Winthrop, undated

As the century turned, Fred and Tina's departures were not the only blows to family solidarity. Beekman would spend the thirteen years from 1900 to 1912 in the Philippines, Cuba, and Washington, holding a series of increasingly weighty political appointments. Grenville, though he turned to his mother for help in raising his daughters after his wife died in 1900, was becoming lost in the arcane world of art collecting. And Dudley was stricken with wanderlust, more taken with stalking big game than tracking a wife.

Dudley's hunting expeditions extended as far afield as Mexico, Europe, and Ireland.[36] By the mid-1890s he had become a regular at the Okeetee and Pinelands Clubs in South Carolina, havens for wealthy quail shooters from the North.[37] In 1892 he went to Wyoming with Fred, and in 1896 he spent a year in the Wild West, following in the footsteps of his friend and soulmate Teddy Roosevelt, who had played cowboy in the Badlands during the 1880s, riding a hundred miles a day, pounding after stampeding cattle and turning from a "bespectacled dude" into a "rugged, bronzed" and "very powerful" man.[38] Dudley's year was spent in Wyoming. One of his greatest moments was hearing the commander at Fort Washington say that his Uncle Fred, the slain Civil War general, was "as plucky as anybody he had ever seen."[39] In 1898 when the Spanish-American War broke out, Dudley had a chance to prove his own mettle—though his service may not have been as rough-and-tumble as the story my mother was brought up on. War fever broke out that spring when the battleship *Maine* was blown up in Havana Harbor. Asked by one General C. C. Coppinger if he wanted to join the army as a captain and be his aide-de-camp for the duration, Dudley readily accepted. The press was quick to ridicule him as "another wealthy society man" who was "to wear the blue." His only credential, the clipping in Fred's scrapbook noted, was his "fast" friendship with Coppinger, whom he had met in the West. Otherwise, it continued, he had had "no experience in military affairs" other than coming "from the old Winthrop family, which has furnished warriors to the country before." Whether he was ever a member of Roosevelt's Rough Riders or had actually stormed up San Juan Hill (the story my mother had heard) remains unclear. His nephew, Robert Winthrop Kean, claimed that he spent the brief war on Long Island and never left the United States at all.[40]

Meanwhile, there was Robert Winthrop and Company to attend to. It was no mean responsibility: the family fortune could wax or wane depending on the company's performance. Yet none of the sons seemed nearly as dedicated to the hustle and bustle of Wall Street as their father had been. Dudley had become head of the firm when his father died in 1892, but as my mother put it, he "was altogether too busy with his slaughtering" to pay much attention to business. In time, he left the company to be run by his partner, Mark T. Cox, and Cox's successors, his nephew

Dudley Winthrop, 1861-1912, president, Robert Winthrop and Company, 1892-1912, official portrait now at Wood, Struthers and Winthrop (courtesy Wood, Struthers and Winthrop Collection)

Charles W. Cox and W. J. Wilson.[41] Grenville, my mother said, "was altogether too busy with his beauty" to take a hand. As for her father, Fred, working at the company "had nearly killed him." Beek was unavailable while abroad on his various diplomatic assignments, though, when these ended, he did take up the reins. He would remain senior partner of the firm for twenty-five years, until his retirement in 1939.

If Dudley, Grenville, and Frederic seemed to have preferred the company fruits to the labors that kept them growing, their mother was apparently not so blasé. My mother described a quaint Kate Winthrop playing the stock market the way others of her class would play bridge.

> Grandma Winthrop was smart. When she was 35 years old, she retired, put on a little lace cap and sat by the fire. That's what my father said. At the age of 35, she said she was too old to do anything any more. They had lovely little coke fires in those days, and she'd sit by the fireplace, next to the coke fire, lace cap on her head—and invest.

In truth, it's unlikely that anyone in that day and age would have taken seriously the financial wheeling and dealing of a woman. Wall Street chronicler Henry Clews thought women "complete failures" as speculators, for they lacked the "mental qualities required.... They jump to a conclusion ... [and] are entirely unable to take the broad view of the whole question."[42] Another story, however, partially corroborates my mother's tale of Kate Winthrop as financial kibitzer. Winthrop historian Lawrence Mayo wrote that Kate Winthrop vowed to leave to each of her sons the same amount of money that she had been left—$8 million—and did.[43] To some degree, the story may need to be taken with a grain of salt. Kate Winthrop was just as concerned about the financial well-being of her daughters as that of her sons, and her will divided her assets (other than Dudley's portion) equally between her daughters and living sons.[44] Moreover, between the first reading of the Dow-Jones average in 1896 and the date of her death, in 1925, the average had quadrupled in value.[45] Is it such a surprise, then, that her assets had apparently quintupled over that same period?

— • —

To return to the pivotal year of 1900, Fred may have officially severed his ties with the firm, but his stay in Boston turned out to be sharply abbreviated. That spring he was back in New York, no doubt under his mother's watchful eye, for he had been taken with some illness and needed to be hospitalized. This wasn't the first time this seemingly fit young man had succumbed. His doctor had warned him off crew his senior year at Harvard, saying that the "strain and tension" of training was too much for his constitution.[46] This was followed by the blood poisoning attack, and with it, his unhappy dream of a visit from an unsympathetic Dorothy. In spring of 1900 the real-life Dorothy proved kinder. "I'm sorry you're having such a horrid time," she wrote him in May.

Once recovered, he returned to Boston, perching here and there for the next couple of years—the Union and Somerset Clubs in Boston, the Myopia Club in Hamilton, interspersed with a series of other addresses. Just before moving north, he had apparently purchased a fifty-two-acre farm near Dedham called Fairview. This evaporated mysteriously, for in the summer of 1900 he rented a house at Manchester-by-the-Sea with his brother Gren. Here at last, he hoped, he would have a clear path to Dorothy's door, for the Amorys had taken a house at Pride's Crossing nearby. Finding her suitor so close, and with nothing to do but pursue her, must have made Dorothy uneasy. Fred seemed to see no more of her than he had when he was commuting from New York. At the end of September she served him up with this curt note:

The senior Amorys rented a house on the North Shore with the Jeff Coolidges around 1900. Clockwise, starting at top left: *Libby Amory, Ned Amory, Amory Coolidge, George Amory, unidentified young man, Dorothy Amory, Clara Coolidge, Jeff Coolidge III, Jeffie Coolidge, Jr. "Jeff and Amory were little dears" (caption in Libby Amory's scrapbook)*

THE LONG COURTSHIP

Far right: *Mary and Frank Curtis in 1898. Dorothy wrote of Frank during their trip to Egypt, "He is too indifferent to be bored...."*

Right: *Helen R. Curtis, "Great Aunt Helen," dressed as Katharine de Medici at the Artists' Festival, April 5, 1893*

I cannot change my answer of Tuesday, and I do not see how you can think me considerate, when I am so cruel to you. Of course I like to see you, and would like to still more if you were only a friend.... If you only knew how unmoved I am, you would hate me.

Then, in a reversal of the usual scenario in which the young man is exiled to Europe to forget his unsuitable lady love, Dorothy was dispatched abroad for the fall, winter, and early spring of 1901. Her chaperone was her mother's sister, Aunt Helen Curtis, and her companions were Aunt Helen's children, her cousins Mary and Frank. From the Grand Hôtel des Palmes in Palermo, Dorothy wrote Fred the only letter she would send him during the entire trip:

I am not going to write you again, and hope you will try not to think of me. It can do no harm, and might do good, and I would be even happier if only you were happy, because I do feel badly for you, though I cannot help it.

Meanwhile, she deluged her mother with letters, mentioning Fred only twice. Once it had to do with a lost box, and the other time it was in connection with a letter he had written her about his trip to Washington. It must have been glamorous for he attended a dance at the White House and the inaugural ball for President McKinley and Vice President Roosevelt. There were evenings with Senator John Kean and his family, dinners at the British embassy, and he often escorted the daughter of the secretary of state, "Miss Hay." But all Dorothy passed on to her mother was

REARED *in a* GREENHOUSE

that "some lady" had mistaken Margaret Winthrop, Fred's third cousin once removed, for his sister and had "thought him the nicest and most devoted *brother* she had ever seen."

Dorothy was much more expansive about her own adventures. Her first letters told of Palermo in late November: "The carts here are so attractive, all handpainted, drawn by mules or donkeys so gaily harnessed with tall red plumes. The tiniest donkeys drag the largest loads, and it is very common to see one poor little skinny horse drag 10 or 14 people! … Such an excitement this a.m. [in the hotel]. The monkey escaped, all the men after him, then he jumped into Aunt H.'s window so 7 men flew upstairs after him, but couldn't catch him (how they made the room smell of garlic). So Frank turned them out of the room, talked monkey talk learned in Japan, and the monkey came right to him!"

Aunt Helen kept stealing the limelight: "Last night we went to the Opera, *Manon*, which was lovely.… One man … kept his opera glass right on our box. Mary and I did not know whether to take the credit, or give it to Aunt Helen, who kept tilting dangerously towards the edge of the box. Poor thing, she struggled so hard to keep awake."

Aunt Helen wasn't shy when it came to comfort, no matter what the public conveyance. Dorothy wrote her mother of the nine-hour train trip from Palermo to Taormina. Aunt Helen had been packing since August, so she was prepared. Off came her bonnet, on went a padded jacket and a pair of slippers, and then, "she undid and held up a huge pair of black corsets, just as we were drawing up to a station." Everyone laughed at that, even Aunt Helen.

In Taormina, Dorothy's main topic was a prince (not further identified) who entered their lives, first inviting her and Mary to look at the moon from his terrace.

> We three gazed at the moon shining on the water and on Etna, most romantic! Then he invited us in to see his apartments, very antique, he said. We didn't know whether we ought to go or not and felt as though we were being waylaid like princesses in fairy tales and I was sure I heard him lock the door behind us! However, his rooms were very pretty and he showed us many photos of his daughter and wife of whom he was very proud. Then he said he would show us his wife's room "tres antique." We couldn't refuse but were quite surprised to be ushered into his bedroom with his pajamas lying on the bed!! … Then, we went back to his parlor and had to admire his children all over again, and I tried to be very polite and make out that he looked young to have grown-up children, instead of which my French, not being as fluent as might be, I said "How old-looking your children are."

Egypt was to be the climax, Aunt Helen's idea. There, in "fascinating" Cairo, Dorothy couldn't contain her excitement about shopping. "What a day we have had! I don't know where to begin, but I will start by telling you I have spent untold sums! … I hope you will approve!" She bought $40 worth of crêpe de chine, "*so* pretty," $40 worth of "Maltese" silk, and a lovely gray wrapper for her mother.

One day outside the shops they discovered a parade of men, singing and laughing, and bearing a body covered with a "gay" cloth. "They were laughing," Dorothy wrote her mother, "because it was a woman and she has no soul." Even as brides, Dorothy discovered, Arabic women seemed more chattel than soul. She and Mary had been taken by their dragoman to view an Arab wedding. They had been marched through the courtyard where the men were gathered and up a flight of stairs, where they "were freely handled by the women, showing us the way, and just as I was going up to a bride, a tall Nigger eunuch grabbed me and pulled me away and an Arabian woman grabbed my other arm, and pulled the other way, then such a storm in Arabic as they had over me."

It turned out that there were not one, but two brides, and the eunuch and the woman were fighting over which would get Dorothy's flowers. Next Dorothy was treated to a viewing of the unveiling, when the bride and groom would see one another for the first time.

> That is all the ceremony, then they retire to bed … and leave all their guests to sit around or do as they like…. We were … shown the two bedrooms. One had a bed beautifully hung in satiny stuff embroidered in gold, quill to match, also steps to match, to climb up into the bed with. One large pair of slippers and one small pair were neatly laid out and their nightgowns hung up. They also had gold embroidered towels…. The brides, and in fact all the guests, were dressed in an attempted European style…. After a while, the poor brides looking ready to cry, were hustled from room to room.

But Assouan (Aswan), not Cairo, was their final destination, and getting there meant "doing the Nile" aboard the *Mayflower* and then the *Ibis*. For once, Dorothy indulged in a few complaints. Ship life, for instance, she found distasteful: "We *freeze* from sundown till about 9 a.m. and the rest of the day is hot and glary…. Our bath is of Nile water, so dirty, you can't possibly see the bottom." The tombs weren't much better: "all alike to those who do not know hieroglyphics…. [They have] no modern improvements … except bad air, which smells and feels old enough!" Their fellow travelers were the worst of all: "the stupidest set of people. There is an 'Honorable' and her friend, both very dressy and swell, two Englishmen going shooting, one's an Earl … there is a Mr. and Mrs. Steer, both commonplace. They are newly married, we think, she an old man's darling! The only other people are two deadly Englishwomen who are indefatigable sightseers and write home, copying Baedeker. Wouldn't you like me to? … The English swells don't even bow, just stare and take our best seats."

But these were brief clouds and mostly Dorothy stayed sunny. The donkey trips were entertaining: "Almost every day we land and gallop across the desert [on little donkeys], to see tombs, which is *great* fun." The sights of the evening, thrilling: "I never imagined such brilliant coloring, the sunset was *wonderful*, and then we rode home by moonlight, though tall palm trees, along the banks of the inundation of the Nile. Too weird and beautiful." The sunrises, challenging: "[We climbed] a *very* steep hill for more than half an hour. [Even] Aunt Helen did it and is not dead [because] to save her strength, [she] was borne aloft on a chair to the foot of the hill."

A page from Dorothy Amory's scrapbook, showing scenes from Egypt, winter of 1901

Dorothy's good humor was severely tested once they got to Assouan. Mary had come down with bronchitis and they would be marooned there for more than a month. Because she was sharing a room with the invalid, Dorothy also shared part of the treatment—the lighting of a hot fire in the room at five each morning. "Won't I roast!" she wrote. Luckily, she was spared the rest of the therapy: the doctor "sort of handles her [Mary] and stroked her hair once!" and directed that she be "blistered like a horse to prevent more thickening at the bottom of her lungs." In Mary's view, the doctor was just keeping her delicate to "so as to get his large fees!"

Aunt Helen was forever putting the blame for their extended stay on her daughter: "She says for years Mary has caused her such worry by not wearing proper clothes in winter and by having such bad colds. She said she couldn't stand it many years longer." Dorothy, however, thought the fault lay squarely on Aunt Helen: "I have thought Aunt H. *very* neglectful of Mary as she only sees her 3 or 4 times a day for a minute at a time.... She said to me she was sorry she couldn't do anything for Mary, but she was too old, she couldn't read to her and saw her presence made Mary nervous so she didn't sit with her.... She thinks Mary does not enjoy having her in the room." How lucky she was, Dorothy wrote Libby Amory, to have the mother she had: "I am more and more thankful you are what you are, and that we are sympathetic, and I don't take any of the credit."

While Mary languished, Aunt Helen trotted off each day on a donkey and occasionally helped out when Dorothy and Frank played tennis. "First she sat and watched us till a ball hit her, then she *ran* after our wild balls for exercise!" Frank, meanwhile, did little all day except "loaf around and read.... I never imagined such an indifferent person.... He is too indifferent to be bored, even!!"[47] When mealtimes rolled round, announced by a clanging gong, Dorothy would go and collect Aunt Helen and generally Frank. The meals themselves were "rather quiet as Aunt Helen is really very deaf and can hear nothing that is not said right to her rather loud.... Then she talks so low we can't hear her. However, if the person in the middle acts as Central, we have a very pleasant time." Modestly, Dorothy decided that Aunt Helen appreciated her being with them: "I am so *calm* and *phlegmatic*."

When a small shower washed the sand over the railroads, blocking all traffic from Cairo and washing away the telegraph poles, it began to seem as if their stay would never end. "We can get no food from Cairo and this hotel is running very short! Perhaps there will be a famine caused by a shower!"

But at last they boarded the *Mayflower* for Cairo where Dorothy summed up her views on the trip so far. It was the here and now that had caught her fancy: "I do not like Egypt as much as Sicily, but I am so glad to have seen it. I think modern Egypt and its history is thrilling, more so than ancient Egypt. All the temples and tombs are exactly alike except for size and shape. I am told some are a degenerate style of architecture but I see little difference. Isn't it scandalous my feeling this way!"

Things turned more conventional in Europe—the route home would include Naples, Sorrento, Rome, Paris, and London. And Dorothy was very much the carefree young lady as she hit the highlights. She found the Colosseum "wonderful" and at the Vatican, "I adore Raphael." Of course, she couldn't travel alone to Paris (the Curtises weren't going), so they hired a "strange fat female" to accompany her. Brother George was waiting for her: "We are so gay and I am having such fun!!"

Fred wouldn't have liked to know about the fun she was having:

This a.m., I go to the Louvre with Mr. Daesel, I wonder how it will seem, admiring Venuses etc. with him! Wednesday Mr. P., Mr. D. and Mr. N. dined with us and we went to the theatre. Pretty, dining at a restaurant alone with five men.... Yesterday Mr. P., Mr. D. and I rode bicycles to Versailles and Mr. N. took me in an automobile. We had a wild goose chase for machines, Mr. D. got awfully discouraged, it rained, we got covered with mud, didn't get lunch till three, it cleared, every one was cheerful, the palace was *too* interesting, got home by 6:30, automobile broke. We mended it with my hairpin, which saved us from walking home. Altogether, I had a splendid time.... I love writing you everything, but must dress for Mr. D. The crowd are very nice to me, I like them all and love Mr. P.

Dorothy in London, spring 1901

But Dorothy seemed just as excited about her purchases as her conquests: "I am very extravagant, and it is such fun. I have got more hats than I need.... I wish to prepare you for the worst so that my return home won't be marred a bit by foolish purchases." From London came more on hats: "Your letter saying I needed no hats arrived too late. I have bought four, I can set up a hat shop! I didn't mean to get so many, but circumstances led me into it."

On April 25, 1901, Fred showed up in New York City to welcome Dorothy home. His diary describes his reception: "Dorothy and George arrived last night on the *Teutonic*. I went to the Holland House and Waldorf to find them, and finally found them at the Manhattan." He returned to Boston with them on the one o'clock train, but the next day, and the day after, when he sought Dorothy at home, she was out.

— • —

The summer of 1901 was a repeat of 1900, with Fred ensconced on the North Shore in a house near the Amorys. He would pine after Dorothy at polo, at tennis, at home, at the club, where she was always decked out in the beautiful finery of the day. In June, Fred wrote in his diary, it was "a low-neck dress of light silk with little flowers arranged in rows. The dress was full in the skirt and had black satin bands over the shoulders." In August she appeared "dressed in white with a large pink bow and a large black and white hat."

In September, for a brief minute, he thought at last that she had come around. They were sitting on the piazza late one evening. He was waiting for his horse and buggy to take him home. Suddenly she took his arm. "I may change. I may change," she said to him. "I went home thinking we were engaged," he wrote in his diary, "but received a letter breaking it."

Dorothy knew she was playing with his feelings and hated herself for it. But what could she do? Was it kinder not to see him at all, which made him miserable, or to see him and rebuff him, which had the same effect? The warmest thing she could say was that she was "grateful" to him for taking it all in "the nice way" that he did. His resolve only hardened. In a lengthy letter dated November 30, he wrote: "I have made up my mind to win you if I can, because I know it means my happiness or the reverse. I have staked everything on this and it is win all or lose all. I am going to wait and hope. I can do nothing else.... It may be as you say that if I had an absorbing occupation I might be better off, although I doubt if in my state of mind I could have an absorbing occupation.… I don't want you ever to feel badly on my account."

Finally, in despair, Fred decided he had to get away. With Dorothy's brother Billy as his traveling companion, he spent four months from January to May 1902 in Europe and Egypt. On the eve of his departure, Dorothy's mother told him she thought he was wise to leave. Libby Amory must have felt sorry for him, for she took him into her confidence. She assured him "that she would be my friend," he wrote in his diary, "that she didn't understand Dorothy.… She said Dorothy told her last night she liked me better than any man she ever met."

Free from her persistent suitor, Dorothy had a gay winter, the high point of which was an extended visit to the resort of Aiken, South Carolina, with a bevy of Boston girls and her mother as the chaperone. In a letter to her son Billy, Mrs. Amory sounded amused about the sins from which she was supposed to be protecting her charges. The main danger was bridge, which the girls "played all the time.… Last Sunday the ministers of the different churches all preached against it," only to find themselves in an "awkward" spot when some one hundred well-meaning vacationers decided to raise money for the church—through a bridge tournament. Fred's fears about Aiken didn't have to do with cards. While still in Boston, Dorothy had written once or twice, twitting him about a certain unchaperoned Miss Hedley, who seemed to be constantly in the company of Billy and Fred on their travels. "Do tell me about Miss Hedley," she wrote, "is she attractive and what is her age and which is she after, you or Billy?"[48] But once she arrived in Aiken, the letters stopped. Fred heard from a mutual acquaintance that she was "so much admired" there. "I imagined," he wrote her, "perhaps you had found someone else that you cared for more than for me, and the thought haunted me and kept me awake for nights."

Clearly, the European cure was not working for Fred. He dreamed that he and Dorothy were running away from something, hand in hand, through an old barn. They mounted some high stairs without any rails and at the top they found the land-

Fred Winthrop in Egypt, winter of 1902

ing was only loosely nailed and their weight made the whole thing topple over. "I said," he wrote her, "'You will say yes now, won't you, because we only have a few seconds to live.' You did say yes, and we found ourselves standing on the ground with the broken stairs all around us." Today, that dream seems an eerie harbinger of what little time they would actually have together. Even Dorothy had seemed to sense something ominous, writing in an otherwise exuberant letter to her mother in 1900 from Dark Harbor, "I do certainly have a perfect time, but I am still young and will be sure to have sorrow later."

At the time, though, Fred's dream plainly reflected the pressure he knew he was putting on Dorothy. He

REARED *in a* GREENHOUSE

appealed shamelessly to her kind-heartedness, threw himself upon her mercy. Writing on the eve of his return home, he begged her, "Please, please try to say yes." She felt other pressures as well. After all, she liked the man, he was gentlemanly, obliging, and loved her passionately. Her mother approved, and she deeply respected her mother's opinion. One fact stood in the way: she still didn't love him. Her instant retreat in the fall from her hint that she "might change" suggests that she had been terrified of the prospect of marrying him. But at that moment something had also changed within her: from then on, every night, she began to pray for him.

Fred had been home from Europe for about a month when something seemed to give way. On June 17, seeing him on the same train, Dorothy would hardly speak to him. Soon thereafter, inexplicably, she said "she wished she could love me but that she would marry me anyway when she was twenty-five [she was then nearly twenty-four]." A week later she confirmed the agreement, promising that "she would never say no to me again" and confiding that she'd prayed for him every night since the fall before.

Their relationship, however, would rise and plummet more unpredictably than ever before. He took her for romantic moonlit drives through the dense Chebaco woods that ran between Manchester and Hamilton. On one of these drives, three weeks after she'd agreed to marry him, she allowed him to kiss her—and repeated once again she did not love him.

He chose her engagement ring and she chose the size. But she couldn't bring herself to set a date. On July 7 she said she couldn't marry him in the autumn. On August 19 she said she didn't know how she was "ever" going to marry him. On September 17, during another evening drive through the Chebaco woods, she warned him that he "would have to make her" marry him.

The dates kept changing. As if this weren't enough to distress Fred, Dorothy was just as skittish about letting anyone know of the engagement. She warned him not to be too attentive to her in public. He had written his brother Beek in the greatest of secrecy, and Beek had replied in like vein, saying he'd resisted sending a cable for fear someone might open it and solemnly promising not to tell a soul. Dorothy told her mother on September 21 that she had promised to marry Fred; the only effect of this news was that Billy started acting like flypaper, refusing to leave them alone when Fred came to visit. In mid-October she gave Fred "permission" to tell his mother of their engagement while he was visiting her in Lenox; but when he told her, the upshot was a cross note from Dorothy berating him for doing so.

It was all very discouraging. Sometimes she was kind but all too often she would be "cold and distant." He'd go see her and she'd be out. Then he wouldn't go because he was "afraid of boring her." For Dorothy, perhaps the torment was worse. Twice, she was on the verge of making it official, only to stop in her tracks, unable to go through with it. "She said," wrote Fred in his diary, " 'Don't you suppose I do love you a little? I suppose I do.' " But supposing wasn't knowing. Soon thereafter, she went to her room to get a picture of herself for Fred's birthday, on November 15. She wept, she confessed to him later, because she didn't love him.

Finally, on December 2, Fred was given permission to tell her mother they were officially engaged, and she agreed they would announce the engagement the following Monday. Wrote Fred, describing the moment he'd awaited so long, "She forced herself to do this, like the dear good brave girl she is." And on that joyless note, Frederic Winthrop ended the diary saga of his courtship of the beautiful Dorothy Amory.

The Amorys had assured Fred they were delighted by the match, and when Dorothy went to New York to be officially presented to the Winthrops, she took them "by storm," Fred proudly wrote Mrs. Amory. "My mother and sister Kitty think she is the loveliest person they ever saw. And the rest of the family are just as enthusiastic. I knew they would be." Self-deprecating as always, Dorothy acknowledged she had made a hit:

> If I stay here much longer, I will have my head turned. Everyone says such nice things, and Fred's family are *too* lovely. Of course, I know they were more than ready to like me on Fred's account. All the same, it is pleasing. Even Dudley, who seldom says anything, told his mother that he thought they would never be ashamed of me! Fred considered that splendid!

— • —

But what of Dorothy? Did she, in time, really come to love her serious and persistent suitor? With the curtain drawn—no more diary and very few letters—the evidence is scant. What little there is, however, suggests that, as Fred relaxed and she grew to know him as her fiancé and husband, she discovered that she could at last love him. On January 6, 1903, a month after the engagement was announced, her old humor had returned. She wrote him in New York: "Dearest Fred, Anne Tucker sent me some gold plates which are *sights*!.... Well, Fred dear, I hope you are missing me *horribly*. Are you as much as you thought you would? I *hope* so.... Good bye to my dear heart." Shortly before the wedding, she wrote him in terms that suggested her heart at last was his. She had this note hand-delivered to his apartment at 1 Marlborough Street, where he lay, once again, ill:

> You *must* pass the night here dearest Fred. I order it, and have ordered a cab to be at 1 Marlborough St. at 6:30 so you can bring your bag in it. I am a silly old fuss, but I do hate to have you feel sick, and night air is very bad for gripe [*sic*], so we expect you to pass the night. And you *must*! I won't marry you if you won't do that much for me! Dearest dearest Fred Your Dorothy[49]

REARED *in a* GREENHOUSE

A Winthrop and Amory Union

chapter FIVE

Dorothy Amory Winthrop on her wedding day, January 20, 1903

Fred Winthrop, 1903

T̸he wedding took place less than two months after Dorothy finally gave in to Fred—on January 20, 1903, at Emmanuel Church in Boston. To the mother of the bride, "When I remember how breathless I was, and doing chores until it was almost too late to scrabble into my clothes, and yours too!" it was all a haze of confusion.[1] On the society pages, however, all seemed smooth. "The eminent social station of the two families and the personal popularity of bride and bridegroom were evidenced in the large and brilliant attendance of wedding guests," reported one. Wrote another, "The Winthrop-Amory wedding … was, we think we can truly say, the largest and smartest of the winter, for the connection on the Amory side is unusually distinguished and the Winthrops brought over a brilliant New York clientele."[2] The occasion was marred by one minor chord: the bridegroom was still ill (malady unidentified) and it looked as if the festivities might have to be postponed. Luckily, all ended on a triumphant note: "He insisted it should go on, and pluckily remained at his post until the last guest had left."

For the smart set of that period, honeymoons took months and spanned continents. Although Fred Winthrop's illness delayed their departure, by January 31 Dorothy and Fred had visited Aiken, South Carolina, and were preparing to leave their next stop, Washington, D. C. Dorothy was concerned about her husband's health. "It is hard

REARED *in a* GREENHOUSE

to tell whether he is much stronger, but I think he must be, he eats such a lot," she wrote to her mother. But otherwise her letter exuded the spirit of old:

> The last evening we were at Washington, we decided to have a treat, so we had tea upstairs, and ordered scrambled eggs and hash and I put on a wrapper! We had a lovely time and just as we finished, we received Mr. Watress's card saying he was dining downstairs and wouldn't we come down, so I hurried into a dress and we sat with him and Mrs. while they ate butterballs and drank champagne. Thought we had had a better meal!

Dorothy and Fred on their honeymoon

In April they were in Florence. "We are having a very interesting time and trying to learn something about art," Dorothy wrote her mother. Then on to Paris in May, where the letters took a more domestic turn, focusing on towels and shams for their house, the prices, and such. "I haven't been homesick at all!" the young bride wrote. "I am so glad we are so near this summer, we must always be."

Nothing would have pleased Libby more. She and Dorothy had such fun together, and being in touch with her daughter lifted her spirits, even about gloomy subjects like her husband Ned's own illness. "With me to bully him and feed him in slops, he will improve," she wrote Dorothy the summer of her return.

Dorothy and Fred had no home of their own in which to settle when they returned from their travels. In one letter to her mother, Dorothy had queried: "Has Bobby Shaw's place been sold yet? I think Fred hankers after it a little. If we got that, we would let the little farm house to Marjorie. You would *have to* settle in Hamilton, I suppose, nearer the station."

— • —

Dorothy Winthrop, May 1903

The place Fred was considering, a barely finished hilltop mansion that had been planned for polo-playing Robert Gould Shaw II and his bride, the Virginia-born beauty Nancy Witcher Langhorne, was in Hamilton right across the Ipswich River from Ipswich. Neither town was among the most fashionable on Boston's North Shore. By 1890 Boston's elite had more or less completed their colonization of this stretch of land. But the choicest spots for summer "cottages" were the seaside resorts of Beverly, Manchester, and Magnolia. The meadows and glens of Hamilton, Wenham, and Ipswich, being inland, were off the beaten track and attracted far fewer persons of note.

With one exception. In 1882 Hamilton had begun to draw a certain species of prominent Bostonian, a type that thought hammering on horseback across rough fields and over stone walls chasing a fox was the height of glory. These were the pioneer members of the newly formed Myopia Club, a group of men looking for some place to indulge in their anglofolly, a sport only recently imported into this country by the summer crowds in Newport and Long Island. Myopia had been established in 1878 in Winchester, Massachusetts, on the country estate of wealthy Boston lawyer Frederick O. Prince. His four sons had named it in honor of their near-sightedness.

The move to Hamilton was prompted by the town's open countryside, which promised miles of uninterrupted galloping. What's more, the dozens of stone walls and streams presented opportunities aplenty to rise with the steed—or hurtle to the ground and sport the huntsman's badge of honor, a broken collarbone or head. One of the town's more prosperous residents, a Salem leather merchant by the name of John Gibney, was persuaded to rent his several-hundred-acre farm to the hunters, and on his death in 1891, the year that Fred first glimpsed Dorothy, Myopia bought it. The rambling century-old farmhouse[3] was altered to make a clubhouse and the club was incorporated officially as the Myopia Hunt Club. Those who escaped injury in the hunt were soon courting it on the polo field, and the local residents enjoyed watching the players wield their mallets as much as they did watching the huntsmen "risk life and limb in their almost hysterical enjoyment of the transplanted ancient sport" of fox hunting.[4]

In 1900, most of the people of Hamilton were engaged in nineteenth-century trades—farmers, stone masons, carpenters, storekeepers, blacksmiths, harnessmak-ers, wheelwrights, stablemen, ice dealers, milkmen, and railroad workers.[5] The com-munications revolution, however, and the establishment of public services made it possible for people like the Winthrops to imagine sinking roots in the country beside the Hamilton natives. The railroad had come in 1839, replacing the stagecoach as the means of public transportation into Boston, and Western Union was available by the 1870s. The first telephone was installed in the 1880s; the first volunteer fire depart-ment was established in 1896; the first "carriage without a horse, propelled by elec-tricity or steam," went through the town in 1897; and by 1902 "automobiles were quite plenty." You could get nearly everything you needed from the little shops that had begun to cluster around the depot in the mid- to late 1800s. This was South Hamilton—today's town center—which lay on Bay Road about a mile south of the historic center with the Myopia lands in between. You could find "ladies' and gen-tlemen's fine boots and shoes, gents' furnishing goods, hats, caps, umbrellas" in the clothing store of Frank E. Miller; "all kinds of temperance drinks, cigars, tobacco, confectionery, crockery, glass, tin and woodenware" in Samuel A. Waitt's poolroom; and "dry and fancy goods, ribbons, laces, thread, soda and soft drinks, confectionery, fruit and cigars" at Hanna Crosby's variety store. Heinrich Bernhardt had a hair-dressing establishment and Sing So Ho, a Chinese laundry.[6]

In one particular, Hamilton's rich newcomers tried to set back the clock, hoping to preserve the splendid rural prospects from too many commercial incursions. Many of them displaced old-time landowners, the families who had farmed some eighty or ninety acres for years but who, sniffing a profit, gladly sold off all or part of their farms to the city folks. Between 1885 and 1905 the number of farms in Hamilton

REARED *in a* GREENHOUSE

would drop by one-third, from ninety-three to sixty-two. But this did not mean the end of farming, just that the "gentleman" farmer had replaced the hardscrabble farmer.[7]

Among the thirty or so men who had been drawn to Hamilton's open fields and closed country club was an assortment of able businessmen and public figures.[8] Dolph Agassiz, the old friend to whose house bachelor Fred had so often repaired to mend his shattered psyche, was rare among the group for the scholarly strain in his background. His grandfather, eminent Swiss naturalist Jean Louis Rodolphe Agassiz (1807–73), had revolutionized the teaching of natural history at Harvard. His step-grandmother, Elizabeth Cabot Cary, a Brahmin bluestocking, became, after Agassiz' death, the first president of Radcliffe College.[9] Others were Frederick H. Prince, of Myopia founding fame; eight-term congressman August Peabody "Gussie" Gardner, who married Senator Henry Cabot Lodge's daughter Constance and who was Dorothy's first cousin on both sides; and George von Lengerke Meyer, who served as ambassador to Italy and Russia, U.S. postmaster general, and secretary of the navy.

No one lived very far from anyone else in Hamilton, but if the Winthrops bought Bobby Shaw's place, their closest neighbors would be Charles Goodnough Rice and his wife, Anne Proctor Rice. The Rices lived year-round on Turner Hill Farm, a seven-hundred-acre estate in Ipswich they had bought shortly before the turn of the century. They were very much in tune with the retiring Fred Winthrop. C. G. loved polo, but also work and quiet. Anne loved riding, but also children and flowers. He was content to pursue his thriving business concerns—he was both president of the N. W. Rice Company, which imported hides and other leather products, and of the U. S. Smelting, Refining and Mining Company of Boston. She wanted to have a home that would welcome the world. And the house they built, the baronial, Elizabethan "mansion house" that outshone anything else in town, would perfectly serve that purpose.[10]

If the Rices promised to be *gemütlich* neighbors, the Appletons, who also lived near the Shaw property, must have whetted Fred Winthrop's historical appetite. Three hundred fifty years earlier, the Appletons and the Winthrops had been neighboring country squires in England. The "Appultons" were prominent citizens in Little Waldingfield, Suffolk, when Adam Winthrop, Governor John Winthrop's grandfather, bought nearby Groton Manor in 1544. In 1630 Governor John Winthrop had hoped Samuel Appleton would be in his party on the *Arbella*, but Appleton was unable to settle his affairs in time. In 1635, at the age of forty-five, Samuel Appleton brought his wife and five children to New England. Within a year he had received a grant from the Town of Ipswich of "Mr. Appleton's farme"—a 770-acre spread of "medow and upland."[11] At the time Ipswich was considered "the most remote and isolated settlement in Massachusetts Bay."[12]

The Winthrops and the Appletons had missed renewing their old country status as New World neighbors by a scant two years. In 1633 John Winthrop, Jr., led the expedition that settled the lands in and around Ipswich (then called Agawam). On

John Winthrop, Jr., 1606-76, founder of Ipswich, Massachusetts, and first governor of Connecticut (courtesy Harvard University Portrait Collection, gift of Robert Winthrop, representing the Winthrop family, to Harvard University, 1964)

A WINTHROP AND AMORY UNION

arrival, he secured for himself two choice parcels of land, including Castle Hill, a promontory commanding a beach view that remains today one of the most spectacular on the North Shore. He had a house built for himself and his family, laid out the town, and was expected to stay and govern (he was even called the "Sagamore [Chief] of Agawam" after the Indian chief there). But Winthrop was a restless sort, other responsibilities beckoned, and by the end of 1634 his involvement in the town had petered out.[13] Within a decade he had sold all of his property in Ipswich.[14]

When Fred Winthrop was eyeing the Shaw place, Samuel's lineal descendant Francis R. "Frank" Appleton was still farming Appleton Farms, the eighth generation of the family to work the land. His father, Daniel, from whom he had taken over around the turn of the century, had been a pioneer cattle breeder who raised prizewinning Jerseys. Frank would diversify the herd, increase the farm size from 770 to a thousand acres, plant pine groves on the hills and line the avenues with maple trees.[15] Today the place stands as the oldest farm continuously in the hands of one family in the country—celebrated "not [as] another summer estate, but ... a living farm."[16] And the Winthrops and Joan Appleton (Frank Appleton, Jr.'s widow) remain close friends, even if my mother's brother Fred used to josh Frank, Jr., that the Appletons had come over in "steerage."

—— • ——

Apart from Dolph and the Appletons, hills and horses, surely what Frederic Winthrop liked above all about Hamilton was Bobby Shaw's place itself. This was a beautiful 140-acre estate with the Ipswich River running through it. The property belonged to a glamorous young couple, Bobby Shaw and his wife, Nancy. They'd met at a polo match, and while she sized him up as a "rather spectacular young man ... who rode a one-eyed pony," he decided then and there that he would marry her.[17] And so he did, in 1897. As newlyweds, Nancy and Bobby cut a swath among the North Shore young. In October 1901 they entertained Fred and Dorothy at a luncheon honoring a certain Mrs. Astor (the hostess little imagining that she herself would soon be sporting that name). But already their marriage was on the verge of dissolution. Bobby was an alcoholic, and on the second night of their honeymoon Nancy had fled. The senior Shaws had settled the Hamilton estate on the couple, in hopes that it might repair their marriage. Instead, matters only grew worse. Nancy and Bobby were divorced in 1902, and the place was up for sale the next year.[18] Nancy went on to become the fabled Lady Astor. Her marriage in 1906 to Waldorf Astor brought her access to the Astor millions and a seat in the House of Commons—the first ever held by a woman—inherited initially from her husband but earned in elections thereafter. Though her stay in Hamilton was brief, Nancy's name lives on. Today, the site at the end of the Winthrops' front driveway where she and Bobby had roosted in a cottage waiting for the big house to be finished is called "Nancy's Corner." Located at the intersection of Cutler Road and Highland Street, it serves as a parking lot for Appleton Farms Grass Rides, one-time Appleton lands that now belong to the Trustees of Reservations.

Lady Astor, the former Nancy Langhorne Shaw. She fled her Hamilton home when her new husband Bobby Shaw proved a drunk and a boor, leaving it available for Fred Winthrop to buy. (Courtesy Library of Congress)

REARED *in a* GREENHOUSE

The house on the hill over-looking the Ipswich River that Fred Winthrop bought in 1904 and which remains in the family nearly a century later

The marriage broke up just as construction was more or less complete on a "modern house and stable," as a press clipping described the rambling English arts and crafts style house and stables below. It was one of the first commissions of Guy Lowell, one of Libby Amory's relatives, who was then still working on his architecture degree at Harvard. In time, Lowell would become one of Massachusetts' best-known society architects. But he was just cutting his teeth on the Shaw commission, and it was hard to tell what it would look like upon completion. When she was fifteen, my mother wrote a little history describing the condition of the house when her father bought it:

> Only the first floor had been completed when young Mr. Shaw and his wife quarrelled and divorced, so old Mr. Shaw sold the place to Father after finishing the house as cheaply as possible. The third floor was just a large attic, which Father built over later.[19]

The Winthrops most likely didn't mind, and in the fall of 1903 Fred consummated what the press dubbed one of the "most important" real estate sales of the season. The house on the hill overlooking the Ipswich River became theirs for the then-handsome sum of $55,000. Fred called his country home Groton House Farm, after Groton Manor in England where his Winthrop ancestors had resided. In the 1930s it became the home of Frederic's son, Frederic, Jr. Today, Groton House, surrounded by its beautiful rolling hills, river, stables, and hemlocks, remains the residence of Mrs. Frederic Winthrop, Jr., and still stands always open and ready to receive all of her family, her sons and daughters, their spouses, and an ever-growing flock of grandchildren and great-grandchildren.

The Ipswich River view is beautiful year-round.

A WINTHROP AND AMORY UNION

During the summer and fall of 1903, while they were waiting to settle on their new place, Fred and Dorothy rented the "small Quincy A. Shaw, Jr., cottage at Pride's Crossing."[20] It was just a simple clapboard house, but with room for their several large dogs, and they had their horse and buggy to take them about. Dorothy, already pregnant, looks shyly radiant sitting on the porch with her long hair drying in the sun, as if she is completely at home in her new life.

As the Winthrops were taking possession of the Shaw place, Dorothy's sister Clara Coolidge was becoming mistress of a seaside mansion that would place the Winthrop house in an architectural shadow. Her husband Jeffie had hired famed architects McKim, Mead and White to design a glorious brick and white marble edifice in the English Palladian revival style, with two pavilions and Roman columns. The land was in Magnolia, about fifteen miles from Hamilton, at Coolidge Point, a spectacular promontory into the ocean that Jeffie's father had purchased in 1871. The house would be dubbed locally the Marble Palace and—though it was torn down in 1958 and the land on which it sat turned over to the Trustees of Reservations in 1990—the structure is well remembered even today in architectural circles.[21]

By 1903, Clara and Jeffie had three sons—Thomas Jefferson III, Amory, and Billy—with a fourth soon to come. Their new house was planned just for the summer, but what glorious summers it offered. You could hear the calls of wheeling seagulls and smell the boxwood hedge that set off a gracious staircase leading to the front door. And from the windows, you looked out on the magnificent lawns, speckled with the shade of towering elms and oaks and stretching seaward on all sides, finally ending in rocky cliffs which fell abruptly to the waters of Kettle Cove and the Atlantic beyond.

Both Dorothy and Clara had come a long way from the string of modest summer homes in which they had grown up. Their new residences made Mrs. Flint's in Lenox and Mosquito Hut in Wareham look like maids' quarters. Libby Amory, who later referred to herself as "dirt-sprung Grandma," was probably not all that impressed.

Though the Amorys spent summers in cottages on both properties, they also continued renting places here and there rather than living off their well-married daughters.[22]

— • —

Groton House Farm was a beautiful setting in which to begin a new family, and sure enough, the children soon began to arrive—Robert, on January 21, 1904; Dorothy, on May 21, 1905; and Frederic, on June 30, 1906—all three in just two and one-half years. In those days of birthing at home, with the horse-drawn doctor and his useless black bag in attendance, the advent of each new baby was a grave worry. Robert's birth, in Libby Amory's words, was "terrible hard."[23] Labor lasted more than two days, with Robert weighing in at a whopping ten and a quarter pounds. Afterward, all wasn't well with the mother. In February phlebitis set in and not until March could Dorothy even be carried downstairs. By mid-March she went to lunch with her mother—"out for first time" in almost two months.[24] It was a desperately anxious time for Frederic.

Despite the physical repercussions, Dorothy Winthrop was an enthusiastic mother. For all three children she kept extensive records chronicling weight, ounces of formula, cries, smiles, teeth, turnings over, sittings up, standings, crawlings, and first steps. Robert must have been the most placid baby on record (or had the most adept nurse), for his mother didn't "hear him cry from July 3rd to August 19 except for one bad burp." He remained a model child until little Dorothy made her appearance on May 21, 1905, at which point he started to become headstrong.

Dorothy junior initially seemed just as cheery as Robert: at five months "laughed out loud when tickled with powder puff," loved to play and coquette, and later became "very fond of trying on new bonnets." Her mother never seemed to worry about her, although Dorothy's physical development was sluggish. At ten months she was "very fat and helpless" and couldn't roll over "or move if put on her back." By mid-June 1906 she had finally "turned onto her face in bed," though she "couldn't get back."

At that point Dorothy senior herself had once again become decidedly larger, for her third child was about to arrive. Compared to Robert and Dorothy, who was a relatively dainty eight pounds, fourteen ounces, at birth, Fred would prove the champion, weighing an immense eleven pounds, five ounces, when he emerged on June 30, 1906. It was a misleading start. In a week his mother began noting digestive problems. By the end of the first month he had barely regained his birthweight, and the parents became so alarmed they called two doctors. "Poor little Fred has been *very* sick," wrote Dorothy to her mother on August 1.

Jeffie and Clara Coolidge and their four sons in 1905. From left, Billy, 4, Jeffie, Jr., Clara with Linzee on her lap, Amory, 10, and Jeffie III, 12

Below left: *New parents Dorothy and Fred Winthrop with first-born Robert*

Below: *Soon there were two, Robert and Dorothy, and a third, Fred, was on his way.*

A WINTHROP AND AMORY UNION

It took some sleuthing on the part of the parents, with the aid of one Miss Carlisle, to get to the root of the problem. As Dorothy continued in her letter to her mother:

And the *whole* trouble has been that our milk pails have been *filthy*. We only found out on Sunday, we ought to have found out sooner by investigating personally, but Fred asked Charlie [a handyman] and he said everything was clean. Charlie is now furious because Miss Carlisle went up herself, and looked at everything and found him out. She brought back the pails and both doctors said that that was more than enough to make any baby *very* sick and that it was a wonder the other two weren't upset.

The doctors ordered the parents to get some clean supplies, but no one was around to help. First, they asked the chauffeur in the hire of Dorothy's brother George, but he pleaded "a terrible headache." Taking matters into their own hands, they "harnessed up and went … down a side road" where the suffering chauffeur was spotted strolling with a girl. As soon as he saw them, "he put his head down and put his handkerchief up to his face."

It all ended well. "Thank goodness the baby is straightening out, both doctors were surprised and delighted to find him so much better," Dorothy wrote her mother. "I don't think I ever was so happy; as last night I was so worried." Fred the Frail was soon the most boisterous of the lot. At nine months, his mother wrote in amusement, "Cannot be left alone in his high chair as he tilts it off its legs."

The likes of milk pail Charlie and the reluctant chauffeur seemed to come with the territory in Hamilton. One local observer commented, "It is like drawing teeth to make Hamilton people do anything for you.… After days of delay, you must keep your eye on them or they will slip out from under your hand, leaving your potatoes half hoed, your furnace half mended, your awnings half hung. When you can catch them long enough to scold them about it, they seem to think it is a good joke and laugh."[25] For the Winthrops, the servant problem also included Julian. This hireling had been allowed to stay in a house on the place for next to nothing on condition that he fix it up for the Amorys. Dorothy wrote her mother in exasperation that Julian hadn't "done a thing but stick nails everywhere and tear the paper… and then … [left] some old rat-eaten paper which he found in the attic for you to put on!!" And then there was the "servant smell" in Robert's room, on which Dorothy remarked with distaste.

Fred and Dorothy tried to crack down. She wrote her parents, "Of course, it is much more Christian to be like you and Pa and not mind any imposition and be very easy going and be *done* rather than risk any disagreement, but Fred isn't made that way, neither am I." It's unlikely, though, that their sternness amounted to much. Fred groused that he had to do all the dirty jobs around the place himself because the men refused to do them.[26] Dorothy was probably an even softer touch. She even once offered to let an employee wear her furs when it was especially cold. "The servants adored her," my mother recalled later.

Though managing the place was no mean task—an unfinished house with vast rooms and stately halls plus acres of unlandscaped grounds and gardens—Fred Winthrop had more time to cope than many of his male contemporaries. Unlike his

Fred Winthrop ran a working farm, enjoying the exercise and training son Robert in the ways of the land as early as possible.

REARED *in a* GREENHOUSE

"merchant" friends (then the term for a businessman), Fred had permanently with-drawn from office life when he quit Robert Winthrop and Company in 1900. He list-ed his occupation as "gentleman" in the 1904 Hamilton voting records, changing it to "retired" the following year.[27] "Gentleman" was in fact a recognized career at the time, indulged in by some fifty members of Boston's Somerset Club.[28] But Fred Winthrop was still only in his midthirties when he became a "retired gentleman" and assumed the task of land stewardship as a gentleman farmer. Like the Appletons and the Rices he undertook serious farming, making his family—in my mother's words—"live off the land." This meant that in years to come, several times each win-ter up from Hamilton to Boston would trundle "a farm wagon, pulled by the two farm horses, piled with vegetables, horrible root vegetables—turnips, carrots, acorn squash"—crops that would leave a permanent bad taste in my mother's mouth. (In later life, only cabbage among the winter crops would sound good to her, perhaps because that was the only one her family didn't grow.)

In the beginning were the dogs. At left, Robert is over-shadowed. *At right,* a photo from Libby Amory's scrapbook captioned "Dorothy and her family."

Fred was also mastering a pair of other skills—nurturing dogs and rearing children. In the beginning were the dogs: page after page of Dorothy's scrapbook is devoted to Great Dane Ada, head erect and tail pointed behind; on her hind legs; nose in the ground; searching for prey; with her canine friends, May, Bill, and Sammy. After the children began to be born, they would be accorded a place in the pictures, though often dwarfed by their four-footed friends. Libby Amory picked up on the spirit of canine worship. Her own scrapbook, interspersed with photos of her children and grandchildren, contains a gracefully posed picture of Dorothy, properly hatted, alone with four large dogs, with the caption "Dorothy and her family."

Fred Winthrop, the proud papa, with Robert and Dorothy

Fred sometimes played the reluctant father, one day refusing to take baby Dorothy in his arms when a friend was visiting. "I don't have anything to do with the baby," he explained. "That's

A WINTHROP AND AMORY UNION

Top: *Robert was the merriest child imaginable.*

Above: *Little Dorothy was a more sober sort.*

because she'll rule you when she grows up," the friend had laughed.[29] The scrapbook, however, belies any misgivings on his part. He's certainly every bit the proud papa, standing with Dorothy senior and little Robert in the summer of 1905. And the next summer, there is little Dorothy cradled in his right arm while he looks happily at Robert, held firmly in his left.

By the fall of 1906 life had settled into a routine in the Winthrop household, insofar as any routine is possible with three children under three. They must have made a wriggling threesome, all eyeing each other with varying degrees of affection and curiosity. As the eldest and heir presumptive, Robert was the apple of the family camera's eye and the star of his mother's scrapbook. He was the merriest child imaginable, little bow mouth turned up in a smile, eyes just laughing slits, running, laughing.

Dorothy was quite different. She had a nature "very sweet and affectionate," her mother wrote, but "not so jolly as Robert.…When she gets mad, she gets *very* mad. Very decided.… More obstinate and contrary than Robert and *screams* as though her heart would break if you forbid her severely." She idolized her big brother. At ten months, her mother wrote, she would lie on the bed and watch Robert "for ¾ hour." At two, she "has to do what he [Robert] does." Dorothy's somber side, however, dominates her mother's scrapbook. In most of the pictures, the pudgy face is intent,

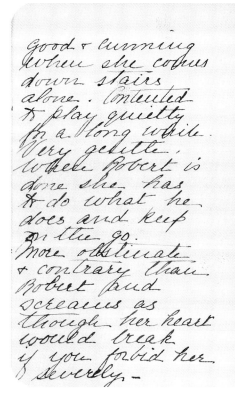

Dorothy Winthrop's comments on baby Dorothy in her baby book

REARED *in a* GREENHOUSE

Far left: *Three little ones under four were a handful, best managed by three nurse-maids.*

Left: *Frederic and Dorothy Winthrop, September 1906, at Wareham. Just the two of them, alone, for once.*

mouth downturned and eyes startled, and the squat small frame is like an over-stuffed Miss Muffet, so many clothes must she wear.

Thanks to all the servants—when needed, the Winthrops could muster one per child—Fred and Dorothy could carry on with family visits whenever they chose. In early September 1906, they took off to Wareham, where Billy and wife May had taken over Mosquito Hut. Billy had become engaged to Wareham neighbor Mary Stockton in the summer of 1903, seemingly more to the delight of his mother than to himself. "Bill doesn't seem in the least excited," Libby Amory had written Dorothy, "but I am…. [The ring will be a color] better than a diamond—and not very large— that he calls vulgar and May wouldn't like it either." Now, no longer newlyweds, they were settled in nicely, enjoying the lazy summer days by the ocean just as they had in their youth.

Just how inundated the Winthrops had become by children is suggested by two pictures taken during that visit. For once Fred and Dorothy are standing side by side, with no children, no dogs. In one picture he's holding a tennis racquet and she's grinning broadly; in the other she's looking up at him happily while he smiles contentedly at the camera.

They were to spend that fall and early winter in Hamilton. It was so beautiful. The Winthrop side of the family descended on them at the end of a warm, leafy September—Fred's brother Dudley

Below left: *"Sweet May with Robert" (caption in Libby Amory's scrapbook, January 1906)*

Below: *Billy Amory in Wareham, September 1906*

A WINTHROP AND AMORY UNION

In late September 1906, the Hamilton Keans and Dudley Winthrop came to visit. Photo at left, from left, *Hamilton Kean, Fred Winthrop, Kitty Kean, Dudley Winthrop;* at right, *Kitty and son John.*

along with his sister Kitty Kean, her husband Ham, and their sons. For Thanksgiving, someone produced illustrated poems for both Mr. and Mrs. Winthrop, celebrating their domestic bliss. Fred's went like this:

> *Mr. Winthrop*
> *What a turmoil, what a clatter!*
> *Goodness gracious! what's the matter?*
> *Freddy's tumbling down the stairs.*
> *Robert will not say his prayers.*
> *Dorothy alone is good.*
> *Minds her Ma, and eats her food.*
> *And you say, when stunned by noise,*
> *How could I ever wish for boys!*

Dorothy's poem was more muted, making the point that though some say country life is "very slow and dull," at Groton Farm there's "enough to fill one day." Dorothy, posing by the steps with Robert and little Dorothy, looks as if for her the country certainly does offer enough. Even little Dorothy seems content, caught for once with a smile on her face, while her mother, serene and beautiful, holds her close.

Winter came on, putting a cold, white cap on their house and laying feathery white lace over their beautiful river view. Farms Road and the Appleton Wood Road leading off it were buried in virgin white. Robert made a tiny figure standing alone in the winter landscape. Fred took him ice-sledding, with Ada dragging him over the frozen pond.

January seemed a good time to have a professional photographer come around to capture Dorothy and her children. It couldn't have been easy, making three squirmy little ones look their best. Only once did he catch a group photo with smiles, and that was of little Fred on his mother's lap. The picture of the three children with their mother is at best pensive. And there is one shot of little Dorothy with such a sad, far-away gaze, it's almost as if she's wondering fearfully what life holds in store.

— • —

In early February 1907 Fred and Dorothy escaped the winter, heading for Puerto Rico for a three-week visit with Fred's brother Beekman, who was finishing up a three-year term as governor of the island. It was a "horrid" trip, wrote Dorothy to her mother, for the "little tub" they were on "tossed and rolled a great deal." Such thoughts soon vanished, however, in the sumptuous quarters of her brother-in-law and his wife Melza. The couple were installed in the governor's old palace, La Fortaleza. "Fifty rooms in all!" Dorothy wrote her mother, astonished. "The ground floor is taken up in offices. I haven't yet succeeded in counting the parlors." President Roosevelt and his wife Edith had been there in November and Secretary of War William H. Taft would stop by in April.[30]

Between 1897 and 1900, while Fred was weaning himself from New York to devote more time to Dorothy in Boston, Beek had been at Harvard Law School. He made the *Harvard Law Review* and graduated second in his class. In 1900 he was whisked away to the Philippines for the first phase of a thirteen-year

A WINTHROP AND AMORY UNION

Two of the 50 rooms in La Fortaleza, where Beekman Winthrop exercised colonial rule

Beekman Winthrop logged in a parade of distinguished visitors during his last year as governor of Puerto Rico, among them President Theodore Roosevelt, Roosevelt's wife Edith, and Secretary of War and president-to-be William Howard Taft.

career in government. It was a time when most Americans, including President McKinley himself, thought of the Philippines as a place "somewhere around the other side of the world."[31] But when William Howard Taft, the 325-pound leviathan who had been appointed the first civilian governor to oversee the transition and "civilizing" of the islands under U.S. tutelage, invited Beekman to serve as his private secretary, Winthrop quickly accepted. One lengthy profile raised a passing question about his choice of career: "It wasn't a job that a well-to-do young lawyer with good family connections might be expected to crave." But on balance, the reporter gave "young Mr. Winthrop" full credit: "[He] swallowed the disagreeableness, spent the thousand dollars [stipend for the job], and some more, in such creature comforts as were attainable, and buckled down to work."[32] Beekman would spend the next four years serving in quick succession as assistant executive secretary and acting executive secretary of the Philippines and finally as judge of the Court of First Instances.

In 1904 President Theodore Roosevelt, like Taft a personal friend, appointed Beekman governor of Puerto Rico. The inauguration ceremonies were, wrote one jaundiced observer, "as elaborate as could be expected in Porto Rico." But Winthrop's performance quickly overshadowed this unpromising start, and soon the press was calling Winthrop "one of the hardest working officials of the government service." Reporters commended him for immersing himself in his job, learning Spanish and studying "native conditions."

Just before the Puerto Rico appointment in 1903, Beekman married. Far away in the Philippines, he had not been among the "brilliant New York clientele … brought over" for Frederic's own January 1903 wedding in Boston. Fred and Dorothy, however, did make it to New York for Beekman's, on October 3, 1903. Beekman's courtship of Melza Riggs Wood seems to have been as effortless as

REARED *in a* GREENHOUSE

Frederic's of Dorothy had been labored. The wooing and winning of Melza took place half a world away, with Beekman in the Philippines and Melza in New York. The two probably knew each other well, however, for they were close neighbors in Murray Hill. Melza may also have been attracted by the idea of marrying into a large, intact family, for many members of her family had succumbed to scarlet fever.

Beekman was back in Cambridge during Harvard commencement weekend in 1905, but this time on official duty with not a moment to spare for family. By then governor of Puerto Rico, he appeared on the doorstep of Bishop William Lawrence in hopes of conferring with William Howard Taft, then secretary of war who in turn was there hoping to have a word with his commander-in-chief, President Roosevelt. The president was staying at the Lawrences in connection with his twenty-fifth Harvard reunion. All were at the Lawrence table save the president, who sat on a sofa behind Beekman's chair, while Taft and Beek tried to gobble down supper before rushing to catch a 7:30 train. Said Mr. Taft, "Winthrop, don't you want to do a little telephoning for me just for the sake of old times?" The bishop's daughter, Marian, who was watching the scene unfold and who afterward preserved it in her diary, wrote that "of course Winthrop jumped up … flew to the telephone, where he spent the next course or two of the dinner." By the time he returned to the table Roosevelt had taken his chair, and anyway, it was time to catch the train. The "huge unwieldy" Taft, the diary continues, made "the most deliberate of good-byes all round, while Beekman Winthrop collected all the baggage, umbrellas, etc." Then they were off, Taft still "smiling and deliberate and lumbering, and poor Beekman Winthrop looking distraught." That would have been the end of it, except that Taft had forgotten some papers. So back thundered the carriage, through the front door burst Beekman, "with bows and apologies, still smiling, grabbed some papers off the mantelpiece," and murmured to another lowly factotum to "telephone the Back Bay Station to hold the train." Whereupon he made "more bows and apologies and was gone."[33] No doubt when he got back to Puerto Rico, Beekman laughed about that comedy of errors. Both he and Melza gloried in the unusual.

The press was as impressed by Melza as it was by Beekman. They praised Melza's Spanish and her hospitality, writing that she "knew the Latin heart" and through her charm was able to "[persuade] the women to trust her, and come to her teas and receptions…. Soon she had the governor's old

This photo of Beekman Winthrop appeared in the New York *Independent of June 16, 1904, and the* New York Sun *of November 8, 1904. The latter said that Winthrop was the first U.S. colonial envoy to converse with the local people in their own tongue and credited him with establishing conditions that allowed the Puerto Ricans to exercise their "love of order, peace and justice."*

Beekman Winthrop and Melza Wood in Lenox, visiting his mother Kate Winthrop and brother Grenville, shortly before Beek and Melza's wedding in October 1903

A WINTHROP AND AMORY UNION

San Juan, Puerto Rico (from Dorothy Winthrop's scrapbook)

palace filled with native officials and their families." It didn't take long for Dorothy to recognize her sister-in-law's diplomatic talents. Unaware that Melza always "received from four to five," she had descended from the *de rigueur* afternoon siesta too early and found herself in the presence of a visitor. There was nothing for it but to go in and bow. The butler explained to the visitor in Spanish that the unknown young woman was the governor's sister-in-law, but after that, the two could do nothing but sit and smile at each other. Finally, Melza appeared and broke the conversational ice with a flow of Spanish. Later that evening, at a costume ball, the Winthrop party sat in the governor's box where Melza astonished her Boston visitor, chattering in "first Spanish then English with perfect ease." "Everyone is so enthusiastic about Melza," she wrote from Cuba, where they went after they had left San Juan. "And they ought to be. Her tact and never failing interest in everyone are wonderful."

Dorothy found the Puerto Rico weather "perfect," the place "beautiful" and "fascinating," though the abundance of poverty in San Juan came as something of a shock. For the visiting Winthrops, the pace was also a little languid. "We do nothing

Scenes from the interior of Puerto Rico (from Dorothy Winthrop's scrapbook)

REARED *in a* GREENHOUSE

in the mornings and retire from two to four, then generally go to the club ... or we have refreshments downstairs, and generally lots of callers." The practice of leaving cards, which had become a suffocating social ritual in the United States at the turn of the century, had invaded the colonies, with the governor's sister-in-law and houseguest a particularly tempting target. "All leave cards for me," Dorothy continued in her letter to her mother, "so I have quantities of calls to make on all sorts of people, those who can speak English and those who can't. As ... it is etiquette to make quite a long call, and we never start out till 4:45, I don't see that I will ever return them all!"

The Amorys spent lots of time visiting their Winthrop grandchildren and were glad to supervise the household while Fred and Dorothy were in Puerto Rico. At left, *Ned Amory with daughter Dorothy and granddaughter Dorothy;* at right, *Libby Amory with granddaughter Dorothy.*

Beyond the governor's palace and the homes of a few wealthy locals, Puerto Rico was a primitive place, a land where years of Spanish misrule had left a people in terrible poverty with little in the way of industry or infrastructure to offer them a way up. Beekman believed, in the turn-of-the-century tradition of colonial noblesse oblige, that America had a responsibility to bring its civilizing powers to bear, and became "an ardent friend of good schools, good roads and good government." And the young American governor was winning press plaudits for "ruling wisely, in a not altogether harmonious population ... [and] bringing order out of the chaos left by long misgovernment." But Dorothy didn't care much for the affairs of state in which her brother-in-law was engaged. Only the trappings of his life amused her. "Today the 200 men from the Chamber of Commerce arrived and all swarmed over the Palace to see it," she wrote her mother. "As it had been pouring all night they brought in lots of mud!" Another day, they ventured into the interior of the island, arriving at "a little town where we were the second automobile that had ever been there and it was too funny, the excitement we caused. Everyone from every direction came running to see us and surrounded our car until driven off by the policeman."

While their parents were away, Robert, Dorothy, and Freddy had been left under the supervision of the Amorys. They were doting grandparents and what little concern Dorothy had about the three was blithe.

> I do not worry about them as I know they are all right *as I trust you to cable*, but I *long so* at times to see them.... Of course the children do not even notice we have gone, I suppose! ... I wonder if [they] will be glad to see me! I suppose May will coach them to appear to be.

She was full of the news of Beekman Winthrop's next move. "Isn't it *splendid* Beek and Melza are going to Washington!" she wrote enthusiastically, referring to her brother-in-law's upcoming appointment as assistant secretary of the treasury. Beek and Melza were to spend the next six years in the capital. First he would serve in the Roosevelt administration, then in President Taft's as assistant secretary of the

*Robert and Dorothy in
Boston in March 1907*

navy, ending his public service career when the election of Democrat
Woodrow Wilson in 1913 would remove all his influential friends
from office. "It will be fun to visit them in Washington!" Dorothy
wrote, anticipating another glamorous trip.

But it was not to be. In March Fred and Dorothy arrived back in
Boston for more winter. Little Dorothy was enveloped in bonnet and
coat, posed in the bleak city setting to be photographed, and the pictures were pasted in the family scrapbook. In April the family went
down to Hamilton where snow still lay cold on the wintry ground.
Outdoors, the children were bundled in a cart and looking cross,
photographed again. Next come photos of the children out with their
father and Ada and of Robert pushing a wheelbarrow. The last picture on this page is of Dorothy and Robert in their underwear, standing on a bed, staring at the camera. The next page is blank, and the next, and so on
to the end of the scrapbook, nothing but page after page of empty gray.

IN HAMILTON, APRIL 1907.
Photos from left, *Fred, Dorothy and Robert;
Robert and Dorothy with their father; Dorothy and Robert.*

REARED *in a* GREENHOUSE

The Tragic Death

chapter SIX

Dorothy Amory Winthrop, taken in the New York studio of Davis and
Sanford probably shortly before her marriage. This was Fred's favorite
picture of her. He had multiple copies made, from miniatures to very
large, and two portraits painted using the photo as a model.

O*f her mother,* my mother retained only two impressions. One was clear but fleeting. "I remember coming down stairs and eating breakfast in a high chair. I was two. I remember, my mother was dressed all in white. That was my birthday party, and I remember it so well."

The other—as horrifying scenes are wont to do—remained etched in her memory for a lifetime. The incident occurred less than two months after my mother's second birthday, on July 18, 1907:

> We were all out in front of the house when it happened. It was a riding accident. Groton House was slightly different in those days from the way it is now, but we were all out there, outside what we called the den, and my mother and father started off riding. They didn't get any farther than half way to what is now the swimming pool—there was a road that went there in those days—and my mother's horse began to buck most terribly, and my father leapt from his horse to assist her. He grabbed her horse by the bridle and then helped her down, off the horse. But the pommel had upset her insides. That's what had happened. The pommel. She was riding sidesaddle and the horse had bucked most awfully.

Robert, then just three and a half, remembered running into the house to get a glass of water for his mother ... but, poor, frightened little boy, spilling it all before he reached her.

The story appeared two days later in the *Boston Evening Transcript*, a more violent version describing Mrs. Winthrop as having been "pitched from her saddle facedownward." That she was thrown from her horse immediately became the official version of the story, perpetuated when Lawrence Shaw Mayo included it in his definitive family history, *The Winthrop Family in America*. Near the end of her own life, my mother reread the Mayo account and found with consternation that the accident was not described as she remembered it. A phone call to her brother Robert revealed that he, too, found it faulty. They were astonished to discover that both had the identical memory of the event: that their mother had not fallen from her horse, but rather that their father had taken her in his arms and helped her to the ground.

My mother remembered nothing beyond those brief terrifying moments to which she was witness, nothing of the anxious days that followed while her beautiful mother lay hovering between life and death, nothing of her father and grandmother who took turns sitting by her bedside during those hot July days, fanning her, nothing of the doctors who came and went with their black bags and were of little use except to provide morphine to ease the pain.

A detailed account of those days, however, remains in the form of papers prepared by Libby Amory. The most poignant is her own day-by-day account written on notepaper edged in black and enclosed in an envelope with this in ink on the outside: "A little remembrance of the tragic death." Then in pencil, "She was under morphine for days to allay pain."

Libby was visiting her dearest friend, Mrs. Arthur (Fanny) Blake, in Mattapoisett, Massachusetts, when, on the morning of July 19, 1907, she received a telegram from her son-in-law Jeffie Coolidge in Magnolia. "Dorothy fell from her horse yesterday morning. No bones broken. She was badly hurt, however, but is better today. Hope you will come right home as she would surely like to have you."

On receiving the telegram, Libby went immediately to the little cottage on the place that the Winthrops kept available for the Amory grandparents and that had brought true the wish Dorothy expressed during her honeymoon that they should "always be" near. At the time, Dorothy surely had no idea how important her mother's proximity would prove, nor how short "always" would be. But when Libby arrived in Hamilton on the evening of July 19, she must have shuddered at what she learned.

Thursday morning, Dorothy thrown from her horse near the house. Fred carried her home, laid her on couch in den, gave her brandy thinking she was knocked out only. Dr. Tucker arrive in $\frac{1}{2}$ hour, he immediately summoned Drs. Porter,[1] Quimby and Harrington from Beverly Farms and Ipswich. They said it was an even chance, not till p.m. did they get her upstairs, cut off her clothes—

Friday p.m., Dr. Cabot and assistant came from Boston to remove kidney and spleen but as no worse, waited till morning and it was not done.

With Groton House full of medical staff and Fred distraught, Libby agreed to have the three little grandchildren and two nurses come stay with her. Dorothy was

THE TRAGIC DEATH

reported to be "better but suffering more." On day five after the accident, Libby was finally allowed to see her daughter.

> Told I could see Dorothy and sit by her bedside and not talk, as she has a little pleurisy. I sit fanning her, she looking lovely, difficulty in speaking, but asked after children. I said they loved it at my house. Then she pulled me to her face and said she felt weak but thought it was the morphine she had been taking.... The nurse praised me, and said I was splendid at the bedside and to come in afternoon. I was quiet and knew how to fan her.... Suddenly realized how perfectly wretched I had been, and how very happy I now was, at seeing her.... She said to nurse that she had never before felt so very weak and Dr. Quimby came and took a drop of blood from the back of her ear. He said it was natural to feel weak for she had had no food to speak of—while there, the nurse injected morphine and after a while sent me away.

The news that evening must have been reassuring. The nurse called her on the phone to say Dorothy was feeling *so* much better and had had a sound sleep.
Her relief was short-lived.

> I was waked in the night by the sound of men talking in my little stable and an auto stopping and then rushing on ... it was 1½ o'clock. Then, with beating heart, I threw something on.... I went up D's avenue and met an auto coming down, it was Dr. Harrington. I held up my hand, he said they were summoned to operate but as she held her own, waited till morning. We returned, but not to rest!

The operation they were contemplating was removal of three or four ribs. Libby recoiled at the prospect. "I felt I would rather have her die."[2]
That day Libby was told to stay at home since Dorothy needed to be kept quiet. Later on, the report was that she was doing "*very* nicely." Then suddenly, it was the beginning of the end. A phone call came, a little after 5:00 p.m., asking for "hot water bottles at once, she was worse."

> I sent one, and walked up the avenue, feeling like one in a dream. Dr. Jackson, from Beverly Farms, overtook me in his auto and I got in—I waited in the large hall upstairs, and coming and going out of my darling's room were 2 nurses, Drs. Jackson, Porter and Quimby. I saw nothing of Fred; he never left her side. About 5, Dr. Quimby tapped her lung, when it collapsed, letting air into heart, and she sank— everything was done—and Dr. Jackson told me if they could pull her through this crisis all would be well, not long after he said to look in as it seemed to frighten my darling. Dr. Porter came to me and patted me on the back but said nothing, I knew all was lost—about an hour before she died, they told me to go in, she pressed my hand affectionately but said nothing except to poor Fred who knelt beside her pillow. I heard mostly what they said, she was happy and cheerful, but did not feel the way the living felt; partly dazed by morphine, partly by the dying stupor, her speech was painful—but she talked cheerfully with Fred—She said, "You will be good to the children, won't you. I am glad you have *three*—I should not mind dying except for my family." Finally, she grew weaker, her eyes closed more and the doctor took Fred away, he could not stand and would have fallen except for them—I remained kneeling by the bed, when suddenly she struggled to get her arms up and waved them about her head, and all was over!

I could not feel that our darling, so full of generous feelings and so dear, was extinguished for ever—she left her body on the bed, but *that* was not *Dorothy*. Where has she gone!

The date was July 23, and the record appears in Libby Amory's "Stardrifts Birthday Book:" "Dorothy Winthrop died 1907 at 11:30 o'clock p.m. Tuesday."

In the envelope that contained her account of the last days of her daughter's life, Libby also put a handwritten text of two hymns, "O Love Divine, That Stooped to Share" and "Abide with Me," which were read at Dorothy's funeral at her home in Hamilton. "The coffin was at the end of the hall, entirely hidden, a huge bank of flowers sent by friends, was all that could be seen. Friends sat in the Hall, the family in the library."

On another envelope, which remains sealed to this day, Grandma Amory wrote:

A white rosebud taken from off my darling's coffin, when waiting at Hamilton station—
    The early morning of Saturday, July 27th, 1907. Ned and I and George watched the train out of sight, that bore her and the Winthrop family to N.Y. where our darling was placed in the family Tomb, in Greenwood Cemetery. *Just* 29 years old.

For months afterward, letters of sympathy poured in for Fred and his mother-in-law Libby. Each preserved them, Fred formally, in two bound volumes with red leather backings that read "Winthrop Letters to F. W.," and Libby, with a more personal touch, simply tied by a ribbon and a handwritten note on top. Libby hid her grief from the world, saving it for her departed daughter and herself alone.

Darling—In the Eternity where things that cannot be spoken, shall yet be known, you will find out what peace and comfort your endless, patient sympathy that never forgets nor leaves undone, has spread over the heartache that will never quite cease while there is anything left of me—

_____

I love her endlessly, she was my darling, my delight, my joy, ever since her birth—I only feel now that I did not love her half enough while she was here—

Fred's misery seemed even more raw. For Libby, there had been a lifetime of nurturing and companionship. For him there had been seven long years of uncertainty and less than five "of perfect happiness and contentment." Without Dorothy, he thought life no longer worth living.

My dear Mrs. Amory,

You say that you were selfish in speaking of your sorrow. Dear Mrs. Amory you are one of the most unselfish people I have ever known, and I can never forget how wonderfully kind and considerate you have been to me through all this.
    Dorothy was an absolutely perfect person, and I never saw anything about her that I could wish changed in the slightest degree. Of course our life together was to me, one of absolute happiness and contentment. We often said how happy and fortunate we were.

· 103 ·

THE TRAGIC DEATH

She was my life and more, she was my religion. Everything for me revolved around her. I loved her with my whole being, and I think she knew it, and knew too that I was absolutely true and loyal to her in thought, word and deed. I could not have been otherwise.

I would gladly have lost all my friends, family and children if I could have kept Dorothy, and if it was not for my children and my duty to Dorothy through them, I know that I would not be here. I must live out my life for the sake of the children and make the most of it, but I want you always to remember that my feelings for Dorothy can never change as long as I live.

Affectionately,

Fred

Dorothy Winthrop's internal injuries would surely not have been fatal today. Modern medicine would most likely have saved her life, and my mother's story, and stories, would have unfolded quite differently. With four doctors in attendance, Dorothy Winthrop was doubtless provided the best care possible in those days. But the turn of the century was still the medical dark ages, and even generous-hearted Libby Amory may have harbored some doubts as to whether the doctors themselves had not played a role in the death of her daughter.

She was well aware they hadn't been entirely straight with her about her daughter's prognosis. While they were reassuring her that "the first two days it was an even chance," they were giving her son-in-law Jeffie a far more pessimistic picture. For the first two days, they told him, Dorothy had "one chance in *ten* of recovery,"[3] for the next two, "an even chance." In the last two days, he was told "it was hopeless, for the lungs filled."

Libby no doubt forgave the doctors for the white lies they told her, well aware that they were only trying to spare her worry. But what of her comment that, when Dr. Quimby tapped Dorothy's lung, it "let air into heart, and she sank—everything was done"? Did she suspect a mistake had been made? If so, did she forgive the doctors for this too, fatalistically aware of the medical limitations of that day?

Fred Winthrop appears not to have accepted so generously the failure of this last-ditch effort to save his wife's life. Nor did he appreciate the extraordinary personal and professional sacrifices made by his chief physician, Dr. Porter. Rather, his attitude was such that Dr. Porter was moved to write his client a lengthy letter, explaining his medical decisions, pointing out the extraordinary amount of attention he had given to the case, and justifying the bill (for $1,250) he was sending. It may have embarrassed Dr. Porter to write such a letter. But it should have humiliated Fred Winthrop even more to discover that this was not the first time he had offended the doctor; on an earlier occasion, Dr. Porter wrote, he had been "hurt" when Mr. Winthrop had sent him only $30 for an operation on a servant. Yet despite this behavior, the doctor had given his all for Dorothy.

The day before she was injured, on her birthday, Dorothy and Fred had visited Clara and Jeff at Coolidge Point. From Hamilton to Magnolia and back was a long trip in those days, and the couple would have had lots of time to banter on the way. No doubt Fred had loosened up a lot since his courting days and often exchanged with Dorothy the straight-faced little jokes that people would remember him for later.[4] One of their recurring topics of conversation was her perfection. That it was real, he was sure. That it was not, she was equally certain. He'd insist on its existence, she would reply that he "would find her out, and she was not as nice as I thought her," and he would rejoin that he thought he knew her "much better than she knew herself." They had this little discussion often.

Six years after her death, in 1913, Fred wrote to Mrs. Amory, describing that last little chat and reiterating his certainty that he knew Dorothy to the core. "I don't think *anyone* knew Dorothy as well as I did," he wrote her mother. "I watched her grow up from the time she was a little less than thirteen years old.... I do not believe that there ever was such a perfect person as Dorothy."

But knowing a character is not understanding a heart, and to his own dying day Fred may have had a tinge of worry about whether Dorothy's happiness had matched his. "I hope she was happy with me," he wrote in the same 1913 letter, "and I believe she was."

As for the Amorys, they must never have doubted for an instant the depth of Dorothy's love for them. An undated letter from Ipswich, written to thank them for a pearl necklace, was typical of her devotion.

> Dear Papa, I wear your and Mamma's present night and day and have only taken it off for my baths since Friday. Truly, you can't imagine how excited and pleased I am. There is nothing so lovely as pearls and I have always admired them so much on others and now to think that thanks to you and Mamma, I own some myself, and such lovely ones too! ... I really can't thank you as I want to, but then, I have so much to thank you for, there is no use trying to thank you enough!

— • —

When recalling her mother's death, my mother never spoke of her own loss. Rather, her thoughts were for her father. "He was nine years older than she was. She was twenty-nine and he was thirty-eight. It was a terrible thing." Terrible it was—but not just for Fred. The gloom that overtook Fred Winthrop when Dorothy died never entirely lifted. Reserved by nature and now grief stricken, he couldn't have been much of a companion to his three little children. Yet it was now this austere and distant figure who would dominate their lives.

After Dorothy's death, no one—not even his mother—knew how to deal with Fred. He had remained in New York after the burial in Green-Wood Cemetery while the children returned to Groton House to be with their Amory grandparents. In her anxiety Kate Winthrop wrote to Libby, sharing her impressions of his state of

Right: *With her mother gone, little Dorothy tentatively makes her way in the world.*

Far right: *"Not pretty but bright looking," wrote Grandma Amory in her scrapbook under this photo of Dorothy.*

mind: "He cannot sleep or scarcely eat … no one can help him—he wants Dorothy and only her—his whole life has been devoted to her and now she is gone, what can he do? … nothing will help him but time … the children will interest him later. Now he can only grieve and he must be allowed to do as he wishes."[5]

His return home in early August failed to revive his spirits—he continued to look "unhappy … hollow cheeks, no sleep, forlorn and wretched."[6] Though skeptical about religion, he arranged for all three children to be baptized. A German governess was hired, known always as Fräulein, and although Dorothy grew to depend on her, she described her later as "strict and severe." There were also maids, no doubt in abundance, and my mother would speak particularly of "loving" one "dear little Annie."

But her main recollection of her early years, especially during the bucolic summers in Hamilton, was of running free with her brothers, with no one paying them much heed. They were an inseparable trio—"We three," as she came to call them—making their own fun and fighting their own battles. There never seemed to be any supervision while they played around the Ipswich River that ran its muddy course down the hill from the house. Where was the nursemaid the day that little Robert fell into the muck? My mother described the situation to us:

REARED *in a* GREENHOUSE

The river had a plank out over two uprights, like a seesaw. If you went out over the river at one end of the plank, somebody had to be on the other end to balance it. So there was Uncle Bob [brother Robert], fishing away, ever so happy, on the end of the plank, and for some reason or other, Uncle Fred [brother Fred] and I, who were holding it in balance, got off, and of course the thing tipped off and Uncle Bob fell into the water. Well, Uncle Fred and I screamed and yelled, so distraught. I remember standing on the bank in absolute agony, and Uncle Bob—he appeared, he popped up—said, "We must go into the house and I must put on some dry clothes," so we all crept up the stairs, and nobody saw us, and we got him into the bathtub, and took off all these muddy old clothes, and put on nice clean ones. We were so stupid, we just left all those dirty old clothes. We thought nobody would notice. But of course they did!

Another time, the family Great Danes stood *in loco parentis*. Two would keep guard while Robert was fishing off a bridge. But once they weren't alert enough: a collie from a farmer's house rushed at Robert and bit him. "His dogs, one on either side of him, made sure that he got home and as soon as he was safely in the house … they … went back and killed the collie."

In my mother's stories, Freddy comes across as the most adventurous of the three.

He was a naughty little boy, used to climb around the roof, out one of the windows and around the roof. He did the most daring things, terrified me. Once, probably to escape the governess, he climbed way up to the top of a heavily leafed maple tree where no one could find him. The governess searched frantically for him, calling for him and looking. What finally brought him down, I think, was that he was hungry, and it was supper time.

Stern as he was, their father never interfered with Freddy's ventures. "He didn't want to scare him, didn't want to stop him, didn't want to take away his courage,"

Below left: The Winthrop children seemed to fend for themselves.

Below: Periodically, "we three" were spruced up for a professional photographer. Here are "we three" in December 1912: Freddy 6, Dorothy 7, and Robert 8, photographed by Bachrach.

THE TRAGIC DEATH

Freddy was a naughty little boy who used to climb out of the windows and around the roof.

President Howard Taft, 1910. President Taft came calling on the Winthrops that summer. On the Winthrop terrace, where the chairs were slender, he needed two to sit on. (Courtesy Library of Congress)

recalled my mother. Instead, "he just stood there and shut his eyes."

Her father came bounding to my mother's rescue, however. Groton House had a skylight, unprotected, on the floor in the hall above the great staircase and she had ventured out on it. The crash of shattering glass brought Fred to her side in a flash. He swept her up in his arms, rushed to crank up the phone and called the doctor. When Fred senior wasn't around, it was Fred junior who came to her aid. My mother remembered her doll carriage rolling down the hill toward the river. In a little box in the carriage was a "very very precious" tooth that she'd just lost and for which the tooth fairy was going to give her ten cents.

> It was terrible. There was nothing I could do about it, but Uncle Fred rushed after it as fast as he could. Of course he couldn't catch it and they said to me, "Aren't you glad that your brother Fred didn't fall into the river, too?" I said "Yes, I'm awfully glad, but I wouldn't have minded if it had been Robert."

So the summers went on—1908, 1909, 1910. Robert, Dorothy, and Fred would play around the U-shaped barn[7] and visit the beautiful carriage house full of every kind of carriage. They still went most places by horse and buggy, because, recalled my mother, "We didn't have automobiles, and if you did, they broke down."

One summer afternoon around 1910, when Robert was about six, an imposing visitor came by for tea. It was President William Howard Taft, the bulky chief executive in whose administration Beekman Winthrop was then serving. Dorothy may not have been trotted out to meet him, but her brothers were, and she was certainly told about the interchange between Robert and the president:

> They had arranged for tea on the terrace, but the only sort of chairs we had were rather slim gold chairs. President Taft was very well fed and so we arranged two of the chairs together for him to sit on. The boys were asked to appear, all clean and nice, to meet the president. And he looked at Robert, and said: "Now, little man, what do you want to do when you grow up?" Everyone waited, expecting Robert to say that he'd like to be president—but not at all. He answered, "I'd like to be a carpenter."

— • —

On July 12, 1911, Frederic Winthrop took a second wife, Sarah Barroll Thayer. The marriage of the two—the attractive young socialite and the wealthy widower—once again had the Boston press atwitter. In a newspaper story Fred clipped, the bride's appearance was lyrically noted, and great accent was placed on her place in the best circles: "one of the prominent young women in the Newport summer set ... a very prominent member of the Vincent Club, and one of Boston's best known and most beautiful society girls." Her bent for good works was also noted. Said an article, "She is remembered gratefully by countless little sufferers at the Children's Hospital." Again, there was a snag at the wedding, this time not the illness of the bridegroom but the death earlier that year of Sally's father, the millionaire businessman Nathaniel Thayer, Jr. Thus, unlike her sisters' brilliant weddings (Cornelia married Count Carl Moltke, whose posts would include Danish minister to the United States and foreign minister of Denmark, and Anna wed William W. Patten of New York City), Sally's was a quiet home affair.

The Thayers had won their place in society not only through the longevity of their line (the first Thayers—then called Tayers—had settled in Braintree in 1630, arriving as early in America as the Winthrops) and the correctness of their religion (great-grandfather Thayer had been a Unitarian minister), but also through their business acumen. The Thayer fortune was founded by Sally's grandfather, Nathaniel Thayer, Sr. (the son of the minister), who, with his brother John, established and ran with great success the banking house of John E. Thayer (later to become Kidder, Peabody).[8] He was said, in a news clipping in Fred Winthrop's scrapbook, to have left the "largest fortune ever accumulated in this State up to that time … estimated at $12,000,000." His son, Sally's father, was one of those men of many hats, with directorships in a dozen or more of America's flagship companies, trusteeships in all of Boston's best health and educational institutions, and the inevitable multiple club memberships. On the female side, her paternal grandmother was Cornelia Van Rensselaer, whose family history could be traced back to colonial days. Years later, my mother would laugh at what she considered the pretensions of the extended Thayer family: they built themselves "palaces" in Lancaster, she told us, and vied with one another in the grandeur of their picnics. But in those days she knew nothing of such things, for she was only six when her father remarried.

Sally Thayer knew what it was to lose a mother. Her own mother, Cornelia Street Barroll, had died when she was born, leaving three little girls under the age of four. Fortunately for Sally, she'd had a good stepmother. Pauline Revere, whose ancestry was obvious from her name, had been considered *nouveau* when the widower Nathaniel Thayer, Jr., had taken her for a second wife.[9] But she soon overcame the gossip with her wonderfully warm-hearted ways, and her three little stepdaughters grew up bathed in surrogate mother love. My own mother remembered that

Sarah Barroll Thayer wed the widower Frederic Winthrop on July 12, 1911. The accident that took his beloved Dorothy's life had occurred almost exactly four years earlier, on July 18, 1907.

Pauline Revere Thayer, Sally Winthrop's stepmother, in her younger years. "Everyone loved her," my mother remembered. (Courtesy Eleanor Winthrop)

THE TRAGIC DEATH

Dorothy, about 6, when the new "Mama" entered the family

Sally and Fred Winthrop, shortly after their marriage, with Dorothy, Fred, Jr., and Robert. This is a rare picture of Sally with Fred and of Sally with her stepchildren. Sally looks unhappy in all the candid photos we have.

moment of hope when the new "Mama" entered their lives. She remembered running to the lovely young woman and crawling into her lap. But the reaction was cold, and Dorothy felt she wasn't wanted. She may have read her stepmother's reaction incorrectly, but the impression was indelible and it colored her feelings toward Sally for the rest of her life. Probably Sally's reaction wasn't intentional. She was adored by her own children, and her letters to Dorothy in later years reflect a kind-hearted woman who appeared sincerely to love her stepdaughter and want the best for her. But she was seventeen years Fred's junior, naturally shy and insecure, and her new husband seemed not to warm to her presence.[10]

Little wonder, then, that a great divide grew up between Dorothy's children and Sally's. My mother described the situation that developed:

Robert, Freddy and I lived in three bedrooms on the top floor of Groton House. Katharine and Nat lived on the second floor. Then at a certain age they went up and we came down. But we all ate at the table together, we all had the same meals. My father and stepmother sat at either end of the table looking very severe, and all of us sat up very nicely and behaved very properly and it was all very dull.

The age difference between the children partly explains the gulf. When Nat was born, Freddy, Dorothy, and Robert were already six, seven, and eight. There was an even greater gap between the three and Sally's second son, John, who came a year later, and Katharine, born the year after that. (Refer to Chart 5.)

Dorothy was eight and probably visiting her Grandma Amory when she learned of Katharine's arrival in a letter from her father: "Your little sister is very red, very ugly, and cries a great deal. Her name is Katharine, the name that Grandma Winthrop was baptized." Katharine turned out to be a sickly infant, a fact that always amazed my mother when she thought of what a marvelous tennis player her younger sister would become: "Can you imagine? I think she weighed ten pounds when she was born, but she didn't regain her birth weight for ten months. She couldn't digest milk of any kind." A certain Dr. Smith of Ipswich finally put her onto "a kind of malt ... used in making beer, which she could digest, and she flourished on that." It wasn't just her size that won Katharine attention. "She was full of fun from the time she was a little one," my mother said, "and she knew just how to get her way in a sweet manner."

More than the age difference split the Amory from the Thayer children. One story has it that Fred Winthrop sternly informed Sally that she was not to have anything to do with his first three children, that he was to be solely responsible for their upbringing.[11] This could explain why Sally seemed to freeze when little Dorothy jumped on her lap. The story has a ring of truth: when Sally would suggest she buy something nice for the three older ones, especially Dorothy, Fred Winthrop would say no, he preferred to buy them their clothes himself. As a result, little Katharine was dressed beautifully, while Dorothy had the wardrobe of the proverbial poor little rich girl.

> I had two dresses, and my brother Freddy was not at all pleased with this, especially one that he thought was particularly ugly. So he took his scissors and he cut it right up the front, from hem to neck. But we had a wonderful waitress, who saw what had happened, snatched the dress, ran off with it, and sewed it all up.

Though my mother's two-dress story became a running family joke, it unwittingly revealed an unpleasant truth about Fred Winthrop. As with Dorothy's doctor, Fred Winthrop was miserly with his children. When Dorothy and her brothers visited their Winthrop grandmother in Lenox, she would "take one look at our wardrobe, and—she was old, too—she would take the next train into New York and she'd buy us half a dozen of everything. All the same."

The overriding problem, however, was that though the second family appeared to come first with regard to living arrangements and clothing, they came second in Fred's heart. In the Winthrop household no one could forget that Sally Thayer had a revered predecessor. Dorothy's portrait—a copy of the photograph taken just before her marriage—was prominently hung and beneath it, shrinelike, stood a vase, always with a single fresh-cut rose.[12] The portrait shows a beautiful woman in profile, brown hair swept high, features perfect, eyes somewhat melancholy as they look past the gilded frame into the distance. She is wearing a white chiffon dress, with a flower of the palest yellow nestled at the low-cut square neckline.

Libby Amory had had great hopes for the new marriage. Her scrapbook contains a sweet picture of Sally and second-born John, with this written beneath a picture of three Winthrop "chicks" on the opposite page: "I feel very happy for Fred and to think that the children will have a kind friend—for every one praises Sally." She had tactfully suggested to Fred that, when Sally became his wife, he should take down Dorothy's portrait. A sensible proposal, if the marriage were to get off to a good start. But Fred, determined at any cost to keep Dorothy's memory alive, did not heed her advice:

Sally Winthrop and her three children, John, 1, Katharine, a few months old, and Nat, 2. Sally was 29, the same age as Dorothy at her death. She and Fred had been married three years.

Dorothy Amory Winthrop, portrait done posthumously by Church, 1910, based on the photograph at the head of this chapter. The story goes that this portrait was an icon in the Winthrop household and that a fresh-cut rose, placed daily in a vase, stood below it always. (Courtesy Standish Bradford, portrait photographed by Philip Reeser)

THE TRAGIC DEATH

*"I feel very happy for
Fred to think that the children
will have a kind friend —
for everyone praises Sally"
(caption in Grandma Amory's
scrapbook opposite this picture
of Sally Winthrop with son
John)*

My dear Mrs. Amory,

I expect to put a photograph of Dorothy in each of the children's rooms, and one in my
room. I do not think Sally will mind. I want the children to see and know her as well as
possible....

    I loved her as you know with every atom of my being, and she was more, much
more, to me than life or all else that the world contained....

    Of course dear Mrs. Amory I do not mind your suggesting putting away the pictures,
but until I think Sally would mind, I shall keep them.

Affectionately,

Fred

How could Sally not have minded? She adored her husband and did her best to
please him.[13] But everywhere in the house were constant reminders of a rival who
could not be unseated, a predecessor whose youth and beauty would remain frozen
in time and perfect forever.

— • —

If her stepmother was unable to give her the mothering for which she longed,
Dorothy still had her grandmother, Libby Amory. In the letter about Dorothy's picture, Fred Winthrop had pleaded with his first mother-in-law: "If you can, I wish
you would talk to them about her as much as you can. I find it very difficult to speak
of her much yet, even to our children." Little did he think that for her, too, speaking
of her daughter might bring unbearable pain. Fred relied on Libby for more than
talking to the children. During the first years after Dorothy's death, he had kept her
close at hand to be their friend and companion. During the summer after Dorothy's
death the Amorys moved into Groton House with Fred and his children. In Boston,
Fred and his children moved into the house at 280 Beacon, next door to the Amorys.
Here a door was built between the adjoining houses so that the grandchildren could
scurry easily back and forth between the relaxed Amory home and the more formal
Winthrop household. It was probably here that Miss Litchfield, who had been one of
Dorothy's teachers, found Libby, in her late sixties, on the floor playing with her
grandchildren.

    Fred Winthrop's remarriage changed all this. In Hamilton, my mother said,
"when the new Mama showed up, Grandma disappeared." In Boston, too, "when the
new Mama came, we moved away." Moved they did, both away and up, from the
solid respectability of Beacon Street to the grandeur of a twenty-two-room mansion
at 299 Berkeley Street. Theirs would be the only house in Back Bay that stood alone
on its lot surrounded by "light and air," according to the press clipping in Fred's
scrapbook describing the $165,000 purchase.[14] A large photo above the story shows a
gloomy, ivy-covered mansion of the Dutch Renaissance style.[15] The house would
remain the Winthrop family's in-town residence for the rest of Fred's life. With so
many familiar things gone (even the maids who had loved her mother and whom she

REARED *in a* GREENHOUSE

loved in turn), little Dorothy clung ever closer to her grandmother. As she put it, "When Grandma disappeared, I just followed."

Without doubt, Libby Amory would become the central person in Dorothy's youth, the one who took an active interest in her growth, the one who was always available, the one who offered the kind of humor and sympathy she needed. Libby's was an indomitable spirit, and the good measure of common sense she brought to every situation must have given Dorothy strength no matter how difficult things were at home. Through the years Dorothy and her grandmother shared meals and car rides, theater trips and card games. And when they were apart, there were letters back and forth chronicling events large and small.

Dorothy must have been seven when she got her first letter from Libby. Her husband Ned had been growing frailer, and for Libby it was a terrible worry. First it was just "attacks of vertigo," and she would sit up at the library window, sometimes as late as midnight, waiting for him to get home after his evenings out at whist. As time went on, however, "he felt he was gradually losing his mind—having occasional lapses of memory." Then he started to have epileptic attacks and hardening of the arteries.[16] The end couldn't be long in coming.

Frederic Winthrop Purchases the Magnificent Residence at 299 Berkeley St, Once Occupied by Ex-Gov Draper.

PHILLIPS ESTATE SOLD BY J. SUMNER DRAPER AND MARK TEMPLE DOWLING.

The Boston press made much of Frederic Winthrop's purchase of 299 Berkeley Street. The story that accompanied this picture pointed out that there were 22 rooms and 5 bathrooms and the interior finish was of "the very finest hardwoods.... Fitted with every modern improvement," the house was one of the "most up-to-date private residences in the entire Back Bay."

DEAREST DOTTY,

Is it a bore or trouble to you to write to me? For, if it is, I will trouble you no longer. I so often think of you all! For it is many years since I have been able to go down and see you, for grandpa has not been well enough, and I could never leave him for such a long time—I have seven very delightful grandchildren [her daughter Clara's four boys and Robert, Dorothy and Fred], and think I am a very lucky person, don't you?

I am going to Cambridge tomorrow afternoon to see Jefferson play football, for he is one of my darlings. I have another dear boy out at Cambridge this winter, Amory, you know him too. Both these boys are playing football and getting very tired every day....

Grandpa is pretty well just now, but always suffers. He went to War when a very young man, he was not killed, but he has been sick ever since—and so brave, struggling to do things, and never speaking of his troubles.

Meanwhile, two far younger male relatives of Dorothy's were also ailing. In mid-April 1912 Fred Winthrop was called to New York to be with his oldest brother, Dudley, who had been failing for several months with a serious heart condition.

THE TRAGIC DEATH

T. Jefferson Coolidge, Jr., in his official portrait at the Bank of Boston (courtesy Dr. Catherine C. Lastavica)

On April 14 he was unconscious all day, though on the fifteenth, he regained consciousness and seemed no worse. At this very time Fred received a telegram from Sally with more bad news: his brother-in-law Jeffie Coolidge, who had been diabetic for some years and had recently contracted tuberculosis, was dead.[17] Fred wrote Libby that he couldn't go to Jeff's funeral, as "Dudley cannot live but a few hours ... although I am afraid that his wonderful vitality may prolong his ... suffering for a longer time than the doctor thinks." The doctor was wrong; Dudley Winthrop lived only a short time more. Jeffie and Dudley died within two days of one another, T. Jefferson Coolidge, Jr., on April 14, 1912, and Dudley Winthrop on April 16. Jeffie was forty-nine, Dudley fifty-one.

A man in his prime, Jeff Coolidge had, with his father, founded the Old Colony Trust Company, then the largest trust company in the country outside of New York and Chicago, and had served as its president, chairman of the board, and chairman of the executive committee. He was honored in death with a splendid funeral at Trinity Church and a letter of consolation to his father from President Taft. For his widow Clara and their four young sons, his death was a devastating blow. For Libby Amory, too, it was crushing, for she had been fond of her son-in-law and had relied on him in many ways. Her main responsibility, however, remained Ned. By November, six months after Jeffie's death, he had become bedridden. The next summer, 1913, she and George would give up their usual escape to the country so that he could remain at home. "Dear Ned, breathing quietly his life away, and mine too," Libby wrote in her diary.

Mother and son George were at Ned Amory's bedside on November 5, 1913, when the end came:

> Geo and I watched our dear one breathe his last—now I must face great loneliness after nearly fifty years living for him—but how happy I am that his sufferings are over—what a terrible year and how dreadful! and how patient and sweet he was. I have always hoped and hoped I should outlive him, for he was so absolutely dependent on me—I can live along for a little while and then join him....
>
> How I wish I could see him just for ten minutes to tell him how I cared for him, for we were both too reserved.

Ned Amory, during his late years, with charcoal drawings of Libby and of Dorothy as a baby on the wall behind him

Considering how modest he was, Ned would have been astonished at his funeral, Libby wrote her niece Mary Curtis—surprised "at all the lovely flowers in the church and all the gentlemen who came to honor his memory." Libby had been urged by her sister Clara Brooks to place on the coffin the flowers sent by the immediate family. "But I didn't," she continued in her letter to Mary, "and I'll tell you why."

> In 1862, when he was a senior and I a bud, he sent me a bouquet of white roses for my first party and as I liked him then (and meant in my heart to marry him) I kept one rose all those years in a little box—I now found little but a dried up stem and yellow powder. Still it was full of sentiment for me, so this I placed in his hand, and that was the only flower about him when he was buried—I gave it back after fifty-one years!

As people often did in those days, Libby wrote a remembrance of the husband she'd loved so long and well.

November 1913

Charles Walter Amory was very shy, retiring and modest—he was inclined to be melancholy at times, a little morbid, but as he grew older he was less so—so sensitive that anything like sending away his nice agent at the mill on account of failing health, would trouble him so that he could not sleep and because really ill they allowed him to pension him till he died. He was active minded and needed to be occupied to take his mind from himself for he was never feeling well…. He never spoke of his torments and spoke cheerfully when others mentioned his poor health and … never liked to be pitied. He took it as a cross necessary for him to bear….

Grandma Amory steps smartly down the stairs with little Dorothy and Fred, September 1908.

As she entered old age Libby had sustained three mortal blows—the death of a daughter, the death of a beloved son-in-law, and her own husband's departure. These losses placed her, a woman of seventy, in a pivotal family role. Personal tragedies and grave responsibilities, however, seemed never to engulf or diminish her. Her eyes were on the future, especially that of little Dorothy, her daughter's namesake.

Libby tried to pass on to Fred some of her indomitable spirit. She was concerned for what seemed his continuing apathy about his new marriage. "I hate to have you say that you never can be happy again!" she wrote. She tried to buck him up, to make him look ahead and think about his children: "The lovely vision of your youth can never return, but you are still young and have much to live for, in the children and in Sally, who is so good a woman. In trying to promote their happiness, you will find your own."

Libby also forced herself to do what Fred couldn't: she spoke and wrote to her granddaughter about her daughter, knowing that such a legacy would strengthen young Dorothy's spirit and warm her heart:

Dorothy, 7, staying in Boston at her Grandma Amory's. She had short hair in 1912 — the only time in her life.

DEAREST DOTTY,

Here I am staying with Great Aunt Clara [her sister, Clara Brooks] in Medford—it is a very lovely home with kind hearts living in it. Your Mother used to stay here with a girl cousin 2 years older than herself named Helen—they had a perfect time playing about in the Autumn, having a bonfire and burning up all sorts of things….

There is a pond here that the two little girls used to bathe in, and go out in an old wide flat bottomed boat for fun—

Now there are no children playing about—only two grey-haired sweet old people—living in their children's life, and happy in this lovely place.

· 115 ·

THE TRAGIC DEATH

Dorothy Winthrop Bradford
and Her Extended Family

In Sickness and in Health

chapter SEVEN

Dorothy Winthrop, April 1915 (almost 10),
professionally photographed

*M*onday, *January 25,* 1915: "First day sick." So begins Dorothy Winthrop's diary. She was nine years old and her journal was just a few loose pages held together by a safety pin. She continued in fits and starts, not becoming a serious diarist until the age of twelve, when she acquired a red, gold-trimmed "standard diary and daily reminder" for 1918, a gift from Fräulein. By now, the handwriting had become large and clear, though crudely formed. The entries are crisp—short, well written, and full of whimsy. Within a year they would begin to express personality.

"Sick," however, turned out to be an omen, not only for Dorothy but for others. Over the three years, it seemed as if she were always sick: "headache—bad cold—I feel like a rotten potato"; "church, felt faint! awful!"; "sick in bed with grippe. I don't believe I will be out more than once before Christmas." And apparently she wasn't, as the entries from then on are merely "Ditto," "Ditto," Ditto."

The fall and winter of 1918 was a terrifying time to be sick, for an influenza epidemic was sweeping the world. St. Mark's School was closed that fall, and Frederic Winthrop set his marooned sons, Robert and Freddy, to splitting wood.[1] Dorothy got sick in December. A doctor and a trained nurse came round and flowers poured in.

This was not the usual response to her illnesses. Most were met with skepticism. "Father said 'I flopped down like a sow' when I felt the slightest bit sick, and 'Mama' said I put it all on and was not sick," she wrote in her 1917 diary. "Katharine told Grandma Amory that I was only pretending to be sick. She said 'Mama' had told her."[2] No wonder she began keeping her illnesses to herself.

Over Christmas 1917, her father took Robert and Fred south—the boys' first trip to the plantation in South Carolina that Dudley had bequeathed to brother Fred on his death—leaving twelve-year-old Dorothy behind with Fräulein, her stepmother, and her young step-siblings. When Dorothy discovered she had a temperature of 102 degrees on Christmas Eve, she said nothing. On Christmas Day, her diary entry is blank. "I am afraid to tell anyone but Fräulein when I feel sick," she wrote a week or so later. Once again her fever had hit 102 degrees, and once again her stepmother had been unsympathetic. She was "mad that I should be sick," wrote Dorothy. Nor did Fräulein dare get sick. Only once did she take to her bed, and that time "'Mama' gave orders not to send anything up to her unless she came down to the dining room herself." The memories festered. Two years later, at the ripe old age of fourteen, Dorothy looked back on those days "when I was a little kid" and remembered being "terrified" when she didn't feel well.

The second Mrs. Winthrop's impatience was taking its toll. Dorothy had always been careful to put the word "Mama" in quotation marks when referring to her stepmother in her diary, making it emphatically clear that this was in no way her real mother. About this time, however, she found a new name—the impersonal "Somebody." It stuck for a while, until she found other, equally remote names. Grandma Amory's flickering hope for family happiness when the new "Mama" arrived some six years earlier had turned to ashes.

Sarah T. Winthrop with son John, about 1

Perhaps Sally Winthrop's reaction to Dorothy's health was just a symptom of deeper trouble. After all, Fred had warned her against becoming involved in her stepchildren's upbringing. Moreover, three years into what was turning out to be a marriage of unrequited love, she was to suffer the greatest grief a mother can endure—the death of a child. Her second son, John, born June 14, 1913, seemed to be in perfect health. Then suddenly, as my mother remembered, "When John was just short of two years old, he suddenly, very suddenly took ill. He was perfectly all right at 6:00 a.m., at eight o'clock he was having convulsions. He died that afternoon."[3]

Dorothy's diary entry about her little stepbrother's death was brief, as might be expected from a child of nine. "John died suddenly. We went and stayed with Grandma." For her stepmother, it wasn't so easy to go on. The loss of her boy would become a barb that she would sometimes aim at others. Two years later, Dorothy noticed the short step between her stepmother's heartache and her ill temper. It was in late May of 1917 at the funeral of another close relative, Dorothy's twelve-year-old first cousin Linzee Coolidge. "Near the end, 'Mama' cried so hard that she sat down on her seat and hid her face in her hand. She must have been thinking of little John. Afterwards she was very disagreeable to us."

Linzee Coolidge, at 12, the way he would be remembered

Grandma Amory wrote to Dorothy about the different way in which Linzee's mother, Dorothy's Aunt Clara, had reacted to her son's death. Widowed five years earlier, in 1917 Clara Coolidge was reigning over an emptying nest (refer to Chart 9). The year before, her oldest son Jeff had graduated *magna cum laude* from Harvard; the second, Amory, was heading into his senior year at Harvard; and Billy was off at St. Mark's School. By 1917 only Linzee remained at home. Born March 21, 1905, he was exactly two months older than Dorothy and, like her, a favorite of Grandma Amory's. "We always breakfasted to-gether, he and I, at 8:30," she wrote Dorothy after his funeral, "and had a cheerful time. He was a fine little fellow, with a lovely nature, and a very manly spirit." Aunt Clara, she wrote, was weathering her loss with courage. "She will never be so happy again, but she is brave and unselfish, and tries her best to keep up for her boys."

Linzee's illness had lasted three distressing weeks. On May 1, 1917, Dorothy and Fräulein saw him in the Public Garden "rowing around in the pond with his shirt sleeves rolled up, no collar or tie, no coat or jacket on. It was a damp chilly day. When Fräulein saw him, she said he would surely get sick." Four days later Dorothy went to bed with one of her frequent illnesses. Soon she was well. But Linzee was getting worse.

May 21 was her twelfth birthday. She had no family around, no party, no friends. "With Fraulein alone all day," says the diary. "From Fraulein, I received a postcard and a beautiful silver bookmark. From Father, five dollars, from Freddy a letter, and from Grandma A., an umbrella, a hat pin, a letter, and twelve candles." Grandma Amory did her best to make her granddaughter feel special on her twelfth birthday: "Tomorrow you will be in your last year before your 'teens'—how girls do grow—faster than flowers—I don't know about vegetables." But Grandma Amory couldn't be with Dorothy that day. All her time was spent at her daughter Clara's. "It is very touching," she continued to Dorothy, "to see Linzee's little dog, sitting in front of the house, day after day, watching the front door, for he knows Linzee is inside and he expects him to come out—sometimes he sits on the grass, sometimes under the trees, but he never leaves his watch."[4] The next day, at seven in the morning, the dog's watch ended. Linzee had died.

Today's explanation of Linzee's death is that he had tubercular meningitis.[5] The view of the time, however, was more simplistic: Linzee had caught cold because he was rowing in the Public Garden with his coat off.

The most haunting death for Dorothy, though, was her mother's. At thirteen, in the still childish handwriting of her 1918 diary, she recorded the events of the week of July 17 to 23: her mother's birthday, "our darling mother['s]" accident, her death. "This week's awful sad. I can't explain, but today is the saddest," she wrote on the 21st. The day before, she copied a poem entitled "To My Mother":

O gentle child beautiful as thou were
Why didst thou leave the trodden paths of men?
Too soon, and with weak hands though mighty heart
Dare the unpastured dragon in his den?

— • —

Sadness passes quickly for the young, and Dorothy had lots of new interests in her life. In the fall of 1916, she finished Miss Newcomb's School and entered the May School. She had been placed in Class II because she "passed her examinations very well, and seemed in some studies more advanced than most of the children who are coming into our first class." She was already a great little reader. Sick in bed at age nine, she had lost herself in the *Cricket* books, stories about a little girl like her. Miss May's, as the students called their school, assigned her the usual required reading for the summer before she entered. She was also expected to make two pillow cases entirely by hand. Thankfully, considering her adult sewing skills, the basting could be done for her "if necessary." The hems were to be two-and-a-half inches wide.

Dorothy did well that first year, straight A's in "deportment" climaxed with an end-of-year honorable mention in desk tidiness. Her other A's were in arithmetic and French; the rest of her marks were B's. The next year Dorothy did equally well. Only spelling would bedevil her. "It a very winddy day," she had written on March 26, 1915, and so it would continue for the next four days: "winddy … winddy … winddy … winddy."

Her father had chosen Miss May's for several reasons. It was the school her mother had attended when it operated under its original name, Miss Folsom's School for Girls. It was small, with fewer than 150 students spread over seven classes. Located at 339 Marlborough Street, it was close to Grandma Amory's, and Dorothy would drop by after class almost every day before trudging home to Berkeley Street. It was not fashionable, like Winsor School where Katharine would go, catering mainly to girls whose fathers were professionals (doctors or lawyers) and even accepting "Jewesses," as my mother would put it in her old-fashioned way.

In addition to school, Dorothy always had an activity designed to improve or amuse her: music lessons, German lessons with Fräulein, baseball, luncheons, drives with Grandma, theater outings, walks and playing in the Public Garden with friends, the

Two of Dorothy's childhood — and lifelong — pals in the Public Garden (c. 1915): left, her cousin Jean Sears and right, her cousin through her stepmother, Mabel Thayer (later Mabel Thayer Storey)

"On Sundays, these chicks lunched with me and I tried to give them a good time," wrote Grandma Amory in her scrapbook above this 1916 photo. "You did, dear Grandma," was added below, in my mother's mature hand.

dentist. Often on Sunday, Grandma Amory would take her to the Arlington Street Church—a responsibility her father, having lost his spiritual appetite on his mother's strict diet of Episcopalianism, was happy to abrogate. Grandma Amory was a Unitarian, and she must have made church a fun outing for Dorothy. They sat together in the Amory pew. Dorothy wrote of "a beautiful Easter Service," of copying hymns "our dear Mother liked," and of being read hymns by her grandmother. On Sundays, too, when the boys were younger, Grandma would invite them all to lunch. "I tried to give them a good time," she wrote under a photo in her scrapbook of the three sledding. "You did, dear Grandma," was added, in my mother's mature hand.

Like other Boston families, while sheltering their daughters at home, the Winthrops would dispatch their sons to boarding school—the earlier the better. In 1916, Robert, age twelve, entered St. Mark's School while Fred, only ten, was sent to Fay. Both schools were in Southboro, Massachusetts, a few miles west of Boston.

Robert took to life away from home with gusto. Less than a month after his arrival he was writing Dorothy enthusiastic letters about the "beautiful" place and the "swell" gym. He basked in the company of "a hundred and fifty boys all bellowing and shouting on all sides." The camaraderie didn't do much for his scholarship; by the end of his second year, he stood seventeenth in his class of thirty-four boys, a ranking that pleased him more than it did his father.

Unlike Robert, Freddy was petrified at the thought of boarding school. His physical handicaps may have had something to do with this. He was partially deaf, no one knew why.[6] And when he was eight, the oculist discovered that he "was almost blind in his left eye," in this case perhaps the aftermath of undulant fever, which later

REARED *in a* GREENHOUSE

became the explanation for the mysterious illness he had contracted from Charlie's filthy milk pails. Dorothy herself wore glasses in those days, and Grandma Amory worried about both of them, warning Dorothy in an August 1917 letter, "It is up to you to see that Freddy wears colored glasses on the water (you too) or his head will ache—he is such a little Careless."

Freddy did his best to compensate for his infirmities. Fortunately, he had talents that required neither sight or hearing. He could walk down the hall on his hands and open doors with his feet. But acrobatics didn't translate into social courage. On the eve of his departure for Fay School, Dorothy wrote in her diary, "He was weeping in bed, and I told him to look at the new moon. He said, 'I am going tomorrow, but I shall return when that moon is full.' "

From Fay, he was soon writing Dorothy letters filled with misery. Longing to be home with her and Fräulein, he urged her to intervene on his behalf—and threatened dire consequences to his father if he didn't listen. "Beg Father and Grandma to take me away and tell him he must or he'll find something out when I'm older will you please Dearest Dot." His imaginary plot so captivated him that he wrote her a verse about it.[7] The poetry was no more successful than the conspiracy.

> *There once was a boy named Fardy and had a sister named Dardy*
> *His pa sent him to a school called the fay*
> *And wanted him there to stay*
> *But Dardy and Fardy did fight away*
> *Until his pa said I will take you away.*

In another letter he asked his sister if she could separate the word "Ihatefayschoolverymuch." Another was signed "Hatfully yours."

His despair lingered into his second year there. Once again he was looking for a way to escape, but this time he would rely on himself, not on the dubious support of his sister. In a letter from October 1917 he described his plan:

> Dear Dot… Two boys and I have a club. We only take boys who don't like the school. One comes from Lenox Uncle Gren knows him. The other is from denver, Colorado.… If father does not keep his word in taking me away in two weeks if I don't like it here I will write for all my mony and walk away. I will by a loaf of bred and take the train to the Back Bay Station and walk to Grandmas house and live there till you come and get me. do you see Father can't say anything because he did not keep his word. Tell Fraulein I don't eat hardly anything and cry every evening for homesicknes and I dream that I am home with you and Fraulein and when I wake up I am mad.

Nothing seemed to go well for Freddy at Fay. "Exams begin tomorrow and my legs are shaking I am so scared," he wrote. As for deportment, "I am a very bad boy for I had fifteen marks yesterday."

— • —

IN SICKNESS AND IN HEALTH

Grandma Amory invited the Winthrop children to Mattapoisett for the summer of 1915. At left, *Freddy and Dorothy learning to dive;* at right, *"Fred, D. & shark!" (caption in Dorothy's scrapbook)*

"Played" is how most of Dorothy's summer diary entries begin. During the summers of 1914 and 1915, Grandma Amory took the children for long visits in Mattapoisett, where she was visiting her friend Fanny Blake. For Grandma, it was a "nice rest," as she had been feeling "debilitated."[8] For the children, it was a wonderful change from land-locked Hamilton and they learned to swim and fished the sea.

Thereafter, summer meant Hamilton, and Hamilton meant back to nature, to the endless grassy fields surrounding Groton House and the muddy Ipswich River. It meant returning to the great rambling house and plain little Hamilton with its drug store and post office and Chittick's hardware store and the trolley car that ran through the center of the village toward Salem. It meant trotting about the country-side with horse and buggy. And sometimes being allowed to sit next to Grandma Amory's chauffeur, Nicholas, and to "drive" her car, identified only as a "buble."

Summer also meant gardening, a lifelong hobby Dorothy (with a little initial help from Fräulein) had taken up at nine, and time to devote to her birds. She had four feathered friends as pets, all named after members of her family: two canaries, Dotty and Bob George, and two wild birds, a cedar waxwing named Libby and a hermit thrush named Freddy. Libby (a male) was particularly troublesome. After escaping from his cage he flew about the hall and broke his wing. He would die but not be forgotten, for his little corpse was stuffed and placed in a glass case which came to reside in our house for many years.

REARED *in a* GREENHOUSE

Summer also meant endless hours with Freddy, the two of them speaking in code and playing imaginary games. "Just you wait till Easter and then Summer comes," he wrote to her from Fay School, during his agonizing first winter there. "Hamilton Lodge. Diamond D. stands for your bike and Diamond F. stands for mine. They are our two horses." Robert was usually above all this, although on one rare occasion, stuck for the afternoon with Dorothy and her friends, the Rantoul sisters, he proved "very affable." Freddy, on the other hand, would tag along everywhere with Dorothy, even when she would visit her best friends and second cousins once removed, Emily and Jean Sears (refer to Chart 13).

Freddy and Dorothy, summer of 1916. In the fall, he would be sent to Fay School, much to his and Dorothy's distress.

More than anything, for Dorothy, summer meant seeing the Searses. As she reminisced years later: "They lived in Beverly, and there I was, this little waif over there in Hamilton. Saturdays, they would send over their touring car, and it would come and take me over there to play." A remarkable friendship developed between Emily Sears and Dorothy Winthrop. They were best friends from childhood all the way into their eighties. It didn't matter that Dorothy would remain a "little waif in Hamilton" while Emily would be whisked off into the larger world of public affairs after her marriage to Henry Cabot Lodge. Their relationship never skipped a beat. Emily would always call Dorothy when she and Cabot returned to the house they built in Beverly. And Dorothy would hear about each assignment—their life while Cabot was a senator in Washington, ambassador to the United Nations under President Eisenhower, Richard M. Nixon's vice presidential running mate in 1960, and ambassador to Vietnam.[9] The two women's lives might have been totally different, but their outlooks were much the same. Both born to society, neither particularly cared for it, shunning the bridge and the golf that seemed to consume so many women of their generation. They shared an interest in world affairs and in books and secretly leaned away from their Republican roots toward the Democratic party, a disloyalty they gloried in discussing out of their respective husbands' hearing.

Far left: *The three Sears children: Emily, Jean and Harry at Woodlea, Bryn Mawr, in 1918*

Left: *Emily and Henry Cabot Lodge on election night 1942 as he is reelected to a second term as U.S. senator from Massachusetts. He was only 34 when he first won the seat. (Courtesy Harry Lodge)*

In Sickness and in Health

Even as children, Emily was the irrepressible one. At the tender age of nine, she had decided something needed to be done to give her cousin more rein at home. So she and her sister Jean, then seven, took it upon themselves to intercede on her behalf with Dorothy's Aunt Clara. The two young girls wrote a letter to this rather imposing aunt, pointing out that Dorothy's upbringing was far too strict and asking her to intercede with her father. It's unlikely that this had any more effect on Dorothy's life than the next ploy Emily came up with. This time she tried teaming up with Grandma Amory, urging Dorothy to put on a little lipstick, dress up a little, and kick up her heels. Dorothy never bothered with lipstick, cared little for clothes, and kept her heels severely beneath her.[10]

In vain, Emily tried to find other ways to lead her cousin astray. Dorothy wrote in her 1918 diary about a hot June day when they were all playing together in a large hole that they had filled with water. Emily, another friend called Cintra, and Harry "were jumping about in the muddy water. Harry had a silk suit on and he lay down in the hole! Emily and Cintra took off their dresses and shoes and stockings and it's too bad they didn't put on bathing suits, because they got splashed from head to toe." Dorothy stood aside, pleading a cold.

In later life, Emily voiced some compunction about one of her deviltries. One day she had told Dorothy that the water she had just drunk from a hose "was poison and that she was going to die." A man on the place came right over and reassured Dorothy that this wasn't true, but Emily was one step ahead of him. As soon as he had gone, she informed Dorothy that the poison acted only on women, not men, and that she was still going to die. "It was the worst thing I have ever done in my life," she recalled much later. "Oh, it was just terrible."

On occasion, they tried to be good. During the summer of the mud bath they started a club called "The Righting Wrongs Club." They included Grandma Sears, electing her, "in a fine ceremony," to the "permanent" job of Queen. Grandma Sears entered into the spirit of the day. "She came all the way into the cellar and accepted. Then we knelt before her and she blessed us!!!!!" Whether it worked was another question. Dorothy feared that "we wrong more rights than otherwise."

In France during the war, Frederic Winthrop found this patriotic picture of Dorothy, 12, when he opened a miniature leather frame inscribed with the message "The girl I left behind."

— • —

"My heart is broken." So Dorothy described her feelings on April 3, 1918, the night her father took the midnight train to New York with "Mama" to go to war. His would be a modest role in World War I, a four-month assignment as a captain in the

Red Cross in France. It was the first glimmer in her diaries of a larger world, the first we hear of the war that for three and a half years had been destroying Europe and killing millions of its people. Robert and Freddy had been allowed home from boarding school to say good-bye.

While he was away, Frederic Winthrop wrote Dorothy several letters. One of the first thanked her for a little leather-bound picture frame with "The girl I left behind" embossed on the front. Inside, opposite the picture of "my darling little daughter," was a small American flag. His letters show how the memory of Dorothy's mother, now dead more than ten years, still haunted him. He began shifting some of the weight of his grief to his daughter.

"During the war, everyone had a potato field." (Caption in Grandma Amory's scrapbook under this photo of Dorothy in the summer of 1918)

> Your letter made me realize that you were growing to be more and more like your dear mother.... She was the dearest, the best and the finest person that ever lived.... I have never known anyone who could compare to her and I knew her *very very* well, and watched her grow up from a beautiful and perfect girl of just your age to a beautiful and perfect woman. My eyesight was all blurred reading your letter, it made me think of her so.

It must have been a heavy burden for Dorothy, feeling she had to live up to her father's ideals.

Some letters were lighter. He described an old man who had a tame young boar for a pet and a bird market in Paris with hundreds and hundreds of birds for sale—canaries, parakeets. Of the war he wrote little. The most exciting tale was of a German aircraft that flew overhead while he was breakfasting in a French restaurant. He described how it began "to fall, turning over and over" after antiaircraft guns shot at it, how he and two men jumped into an automobile but on arriving found the plane had "been righted and had sailed away, in time lost to sight." It was about as close to the action as he got. "I am not doing much work that is worthwhile," he wrote, and "I miss you all *very* much, even more than I thought I should." His assignment was a disappointment, and at the expiration of his four-month tour he returned home.[11]

If her father's absence was the most traumatic part of the war for Dorothy, the departure of Fräulein was a close second. Fred had arranged for Dorothy to stay with Grandma Amory during his absence, writing her that he thought his daughter would be happier under her "loving and sympathetic care" than at 299 Berkeley Street. "I know I will be," Dorothy wrote in her diary. When Fräulein wanted to move in as well, Grandma Amory put her foot down. In her view, Dorothy at

Freddy and Fräulein, with Freddy "the way he looked when Fräulein was around," as attested to 80 years later by brother Robert

thirteen was quite old enough to walk to school unchaperoned. Moreover, Fräulein, a German, was one of the enemy. Dorothy wrote her father in distress. "I do sympathize with you about Fraulein very much," he wrote back.

Fräulein left Dorothy a loving note in German, dated April 18, 1918:

> *To my Dear Dorothy,*
> *May your life be joyous and happy.*
> *May no suffering distress your heart.*
> *Luck be always your guide.*
> *May you never be struck by sorrow and pain.*
>
> *Dedicated to you by your dearly loving Fräulein Wilhemine Hofmeister*[12]

As it turned out, the departure of the caring but strict Fräulein was a release. For a full year afterward, my mother claimed, she never once brushed her teeth. But she had also benefited from Fräulein's tenure: she had learned both to speak and write German fluently, a skill that stayed with her to the end of her days. And at twenty-five, she came to the conclusion that, on balance, she felt sorry for Fräulein: "[She has gone through life] all gloom and all self-pity, going over and over in her mind her trials and troubles and feeling no one understands her suffering for no one has suffered as she. She must get a certain satisfaction from this attitude, for if a thing really hurts, one would do all in one's power to chase the memory of it forever from one's mind. Yet, in spite of a feeling of impatience, I am sorry for such miserable people."

The Winthrops went most places by horse and buggy. They did have a car but it was always breaking down. Pictured here, Fräulein with Happy, c. 1915.

Fräulein's farewell during World War I did not mean that the older Winthrop three were rid of hovering mentors. No sooner had she gone than one Mr. Hicks, whom everyone called "Hixie," appeared to tutor the boys during the summer of 1918. Perhaps Hixie had been hired in response to the boys' academic performance. Or perhaps it was because, with their father in France, it had been decided that a male hand was needed in the home. This gentleman did not meet anyone's expectations, however. For fun, just before he was to leave in September, he and the boys had an odd sort of party which Dorothy's diary called a "barn fire." Hixie "swated R. over the back and pushed him in the fire and hurt him…. Hixie said he'd go through the fire for $50 and father said 'He must be hard up for $50.' Hixie is a nut." Then, in large letters on September 6, "Mr. Hicks left! Hixie is gone!"

His epitaph was a poem, signed by "we three"—R. W., D. W., F. W.—which went as follows:

> *Everyone works but Hixie,*
> *He hangs 'round all day.*
> *He lies upon the sofa,*
> *And writes to Anno Gray.*
> *Mama is shelling peas and*
> *Nat is taught by sister Dor.*
> *Everybody works in our house,*
> *But my tutor.*[13]

World War I exacted its dislocations on the Winthrop children, but there was also a thrilling moment: President and Mrs. Woodrow Wilson invaded Coolidge Point during the summer of 1918, with a military entourage of fifty bivouacking troops and a fleet of submarines. My mother never forgot it: "It was felt that President Woodrow Wilson really needed a rest, and so they took over Aunt Clara's big beautiful house. It was very exciting for the rest of us, because there were submarines and all kinds of boats out in the ocean protecting him, and a whole lot of soldiers living on the place."

"We three," Fred, Dorothy, and Robert, in 1918

Even if the Winthrop children had already seen another president close up—the substantial William Howard Taft, occupying two of the chairs on their Hamilton terrace—they were thrilled to see President Wilson driving down their Aunt Clara's driveway. "President W. waved his hand and took off his hat … !!!!" wrote an excited Dorothy in her diary. She would remember that day nearly seventy years later: "Along came this open automobile, President Wilson sitting in the back seat. And there we were, three worthless little children. And he took off his hat to us, as if we'd been the King and Queen of England. So that was Woodrow Wilson. And although I didn't know him very intimately, I felt as though I had met him."

At the time, however, it was the soldiers who most caught Dorothy's fancy. She reported she gave the soldiers some "grub" because the food train was late.

IN SICKNESS AND IN HEALTH

Then a couple of days later: "Hung round soldiers (interesting!) Ha! Ha! There are 50 of them."[14] On July 30, 1918, when Fred Winthrop came home from France, she greeted his return with an exuberant "I'm as happy as happy can be—because *FATHER* came over to Magnolia with the boys and hurrah! He is home from Europe. My darling dearest Pop!!!!" A few days later she was fretting over him. "Father's hair is getting gray.… He is much thinner and doesn't seem very well." Up and then down: No doubt about it, Dorothy was about to climb aboard the roller coaster of her teens.

Mea Maxima Culpa

chapter EIGHT

Dorothy Winthrop, undated, probably age 13 or 14

In her seventies, my mother would comfort my daughter Dodi when she was downcast, saying, "When I was young, I was unhappy just like you." At other times she would say that as a teenager she had been "bad … disagreeable … horrid." To me it didn't ring true, for there was nothing about her adult personality that suggested such a person. The journals from her mid-teens, however, are full of self-castigating remarks: "No pluck is my middle name," she wrote, and "Rotten fun is my middle name." "Dorothy Tactless Winthrop," she called herself. "I have the manners of a cow….When I'm peeved, I'm dangerous!" The seemingly self-assured young girl of the first diaries had become an introverted and troubled teenager. The change began at the age of fourteen: "I HATE this diary! What I say is so idiotic! A poor success," she wrote. She cut out great sections of pages and blotted out others. She was indeed unhappy, though there is little evidence that she was bad or horrid.

Dorothy channeled all her energies into exorcising the "bad" in herself, for what could one do about being unhappy? The golden rule was, as her father put it, doing "what was right for the sake of … parents and ancestors." Dorothy agreed wholeheartedly. "If Father doesn't want me to do a thing, I don't want to do it. Of course, there are exceptions, but I think he knows what's best, better than I do," she wrote when he forbade her to go to the "Saturday evenings," a regular dance group in Boston. Grandma Amory's word was equally sacred, and when all her friends were getting confirmed, Dorothy didn't, explaining to one, Nancy Murray ("Goaty"), that she couldn't "because Grandma didn't want me to until I was 21 and not then unless

I wanted to." Once she even reminded her grandmother that she had forgotten to enforce a rule about Dorothy's going out to dinner. Later in life she realized there was security in being obedient. As she wrote me in September 1955, "Life was easy in my parents' day for things were either definitely black or definitely white and one grew up knowing which was which."

As obedient as she was, in the spring of 1919, as she was turning fourteen, her "sins" were haunting her. "A" in deportment was no longer good enough. She listed the four wickedest moments in her life:

Christmas 1916
Hayloft 1918
Cellar 1918
March 21, 1919

Her regular diaries for these years hold no clues to these incidents. A hint of what happened at Christmas 1916, however, can be found in the special diary she kept for cataclysmic family events, her "Good Luck Diary." Apparently what she did was to return her father's Christmas presents. The entry for December 25, 1916, reports, "He said 'Your dear Mother would never have done it; she never did anything to hurt anyone's feelings and she would not wish you to.' Father, forgive me, for I knew not what I did."

The memory festered on and more than two years later, in 1919, she revisited it in her regular diary. "I can't help thinking of Hamilton Lodge, etc. and Christmas 1916 most. It really was awful. I would not have done it, but I was told to. I won't tell who told me, but Pa still thinks I am to blame entirely." Later she wrote, "I don't know whether to tell Father that Christmas 1916 was not all my fault. He told me never to mention it again, so I don't know what to do."

Whose fault was it? The "Good Luck Diary" tells us. In a hand more mature, Dorothy wrote opposite the entry about the returned gifts: "In all justice, mature judgment and bitterness of heart, I blame Fraulein and only Fraulein for what I did." Even if she exonerated herself, one can only wonder at a moral sense so overwrought that it turns a child's innocent gesture into an act of cruelty too base to be discussed.

In the summer of 1919 she sought salvation in scouting. For her, the Girl Scouts would have little to do with making campfires and knots; her friend Goaty had explained to her that the purpose of Scouts was to do good and give one honor. But she hesitated about joining: "I doubt if I am good enough to be a

In 1919 Dorothy sought salvation in scouting.

The Winthrop mansion at 299 Berkeley Street loomed gloomy and silent.

Scout—when I remember Hamilton Lodge." Her desire to improve herself won out. "I need something to give me honor," she explained.

A year and a half later, when she was fifteen, Dorothy's self-doubt peaked. She recorded the anatomy of her various alleged crimes. Her first misdeed consisted of having done her homework for the Girl Scouts during cooking class. When Goaty, to whom she was "endlessly thankful," pointed out this was wrong, she apparently went right on—but in retrospect, she felt terrible about it. "Now I see how very dishonorable it was and what a low-down sneak of a cheat I was and still am." On the very same day she forgot her father's birthday at least until the afternoon, when she remembered to get him a card: "I've gone from bad to worse." The next day she slipped in between Goaty and another girl walking side by side, an incident that prompted her to call herself the "meanest, most dishonorable nastiest girl." Dorothy deliberately set for herself a two-week course of self-punishment in the hope that "if I punish myself for each thing I do that is horrid and not nice, I may remember to improve." The punishment, designed to fit the crime, was not to sit next to Goaty for the coming two weeks. She backslid twice, but she did so deliberately and was prepared to accept the consequences: "I've added on this Mon. and Tues. to the two weeks I was originally going to punish myself … after that, I think I won't punish myself any more for that."

By today's standards Dorothy would be considered not only not badly behaved, but preternaturally good. Others spoke well of her. Cousin Jean Sears, Emily's mother, believed "that if anyone deserved to be happy," it was Dorothy, who was "always so uncomplaining." Her friend Goaty reassured her that "if there were many like you, this world would be a better place."

In a sense, Dorothy's belief that everything was her fault gave her a kind of strength, because she knew that if the blame was hers, so too were the means for improvement. For all her self-criticism, at her core lay a hope, perhaps even a faith, that she was strong enough to overcome her faults: "This may be conceited, but I don't think I'd do such bad things as I have done, again. Of course I might. When one is bad it's hard to get right.… I do so want to be good."

— • —

Dorothy's sins were one symptom of a more fundamental trouble: a biting loneliness. She was still only thirteen when she wrote in her diary that, though she'd had "more fun [this spring] than any other spring I can remember ... at times I feel awful blue and then I'd like to bust. I want to tell someone lots of things which trouble me." Her only outlet, it seemed, was her diaries. "Dorothy Winthrop Very Private," she wrote on the front of one of her 1920 diaries, and "Private Property of Dorothy Winthrop or Dossify Scatterbrain, 299 Berkeley St.," on another. She seldom found a sympathetic ear at 299 Berkeley Street. "Supper alone," she wrote at one point in 1919. "I often have supper alone these days." It was not just that her father and stepmother would leave her to sup at a lonely table. She couldn't confide in either one.

The tension between Dorothy and her stepmother was growing. The secret nickname YOW (standing perhaps for You Old Witch) replaced "Somebody" as a secret code name. No insult was strong enough, she seemed to feel, in light of the way her stepmother treated the Amory side of the family. Sally Winthrop, for example, fed her own children well, while Dorothy and her brothers ate food that was "so bad, we went without supper! I used to be sick all the time, the boys weren't so often.... Of course, now we eat with Father and get good junk." Another sore point continued to be Sally's reaction to Dorothy's illnesses. No longer terrified to admit she was sick, Dorothy was mad. Why should Nat be allowed to stay in bed all day when he was "only tired" while she herself was made to feel like a faker when she was genuinely sick? She resented her stepmother's saying she and her brothers had been "petted and spoiled."

Sarah T. Winthrop, c. mid-1920s (courtesy Eleanor Winthrop)

Her stepmother downplayed Freddy's misery at Fay. She did concede that "home-sickness was an unpleasant feeling, but she thought it quite natural for little boys as young as Fay school boys to be so.... It was easy to see by the way she spoke that she had no sympathy for Freddy." When Freddy moved on to St. Mark's, things went much better for him. Sally Winthrop continued to be a wet blanket, however. "When Fred stood 4th in his form, thrilling everyone, YOW's comment was 'If he could do so well once, he should always do as well.' And when Robert stood 5th, she said, 'If a boy loafed all his life, he was bound to make an effort once.'" And she refused to acknowledge their social successes. When Dorothy told Freddy that Dr. Thayer, headmaster of St. Mark's, had said he was the most popular boy in his class, her stepmother took issue with her. "I think you made a mistake. Dr. Thayer said the most popular in his form, and that ought to be good enough."[1]

Though on balance Dorothy thought her stepmother was "horribly nice" to her compared with the way she treated Robert and Freddy, Dorothy herself was not immune to criticism. "She thinks I wear too many clean clothes, but I only change twice a week and I wear two or three waists a week.... She is very clever and has a calculating … brain.… Nothing goes on about her that she doesn't know about." The worst fights were over the car, which Dorothy's stepmother sometimes let her have for afternoon expeditions (with chauffeur, of course). Nat and Katharine would complain that Dorothy "always" used the car. Dorothy would decide not to use it because she didn't want to be accused of "hogging" the car. Her stepmother would say she was glad to let her stepdaughter use the car, but, wrote Dorothy, "I see now, at heart she isn't." Then the inevitable mix-up would occur and everyone would blow up. Once Dorothy was fifteen minutes late, and her stepmother "was mad … she was white with rage." Other times it was Dorothy who lost control. These scenes often filled her with shame. Once she wrote, "I screamed and hollered and explained and made a fool of myself. I wish I wouldn't always holler. I do *not* want to."

Within a few years, however, Dorothy had begun to overcome the hate demons— or maybe, as she and her brothers grew older, their stepmother was becoming more lenient. Whatever was happening, the wall of anger between the two began to crumble by the time she was fifteen. "Sometimes I do think YOW is perfectly disgusting and sometimes I don't think her half bad," wrote Dorothy in her 1920 diary. "I don't know why," she wrote in 1921, "but the last year or so she has been half decent to us. Perhaps she's softening."

When her stepmother, too sleepy to be angry, let her in "late" one evening (9:10), Dorothy felt remorseful: "I'm sorry I kept her up, because she said she was tired." When her stepmother didn't criticize her for going to bed sick, Dorothy allowed that "she hasn't blown me up for ages!"

It was one thing to admit to herself that her stepmother had some good points. It was quite another to become her friend. Sally Winthrop tried one evening, when they were having supper alone together, to bridge the gulf between them. Dorothy remained aloof. "She asked me lots of questions. I don't like her to know how I feel on certain subjects, but I can't refuse to answer." Still, Dorothy made reciprocal gestures of kindness. On March 12, 1921, the sixth anniversary of her son John's death, Dorothy gave her stepmother flowers. Every year she made this gesture, and every year, doubtless making her stepdaughter squirm, Mrs. Winthrop wept. This year, the scene was more restrained. "YOW thanked me for the flowers. She didn't cry." Sally's tears were unshared. While on the anniversary of his first wife's death the deepest gloom would settle over Fred Winthrop, it appeared he didn't even remember John's passing. This, at least, is the implication of a note Sally wrote Dorothy three years later, in 1924, thanking her for the flowers and apologizing for crying. "You can't possibly know how much they mean to me," she wrote. "My Johnnie was so little and the years go by so fast that I love to feel that someone else remembers him and thinks of him sometimes."

On July 12, 1921, Dorothy abandoned her secret name for her stepmother: "Father and Mama's 10th wedding anniversary."

Dorothy's father, instead of providing a steadying hand, got caught up in the bickering between his daughter and his wife. His rule that Sally should take no role in bringing up his first wife's children was proving impossible to comply with. He was furious when she did nothing, and even madder when she did something he didn't approve of. "Why doesn't anyone try and make her comfortable!" he fumed to Sally one day on finding Dorothy sick in her bed, untended. That time, he brought his daughter pillows and wheeled her to the window.

The arguments between Fred and Sally could be petty. One evening in early February 1921 it seemed as if dignity and restraint had taken their leave of the Victorian mansion at 299 Berkeley Street.

> When I came home from Grandma's, I rang the bell four times but no one answered so I banged the door and Father let me in. Father was mad because all the maids had gone upstairs and YOW was mad because Father was, and I was mad because I had rung and no one had answered, so that Father had become mad!!!!

It was a house swarming with staff, eight maids and a butler,[2] and though Fred presumably wanted them on tap at all times, Dorothy was mortified that one of them had been present for another family flare-up that winter. "YOW said there was no use telling Father anything. He always forgot and she wished he would remember, and she complained about and slammed him until I could have killed her. And she did it all in front of Eva."

Fred Winthrop would be forever haunted by the loss of his beloved first wife, Dorothy.

For a man of Fred Winthrop's reticence and self-control, these quarrels must have been embarrassing. Evidently, rather than risk confrontation, he would retreat into his shell. He didn't do this only with Sally. When Dorothy went out to supper too often, or came home too late, she met with an angry curtain of silence: "He hardly speaks to me now. I know he hates to see me round. I deserve it, but I'd rather he blow me up and get over it, than brood all day long and barely notice me."

Equally unnerving, her father was unpredictable. Sometimes he was simply forgetful, both about his promises (to give her music lessons) and about his threats (one list included forcing her to drink one quart of milk a day, having her hair treated, and dropping dancing school and Latin). Other times he made an effort, staying at home when her friends came to dinner and trying to get to know them. In one instance he spoke to her angrily on the phone when she was late getting home, but when she got back, he turned to the subject of his own youth—how terribly shy and self-conscious he had been and how he thought he had improved.

This was not the only time that Frederic Winthrop bared his tortured soul to his daughter. Seemingly oblivious to how his black gloom might affect her, he told her during her sixteenth year that "he'd just as soon die and have it all over with." It was in late July, and he and Dorothy were visiting his brother Gren in Lenox. There, in the beauty of the Berkshires, Dorothy listened with growing distress.

> Then he said, "Your mother—" but his voice failed him and he could say no more. Poor darling Father, I feel so sorry for him. It was all I could do to keep from crying. After a while he said "Strange, I can't speak of her after fourteen years." Oh Father, Father, Mother. I could not help myself any longer and two tears got the better of me. I tried not to let Father see and thank God I made no noise. I feel sorrier for Father than anyone in the world and darling Mother we all want.

Dorothy never found fault with her father for not trying to conceal his moods, nor did it occur to her, apparently, that in his obsession there was a hint of morbid self-indulgence. She only felt sorry for him. This was strange, because she once wrote disparagingly of a family that had lost a daughter: they "live in the past and are morbid about [her]. Her room is not touched, the door plate of the house she died in hangs in Mrs. H's room. Mrs. always talks about her." In general—her father's case excepted—Dorothy adhered to her headmistress Miss Degen's decree that such sorrows should "be taken with the day's burden. One should not live in the past with the dead, but pluck up courage and go on with life."

Despite his moods, Dorothy idolized her father. "I have the most perfect Father imaginable. He makes me want to do right and he is so just and nice to us all. He is a model of unselfishness and he just seems to live for his children. Nor does he spoil us, in spite of all the things he gives us."

On November 15, his fifty-third birthday, Dorothy gave her father an ashtray. It was a modest gift, and the birthday was of no particular consequence. Fred Winthrop's thank you note, however, was heavy with significance; a less sympathetic daughter might have been embarrassed reading it: "My greatest concern in life is for the welfare of you children, and I want you always to feel that you can consult me about *anything*.... The best that I can hope for is that you and the boys will always remember and believe that I am the best friend you have. You are a dear friend and I love you very much." Though he invited her confidences, Dorothy kept many things to herself. At the St. Mark's–Groton football game in November 1921 she felt she was about to faint. Not wishing to bother her father, she didn't say a word, but tried to slip away "unobserved." When he realized what was happening her father took the situation in hand, bringing her back to the car for "some rare ... whiskey[3] and [making] no fuss. He is at all times unselfish and he lives for others. A perfect father."

— • —

During her early teens Dorothy's need for her real mother was reaching a painful climax. Sally Winthrop remained an unwelcome interloper: "I don't feel I can ever love her. My blood boils when I think that she sleeps in my mother's room and in her bed and uses her towels, sheets and pillow cases, etc." She wanted someone she could confide in.

> Whenever the girls speak about their mothers and say that they told their mother this and that (because they always tell their mother everything), it makes me feel queer, I can't explain and wish I had someone to tell things to. I don't tell anyone and oh! sometimes how I long to. Doubtless if Mother had lived, I should not be so bad. Mother darling, Mother come to us again.

Even from her grave, her mother became Dorothy's conscience.

> When I've done wrong, it is when I think of Mother that I feel most miserable. I'm not worthy of her and it is she that makes me want to do right, almost even more than Father. If I imagine that Mother is looking at me, I stop being bad.

Fred Winthrop sent mixed messages, in some instances telling his daughter she was becoming more like her mother and in others, suggesting she wasn't living up to her mother's perfection. Assuring Dorothy she was worthy to take them over, he began to dole out her mother's possessions, but it was with a grudging heart. Meanwhile, Dorothy would seize on and record the minutest detail of any encounter with her mother that anyone told her of. At the Searses', she talked to a "lady who knew our darling mother. She has a daughter Dorothy and a son Jack." It was a painful process. Conversations with such people, she wrote, "made me feel as if I would go home and really speak to Mother.... Although I barely remember her living, I can't grasp that she is dead and that I won't see her until I die."

A certain Mrs. Fitzgerald conjured up another vision of Dorothy's mother in a letter she wrote Libby Amory about a visit to Green-Wood Cemetery in Brooklyn. No doubt, Dorothy, knowing nothing of the place, just that Winthrops had a burial site there, craved to learn more.

> She [Mrs. Fitzgerald] sat three hours by Mother's grave thinking of when she knew her. She said it looked lovely with trees, grass and flowers. I wonder if anyone ever goes to it, I mean of my relations from New York. I wish I could go. I'd like to go alone and stay just as long as I liked. Perhaps it is foolish, but I want to ask to be forgiven there for all the bad things I've done and to ask for help to improve. I'd never want to leave it when I once got there.

After writing of Mrs. Fitzgerald's visit, she wrote a poem that began

There's a sacred spot in Greenwood
That I'm longing for to see.
I would plant it round with flowers
For it is sacred to me.

Elsewhere, Dorothy wrote another poem:

In Greenwood, she's softly sleeping
Where the flowers gently wave
Lies the one we loved so dearly
"She will never be forgotten"
Never will her memory fade
Sweetest thoughts will always linger
Around the grave where she is laid.

Sometimes she would gaze at her mother's picture and wish for the impossible: "Oh give me my life again with Mother in it. I want my Mother. The boys need her and I know want her. Oh let us again live our life with Mother darling. Mother, we want you."

— • —

Grandma Amory was surely aware of Dorothy's suffering, for she herself never got over the sorrow of her daughter's loss. But it wasn't her way to brood, and anyway she had a job to do—helping raise Dorothy. Unlike Fred and Sally Winthrop's, however, Grandma's idea of discipline was a dash of correction, administered with a pinch of humor and a large measure of love. For someone like Dorothy who was eager to please, the approach worked wonders. "Scrabble up to bed," Grandma would warn her granddaughter and Dorothy would trot obediently off, happy to comply. Grandma Amory's sternest words were reserved for Dorothy's attire. Neatness and cleanliness were very important to her. When people had told her what beautiful daughters she had, she was in the habit of replying, "Thank you. They are very clean." Dorothy's clothes were neither neat nor clean and she made no bones about telling her. After reassuring her granddaughter that she was "only writing to tell you how much I love you and desire your well being," she got right to the point.

> Now I am going to scold you. I heard you were at the club with that shabby and dowdy-looking khaki skirt—I was sorry you did not take the trouble and interest to be well dressed, why not put on one of the summer dresses I got you or a *clean* white skirt and waist? as you have plenty. You have to look after your appearance yourself now, for men don't know or notice, but women do—I used to be *so* particular that my girls should be neat and well dressed. Now my ambition falls on you.
>
> I think it is just as important to be … well dressed as to know the multiplication table. I wish you would give that girl scout suit to a beggar.

Once again, Dorothy was compliant, for three days later another letter went to "dearest Dar," complimenting her for being "a sweet thing to take my scolding so amiably!"

If criticisms flew thick and fast at 299 Berkeley, Grandma Amory and Dorothy were almost never cross with one another. In the only recorded instance of Dorothy's feeling put out by her grandmother, she was just as angry at herself for being peeved: "Grandma stretched over and took a drink from my glass of milk. I didn't like it and it made me feel disagreeable. I'm mad that it did. Grandma does so much for me and is so nice to me, I shouldn't mind if she does drink my milk (she gave me the milk in the 1st place, so it wasn't really mine)."

Mostly they just chatted. Grandma gave her insights on the Amory side of the family: "she told me lots about Mother and Grandpa." She was provocative: "I am glad you saw Hamlet. There is always a question whether he was really a little crazy or only pretending to be at times so he could more easily revenge his father's death...." And kind: she "comes upstairs ... and entertains me," wrote Dorothy, during an episode of chicken pox in 1921 when Grandma had taken her in. "[I'd have been] bored stiff if Grandma didn't pay so much attention to me."

Grandma Amory tried to make up to Dorothy for the cold shoulder her illnesses met at home—even if it required the most extreme effort. On one such occasion Grandma Amory was nearing her seventy-eighth birthday. Dorothy and her school friends were at one of the Boston armories practicing for a rally.

> It was hot and stuffy and pretty soon I began to feel queer.... I began to feel worse and worse.... I soon said I wished Dinkey Smith would take my place.... Olga Leary ... led me to the First Aid place where they put me on a cot. Olga meanwhile telephoned Grandma.

Pretty soon the cots in the first aid station were full, and others affected by the heat kept arriving. One Mrs. Seaver offered Dorothy a ride home, which she gladly accepted. Meanwhile, Grandma Amory had been contacted and was hurrying to fetch her granddaughter. The day was hot, and she was most likely wearing one of her long black dresses. The attempt started badly, with Grandma unable to find her car and having to settle for a taxicab. The driver, of course, took her to the wrong armory.

> Finally, she found the right one and pushing her way through an immense crowd, she at last reached the First Aid, only to be told I'd gone. Then someone said a friend had gone with me, so Grandma pushed back through the crowd, expecting to find me on the sidewalk, waiting for her, but no, I was not to be seen. Then she thought I might be in the cab, but she could not find it, so a little boy led her to it. No, I was not there, so poor Grandma pushed her way through the crowd again and received the same information at the First Aid. Then Grandma felt in her bones, that the "friend" had taken me home, so after pushing her way for the fourth and thank goodness last time through the crowd, she drove to the nearest drug store.
>
> She tried to telephone but was unsuccessful as she didn't know how to use a public pay phone. However, a girl telephoned home and hearing I was safe, dear Grandma hurried to me. Oh, I am so very sorry for her and I shall never forgive myself for causing her all that trouble in the intense heat. My darling Grandma. She is indeed the most perfect person on this earth.

Dorothy, 17, and her two step-siblings, Nat, 10, and Katharine, 8, in October 1922

As they grew older, the tables turned and Dorothy began to worry about her grandmother's health. She had glaucoma. Easily treated today, glaucoma then meant blindness. Grandma Amory set herself to tackling typing and Braille so as to be able to keep up with the world—and her grandchildren. My mother remembered that, when her grandmother couldn't sleep on a cold winter's night, she would snuggle under her covers and pass the time "reading" her books in Braille. Grandma Amory never let her ailments conquer her spirits. "What do you think has happened to me?" she wrote Dorothy after an attack of pleurisy. "The doctor discovered that my rib was broken!! It is a little uncomfortable but not much and next week I expect to be up and dressed for several hours.[4] But what is much worse than my rib, is that Sarah [a maid] is going to get married this fall! I shall miss her, she is so neat and nice."

Like Fred, Grandma Amory sought to encourage Dorothy by assuring her that she "was getting more and more like Mother all the time." Dorothy, of course, didn't agree: "I wish I was … I am bad and have a million faults." Whether she was or wasn't, however, was beside the point. Dorothy's role model, the person she would try to be like, was not an exquisite picture hanging eternally beautiful and mute on the wall. It was Grandma Amory, rattling the cages of old age, forever speaking her mind, living just down the street.

— • —

One of Grandma's lessons was how to stay cheerful and calm when all about you was commotion. Dorothy was inching her way toward controlling herself, and not just with her stepmother over the car. When brothers Robert and Freddy fought, it was Dorothy who would step in and try to referee.

> O, I wish they wouldn't fight. They don't if I stand between—and it seems cowardly of me to take advantage of being a girl, but I can't bear to see them come to blows and that is the only way I can stop it.

At other times she would intercede between the younger two, protecting Katharine from Nat. He was "a pest, a terrible pest," she'd say in years to come. Her diary confirms the squabbling: "Nat was giving Katharine a kick so I grabbed him, until Katharine got safely downstairs and [I] received the kicks myself. I dodged all but one, much to N's disgust!!"

Despite their separate upbringing, Dorothy couldn't resist her little sister. Katharine made her laugh. "All through the prayers [at church one day], she whispered and brushed her face with my hair and finally asked if they wouldn't wake up soon.… Katharine is killing. I like her." Years later, she recounted another incident

REARED *in a* GREENHOUSE

she thought just as comical, when Katharine had tricked their old-fashioned father, gradually snipping away at her hair each month against his orders while my mother had obediently kept hers long. "He never noticed [that it was getting shorter]," my mother related, "and finally, it had gotten short enough to be the fashion."

Meanwhile, she tried another lesson on herself: to see some good in Nat. "[It] was really awfully nice of him," wrote Dorothy of an occasion when he waited for his little sister to catch up. "There is lots nice about him, but he does make me so mad at times. Most likely he is much nicer than I think." When it came to studies, Dorothy reached the reluctant conclusion that Nat and Katharine "are the family stars." Both did well at school, Katharine being described by one teacher as "very bright and [with] a great mathematical mind."

The main fault lines between the three older children and the two younger remained firmly in place, however. Her two older brothers had the central spot in Dorothy's heart: "I wouldn't swap them for the world. I love 'em both and think they're fine." Even so, one was more equal than the other: "Freddy is really the finest of us three." Freddy was also more like Dorothy. "Freddy is reserved and retiring, while Robert somehow pushes himself forward, so I prefer Freddy in that way. I think Robert is girl crazy, Freddy is not." Like her, Freddy had known unhappiness: "He has had to suffer a great deal, with his eye and homesickness at Fay and many more things, but he bore them wonderfully. Why does the best one always suffer most?"

Dorothy and Katharine enjoy a playful moment.

While Freddy and Dorothy must have swapped stories of their woes, Robert was off in his own world, oblivious to much of what Dorothy was going through at home. His main battle seemed to be with books, for he was often the target of paternal wrath over unfulfilled academic expectations. He was up at five or six every morning to do his work, he wrote Dorothy, sending her one of their father's letters to show her "what I am up against. He thinks I ought to stand first!" By the time he was seventeen, however, Robert was golfing with his father and partying with the girls. He "liked 'em fast," wrote Dorothy, and had a "gay time" with his circle of friends—John Sherborn, Alice Herrick, Dolly Duane, and Dolly Thayer. Only the sixth-form dance was a bust, because "many NY girls gave out [and the boys had to] ask … Boston girls up instead."

"We three"—Dorothy and her "own native brothers"—shared a string of adventures. One was a canoe trip she and Robert took on a cold March afternoon: "The current is awful. We shipped water and nearly upset. Ice is floating all over and we paddled on lots of meadows. Wonderful fun." Another involved a certain Mr. Barret from Chicago, who—from his spot under an umbrella on the river bank—threatened to have the three young Winthrops arrested for wading past a dam he'd built. They just laughed at him. "Around here everyone is neighborly and no one thinks anything of someone riding through their grounds or carrying canoes round dams, so this old crank is great fun, because he is so fussed."

"I love 'em both and think they're fine," wrote Dorothy in her 1920 diary of brothers Robert and Fred. At left, Freddy, summer of 1922 at Squam Lake; at right, Robert, sixth former at St. Mark's, 1921.

Their most memorable adventure, however, was a conflagration in their playhouse during the summer of 1921. Dorothy and her brothers had lit a fire in the fireplace and were sitting around talking when Dorothy noticed something amiss.

> Suddenly in the corner, where the chimney was, I saw the wood turn light and red, and even as, in terror, I yelled "Look," the glow spread. I was paralysed with fear for what could that mean but that the little house was on fire? After my cry, the boys gave one leap and tore into the workshop, with me at their heels…. Fred tore up the ladder, Robert after him.

Robert lost his balance trying to swat out some flames and fell backward onto the floor. Before he could move, a flaming hammock had landed on top of him. Luckily, he was able to get up and stomp it out with his boots. But by then a flaming tennis net had fallen too.

Fred, meanwhile, was missing. They called to him and heard "a muffled reply." Supposing he was all right, they dragged the burning objects out onto the wet grass and extinguished them. Suddenly Fred appeared with the story of what he had been doing. He had reached the loft to look for water, but there being none, he had thrown down the burning hammock and net, thinking they could be more easily extinguished below. Barehanded, he had "smothered all fiery gleams,"

> Then choking, suffocating, and his cheeks streaming with tears, he had felt all in … he could not get to the trap door, so he had just reached the window and stuck his head out … but hung suspended in the middle [and w]hen he'd gotten back some breath, he had climbed down to us.

"My brothers are wonders," she wrote afterward. "They saved the house! Especially Fred. He was so quick in getting up the ladder and throwing junk down. I love 'em both and I'd give 'em both a medal for bravery and presence of mind."

Hamilton wasn't always so exciting. "We three" would disappear into Fred's room after dinner to play poker "with awful old cards" and drink coffee milk shakes. "The boys," Dorothy recorded, "smoke cigarettes" and sit around and swear at Hamilton.

— • —

At fourteen, Dorothy was finding school engrossing. Her diaries brim with gossip of her schoolmates. "Walked with Emily Sears, Ruth Bremer, and Nancy Murray … saw Isabel Thorndike (a nut) … fooled with Jean … walked home with Helena Lodge [sister of Henry Cabot Lodge] … saw Louise Brown with her feller. She is a fish…. A secret is brewing which Harriet Rantoul and I alone really know about. Helen Partridge got my goat trying to find out…. Pit was absent." They played beacon, hide-and-go-seek, prisoner's base, truth, and ball in the backyard.

A special friend was emerging, one who would serve as Dorothy's polestar as her teens progressed, one who would remain her friend for life. She would lead a colorful life, this new friend: marriage to Shakespeare scholar Theodore Spencer, a divorce and conversion to Catholicism, a move to a Swiss nunnery where she took the veil, and finally a return from the religious order to settle in Vermont near her son John, who had become a professor of history at Middlebury College. In our family, we referred to her as Nancy Murray Spencer Murray, to celebrate her maidenhood, marriage, and return to maidenhood through religious vows. But at Miss May's she would be called Nancy Murray or simply Goaty, as in Nanny Goat. Dorothy sang Goaty's praises. On St. Valentine's Day, Goaty got twelve valentines: "very popular…. I just love Nancy Murray…. Goaty dances speedily…. Ruth is nice, but Nancy is best."

Nancy Murray, Dorothy's new special friend, in 1919

Dorothy was emerging as a leader in school. Here she is with Nancy Murray (left) and Juliet Greene.

Meanwhile, a part of Dorothy still reached out to those like her with secret sorrows. She had a dream about a girl, which lingered for days. The figure in the dream "was sad and it seemed that her sadness was somehow connected with the War." Shortly thereafter, in school, Dorothy saw a new girl whom she "recognized … with a shock" as the girl in her dream. Not only that, a woman was telling the girls about the war and all the suffering in Europe—and the girl herself started to cry, just as she had during Dorothy's dream. Four days later in French class Mademoiselle had the class in "rapt attention," when Dorothy heard a "sound like a sob" behind her. She looked to see where the sobs had come from and "there … was the girl of my dream!" The girl continued to haunt her: "The memory of my dream girl will not leave me. I cannot get away from the thought that she is sad.… Poor dear girl. My heart is breaking for you."

Most of the time, however, Dorothy was having fun—so much that her academic record for 1918–19 turned out to be her worst ever. She did retain her A average in deportment, but there were gentlewoman C's in Bible, French, and history, and several D's in exams.

The fall of 1920 was an auspicious start of a new school year: "There is heaps of difference between this year and last, because last year I didn't look forward a bit to good times during the school year, for then I had no friends, but now I am looking forward and especially after I move to 299, when I'll be near everyone!! and walk to and from school!! with them!!!!" During this year and the next, her school record gave the lie to the picture she painted of herself in her diaries as a brainless, clumsy, tactless spoil-sport. In 1920–21 she chalked up A's in German, history, physics, French verbs, and Bible, and a record in exams that matched that of her regular work. Her father was impressed, Freddy wrote her, calling her "con she en shus." In 1921 the school magazine, *The Maze*, finally accepted an article she had written entitled "Ten Commandments for Mayites," which listed the "Thou shalts" and "Thou shalt nots" of school life: "My brain worked, my heart beat, I read the writing, my brain reeled, my heart pounded.… I felt gratified after four years of continuous failure."

The inept athlete also served as captain of her class basketball team and treasurer of the Athletic Association and was commended for her school spirit. She was dubious: "I don't know as how it is school spirit, but I'd walk to kingdom come to see our team, our glorious team play."

Neither was she "rotten fun," as she wrote she was. Emily Sears Lodge recalled that Dorothy couldn't suppress her sense of humor even when she had to. "I used to hold up my book and make faces at her and it would make her laugh until the tears streamed down her face and she sometimes got in trouble." The Sears sisters left

Miss May's to study in Europe, but other girls took Emily's impish place. And when they "try and make me laugh," wrote Dorothy ruefully, "I always do." She laughed so much that she was made to recite her French lessons facing the blackboard. Even then, she couldn't resist peering around, and every time she did she would start laughing again.

The opera singer Mademoiselle Cossini with the Sears girls, Emily, left, and Jean on the French Riviera in 1920

She returned the favor, playing tricks on the girls. On false pretenses she won the sympathy of Ethel Cummings, school president, pretending she was upset when scolded for taking part in a food fight. Her shame was fake: "[I] wet my eyes and rubbed them until they were very red and walked through room 6 on Jean's arm snuffling and applying my handkerchief to my eyes." Ethel spoke to Dorothy in a "condoling, pitying tone." Dorothy didn't let up, answering with "a martyred smile on my map." Afterward, feeling guilty, she confessed, much to the displeasure of her teacher.

Giggles aside, Dorothy was emerging as a leader, an older girl to whom the younger girls looked up. Two of them begged her in a letter: "We want your picture as we like you very much. We think you are pretty." Dorothy protested she was unworthy of any of these compliments. Sternly, she reprimanded her admirers.

My dear Emily and Anne

Please do get over it. It is a silly way to like a person for you might be disappointed in her when you got to know her. I really feel that sensible and not too sudden friendships are always more lasting and give more pleasure and happiness to all concerned than the other kind of affection. Don't you?

I really think you are both much too nice to have crushes. Please forgive me if I sound angry or unkind, because I feel far from it.
Your loving friend,
Dorothy Winthrop

By her mid-teens Dorothy's world was opening up, beyond home and school. The Searses reappeared in the summer, showing off trunkfuls of "lovely and numerous" new dresses from Paris and accompanied by a glamorous opera singer named Mademoiselle Cossini.[5] Dorothy was learning to drive, practicing in Wareham on Uncle Billy Amory's new car. It was, she wrote, "one of those queer Fords he'd fixed

up all peculiarly himself. It had two very broken down but comfortable front seats. A box and gas tank in back, and canvas mud guards." It went like a wild bronco: not only did it "jump and skid all over; one had to drive it very fast or it would stop."

One would have thought Dorothy Winthrop had everything. But the fact remained that she was a mere girl, and her greater family circle was dominated by boys and men—her three brothers, five uncles, and seven male first cousins (only two female first cousins). Among the assortment, her father's three brothers—Uncles Dudley, Grenville, and Beekman—would receive top billing in her stories, and all three made their debuts in her diary between 1919 and 1921.

Strictly speaking, only Uncle Dudley's ghost appeared, for he'd been dead eight years when in 1920 Dorothy was at last inducted into her father's plantation in South Carolina. Uncle Dudley had bought the place, the rumor went, when the Okeetee Club where he lodged for his hunting and shooting was opened to women and children.[6] He'd bought it for his old age, my mother told us, but he died before he was old and left it to her father, because he was the only brother with sons. The place reeked of manliness—plenty of shooting and no hot water, lots of cigars and little landscaping. Fred was maintaining his brother's pecking order, to wit, in my mother's words; "At the plantation, first came the Winthrop men, then Richard [the 'darkie' who led the quail hunts], then the dogs and the horses—and finally the Winthrop women.... Women could come only on sufferance."

If not at the plantation, Dudley had room in his life for a woman or two. A certain May Bird "adored him," my mother said. May Bird was reported to be "a snappy lady" who had "left in a huff" when Dudley's groom failed to show up to take her horse.[7] But my mother's recollection was of a later time and was more pathetic. After Dudley had died and left May Bird without a suitor, my mother would see May Bird in church on Long Island, becoming more and more nearsighted, and hear Aunt Melza, Uncle Beek's wife, say, "Poor little May Bird, poor little May Bird." Uncle Dudley also had, my mother's brother Robert discovered, another woman, "a shady lady who lived in New York, well out of the way uptown." Her existence became known, he told me, when it was learned that Uncle Dudley had left a $200,000 trust in her name.

REARED *in a* GREENHOUSE

Although Dudley suffered the odd woman, he found children beyond the pale. People told stories about how he would sic his dogs on the little black boys on the plantation and laugh as they went scuttling up a tree.[8] My mother's story wasn't much nicer.

> He thought children were awful. Once, on entering the house of some friends, he sniffed and said, "Damn baby in this house. Damn baby in this house." His friend said, "Oh no, Mr. Winthrop, oh no. There's no baby in this house." But Uncle Dudley insisted, "I say there's a damn baby in this house." And lo and behold, he was right. He could smell it. There was indeed a damn baby in that house.

Dorothy might have been intimidated by Uncle Dudley himself, but she was enraptured by his legacy. The plantation was wild and inaccessible land, a sportsman's dream. Huge fields lay open, mostly yellow with tall grasses, some still poorly cultivated with cotton. Stands of tall pine and oak were everywhere, and along the river the swamp lay wild and spooky, Spanish moss dripping to the still, muddy waters below, deer and wild boar, turkey, and quail hiding everywhere. In 1906, when Dudley started buying up the place, land in that part of South Carolina had been dirt cheap, as low as $4.50 an acre. Over a four-year period, he purchased nearly ten thousand acres—properties named Joint Stock and Stevens, Oakland and Greenwood. Today Groton Plantation is a thirty-three-square-mile stretch of country on the Savannah River, halfway between Augusta and Savannah, Georgia, and directly west of South Carolina's capital, Charleston.

In December 1920 Dorothy was finally allowed to join her brothers and father for the annual Christmas trip to the plantation. She was thrilled:

> Dreadful 10-mile drive until we reached the place which is too lovely in spite of the awful roads. I think I like bum roads. It makes the place more wild. Here there is an artesian well, the water comes from 900 feet underground and would shoot from 40 to 50 ft. high, if pipes didn't prevent it. The water is warm, where the well comes up, but by the time it reaches the faucets, it is freezing. There is no hot water here, excepting a canful every morning. There are six darling log cabins in an enclosure.
>
> Everywhere there are lovely and queer trees and shrubs.

MEA MAXIMA CULPA

In Dudley's day, the planta-tion was wild and inaccessible, a sportsman's dream. Today in Winthrop hands for more than 90 years, it has gained renown as the oldest single-family-owned hunting preserve in the region. Photos from top: Freddy, Jr., Dorothy and Robert in swamp, January 1, 1922; one of the sheds where the "hunters" would picnic; hunting quail, early spring 1934.

Frances, a darkie, came in at about 7:30, lit a roaring fire and left some hot water. After getting dressed and washed and frozen, we all go over to the dining room and eat. At 9 or so, we all start off riding, Robert on Maimy, Fred on Elmo (a lovely horse!), Richard, the dog man, on a mule, and I on Happy. Poor old Happy, how I love him. We shoot all morning, come home for lunch, start off again at 2, and come home after dark. We ride all day and are still on Father's place, which is 25 square miles. There are lovely woods and pine woods everywhere. There are ditches in many places, which cross the roads and are up to the horses' middles, and in order to keep our feet dry, we hold them up high. It is ideal here. We come home for supper and after reading in the biggest house, I come to my room, undress, take a freezing bath in a freezing room and jump into a freezing bed and freeze all night.

When it rained they read and took soaking walks, and when it cleared again Dorothy rode a mule and jumped her horse. They watched some cotton ginned, rode to the "three bridges" where they had their first picnic lunch (ham sandwiches, corn bread, sweet baked potatoes, and cocoa), and saw the road on which Sherman's army had reportedly marched its devastating way from Atlanta to Columbia and which Dorothy found "small and not nearly as good as the worst roads in Hamilton!"

The following year, 1921, Dorothy's diaries contain the first mention of her second Winthrop uncle, Uncle Gren, together with his daughters Kate and Emily. My mother often compared Uncle Dudley with Uncle Gren: "Uncle Dudley was short and wide. Uncle Gren was short and skinny. Uncle Dudley loved to shoot and kill. Uncle Gren wouldn't kill anything. Uncle Dudley was always busy with his slaughtering and Uncle Gren was always busy with his beauty."

By the time Dorothy was sixteen, Uncle Gren had been a widower for over two decades and was immersed in his art collecting. He wintered in New York and sum-mered in Lenox, Massachusetts, on a manicured estate my mother remembered vividly: "He collected birds, marvelous pheasants and other exotic birds, and had them running around everywhere. He beautified the place with wonderful planting and created vistas all about, with statues at the ends."

When visiting the family in the summer of 1921, Dorothy wrote about her only female cousins, his daughters Emily and Kate, who had been only seven and one when their mother died. Naturally, Dorothy sympathized with them.

In his [Uncle Gren's] bedroom is a large portrait of Aunt Mary. She has been dead for 21 years. Poor Emily and Kate. I pity them … they have never had a mother … they are prettier and sweeter than ever. Emily is my favorite cousin and Kate my second. They both sing well and sculpt and draw…. I love [Emily] more than ever…. She is really lovely in looks and in her own self too…. She doesn't look anywhere near 28.

That summer at her Grandma Winthrop's in Lenox Dorothy met two other cousins, the van Roijen brothers, for the first time. They were just about her age: Herman had turned sixteen in April and Robert was fourteen. These were the sons of her father's sister Tina and her Dutch diplomat husband Jan Herman van Roijen and this was their first trip back to the States in thirteen years. After such a long separation, Aunt Tina and her mother were happy to have a long visit in Lenox. To Dorothy the van Roijen boys—"[they] spoke with an accent"—were of great interest. She and Herman hit it off particularly well.

Finally, also during the summer she turned sixteen, Dorothy had a chance to become better acquainted with Uncle Beek, who, now retired from government service, was ensconced full-time at Robert Winthrop and Company. He and his wife Melza had been invited to join the Fred Winthrops for a vacation at New Hampshire's Squam Lake—a sort of "Plantation North," a place where the starched and corseted could put on their oldest tweeds and khakis, stay in camp houses like the Winthrops' with a "big fireplace and a dining room, sitting room, and piazza all in one," take walks, pick blueberries, and go boating. The only difference was that the real plantation was exclusive Winthrop territory while *tout* Boston seemed to have gathered at Squam: the Porters and Mandells, the Higginsons, Walcotts, and Websters, the Coolidges and more of the Coolidges. The spartan Boston regimen had marched up there, too. Fred Winthrop started his day at seven with sitting-up exercises and a swim, at which point the entire family would fall into step. "Breakfast at 8, lunch at 1, sup at 7, and go to bed by 9," wrote Dorothy.

Bobby and Jan Herman van Roijen, about 3 and 5, when their father, Jan Herman van Roijen, Sr., was Dutch minister to Japan

Squam Lake was a sort of "Plantation North." At left, Nat, 10; at right, Katharine, 8.

Dorothy was forever bemoaning her bad shots, and bad temper, on the tennis court. Here she is with Robert.

Dorothy described her father and Uncle Beek as "real wonders at tennis ... Father has only played once or twice in 15 years. He once beat a tennis tournament as minus scratch.... He was runner-up in championship of the Philippines, when Uncle B. was governor there." As for Dorothy, she was allowed to join the men but "Father kept correcting me, which I took with very bad grace.... After the sets, Father said he had not meant what he had said unkindly, but it was the way he was made; he played hard and he fought hard." In Fred's world, as at the plantation, women were included only on sufferance.

——— • ———

On the Amory side, Dorothy had her three male Coolidge cousins (Jeff, Amory, and Billy) and two uncles (Billy and George), but only the latter made it into her diary and stories. By the time Dorothy was in her teens Uncle George had settled into his life's work, which he described in his Harvard class report as "unoccupied."[9] As my mother would put it, genteelly, "He had a lot of lost weekends. He loved the bottle and he loved to gamble." The first story about him in her diaries, dated January 1921, corroborates this:

> Last Sunday early in the morning, Grandma awoke and heard many voices below stairs. She got out of bed and found the hall full of firemen! Pretty soon Sarah [a maid] arrived to see if Grandma had been burnt yet! This is how it happened: Uncle George came in late and dropped a match or a cigarette stub on a pile of papers in the back hall, and they burst into flame. He called the firemen because it got beyond his control, and now there is a very thrilling hole in the wall and charred wood all around.

Dorothy might have been thrilled, but her father had "no use for Uncle George and thinks he is crazy." George was already on his black list for having cruelly teased Dorothy senior when she was a child. He had thrown her pet bird into the fire and made sure she watched while it burned alive. Fred senior must have been equally disgusted later, when Uncle George would set his Dobermans onto Freddy junior, yelling "Sic 'em, Sic 'em," and sending Freddy scuttling to the top of a car to escape them. In 1921 her father told Dorothy about Uncle George's fake suicide—he had phoned a friend at 2:00 a.m. and said Mr. G. G. Amory had shot himself in the Hotel Touraine—and how this had embarrassed his poor friend, who had quickly called a doctor to go to his rescue. Dorothy herself saw Uncle George later that year with "his mouth all swollen as if he'd been hit, his eyes ... bloodshot.... Father said he was drunk and he thinks that must be awful for poor Grandma."

Grandma Amory certainly had a cross to bear with her son George. She thought her husband might have been partly at fault, being "over-indulgent to his children or

REARED *in a* GREENHOUSE

any young person.... This I had to combat." But she herself coddled her son, keeping him under her roof and advancing him money all her life. True, she had little choice, for in addition to being "unoccupied," Dorothy learned from her father, Uncle George "had gambled away every cent that his father had left him (a great deal) in a very short time and then had boasted about it." Nevertheless, Grandma Amory seemed unnaturally restrained, considering the way her son behaved in her house. Uncle "Raisin," as Emily Sears Lodge called him, would poke around his rice pudding, picking out all the raisins and throwing them on the floor. His mother would simply watch him and quietly say, "George I wish you wouldn't do that."

This picture from Libby Amory's scrapbook is captioned, "George Gardner Amory on polo field at Narragansett Pier. George seems to have no other interest."

My mother remembered how helpless her uncle was when his mother died and he had to fend for himself. He claimed, perhaps correctly, that because during her lifetime his mother had provided him all the money she intended to give him, that he was terribly hard up. So when he phoned my mother from Manchester, a five-cent call, he would always reverse the charges.

Fred Winthrop also conceded to Dorothy that Uncle George was "sometimes ... kind and [had] some good points." Though none of the family stories reveal such worthy traits, some show Uncle George engaged in innocent pastimes. Everyone thought it was funny when Uncle George and his "sort of girlfriend," as my mother called a certain Miss Blake, would "hitch up their horse and carriage and trot around the neighborhood, announcing to everyone that they were engaged. The last thing they were!"

My mother's brother Robert thought it comic when, at a dinner, Uncle George lavishly complimented a Wesson Oil fortune heiress on her jewels and then added, "You know, no matter how common and vulgar a person is, if they're rich enough, I like them." One of his great-nieces was amused by a similar party tale. In this instance, George had crashed a dinner to which a cousin had refused to invite him. He arrived at the back door, outfitted as a cardinal, red robes and all, and the Roman Catholic help all crossed themselves and let him take over in the kitchen. From there he infiltrated the dining room and began serving the guests their meals.[10] At least it was better than the way he had dressed in a story told by my mother's brother Fred. While watching the Harvard-Yale crew races, George fell overboard, and when another boat came to his rescue it hauled out of the river his perfectly naked body.

— • —

While Grandma Amory was doling out an allowance to Uncle George, Grandma Winthrop was expanding the family holdings on 37th Street in New York. In the twenty years since Fred Winthrop had moved to Boston the Winthrop settlement on her block in New York had greatly expanded. Uncle Beek and Aunt Melza had moved into 36 East 37th Street and Aunt Kitty's younger son, Winthrop—the first among Grandma Winthrop's eleven grandchildren to be married—had moved into another nearby house with his wife, the former Elizabeth Stuyvesant Howard. When Dorothy visited her grandmother in 1921 she noted the living arrangements in her diary:

> Grandma and Aunt Melza and Uncle Beek live side by side. A little ways down the street and on the opposite side, are Emily and Kate and Uncle Gren and Aunt Kitty and Uncle Ham and John … side by side. And behind Aunt Kitty and Uncle Ham and John are Elsa and Winthrop.

On Friday, February 4, 1921, Grandma Winthrop turned eighty-three, and as always the family gathered about. Her impeccable instructions indicated that her dinner was at eight, that there would be a dozen at table, and that there would be fifteen separate things to eat. The fare included soup, fish timbales, pheasants, potatoes and macaroni, currant jelly, bread sauce, green beans and spinach, small cheese pâtés and salad, ice cream and birthday cake, topped off with fruit and candies and washed down with sherry, claret, and whiskey.

Age had in no way diminished Kate Winthrop's prowess as a dowager hostess, and her official family birthday celebration was among the smallest parties she gave in the course of that week and the next. Her ladies' luncheons had grown as her women friends graduated to widowhood, and on her birthday, eighteen ladies congregated to fete her. The following Thursday, there were twenty-three ladies for lunch, and on Friday, seventeen. After a relatively quiet weekend (dinner Sunday night alone with Grenville), she was at it again: ten for lunch Monday and sixteen on Tuesday. Indeed, all that had changed in more than two decades of entertaining was that the food was more soothing,[11] with more poached eggs and the like.[12]

Dorothy wasn't in attendance for any of this, and though she wished the Winthrop clan all lived closer by she had no interest in moving to New York to be with them. Overhearing a conversation between her father and her stepmother about a possible move there, she wrote in her diary, "If the family do sell 299 and move to New York (which I doubt), I'll [stay] in Boston and live with Grandma, so let them move if they want to!"

Reared *in a* Greenhouse

Grandma Amory's Medicine

chapter NINE

Grandma Amory's note atop the bundle of letters Dorothy
wrote from Italy, Egypt, and France in 1900-1

At sixteen, something very odd was happening to Dorothy. In January and February she seemed to have lost her verve for writing. Her diary entries are short and melancholy. She complained of headaches and an inability to concentrate. If she could keep her mind from wandering, she wrote, "my silly blockhead would be filled quicker with my lessons." A Mrs. Shirley was engaged to come to the house and massage her head. In March matters grew worse. Her father was in South Carolina and Grandma Amory was not well. Dorothy found no pleasure in anything she did. Bouts of feeling "limp and worn out" were punctuated by isolated attempts to perform in school and fulfill social obligations. At a "St. Mark's musical [she had] enjoyed standing in a dim religious light" where she hoped she could avoid observation and the dancing. Two weeks later, she struggled up for another dance so as not to annoy Mama, who had taken a lot of trouble in making arrangements.

> Rose at 7 and lay on my bed when I was all dressed. Felt shaky when I went down a little after 9 and didn't think I'd stick it out for long.... I was busy introducing.... I enjoyed "introducing" because then I forgot about myself ... [also, that way] the poor unfortunate gents would not have had to dance with me.

April was even crueller. She had dreamed of completing eleventh grade with good marks, perhaps even the French prize. Instead, she felt so sick she never went to school at all. As the days wore on she "felt discouraged and as if I'd never get back to school." On Monday, April 3, she tried returning but "began to feel worse.… Grandma took me for a little drive and then took me home.… Poor Grandma, she's been sick all winter and never complained. I shouldn't complain. I haven't been sick long." As in her earlier years, she was suspected of making it all up.

> Mama took me to Dr. Frothingham. I felt so sick just before we went but I got feeling better and better and felt almost fine on the way home. Dr. Frothingham says nothing is wrong with me and I must not give in to myself. He seemed to think it was my imagination. I wish I had such a vivid imagination when it comes to writing for the Maze. I don't give into myself entirely … although I am a pretty bad egg.

Two incidents, uncannily similar, took place in April that temporarily diverted Dorothy's attention. The first, on April 18, concerned a classmate, Elizabeth Jackson. That afternoon in gym class the girls were climbing ladders and Elizabeth was the only one who managed to land properly on the ground.

> At about ten o'clock tonight, she went walking in her sleep and jumped out the window and landed on a brick backyard 28 feet below. She hit on the lower part of the back of her head and her shoulders. The servant found her and roused Mr. and Mrs. Jackson, who immediately took her to the Peter Bent Brigham Hospital where she was taken to the operation room and ex-rayed. No bones were broken, but she is unconscious.… Mr. Jackson has been sick for a month, came down for the first time today, and of course this dreadful accident will set him back.

Only six days later, much to everyone's amazement, a St. Mark's student followed Elizabeth's tracks.

> Late last night Degan, a third former at Saint Mark's, fell out of a 3rd story window onto a hard gravel road, while walking in his sleep. He broke one arm very badly and had some cuts and bruises. Unlike Elizabeth, he awoke on hitting the ground and hollered. The strangest part was that Mrs. Thayer [the headmaster's wife] with some others was discussing Elizabeth Jackson's fall when the night watchman came running in to tell her about Degan. I suppose Degan may have been thinking sub-consciously about Elizabeth walking in her sleep when he did likewise. Poor boy.

Dorothy hoped "window-falling" wasn't contagious, adding, however, "I don't think I'd mind very much if I caught it just now. Only it might be disagreeable to some and discombobulate the household."

Her father, clearly worried, was by turns encouraging and solicitous. His concern only undid her more.

> Father said you must eat so you can resist. I said I didn't want anything and in spite of trying not to two tears came into my d—— eyes. Then Mama asked if I didn't want to go upstairs so I left and lost all control of myself and burst into tears. I have not really cried in four years. I don't know what's the matter with me. After dinner Father came upstairs and asked how I felt. I said sea-sick and he said he would do anything

I wanted to make me well. He said Dr. Frothingham was a good Dr., but if I wanted to try another or a specialist he'd let me. I said I was quite content with Dr. F. and anyway Father knows better about these things than I do. He said the way to get well, was to eat, rest and exercise.

Her tears flowed again, and just as uncontrollably, when Mademoiselle came to the house to urge her to return to school.

She begged and begged and really seemed to care. I cried; I don't know why, but no matter how hard I tried not to the tears ran down my cheeks. Mlle said "Oh Dorothy, *je n'avais jamais pensé que vous ayez peur—que vous étiez un lâche.*" ["I never thought you'd be afraid—that you'd be a coward."] That did more good than all her begging. She kissed me good-bye and said she loved me. I felt I could not bear all her kindness.

Her father continued being attentive, leaving it to Dorothy to decide when she planned to return to school. Her stepmother, however, was unmoved. "Mama hates having me hanging around the house." Dorothy was baffled. She hated staying home but she couldn't face school and "the fear of feeling sick away from home."

There was a moment in 1921 when she began to wonder if she were going crazy. And in a way, she probably was. The headaches and stomachaches, uncontrollable crying, withdrawal from the world, all with no identifiable physical cause—these are the symptoms of clinical depression, or as they called it then, a "nervous breakdown."

But if this was the explanation, what was the cause? Was it, to invoke one of my mother's favorite debate topics, heredity or environment? She accepted that there was a degree of mental instability in the family. Grandma Amory knew of many such cases, and had listed them on a three-by-five scrap of paper that my mother saved in an envelope labeled "Grandma Amory's clippings." In later life my mother decided to bring the list up to date. The new candidates included not only a niece and two cousins—but also herself. My inclination is to think that the environment—299 Berkeley, dominated by her impatient stepmother and her morose father—was the more likely culprit.

There was also the fear, perhaps subconscious, that her mainstays—her father and her grandmother—could die and leave her all alone. Fred Winthrop continued to talk as if his life were over. Hearing him repeat this idea over New Year's, Dorothy had protested, "You always say you are so old and you are only 53." Her father's answer was glum: "I feel old. I've lived my life, it was a short one, but...." Meanwhile, she was worried about her grandmother's frail condition. She had been only eight the year she'd prayed and prayed that her grandma might live another two years. At nine she'd asked her grandmother if she could stay and live with her for five years. When she was ten, Dorothy got a cheerful note signed "wretched Grandma" reporting that her "library was full of carpenters and painters and the smell of paint is not agreeable" and that she was sick in bed. During the influenza epidemic, Grandma joked about being a "decrepit old critter" who was forbidden by the doctor to walk over to her granddaughter's house. But, as was her way, she made light of it all in hopes that her granddaughter would not worry.

If Grandma and her father were to die, none of the other members of Dorothy's family could have given her any real support. Robert had the maturity, but he was engrossed in his own world. And Freddy, still young, was more dependent on Dorothy than dependable.

Robert's world of sports and fast parties must have seemed inaccessible to Dorothy. He wrote her an exuberant letter about his sixth-form dance at St. Mark's that winter: "You ought to have seen the New York girls, they were so *fast* that nobody bothered to look at the Rhodes(es) [no doubt, Bostonians]. A lot of them smoked and would have drunk only there was nothing to drink." He went on to describe the event, which included dancing till one in the morning, then skating, escorting the girls to the 11:27 train the next morning, tobogganing and sledding, dancing all afternoon and having tea ... and dancing the evening away at school. "The only thing left now is the *cost*!!! I shouldn't be surprised if it was $25 or $30 per!!!!!"

If Dorothy felt strait-laced next to Robert, she remained Freddy's confidante, confessor, and banker of last resort. He had long since gotten over being traumatized by school. But he still rambled on to her in his letters, certain that she would loving-ly accept whatever he had to say.

> I wrote a letter to you and forgot to mail it. It's lost I guess. If you try hard you can read this. I have nothing to do so I am writing to you in study hour. Now don't slap my wrist. If you can't read this send it back and I will recopy it. I am using this paper because it does not look so suspicious....
>
> I debate Friday for the second and last time. Don't tell Father he would get sore but I have only been to extemporaneous speaking once. Other times I have skipped and gone down to the cottage. I hate it.

Another letter goes on,

> My golly, I'm the worst brother you every saw, I guess you're saying. Well no, I guess not, because you have such a good disposition.
>
> Please send me a forty dollar cheque....

Even with all his self-admitted faults, Dorothy saw only the good in Freddy. Once again in her diary she revisited the legend of his bravery.

> My father said Fred was the bravest chap he had ever seen when he had his eye oper-ated on. They took out his whole eye, cut a muscle and then put it back. Father said Fred never budged and he was not completely out. Also, when he had his tonsils out ... they brought Fred into the room and then began making preparations, of course, he saw it all. Poor little fellow. The suspense must have been awful.... I love and admire Fred.

— • —

Not surprisingly, death had become an obsession for Dorothy. When an uncle died she wrote of its mystery and finality: "Death is a very hard to thing to realize. I can't believe he is dead! I wish I knew what came after death." She wondered—doubtless thinking of her mother—if the "dead can guide and help the living … if we meet after death."

Grandma Amory, sensing her granddaughter's need, found a way to penetrate the veil, to bring Dorothy's mother nearer. She had carefully stored all the letters she'd ever received from her daughter, Dorothy senior. And on May 11, 1922, ten days before young Dorothy's seventeenth birthday, Grandma Amory handed over these precious remnants of days gone by. Dorothy's diary captures the moment:

> Today Grandma gave me a box of letters which our darling mother wrote to her, some letters which were written to Grandma when dear Mother died were there too, and some pictures and other things of Mother's. I love them all.… I read some of the letters aloud to Grandma and I cannot describe the look on her face. She looked so sweet and sad and happy at the same time. I think she must have been living in the past. She said she had often read the letters over, but last year she tied them up for me as her eyes are failing.

The bulk of the collection consisted of the letters that Dorothy Amory wrote when she went abroad in 1900 with her Aunt Helen and her cousins Mary and Frank Curtis. So it may well have been the exotic world of her mother's Egyptian travels that young Dorothy entered that morning. Perhaps she read her mother's tales of the prince, the native wedding in Cairo, the stuffy British and the common Americans tourists, moonlit donkey rides over the desert, ancient tombs, Mary's bout with bronchitis, Frank's limp outings on the tennis court, and the final, ecstatic shopping sprees for hats and wrappers in Paris and London.

But surely what interested her most was the palpable warmth that had flowed between her mother and grandmother. Part of Libby Amory's plan in arranging for

Helen (left) *and Elizabeth Gardner, 1866. Both sisters would marry the following year, Helen to James Curtis and Libby to Ned Amory.*

Dorothy to travel with the Curtises had been to give her daughter an eyeful of the strained relationship between another mother and daughter, Libby's sister Helen—by then twelve years a widow—and her daughter Mary. As my mother would later tell us: "My grandmother and mother were very close … and my grandmother thought that my mother should know … that really and truly all families were not as happy as hers." Libby Amory had no illusions about her sister Helen. My mother would say, "If you want to know about queer people, Great-Aunt Helen was queer.… She liked to do what she liked to do. So she would put on … her dressing gown … she had a long pigtail behind, and she'd go wandering through the woods talking aloud to herself. She was known as the Witch of Pride's Crossing."

At the time she was given her mother's letters, Dorothy junior already knew plenty about the bad blood between her cousin Mary and Great-Aunt Helen. She had been present

Reared *in a* Greenhouse

Cousin Mary Curtis in 1905
(at left) *at the millinery booth
at a bazaar in aid of Sharon
Sanitarium at Horticultural
Hall. She was nearing 30,
still lived under her mother's
roof, and according to my
mother, didn't have much fun.*

when Mary, then in her thirties and still living at home, had rushed over to her Aunt Libby's, Grandma Amory's, to complain about her mother's treatment. Mary had organized a dinner party, complete with an excellent wine from the premier Boston grocer S. S. Pierce, but when the guests filed in to dinner the wine had vanished. Her mother had returned it—and the party was spoiled. No sooner had a distressed Mary gone over to her Aunt Libby's to relate this sad tale than Helen herself appeared, sputtering furiously to her sister about Mary: "What did she mean by having wine delivered to the house?" When my mother told us this story, she would add, "Of course, my grandmother scolded her sister quite properly. But it didn't do any good. She continued to be as queer as ever."

Though Dorothy junior had personally overheard Cousin Mary and Great-Aunt Helen's tiffs, her own mother's voice remained muffled, coming to her secondhand from tales her grandmother, father, and friends told her. Now, as she read the letters aloud to Grandma Amory, it must have been as if her mother was speaking through her—laughing at preposterous Aunt Helen and sympathizing with poor Mary. "Aunt Helen … mortified Mary so by her costumes. She generally wears the funniest little poke bonnet with bows and a low neck and a shawl like the white queen. Yesterday, she appeared with a pigtail not even turned up! She looked as though she had slept in it…. Aunt H. has appeared in blue goggles. What next?"

It was also as if her mother's sweetness to her own mother—Grandma Amory—was filling the room. Commenting on their travel plans, which kept shifting with Aunt Helen's whim, Dorothy wrote her mother: "You are *so* different. I long for your letters."

Dorothy Winthrop, May 1903

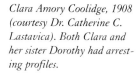

Clara Amory Coolidge, 1908 (courtesy Dr. Catherine C. Lastavica). Both Clara and her sister Dorothy had arresting profiles.

That May morning as Dorothy and her grandmother read over the letters from the missing generation, it was the most private of times. The circle grew by one after lunch, when Dorothy's Aunt Clara came by. Dorothy must have often wondered whether in Aunt Clara she was seeing an older version of her mother. "Handsome and generous," she'd written once in her diary of her aunt, "good looking." Aunt Clara had surely read these letters with her mother before, but she settled in comfortably as Dorothy continued reading aloud. Suddenly, Dorothy's father appeared at the door: "I quickly stopped and Grandma covered up the other letters. I hope he did not know. It would have made him so sad. Also, Father's love for Mother was so deep that he could not understand our reading the letters out loud."

Dorothy was shielding her father from sadness. She did it to be kind, but the effect was also to exclude him from the healing world of womanly chatter. With lives centered at home, and time on their hands, upper-class women of that day could talk on for hours. The words flowed easily, rippling with laughter and washing away the sharp stones of painful memories. Few men fit comfortably into this world, particularly men as reticent as Frederic Winthrop. So he would remain apart, a taciturn figure alone with his grief.

And what of Dorothy? She was almost as reticent as her father, writing little in her diary of her reaction to the mother she was meeting, other than to repeat how much she loved her and longed for her. Was she surprised at the differences her letters so vividly showed—at her mother, the frivolous shopper? her mother, the unscholarly sightseer? her mother, the outgoing, carefree young girl who so easily unburdened her soul? Did she recognize that she also shared many of her mother's most beguiling traits: her irrepressible sense of the ridiculous? her reluctance to complain? her modesty? her love and appreciation of those closest to her? Did Dorothy wonder whether she would have been more like her mother, more lighthearted and gay, had she grown up with Dorothy senior?

Getting Well

chapter TEN

Photo of Dorothy Winthrop from her school year book

Dorothy started down the long road to recovery the day after she and her grandmother sat reading her mother's letters. Perhaps they were the tonic she needed. Or maybe it was some bracing words from her father. A few days earlier he had assured Dorothy that Miss Degen was very understanding about her long absence from school, adding, "Now I want you to return to school no matter if you do feel rotten.... The only way to get well is to fight against yourself." Whether it was her mother's cheerful tone or her father's forceful charge, Dorothy made herself go back to school on May 12. It was an "awful effort," she wrote, "but I am thankful that father made me do it." In the same breath she wrote, "Read dear Mother's letters; my only comfort."

She not only finished out the year, but she did so with distinction, receiving a "mention" in studies and the French prize she had so hoped for. She was also elected school president for the coming year. She took it all soberly, especially her upcoming term as school president, which she saw as a chance to turn over a new leaf: "I shall not lie imbedded in the memory of past sins, but do the duty that comes next, earnestly endeavoring to make good and live it down."

Still, when the school year ended in May, just two weeks after she had returned, she wrote, "Today was the last day of school. God be thanked. I have been longing for it. Now I can go into the country for a good and long rest (how pleasant that sounds) for almost four whole months."

On May 21, 1922, Dorothy turned seventeen, and her grandmother and her father seem to have decided that this was the year she should have the rest of her mother's things. One day in mid-May Grandma Amory turned over a lot of pictures of Dorothy's mother. Dorothy was grateful, but also felt guilty: "I see no reason why I should have all the pictures of our dear mother that Grandma gave me and the boys have none. They are more worthy to have them, so I shall divide them up. Mother was beautiful." At the end of May Grandma Amory made a second gift to Dorothy, "a little black trunk full of old treasures … fans and jewels and a pair of dear Mother's slippers as a baby and the dress in which she was baptized." They sat together at the head of the stairs while Grandma Amory told her granddaughter about them.

On her birthday, Dorothy's father took his daughter to the little room in the attic where her mother's things were kept. "As soon as he was in there he tried to speak but he could not. He ran his hand through his hair and his whole face and position expressed the deepest grief and suffering I have ever seen." This was the second time that Dorothy had witnessed her father weeping when he tried to speak of her mother. The first had been the summer before, in Lenox, when he had said his life was over. This time, when he got control of himself, he told her that she could get the key from him any time and take anything she wanted, or wait and divide the things with the boys. She opted to wait.

On July 19, two days after Dorothy senior's birthday, Fred gave his daughter the key to the attic closet, and she and her brothers went up and divided "our dear Mother's things. The boys were very unselfish and gave me the lion's share. There were many picture frames, gloves, fans and workbags and boxes and umbrellas and parasols. There were also three trunks and some clothes which we did not touch." Among the things were some diaries and "three little books telling about us." Dorothy studied the books closely, noting, "The last entry was July 10th, 1907 in Robert's little book and the middle of July 1907 in Fred's…. She must have loved us very dearly…. She loved us when we were babies. I wish we still were babies with her."

The four-month summer vacation passed all too quickly, but not as quietly as Dorothy had anticipated. The summer held trips to Wareham in July and to Squam Lake in August. At Squam Lake Dorothy had two guests, the Sears girls. Fred Winthrop and his wife were taken with the well-bred sisters. They are "ladies … and good sports," her father said. When the adults weren't looking, however, they and their hostess were engaged in mischievous pranks. The girls made apple-pie beds for the boys, and Robert dumped water on them and put crumbs in their beds. The girls tied knots in the boys' pajamas, and in revenge the boys set an alarm clock for midnight outside the girls' bedroom. The girls peppered the boys' pillows and pajamas and bureau drawers, salted their beds and toothbrushes, and put paper under their bottom sheets and wood under their mattresses.

Emily and Jean Sears, September 12, 1921. This photo, sent to "dear Dorothy with a great deal of love, from Emily and Jean," was mysteriously captioned "Keith's Dolly sisters."

GETTING WELL

A glamorous Nancy Murray

Emily and Jean's role in all this is a little unclear. Dorothy found them "so ladylike and dear," moaning "I talk so loud and boisterously.... I wish could be like them." The evidence from the diaries suggests, though, that when the Searses disappeared, so too did the hijinks.

For Dorothy, passing the hours with her brothers and the Searses—this was summer's greatest joy. And parting from them all in September, autumn's heaviest sorrow. In elegiac cadences, she mourned Freddy's departure. "My best beloved left me today to go back to Saint Mark's.... We played our last tennis together for ages. At 6:30 I left my best beloved and came home, 'alone, alone, all alone on a wide, wide sea, and never a saint took pity on a soul in agony.'" By the next sentence, she had miraculously recovered. "Anyway, I'll have Robert over Sundays." (Robert was a freshman at Harvard.)

When Dorothy returned to school in the fall of 1922, her goal was to prove "worthy" of the post of school president. She took her position so seriously that Sister Amy's Bible class, which offered moral pointers to the young, turned out to be the most meaningful part of her school life. The girl who couldn't stop giggling in class had vanished. In her place had risen one who exemplified the Shakespeare line in her May School Class Book: "Those about her, from her shall read the perfect ways of honor."

Dorothy's first instinct was to reach out to the outsiders: "There is an awful lot I could do in the school to make the new girls and even the old girls who are lonely and unpopular, happy." But this, like everything else in the job, was hard for her. Simple events, such as overseeing lunch during a teachers' meeting, presented quandaries—in this case whether to start the meal with grace or not. After deciding against it, she worried whether she had made the right decision. Another day, she had to run a class meeting to decide about Halloween activities: "Everybody talks at once and we get nowhere. I hate to say 'sssh' because then they will all expect I have something to say ... and I never have.... I'm a bum president." As late as March she was "scared to death and trembling like a leaf" when she had to interfere and reprimand a group of girls who were cutting up in study hall. Her responsibilities were bringing out the puritanical in Dorothy: "I wasn't mad," she wrote of her reaction to the study hall mischiefs. "I was disgusted that the girls had no more honor. They were on their honor to behave orderly."

As her friends grew naughtier, Dorothy grew haughtier. "She doesn't seem a bit ashamed," Dorothy wrote of her friend Elizabeth Ferguson, who had climbed onto a six-foot bookcase at a dance and there smoked her partner's cigarette. "I am sorry for I like her," she wrote of another friend who, perhaps at the same dance, had smoked a cigarette behind her fan. Dorothy even felt herself drifting apart from her old friend Nancy Murray, for Nancy was losing interest in school, spending time with gentlemen callers and wearing makeup and jewelry—"her face [was] covered with powder and earrings in her ears." When she discovered Nancy had skipped school but then gone to her skating lesson, Dorothy wrote primly, "I always feel that if one isn't well enough to go to school, one isn't well enough to do other things that day; but I really think I may be narrow-minded in this respect."

High-minded as she appeared, Dorothy continued to fret. Her friends' ignorance of her errant ways made her feel "wretchedly because I live a life of deceit." Sister Amy's Bible classes came as a godsend. Nothing could keep Dorothy from attending, not even the terrible headache she had the day of the first class. Particularly pertinent was Sister Amy's disquisition on the qualities required by a school president. One can almost imagine Dorothy scribbling busily to take them all down. A president should not be concerned with popularity, said Sister Amy, but should have "high ideals and principles … dignity, consistency, tact, sincerity, broad mind, courage of convictions and executive ability." The classes lasted only a few weeks. When they ended Dorothy purchased a small Bible together with a "Teachers Testament, which explains lots of the New Testament and has some nice hymns in back."

Being school president may have been more of a strain on her than she could manage, for the sick spells, which had abated during the summer, returned in late November 1922. This time her father's solution was to take her south with the family in December. "I have so much to do in school and have so many interests there and I don't want to shirk my duties," she wrote, "but, on the other hand, I don't feel very well these days and it will be a great rest down there." Her father's words of consolation were well meaning but ill chosen: "You aren't doing the school any good and it's not doing you any good."

— • —

It was her third trip to South Carolina, that 1922–23 Christmas season, and her attention was shifting from the exotic rigors of the place to the "darkies," to her, the equally exotic people who lived there. Her first glimpse of them en masse had come the Christmas before, when 150 of them had gathered at the Winthrop compound for presents—"toys, cookies, oranges, and candy"—followed by singing and reciting. This year the crowd had swelled to three hundred. The feast included three pigs and one ox and the dancing was accompanied by drums and cymbals.

The speechmaking was an important part of the festivities. It was hard to silence the revelers. A certain John Brown, the master of ceremonies, was having a terrible time making the introductions. "First he put up a pole on the end of which was stuck an old newspaper," wrote Dorothy. "He made a request for silence which had no result and then he did it again": 'Good people can't you keep quiet? You aren't worrying me, you are worrying Jesus and Mr. and Mrs. Winthrop.' "

That anecdote captures the naive awe with which the blacks of the 1920s still viewed the rich northerners who had come and essentially replaced the slave-holding antebellum gentry as their providers. The blacks weren't universally submissive, however. One of the speakers that day was a Brother Ruth ("about ¾s white"), who "talked a lot about the negro race being the strongest and being as good as the whites, etc." His was not the reigning view, however. Most believed that they were powerless—and that the Lord had chosen the Winthrops to come help them. "They said," she recorded, "'De Lord send away up to the Norf fo de northern gentlemen to come way down here to us. He was Mr. Dudley Winthrop and when de Lord called him away he done send way up norf and bring his brother here to us.'"

When my mother reminisced about the plantation, she would lapse into the local black dialect, which, though she meant no disrespect, sounds almost racist by today's standards. She loved to tell the story of the proud father who—when she asked him how many children he had—answered, "Wha, mizz Dorthy, I has twenny-two—no! twenny-three—head a' chillen."

THIS IS THE FAMILY FROM "WAY UP NORF" SENT BY THE LORD AFTER HE CALLED MR. DUDLEY WINTHROP AWAY, OR SO SAID THE PLANTATION BLACKS OF THE WINTHROPS IN THE 1920S.

Right: *The Winthrop family on the steps of the main house in the Groton Plantation compound, winter of 1921-22:* from forefront up the stairs, *Katharine, Nat, Freddy, Jr., Dorothy, Robert, with Sally and Fred, Sr., behind.*

Far right: *"The Winthrop men" in the early 1920s, Robert, Fred, Sr., and Freddy, Jr., by the steps of the main house*

Right: *Katharine, 7, and her father, 1922-23, on the steps of the main house*

Far right: *Sally Winthrop and son Nat, with Fred Winthrop's feet, in the living room of the main house, 1926-27*

REARED *in a* GREENHOUSE

DOROTHY WAS SHOCKED BY THE CONDITIONS
OF THE PLANTATION BLACKS.

Far left: *The Oakland School*

Center: *Frances, who came into each room each morning, lit the fire, and left a container of hot water, posing with her son*

Left: *Frank, the cook, and the Winthrop's Christmas turkey, Christmas 1926*

Left: *Making sausage, 1922-23*

Far left: *"Bill Frazier has had eight wives!" (caption in Dorothy's scrapbook, 1922-23)*

Left: *Richard's boys and ox, 1921-22*

GETTING WELL

If their dialect amused her, their poverty did not. Among her various school papers was an A minus composition she'd succeeded in writing the previous March, despite her gloom, full of close, shocked observations of the plantation residents' poverty. She wrote of their "dirty little huts … their cooking outdoors … they not infrequently eat hares and crows and I have heard of more than one who liked 'rat pie'.… Their clothes are often so old that they are held together by bits of string and nails. The Doctors … do not seem to care how much the sick or hurt Negro suffers." The main cause of their poverty, she thought, was their inadequate education. Teachers began classes at any old time of day and were frequently absent for weeks at a time and the children were "taught … trashy poetry and songs.… Many finish their school career almost as illiterate as when they began."

The whites, she thought, took advantage of the blacks, exploiting their ignorance: "The northern and southern white … instead of trying to help the Negroes and teach them frugality … try to get all the money they can out of them." There was the man who had "bought a lot of Bibles for eighty cents up in the north, painted picture of black angels in them, and sold them down south for eight dollars each." There was another who "peddled elaborate tombstones," many of which were still standing in the corner in various huts. There was yet another who had sold lightning rods "for huge sums." She was not amused. "I think it is not so much a ridiculous as a pathetic sight, to see two or three large rods perched on the roofs of many of the small, rickety huts."

— • —

Dorothy continued trying to be as good at home as she was at school. But it was hard to be pleasant when the weather was lousy and you were sick—the situation to which Dorothy returned after Christmas at the plantation. In January she was home with a grumpy Robert who had a broken leg, in February an intestinal grippe was "flying around Boston," the snow was fierce, and Cousin Mary Curtis, who had finally moved away from her mother to buy a house in Hamilton, phoned that the roads were impassable—not even sleighs could get through. The water by Dorothy's bed froze, she was sick, and no one would go near her, "excepting the boys. I guess it's because I'm disagreeable." Fortunately, Grandma Amory again came to the rescue, putting up her ailing granddaughter. "Grandma sits with me hours on end," wrote Dorothy gratefully. How eager she was to repay her grandmother's many kindnesses shows from a little poem she had clipped and pasted in her diary at this time.

From "The May School Class Book," Class of 1923

DOROTHY WINTHROP
229 Berkeley Street, Boston
"DOT"

March 21, 1905

"Those about her, from her shall read the perfect ways of honour."
— *Shakespeare*

Term — Seven years.   Class IV — Class Representative, Lower School Basketball team.   Class VI — Treasurer of Athletic Association, Class Basketball team (Captain).   Class VII — Secretary of School Club, Exchange Editor of the *Maze*, Class Basketball team (Captain).   Class VIII — President of School Club, Hockey squad.

18

REARED *in a* GREENHOUSE

GRANDMOTHER AND ME

Grandmother dear is a very old lady
Grandmother dear can't see
But when she drops things or loses her spectacles
Grandmother's eyes are me.

Grandmother dear is a very old lady
Sometimes she never hears
But I always run when the postman comes ringing
I can be grandmother's ears.

Grandmother dear likes the house all-tidy
Everything dusted and neat
So I work with my little red broom and my duster
I can be Grandmother's feet.

Grandmother dear is a very old lady
Can't walk, can't hear, and can't see
You never could tell though, the fun we have playing
Grandmother dear and me.

During that gloomy winter Dorothy returned sporadically to school, but it seemed almost as if they were forgetting her there. On Valentine's Day, which the girls always celebrated with a snowstorm of cards to each other and which Dorothy spent miserably in bed, Nancy Murray sent her, along with her homework, one lonely valentine. "I expected and was looking forward to getting at least a doz. valentines." Whether for her health, or because it was the thing to do, in March her father decided to take Dorothy along on a six-month European trip with his wife, Nat and Katharine. Her school chums planned a gala send-off, a luncheon party at Nancy Murray's, but, feeling "rotten," she bowed out at the last minute. The girls came around to her house anyway to say good-bye, and after they left, she got up from the sofa and watched them walk out of sight: "As they turned up Dartmouth Street ... I began to miss them terribly and felt ... desolate and lonely. I shall never go to school with them or know them in the same way again, but I shall never forget and always love them."

From "The May School Class Book," Class of 1923

Class Statistics

Most attractive	NANCY MURRAY
Most pull with faculty	LAURA BRANDT
Most school spirit	DOROTHY WINTHROP
Most popular	DOROTHY WINTHROP
Most tactless	ELINOR HUGHES
Most tactful	NANCY SMITH
Most conventional	LOUISE THAYER
Most talkative	PATTY PENMAN
Most considerate	DOROTHY WINTHROP
Most efficient	NANCY SMITH
Best mannered	DOROTHY WINTHROP
Best dressed	NANCY SMITH
Best sport	DOROTHY WINTHROP
Best student	ELIZABETH GARRETT
Brightest	ELIZABETH MOORE
Wittiest	NANCY MURRAY
Stubbornest	ELIZABETH GARRETT
	ANNA JACKSON
Noisiest	ELIZABETH MOORE
Frankest	NANCY MURRAY
Tidiest	NANCY SMITH

GETTING WELL

Though she would miss the spring term, she was officially counted among her graduating class of 1923. In her May School Class Book lay a minefield of "mosts," with Elinor Hughes selected "most tactless," Laura Brandt "most pull with faculty," Louise Thayer "most conventional," Elizabeth Garrett "stubbornest," and Elizabeth Moore "noisiest." Dorothy's five "mosts," however, were all friendly fire: "most school spirit," "most popular," "most considerate," "best mannered," and "best sport." It was a salvo of praise that should have convinced even skeptical Dorothy of her own worth.[1]

After Europe, during the spring of 1924, Dorothy returned to Miss May's to finish up her schooling. She enjoyed the classes, and despite a disappointing senior class—she disapproved of "the restlessness and inattention of the girls," who seemed "to get worse every year"—it all ended well. Dorothy received her diploma, the French medal, and a special commendation for returning to make up missed work. She was also singled out at graduation with a bittersweet reminder. Miss Degan said that giving her a diploma was a special pleasure, for Dorothy Winthrop was a second-generation graduate of Miss May's—attending the school that her mother had gone to before her.

A Trip Abroad
chapter ELEVEN

The Winthrops, Pattens, and Moltkes at Hill Hall in England

The Winthrop family's European tour began in March 1923 and lasted six months, a stately sweep northward that commenced in Rome, passed through Paris, and glided to a finish in London. Along the way familiar faces were everywhere, and their social life proved as conventional as their itinerary. For Dorothy, though, it was a heady experience.

Off to Europe: Sally Winthrop with her children, Nat, 10, and Katharine, 8, in March 1923

They sailed from Boston on the *President Wilson*. The weather was terrible, with gale-force winds and fog so thick that Dorothy thought the ship might not set sail till morning. It did, however, and as it lurched and bucked in the late March seas she made a note in her diary: "Sea-sick!" Sharing a stateroom with Nat must have made matters worse, for she was trapped with him, too sick to move from her bed. Katharine and her mother had a second cabin, and her father, a third.

As Dorothy lay there wishing she could die, she was unaware that there were others at sea that night—not far from the *President Wilson*—who were quite certain they would. The crew of the *Giulia*, an Italian freighter, was radioing a frantic SOS into the stormy night as their ship foundered in the high seas. Picking up the signal, the ocean liner changed course and headed toward the distress signal, which came from somewhere south of Newfoundland and east of Nova Scotia. By morning, the *President Wilson* had arrived at the scene and the passengers rushed on deck to see the disaster. Dorothy

Reared *in a* Greenhouse

was awestruck: "She rose and righted herself with the swell and the water came pouring out of deck doors and windows in sheets; then, with another wave, she rolled back onto her side ... until we thought she must ... sink." The *President Wilson* lowered one of her lifeboats, but the high seas prevented the little boat from getting close to the wallowing freighter. The men clinging to the upper side of the vessel were desperate and decided to swim for it, clambering down a rope ladder and leaping into the sea where they attempted to reach the lifeboat. The first two made it, but a third, "weakened by 36 hours exposure and lack of nourishment, died of heart failure when he struck the water." By afternoon, with the aid of an American freighter which had arrived on the scene, the rest of the forty-man crew had been saved and the great adventure was over. It made a deep impression on Dorothy: "I used to think the ocean was very dangerous but lately I have thought men had overcome nature's inventions. I find I am mistaken. I thought men considered they no longer needed to consider God as they had become so powerful themselves but I find we are as much at God's mercy as ever."

The full story came out a few days later, from the first mate. The *Giulia* had set sail from Canada in a snowstorm, the day before the *President Wilson*'s departure. The next day, high winds and waves were battering the freighter and causing it to list. Finally, under pressure from the heavy cargo of grain, a partition gave way and the "cargo shifted to starboard. Water rushed in wherever it found an opening and soon the fire in one of the engine rooms was extinguished." The crew rushed to save the ship, some to shift the cargo back and others to man the pumps. This was the frantic scene that led to the SOS picked up that night by the *President Wilson*.

Dorothy soon settled into a shipboard routine, reading and writing and making new friends. She found several other girls ranging in age from seven to fifteen, all of whom, like her, had abandoned their desks and notebooks for education of another

To the rescue! The President Wilson *had five Winthrops aboard.*

A TRIP ABROAD

sort—history to be imbibed at cathedrals and castles, at museums and monuments. The routine was short-lived: on March 29, only nine days out of Boston, the *President Wilson* briefly put to shore at Algiers. They docked long enough for Dorothy and her father to take a quick guided tour of the city. Dorothy—who kept two diaries on this trip, her regular journal and a more formal account, "My Trip," in which her words trudged as diligently across the page as her own mother's had tripped lightly in her letters from abroad twenty-three years earlier—couldn't believe what she was seeing:

> Wherever we looked were squalor and filth and smells, but cheerfulness withal.... Every now and then we came upon piles of swill thrown in a corner of the street, but no one seemed to mind.... Never have I seen as many cats as we saw in Algiers, they lurked in eerie corners and lay about the streets in swarms.... The inhabitants of these dark and gloomy slums were of the greatest interest to us, but they did not glance at us twice, as no doubt they were used to well-dressed, inquisitive foreigners visiting their quarters.... In spite of the filth and poverty, the Arabians, dressed in their flowing robes and turbans made of material suspiciously resembling bath towels, or wearing full bloomers and tight, red caps with black tassels ... went about their tasks or pleasures in the narrow dirty streets of their native city. No women were abroad that night.... [Most] pathetic and disgusting [was] a full-grown Arab moving swiftly on hands and knees across a muddy pavement. He had both legs and feet, but they were helpless, useless to him. It was bad enough for us to have to walk in the dirt with stout shoes on, but to have to crawl on hands and knees in ... that disgusting filth was worse than my wildest flights of imagination.

Like her mother before her, Dorothy stopped in Naples, Pompeii, and Rome. Unlike her mother, however, who had scorned the industrious diary keepers, Dorothy out-Baedekered Baedeker in her methodical description of every detail:

> The vomitorium itself was a large, rectangular basin about as deep as to a man's middle. Around one or two sides, its columns were built a few feet apart. One side was against a blank wall. During a feast when the old Pompeiins became too full to eat any more, they used to stand between two columns and empty their stomachs into the vomitorium with the aid of a feather and some pine oil. After a visit to the vomitorium, they would return to the banquet table in the dining hall and eat good things until they once more found it necessary to empty their stomachs, before they could put any more in. What awful pigs the old fellows used to be!

When it came to choosing between monuments and man, Dorothy was her mother's daughter. As Dorothy Amory had preferred modern day to ancient Egypt, Dorothy Winthrop amused herself imagining the men sitting around the baths in Pompeii, "some in their togas and tunics, discussing the topics of the day, others splashing or calmly sitting." Both also had firm opinions. If in Egypt Dorothy senior had flinched at the close air of the tombs, in Rome Dorothy junior had equally pronounced reservations about the churches, which she found "overdecorated and too full and crowded for their size." But the daughter didn't view traveling as a lark the way her mother had, dismissing great works of art with a blithe, "I never know what the subject is! and when I am told, always forget." To Dorothy, the object of travel was to learn—to observe, record, and remember: "The more one knows of history and art, the more one appreciates it, so if I in my ignorance liked it, what would it not be to one learned?"

So different, the two would have made delightfully contrasting traveling companions. At least, this is what Dorothy thought, after she got home and reread some of the letters her mother had written on her trip abroad with Aunt Helen and Cousin Mary Curtis in 1900. "They are lovely letters from a lovely person.... Oh darling Mother, if you had only been with us this time."

In April the Winthrops settled in for a two-week stay in Rome's Palace Hotel. "Service is 100 percent better than the Grand Hotel but the view doesn't begin to compare with Naples," wrote Dorothy, who was also learning from her travels about matters more practical than art and history. The first full day held family reunions for both her stepmother and her father. On Sally's side, her sister Nina, Countess Moltke, had arrived, doubtless exhausted, after a three-day train trip from Germany, the last night upright as there were no sleeping accommodations. While Sally and Nina caught up with one another, Fred Winthrop took the younger generation to visit his sister, Tina van Roijen. The van Roijens had been ensconced in the Dutch minister's elegant residence in Rome for the past four years. On the day of the Winthrops' first visit, however, the family had just returned from a visit to Sicily, and all but Uncle Herman were "invisible," immersed "in their bathtubs." Two days later, August 8, was Herman, Jr.'s eighteenth birthday, and Dorothy had her first taste of social life among the young European diplomatic set. She took to it immediately.

> After dancing for a while in Herman's sitting room under the eye of a handful of governesses who had come with their charges, we all trooped down and had tea and birthday cake.... The girls and boys (about 12 in all) were of every age and nationality. Two girls wore socks but had just as good a time as the older girls. Foreign boys aren't such snobs as American ones! American ones scorn all but girls their own age or older and the faster the girl the better! ... They all spoke English, French and Italian with equal ease.... They were very intelligent and discussed lots of high brow stuff. An Italian youth and the Belgian had a very heated discussion in French on the relative merits of Italian and Flemish art!

Far less to Dorothy's liking was a dinner party for twenty given the next week by the van Roijens in honor of the Japanese minister and his wife. She had put on her best dress and had had her hair waved, the first time ever. "There were lots of old swells there," she wrote, and, as the youngest guest, she "felt dreadfully out of place." Her dinner partner was thirty-year-old Copley Amory, Jr., second secretary of the U. S. embassy and a cousin. Her acute discomfort did not prevent her from studying the dinner etiquette of the diplomatic set: "The men do not definitely separate from the women after dinner, neither do they talk with a single lady later. Conversation is more general."

The Winthrops found other friends and relatives in Italy, though not as exalted as Aunt Nina Moltke and Aunt Tina van Roijen. In Rome, the Squam Lake Coolidges were off to be blessed by the pope and obligingly took along some relics for the Winthrops' maids, so these could be blessed, too. In Florence Dorothy and her father looked up some Taylor cousins, Netta della Gherardesca and her two daughters, Lotti and Clarigi. "Netta," *née* Harriet Taylor, was Fred Winthrop's first cousin, whose marriage twenty years earlier to Count Giuseppe della Gherardesca had been hailed by the press as a match of "international significance." In Venice the closest Dorothy came to a relative was her grandmother's evocation of Great-Aunt Helen Curtis. "You saw the Campanile in Venice," Grandma Amory wrote her granddaughter. "Aunt Helen went to the top of it one day. That night it fell to the ground. I don't know what she did to it. But they had the plans and rebuilt it."

Their connections in Italy may have been more numerous, but it was the Americans in France whom Dorothy most wanted to see. At the Hotel Lotti in Paris, where they arrived on May 3, she found letters from her beloved friends Emily and Jean Sears, inviting her to dine that very night. They sent their maid to escort her, and she "took me ... on the subway" to their apartment near the Bois de Boulogne. "I LOVED seeing them ... we giggled all evening." The Searses would leave Paris on Dorothy's birthday, less than two weeks later. "Sears gone to England," Dorothy would note dolefully. "Paris has lost half its charm."

To the American woman traveling abroad in the 1920s, the heart of Parisian culture was its dressmaking salons. For the Winthrops there was important shopping to be done. Dowdy young Dorothy would need a new wardrobe, for she was about to turn eighteen and would be coming out soon after the family returned in October. She and her stepmother headed straight for Ytebs at 14 Rue Royale, hiking up three flights of stairs to the wonders of Paris haute couture. Dorothy wasn't especially interested in the clothes. The models, however, intrigued her: "so funny. They must have been double- or triple-jointed, for they wiggled and squirmed everywhere, hips, stomach, shoulders and all!" Even more absorbing was the family who ran the establishment. They were White Russians, Guillenchmidt by name, who had fled their country during the Russian Revolution and were attempting to make ends meet in a new country. Grandma Thayer, Sally Winthrop's stepmother, had discovered them earlier and, to help them out, had suggested that her stepdaughter try them the next time she was in Paris. Like her step-grandmother, Dorothy was deeply moved by these "poor Russian refugees who are most of them making such heroic struggles."[1] Even her father got caught up in the shopping, but he headed instead to the more plebeian Bon Marché. This large department store suited Dorothy, too, with its huge variety "of commonplace and fascinating things."

Dorothy's first impression of Paris had been one of disappointment. During the train trip there, she had spent the day gazing pleasurably out of the train window at the passing French countryside—"flat, fertile valleys with mountains, some snow-capped ... and slightly rolling country with scattered houses ... and men and women working in the fields." Paris, by contrast, "was just an ordinary dirty, noisy city full

REARED *in a* GREENHOUSE

to the brim with automobiles and devoid of traffic reg-
ulations." Having studied her art history, however, she
was soon soaking up the city's treasures. After a first
trip to the Louvre with her father, she returned alone
and "wandered around by myself and took as long as I
wanted in each room. I didn't really take as long as I
wanted for that would be *weeks*!" As for the opera, "it
took so long for them to sing at each other that it
became tedious.... The music was too loud and the
tunes not pretty to my mind."

*The French countryside was
still scarred from World War
I, five years after the fighting
had ended.*

On June 1 she and her father set out for a tour of the French battlefields. She had
been too young to comprehend the enormity of World War I while it was being
fought, but now this trip made a powerful impression on her. The devastated land-
scapes remained vivid in her mind long after memories of Paris had faded.

> We saw remains of trenches and shell holes, in one the wheels and framework of a
> German cannon ... many bullets and hand grenades ... a German gas mask.... The
> whole countryside ... was as rough as rough could be ... everywhere ... remains of
> barbed wire entanglements.
>
> In the fields between Soisson and Rheims, we saw men clearing the barbed wire
> etc. away and digging up the ground with hoes, leveling the mounds and filling in
> shell holes and trenches. We passed village after village where men were busy build-
> ing up new houses on the site of the ruins. The French are a wonderful people. They
> returned to villages in ruins or completely wiped away ... and set to work to rebuild
> their homes and cultivate their fields.

Many years later, the sights of that visit came back to my mother when Hamilton
was under siege by gypsy moths. She wrote a letter to the local paper recalling how,
shortly before World War I, "for two long summers not a leaf did they [the gypsy
moths] leave on a single oak tree, anywhere in town. Some oaks looked dead and
some did die—but the woods were still there." Shortly after the war, she continued,
she had visited the battlefields of France. "There, in France, acres and acres of woods
had vanished. As far as the eye could see, the stumps of trees were all that the shells
of war had left. So I am grateful it is only gypsy moths we have here."

— • —

It would have been a miracle if Grandma Amory hadn't missed her granddaughter.
Dorothy had spent three and a half months with her earlier that winter. In her first
letter to Dorothy she wrote that "your father was an angel to let you stay so long with
old Granny." Dorothy viewed her return home as a chance to look after her grandma's welfare: "Next year I shall be devoted to her and we'll have great fun reading
and doing things together.... I'll be her eyes and try to repay her a little for all she
has done for me all my life. She is my second mother, if anyone is, and I love her very
much."

Hill Hall, where the Winthrops, Pattens and Moltkes gathered for a summer "house party" which none of them ever forgot

Grandma Amory had never hidden the truth of her waning strength from Dorothy. But she made light of her "unfortunate" age, as in this letter from the summer before about her abortive efforts to paint the boys' bedrooms:

> I am still exhausted and do nothing but lie down. Perhaps I did not tell you why I am tired. Well, I felt like doing something, as I cannot read or walk, and so bought some paint and thought I would beautify the shabby little rooms where I put the boys. I managed to scrape off the old paper by standing on the bureau, but in doing it, I had to use water to soften the glue, and it fell down all wet and now is fastened onto the floor and will have to be scraped off. Then I began to paint and got interested, but my unfortunate age hampered me, I became exhausted, and am trying to feel like moving again.

The warning signs were clear enough, but it was still a shock when—just after arriving in Paris—Dorothy received news from Freddy that Grandma had had a "very slight stroke of paralysis" and could "only walk with difficulty." He and Robert had been visiting their grandmother when it happened. Fred Winthrop was clearly upset, breaking out of his shell to write Mrs. Amory of his "deepest affection … much more than it is in my nature to show, I am sorry to say, but it is there nevertheless." He told her how "wonderful" she had always been to him, in his years both "of happiness and of sorrow." For everything, he wrote, "I can never forget nor can I ever begin to repay."

Dorothy longed to be with her grandmother, but a reassuring note from Grandma herself soon put her worries to rest:

REARED *in a* GREENHOUSE

Here I am writing on Sunday and sitting at the typewriter, arrayed in a lovely grey satin robe with chiffon sleeves that Molly got for me at Jordan and Marsh. I have no pain and never felt better and can hobble across the room with a crutch, in fact am having the time of my life for nothing is expected of me and friends send me flowers with messages of sympathy, whereas I suffer less than any of them. Some cannot come up the stairs. Two are in bed with broken hips.

ENOUGH OF MYSELF.

Other notes followed: "I have just breakfasted but not yet dressed.... I take life easily and grow fat. But miss my girl!" And mostly the spotlight was on others, colored by whimsy: "George has just come up and says that Harding is dying in San Francisco, he has been to Alaska and ate some fish out of the bay and got ptomaine poisoning"; "P. S. Seven hundred Fords are being turned out each day. Horrid"; "You say that Emily Coolidge has New England conscience. Poor thing. I consider this a mild form of insanity."

— • —

After a month in France the family packed up and headed across the channel for a summer in England. This was the summer of "Hell Hall" and none of my mother's generation ever forgot it. Grandma Thayer had rented an enormous mansion in Epping, about fifteen miles outside London, for "all her step-children and all her step-nieces ... everyone she could think of," as my mother later described the cast of characters. "It was Hill Hall, but we called it Hell Hall ... there were 21 of us at every meal."[2]

It took about three weeks for the entire ménage to assemble. When the Winthrops clambered off the train in a pouring rainstorm on June 15, they were greeted by Grandma Thayer and Jean Patten, followed soon after by Jean's sister, Nan. The girls, who had gone to school with Dorothy, were the daughters of Anna Patten, Dorothy's stepmother's sister and therefore—technically speaking—her cousins. Dorothy would have none of it, as she had made clear in an earlier diary: "It is an absolute *fact* they are no relation to me and no one can truthfully say they are. ... I am not her [Jean's] cousin. I am her aunt's husband's daughter." Nat and Katharine were more enthusiastic than Dorothy, greeting Nan's arrival with "wild shrieks" and "jump[ing] about with excitement." Nan had come from Denmark with her Aunt Nina, Countess Moltke. Soon the countess and

The Patten sisters. They were, maintained Dorothy staunchly, "no relation" of hers, for she was their "aunt's husband's daughter." At left, Nancy Patten, who married a Groton School teacher, Fritz DeVeau; at right, Jean Patten, who married a papal guard with the surname Pellegrini-Quarentotti and moved to Italy.

A TRIP ABROAD

Aunt Nina Moltke, 1924.
She was a beauty.

The Winthrops, Pattens, and
Moltkes assembled at Hill
Hall under the aegis of
Grandma Thayer in the
summer of 1923.

Dorothy's stepmother were joined by Anna Patten, and the trio of Thayer step-daughters was complete. The sisters must have made a striking threesome—particularly the countess, a grande dame remembered in her later years as imposingly bosomed, often with ashes from a dangling cigarette drifting into her cleavage.[3] Anna Patten carried less gravitas than her sister Nina in the family circle, for she staunchly disliked her stepmother, a sentiment she directed with equal zeal at her own daughter Jean.

Anna Patten, when she arrived, was escorting her sons Billy and Arthur. Billy Patten was a charming but sickly boy who would suffer all his life from asthma and allergies, a condition so intractable that his mother once accepted a friend's misguided suggestion that he sleep in the stable.[4] Mrs. Patten had other problems with her son Arthur, one of which was that she took exception to his doing needlepoint after dinner.[5] A few days later Count Carl Moltke arrived with his son, Carl Adam. Now there were seven males and eight females in residence.[6] Not surprisingly in a household dominated by Thayers, Fred Winthrop slipped regularly off to London. On July 5 he did so again, this time returning with Dorothy's "beloved brothers." This bolstered the male contingent and, in Winthrop eyes, improved its quality immeasurably.

Even by Thayer and Winthrop standards, "huge and rambling" Hill Hall must have seemed palatial. Downstairs had a dining room, smoking room, music room, morning room, library, billiard room, two dressing rooms, and a large hall. Upstairs were bedrooms where the grownups slept, and in the attic, more rooms for "the young ones." Construction had begun nearly four hundred years earlier, in 1560. "Queen Elizabeth once slept in the room now occupied by Mama," Dorothy noted. "It is said she rode her pony upstairs and kept it in the 'barn' in the boys' room." The grounds matched the house for splendor. Ten white peacocks strutted about the lawn. Lebanon cedars and other fine trees were everywhere, and beyond the lawn stretched green pastures dotted with grazing cows and horses. Dorothy counted three tennis courts, two hard and one grass, and a squash court.[7]

There were a few thorns in this pastoral setting, the sharpest of which was Arthur Patten. Not that he wasn't provoked. It all began one day when Nat and Bobby Moltke pretended they were going to feed him to the swans. Dorothy, as usual championing the underdog, hurried to rescue him. His thanks were highly unusual. Whether it happened on the great staircase or in the nursery where the younger children were kept, it became the moment that defined that Hell Hall summer. When he saw her Arthur made a beeline for Dorothy, threw himself into her arms,

REARED *in a* GREENHOUSE

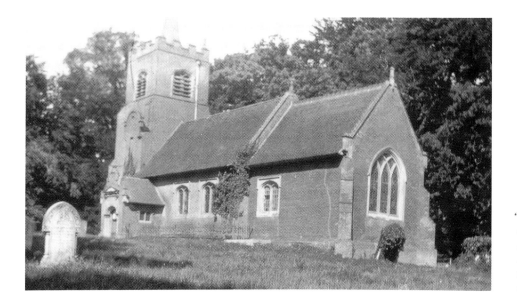

"The dearest little church you can imagine," wrote Dorothy of the church near Hill Hall where she escaped the Thayer hoards one evening.

wrapped his legs around her—and bit her, deep in the neck.[8] If that didn't finish him with Fred Winthrop, another act did. As they all sat around the dining room table, he filled his spoon with oatmeal and—taking careful aim—let go, splat, right into Fred Winthrop's eye.[9]

As if there weren't enough people in residence, the neighbors kept coming around. One frequent visitor was the rector of Stapleford Tawney church, Sidney M. Stanley, and his daughter Joan, about Dorothy's age, dark and jolly, and an excellent tennis player. Dorothy found another neighbor, a Sir Drummond Cunliffe-Smith, "an ancient man … [who] seems half crazy." "Very kind but stupid," she decided later, after an afternoon of tea and croquet at his house. The tea party had been something of a disillusionment for Sir Drummond, too. He had been very excited about getting to know these Americans, the rector told Dorothy later. But after they left, he turned to the rector and said with surprise, "Oh, those Americans, they're just like anybody else."

Gathering her stepdaughters together for this mammoth family gathering was typical of Pauline Revere (Grandma) Thayer. She had, my mother remembered, "a great big heart and was good and kind to everybody." That summer, however, she was "all nerves" by the time everyone had assembled. She was recovering from a recent illness and Countess Moltke worried she was pushing herself too hard. Dorothy was concerned, too, writing that Grandma Thayer refused "to take it easy and gradually regain her strength. She says 'I'm not an invalid, so why lead an invalid's life?'"

The air was thick with Thayers, too close for comfort in the opinion of Dorothy, Robert, Freddy, and their father. Dorothy tried to make her escape at a little church near the Hall. "It was the dearest little church you can imagine," she wrote, "full of little wooden pews, excepting for the Hall pew, a big square sort of box, where we sat." One evening, after an endless round of tennis, bridge, visiting, sightseeing, all with ever-changing combinations of Pattens, Winthrops, and Moltkes, Dorothy had slipped out alone for the evening service. "I left purposely a little bit late," she wrote, "so I could sit by myself in one of the pews and not with all the others in the Hall pew."

Her father and brothers had a better solution. They left entirely, for Paris, abandoning Dorothy to the Thayers.[10] Robert soon wrote her, "I hope you won't be rash and murder anybody while your guardians are away."

— • —

WAIT STILL WINTHROP, 1642-1717 (left),
one of the judges to find the defendants guilty in the Salem witch trials
FITZ-JOHN WINTHROP, 1638-1707 (right),
governor of Connecticut, the third generation of Winthrops to hold the office of colonial governor

According to historian Richard S. Dunn, the two were "conspicuously weaker men than their father and grandfather [Governor John and Governor John, Jr.] ... they were narrow and parochial, half-humorous and half-ludicrous ... by the third generation, the dynasty was in decay" (Puritans and Yankees. The Winthrop Dynasty of New England, 1630-1717). *Louis Auchincloss in his* The Winthrop Covenant (*Houghton Mifflin. Boston. 1976) creates a memorable scene of Wait Still, sitting up "round and solid on that vast soft bed," wearing his "immense white perruque," his "small black eyes" peering with "odd suspiciousness." With him was a worthy cleric urging him to repent publicly for his role in the Salem trials. "'Do you want me to make a monkey of myself?'" sputters Wait Still. "'Those Salem defendants were the vilest old crones, the most dog-like peasants.'" Then, in the Auchincloss rendering, "[He] rose to his knees ... his short stout arms ... stretched above his wig ... his face.... an alarming scarlet [and screamed at the reverend] 'Get out of here you witch.'" Death by a "stroke of apoplexy" came a few days later. (Both pictures courtesy Harvard University Portrait Collection, gift of Robert Winthrop, representing the Winthrop family, to Harvard University, 1964)*

REARED *in a* GREENHOUSE

For a Winthrop, a trip to England would not be complete without a pilgrimage to the ancestral home in Groton—so Fred Winthrop took two, the first to give his Thayer family a chance to pay homage, the second to provide exposure for his Amory children. Though a mere female, Dorothy was suffered to go both times.

Next to Winthrop, "Groton" was the name most revered by Fred and his brothers. It conjured up memories of Groton Manor, the former monastic lands that the first Adam Winthrop, grandfather of Governor John Winthrop, had bought in 1544 after King Henry VIII's religious reformation, signaling their ancestor's ascension into the land-owning bourgeoisie and allowing him to assume the title "Lord of the Manor." Over the years, the Winthrop brothers had, one by one, created their own Grotons in the United States. Fred called his house in Hamilton Groton Lodge (later changed to Groton House), and the place itself Groton House Farm; Dudley called the plantation he bought in South Carolina Groton Plantation and his place in Old Westbury, Long Island, Groton Farm; and Grenville's grand estate in Lenox went by the name of Groton Place.[11]

Adam Winthrop, 1498-1562, first Lord of the Manor (courtesy Harvard University Portrait Collection, gift of Robert Winthrop, representing the Winthrop family, to Harvard University, 1964)

Through the centuries, several American-born Winthrops had returned to their sacred English roots. Little did it matter that Groton Manor had remained in Winthrop family hands for only three generations—bought by Governor John's grandfather Adam in 1544 and sold in 1630 by his son John on his father's behalf to help settle bills arising from his colonial responsibilities in New England. Governor John's grandson Fitz-John (to become the third consecutive Winthrop colonial governor) was back in less than sixty years after the sale. Officially in England to adjudicate the Connecticut charter, he shopped for a camlet cloak and two wigs for bulbous-nosed brother Wait Still, discovered a certain Madam Rawlins to whom he confessed "a passionate love for your person," and squeezed in, "with greet Duty and affection … [a] visit [to] the tombe of my Ancestors"[12] just before his return. About thirty years later, in 1728, came the next Winthrop devotee, the disreputable John of the fourth generation, Fitz-John's nephew and Wait Still's son. John was the ultimate Winthrop disgrace, the one who returned to England permanently, abandoning a wife and seven children after piling up considerable debts and ill-will in America. When he arrived in Groton to view the "Ancient House, arms in the window, the House and Church, the Tomb, and adjacent Lands," he was given a royal welcome. "The bells rang for joy of our arrival," he wrote, and he was entertained during his five-day stay with "dancing, musick, and mirth," dining "splendidly" and taking "a whett" (an appetizer) in Boxford.[13]

Wait Still's son John Winthrop, Fellow of the Royal Society (F.R.S.), 1681-1747, brought the dynasty to further disrepute, fleeing his debts and his family for England, where he lived out his life. (Courtesy Harvard University Portrait Collection, gift of Robert Winthrop, representing the Winthrop family, to Harvard University, 1964)

A TRIP ABROAD

Robert C. Winthrop, 1809-94 (courtesy Massachusetts Historical Society)

"Groton Church, Suffolk County, England, with the tomb of Adam Winthrop, 1562, and his son Adam Winthrop, 1623, Lords of the Manor and Patrons of the Living" (caption in Robert C. Winthrop's Life and Letters of John Winthrop, *1864; photo courtesy Massachusetts Historical Society)*

By 1847, when the next recorded Winthrop visitation took place, the bells were silent, the dancing had ended, and Groton had become "too inconsiderable" to warrant a spot on local maps. This suited Fred Winthrop's eminent Boston cousin Robert C. Winthrop just fine, for he was drawn to the peace of the place, the "matchless verdure of an English summer," the "quiet loveliness." Always the historian, Robert C. Winthrop had even chosen to come on a Sunday, so he could attend the service at the church where his Winthrop ancestors had worshiped. As he joined in the "grand old service of prayer and praise," Winthrop thought he could almost imagine that "the venerable walls gave back an echo of welcome, as to a not unrecognized voice."[14]

In the early twentieth century travel to Europe became easier, and the Winthrop trickle became a rivulet, with four visitations to Groton in a little more than a dozen years. First came Fred Winthrop's New York cousin Bronson, in 1909, who popped by to have tea with the vicar and his daughter in the rectory gardens. No doubt Bronson was more amused by his encounter with Lady Astor at the races with "all England's best." The former Nancy Langhorne Shaw, who had abandoned what would become the Winthrop estate in Hamilton and her drunken husband Bobby Shaw and snagged one of the world's richest men, Waldorf Astor, was feeling her oats at the races, as their horse had beat the king's. "Mrs. A. was told not to make such a noise while standing next to the saddened king," Bronson's traveling companion wrote in his diary, "but she gaily told him that she was pleased as 'It is not often we get ahead of Your Majesty.' "[15] Two years later, Fred Winthrop's brother Grenville would have his sojourn in Groton, and for once a Winthrop was to put his observations of the quaint old village to some practical use. After visiting the "charming English town," he would come home and attempt to "reproduce its atmosphere" on the grounds of his estate in Lenox.[16]

And now it was Fred Winthrop's turn. His first visit, this one with his Thayer family, included the "old, old church where John Winthrop's ancestors used to worship." Dorothy wrote, "It was quite large and restfully plain." The church was located in Lavenham, a village in Suffolk about fifty-five miles northeast of London, with

a "Guild Hall 300 years old, the floor of which sagged!" Here John Winthrop's grandfather Adam had been born, and from here Adam had set out to London to make his mark in the textile trade. The other attraction was a church at Groton Manor, to the south, where the Winthrops motored next. According to Dorothy, it was "a pretty, little church … dear inside, but very musty." Adam Winthrop's tomb was "in a corner by the Church's side door," and "the coat of arms was on the tomb and other places." So ended their first visit to the ancestral home.

Scenes from Dorothy's scrapbook

Fred's second pilgrimage to Groton was made with his Amory family. A man led them to the "very spot where John Winthrop's house, which burnt down 150 years ago, stood. Beside it was a mulberry tree, several hundred years old, which still stands and twigs of which we plucked to press. Nothing now remains of the Manor but a grass grown hole in the ground where the cellar was."

That was it: an old church, an old tomb, and a spot where a house had burned down. It left Dorothy with a feeling of wistful nostalgia: "Wouldn't it be nice if we still lived on the old place and it had never been sold, but had gone from Father to Son for all these hundreds of years."

— • —

The Winthrops' final moment in England came on September 16, two months after the family trip down Ancestors' Lane. Dorothy's two older brothers had returned to school, so Freddy was not with them when the family set off to have lunch with their Grant Forbes cousins in Oxted, Surrey, about fifteen miles south of London. Cousins there were aplenty, for Margaret Winthrop Forbes, granddaughter of Robert C. Winthrop and daughter of his son, Robert, Jr., was Fred Winthrop's third cousin, and there were ten children, all Dorothy's fourth cousins on the Winthrop side.[17] Moreover, Margaret Winthrop Forbes' paternal grandmother had been a Gardner (Libby Amory's second cousin Eliza Cabot Blanchard); her ten children were thus also Dorothy's fourth cousins once removed on the Gardner side.

Margaret Winthrop had grown up in Boston, a contemporary of her third cousins once removed, Dorothy Amory and Mary Curtis, and a close friend of Eleonora Sears'.[18] Eleo, as the press always called her, was a champion tennis player, long-distance swimmer, golfer, squash player and skater, who built herself extensive stables in Beverly Farms and sported a trademark leathery tan year round. She and Margaret Winthrop, it was said, were the first women to ride astride, scandalously breaking a second taboo by choosing Sunday to ride through Myopia. Eleo never tied the marital knot.

Margaret Winthrop, June 1901, from one of Dorothy Amory's scrapbooks

Margaret, on the other hand, did marry, and into the Forbes clan, two branches of which had more money and were more eccentric and numerous than the Boston Winthrops (Grant was from the third branch).[19] Born in Shanghai, James Grant Forbes went to school in England and graduated from Harvard. Margaret and Grant lived in the United States for the early years of their marriage, but after their third child was born, they went to Europe, where they made Paris their home. During World War I, after several more children, they moved on to England where they rented Barrow Green Court, the place where Dorothy and her family met them that day in 1923. Grandma Amory had written that she hoped Dorothy would have a chance to visit Margaret Winthrop, for she'd heard the house was "charming and the children handsome, six girls." She was less charitable about Margaret herself: "What a different fate [from Grandma Amory's own] poor thin and worn out looking chamber-maid … who brings wild flowers every other day to decorate my little parlor [but] has had 13 children and a husband who was not kind and, now they are grown up, she has to work." Not so for Margaret Winthrop Forbes, who had "two superior English Governesses to bring up her children and … plenty of money and goes off for fun, when she wishes to."

Even if Freddy had been in Oxted that day, it's unlikely that he would have noticed the second daughter, eleven-year-old Angela, among the hoard of Forbes children. Dorothy didn't single her out either, though she carefully listed the names of the six girls and four boys. She found all but the oldest two ("they were too small") "fine specimens … and sturdy.… All had perfect manners and seemed very nice and very pleasant."

Angela had grown into a beautiful young woman of nineteen when she and Fred finally met. It was on his home ground in Hamilton, where Angela had come to stay with her godmother, the Winthrops' neighbor Anne Rice. The two took horseback rides together in Hamilton and had a clandestine meeting in New York, where he squired her about. She was expected at the tony Tuxedo Ball, but a night on the town with Fred Winthrop had sounded like too much fun to miss. Telling no one, she slipped away. She couldn't stay long, for she might be missed, so at the Empire State Building she abandoned Fred for another young gent who returned her to Tuxedo, if not for the ball, at least for the luncheon the next day.

Angela and Fred Winthrop at the time of their marriage (courtesy Freddy Winthrop)

Two years later, in 1933, Fred was in England and looked up his intriguing cousin, now living with her family in another rented house, Squerryes Court, in Westerham, Kent. He took a fall on a walk in the woods, which skinned his shin terribly and caused him to postpone his departure for several days. Angela proved an attentive nurse; it was her ministerings, she claims, that led to a proposal of marriage before his stay had ended. She said yes, but he was in such a hurry to get on with his trip that they were married—"indecently" fast, her mother thought—within the month. The date was July 4, 1933, ten years from the day that Dorothy had—unbeknownst to either of them—first met her sister-in-law to be.

REARED *in a* GREENHOUSE

Angela and Fred Winthrop's wedding, July 4, 1933, in England (courtesy Angela Winthrop, rephotographed by Philip Reeser)

My mother couldn't go to the wedding, for she was soon to have her second child. But Angela wrote to tell her what the ceremony would be like:

June 26th. 1933

DEAREST DOROTHY

We are being married in a tiny little village church … where we have all been on Sundays ever since we were quite small. My five younger sisters are going to be brides-maids—though the three elder ones have got to disappear for half the time because there is literally no room for them in the chancel!

We are not having a real reception, I'm sorry to say. Poor Father can't rise to it this year[20]—so we are just having an informal lunch party for relations and intimate friends. Afterwards we plan to go to Paris, and then motor in Germany. I expect we shall be back about the beginning of August to spend a last week with the family before we sail for home. We should arrive towards the middle or so of August. I am so looking forward to seeing you again—especially in the capacity of a sister-in-law.

The double-cousinage of the bride and groom might be dismissed as one of those genealogical curiosities but for one thing—the "new" Boston line, founded at the turn of the nineteenth century by Thomas Lindall Winthrop, had nearly petered out. His only male descendant four generations later was Margaret's brother Robert Mason, who was living out his days as an aging bachelor in southern France with no intention of reproducing himself. Luckily, another "new branch" had begun when Fred Winthrop, Sr., moved to Boston from New York. Angela, by marrying his son, Fred, Jr., would have children who would again bear the august surname of her great-great-grandfather Thomas Lindall Winthrop. (Refer to Chart 14.)

Angela proved to be an effervescent addition to the family, attracting the world to Groton House with her irrepressible wit and infectious laugh. Her only drawback,

Thomas Lindall Winthrop, 1760-1841, lieutenant governor of Massachusetts, 1822-32, president of the Massachusetts Historical Society, 1835-41, father of Robert C. Winthrop, and "my Winthrop ancestor," as Angela Forbes Winthrop likes to say. (Portrait by Charles Osgood, courtesy Massachusetts Historical Society)

A TRIP ABROAD

it seemed, was that one could never expect her at the appointed hour. Winthrops prize punctuality—so compulsively that, like their thriftiness, it could be considered as much a vice as a virtue. It just so happened, however, that on that day in 1923 when they were making their first formal call on the Forbes clan, it was Dorothy, her father and her Thayer step-family who arrived late, an hour behind schedule. Naturally, it hadn't been their fault. The train had been delayed. Dorothy wrote with chagrin, "From the station we could find no conveyance so we had to tel. them our plight and Mr. arrived in his car and drove us back. We made lunch an hour late, but they were so nice about it and so kind they really made us feel it didn't matter." Thinking of Angela today, one wonders: Could it be that they hadn't even noticed?

Coming of Age

chapter TWELVE

Dorothy Winthrop out West in 1926.
My father kept this picture on his desk.

Dorothy returned home from Europe on October 1, 1923, a debutante. Cinderella would have to cast aside her "dowdy-looking khaki skirt" and step out of the "dim religious light" onto the dance floor. No more succumbing to the "limp and worn out" feeling, no more pity for "the poor unfortunate gents" who might have to dance with her. It was time for Miss Dorothy Winthrop to make her entry into society. She was too down-to-earth to find much of it magic. Her ball gowns were only by Ytebs of Paris, not by wand of fairy godmother. Her transport was by family car, not by pumpkin coach. And there was no Prince Charming—at least she didn't recognize him at the time. She took it all in sensible Boston stride, finding the parties "very pleasant," the people "very attractive." One gown truly caught her fancy. It was vintage Gay Nineties and had belonged to Grandma Amory. Dorothy wore it at a "delightful" dinner at the Pattens, where everyone sang and was "merry."

> [The dress] Grandma wore 30 years ago [was] made of beautiful old pale mauve brocade, very tight-fitting at the waist, having a long full skirt, sweeping out behind and large leg of mutton sleeves. I fell in love with it and wish people dressed in that style now. It is infinitely prettier than the modern fashions and gives one an air of distinction and of being well-groomed. But modern dresses are easier and more comfortable!!

In the 1920s coming-out was a full-time occupation, lasting nearly a year. Dorothy missed most of her debut year, being in Europe for the summer, in South

REARED *in a* GREENHOUSE

Carolina for the Christmas season. That left her with barely four months to get launched and advertised in order, as they hoped back then, to find a suitable mate.

Some tsked that she was tossing away her chances by her absence over Christmas. She scoffed. "Many women say my place will be filled as coming out is a competition, but that is not the way I'm coming out. Some actually think it will make a difference in my getting married!! … I cannot see how my being away 6 wks is to make any difference in the friends I make in the long run." As for "the social stuff," Dorothy didn't care a fig about missing it: "The only reasons I'm sorry to leave Boston [are] first—to leave Grandma; second—not to be at Grandma's Thanksgiving lunch; and third—not to see Emily act Jean Marie."[1]

Four months of exposure was probably enough anyway, for the invitations came fast and furious—from all the right people to all the right places. Like their hats, Bostonians tended to have their friends, but for debutante parties, they branched out, inviting people they knew only slightly, if at all. "I thought I knew most everyone in Boston," wrote Dorothy after one particularly crowded tea, "but I've changed my mind." She was rather disoriented at one event, noting it was "so jammed … one couldn't see anyone there one knew." Many of the new faces belonged to extra men who were "put on the list" for parties. They were invited in droves, the purpose being to create a ring around the ballroom that would yield up lines of eager young men who would cut in and give a whirl to even the homeliest deb at the party. These boys were mostly upperclassmen from Harvard, and most were members of a club, preferably the Porcellian. Though their backgrounds may have been unknown, their prospects were good, and without them the coming-out season would have failed. If things went well, some of these outsiders would become the next generation of insiders, marrying Boston girls and pumping new blood into the old vessels of Boston's finest.

Most everyone she met made a good impression on Dorothy. Two of her girlfriends were "too sweet to me and really made me feel welcome back to Boston. Nearly all the others were awful nice, too." Among the men, at least some whom she had registered pleasure at seeing again after Christmas turned out to be winners. "Mr. Hamilton Potter" made an excellent impression: he came "right up and spoke to me, which was awfully nice of him. He is one of the nicest people I have met this winter and he looks like a gentleman."

One "H. C. Lodge" first appeared in the pages of Dorothy's diary at Emily Sears' coming-out party. Emily had told Dorothy when she returned from Europe that she had encountered "the most attractive man." On meeting him at the party, Dorothy agreed. He was "very handsome and he danced often with Emily." The next time Dorothy saw them together, at an after-dinner mah-jongg lesson, she still found him "very attractive and interesting" but noted he was "nervous as a witch. He works like a slave."

Emily Sears and Henry Cabot Lodge, Jr., tie the knot at an event of "national interest" at the Sears home, The Cove, in Beverly, Massachusetts, on July 1, 1926.

COMING OF AGE

At the time, Dorothy had no inkling where these traits would lead him. But she quickly caught on to where his heart was headed. The courtship of Emily went on for two years, and the wedding, an event "of national interest" with a reception at The Cove (the Sears summer home in Beverly) of "400 Boston, New York, and Washington society members," took place on July 1, 1926.[2] The match was magic. Cabot sailed ahead, powered by his "tremendous fortitude … energy … intelligence … and charm." But it was my mother's opinion that "he got where he got partly because he had the most wonderful wife that anybody ever had. She was really charming, really and truly charming, and delightful. And so good with him."[3]

Emily's coming-out party had certainly done its job, introducing her to the dashing young man who would whisk her away. Whether Dorothy's marked the first meeting with her own future husband, we don't know. Certainly he was present at the Hotel Somerset ballroom on the night of January 24, 1924—one of many in attendance at a debut that sent the local press into a breathless tailspin. The clipping tucked into Dorothy's diary read:

> The dominant note of the past week was "on with the dance," every night a star event, the Frederic Winthrops' ball for their debutante daughter, Miss Dorothy Winthrop, coming on Friday night at the Somerset bringing a high and colorful light with the distinguished family connection and wide and notable Boston acquaintance gathering to honor the young girl making her formal bow to society.

Nature had smiled on Dorothy that January night, providing "nice, mild" weather, a rare occurrence in midwinter Boston. The "distinguished family connection" came out in force. Twenty-four families sent flowers—the Higginsons and Saltonstalls, the Websters and Ayers, the Masons and Murrays, the Coolidges and Thayers—adding their congratulations to the obligatory bouquets from her own family—Aunt Clara, Uncle George and Grandma Amory, all the Searses, all the Keans, the Emmonses and the Jacksons, and Uncle Billy and Aunt May. Every one of her "dear Mother's friends … who were not away" showed up. Some, like Mrs. Moses Williams, had sent flowers. Others, like Mrs. F. Murray Forbes, Mrs. R. Homans, and Mrs. Robert Warner, just came. The ushers' list featured Ed and Jimmy Bangs, Columbus and E. Iselin, Dick Trimble and Dick Tucker, Buff Bohlen and Buck Wallingford, and of course, brother Robert and cousin Billy Coolidge.

Dorothy set a tone of understated elegance by choosing to hold a single rose, a bud selected from the bouquet Grandma Amory had given her. Rose in hand, she stood to receive while the other flowers lay banked high behind her. Mama and Aunt Clara were with her in the receiving line, but only Aunt Clara's appearance earned mention in Dorothy's diary: she "looked *very* handsome in a deep blue dress with a pearl and diamond dog collar." The three had lined up promptly at 10:00 p.m., but the guests were fashionably late, and "there was no one to receive until eleven or after and then until twelve a steady stream." Grandma, who "looked sweet," had arrived on time with Uncle George and Aunt Clara and didn't leave until 11:45 p.m., just as the last surge of young people was passing through the line.

Other balls were "jammed—dance[s] of quantity and not quality." At Dorothy's dance, "the hall was not crowded and there was plenty of fresh air and good music." Dorothy seldom found a partner who knew how to waltz, but that evening she had "great good luck … waltzing with Messrs. Harry Atkinson, Elliot Perkins, Standish Bradford, J. Brooks Fenno, and one or two others—but best of all, Father (who with R. next was the handsomest and finest looking man in the room)."

There he was, Prince Charming, in the person of Standish Bradford, tucked into a list of waltz partners and ranking well below her father. He was one of the Harvard boys invited, not a genuine Boston Brahmin. But it would have been impossible, on the surface at least, to tell the difference. He was a tall, handsome blond; a direct descendant of William Bradford, governor of Plymouth Colony; a graduate of Groton School and a Harvard senior; a member of the Porcellian Club and a center on the football varsity.

Standish Bradford next appeared in her diary on May 27 of that year, at the Hamilton wedding of Anna Agassiz, daughter of her father's old friend Dolph, and Gordon Prince, son of Myopia co-founder Frederick. Again, he was only part of a list ("most of the Porcellian Club was there, young, old and middle aged—Hugh Whitney, Standish Bradford, etc."). The wedding itself was more interesting, for the bride and groom "flew off in an aeroplane."

It would take two years for Standish to move from bit player onto center stage in Dorothy's diaries. And it would take another five before they would wed. For when lightning finally struck, her father stepped in, deeply concerned that Standish's connections were only Harvard-deep. It was all very well for them to come to your parties, these boys with no family or money, but not to marry your daughter. For Dorothy, it would be a terrible conflict. But this story comes later, long after the last chord died in the Hotel Somerset ballroom the night of her coming-out. That evening it was all joy—and when the music had ended at three in the morning and the last guest had left, Dorothy finally allowed herself to pronounce something with which she had been associated "a great success." To the world, Dorothy Winthrop was now launched, ready to face life and whatever it might bring.

— • —

For Dorothy and her girlhood friends who did not go to college, the post-deb years, with the Flapper Age in full flower, were carefree. There were parties to attend, weddings to celebrate, new babies to cuddle, friends and relatives whose homes were always open, and exclusive resorts that were always closed except to them and their intimate friends. Dorothy would take a trip out West, three more trips to Europe with her father, visits to the plantation, to Wareham, to New York with Uncle Beek, and to Washington with the van Roijens and their diplomatic friends.

Dorothy loved the trips. She adored her friends and family. But beneath the round of activities was an undercurrent of introspection and indecision. She wanted to do something worthwhile with her life. College, however, was out of the question,

COMING OF AGE

not with a father who believed that "dogs had souls—some did—and horses. But not women." Continuing to paraphrase her father's views, my mother would say, "To go to college for a girl—most ridiculous thing he ever heard of!"

Her father was equally opposed to the idea of a career. Not only was Dorothy a woman, she was upper class: women of her station didn't work. For that matter, not even men need work if they didn't have to. After all, he had "retired" in his early thirties. It was enough just to have "an interest in life, a real all-year round interest … it need not necessarily be work or business."[4] To be sure, her father had plenty of interests to keep him busy. First and foremost were the Massachusetts Historical Society, with a focus on Winthropiana, and a brotherhood of like societies—the New-York Historical Society, American Antiquarian Society, New England Historic Genealogical Society, Colonial Society of Massachusetts, Bostonian Society, and Society of Colonial Wars. Then came the place in Hamilton, where, as Grandma Amory wrote to her friend Fanny Blake in 1928, he "has done so much … and planted millions of trees that it is much improved, though I wish he had had a landscape gardener instead of his own taste, though everyone likes to carry out their own ideas, I suppose." Public service was a distant third. My mother told us that "he was sufficiently interested in Hamilton affairs to attend town meetings, but he never held a position and I don't know that he ever did anything.… He didn't tell us anything, either." But whether as a matter of parsimony or principle, he didn't believe in philanthropy at all. As my mother put it, "He didn't approve of charity. He thought charity did more harm than good."

Dorothy did not have any female role models who would point her beyond friends and family. Grandma Amory's main charitable activity appeared to have been the Maiden Aunts, a sewing circle born after the Civil War and consisting originally of "a dozen bright and merry girls" who met on Thursdays to "sew for the poor, and talk and eat." But few needy were clothed as a result, and she and Dorothy must have chuckled together over the little booklet of poems, entitled *M. A. Sewing Circle 1867–1892*, prepared to commemorate the circle's twenty-fifth anniversary. One verse summed up their dwindling contribution to society: "We met with an honest endeavor/ To cut, and to baste, and to sew;/ How little we thought we could ever/ Come to gossip, eat luncheon, and go." Her mother had never strayed much beyond the carefree life as a single girl, followed by her few short years as a wife and mother.

Dorothy's, however, was a new generation, and a goodly number of her contemporaries were breaking out of the old mold. Two girls from the May School class of 1921, Ethel Cummings and Priscilla Pollard, had announced that were "going to live in New York and be social reformers." When her class graduated, twelve of the eighteen girls headed for college, leaving only Dorothy and a few others, including Nancy Murray and Nan Patten, behind.[5] Some people were even questioning how long families could afford to keep their daughters at home. Dorothy reported one conversation, shortly after her return from Europe, between Miss Degen and a Mr. Kempton, who said that "in about 10 years, there would be no people of property; all would be equal; and every girl should be prepared to do their own work or earn a living, for no property or money owned by anyone is to be depended on 10 years hence."

This dire prediction never came true for Dorothy, but she was as precise about her finances as if it had. On her trip out West, for example, she recorded her expenditures to the penny—post cards, $.27; taxi, $.32; lunch, $.71—and she calculated the tips she gave according to these same painstaking standards. But this stemmed more from her orderly nature than from any fear that she would soon run out of pennies.

Had she had a job, Dorothy might have found it less difficult to invent her life. All that empty time on her hands was a challenge, particularly as she was constantly worrying about how to justify her existence. She began to keep a philosophical journal in addition to her daily diary. In November 1921 she described herself as "continually tormented by unanswerable questions ... thinking does not seem to get me anywhere. My whole mind is a question mark!" Once she wrote Nancy Murray (a copy of the letter was in her philosophical journal):

> Why is there a world? What's it all leading to? Why am I here? What am I meant to do here? Before I was born, there was an infinity of time and after I die there shall be an infinity of time. Schopenhauer says, "Life is a uselessly disturbing episode in the blessed repose of nothingness."

Her Unitarian upbringing, the prevailing rationalism and skepticism of the day, had disabused her of any notion that there was a personal God.

> People are *sure* there is a universal God or they are *sure* there is a personal God, or they are sure of both. How do they know? They *don't*.... I think that life is much simpler to religious people than to such as I. They do not let their minds roam and inquire into all these problems, but they cling blindly to their faith.... The Christian God, I think, is a product of men's minds. Men wrote the Bible; I don't believe it was divinely inspired.

Nonetheless, she continued to plumb the depths of conventional religion, searching for guidance on how to live. Sister Amy's Bible classes were still on her schedule. She went to church regularly, filling the pages of her diary with unfathomable questions raised in the sermon. In 1925 she attended a summer religious conference at Northfield School in Massachusetts and took copious notes, urging other like-minded young women to attend. Prayers were not a way to get what you wanted; rather, they

> are a good thing in that they lift the mind from sordid things.... If we pray to be good every night, there will probably be some result ... because we remind ourselves, perhaps unconsciously, to fulfill this desire. Though I cannot conceive of a personal God, there is surely Something at the back of the world keeping it going—call it Nature or what you will.

This something, Dorothy thought, might explain some of the weird coincidences and dreams she'd had over the years. When, at fourteen, she was haunted by the dream of the sad girl who later turned up in her class, she had written in her diary,

"Of course dreams don't necessarily mean anything." But wasn't it odd that at about the same time, also in January 1919, she and Grandma had both dreamed about Linzee Coolidge, then two years dead, on about the same night? Grandma saw Linzee Coolidge standing on his bed watching some flies, while Dorothy saw him in front of the front door at Hamilton cutting grass and playing with them. And wasn't it just as weird that her father had dreamed he had seen President Theodore Roosevelt's daughter, Mrs. Alice Longworth, dressed in deep mourning, only to discover the next day, January 6, 1919, that Teddy Roosevelt had died? These coincidences, though they made no sense, spooked her. The next January, in 1920, overhearing her father telling her stepmother about a peculiar series of events in the Winthrop family history, she'd written, "It is mighty queer, but every time one of the Winthrop family move houses, someone dies. Grandma Winthrop moved three times since she married Grandpa, and the first was a baby, then came Grandpa, and Uncle Dudley. When Uncle Gren moved, Aunt Mary died, and when Father moved to Hamilton and the second time to 299, I remember wondering if I'd be the next one, when we came to 299."

Grandma Amory no doubt assured her it was all poppycock. She had told her granddaughter about a spiritual hoax she had witnessed while she and Grandpa Amory were visiting Robert C. Winthrop's son John and his wife Isabella in Stockbridge. Ouija boards were the rage at the time, and author Harriet Beecher Stowe and a local minister and his wife had joined the group for an evening of conjuring. Mrs. Stowe's son was dead, and so it was he they conjured up. She had wept when he assured her, "Don't worry about me, Mother, I'm very happy." Then the minister asked a question. To this, the "son" retorted, "Don't bother me you old bald-headed priest; save your breath to cool your future hell!"[6]

Spirits or no spirits, prayer or no prayer, God or no God, Dorothy nonetheless had strong moral convictions. Later in life, my mother would describe morality's survival in a godless world this way: "I always liked the idea that originally our moral ideas came from religion, but then, as we slipped away from religion, the moral ideas remained as a kind of interest. The capital had been spent, but the interest is still there." With her convictions to guide her, nineteen-year-old Dorothy decided that the best she could do was take a sort of "less is more" tack.

> I suppose [we are] meant to fit in with the general scheme of things and help nature in her work of progress. [We] should try to improve the world, though ever so little, by right living, by good example and influence. Everyone cannot do great things and exert tremendous influences, but everyone can do the little things and quietly influence for good those with whom they come in contact.

— • —

Nineteen is very young to dedicate oneself to such a self-effacing ambition, and Dorothy still had some living and learning to do before she would figure out whether and how to settle into such a life. She became a volunteer, like many of her friends. The girls dutifully made surgical dressings, packed candy and nuts at the Junior League, and sold tickets and typed letters for the Society for Prevention of Cruelty to Children. These efforts must have seemed puny, even if all she wanted to accomplish were "little things." But the SPCC offered something else, a shocking view of abused and abandoned children, which instilled in her a strong urge to make a more meaningful contribution. In time, the typist for the SPCC would follow the lead of the family planning pioneer and become the Margaret Sanger of the North Shore.

For the next couple of years, however, it appeared as if her course would more likely follow the wandering path of the social butterfly. She seemed always to be out—one of her friends said she was the hardest person to get hold of that she knew.[7] She went about her social life scientifically, noting the "Misses" and "Messrs" she encountered on her rounds as meticulously as she accounted for her money. In a little homemade notebook, sheets of folded, lined paper sewn up the middle with her name stamped on the cover, she logged all the large parties she attended over the two-and-a-half-year period between October 6, 1923, and May 8, 1926 (there were seventy-seven of them, some lasting two days). Then she recorded the names of anyone noteworthy there (mostly the men), anything memorable about them, including their Harvard class and final club (if it were the Porcellian), their relatives, their looks, and their first names if she got them. They ranged from "Clark, short, drunk, awful" and "John Smith—pasty face" to "Blainey—spectacled beanstalk" and "Theodor Spenser [*sic*]—Philadelphia, very tall and blond, genius in art, lit. and music [to marry Nancy Murray]." There were also the impressively named "Winthrop Churchill" and "Robert Winthrop Storer—No relation of Winthrops or Storers" and the less notable "Blake—not much."

If she flitted from one engagement to another, at heart Dorothy was drawn more to the glow of a lecture than to the glitter of a party. She would have thrived in college. "Books fascinate me," she wrote one afternoon after rummaging in a second-hand bookshop, "but I never find time to read and I read slowly without grasping everything." Luckily, Boston itself was filled with worthy elders bent on improving minds, and even before finishing school Dorothy had begun to attend the various lecture series for adults that were so much in vogue in those days. She would carefully inscribe the high points in her diary after each lecture. This is what she wrote after a talk on the English diarist Samuel Pepys:

> The majority consider him and his diary as a joke, for he records all his little foibles, fancies, and vanities. He could not overcome his love of drinking and going to the theatre and he somehow generally gets around his good resolutions. However, all through his diary, not ever by him intended for publication, one feels his great gusto, his great love of life. He made the best of everything and saw the bright side of everything.

In later life my mother would say, "I'm never bored," and even in her teens, everything piqued her curiosity. It was not just the formal opportunities to which she

Roughing it out West, summer of 1926. At left, the Saltonstall twins, Harriet and Caroline, just after an icy dip in Lake O'Hara, August 17, 1926. At right, Dorothy wading in the high Sierras in the Tuolumne meadows between Yosemite and Mono Lake.

gravitated—the art classes and French lessons, the foreign policy luncheons on Mussolini and discussion groups on Egypt, the talks on Plato's *Republic* and Whistler and Emerson. They went to a dog show "where we lost our hearts to some Great Danes." She went to a flower show with Grandma: "Never realized how many members of the orchid family there were." Even the dentist was a source of education: he "explained the two kinds of decay to me." Only the movies left her cold.

More scholarly than many of her friends, Dorothy was also more of a country bumpkin. Of course, not all her friends had a magnificent country estate to which to repair, nor a father who was always around, a companion with whom to ride and chop wood. Dorothy had a love affair with the country. Even such a quiet place as Hamilton had its adventures. In April 1924, she was in Hamilton with her brother Fred, who was recuperating from mumps. It was the windiest spring she'd ever known. One day, she and Fred were out riding when they spotted "volumes of smoke" right across the hill from Groton House. Four rescue squads were swiftly on the scene—the Hamilton, Wenham, and Ipswich fire departments and the Rices' (their neighbors') private fire department. When Dorothy and Fred inspected the damage the next day, they learned that a broken wire had started the fire but the terrific wind had soon spread the flames. "All, all was charred and black from the stable, the whole length of the front drive to the main road.... In a short time, we had lost *thousands of dollars worth* of pine trees. Had the wind been in the other direction, the house, stable and barn would have gone."

Dorothy would record one more bout with the elements before ending her 1924 diary. It was July 17, her mother's birthday, and she and her father were motoring back to Hamilton after a trip to Magnolia where they had gone to give Grandma Amory some flowers. The sky was growing so dark and the wind so violent that her father decided they should wait at Myopia rather than trying to get home. Soon the rain was coming in sheets, and after crawling along with their car lights on, Fred finally stopped under a tree. Then the hailstones came, as big as her father's thumb, and soon the fields looked as if it had been snowing. Thunder was crashing, first on one side and then the other. But it took a blinding flash of lightning to finally alarm Frederic Winthrop. "It stretched from heaven to earth and found its mark in the middle of a pasture just across the fence from us.… We were literally so blinded by the light that for a few seconds we could not see a thing." What it could have done to them became all too evident minutes later when, driving again, they spotted "billows of smoke" where an earlier bolt of lightning had hit a stable. As they looked through the "lurid light on the dark and dismal landscape," three horses came galloping toward them, "heads erect and tails streaming," chased by a bareback rider who was driving them to safety. When they finally arrived home, Dorothy and her father found there had been yet another close call. Lightning had struck their chimney, and the chauffeur, who was walking through the door below, had been knocked over by the shock.

In 1926, the summer she was twenty-one, Dorothy was invited on a trip out West and to Alaska and Canada with her Aunt Lena Saltonstall and twin daughters Harriet and Caroline. It was a complete eye-opener. She had roughed it before, had washed in cold water at the plantation, but never before in waters as icy as in the glacial streams of Alaska. She had been out in the rains and the winds in Hamilton, but these were nothing to the torrential downfalls they encountered riding in Canada near Lake Louise. She had seen the damage in Hamilton after fire swept their property, but it paled beside the great charred tree trunks left by the great western forest fires around Crater Lake. She had been treated with southern hospitality, but she found western hospitality beat it hollow. She'd known the peace of Hamilton and the plantation, but it didn't measure up to the tranquillity and repose of the vast mountains and valleys of the West.

Mr. and Mrs. Partridge in front of their house, August 8, 1926. She was, wrote Dorothy in her dairy, "the dearest old lady I ever hope to see."

She was filled with "deep feelings" that she found difficult to verbalize but easy to write about. And write she did, with complete abandon. Here is her enthralled description of an old couple they met in Alaska:

> I shall never forget that low, rough-beamed room and Mr. and Mrs. Partridge standing there in the mellow light, the dearest old lady I ever hope to see. So frail and dainty in her black lace dress greeting every one with such a pleasant smile.… Hardly anyone was left when Mrs. Partridge played "Abide with Me" and the little group around her sang it more sweetly than ever I had heard it sung. I felt more uplifted than I ever felt in any church.

And thus she described an evening in the wilds:

After supper the rain let up, a gorgeous rainbow appeared over the mountains and the last rays of the sinking sun bathed the peaks in a soft and tender glow. H. and I sat on the steep bank of the gully with the torrent rushing by below, until the chilly night air drove us to bed in our cozy tepee tent.

Dorothy felt ready, at times, to give it all up as a bad job.

Oh, my dear, I want to throw away my pen in disgust when I try to describe today.... How can I convey the deep, deep, blue of the sky the glory of the forest or the grandeur of the canyon ... I am helpless ... at a loss....

— • —

While Dorothy was gingerly feeling her way in the world outside the May School, her siblings, too, were moving along. Between 1924 and 1926 Robert would graduate from Harvard; Fred would be well into his own Harvard years; Nat would enter St. Mark's; and Katharine would soon be leaving Boston for Foxcroft School, in Middleburg, Virginia.

Robert, the eldest, was a star, socially in demand. "No sooner does Robert return than off he flies," wrote Dorothy. But he took it all lightly, having joked in an earlier letter to Dorothy, "Dear Madame:— ... Friday evening very gay affair?!? One beautiful damsel, Izzy Turnpike, 16 hands high and weighs eight stone, has broken a flock of hearts. One can only dance 3 knots with her before being cut down by ennuis!?!"

By contrast, he was serious about his rowing responsibilities. His father had encouraged him to take up crew because "gentlemen were oarsmen."[8] He had been made varsity stroke in his sophomore year and would be varsity captain in his senior. His picture made the Sunday, March 28, 1926 *New York Times*, a handsome, reserved but eager young man, leaning forward in the shell, hands firmly on his oars, "starting to buck the ice cakes of the Charles at the opening of spring practice." Not all was glory, however. The crew he captained never beat Yale and the coach quit in a mysterious tiff with the Harvard powers. In another of Dorothy's clippings, a June 3, 1926 story in the *Telegram*, Robert, as captain, diplomatically attributed the leave-taking to "lack of cooperation" between crews and coach. The author suggested, however, that the coach had proved "too democratic for

Robert, August 27, 1926. A couple of days later, he was off to Trinity College, Cambridge.

REARED *in a* GREENHOUSE

Harvard" because he had accepted an invitation to a sports writers' dinner. "Harvard Wants Only an Aristocrat Crew Coach," was the headline.

After graduating in 1926 Robert set off for England for a non-credit postgraduate year at Trinity College, Cambridge. He had intended to continue his rowing, but on arrival discovered that the stroke was different. "*Hell!* is all I can say when it comes to English rowing." He was expected to learn it in a week, competing against candidates who had been carefully groomed for a year. Instead he turned to hockey, a sport for which he was even more unqualified. He hadn't been on skates for five years and was "rotten." But when university team captain Murray Forbes (first cousin of the Forbes children Dorothy had met in England three years earlier[9]) spoke of the fine trip to Antwerp, Paris, and St. Moritz planned for the squad during Christmas vacation, he swaggered up to Murray and bragged, "You may not be aware of the fact, but I am a pretty sweet hockey player myself." Even when he learned the truth, Murray signed Robert up, for there were few candidates to choose from. As Robert wrote Dorothy, the team "consists only of Americans and Canadians, for Englishmen don't skate."

At the end of his first term at Cambridge Robert had met only a few Englishmen. He took the British snubs in his stride. "There is a saying," he wrote Dorothy, "that if an Englishman is especially attractive and nice to an American, he is [really] either a Scotchman or an Irishman." He learned from a friend at Oxford that things were different there. At Oxford, "as soon as the Englishmen found out that you weren't an objectionable Rhodes scholar, they took you in immediately." He accepted an outsider's being cut dead at Cambridge philosophically. "To be an American here," he wrote Dorothy, "is almost as bad as being a Jew at Harvard."

He and his friends had their own prejudices against the British. Robert had donned his cap and gown "as naturally as I do a hat at home," but hoped he wouldn't "come down" with an English accent and hated the English food. Tea, he wrote, consisted in "eating enormous quantities of heavy rich cakes" and lunch was "a big indigestible [meal] at one o'clock." Saturday evenings he and his friends would escape the common fare, instead "din[ing] together in our rooms on game birds and good wines, and then go to the theatre." But they hated a master's tea-dance for which they "screw[ed] up [their] courage, put on dark suits" to attend. "We had an awful time weathering it, for there must have been at least 20 old gray-haired fossils there and the master's daughter is a fright. She is plain ugly, having just half as many teeth as she ought to have and speaking in a most annoying drawl."

The vacation hockey trip was much more to Robert's liking, especially St. Moritz. Though "ultra-fashionable ... and frightfully expensive," it afforded late night dancing and many a "slight libation." For New Year's Eve, Robert and his teammates dressed up as ministers (putting their collars and waistcoats on backward), met "several girls," and then spent the next two days "recovering." But they also had to put in periods of "rigid training" and, somehow, easily won their big Oxford match. They knew they had to. Otherwise everyone would accuse them of having gone to Switzerland just "to have a good time."

Freddy and Robert Winthrop, two stalwart Harvard oarsmen, c. 1925

Meanwhile, in June 1924, Freddy finished St. Mark's. Fresh from her own belated graduation, Dorothy drove to Southboro with her stepmother for the ceremony. "I can't believe Fred is no longer a school boy!" she wrote. Fred had gotten his athletic "SM" at St. Mark's, and at Harvard he would follow in Robert's footsteps, sitting at bow on the freshman crew as had Robert two years before.

Fred, however, did not share Robert's flair with the girls. During his last year at St. Mark's he had invited Jean Sears to the school dance. He had fallen "in love" with his cousin Jean when he was twelve, bashfully confessing his attachment in a note to Dorothy with a heart enclosing the initials J. S. and F. W. Although Dr. and Mrs. Thayer, the headmaster and his wife, "awaited the girls with open arms" and offered them a "very good" tea on their arrival, Fred wrote Dorothy, "I did not have any. I stood around and looked and felt simple." Jean, throughout her life less exuberant than her sister Emily, seemed as awkward as her escort. At dinner, instead of waiting for the obligatory grace, she "immediately plumped herself down into a chair to which she was shown. She didn't stay there long, for she was "roused up by Mrs. Thayer who in a loud stentorian voice bellowed 'Grace.' " With this, wrote Fred, "she almost sank through the floor."

If Fred was less social than Robert, he was also less cavalier about his studies. During one vacation at Harvard, he apparently decided to stay on campus and work while his classmates went off to play, writing his sister:

> It is really pretty disorganizing to my work to have vacation come. I hope to accomplish a good deal during it, but it certainly gives you the wanderlust to hear everybody talking about Aiken, Bermuda, Hot Springs, St. Louis etc. Well, everybody will have cleared out by this afternoon and I can concentrate undisturbed. I have just four weeks from Monday which is just about four weeks too short. I wish I could have started right after divisionals last year for with my sieve-like memory, I have to learn everything all over again not merely what I did not know. Anyway, I am trying to make a real drive, which I hope will bring me sailing through. If not you may be able to find me digging ditches in Kamchatka.

Fred may have felt bleak about his studies, but he didn't share his sister's sober view of religion: "I went to church, get that, with Aunt Clara and Billy. Sherrill certainly shoots some sermon. I felt like a Christian for at least 15 minutes."

In 1926, shortly before Robert left for Cambridge and while Dorothy was heading west with the Saltonstalls, Fred took a trip around Europe with his friend Paul

Nitze, who would become the eminent arms negotiator and foreign policy elder statesman. At last Fred seemed to relax and enjoy himself. He had a birthday party on board ship with a menu that included "Hors d'Oeuvres à la Winthrop," "Roast Golden Pheasant," "Nitze Bread Sauce," and different wines with every course. But, like Robert, he was very particular about those with whom he associated: "The people on board are … mostly big butter and egg men and women except those that are Israelite.… The best pair, however, are two from New York by the names of Wopsy Abrahams and Billy Shapiro."

Paul Nitze, 24, great friend of Fred Winthrop and future pillar of the U.S. foreign policy establishment (courtesy Paul P. Nitze)

He covered a tremendous amount of ground: London, Paris, Venice, Amsterdam, Rotterdam, Cologne, Munich, Prague, Vienna, Salzburg, Berlin, Helsingfors, the North Cape. He found to his surprise (memories of Fräulein?) that he liked the Germans: "Strange as it may seem they have been nicer to us than any other place.… These south Germans are a jolly bunch and all very pleasant even if not very attractive." What he most looked forward to, however, was Lapland, where

"Freddy the fop!" (Dorothy's scrapbook caption, November 28, 1926)

COMING OF AGE

Miss Eleonora Sears is at the left and Miss Elizabeth Ryan at right. Their companions, who acted as pacemakers, are Henry Sheldon and Frederick Seymour.

Globe - Nov. 30, 1926

Frederic Seymour alias Fred Winthrop
Henry Sheldon alias Paul Nitze.
gus Leonard alias Bill Wister? — *also Chip Bohlen*

At right, *Fred Winthrop, 19, pacing Eleo Sears, woman on left, on one of her legendary long-distance walks*

there wouldn't be any people at all: "I feel [Lapland] will be the best of the whole trip. The salmon are plentiful and the air is black with ducks while the lakes and rivers are ideal for the canoeist."

Late in the fall of 1926 Fred took another trip, this one shorter but more celebrated. Eleo Sears, fading athlete, had given up riding astride around Myopia and playing championship tennis and taken up the sport of walking. In her sturdy brown oxfords, however, walking was anything but sedate. She strode manfully from Providence to Boston, paced by Harvard students. Fred Winthrop and Paul Nitze were tapped for a particular walk and appeared, under the aliases Frederick Seymour and Henry Sheldon, in the *Boston Globe* of November 30, 1926, marching alongside a hatted, scarfed, and sensibly shod Miss Eleonora Sears and companion Elizabeth Ryan. Another account, however, divulged that she was "followed by her limousine in low gear, chauffeur at the ready with fueling drafts of hot chocolate."[10]

Though Dorothy might no longer have thought of Nat as a "pest," neither was he a pen pal like her other two brothers—or indeed Katharine. Thus, the evidence is thin on what he was up to during these years. What we know is from Eleanor, his future wife, who offered an anecdote on his schooling before St. Mark's. He had gone to the Charles River School, she said, an "outdoor" school where his mother had sent him because he seemed to have too many colds. It worked, he had told Eleanor, for instead of having many colds, he had one continuous cold all winter.

The most athletic of the Winthrop five was surely Katharine. In 1925, at the age of eleven, she had been singled out in the August issue of *Women's Sports* as a possible " 'Helen Wills' in the making." At thirteen she amazed the crowd at the Essex County Club by playing four tennis matches in one day and winning three. As reported in the September 10, 1927 *Boston Advertiser*, the sun was sweltering, the competition was older than she, but for her fourth and final match she "wiped the perspiration from her forehead, gripped her racquet and went through the wire gate, from which, to the long and thunderous applause of the spectators, she emerged a winner." The following summer at Longwood Katharine prevailed against a seventeen-year-old Toronto girl during a protracted, come-from-behind match. By 1928 she was state girls tennis champion, pictured in an unidentified newspaper clipping in Dorothy's scrapbook at the Monserrat Golf Club's annual junior tennis tournament. Wearing a square, nearly knee-length tennis dress, her stockings wrinkled at her knees, she stood poised to serve with a big smile on her round face.

Katharine, almost 14, at the Montserrat Gold Club's Annual Junior Tennis Tournament in Beverly, Massachusetts, early July 1928

Katharine was as full of bubbling assurance in her studies as she was in tennis, writing to Dorothy, who was traveling in Europe, in January 1927: "We are going to have exams.… I find I am a little behind but as I am so bright it is easy for me to catch up. I am still at the head of my class, *of course*." To her, everything was a lark. She poked fun at family sentiment, starting an April 1927 letter to Dorothy, "My own sweetheart: I yearn for thee night and day: I crave for a sight of those beautiful eyes and a kiss from those fragrant lips. My eyes are swollen by weeping for thee." She tried to horrify her older sister, continuing, "Saw Ellen Taintor in a car with four boys going b*rrrr* (that means fast and she had her arm around their necks). You are shocked, you are asking me to tell you no more of those immodest scenes." She even made fun of the Winthrop name. One envelope with her return address read, "From Katharine Lovely Winthrop, Daughter of the Pecan Peddler." But outside the family, she was cutting quite a swath. Freddy described her at a dance: "She is quite a belle, hair up, fingernails polished, nifty stepper."

In her mid-teens, Katharine went off to Foxcroft, a boarding school for upperclass equestriennes in the heart of the Virginia hunt country (no buttoned-up Boston finishing

Katharine, undated

school for her). She survived hazing ("Luckily, I didn't have to darn any stockings, but had to do about everything else"), laughed at her roommate ("She stands before the mirror for half an hour training her eyebrows!"), and overate ("The food is awfully good to taste but poor for the figure"). Home still had some allure, particularly after she acquired a Chevrolet convertible coupe, black with red wheels. "It leaves your Franklin in the ditch for looks," she wrote Dorothy in April 1931. "I can't wait for June to get home to drive it and of course see the family."

Nat and Katharine were developing perfectly well, it appeared. Fred Winthrop, however, remained unshakably partial to his first three children. Surveying his brood in 1924, he told Dorothy that "the more he saw of different families the more pleased he was with his and he felt no one had better, more satisfactory children than his three older ones."

The Startling Elopement

chapter THIRTEEN

Grenville L. Winthrop feeding his pheasants at the Rock Pool, Groton Place, Lenox (Winthrop Scrapbook, Fogg Art Museum Archives, courtesy Harvard University Art Museums)

September 6, 1924—a date engraved in Winthrop family history, the day that Kate and Emily, Uncle Gren's daughters, eloped with the electrician and the chauffeur. This is how my mother used to describe it:

> We [Fred, Robert, and Dorothy] were all going out to supper in Manchester with Grandma Amory and the telephone rang—"Long distance from Lenox." My Grandmother Winthrop lived there and she was very old. But we had to hurry off or we'd be late for supper, so we went and we kept worrying that there was something wrong with poor old Grandma. But when we came back, nobody said anything, nothing was said, nothing was done, and we all went to bed....
>
> The next morning we were sitting around the breakfast table, and there was Nat, and my father said, "It's perfectly all right ... there's nothing the matter with Grandma." So I said, "We thought that maybe, maybe the girls had eloped." And Nat clamped his hand over his face and ran out of the room because he was laughing so hard. He knew.

Dorothy's 1924 diary gives a more complete rendition of the scene. Her comment "met with a most unappreciative response.... Father and Mama looked like the blackest of thunderclouds, Katharine stared into space with a set jaw and Nat whisked out a large handkerchief and rushed from the room, apparently to blow his nose, but in reality to disguise his laughter. Directly after breakfast, I was told the cause of his unnatural behavior.... *Emily and Kate had both eloped* with two terrible men and Father was going right up to Lenox."

Dorothy's suggesting that an elopement might have been behind the mystery phone call was not so far-fetched an idea. The family had been buzzing with the possibility for some time. During a visit to her uncle's the previous October Dorothy had found her two cousins, by then twenty-three and thirty years of age, still tethered to the gateposts of their palatial Lenox mansion. Emily seemed the more quiescent. She had a white marble studio on the place, and her bronze bust of her father had been exhibited at the Lenox Arts and Crafts show. She "sculpts very well," Dorothy wrote. Kate was more sporty. "She hates sculpturing. She loves swimming and riding but never gets a chance to do the latter. It is pathetic, the way they were brought up." Kate, as a full-grown woman, was still riding on a little pony.

Pathetic it was, for their father did not let the girls go to school in New York. Who could tell what kind of people they might meet there? Not even when Emily, at that time eighteen, came to visit the Fred Winthrops in Hamilton was she allowed to meet the local gentry. As my mother recounted later, her stepmother Sally had gone to considerable trouble to have nice people over and to arrange for her young niece to be included in parties. But Uncle Gren had "insisted that he know who the guests were to be, and Mama was so disgusted that she said she'd never do another thing for either of his daughters."

Dorothy's sympathies were not all with her cousins, however. Three months before the elopement, at a dinner on Long Island with Uncle Beek, Uncle Gren, and Grandma Winthrop, Dorothy had heard some disagreeable reports about them. "Emily and Kate are very mean to him," she wrote in her diary afterward. "They bobbed their hair and bought automobiles and got licenses without consulting him and they knew he hated bobbed hair. I should think they'd love him enough to at least talk over their plans with him." In late July, Dorothy became incensed, this time over the way her cousins were treating their grandmother in Lenox. "She must be lonely, especially in the evening when no one is there," Dorothy mused, thinking of her grandmother alone in her summer place, Ethelwynde, next to the Lenox Club. "Uncle Gren is devoted to her but Emily and Kate are mean and pay her no attention.... Kate is nice to me, but I'd rather have her nice to Grandma who needs her."

Grandma Amory and Uncle George didn't share Dorothy's indignation when she relayed these reports. To the contrary, they were "much amused and said they'd no doubt elope with the chauffeur. [Grandma Amory and Uncle George have] often said before that [Kate and Emily would] end up by eloping, but now they are convinced, and although they are only joking, it annoys me."

When disaster actually struck, Uncle Beek rushed from New York, Frederic tore over from Hamilton, and sister Kitty raced up from New Jersey. Just as fast came the press, to lap up

Grandma Winthrop, who, Dorothy thought, must be lonely in her old age

THE STARTLING ELOPEMENT

this delectable tale of double mésalliance, reporting that Emily had married her chauffeur, Corey Lucien Miles, and Kate had married an electrician, Darwin Spurr Morse, "who was once Uncle Gren's chicken man." The *New York Times* ran the story on the first page, noting that the "joint runaway marriage" was "one of the most startling of its kind society here has known in many years." The *Boston Herald* pursued the saga for days, pinning down details of the ceremony, the flight, the background of the grooms, and the consequences for the young women. Dorothy followed diligently along with her scissors, clipping each new story as it appeared. For the reclusive Grenville Winthrop, headlines such as these must have been devastating:

2 DAUGHTERS OF AGED LENOX MILLIONAIRE IN ELOPEMENTS. EMILY AND KATE WINTHROP ARE WED TO CHAUFFEUR AND ELECTRICIAN. FATHER PROSTRATED. SOCIETY ASTONISHED

ELOPERS REPORTED OFF FOR MONTREAL. MORSE RESIGNS JOB IN LENOX BUT MILES HASN'T—YET

QUIT PALACE FOR LOVE IN COTTAGES

The first of the articles appeared on the day of the event, just after the fugitives had sped off. According to this account, the two couples had been secretly married

The double elopement of Emily and Kate Winthrop to the chauffeur and the electrician made quite a splash.

REARED *in a* GREENHOUSE

at the hundred-year-old parsonage of the Congregational Church in the little village of Interlaken, near Stockbridge. The ceremony took place at nine in the morning, performed by one Reverend John P. Trowbridge, seventy-four, who had admitted that he was sworn to secrecy by the bridegrooms after making arrangements for the wedding a few days earlier. The wedding party was very select, with the only family present being four relatives of Morse's, including his mother, his sister, and his cousin, the proprietor of the local garage where the girls kept their cars, who acted as best man. On the minister's side, two of his neighbors were in attendance, including a Miss Heath who had decorated the old-fashioned parlor of the parsonage "tastefully" for the festivities. Mr. Trowbridge disclosed later that his fees for marrying the two couples were the highest he had ever received.

The wedding had been timed to take place while the brides' father was away on a business trip. When sixty-year-old Grenville arrived back at the Hillsdale, New York, train station late that same afternoon, he was met by a strange chauffeur in an automobile from one of the public garages in Lenox. His own chauffeur, he was told, had been "suddenly called away." At home, Miss Helen Holmes, who had been with the family for some twenty years, first as the girls' governess and instructor and later as their secretary, informed him of what had happened. They had told her of their plans but sworn her to secrecy; she was reported to "feel the elopement of the girls almost as much as does their father."

Accounts varied as to what happened next. One, which reported correctly on the galloping arrivals of Fredric, Beek, and Kitty, said there was a "family council at Ethelwynde, the Lenox villa" of Mrs. Winthrop, at which "the sensational elopement" was said to have been "discussed in all its phases." The press, not privy to these high-level deliberations, were free to speculate on the abandoned father's state of mind. The *Herald* of September 5 described him as "grief-stricken at the loss, there having existed great companionship between the father and his daughters, since the death of the mother several years earlier." (Dorothy must have scoffed at that one.) The *New York Times* of September 8 pronounced that he was "treated for shock," a dramatic tale echoing the *Herald*, which the day before had reported that

"Groton Place, Moonlight," etching and aquatint by Julius F. Gayler, where "millionaire Winthrop brood[ed] over elopement of daughters" (courtesy Harvard University Art Museums)

"he broke down completely and was under the care of his physician." On the eleventh, the *Herald* stated that he was angry at first, then forgave his daughters while insisting that his new sons-in-law "would get a frigid reception." Most poetic, however, was a photograph of his mansion and its wide expanse of law provided by International News Reel. "WHERE MILLIONAIRE WINTHROP BROODS OVER ELOPEMENT OF DAUGHTERS," the caption read. "Silently, a lonely father strides through the great halls of this palatial mansion at Lenox. Grenville Lindall Winthrop debates whether or not he will take unto his aristocratic bosom his chauffeur and electrician sons-in-law."

Above: *Kate and Darwin Morse, about to set off on their honeymoon in her very own car, variously dubbed "expensive" and "high-powered" by a titillated press (courtesy Thomas S. Morse)*

Above right: *Kate and Darwin Morse as newlyweds in Santa Barbara, California, late 1924 or early 1925 (courtesy Thomas S. Morse)*

Shortly the young women and their husbands, or at least Kate and Darwin, were discovered in the Hotel Vermont in Burlington, Vermont, where they had spent the second night after their wedding "in a tiny room." From there they "leisurely" motored to Montreal. There was considerable speculation about what would happen after the honeymoon. Would Emily have to move into the "humble home" of Corey Miles and enjoy "love in a cottage"? Would Kate be taken to the "modest little home" of Darwin Morse, an "heiress' love nest"? Thanks to their mother's will, the girls each had either $1 million or $3 million (depending on the account) and so they settled in neither spot, but rather in Santa Barbara, California.

Most interesting to the press, however, was how these romances had started in the first place. Amid all the hoopla one story, from an unidentified clipping in my mother's scrapbook, seemed to hit on the real reason for their secret affairs. "Seldom if ever," the report read, "did the daughters assume the hostess role for coteries of youthful guests; indeed young people were taboo, evidently, and hospitalities were confined almost entirely, so it is said, to gatherings of the older circles." Where else were the two women to find companionship, then, except on the grounds of Groton Place?

Kate's romance with Darwin Morse appeared to have had its origins in their mutual concern for chickens. He had been the "chicken man" on the estate, and as all the fowl had been under Kate's care, naturally they were "much in each other's company," according to the *Herald* of September 7. About three years before the wedding, this report continued, "Morse suddenly left the estate and gossip had it he had been summarily discharged when Winthrop, while inspecting the chicken farm one day, came on his daughter and employee in each other's arms." They saw each other clandestinely thereafter. Kate would sometimes give Darwin a ride in her car after he finished his job, and sometimes she and her sister would be "conveyed" to the movies by Miles, where Darwin would be. Neither man "ever sat with the

REARED *in a* GREENHOUSE

Winthrop sisters during the performance." Similarly, Emily's attachment to Miles appears to have arisen from his role on the place. He was said to have taught both women to drive, and during the summer of 1924 he and Emily had frequently been seen together in her car in out-of-the-way spots in the Berkshires. This caused little stir because he was the family chauffeur.

An editorial in the *New York Times* (September 8) was of the opinion that "as a prospect … the electrician is somewhat superior to the chauffeur." Darwin Morse, in fact, did have the edge. He came from an established Lenox family; his father, owner of the Thomas S. Morse auto agency, had been in the vanguard of the transportation revolution, receiving press notice in 1904 when he sold Edward R. Wharton, Edith Wharton's husband, his first Lenox-based car. By the time Darwin grew up, electrical work had become a promising career for an upwardly mobile young man. After his peremptory dismissal from Grenville Winthrop's employ, Darwin had gone to work for an electrical company, first as a common laborer and later as an electrician. He was also a master of the Lenox Grange, a member of the Lenox fire department, and a deacon in the Lenox Congregational Church. With his marriage Morse resigned as master of the grange—a move the report noted that "was accepted last night with keen regret." He also resigned from his job with a note saying, "I was sorry to leave you so suddenly, but conditions seemed to warrant it," and quit the fire department, this note saying, "I expect to be absent for some time."

Unlike Morse, who had been born and raised in Lenox, little was known about Corey Miles, who hailed from Milton, Vermont, and who had arrived in Lenox about eight years earlier. After swift investigation, reporters discovered that he had first found work as a chicken man and then had moved on to become a chauffeur for novelist Edith Wharton's sister-in-law. He had been in the Winthrop's employ for about a year at the time of the wedding. This, moreover, was not his first marriage. The first wife was said to have been in a musical comedy company; the couple had reportedly lived on the Winthrop estate before separating. When, a year before marrying Emily, Morse had gone to file for divorce, it was discovered that his first wife had died.

Eventually, the tangled situation would sort itself out as Grenville and his daughters became more or less reconciled. But that was several years away.

— • —

What had brought the Grenville Winthrop family to such a pretty pass? Grenville Winthrop and Mary Trevor's married life had begun full of beauty and hope. Their wedding took place on June 2, 1892. Grenville had waited until he was twenty-eight to marry; she was a Murray Hill neighbor, spending her winters with her widowed mother on 37th Street. Like Grenville she was rich, an heiress to several million dollars under the will of her father, John B. Trevor. The wedding had been "a brilliant gathering of prominent society people." (Weren't they all?) Guests came to the Trevors' summer home in Yonkers on a special train from New York, and eleven

Yonkers police were on duty in the house and on the riverfront grounds. Howard of New York had been hired to display the gifts, and among the silver pitchers, exquisite screens, and asparagus dishes were the works of Thackeray and of the Boston Winthrop scion, Robert C. Winthrop. Exactly nine months later there entered into the home of Mr. and Mrs. G. L. Winthrop at 10 East 37th Street "a sunbeam, in the shape of a daughter," Emily, and six years later, in December 1899, a second ray of light, her sister Kate.

The news story of Mary Trevor Winthrop's death, on December 1, 1900, suggests that the couple's relationship had not lived up to expectations. When Mary died it was not at the address in New York where she and Grenville had made their home but rather at Glenview, where the wedding reception had taken place. Fred Winthrop's diaries indicate that the separation had come even earlier, during the summer of 1900. Grenville had taken a house at Manchester-by-the-Sea with Fred that year, presumably trading domestic trouble for the lugubrious company of his perpetually rejected suitor-brother. When Mary Winthrop died the press did not speculate about the cause of death—"she had been ill but a few days and her death was entirely unexpected." But the family whispered that she had suffered a serious postpartum depression after Kate's birth, and that the death had been a suicide.

Grenville never married again. Even before his wife's death he had been smitten by another: art. As a Harvard student some fifteen years earlier he had come under the spell of Professor Charles Eliot Norton. Norton's fine-arts courses, Harvard's first in the field, were considered a "snap" but had a lasting effect on whoever took them.[1] In the Victorian period, art was dismissed as frivolous unless it could be ascribed some higher moral purpose, and Grenville Winthrop, under the influence of Norton, took it as a kind of gospel that beauty was the highest value in human life—"better than the good, because it includes the Good."[2] By the late 1890s he was already feverishly gathering clippings on art collecting—much as his brother Fred was compulsively clipping anything that appeared in the papers about the life, marriage, and death of Winthrops or Taylors.

When Grenville decided to make Lenox his summer home, it was most likely to ensure that his daughters would remain within easy reach of the steadying hand of their Grandma Winthrop. Kate Winthrop had joined the ranks of Lenox's fashionable summer colony around the time of Mary's death, finally abandoning the Long Branch section of Elberon on the New Jersey shore, where her father, Moses Taylor, had built her and her family a summer home next to his in 1879, but which had gradually become the "Jewish Newport."[3] The real Newport was no alternative for either Mrs. Robert Winthrop or her son Grenville: it was too showy, too social. Lenox itself, however, had not escaped the architectural excesses of the Gilded Age. As one writer put it, "The town was … an inland Newport where blue mountains were the equivalent of sand and rolling surf."[4] As in Newport, the rich competed in buying up the most magnificent view and building the most eye-catching dwelling. Among the ninety-three "cottages" that went up in Lenox and Stockbridge between 1880 and 1910, there was the immense crenelated and turreted hunting lodge Shadow Brook of Anson Phelps Stokes; the vast rambling Elm Court of Mr. and Mrs. William Douglas Sloane (she was Emily Thorn Vanderbilt); Giraud Foster's white-marbled Bellefontaine with its long elm-lined driveway; and the Italianate villa Wheatleigh, built by railroad magnate H. H. Cook for his daughter when she married the Spanish count Carlos de Heredia.[5] These mansions could breathe. Set amidst manicured gardens, they were protected from their nearest neighbors by acres of open country.

Grandma Winthrop did not indulge in the luxury of country squiredom. She was almost sixty when she moved to Lenox, and a house on a narrow wedge of land with neighbors close by suited her fine. True, she had the requisite view—a fine sweep across the Berkshire hills to Bald Head mountain (the peak of which Grenville would purchase later, to preserve the forests and scenery and eventually donate to the Audubon Society).[6] Her neighbors, particularly the extremely stuffy Lenox Club, were also all that she could have wanted. The "cottage" itself, however, almost lived up to its name: an ordinary-looking Victorian, painted yellow, with wrap-around veranda, gables, and wooden trim, reminiscent of the somewhat larger and much uglier Victorian house she had left behind in Elberon.

Grandma Winthrop was said to hate its name, Ethelwynde.[7] All Lenox estates seemed be proclaiming by their names that their owners had fled hot, crowded New York for a more rustic clime—with wind (Allen Winden, Windyside, Wyndhurst, Windermere, and Gusty Gables), and brooks (Shadow Brook, Brookhurst, Coldbrooke, Konkaput Brook, and Brookside), and trees (Elm Court, the Elms, Maplehurst, the Poplars, Pine Acres, Oakswood, Merrywood, Chesterwood,

Grandma Winthrop's cottage, Ethelwynde, in Lenox, one of the "wind" grouping of summer homes (Robert Winthrop Kean's Fourscore Years, *courtesy Hamilton Fish Kean II)*

THE STARTLING ELOPEMENT

Above: *Emily Winthrop, about 3*

Above center: *The Winthrop family in Lenox in the summer of 1903. From left: Melza Wood, Beekman Winthrop's fiancée; Grandma Winthrop; Emily Winthrop, 10; and Dorothy Winthrop.*

Above right: *Kate Winthrop, 4, in the summer of 1903 in Lenox*

Linwood and Highwood). Grenville was no more pleased with these whimsical names than his mother. Upon buying his own place in Lenox, about a mile down the road from hers, he changed its name from the Elms to Groton Place.[8]

Ethelwynde may have been unpretentious on the outside, but within certain standards had to be maintained. At Mrs. Winthrop's frequent dinner parties, the table had to be tastefully set and the dowager-hostess had to wear the understated diamond or sapphire. Burglary was always a risk—in 1893, a "gentleman burglar" had made the rounds of the cottages, allegedly inspiring one of his victims to ask politely, "Don't you think you might seek some other employment?"[9] Grandma Winthrop was no safer than anyone else. My mother remembered the night she was robbed: "Someone stole all Grandma Winthrop's jewelry right out of her upstairs safe while she was downstairs having a dinner party. We always suspected the personal maid. Who else would have known where the jewelry was? We always suspected her, because she was French."

The theft was serious enough to interest the local press, although Grenville, acting on his mother's behalf, did his best to keep the whole thing quiet, including the value of the pilfered loot. The local police were not alerted. Rather, Pinkerton detectives were called in from New York. It was a wasted effort, for the culprit was never found and the stolen goods, never recovered.

The cottagers became so apprehensive about theft that they even began counting the harvest of their gardens and greenhouses. The superintendent of Elm Court, the ample spread of multimillionairess Emily Thorn Vanderbilt White, for example, knew if even one peach had disappeared in the night.[10] Someone must have been keeping track at Grandma Winthrop's garden as well. My mother remembered that her grandmother "had a perfectly wonderful garden, perfectly wonderful hothouse—greenhouse—and she grew the most wonderful grapes and all kind of other

REARED *in a* GREENHOUSE

fruits. Sometimes they'd disappear, and then it was discovered that the neighborhood boys would come and take them." Years later, when my parents were dining at the Lenox Club near where her grandmother's house had stood (by then, it had been torn down and another built in its place), my mother remembered the tale of the fruit theft. Turning to the waiter, she asked him if he were one of the little boys who had stolen her grandmother's grapes. How she guessed, she never said, but surprisingly, he confessed he had been.

It was shortly after his mother had purchased Ethelwynde that Grenville Winthrop bought himself a place nearby and hired Julius Gayler, an architect who specialized in the country homes of the rich, to build him a fine new house. The result was big, certainly—the biggest of any of the Winthrop brothers' homes—but unlike most of the Berkshire cottages it does not call attention to itself; rather it stretches long and low, its native stone and cement face unrelieved by any ornament or variation in the pervasive gray tone.[11] It was durable, practical, and relatively maintenance-free—big enough for guests, with eleven bedrooms on the second floor and seven more (for servants) on the third—and equipped with all the necessities of the time, including two artesian wells, three coal-burning steam-heating units, a 350-gallon hot-water tank and a fireproof wall and battened doors to shut off the servant's wing.[12] It also had its vast front hall, a gloomy expanse running the width of the building, where the press would imagine "a lonely father strid[ing]."[13] The walls were paneled in dark oak and the flooring was cold and hard—a burnt-orange and black hexagonal Moravian tile, quite the thing in its day, now more admired for its indestructibility.

If the house itself lacked charm, the hundred-odd acres of grounds became a showplace of unusual beauty. Grenville Winthrop was an artist when it came to landscaping. He lavished years and spared no expense to compose a panorama that met his aesthetic standards. His lands were like a painting to him; he massed darker bushes and shrubs in green, open expanses (one story goes that he employed forty men to mow his lawns)[14] and accented the vistas with spreading trees. The scene was bereft of flower beds, however. Grenville Winthrop would have nothing to do with flowers, nor, curiously, would my mother in years to come. Their reasons may have

Grenville's house in Lenox (courtesy the Lenox Library Association, Lenox, Massachusetts)

been different—hers based on practical considerations and his on aesthetic—but the effect would be the same on their local garden clubs. My mother enjoyed telling of the ladies of a local garden club who came to view her planting at Black Brook Farm. Discovering nothing but a large and messy vegetable garden, they turned up their noses and left, never to return, much to my mother's delight. Grenville told a similar story about himself. After he had shown off his acres to a distinguished club visiting Lenox, one lady smilingly turned to him and asked, "And now, Mr. Winthrop, won't you show us your garden?"[15]

THE STARTLING ELOPEMENT

Top: *Grenville L. Winthrop, about 60 (courtesy Harvard University Art Museums)*

Above: *Edith Wharton at her desk in the library of her home, the Mount, in Lenox, Massachusetts, c. 1905 (courtesy Edith Wharton Restoration at the Mount, Lenox, Massachusetts)*

Grenville Winthrop and his two young girls made barely a ripple when they officially joined the Lenox summer colony in 1902. It was not that the other cottagers were not to Grenville's taste. Had he chosen to socialize, no doubt he would have. Many were urbane and cultured, and most had escaped being typecast as members of the Philistine Four Hundred[16] who, wrote one observer, "would have fled in a body from a poet, a painter, a musician, or a clever Frenchman."[17] Indeed, Lenox had clasped to its own bosom a writer, a sculptor, and a painter. Author Edith Wharton would become the most famous of them all, and at the turn of the century had already made a name for herself with *The Decoration of Houses*. Also in summer residence were sculptor Daniel Chester French, who would create the statue of Abraham Lincoln in the Lincoln Memorial; Frederic Crowninshield, painter of murals and watercolors, whose son, Frank C., would become the famed editor of *Vanity Fair* magazine; and the editors of *Century Magazine* Richard Watson Gilder and Robert Underwood Johnson. In addition, there were the collectors—Grenville Winthrop himself, Giraud Foster, and Robert Warden Paterson.

But Grenville didn't take to society. If his brother Fred was shy, Grenville was downright reclusive, a vegetarian who allowed himself to be served only from his own kitchen, a man so comfortable in his own surroundings that by midlife he would give up traveling, relying on others to scout out the art that he would collect.[18] According to an associate, his happiest moments were spent alone with his art collection in his New York house at 15 East 81st Street—moving "about the shadows, hanging his drawings or cataloguing them, or rearranging the Chinese jades and gilt bronzes."[19]

Edith Wharton knew enough about Grenville Winthrop to expect a soggy hour when he came to call one day in 1902. Though she had often had tea with his mother and counted his older cousin Egerton, Sr., among her most intimate friends, she considered Grenville "(with every virtue under heaven) a rather opaque body." What brought them together that day at her Lenox estate, the Mount, was Sally Norton. Sally was one of Edith Wharton's dearest friends, and Winthrop was bringing news of her father, his old fine-arts teacher, Charles Eliot Norton, after visiting him in his summer home in Ashfield, Massachusetts. Edith Wharton was pleasantly surprised by Grenville that day: "He said such … sympathetic things of his visit to Ashfield that I began to understand the juxtaposition [the friendship between him and the Nortons].… The fact is, I had thought him [as impenetrable].… But I daresay I did him an injustice. He had nice tastes, certainly … but he seems to me to want digging out and airing ."[20] Although Edith and Grenville would work together for the Lenox Library until she sold her Lenox house in 1912, the two would never grow closer. When in 1925 she referred to him in a letter, her comment was emphatic: "I never was intimate with Grenville—that very word is a contradiction!"[21]

The next generation of family found Grenville Winthrop equally difficult to penetrate. Dining with Uncle Gren, my mother wrote my father in 1936, meant "getting all dressed up and sitting stiffly all evening stifling yawns!!" Joan Appleton remembered a visit she, Fred, Jr., and Angela Winthrop had made to Groton Place sometime in the 1930s: "It was a terrible thing. We were hungry, but not until the clock rang the appointed hour could we go into dinner. Fred was falling asleep but we had to stay up until bedtime, no matter what."[22] Like his brother Fred, Sr., Grenville lived by the clock, the minute hand controlling him more than the needs and wishes of those around him.

Despite his reserve, and all the mischievous gossip about the elopement, Winthrop was in fact held in high esteem by the Lenox community. He was best known for his quiet devotion to the Lenox Library, a worthy institution with which he was associated for forty years and which he headed for twenty-eight. Supporting the local library had become a popular philanthropic activity at the turn of the century, sparked by steel magnate Andrew Carnegie, who was establishing libraries all over the country.[23] Grenville's sister Kitty Kean was engaged in organizing the local library in Elberon. In Lenox all the Winthrops, even Emily and Kate, made annual contributions to the library, and Grandma Winthrop gave flowers through the summer and established the children's room. Grenville also benefited the town through his large tax payments; though his house and estate were far from the most extravagant in town, he made Lenox his principal residence and paid among the highest taxes of any of the Lenox gentry.[24]

— • —

On June 7, 1925, less than nine months after the elopement, Grenville and his siblings had another shock. Kate Winthrop, their mother, died. For well over half a century—thirty-three years of marriage and another thirty-three of widowhood—Kate Winthrop had firmly held the reins, setting the standards and providing the funds for her growing family. At her death she left two daughters, three sons, eleven grandchildren, and three great-grandchildren. Only six, however, were surnamed Winthrop: her three sons, Grenville, Frederic, and Beek, and Frederic Winthrop's three sons, Robert, Fred, and Nat.

Robert Winthrop as he looks both in our only existing photos of him and in his official portrait at Wood, Struthers and Winthrop. Not surprisingly, my mother always thought of him as old.

The Grandma Winthrop of my mother's stories is a stiff and corseted Victorian figure—prematurely elderly at thirty-five, seated by the fire in a lace cap. Grandpa Winthrop, even dimmer in memory, seems even older, portly, with a cane.[25] When asked whether her father and brothers had inherited their skills on the playing field from Kate and Robert Winthrop, my mother would laugh: "I'm *sure* Grandpa Winthrop never played sports and I'm sure my grandmother never did." My mother would often compare her two grandmothers, the one "very stern and severe," the other, "very sympathetic, a wonderful listener." Both were towering figures in her life. But whereas Grandma Winthrop used her authority to fashion the world as she wanted it, Grandma Amory directed hers to understanding the world as it was and leaving it to others to design their futures from there.

DOROTHY'S TWO GRANDMOTHERS

At left, *Grandma Amory by the steps of her house at 278 Beacon Street in Boston, in the spring of 1922;
she would turn 80 in June.* At right, *Grandma Winthrop in Lenox in her 86th year, July 24, 1924.*

Grandma Winthrop's household had starched footmen and "flourishing" maids,
for, as Dorothy would write in her 1924 diary, "She is a dear, fine old lady, but she
takes her housekeeping hard, which is too bad." Grandma Amory cared little for formal spit and polish, being more concerned about the well-being of her servants. My
mother told the story of one of Grandma Amory's maids, an immigrant girl called
Mamie Prendergast: "No one liked her at all. She was Irish, she was eighteen years
old. She went straight to my grandmother's from off the boat. She was very unsure
of herself, but my grandmother brought her along. She'd say, 'You can't tell whether
you can do that until you try.' And pretty soon Mamie Prendergast got confidence in
herself and became quite proficient."

My mother's memories played up Grandma Winthrop's imperious ways. But she
always added that her grandmother was "sweet," "kind." Certainly the few letters
she kept from her New York grandmother were loving and supportive.[26] Grandma
Winthrop took pains to sing the praises of the other grandma. "I almost wish I was
a little girl and could be with [Grandma Amory] … as you are," she wrote to eleven-
year-old Dorothy. A few years later: "It will be nice to be with Grandma Amory—
she is one of the best grandmothers I have ever known." When Dorothy was sixteen,
Grandma Winthrop wrote her saying how much her father adored her: "He is cer-

REARED *in a* GREENHOUSE

tainly the best father and his love and devotion to you is very lovely and beautiful." And she added her own affection: "I often and often wish you were here with me dear Dorothy, for I love you very, very much."

Dorothy saw Grandma Winthrop at Uncle Beek and Aunt Melza's house in Old Westbury in June of 1924, during the visit when she had railed in her diary at Kate and Emily's neglect of their grandmother. Grandma Winthrop had come into Dorothy's room for a chat. She spoke of Dorothy's mother, evoking again the vision of earthly perfection:

> She came nearer to being perfect than anyone I ever knew and I don't know of a single fault she had, unless it was that she was too good. She was full of life, too, not one of those mushy good people who never do anything.... Yes, she was too good for this world. She's better off where she is now, wherever it is, better off and happier.

Grandma Winthrop's eighty-sixth birthday, February 4, 1925, was once again a command appearance for the family, and Dorothy, her father, and stepmother all trooped to New York to honor her. Grandma Winthrop wrote Dorothy's place card—"Miss Winthrop"—in her own hand. The only report of illness that winter was of Dorothy's father, who was feeling "wretchedly" at the birthday celebration, who remained bedridden in New York after Dorothy and her stepmother returned home, and to whose side they returned in haste when Uncle Gren called to say that Fred was "much worse" and would have to have an operation. Dorothy stayed with her stepmother throughout. It was an ordeal for Sally, particularly one evening when their route home from the hospital seemed to pass nothing but "an undertaker's shop or a church bearing an undertaker's advertisement." Dorothy doubted her presence did any good. But according to her father, who, as it turned out, suddenly rallied, Sally later said that Dorothy was "the greatest comfort and help" and that whoever married her "would get a star." The old refrain followed: "I was very pleased when he told me, though I don't think I deserved it."

On May 24, Grandma Winthrop was at her writing desk composing a letter to Dorothy and showing her old pique at anything that wasn't quite up to snuff: "If you could see 37th Street now, you will think it deplorable—the street is closed and torn up waiting for a new pavement to be put down—nothing, no vehicle, can enter and in this way it is quiet but so terribly dirty." The letter contains no hint of how little time remained to her. Rather, Grandma Amory's health was the issue. "I hope your Grandmother is better," she wrote. "I have never known a finer person—I know you love her and it has always made me so happy."

The next day, May 25, Grandma Winthrop's granddaughter, Kate Winthrop Morse, gave birth

Place card written for her granddaughter Dorothy Winthrop by Kate W. Winthrop for her 86th birthday dinner, her last

THE STARTLING ELOPEMENT

Emily Winthrop Miles, a woman of many artistic talents. Place and year of exhibition not identified.

to a son, Thomas. He was a great-grandson Grandma Winthrop would never see, for on June 7, 1925, she died.

Edith Wharton, sixty-three and living in Paris and southern France, would remember Kate Winthrop, with whom she'd gossiped and sipped tea in New York and shared tasks in the Lenox Library. A generation older and far more caustic than Dorothy, the author had never held Kate Winthrop in the same kind of awe. "I laughed 'fit to bust' at your handing [*Ethan Frome*] to dear sweet Mrs. Winthrop!" she'd once written her sister-in-law Mary Cadwalader Jones. "What a bewildered hour she must have had, digesting him." When she learned of Kate Winthrop's death, she wrote of her again to Mary Jones, recalling that though she'd been "on very friendly terms with her," she hadn't "heard from her for years." It was not as a grand doyenne that she finally remembered Kate Winthrop: "She was a kindly and pathetic old lady, so helplessly crushed under her wealth."[27]

Perhaps Kate Winthrop was crushed, not only by the money she had inherited from her father but also by the name she had taken from her husband. In her will, trying to balance the desire to provide for all her children and the pressure to preserve the Winthrop name, she created the Male Winthrop Issue (MWI), still a sore subject today, more than half a century later. On the one hand, she divided the bulk of her estate equally between her sons and daughters. On the other, there was the question of the money that would have been left to Dudley, had he outlived her. It was bad enough, say the women, that Dudley himself left the plantation to his only brother who had sons—Fred (who would follow suit into the next generation). It was worse still when Grenville, Fred, and Beekman convinced their mother to leave the one-sixth of her money that would have been Dudley's share only to "grandsons and great-grandsons being persons bearing the family name of Winthrop."[28] Thus were Winthrop women excluded from a nest egg that continues to grow to this day—though it was brought to the family by a non-Winthrop and a mere woman at that.

As for Kate and Emily who, in her view, had sullied the name Winthrop by their unspeakable choices of mate, Kate Winthrop had taken immediate action. On October 8, 1924, two weeks after their elopements, she disinherited them.[29]

— • —

The press picked up the story of Kate and Emily during the summer of Grandma Winthrop's death when Kate returned to Lenox from Santa Barbara with her husband and her two-month-old son, Thomas Spurr Morse. They were staying at her

REARED *in a* GREENHOUSE

mother-in-law's, according to a news clipping, for though her father had written to her offering his forgiveness, he had made it equally clear that he would not welcome her husband. Such an offer, in Kate's view, would never do: "Scorning her father's offer of reconciliation until such time as he accepts his former poultryman as her husband, Mrs. Darwin S. Morse … will not step one foot inside the palatial 'Groton Place.' " Press interest had petered out by September, with a final story of her purchase of a forty-acre farm in Richmond, near Lenox, and its 150-year-old house.

In the summer of 1926 Dorothy received a letter from her father, who was visiting Uncle Gren in Lenox: "I felt so sorry for Uncle Gren, alone in his large and beautiful house. He has had a sad life, poor fellow, and he has always been so good, kind, and considerate and unselfish." Four years later, in 1930, she and her father took "a long, wet drive" to Lenox. By then Emily had left her chauffeur-husband. Dorothy wrote in her diary: "My long lost cousin Emily comes to call and how happy, how truly happy, I am to see her after all these years. She looks as young and as lovely as ever.… I could say a heartful to her. Poor Emily."

It is not surprising, perhaps, that Kate's marriage remained intact while Emily's did not. Emily's marriage might have been triggered by Kate's, who was really in love with Darwin and who confided in her sister that she planned to elope. Rather than remain behind with her forbidding father, Emily may have decided to come along, settling on the only man at hand.[30] It is not certain that Emily even consummated her marriage. As it turned out, she was to live a full life as a single woman. She became

a collector of some note, bringing together several unique collections including six hundred pieces of American glass, now owned by the Metropolitan Museum of Art, and an extensive collection of Wedgwood, Meissen, and Staffordshire china, much of which is at the Brooklyn Museum along with some of her Audubon, Gould, and Elliott prints.[31] More creative than her father, Emily also received recognition as a sculptor, artist, and poet, with shows in many New York galleries.[32]

Kate had a long and happy life with Darwin, who became a pillar of the Richmond community. Uncle Gren finally agreed to see her sons, Tom and Robert, so long as he did not have to see the father. In 1932 Kate and the boys—five and seven years old—went to call on her father and had such a fine visit that they were invited back again. On the way to this second visit, however, they had an automobile accident and one of the boys had to be rushed to the hospital. This was Kate's last attempt to visit the old man. Neither she nor the boys ever saw him again.

Bob and Tom Morse, 2 and 4 years old, sons of Kate and Darwin Morse, in 1929. Three years later, they were taken by their mother for their first and only visit to their Winthrop grandfather. (Courtesy Thomas S. Morse)

THE STARTLING ELOPEMENT

Rumors flew for years that Grenville had disinherited one or the other of his daughters. The true story is far stranger. On the face of it, his daughters were included in his will. The second clause reads, under a trust set up on May 29, 1893: "I give ... all property over which I have the power of appointment ... IN TRUST ... to divide ... into two equal shares ... to my daughter Emily ... and Kate," and in the case of Kate's death, to her children.[33] But according to grandson Thomas S. Morse, though Grenville had set up this trust for his daughters, he had never funded it. Rather, his will explicitly states that he made "no further provision for my daughters as they have been otherwise adequately provided for" (referring to the money left to them by their mother).[34] Instead, the bulk of his estate was disposed of in keeping with the MWI tradition established under his mother's will and carried on by Beekman. (On his death in 1940, Beek had left his estate to his brother Gren.) Being the last male Winthrop of his generation, Grenville passed the financial torch to the only males with the surname Winthrop of the next generation, his brother Fred's three sons. He left the infamous Uncle Dudley's sixth of Kate Winthrop's money equally to the three boys and the income from money bequeathed him by his mother and Beekman to his nephew Robert alone.[35]

During the 1930s Grenville Winthrop opened up a bit with his new niece-in-law, Angela Winthrop, about why he had been so stern with his motherless daughters. He brought the subject up during a visit Angela made while in New York for an operation on Fred's ear. The house itself she remembered as forbidding—all very dark, with red cords over some of the chairs so one couldn't sit in them, and glass cabinets all about with jades: "He was very friendly and nice," she recalled, but "a little pathetic." He volunteered that he had consulted a physician on how to bring up his daughters. "Keep them very quiet," the doctor had urged. "No excitement. And put them on a special diet. If you do this, perhaps they can avoid the same problems their mother had."[36] He was referring to their mother's death, of course, which everyone thought reflected emotional instability of some sort.

— • —

At age seventy-seven Grenville began to fail. He spent from January to March 1941 hospitalized and opened his Lenox house late that summer, not arriving until July 12. When his closest collaborator, Paul Sachs, tried to tempt him with a $3,000 bronze, he demurred, saying that he "must pull in my horns" and make no more purchases until he could settle his bills due to his recent illness.[37] The following spring, a delegation of his Winthrop nieces and nephews and their spouses came to 15 East 81st Street for what must have been a family farewell. He noted them all in his meticulously kept record of visitors: on April 24, 1942, Mr. and Mrs. Standish Bradford, Mr. and Mrs. Fred Winthrop, Mr. and Mrs. Nathaniel Winthrop, and Miss Katharine Winthrop.[38] The last family member to see Uncle Gren before he died was Nat Winthrop. It was January 18, 1943, and Nat, a naval officer, had stopped by his uncle's New York home for a visit. He was by then an old man of seventy-nine, suffering from nephritis. Nat remembered that the two had a wonderful long chat that evening. The next day, January 19, 1943, Grenville Winthrop was dead.[39]

One Friday evening, three or four years after Uncle Gren's death, I was with my mother in the great shed at Tanglewood where she had taken me to attend a weekend of Boston Symphony Orchestra concerts. The immense shell was filled, crowds of casually dressed music lovers mixing with the more formally attired gentry of Lenox and the neighboring towns. Suddenly a woman dressed rather like my mother, in sensible shoes and a button-down shirtwaist dress, came into view. "Kate," exclaimed my mother, in amazement. "Dorothy," replied the woman, equally astonished. And indeed it was Kate Morse, the runaway daughter, now a middle-aged matron living happily with her husband, Darwin Spurr Morse, on the farm in Richmond she had bought twenty years earlier, not far from the grand residence where she had grown up. Kate invited us back to her farm to meet her family. They had two fine young sons, and although no doubt her neighbors remembered the scandalous elopement, the years had long since wiped away any stigma that might have once been attached to this marriage.

Kate Morse, c. 1940 (courtesy Thomas S. Morse)

Nearly forty years later, in the early 1980s, the third Frederic Winthrop, son of my mother's brother Freddy, was in Stockbridge where his job as Massachusetts commissioner of agriculture had taken him to present a series of awards. Among the recipients was one Thomas Spurr Morse. "Thank you, cousin," said Tom Morse, as he came to the dais and accepted his award. Like all of his generation, Freddy had grown up on the legend of the elopement of Uncle Gren's daughters. Young Tom, however, had spent most of his adult life as a pediatric surgeon in Columbus, Ohio, and Freddy had no inkling who this cousin might be. Of course it was Tom Morse, the baby who had been brought back east from Santa Barbara, Uncle Gren's grandson, and Freddy's second cousin. Tom invited Freddy to come home to meet his wife Patricia and their four children. Tom had left medicine to enter the farrier, or blacksmith supply, business, and thus shared with Freddy a great love of farming and animals. They became good friends.

In Lenox today, if you mention Grenville Winthrop's name, someone will remember. The elopement itself has become a delectable morsel of Lenox lore—in the same category as the marriage of a son of Anson Phelps Stokes to a Socialist Jew or the entry in the *Social Register* of a "Miss Rosie Morris, the dog of a Mrs. Morris née Frelinghuysen"[40]—reminders all of those Gilded Age days when the barons of

THE STARTLING ELOPEMENT

summer still lived in their palaces and the year-round residents had jobs as their butlers, gardeners, chauffeurs, and maids. Over the forty-one years that Grenville Winthrop was a Lenox summer resident, however, the fabulous wealth that had allowed the summer cottagers their Edwardian excesses gradually lost its buying power. The income tax and the Great Depression made deep dents; World War II would mark the end of the era of the Berkshire cottages.

When Grenville died his precious art collection was sorted, catalogued, and, in accordance with his will, sent to the Fogg Art Museum at Harvard. Meanwhile, Groton Place was turned over to the Berkshire real estate company of Wheeler and Taylor to sell. Today, during the summer, if you drive past the Lenox Library and the Curtis Hotel and proceed down West Street to number 45, you will see a small sign that reads Boston University Tanglewood Institute. Turn left into the drive and you will see the sweeping lawns and trees and at the end of the drive, Grenville Winthrop's "palace"—still gray and unbending, with a small plaque over the massive front door reading "Groton Place." Inside are the high-school-age BU music students, and administration: forty in a house which, for its first two decades, held, in addition to staff, only three—Grenville and his daughters—and then for its second two decades, but one, Grenville himself. If you roam the grounds, you may discover weed-clogged fountains at the end of what were once long, sweeping vistas. Or you may descend a steep hill to the side of the house and come upon the chicken house, where once, it was said, Winthrop discovered his daughter Kate in the arms of his chicken man. This white two-story building, with pillars on its front porch, housed Winthrop's five hundred fowl, the golden pheasants and the chickens that Dorothy saw so many years ago. Now, if it is summer, you may hear as you walk by, a violin, or a flute, or a horn—the sounds of music students practicing where hens once clucked and roosters crowed.

— • —

Not until Winthrop Day, May 20, 1989, at the Fogg Museum of Harvard in Cambridge did the Winthrop family at large have a chance to get acquainted with the family of Kate Winthrop Morse. This was a day dedicated to celebrating the Grenville L. Winthrop Collection. About fifty Winthrops gathered that hot and sunny May day. Then director of the Harvard University Art Museums Edgar Peters Bowron spoke with the greatest respect and admiration for Grenville Winthrop's enormous talent as a collector of art. It was an education for the Winthrops gathered there. In his own generation Grenville was the odd man out, immersed in a field that left the rest cold. My mother barely spoke to us of his collection, telling us offhandedly, "It's up there at the Fogg." The art world at large was equally unaware of it. Quietly, unobtrusively, he had amassed some four thousand works ranging from Near Eastern and Asian jade and ritual bronzes to English and American painting and watercolors to the decorative arts. The collection was planned specifically so that

Harvard students could have an overview of the world's great art. In its entirety it represents the most important such bequest ever to an American university.[41] Peter Bowron opened his introductory talk at Winthrop Day on this subject, ranking the collection among the finest in the country, along with those of John D. Rockefeller, Henry Clay Frick, Isabella Stewart Gardner, William and Henry Walters, and J. Pierpont Morgan.

There are several reasons for the collection's relative obscurity. Grenville Winthrop's shyness contributed, certainly. So too did his enormous care in ensuring that the works remain undamaged—in the agreement with Harvard, he stipulated that none of the works be loaned. The timing of his death, in the middle of World War II, was another factor. Plans for a separate wing for the collection had to be shelved. Indeed, it was a major effort for the museum even to bring the collection from New York City to Cambridge. Eighteen trucks were needed, special arrangements had to be made to obtain rationed gasoline for the convoy, and when it arrived most of the curatorial staff who would have been responsible for its care were scattered around the world in the armed forces.

My mother ended up with one painting—her uncle's only flagrant fake. Painted in the style of an old Master from the Lowlands, it was a portrait of a bearded gentleman with a great seventeenth-century ruff who bore a curious resemblance to Grenville Winthrop. In fact, Grenville had had his portrait painted this way by Rougeron, the famous restorer, to spoof the Harvard Museum Course students who would come to his house in New York to view his collection. "And what do you think of that?" he would query if the students paused before it. Then he'd stand aside, chuckling to himself, as they puzzled—perhaps weighing manners against erudition—over what to say.[42]

Grenville L. Winthrop, done in the style of a Dutch master by restorer Rougeron — a friendly trap for Harvard art students. The Winthrop crest in the upper left-hand corner would have been a dead giveaway for those in the know about Winthropiana. (Courtesy John Winthrop)

— • —

In February 1925, Dorothy Winthrop was taking an art class in Boston and had just been escorted through the Metropolitan Museum of Art by her Uncle Gren. Her diary entry shows she is well aware of the extent of his collection—she mentions the Bellini, the Botticelli, the Corots, the Davids—but questions its value: "Poor, poor Uncle Gren. What's a collection compared to the love of two daughters?"

THE STARTLING ELOPEMENT

Among the hundreds of letters saved by my mother, only two or three remain from her Uncle Gren. One was written on Christmas Day, 1930, and shows unexpected wit and gallantry. Dorothy apparently had sent him some small gift, for which he thanked her thus:

DEAR ATTRACTIVE TALENTED LITTLE NIECE:

Thanks, many thanks for the "Egyptian Jade, genuine and very beautiful" that you sent me for my collection.

It makes the other stones look shoddy, which demonstrates how important it is always to acquire the best and only the best.

The spirit of contented conjugal happiness with which the artist has imbued the hard stone could not fail to have a good influence upon the young people of today if only they would stop, look and listen before tobogganing to the divorce courts.

I have sent your card to Emily. Your sending that card was only one of your many thoughtful kindnesses.

Affectionately
GLW

Pilgrims and Puritans

chapter FOURTEEN

Standish Bradford, probably mid-1920s

The year 1927 held many a turning point for Dorothy's nearest and dearest. Emily Lodge's first son, Cabot, was born. Nancy Murray married the brilliant and handsome Shakespeare scholar Ted Spencer and on October 17, brother Robert, then at Harvard Business School, informed his sister of his engagement to Theo Ayer, daughter of the Winthrops' Hamilton neighbor Charles Fanning Ayer. "My darling Robert," wrote Dorothy in her diary. "Whatever I want to say would seem so banal and so, so inadequate. But I feel deeply and much tonight."

The year might also have ushered in a new life for Dorothy, for the Standish Bradford who had earned only passing mention at her coming-out party a few years earlier had asked for her hand in marriage. Exactly when, we don't know. Years later my mother would tell us that he had proposed at tea. Her diaries mention two occasions on which he indeed came to tea.[1] But nothing is recorded of anything momentous happening over the teacups either time.

As Standish became a keener interest of Dorothy's, he also became a sharper thorn in her father's side. For four painful years Fred Winthrop would bitterly oppose Dorothy's growing attachment, fighting to head off his daughter's marriage with every ruse he could imagine. Three times he would spirit her off to Europe, make her promise to wait, forbid her to see her suitor, and even threaten disinheritance.

Why was this descendent of the *Mayflower* so unsuitable in the eyes of this scion of the *Arbella*? One could cite certain social breaches. Standish had gone to Groton, whereas Robert and Fred were at St. Mark's. He had been on the Harvard football team, whereas the Winthrop brothers had gone out for the more gentlemanly crew. But these were the rivalries that bound the upper crust. And like Robert and Fred, Standish had also rowed. Better still, he too had been accepted in the Porcellian Club. And the three attended all the same parties, with Standish likely accumulating even more invitations than "girl crazy" Robert who, with his early marriage, would be bumped from the circle of established eligibles.[2]

Olga Gardner Monks as a young woman (portrait painted in 1888 by Dennis Miller Bunker, courtesy Museum of Fine Arts, Boston)

What really mattered, however, was whether the parents knew each other, and in this case they certainly did not. Standish's father, Harold Standish Bradford, came from a comfortable Boston family. But his marriage in 1899 to Mary McCullagh, whose family came from Bray, Ireland, south of Dublin, took place far afield, in East Orange, New Jersey. The local press had described the event as "a brilliant and fashionable wedding." What's more, best man Dr. George H. Monks, the groom's uncle, was married to a cousin of Dorothy's, the former Olga Eliza Gardner, who would become Isabella Stewart Gardner's favorite niece—and "Aunt" Olga Monks to my parents and us.[3] But the Monkses and the Bradfords were no blood relatives of the Gardners. Rather, their common kin, George's father and Harold Standish's maternal grandfather, was John Patrick Monks, a Protestant born in Dublin, son of a roadside innkeeper, who emigrated to Boston in 1830 and fathered eight children. Monks would become a successful lumber and real estate businessman.[4] But in terms of Dorothy and Standish's sharing a relative, the tie was simply that Standish's great uncle George Monks had married Dorothy's second cousin once removed, Olga Gardner. (Refer to Chart 15.)

After their marriage, Standish's parents had settled in his mother's home town of East Orange while Harold Standish Bradford pursued a short-lived career in an uncle's office on Wall Street. By the time Standish was of grammar school age, they

Below, from left to right: John Patrick Monks, Standish's great-grandfather (G. Gardner Monks's Beginnings, courtesy Robert A. G. Monks); Horace Standish Bradford, Standish's grandfather; Harold Standish Bradford, Standish's father, in 1925; Mary McCullagh, Standish's mother, undated

Right: *Mary and Harold Standish Bradford, Standish's parents, c. 1908*

Far right: *Standish* (center) *with brother Tom and sister Barbara*

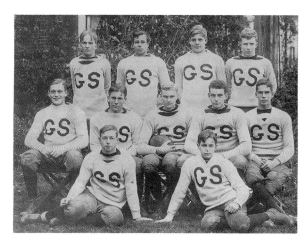

Right: *Standish, undated*

Far right: *Standish Bradford* (middle row, center), *captain of Groton School football team, c. 1920*

had moved back to the Boston area. They first settled in Concord, where his father tried seriously but none too successfully to farm. They then moved to Brookline and he opened a print store on Boston's Newbury Street, again a lackluster enterprise.[5] This choice of vocation met with little favor in Winthrop eyes, Fred disapproving of Standish because his father was "in trade."[6] Even his best man's son (Gardner Monks, son of Dr. George Monks) thought Harold Standish "a bit stuffy and rather narrow minded."[7]

Still, you couldn't deny that the name Standish Bradford had a certain ring, one to quicken the pulse of American history buffs. Not only was he an eleventh-generation descendant of Governor William Bradford, but the Standish signaled direct descent from Myles (or Miles) Standish through Mary Churchill Standish, who had married Standish's great-great-grandfather Zabdiah Bradford. Even though Myles Standish had been no Pilgrim—indeed, he was a Roman Catholic—the Bradfords

REARED *in a* GREENHOUSE

took a liking to his name. Zabdiah's son, also Zabdiah, called his first son Horace Standish Bradford and Horace Standish named his two sons Albert Standish and Harold Standish.[8] When Harold Standish Bradford had a son, however, he dispensed with the Albert, Horace, and Harold, keeping only the Standish. And that was how Standish Bradford came by his name.

For Frederic Winthrop the historian, however, the link with William Bradford may have been more a minus than a plus. The Puritans, led by Governor John Winthrop, represented the proud rich; the Pilgrims, led by soon-to-be Governor William Bradford, the humble poor. No matter that the *Mayflower* had beat the *Arbella* here by ten years, arriving in 1620. Governor Winthrop had inspired his followers with a grand vision; they were to found a "City upon a Hill," a model community that would serve as an example to the godless English they had left behind. William Bradford had no such pretensions; his was just "a small, humble, and harmless band who wished to retreat to a remote corner where they could set up a true church undisturbed." By 1691, perhaps predictably, Bradford's Plymouth Colony and its modest ways had been swallowed up by Winthrop's more powerful Massachusetts Bay Colony.[9] Plymouth Colony would remain forever in the shadow. As recently as 1968, when the Massachusetts Historical Society was spotlighting its collection of the "ancient and honorable body of papers" from the Winthrop family, and particularly the "crown jewel," Governor John Winthrop's *MS History of New England*, the speaker allowed as how "only the Bradford account of Plymouth can compare with it [the Winthrop ms.]." This was an acknowledgment quickly qualified, for he added parenthetically, "if, that is, Plymouth can ever be compared to Boston."[10]

By Winthrop standards, Bradfords had done little to stoke the fires of family fame over the generations. Bradfords were churchmen and military men, judges and a prison warden, farmers and an East India trader. "It is not a striking family," Gamaliel Bradford (one of six Bradfords by that name) had written. Not to worry, thought Edward Bradford, for few American families, excepting the Adamses, had more than one very illustrious member to be proud of anyway. Standish, who quoted Gamaliel and Edward in a short sketch of various family members he wrote, thought that some Bradfords deserved to be thought of, if not important the way the Winthrops thought they were (or the way the Adamses *really* were), at least as "notable." One of many William Bradfords had taken a single silver dollar and an axe to Maine, cleared land, built a cabin, planted corn, and founded the town of Turner. A Bradford daughter, Deborah Sampson Gannett, "to

Governor John Winthrop of Massachusetts Bay Colony, 1588-1649, represented the proud rich, whereas Standish's ancestor, Governor William Bradford, represented the humble poor. (Courtesy Harvard University Portrait Collection, gift of Adam Winthrop, 1840)

escape the daily chores and the mute attentions of a country churl," enlisted in the Revolutionary War under the name of Robert Schurtleff, dressed a bullet wound she received in battle rather than reveal her sex to a doctor, and upon settling down after the war as a "most domestic wife," drew a pension as an invalid soldier for the rest of her life. Another William became one of the first two senators from Rhode Island but grew tired of Washington and retired from his post.[11] And Bradford memory continues to revere the first William Bradford, governor for thirty-six years of struggling little Plymouth Colony. As author Bradford Smith, who was raised on his ancestor, wrote in the prologue to his *Bradford of Plymouth*: "In Bradford, we watch the making of one of the first great Americans.... Winthrop and the Boston leaders tried to reestablish place and privilege as they had known them in England. But Bradford groped toward the new world where all men, or at least all believers, might be free."[12]

— • —

Dorothy and Standish's relationship began innocently enough, probably shortly before Dorothy's coming-out party. A cryptic four-word diary entry—"3 years ago today!"—dated October 6, 1926, hints at the date they met. On January 11, 1924, her list of guests at the Junior Supper Dance mentions him: "Standish Bradford—Pork

In June 1930, the Frederic Winthrops would participate in a day of festivities celebrating the 300th anniversary of the landing of the Arbella. *A replica of the ship, on wheels, was "one of the many curious and interesting floats in the historical procession" (*Herald Tribune — Acme*). Frederic Winthrop played the role of Governor Winthrop and son Nat was one of the colonists. The "pleaſure" of the company of Miss Dorothy Winthrop was "requeſt[ed]" by Mr. and Mrs. William Crowninshield Endicott at a luncheon honoring the "anniversary of the Landing of Governor John Winthrop from the ship* Arbella, *at Salem and his Welcome by Governor John Endecott June 12th, 1630, O.S. [at] The Farm, Danvers, Maſſachuſetts."*

REARED *in a* GREENHOUSE

[Porcellian Club], tall, blond sen." Not exactly compelling, but surely better than the description of one of the other men present: "Colney (?)—short." Something magic must have happened late in the fall of 1924, at least if one wishes to romanticize a stray bit of paper Dorothy stored in an envelope. It contained some lugubrious lines from Matthew Arnold, beginning, "Coldly, sadly descends/ The autumn evening; the field/ Of withered leaves, and the elms/ Fade into dimness apace" and ending, still downcast, "I stand in the Autumn evening./ And think of bygone autumns with thee." Below was Dorothy's startling reaction to this melancholy dirge: "These lines make me think of the happiest month in all the year and of the happiest time in my life—November 1924."

In 1926 Dorothy and Standish were getting together once every month or two. They had lunch several times, once with Grandma Amory and another time with brother Fred and Aunt Clara. There were a couple of canoeing trips, one of which was followed by a climb to the top of Turner Hill. Turner Hill, the crowning glory of the estate of the Winthrops' neighbors, the C. G. Rices, offered bridle paths for riders, strolls for couples, and views for anyone in love with the rolling New England countryside. The wind was blowing when they reached the top that day in early May and Dorothy leaned her head against Standish's shoulder. They had already sat and talked a long time by the river bank. Then they rose, she leaned her head against his wet shoulder, and they trudged along that way, "very close together."[13] For Dorothy, the day brought out a surprising confession in her usually restrained journal: "Had a long talk with R. till 11:30. What shall I do? Turmoil of mind."

Later in the summer they met again, this time on the shores of Lake Tahoe. Dorothy was on her trip out West and was obviously pleased—and surprised—to come upon Standish Bradford in the hotel where they were staying. In the first extended mention of him since the wedding of Anna Agassiz and Gordon Prince, her diary contains this entry:

> Tahoe Tavern is quite a large hotel and who should we see as we entered the hall but Standish Bradford. He is tutoring here and was at the hotel with his charge Peter McBean after playing in a tennis tournament.
>
> After lunch Standish and I mounted two funny old nags and rode up to the top of a ridge behind the McBean place from where we had an extensive view of the lake, blue and green in the sun.
>
> Standish came to the Tavern and we walked out onto the end of a rotting old pier where we sat watching the pink haze of twilight on the hills and the pale green of the horizon deepening over head.
>
> … Standish, Bob, Olivia, Anne and Bill Howard all dined with us and soon after we globe trotters boarded the train for San Francisco.

Dorothy and Standish sometimes went canoeing on the Ipswich River.

· 239 ·

Dorothy (at left) *and Standish on their "two funny old nags" at Lake Tahoe, July 24, 1926*

Below: Fred Winthrop scornfully dismissed the notion that Standish Bradford should marry his daughter Dorothy: "He has nothing to offer except his sweet self.... He does not even earn as much as I pay my butler. He is irresponsible and dishonorable."

Below right: Dorothy Winthrop, painted in 1927 by Hermann Hanatscheck (courtesy Katharine Bradford, photographed by Philip Reeser)

When he received a letter from Dorothy written in Victoria, British Columbia, Standish was elated:

Wednesday, Aug 18th is a day I won't forget for ever so long.... You see I'd begun to think you weren't going to write.... You must know my feeling of jubilation when on the 18th Mrs. McBean walked into my room with two letters—one postmarked Victoria and the other saying I'd passed all my [law school] exams ... 10 more months and I'll be through studies for good and starting to work.

It was a great pleasure to me to have you come to Tahoe and see what a lovely place it is. To have beautiful things in common with someone is one of the pleasantest experiences of life.

As the relationship gathered steam during 1926 and into the winter of 1926–27, he began to write her chatty letters, in one congratulating her for her appointment as director of the SPCC ("I had no idea that the S.P.C.C. performed such a service or that there was so much need for it"). He must have come to dine with the family, for she recollected one Sunday dinner during which they had joked about a tour he would make of the United States to deliver a speech on the evils of divorce.

By early 1927 Frederic Winthrop was making his opposition plain. Over the next four years Dorothy kept a running commentary on her feelings about her father's negative views. In one set of notes, headed "1927–1931—F. W.," she assumes her father's voice:

I [Frederic] always made it very plain to him [Standish] that he was not welcome in my house. I was polite, but cold, to him and always especially cordial to the other guests so he would realize he was not welcome. I made it very plain.

Who does he think he is asking *you* to marry him? He has nothing to offer except his sweet self. What are his prospects? He does not even earn as much as I pay my butler. He is irresponsible and dishonorable.

You will never be happy married to him. I know what is for your happiness far better than you do; and I know you would not be happy.

Her father's animosity must have played a part in keeping Dorothy's emotions at bay. During 1927 she kept her suitor at a respectful distance.[14] At times she said they should not see each other; at others, she relented. Standish took each rejection manfully and he greeted every encouragement with elation. On February 19, 1927, after one rebuff, he wrote her:

I haven't much to say except I hope you change your mind; and that I don't want to lose your friendship for anything. I can't see any good reason why we shouldn't see each other, unless it makes people gossip.... Till then, I want awfully to see you sometimes, for I'm sure my feelings for you won't change. With my love, Standish

During these winter months, full of indecision, she turned to Robert for advice. In a letter dated March 6, 1927, he wrote of his high regard for her suitor—up to a point:

I think Bradford is an exceptionally fine fellow. He has no end of moral and physical courage, and although he does not impress one the first time they meet that he has brains, I am sure that he has an excellent mind. He is very ambitious and conscientious and I am sure will get a very long way.... I know nothing about his family except that they are Christian Scientist and have hardly a cent of money.... I have always heard that [the family] have good blood.

In March began Dorothy's first long trip to Europe alone with her father. Though it was not officially billed as a "forget Standish" trip, Frederic Winthrop's three months with his daughter seemed to have had that effect. On the eve of their departure, Standish thought the relationship had veered back on track, writing Dorothy on March 25, as she and her father set sail on the *Cleveland*:

Dorothy, the European traveler, spring of 1927

You don't know how I enjoyed last Friday with you, I rank it with that day last May that we canoed down the Ipswich river.... I love being with you and I shall miss seeing you awfully. It's probably just as well for me that I'm not to see you, for you take my mind off my work.... Last Friday evening, for example, I sat in my room and imagined all kinds of nice things about ourselves and never did a stroke of work.

But his elation was short-lived. She wrote him very little, and when she did the message must have been that marriage was out of the question and that therefore, for his sake, perhaps they should not see each other anymore. His response was startled but gentlemanly:

I did not feel that you could know you would never want to marry me or I would have taken special care that you should never have felt called on to write as you did. As to your suggestion that we should not see each other, that is up to you....

Writing back on June 10 to explain herself further, Dorothy compounded the confusion.

> Though I can never feel toward you the way you want me to, neither can I ever cease to consider you one of the best and truest of friends. I am glad you see no reason why we should not continue seeing each other as before, because, as long as you understand my position, neither do I see any reason and I should miss seeing you more than I can say. Sometimes, life seems very difficult, Standish, but you are about the most understanding person in the world.

In Europe her father appeared to have won her away from her unacceptable suitor. He was a wise and well-informed guide, and when he imbibed the local beverages too enthusiastically she found it amusing. In Munich, where he had approved of the beer as much as the city and its people, she joked that this was *very* high praise. And in Rothenburg, when he'd enjoyed his wine so much that he had barely noticed the original Dürer on the walls, she simply clucked, "What would Uncle Gren say?!"[15] "It has been a very happy trip for me," she wrote in her trip journal. "I knew I'd love traveling with Father, but I never knew I'd love it as much as I do! And meeting Robert [he joined them in Germany for a brief spell] made everything perfect."

Dorothy and her cousin Herman van Roijen, summer 1927

During the entire summer after their return there was nary a word in her diary about Standish, but maybe that was because now he was off in Europe with the McBeans, still tutoring Peter. "I am so glad you are going abroad," she had written him from Europe on June 10, wishing him well on his way: "It is all owing to my mental influence on the McBeans—of that I am sure!" She wished him good luck on his bar exams as well. "I worked my mental powers very hard on Friday so you would pass!" He would pass, and be quickly hired by the prestigious Boston law firm of Ropes and Gray, where he would remain for his entire professional life.

Out of sight was not entirely out of mind, however, for Dorothy wrote him four long, chatty letters that summer, the first of forty-four that she would write during their up-and-down courtship in the coming years. Her letters were full of family news: Robert is in Hamilton, but there is little for him to do. He is going fishing with Irving Pratt. He is off to military training camp. Fred, just turned twenty-one, sets sail for Nova Scotia with Columbus Iselin (the oceanographer-to-be). Freddy and Robert are going duck-shooting in Maine before college opens. Katharine now ranks second in the girls state tennis championship. And always, the weather report—"so bad we cannot play tennis so exercise ourselves by taking the dogs on walks … but which … increases the time for reading and keeps the country fresh and green."

She claimed she saw no one but the Searses and her Dutch cousins, Bobby and Herman van Roijen, whose father, Herman van Roijen, Sr., had just been appointed minister to Washington and who were spending the summer in Beverly. The van Roijen sons, she could see, were veering off into two different worlds.

> Barbara Forbes is rather taken with the younger boy [Bobby], so the other night promising to be very beautiful with a full moon, she organized a picnic on the Caner Beach and soon she disappeared with him over the rocks and left the rest of us around the fire struggling to keep awake as best we could until they reappeared at 20 to 12 p.m.! They won't hear the end of that for some time! The older van Roijen [Herman] studies law six hours every day all summer [he was enrolled at the university in Utrecht]. He won't practice law, but it is part of his diplomatic training.[16]

She wrote him about mutual acquaintances, and she asked about his doings in Europe. But after her June 10 letter, with its decidedly mixed signals, she avoided discussion of feelings other than noting that she wanted "very much to see you and compare notes on Germany."

Once they were both home again, it was Dorothy who took the first cautious step toward arranging another meeting. In a September 5 letter she wrote:

> If you are not busy this autumn, I hope sometime you can come down here and we can go on the river or take that walk which we never succeeded in taking last autumn. Already the swamp maples are beginning to turn. There is, in all the world, no spot as beautiful as New England, is there?

For the remainder of the year Dorothy's diary was reserved about Standish—the only reference to him being an October 6 entry boxed in red: "4 years ago today."

— • —

If Dorothy was perplexed by her relationship with Standish, she was more troubled yet by the state of the world. Thinking of "all the nations and all this sad, sinful world," she wrote in September 1927, "I am filled with anguish and a deep depression and my soul is tossed to and fro on a dark and troubled sea of doubt." These and many thoughts like it are packed into her contemplative journal. Meanwhile, she was keeping three other notebooks: a journal filled with meticulous notes on all the books she read; a travel journal for 1927, chronicling her trip to Europe with her father; and a five-year daily diary.

Her mind was troubled. At twenty-two Dorothy felt that she had grown beyond her home, her friends, and the "small world" of her childhood. Even Grandma Amory, she believed, would probably not understand the kinds of thoughts she was having. Her moral certitude, the strong convictions she had expressed a few years earlier, had disintegrated. In 1923 she wrote, "I felt I could guide the lives of people and reform the world. I knew I was right and people were stupid. I am humbled now." She turned to modern writers for guidance, but she found them as baffled as she by the great social and religious questions. "I am not lucky to have been born in this century," she lamented. How could one be optimistic when

> the world seems to have gone mad, and when one thinks of the universal unrest and discontent, the wickedness and suffering everywhere, and the stupidity of people who bring so much misery on themselves and others? ... It is horrible to think that we are at the mercy of an all-powerful God who is capricious and self-willed and does with us, his playthings, as his fancy sees fit.

Dorothy's trip to Europe with her father earlier that year had fueled her angst. The two, traveling through France and Germany, had come face to face with the turmoil of post–World War I Europe. Throughout the continent, the reassuring pre-1914 order had been torn to shreds. Germany was only beginning to recover from the horrendous inflation of the mid-1920s, people were poor and scared, and Hitler was already finding scapegoats in Bolsheviks and Jews. The Russian Revolution had destroyed the country's upper classes; those who survived had fled penniless to other parts of Europe or America. The spirit of France and England, which had lost many of their finest young men, was broken.

New England to the core, Dorothy was drawn to the old-fashioned virtues she found in the Germans and English. "The hope of the world," she wrote in her travel journal, "lies in such nations as Germany, England, and America." She admired the British for their modest restraint, the Germans for their "benevolence and integrity.... The middle and lower middle classes ... are fine, simple, respectable, self-respecting and solid folk." She credited German self-discipline for such fine qualities: "They are a methodical and economical people and waste neither time, space, nor energy." She sympathized with Germans as victims of the war. Almost two million German soldiers had been killed and the nation was struggling to survive. Her father fed her sympathies, telling her in words that today seem remarkably prescient, "We must not treat the Germans too harshly. We must not annihilate their strength. Someday they're going to be a bulwark between us and Russia." Perhaps remembering that Grandma Amory had banished Fräulein from the house during the war, Dorothy had sputtered in a letter to her grandmother, "I don't see how people can hate the Germans.... The Prussian officers are no doubt arrogant and despicable, but the majority of the German people are *not* Prussian officers. I wish people at home were more broad-minded and not full of hate."

If Dorothy was conventionally Bostonian about whom she admired, she was equally orthodox about whom she disdained. Among her least favorite people were the Jews, not because of anything they had done—in fact, she was not convinced by tales that Jews were involved in the "ruthless butchery and unjustified massacre" in the Russian Revolution[17]—but simply because of who they were. When Freddy made an airy reference to "Israelites" and Robert commented that being an American at Cambridge was "almost as bad as being a Jew at Harvard," Dorothy didn't raise an eyebrow. At fifteen she herself had berated her Patten cousins as "far

REARED *in a* GREENHOUSE

too democratic" for suggesting that Jews should be admitted into the May School. Her instinct was the same when in 1927 she discovered that Frankfurt was "overrun with Jews":

> I have come to the conclusion that Jews and Gentiles are by nature incompatible and averse to each other in the same way that dogs and cats are. Occasionally a dog and a cat are friends and in the same way there are individual cases where a Jew and a Gentile get along together like brothers. Alas how few.

Grandma Amory understood that Jews were more victim than villain: "I am reading ... a history of the Jews," she wrote her friend Fanny Blake in 1929. "What a horrible time they have had and are still having—what donkeys the English were to try to settle a new lot of people in Palestine, when they did not welcome them— neither Jews or Arabs." Whether she and Dorothy ever explored the topic is uncertain. It may not have been until Jews moved into Hamilton during the 1950s and 1960s that my mother's prejudices faded away—and that she was ready unblinkingly to accept a Jewish son-in-law, my husband.

If, in Dorothy's view, only the Germanic and Anglo-Saxon peoples could show the way, the bucolic countryside offered the only setting in which good could conquer evil. She believed that salvation lay in fields and flowers, hoes and rakes, that cities bred discontent and sin. "The evils of the average city outweigh the good. Look at the city slums, look at the type of people there ... worthless brutes.... Cities are hotbeds of Bolshevism and greenhouses for growing all that is worst, vilest in human nature."

For her, the plantation was the embodiment of purity and peace—her best escape from Boston, which she found "so small and petty, so superficial and artificial." She'd written during her visit there in January, "I hold communion with the fields and the trees and the skies.... I feel as though we could all be good and happy if we all had a Groton Plantation to go to." She seemed to have forgotten the distress she had felt five years earlier over the poverty and ignorance of the blacks in South Carolina.

At this moment in her life, Dorothy's pessimism about the world's prospects may have had more bearing on her hesitation regarding marriage than her father's doubts about her suitor. To Dorothy, marriage was a tricky issue. On the one hand, her instincts told her she had a "duty to propagate our own kind for the good of the world." The world was divided into "two classes—those who lift and those who lean"—and the lifters needed reinforcements. On the other hand, she was reluctant to bring a child into such a dreadful world. It might be better "to be selfish and keep one's unborn children ... safely out of harm's way." Though she was beginning to feel the tug of maternal love—holding Emily's little Cabot filled her with a "yearning tenderness"—she wondered whether marriage could compare with good works in terms of social value. But even good works had their limitations, for many girls who tried soon gave up, disillusioned. It was all terribly confusing: "With no God upon whom to place Responsibility," she wrote gloomily, "we must take it upon ourselves. The progress of the World is up to us."

Doing what? This was the question. Nothing she could think of seemed to get to the root of the problem. She would, during the coming summer, become the leading spirit of the Pena-Tena Club, which ran a "midway" at the Montserrat Golf Club for the benefit of Children's Hospital in Boston. But the club was nothing but a group of prominent North Shore girls. In the fall she would continue her efforts with the SPCC, becoming a director, attending meetings, and spending days and days packing and delivering nuts. Helping poor children, though, wasn't enough. As she wrote in her travel journal, "We busily bail out the boat and keep on bailing as more and more water flows in.… How much better to … find the hole in the bottom of the boat and plug it up."

— • —

Another option might be to help out privately, to focus one's efforts on an individual in need. This idea might have taken shape during her 1927 European trip with her father. The two had returned to Ytebs, the Paris dress salon where she and her family had shopped in 1923, to see how the Russian refugee owners, the Guillenchmidts, were faring. Dorothy must have been haunted all along by the memory of this family, for when Standish had traveled to Europe with the McBeans, she asked him to suggest to Mrs. McBean that she patronize the shop.

Of all the suffering she saw in Europe on the 1923 trip, nothing had obsessed Dorothy like the plight of the Russian refugees: "Millions of Russians have been killed, millions more are starving and many hundred have fled to strange and distant lands to eke out a miserable existence far from home." She also found something romantic in them, especially in their music: "Wistful, pathetic, hopeless and tenderly sorrowful … as though asking, why, why must we suffer." And she admired their courage, commenting later in her letter to Standish about Mrs. McBean, "I feel so sorry for the poor Russian refugees … that I want to do what little I can to help them even if only to find them a new client."

When she and her father themselves returned to the shop, Dorothy was particularly taken with the daughter, Natasha. She had been only fourteen during their first visit, but now she had turned eighteen and Dorothy found her "perfectly charming." Perhaps it was because the Guillenchmidts came to personify Russia to her. Perhaps it was because Natasha herself, had her family not been caught in the grip of the revolution, would have led a life of privilege not so different from Dorothy's. In any event, Dorothy saw that Natasha would have little opportunity to better herself working in her family's dress shop. A solution, she decided, was to bring the young Russian to America for a year to learn stenography.

Dorothy used her own money to pay Natasha's way and expenses.[18] And when Natasha was enrolled in Bryant and Stratton Commercial School early in 1928, Dorothy enrolled with her. That year the two were inseparable. Dorothy took her around to meet everyone. There was a focus on things Russian. They met Dorothy's Russian acquaintances: the Pertzoffs (Olga Monks' daughter had married one

Constantin Alexandrovich Pertzoff) and Tania Makarof. They attended recitals given by the great Russian basso Feodor Chaliapin and the young Russian pianist Vladimir Horowitz. Dorothy also took Natasha to a supper dance, although Boston may not have known quite what to make of this refugee friend of Miss Winthrop's. Although Standish was "so good" to Natasha and looked "after her so well," Dorothy and she slipped out early. "After I left her at home, I was sorely tempted to return to the dance in the hopes of having another waltz with you," Dorothy wrote Standish, "but then I didn't want Natasha to hear I'd gone back after leaving her. It would have looked as though I'd dumped her rather ungraciously!"

Dorothy took her Russian friend Natasha Guillenchmidt everywhere and they did everything together: at left, Natasha at Groton Plantation; at right, Natasha in Wareham with Cousin Billy Amory.

During the summer break they went to Hamilton, where they lived in what Grandma Amory described in a letter to her friend Fanny Blake as "a small shanty on the Winthrop estate." They got their own breakfasts and ate other meals at Groton House, but they seem not to have been very welcome there. During the long summer days Dorothy taught Natasha to drive a car, and Natasha also learned to swim.

Grandma Amory was greatly impressed by Natasha's poise and brains:

> She is only nineteen, three years younger than Dorothy, but seems three years older, more of a woman of the world and self-poised, very charming. Intelligent too. She gets one hundred for examinations.... I am astonished at the many books [she] has read—everything that I have in English as many and more in French, and much in Russian and so on. She … has perfect manners and is quite a star.

When Natasha returned to school in the fall Dorothy did not return with her. She did, however, practice her writing skills, "trying to rephrase" a paper on military defense written by Natasha's grandfather and translated into English by Natasha. In early December she found Natasha in tears, worried about bad news from home. Her brother Peter was ill, threatened with tuberculosis, and needed rest at once. She told Dorothy that she felt homesick for the first time in America. Dorothy did her best to ease her friend's worries, taking her to Washington to sightsee, to the plantation for a family Christmas, and then back to Washington and New York. It was about this time that Standish wrote Dorothy that he had never seen anyone do so much for a friend as she had done for Natasha.

On February 2, 1929, Natasha sailed for home. "I miss Natasha," Dorothy mourned in her diary. "I feel desolate and Boston is so empty. It will get better I know, and the memory of her will grow dimmer—such is Nature's cruelty and kindness—but never fade." The purpose of the trip had been to enable Natasha to help her family. She had prepared well, winning the highest honor in the class with a mark of 99.4 percent. The principal of Bryant and Stratton presented the award to her in Paris. Natasha landed a job with the White Star Line that helped her supplement the family dressmaking income. As time went by, she would contribute more and more to her family's financial well-being. By the next generation, the family was prospering. Peter became an engineer and his son, Michel, spent years in the selective French government service and is now a successful Paris lawyer.

"Adopting" Natasha turned out to be the beginning of a lifelong practice for Dorothy—helping individuals in a quiet, concrete way. The next year it was Fräulein, who had suffered a stroke in February. Dorothy found her a convalescent home, and during the summer and fall she visited and read to her old governess nearly every day. She took her about, once to the Willowdale races, once to get glasses, and twice to town to help arrange for her travel documents. When Fräulein decided to return to Germany for good, she saw her off on the *Cleveland*. It was a bittersweet parting, saying good-bye to this now broken and lonely old woman whom Dorothy had once loved and depended on. "Poor, pathetic, helpless creature," she wrote in her diary, "a hard day for us all."

In later years, among causes of my mother's that I remember, there was Kitty, who used to take care of us and for whom my mother built a little house when she was sick and old and could no longer climb stairs; Van, the Bible teacher and former missionary, to whom she loaned money for the purchase of a house; and Barbara, the recovering-alcoholic hairdresser, to whom she gave money so that a new roof could be put on her shop, with repayment to be made in the form of a weekly hair appointment. There were doubtless many more, but it all began long ago with Natasha and with my mother's longing to reach out and help.

Another Long Courtship

chapter FIFTEEN

Dorothy Winthrop at 23

The epistolary floodgates opened during 1928, with Dorothy and Standish exchanging more than forty letters (twenty-two from each). These sometimes tortured missives chronicle the year's bumpy emotional ride, with Standish ever beckoning and her father restraining her. In the face of parental opposition, she kept wavering: over that year and the next, she would long for Standish, cool toward him, say she loved him, break up with him, and weakly begin seeing him again.

As the year began Standish was still pressing his suit. They went to the theater together, he invited her to go exploring on a snowy afternoon in the country, they dined with his aunt, Mrs. Walter Hempel. And at some point during that spring he repeated his marriage proposal, in vain. The situation came to a head in Hamilton on March 31, a Saturday afternoon, when Frederic Winthrop sat Dorothy and Standish down for a talk. Robert's marriage to Theodora Ayer was less than two weeks away. Though Fred had reservations about the origin of Ayer money, which had come from patent medicines—Extract of Sarsaparilla, Ague Cure, Hair Vigor, Hall's Hair Renewer, Comatone (for dandruff), Ayer's Nose Spray, and Ayer's Cherry Pectoral Plasters[1]—at least it was money. But Standish seeking his daughter's hand—that was a different matter altogether. He had already made his views clear to Dorothy. He had told her that he hadn't approved "at all" of their picnic by the river the March before. Nor had he liked the idea of her dining out alone with Standish in January, thinking it "more comme-il-faut to go to Grandma's."[2] Now he would address them both.

REARED *in a* GREENHOUSE

The upshot, as my mother remembered it later, was an agreement that there should be a two-year waiting period—and if at the end of that period the two were convinced they wished to marry, Standish could then ask for her hand.[3] As she explained it to Standish at the time, however, the agreement was hardly clear-cut. In a letter of April 2 she wrote, "He does not even mean that we will have to wait three or four years before we marry. He may want us to wait that long but he may not.... He is going to continue to think it over, but is not going to make any hard and fast rules." With regard to their behavior in the meantime, he was just as ambiguous. First, he'd promised them that they might see each other if Standish "did not press" marriage for a while. After thinking it over, howev-

Robert Winthrop and Theo Ayer, at the time of their marriage

er, he decided it would be better for them "not to see each other for a reasonable time." Dorothy tried hard to be philosophical: "Father really spoke very reasonably....Three or four or five years seems a long time to wait, but if 'it is the real thing, it will be worth waiting for.' " And: "We must neither of us feel under any obligation and if you find some other girl I shall understand." And: "If we have patience and give this every trial and that includes feeling under no obligation, then someday I feel sure we shall all be happy, you and Father and I." Upon reading over her earnest attempt to put a good face on things, she added a disgusted P. S. This "seems the coldest letter I ever read, but it is far from meant to be so." Standish wrote her back the next day, eagerly grasping at what she had "meant": "Your letter may have seemed cold to you but the things it said and implied left me trembling all over. I was prepared for anything and then you say these things which give me more hope than I've ever had and make me happier."

Theodora Ayer and her attendants the day she wed Robert Winthrop, April 8, 1928

ANOTHER LONG COURTSHIP

The women of the family had little regard for Frederic Winthrop's stance. Sally Winthrop sent a secret letter to Standish right away urging him not to get discouraged and assuring him that "it will all come out right in time." She encouraged Dorothy as well, Dorothy reported to Standish, saying it that "if at the end of a year we want to be married, we should go ahead and do it." When Grandma Amory, who had mused to a friend that "I should like to see Dorothy engaged to a fine fellow before I pass from the stage," learned of the situation, she sputtered to Dorothy, "I do not understand [your] Father at all." At the same time, perhaps to throw a little humor on the situation, Grandma Amory gave Dorothy a poem by Edgar A. Guest, which she pasted into her diary for October 1, 1928.

"So you are to marry," her grandmother said.
"Tomorrow in church you two will be wed.
Then hearken, my granddaughter, hearken to me
And I'll tell you what manner of man is he.

"All men are babies, grown-up, and strong.
They hate to be scolded when they've done wrong.
There is never a man so rugged and stout
But some time or other he'll sulk and pout....

"So pamper him, flatter him, tell him he's great
And mother him early and mother him late;
Coddle his whims and his appetite
And you'll get along with your man all right."

For Dorothy, the conflict was terrible. In another letter to Standish, dated April 15, she confessed to being torn between her fondness for him and her desire not to oppose her father's wishes. Worse, she thought Standish did not know what she was really like: "I am not at all what you think me and it frightens me to think how different I am from what you think." Standish denied that love had blinded him: the "things about you that I love the most are the things that appealed to me before I fell in love with you and I must have seen you clearly at that time." Others were confirming his views. Dorothy's stepmother called her a "prize…. She has one of the most beautiful characters I have ever known." At another point, he wrote her, he had overheard someone say, "You were the 'nicest girl in the city of Boston.' "

The March 31 meeting with Frederic, however, had the effect of subduing the flames. Dorothy disappeared for the summer to Hamilton and her few letters were nonchalant. Thanking Standish for a birthday outing, she commented, "I enjoyed it ever so much and found that getting old is not as bad as they say!!" Later she wrote that "some day soon I hope to ask you down to Hamilton, where the mosquitos are *thick*!"[4] Standish, meanwhile, was steeling himself for the duration. On a small sheet

REARED *in a* GREENHOUSE

of lined paper dated July 22, 1928, he listed "factors influential to my life … in the order of their importance to clarify solutions to my conduct." First came Dorothy Winthrop, then health and work, with ninth and last, religion. A second sheet was entitled "Resolutions [dated] 7.22.28 until Dorothy gives me a definite answer." These included, first, "Be worthy of Dorothy in thought and deed to the point of Puritanism," second, "Abide by agreements with Dorothy both as to the spirit and the letter," and third, "Have faith that she will marry you and that you will make her happy."

If the jaunty air of her summer letters masked Dorothy's earnest attempt to sort out her true feelings, an evening together September 10 stripped the guise away. It had been a clear night and they had been outside together, looking at the stars. That evening she went home and wrote in her philosophical journal: "We found our constellation in the sky this evening. Love shone at the apex with faith and constancy at either end of the foundation, all shining out so bright and true—and towards the center two smaller stars—ourselves—protected and surrounded by faith, constancy and love." A letter from Standish on the same date confirms that she had spoken to him of her love:

During the summer of 1928, Dorothy's letters to Standish were jaunty. In September, she confessed her love to him.

> It is hard for me to write how much your saying you loved me has meant to me.… I do want you to know … that it is the most important thing that has ever happened to me and I am very happy. It scares me to think that a person who loves as deeply as you do should love me, for it seems that I could not be capable of answering such a love in its entirety

Dorothy, however, still hadn't committed herself to marriage. Standish's letter continued,

> I understand that you have not made … any promise to marry me and that you are going to keep an open mind about it. If you decide later that you don't love me, you can tell me with complete assurance that I will not consider that I have been in any way misled.
>   Good bye my lovely precious girl. I love you, I love you, I love you. Standish.

Four days later Dorothy was vacillating again:

> This morning I was completely happy for a few brief moments though I lived deeply and long while they lasted. But then came the thought of Father and how he has suffered and how it may be I who will make him suffer again, I who love him more than anyone in all the world. It is an agony of mind to know what to do and the uncertainty of what is right and what is wrong tortures me. No matter what I do will fill the life of one or the other of those I love with unhappiness.[5]

By this time, everyone seemed to agree tacitly that it would be a two-year waiting period, leading up to a decision in the spring of 1930. In the meantime, Dorothy and Standish would enter into a world of epistolary reverie, where love had no limits and the other, no warts. It was not all "dreams," however; at times, they also wrote of more practical affairs: of how they would have a joint income of only $8,000, of how nevertheless Standish would never allow Dorothy to do housework,[6] of how they planned to settle year-round in the country—a wish apparently as dear to Standish as to Dorothy.

Their dreams—or at least written words—danced decorously on the fringe of the forbidden subject of sex. Dorothy's father had admonished them both that there could be no "courtship" during the waiting period. To Standish it sounded "like a pretty hard assignment," but Dorothy agreed with her father, writing Standish that the "wisest" course for them would be to see one another "in a platonic way." In late October they spent a Saturday and Sunday together which were, in Standish's surprised words, "two of the pleasantest days we have ever spent together ... even though our relationship was for the most part merely one of companionship." Dorothy concurred, noting earnestly that they could not

> always be young and lovers. There must be companionship behind it all, which will go with us down the years. Love is so indefinable and there are so many different kinds and degrees of love. It seems to me that passionate love so often burns itself out unless there is a feeling of friendship and a sympathy behind it.... It is more unselfish than the other.

The "other," most likely, was what they had in mind during an afternoon's discussion of what Standish termed his "despicable" side—that "part of me that makes me temporarily attracted." In a November 26 letter, he thanked her for being understanding about it, noting that "it may be natural as you suggested on our walk but I hate it in myself and think it is despicable. I shall do my best to get rid of it; and I think I can for now that I know about it, I can recognize and check it before it gets started." What about Dorothy's "other"? She must have had a modicum, for she wrote him later, recalling fondly the night he took her arm to guide her through a crowd and how comforting it was.[7] But for Standish, women remained a mystery. "I have read," Standish's letter continued, "that some women are constituted so they do not love as passionately as men do, but nevertheless love very deeply, more so than those who have more passion in their nature. If you are one of the former kind, I am very glad for I feel that is the kind I am more suited to."

If romantic action was tightly bound by lingering Victorian standards, romantic sentiment exploded in some of the letters Dorothy and Standish exchanged that fall.

Standish to Dorothy, November 20: "It is wonderful that as far as I can remember we have never had a disagreement or even a misunderstanding about anything.... You are so exquisite, and to think that you love me is the most wonderful thing that I have ever known."

Dorothy to Standish, November 21, while visiting the Searses in Beverly: "I took two beautiful walks by myself all through the sun-flecked woods. I found a warm sunny spot to sit in and dream. If only I would never have to wake up."

Dorothy to Standish, December 12: "I cannot tell you how happy I was to see you those three times before leaving Boston. Every time I see you seems to quiet me and make me happy.… You are always with me."

Dorothy and Standish spent Christmas far apart that year, she in South Carolina and he in Brookline. Standish gave Dorothy a writing portfolio, for which she thanked him in a note signed "Deepest love from Dorothy." She gave him a book about Lake Tahoe, commemorating their summer meeting two and a half years earlier. Her father, however, remained uppermost in her thoughts, as this note on her Christmas present attests:

My very dear Father,

I made these socks for you out of some yarn which belonged to my dear Mother which I found among her knitting in one of the trunks. I like to feel that she, too, is giving them to you.

From your daughter who loves you more than anyone in all the world.

Dorothy

During the first six months of 1929, Frederic forced on his daughter the cure that had failed for him nearly thirty years ago with her mother—separation. She worked her way up the coast from South Carolina and Washington, ending in New York with her uncles. Then she and her father took another trip to Europe—their second alone together—a three-month sojourn from March to May. Before leaving for Europe, Dorothy saw Standish here and there, and always, the rendezvous made their infatuation blaze hotter. Most memorable was an outing at the Fogg Art Museum at Harvard, where, for the first time, Dorothy met Standish's parents and his sister, Barbara. Barbara "seemed so sweet and I was drawn to her at once,"[8] wrote Dorothy in her diary.

Barbara Bradford, probably in her early teens

They kept their relationship dutifully concealed, doubtless making the forbidden fruit more tempting. Standish had written to Dorothy's stepmother that "I never allowed myself to discuss her with anybody." Dorothy, too, kept her problems to herself, writing on March 7, "Nancy [Murray Spencer] gives me strength and courage, though she knows nothing of my trouble."

Though up till then the intermittent separations had been failures, the three-month sojourn in Europe would finally seem to extinguish the prospects of her marrying Standish. Dorothy's first letter from Paris had some unusually warm and loving passages: "Those were very, very happy times for me and the harmony that was between us will be the happiest of memories to me all my life." But there was an ominous undertone—"All these

ANOTHER LONG COURTSHIP

days on board ship my relationship with father has been as it was two years ago. This makes me happy"—capped with the ending "Good-bye, dear Standish, with my dearest love, Dorothy."

Somehow, Standish was able to overlook her heavy hints. Dorothy's April 3 letter was more blunt: "It would be a sad mistake for us to marry." She blamed "those terrible worldly considerations in which I have been brought up" for her change of heart. Those considerations surely related to her father's threat to disinherit her if she went ahead and married Standish. It was not for herself that this mattered, but for the children they might have: "My nature is such that I do take worldly considerations into account as regards my children, and I do want them to have the best. My happiness depends upon that and that I want to marry primarily for them, not for myself." The other consideration was her father: "I cannot face a break with him and distance, coldness or dislike between my husband and my father would be more than I could bear." She wrote of the "misery" of hurting Standish, who was "so dear and good and wonderful." The letter finally wound to a forlorn end: "Forgive me, forgive me, if only I could have spared you this. Good-bye, dear Standish, from your wretched and loving Dorothy."

Standish was "too confused" to answer her at first. When he recovered from his initial shock, he wrote her full of understanding and sympathy.

Fred Winthrop in Europe, summer of 1929

My poor dear Dorothy, it seems like a tragic thing I have brought upon us by my love … your position was the hardest I knew of, and I don't blame you for deciding as you did.… It was inevitable when I first knew you that your father's money should have influenced me, but the influence worked both ways. I wanted my children to be better off than I was but I rebelled at the thought that people might say I was marrying you for your money. It was almost a pleasure to me to have your father say he would disinherit you if you married me.…

You asked my forgiveness for doing as you have done. I give it with all my heart if there is anything to forgive.… It is possible that you and your father may some day feel that these principles [that governed the decision] … although proper for your father's world, are not wholly adaptable to your world today.… I will live with the purpose of trying to become more acceptable to you.

A final letter passed between them that year, from Dorothy to Standish, dated May 28 from Paris. She thanked him for his wonderful understanding and sympathy always. "It is a terrible, terrible wound that we have both suffered and all we can do is to wait for time to cure it. And we must not probe it open by seeing or writing or thinking of each other.… I cannot bear to feel you will be waiting when I can give you no hope."

What happened between Dorothy and her father, how he brought her to disavow Standish, we cannot know. But it seemed

that her heart was not so much in this trip as in the ones before. The events were repetitious. They returned to Hill Hall after six years. "All quite unchanged ... even Sir Drummie is still around." In London they shopped. In Paris they visited Natasha again, and her family gave Dorothy *War and Peace.* Dorothy left no trip diary, no page after page of enthusiastic observations. She did, however, leave a typewritten letter—obviously meant for her father, though whether she actually sent him a copy it is impossible to know—setting forth the impasse to which he had brought her:

> I have wanted all along to go abroad with you this spring, because I was so happy with you two years ago and I want that happiness once again before I married and left you. Perhaps now I shall never marry.
>
> I do not and never can agree with you as to Standish not being honorable or having the feelings of a gentleman. There is no use arguing this point, but I do know him and understand him and the present situation and I feel I am a competent judge.
>
> As for his retiring and making the break complete and so easiest for me, he has never made me feel under any obligation to him or in the least bound to him. He has suggested my not seeing him.... He has done all that could possibly be expected of him and I was responsible for the rest. If there is any blame it is mine.
>
> I hung on for so long because I felt it would be for my own happiness, though I was torn between my feelings and the ideas you had always instilled in me.
>
> To break with you and to have coldness and dislike between my Father and husband would be almost more than I could bear. Would it be worth it? If in the long run I decide "yes, it would be worth it," you may be sure that anything that could be worth such suffering to me, must be very worthwhile indeed.

— • —

On her return home Dorothy appeared not to contact Standish, nor he to be in touch with her. She did, however, confide in her friend and cousin Jean Sears, a week after her return, about her sad predicament. "Jean knows all now," she wrote. "The depth of her feelings I never quite realized until now." Dorothy believed that perhaps Jean was not fully sympathetic about her worries regarding disinheritance. "She is so lofty, she can never understand my worldly and materialistic nature."

Word of Dorothy and Standish's thwarted love soon spread, and plots were hatched to link the couple under their friends' roofs. But she was guarded, even in her diary. Referring to that starry evening the previous September when she and Standish had "found our constellation in the sky," she introduced a code word, "Northern Cross," which reappeared often that fall: "Red letter evening for me. The Northern Cross shines bright tonight." Jeff and Catherine Coolidge took her to a dance, where she and Standish waltzed. Jean Sears gave a dinner before a Myopia Hunt Club dance to which both were invited. "Stay until 5 a.m.!!!" she wrote, followed by two mysterious symbols placed between quotation marks. After another party she wrote, "No constellation, so leave at once." And another: "How wonderfully bright is the Northern Cross tonight. I have given up worrying and drift weakly along for there are questions I cannot decide."

Early that year on her visit with her van Roijen cousins in Washington, she had met a certain David Karrick, whom (she wrote in her diary) she found "very interesting to talk to on any subject." The feeling was apparently mutual, for that Thanksgiving David Karrick arrived in Boston to take her to the Harvard-Yale game, tea, dinner, even a walk around the basin that she and Standish had often circled together. It isn't clear whether Standish knew of his rival; Dorothy's evident joy at seeing Standish at two holiday parties, however, suggests that the competition wasn't very threatening. In all, Dorothy would see Standish only eight times in the seven months between her return from Europe and the year's end, but each encounter would ensure that the embers continued to glow.

— • —

During the summer of 1928, the summer Dorothy and Natasha were making regular tracks to Coolidge Point, Grandma Amory turned eighty-five. Though nearly all her friends had died, she was too occupied contemplating the foibles of the world to worry much about herself. As she wrote her friend Fanny Blake, "The world was at war and only two men left, they fought together and both were killed, a monkey looked down from a bough and said, 'Oh dear, I shall have to begin all over again.' " The foolishness was greater still at home, on Coolidge Point, where her son George was breeding Doberman pinschers, including puppies with rickets. "We ... live and breathe only puppies," she wrote Fanny. "They are of absorbing interest." George decided to raise another litter "with not quite such a swell lineage but fewer worms." It soon came, as recounted by Libby in a letter to Fanny:

The night was a hectic one and I was exhausted. Our precious dog was in the strain of having many offspring. George was up all night off and on, the chauffeur sat up all night with her in the stable with a candle, they gave mother cocoa. George came into my room and reported every few hours and [so I had] little sleep on this important occasion. At last we have a family of six pincers, five brown, one black, and one blue. This is our life.

When she wasn't worrying about George's canines, there was always her niece, Dorothy's cousin Mary Curtis, whom her sister Helen had so long persecuted, to think about. That summer Cousin Mary was in her new house in Hamilton, ill "with the Trench mouth.... She does not really suffer but has to remain in bed till well as it is contagious. She gets up and takes a bath daily and back to bed where she remains all day alone ... no nurse." The lack of a nurse probably reflected Mary's finances. Her mother was "very dreadful to her," wrote Grandma Amory, telling her "with her New England ... thrift ... her income has been overspent."

The following summer Grandma Amory's first great-grandchild was born. She had been longing—and, with fingers flying and needles clicking, preparing—for this day for years. As she had written Dorothy in 1923, "I am knitting, knitting, as I always like to be occupied. I make baby blankets, for an imaginary great-grandchild,

Freddy and Grandma Amory in the summer of 1928

who never arrives; when it does, if ever, there will be more than a hundred blankets ready. All ugly and badly knit." On July 16, 1929, the baby appeared at last, little Theodora (called Dola in her youth) Winthrop, first daughter of Robert and Theo. Dorothy's diary was bursting with the news of "my NIECE!!!" In September Dorothy, Robert, and Theo took baby Theodora over to Coolidge Point to see her great-grandmother.

Dorothy had to be away from her grandmother for most of the first six months of 1929. She hated to leave her, and after she returned, she visited her often. On November 26 came the first mention of there being a trained nurse on duty. The next day, Grandma was exhausted and went to bed. The doctor ordered her to rest for ten days or more. Dorothy had to go to Boston, where her family had moved for the winter, but she hurried back as soon as she could.

The days went by. In early December Dorothy spent quiet days reading and writing by her grandmother's side. She drove to Hamilton and got her a wheelchair. On the tenth, Aunt Clara took her aside and said, "Grandma needs you now. Father can have you next year, and the year after and after." But for Dorothy, staying with her grandmother was a joy, not a duty. "Grandma is beautiful," she wrote that day. "Sweetness and strength and beauty are hers."

ANOTHER LONG COURTSHIP

Dorothy spent Christmas at the plantation with her family. While there she received letters from Grandma Amory, "the last ... Grandma ever wrote to me." Written in dim, wavery pencil, almost illegible today, they must have made Dorothy anxious to return to her grandmother's side: "It is quite dark and I see nothing," she wrote, and "How Grandma misses you and I hope soon to have you back. I am confined to my room as I cannot walk or breathe properly."

Dorothy hurried back, the day after Christmas, to find this letter from Uncle George, dated December 22, awaiting her.

DEAR DOROTHY:

The Dr. told me yesterday that Ma could not last much longer, it might be a month or it might be four months. She will not suffer at all, and probably pass off in her sleep. She does enjoy having you here so much, that I hope you will be here all you can.... You seem to be the only person who does not tire her. She seems very well and is most cheerful, but her heart is bad and her legs have begun to fill with water.

Back with her grandmother, Dorothy wrote: "I know it is coming, but when I am with her, I cannot believe it."

— • —

The year 1930 began as 1929 had ended—with Dorothy in Magnolia with Grandma Amory, in the house where her grandmother had spent many happy summers. The "farm house," as they called it, was a simple dwelling compared with the edifice across the lawns occupied by Grandma Amory's daughter Clara. It had an ample screened-in piazza but Grandma Amory had for several years been unable to see the acres of manicured grass that led to the blue-gray waters of the ocean beyond. She was able, however, to feel and smell the sea breezes and hear the gulls calling in the distance. They had built her a bedroom downstairs, with windows toward the sea, and here she stayed, serene to the last.[9]

For Dorothy it was a setting of grave beauty:

Jan. 3: Last night, the indescribable sadness of the waves' ceaseless chant and this morning the melancholy warning of the fog horn, but I am at peace and happy for Grandma is better and she is beautiful.

Jan. 4: The spirit of the whole house rises and falls with Grandma's pulse.

Jan. 5: I love the ocean now as I never loved it before for I associate it with Grandma and this, the saddest and most beautiful days of my life—sad because the beauty is slipping from me day by day, hour by hour.

Jan. 11: Grandma says "Happiness springs from within." Grandma is a refuge from the world, a sweet and stabilizing influence on me.

The slow-moving days gave Dorothy many hours to ponder the meaning of her life. On January 5 she wrote:

Ever since I began to think for myself, or at least to think I thought, I have wished to plan my life on the lines of the greatest usefulness I could give to the world.... And so it was, only still this did not seem enough. Others were working out in the world, accomplishing great things for the advancement of mankind and the progress of the world. And there was a crying need for this and I longed to help, and soon I was caught in the maelstrom and rushed headlong on with the crowd—not a leader, of no apparent use, just a fuming, striving scrap of impotent straw or dust caught and tossed on purposeless eddies. There was no peace, no satisfied feeling of accomplishment. I was a misfit if ever there was one, and I was unhappy. My whole mental attitude toward life had changed and finally I felt that my fruitless work, or attempt at work, was doing me more harm than I was doing it good, so I ... decided to neglect the rather doubtful good I did in public charities and devote myself exclusively to those I loved and to self-improvement.... In the ultimate analysis, it was a selfish life, for there was no self-sacrifice, no act of devotion that was not a pleasure and a happiness to me, myself. I was content and yet at times, when I thought of the other girls who were working and amounting to something out in the world, I felt ashamed ... they must scorn one ... whose sphere ... was so small and so private....Then one day I overheard Grandma and Miss Pierce [the nurse]. Grandma said she much preferred my being domestic and doing small things for others that came my way, rather than having me take a job as other girls were doing.... Then she said 'She is unselfish, isn't she?' and Miss Pierce answered 'Yes, the *most* unselfish. She does much more worthwhile things than many of those others do. Just think of all the good she has done in her short life and is always doing!' How pleased I was and how encouraged. No one knows how much those words meant to my weak and doubting heart. Grandma was satisfied with me!

The cold January days passed with Dorothy dividing her time between brief visits to town and a hasty return to Magnolia, where she would read to her grandmother until she dozed off and listen in the evenings to music on the radio. It may have been after one trip to town, where, at a dinner dance, she found the "Northern Cross shin[ing] more brightly than ever," that Dorothy and her grandmother had a last talk about Standish. She wrote him about it later.

When first I told Grandma about you, I asked if my Mother would have been pleased and Grandma said "Yes" and oh, it made me so happy.... She said also, how pleased [Grandpa] would have been.
   I think we, too, can be the tender and devoted lovers that they were all their life.
   When I told her you were not rich, instead of thinking it dishonorable therefore of you to love me, she said, so sweetly, that that must make it very hard for you. Grandma was human—and divine.

By January 25 the family had begun to gather. Aunt Clara came by regularly, Grandma Amory's son Billy and his wife May came down, and so did Dorothy's father and stepmother. Dorothy was especially comforted to see her brother Fred,

Dorothy and Grandma Amory having a lovely time in the summer of 1928

who took this sad occasion to reveal to his sister how much he depended on her. "He tells me more than anyone, and says that it is a great comfort to talk to me," Dorothy wrote in her diary. She went on: "Grandma is most interested in my buying a place on the river and building.... She drew a little plan yesterday. She says if we sell our Hamilton place, I can come and live with her." The next day Dorothy was drawing plans for the house, as Grandma dictated. Two days later Grandma was making plans for Freddy and Dorothy to come down the river in a canoe to Magnolia in October to spend the night with her. "I shall be here, you know," she said.

On January 31 it was all over. The following day Dorothy gazed at the still body of the woman who had nurtured, loved, and raised her: "My darling Grandma. I have never seen anyone as beautiful. I am glad Miss P. tied her hair with the pink ribbons. My darling, darling Grandma."

Even on her deathbed, Grandma Amory's spirit was indomitable. As my mother described it to us later, "Uncle George and the rest of the family were gathered around Grandma's bed and Grandma noticed that George was looking very gloomy. 'George,' she scolded him, 'Why do you look so glum? Why don't you cheer up and dance a jig?'" Among my mother's papers was one that seems to corroborate this story. The words were recorded in school-girl shorthand, the kind that Dorothy might have learned at Bryant and Stratton:

I love you D ... I love you George ... Don't look like that George ... or Dorothy, Billy ... You're forlorn George ... [go dance] a jig with Clara ... Stay Dorothy, dear ...

The funeral service was held on February 4 in Libby Amory's home at 278 Beacon Street in Boston. There was no entry for that date in Dorothy's diary.

Dorothy found her grandmother's death hard to endure. Gone was the one who "understood and cared about the little things in my life as no one else did.... I cannot realize that I must go through life without Grandma's sympathy and understanding. I can never tell her anything any more." Gone was the home her grandmother had opened to her: "I can never again find a home like Grandma's with its atmosphere of *cheerfulness* and *love*. She made it what it was." Gone was the feeling of being "*always welcome*.... She loved me in spite of my faults. No where else did I feel so completely welcome."

At first Dorothy wanted to see no one. Freddy was with her two days after the death and she wrote, "I could speak to him and no one else and it helped." Then she began to find comfort in her family and close friends. She didn't "return home to

299" for nearly a month, spending hours on end with Aunt Clara. The two shared their loss—the granddaughter and the daughter—but the greatest strength seemed to emanate from the daughter. "I do not know what I would have done without her. I wish I could tell her how much I love her."

Uncle George was always around, too, a rather pathetic figure. Wrote Dorothy: "I am fortunate to have her [Aunt Clara] to whom to turn and poor Uncle G. has no one…. I feel we are to Uncle George 'Something better than his dog, a little dearer than his horse.' I find comfort in loving those about me, but he seems unable to." With his mother's passing, George Amory had become a lonely fifty-five-year-old bachelor. He had adored his mother. He once wrote Dorothy he adored her too, because "you are more like your grand-mother than any one I know." Everyone wondered what would become of him.

Family and friends took pen to paper to comfort Dorothy with their memories of her grandmother. Some recalled her youthful spirit: "She was almost the only older person I really *enjoyed* seeing and talking with." Others reassured Dorothy that she had brought her grandmother much joy. Her father wrote, "You have one comforting thought—that you did more to give her happiness during the past ten or fifteen years than anyone or everyone together." Widower Uncle Beek agreed, but with a rather morose afterthought: "You must realize … that your affection and devotion contributed more than anything else to [your grandmother's] … happiness and contentment during these past years…. I only wish that in these sad and lonely years that are left me, I had someone on whose constant devotion and affection I could so firmly rely as Mrs. Amory could on you."

Yet others recalled Dorothy senior, whose early death had brought granddaughter and grandmother so close. Dorothy herself had begun to believe that "in the loss of my dear Mother, there are compensations for me—though never for Father…. Had she lived, I would never have known Grandma quite as I did, and my Mother would now be suffering all as I am, and more."

Of all the letters, none was more touching than the one from Dorothy's stepmother. Sally exhibited only generosity toward the family of the woman whom—after nearly twenty years of marriage—she had still failed to replace in her husband's affections.

> Just a line to tell you that I am thinking of you all the time and wishing that I could do something to help. I think Grandma is the most wonderful character I have ever known. I shall never be able to express how much I appreciate what she has done for me since I became engaged to Father. You can at least have the satisfaction of knowing that you have been the very light of her eyes and although you are going to miss her every hour of every day, I think that thought ought to do a lot to comfort you. I am so glad I saw her last week. She called me in and said she wanted to tell me that she was perfectly happy about you and that her mind was at rest. There are very few really perfect people in this world but she is one of them.
>
> I am very poor at saying what I feel so please read between the lines and try to realize how much I care, both for her and for you.
>
> Don't think of answering this. Much love, Mamma

By the end of May, five months after her grandmother's death when she had finally emerged from mourning, Dorothy could look back and be grateful for what it had taught her. She had gained, she wrote, "sympathy and understanding," a new "strength and self-confidence … from the realization that I could bear up in spite of all," and an increase in her ability to love and feel happy. "I seemed," she wrote, "to emerge from the night into a day of sunshine."

The memory of her grandmother would continue to burn bright, in the form of affection for elderly people. Before leaving for Europe the next year (1931), she called on a Mrs. Hempill, an eighty-two-year-old aunt of Standish ("so sweet and so charming") and on her grandmother's closest friend, Fanny Blake: "I feel so near to Grandma when I see her friends. Even yet I feel she is somewhere and knows all I do and think."

— • —

Dorothy's 1930 diary, even as she stayed vigilant by her grandmother's bedside, had opened with the cryptic "2 years from today." At some point during the previous year her father had apparently changed signals in their pact on Standish. With April 1930 fast approaching and the first two years nearly up, he had extended the waiting period another two years, until January 1, 1932.[10] The details are missing. At what point did he strike this new bargain? During their trip to Europe, when she broke off with Standish (a mere hiatus, as it turned out)? Later at Christmas, when he delighted her with a tea cloth he bought "on the sly" in Paris? What reason did he give for this new delay, and why didn't she register any note of anger at him?

Having secured her agreement once more, her father appeared suspicious that she was not living up to her side of the arrangement. One day he asked her if Standish were often at Mabel Storey's (Mabel, a Thayer "cousin" of Dorothy's, had married Richard Storey, a Groton and Harvard classmate of Standish's). Four days later he personally presented himself to Mabel and requested her not to invite the two together to her house again. Even this didn't seem to anger Dorothy. Her only comment was, "Cannot sleep for thinking and thinking, but calm with strength and hope."

She must have had an iron will to stay calm under the circumstances. She was getting baffling advice from everyone in the family. In November of the previous year, Uncle Gren had suggested, "If one concentrates on something, guidance comes from somewhere, either from some outside power or from within one's own brain." Within a single month, July of 1931, Robert, Freddy, and Uncle Beek all wrote with conflicting counsel. Robert urged further discussion: "I think you have had a very hard time.… I want to see the problem work out in the way that will give you the greatest happiness. I hope … to see you soon for I would like to talk things over."

Freddy, writing from the Los Angeles Limited, wanted her to take the bull by the horns: "As much as Robert and I admire and like Father, in this case we are right behind you." He urged her to do what she wanted, even if waiting another year and a half meant a greater inheritance. He reminded her, as did Robert, that Grandma Amory's estate had left her with an independent income in the range of $20,000 to $30,000, "plenty to live on." Added to "Brad's" anticipated earning power of $25,000 or more a year, Freddy predicted:

> You won't be rich but I am sure happier. This year and a half now is worth about six years on the other side of 50.... Of course, there will be hell to pay, but there will be hell to pay January 1, 1932.... Take this advice for what it is worth and don't get het up unless you intend to act. You will have to get het up Jan 1, 1932.

Uncle Beek thought her father would never get over it if she took the plunge with Standish without his consent.

> First of all, for your own sake and above all for his, you must not do anything which would jeopardize in the slightest degree that *very*, *very* deep affection that exists between your Father and you. You would *always* regret it and it would ruin his life....
>
> Nothing must be done without that consent but you are perfectly free, if you think best, to ask him to give it sooner....
>
> Your father loves you more than you can imagine.... He thinks no one is good enough for you, and at the risk of making you vain, I am inclined to agree with him.

But the summer wore on, "The Northern Cross so bright and people ... so kind," and on August 30 Robert seemed to have had a change of heart. He urged Dorothy to "stand up against Father and show some anger." A day or so later Dorothy spoke. She found her father "as opposed as ever," but he seemed "a little softer. The mere fact of speaking breaks down the barrier. No fear in speaking for now I feel so sure and strong." She still showed no anger, and her father seemed aware of how remarkable her restraint was: "He says he appreciates my never having gotten angry!" It was pity she felt instead, a feeling in her view closely linked to love. "Poor Father. He suffers because he is so indomitable and such a perfectionist." But the relief of talking openly was short-lived. Only a week later, happy after a walk in the woods, she came home and her father once again spoke discouraging words. "Why does he?" she lamented. "It will not change my mind, only depresses me."

Meanwhile, though he was not invited to a dance her stepmother gave, Dorothy went on seeing Standish at other people's houses. It appeared that no matter what, Dorothy had finally decided that she would marry, but not until after her father's new deadline, January 1, 1932.

Her relationship with Standish, she felt, recording her thoughts on a loose sheaf of papers, had easily withstood the test of time:

> The fact of my waiting, although under the circumstances I could not very well have done otherwise, is in itself a great test and trial of the question. I am not rushing things.... Never have I felt under any obligation to Standish and I have accepted the attentions and invitations of other men, which, had I considered myself engaged, I should not have done. The fact that I never cared for these attentions, but only for Standish, I could not help.

She showed herself eminently practical on the subject of the inheritance:

I have considered Father's happiness, the obligation to my family name (which as I am a girl is not very great) and, of course, my children.... I do not believe there would be any sacrifice of my children for if people are what they inherit, Standish must have a pretty fine inheritance to pass on and my children would not suffer from that! Only the question of money for them makes me patient in waiting until January 1, 1932.

She wrote of her change of heart, her shift from her father's belief that marriage must be based on family and money:

I can understand so well Father's old-fashioned point of view ... [but] gradually, my belief in the ideas that had been instilled into me since childhood was shaken, and, I think with the realization of the humble origin of one of the finest characters I have ever known, came the final awakening which shattered forever my earlier notions.

Being unsettled was the worst.

The strain of waiting and of my unnatural position seem[s] to me unbearable at times, as though I could not stick it out. But should I precipitate matters, would not the rupture with Father cloud my happiness and as Uncle B. says "ruin his life"? Yet, if only all were settled! Would it not be easier even for Father to adjust himself to a fait accompli rather than to have nothing definite to which to adjust himself?

Meanwhile, she wasn't entirely open with Standish about the reason for the additional postponement:

Someone told him that Father and I had an agreement whereby after I had waited a certain period Father would give his consent. I denied this. It is so desperately hard not to be able to tell him everything. I am so tired of having to keep things to myself. I am so tired of feeling I must discourage him, so tired of feeling that each time I see him is wrong of me, so tired of subterfuge and silence. I only wish all were settled.

Subterfuge or not, her last two diary entries for the year 1930 indicate that she was secretly preparing for marriage. December 29: "Shop blankets, puffs etc. Very expensive but worth it!! If only I could tell S. about my purchases." December 30: "More shopping for my trousseau!" She must have known this was to be her last Christmas in the Winthrop household, and maybe it was a relief. The holiday couldn't have been very festive. The clan gathered for Christmas dinner at 299 Berkeley. On Christmas Day she and Fred made family calls, to Aunt Clara, Aunt May and Uncle Billy, and the Searses. Fred, Robert, and Theo left on the midnight train for New York. On the day after Christmas her father had still not thanked her for a picture of her mother Dorothy had given him. "Couldn't he," she wondered, "or did he think it his by rights anyway? Oh dear."

The Family Circle Widens

chapter SIXTEEN

Dorothy Winthrop becomes Dorothy Winthrop Bradford,
August 29, 1931.

While her heart sang, Dorothy spent the first six months of 1931 wrapping up her existence as Dorothy Winthrop, revisiting all the old familiar places and silently bidding adieu to her twenty-five years as a single girl. Marriage would mean the end of her foot-loose and fancy-free existence. No more travel up and down the East Coast to visit her extended family, no more long European tours with her father, no more lazy days at the plantation, reading and musing about life, no more dropping by to visit with the Coolidges at the Point, or with her friends Jean, Emily, and Nancy, wherever they happened to be.

That winter she made two trips to the plantation. Conditions there were beginning to appall her. A few months earlier, in October, she had written Standish, "The heat down south was frightful, the hurricane had done a lot of damage, nearly every hog had died of cholera, the rest of the livestock was on its last legs, the darkies were all suffering from malaria and Mr. Maner [the white farm manager] was very, very ill. Mrs. Maner says the summer heat is frightful; 'It takes a heap o' will power' just to do her work and she often just wants to lie down and die." That January she pitied the mules, "mercilessly beaten" by their drivers after straining, pulling, and finally lying down in their harness, "exhausted." Such sights reinforced her certainty that "life is hard for some poor creatures and humans, too. We don't know how lucky we are."

Dorothy also visited Washington that winter, where she had entrée to both the diplomatic and the political sets. All this, too, was winding down, however: the van Roijens were nearing the end of Jan Herman's six-year term (1927–33) as Dutch minister to the United States and Uncle Ham Kean's term as U. S. senator from New Jersey would soon be up. Only David Karrick would remain, her rejected but undaunted suitor. "David has touched my heart," wrote Dorothy. "I do feel honored that he likes me."

She made the best of her last visit. Aunt Kitty Kean took her to the Supreme Court, then to lunch with Uncle Ham at the Senate. Aunt Tina, as always, was "sweet." Her young van Roijen cousins, Herman—in his first diplomatic post as attaché to the Netherlands legation—and Bobby squired her about and introduced her to everyone. She met an Austrian count, the Italian secretary, the Rumanian secretary, the Belgian ambassador and his wife Prince and Princess de Ligne, the German ambassador and his wife, a Baron von Putlitz, and a Count von Putzeler.

All sorts of people also visited the "high class address" where she was staying—the Netherlands Legation c/o van Roijen—including Jean Sears' beau, an Italian named Pio, and a Spaniard, both of whom Dorothy found "unattractive but very amusing." Dorothy, who as usual was chiding herself for not being up to the company—"People often do oppress me with a sense of my own insignificance"—seemed perfectly able to hold her own with these two. Pio had been a young Fascist and sported an autographed photograph given him by Mussolini. To bait him, Bobby van Roijen told him that Dorothy was "an authoress" who might help him publish his story.

Hamilton F. Kean, U.S. Senator from New Jersey (Robert Winthrop Kean's Fourscore Years, *courtesy Hamilton Fish Kean II)*

THE FAMILY CIRCLE WIDENS

Dorothy led him on, telling him that she "got much of her inspiration for writing from listening to Jean play the piano."[1] Perhaps such talk made the Spaniard think that Dorothy had "psychic power." When the party tested her powers, though, it concluded that they were "pretty feeble!"

Dorothy's last tour in Europe with her father—the last overseas trip of her life—would take place in April and May of 1931, this time with Uncle Beek along. Some may have thought it odd that the two previous trips she had traveled alone with her father, but to her it had made perfect sense. As she told us later, "Most people's fathers had their noses to the grindstone, and my father had the liberty to go traveling, and I was all through school and didn't work so I was a convenient companion."[2]

Whether she had actually informed her father of her decision, Dorothy surely steered clear of the topic during the trip. Rather, she remained fiercely loyal to him. "Father is old-fashioned I know and I cannot agree with him in all things," she wrote during that period, "but it absolutely infuriates me to have people criticize him." She felt bad for having disappointed him so that he could never take the same "pleasure" in her again and she didn't blame him in the least for the rift between them. "Father would have been a very different person had our dear Mother lived, even as he is a very different person when he speaks of her and when he relives the past."[3]

Still, it must have been somewhat awkward to travel together. The addition of Uncle Beek probably helped—though it would have done little to make their group seem more conventional. This time the lovely and unassuming young woman would be accompanied by not one, but two elderly gentleman, both with canes, one whose

Dorothy Winthrop with her uncle, Beekman Winthrop, left, *and her father, Frederic Winthrop, in Spain in the spring of 1931*

stern look vied with an upswept mustache, the other whose twinkle gainsaid the downturned white mustache and goatee. For all practical purposes, she was traveling with two fathers. My mother remembered how paternal Uncle Beek had been with her at the bullfights in Spain. Her own father, she told us, would look stalwartly at the scene of chase and slaughter while "Uncle Beek would turn to me whenever there was anything really bloody and he'd say 'Now shut your eyes, shut your eyes,' and after a while he'd say 'Now you can open them again.'"

No doubt for Beek, the trip was a welcome escape, for he had been terribly lonely since his wife Melza died on December 10, 1928, little more than two years before. Dorothy's heart had gone out to him at the time. "Poor, poor Uncle Beek," she'd written Standish. "He has no one left now, for they had no children." And he had reached out to his niece: "Somehow I cling to you as the only hope for the future. Aunt Melza loved you so *very very* much." Two months after Melza's death, Dorothy had seen her two uncles in New York. To her, Uncle Gren—usually the solemn one—had seemed the happier. At least he had his art. Uncle Beek, she felt, had nothing.

To add to his grief, work had just begun on a new house at 117 East 69th Street and now he had to watch it be completed without the woman whom he had dreamed of sharing it with. The house had been designed by Julius Gayler, very much along the lines of the townhouse the same architect had built for Grenville on 81st Street. Grandly reminiscent of the Georgian homes of eighteenth-century London, it too would be set back from the street, Ionic columns by the front door, and would open into a spectacular front hall with a spiral staircase leading to the upper stories.[4]

The trip to Europe turned out to be far more than therapy for Beek and a chance for the threesome to enjoy Europe together. To be sure, it had started conventionally enough, with the usual distinguished circles aboard ship: novelist Henry James, New York banker Tom Lamont and his wife, and distinguished journalist Walter Lippmann and his wife, friends of Emily and Cabot Lodge's. And it had continued with the usual round of churches, views, and paintings. But then in Spain on April 12, as recorded in Dorothy's diary, there was a "riot at midnight before Post Office only one block from hotel and firing on the street. 9 wounded." The Spanish Revolution had broken out.

Uncle Beek had known something was up. Thanks to his years in the Philippines and Puerto Rico he was fluent in Spanish, and when the three went out into the villages, he overheard people saying, "The king must go, we couldn't do any worse. So let's see if we can't do better." The day after the riot the three travelers drove around Madrid and had tea with a Mr. Proctor from Boston, head of ITT, who informed them the king was very worried over elections and might leave the country. They learned that the queen—who was English and popular in the country—and their children had driven to Escorial that morning and taken the train for Paris. "Poor woman in tears," Dorothy's diary continued. "Always noble, good and hard-working.... Huge mob before Palace in Madrid.... Hang King ... in effigy.... Uproar has increased. Red banners everywhere."

By the following day the hotel staff were warning the Winthrops not to go out on the street that day or the next. But the only thing that happened, my mother related to us years later, "was that everybody snake-danced, all night, all day, and all the next night, through the streets, and all the policemen turned their little capes inside out, because the insides were red. And all the donkeys had red ribbons in their hair."

By April 16 the new Republican flag was flying and Dorothy was recreating the scene in her diary. "Everywhere and everyone sports red. Taxis and trucks have red flags and even dogs and donkeys! ... Seems hard to believe, these wild hilarious mobs of yesterday have dissolved and peace restored after 2 days, 2 nights uproar."

Hundreds of Spaniards had fled and hotels were emptied of foreigners, but the Winthrops stayed on as if nothing had happened. After being reassured it was safe they went out on the street where—just to tease Uncle Beek—Dorothy would say, "Viva el rey." "Shhhh," he'd shoot back. They returned to the Prado, went shopping, and—after a decent interval—the men even "interviewed" some of the new government officials. For Uncle Beek, it was a bit of déjà vu. "I shall have seen four rulers in England, two in Spain, two in Portugal, three in Germany, and two in Russia," he wrote Dorothy later. "Of these, one abdicated, two were overthrown by a revolution, one fled, two were murdered. This is a dreadful record."

Uncle Beek headed home two weeks before Dorothy and her father. When the two arrived on the *Bremen* he was there in his car to meet them, along with her brothers Fred and Robert. Some months later, on June 9, Dorothy thought wistfully back on all her trips to Europe: "I am sad to think that my last trip with Father has come to an end. I love him tenderly and have golden memories of our many good times together. He is a very good and indulgent Father to me."

— • —

At some point Aunt Clara Coolidge offered her niece, my mother, a word of preparation about marriage: "The adjustment period of marriage is difficult. The man is apt to be possessive and you feel you cannot call your soul your own." This could not have been easy for Dorothy to hear, for her friends and family had always been the mainspring of her life. "How happy am I in those I love," was the refrain of many a diary entry. She meditated on friendship and its variants. There were superficial friendships that "give us much pleasure … but that mean very little"; friendships that fill us with "such respect, admiration and esteem that we are stimulated thereby"; and friendships that enable us to "unburden [our] weary mind [and find] a relief which can be found nowhere else in all the world." She contrasted her love for her three best friends, Emily, Jean, and Nancy: "I love them all so dearly, but each in a different way.… I love Emily as though she were my sister, Jean as though she were my daughter, and Nancy as though she were my all-wise and comprehending mother, one whose guidance and advice were infallible." At one point, lying in a pine grove thinking about Standish and Nancy, she pondered the pros and cons of romantic love versus friendship: "Which is most beautiful, love or friendship? Does not each possess something of the other?"

Of course, most of her friends were married, and she hadn't lost touch with them at all. It was just that the focus of their lives had shifted to husbands and children. She took it all in good stride, discovering that the men and women who married her friends and relatives had enriched her life.

Not all of them, however. Dorothy was not enthusiastic about Robert's marriage. She shared her father's reservations about the origins of Ayer money, and Theo's pastimes—horses, hunting, partying—weren't at all to her taste. Dorothy's misgivings about Theo would prove prescient. In one of those odd coincidences that seemed to pepper her life, she got an unknowing glimpse of the future on a visit to Long Island with Theo and Robert in the first summer of their marriage. It was a proper Long Island luncheon, a chance for Theo to introduce her new sister-in-law to her friends. Dorothy swam while the others played bridge. Afterward, she dutifully noted the names of those she'd met in her diary, among them Margaret Stone Mann. The years went on. Three daughters—Dola, Amory, and Nina—were born to Theo and Robert. But Theo's interest was straying from her children and her husband southward, to the Virginia hunt country and the dashing master of the Piedmont Hunt, Dr. Archibald Randolph. She'd met him during her Foxcroft days. In 1941 Theo's and Robert's marriage ended in divorce, and Theo became Mrs. Archibald Randolph. And in 1942 Margaret Mann, Theo's guest at that luncheon thirteen years earlier, became Mrs. Robert Winthrop.

Dorothy must have also felt removed from Robert's professional life, for she claimed all her life she never understood high finance. Her brother had stepped into the family shoes at Robert Winthrop and Company in late 1928, six months after his marriage. A year later, on October 29, 1929, the stock market took its historic nosedive. Robert's experience, a year at Harvard Business School and a year circulating as a clerk in various departments at National City Bank, had done little to prepare him for this cataclysm. Unlike many of his friends, however, who had been gambling on the soaring market, his money and that of the family was conservatively stashed away in the family firm. Robert Winthrop and Company, established on Wall Street for more than a half century, had sat out the euphoria, avoiding dangerous leverag-

Theo and Robert Winthrop with daughters Nina, Amory, and Dola in front of their house in Old Westbury, Long Island, c. 1938 (courtesy Amory Winthrop)

ing, and though the value of its holdings dropped precipitously, the family would remain comfortably solvent.[5] The weeks following the crash were a frenzy of activity for the company. A tremendous volume of odd-lot buying had come its way. Back-office clerks worked feverishly, dealing with these small clusters of stocks and snatching a few hours of sleep on office tables or the floor. Even Robert—who always seemed unflappable—would remember it as "a traumatic experience."[6]

Freddy, too, though he remained her pal in a way Robert never had been, had long since fallen out of Dorothy's immediate orbit. He was always off on adventures. Of his escapades the most daring had taken place in 1928—his well-remembered canoe trip from home to New York with his friend and erstwhile traveling companion Paul Nitze. Nitze, though still recuperating from jaundice, had bet Freddy he could "paddle a canoe from the Ipswich River, near Boston, to the New York Yacht Club." Freddy, always game for a dare, had jumped at the chance. They were so cold and hungry that they pulled up on shore in Wareham and broke into the old Mosquito Hut, the summer home of Freddy's aunt and uncle, May and Billy Amory. Here they enjoyed perhaps their only warm night beside a little driftwood fire. After eight days of paddling the two arrived in Manhattan. More than half a century later Nitze—by then a venerable and venerated U. S. arms control negotiator and advisor—would still remember the trip with relish: "We had the most marvelous trip," he told a *Wall Street Journal* reporter, "dangerous as hell, but boy, what adventure."[7]

Dorothy was the only one in the family who'd been given advance notice of Freddy's canoe trip. Standish knew, because they were all talking about it at the Porcellian Club—intelligence that led him, alas, to make an enormous faux pas during one of his rare family evenings chez Winthrop. Nervously trying to make conversation, he had asked, "And how is Freddy getting along with his canoe trip to New York?" His only answer was startled looks around the dinner table and a stunned silence.

Apart though they were, Dorothy remained Freddy's closest confidante and bank of last resort. "I had a nice allowance," she told us later, "but what do you spend it on when you live at home?" Freddy, on the other hand, was in college with lots of temptations and an allowance that he considered not "half big enough. So he borrowed from me, and he borrowed from me, and he borrowed from me." Freddy's debts were the reason a portrait of a stately and demure woman hung above the fireplace in my family's living room. After her marriage Freddy offered to repay his debts, giving his sister a choice between cash or a portrait of an actress, Nelly O'Brien, which Grandma Amory had given him. (May Amory, first in line for the portrait, had rejected it because she didn't want to have a picture of an actress in the house.) My mother willingly took Nelly off Freddy's hands, glad for a remembrance of her grandmother's—even a picture of an unholy actress.[8]

In October 1930 Freddy decided to bite the professional bullet, heading off to New York City for work. "My heart is breaking," Dorothy wrote. But he was back in Boston at every opportunity. They stayed in touch while Dorothy was in Spain, and to Freddy in New York, working late into the evenings in the purchase and sales department of the stockbrokerage firm of G. M. P. Murphy and Company, the Spanish Revolution sounded like great sport—even if he was skeptical about the results. He wrote Dorothy in Paris: "I certainly hate to see the old order changing, giving place to new, which as a rule is infinitely worse."

He reported that the revolution had sparked some Communist doings on the home front:

> There was a miniature community rally on April 30 in front of the Stock Exchange. The whole of Broad St. was soon jammed with people baiting the speaker and generally giving him the bird. One poster read "Morgan will follow Alfonso." May 1st … was very orderly. I got off the subway to see what was happening. Nothing was, so I bought some community papers, from a fellow who said, "Here you are, Comrade" in a furtive sort of way.

Fred Winthrop, Sr., was worried about his younger son, perhaps because he saw in him the same aversion to Wall Street life that had led to his own early retirement.

While aboard the *Bremen* he had voiced his worries to Dorothy: "Father says he has as much love and admiration for Fred as for anyone in the world, but he worries terribly about his future and has a deep concern and tenderness for Fred." As it turned out, Freddy did leave New York in June 1931, when his firm opened a Boston office. But, as he wrote in his fiftieth anniversary Harvard class report, "The year 1931 was pretty depressing in the world of securities; so shortly after having had a prospective investor say to me—'If you're trying to sell bonds, God have mercy on your soul, but don't bother me!'—I left the world of finance." Before leaving New York, however, he and Paul Nitze had another of their escapades. With Prohibition in full swing, they chose to ask a policeman—who would have known if anyone did—where they could get a drink. The policemen rapped smartly on the pavement, a signal used in the force to summon help. "These fellows want to buy us a drink," he said, when his fellow officer appeared. So they set off, Fred Winthrop, Paul Nitze, and two of New York's finest, for the nearest speak-easy and an afternoon of illegal hooch.

By the early 1930s Nat and Katharine, too, had left the family nest, though Dorothy saw them from time to time. Just before beginning her second year at Foxcroft, in September 1930, Katharine was chosen to represent the family at a ceremony in Boston celebrating the three-hundredth anniversary of the city's birth. "K. unveils monument to founders of Boston. She then heads procession between Gov. Allen and Mayor Curley. Is introduced to public by Whipple!! How we all glow with pleasure."

Other family members were dispersing as well. In the case of Dorothy's "cousin" Jean Patten, who married an Italian in June 1930 and subsequently disappeared to Italy, it was no cause for sorrow. Dorothy thought it probably a good thing that there would now be an ocean between Jean and the mother who hated her so. Never mind that the groom was a Catholic and a member of the Papal Guards, and that he bore the tongue-twisting name of Giuseppe Pellegrini-Quarentotti. This simply meant that the wedding would turn out to be one of the more exotic in Dorothy's extended family history.

Jean had her kindly Grandma Thayer to thank, both for her husband-to-be and for her nuptial celebration. Watching how her stepdaughter Anna was treating poor Jean, Grandma Thayer had taken matters into her own hands, arranging for Jean to study at Oxford, far from home. While there Jean had vacationed in Italy, met a Papal Guard, and fallen in love. As my mother would relate it later:

> Jean's mother was simply furious and said, "He's only marrying you for your money," and his family said, "She's only marrying you for your title." The two still wanted to get married but Jean's mother would have nothing to do with it. So my stepmother supplied Jean with a wedding dress and her veil and all that, all those necessities, and Grandma Thayer gave her the reception. Because Grandma Thayer was a great friend of the Archbishop, she arranged for Jean to be married in the Archbishop's palace just outside of Boston.... She was married, early in the morning, in the chapel, then was taken into the Archbishop's private dining room and served the most beautiful breakfast you ever saw. We all went and peeked at her.

· 275 ·

THE FAMILY CIRCLE WIDENS

Sometime later, when the first of Jean Pellegrini-Quarentotti's six children was born, it was not the grandmother, her mother, who would sail off to the continent to be there for birth. It was the great-grandmother, indomitable Grandma Thayer.

— • —

"There is something precious and old-fashioned about him which I love, something chivalrous, seldom met with now." So begins the most romantic passage about Standish found anywhere in Dorothy's diaries. She was writing in February 1931 and she continued ardently:

> If only I could show him my appreciation and my love, for oh, I do love him. In my mind's eye I shall always see him standing in the fast gathering darkness by the snow-covered back street, tall and fair with head bared, his hands hanging by his side, and his clear dear eyes looking into mine as I moved away. I love him, I love him. The more I learn about other people, the more do I appreciate Standish and the more I see I have underestimated him in the ignorance of my youth and the blindness of my point of view.... He was once a wonderful part of my life, now he's my whole life. If only I could show him I love him. What would life be without him, never was there a luckier girl.[9]

Though she was absent for a good part of the first five months of 1931, Standish was never far from her thoughts. While in Europe she bought a going-away dress, a watch for Standish, and a Sheraton sideboard for their new home. (Whether or not her father knew what she was up to is unclear.) As she waited for the *Bremen* to take her and her father stateside, she wrote, "Each day brings me nearer to Standish." And back home: "How much the summer holds in store for me.... We are to be Mr. and Mrs. soon!!! ... I think I have never been happier. Life is sweet and beautiful."

House hunting began in earnest. Dorothy and Standish settled on Black Brook Farm, a place that had belonged to Nathan Matthews, Democratic mayor of Boston from 1890 to 1894[10] and an enthusiastic arboroculturist in his later years. The place, seventy-five acres protected by another seventy-five acres of woodland belonging to Harvard University, came on the market after his death in 1928. The dwelling was an old farm house, but the property was beautiful: "acres of beautiful trees, shrubs, and pines, a pond, lovely paths and trails with laurel and rhododendrons."[11] Better still, it was located only three miles from Groton House Farm. The best way between the two places was to go down the back drive of Black Brook Farm, left onto Farms Road, past several little houses to an unpaved stretch of road through the thick Appleton Farms forest, ending just across the road from the stone pillars that marked Groton House's long front driveway.

At the other side of the property, the front drive, two stone pillars with crumbling stone steps are reminders that here, many years ago, resided a bit of Hamilton history. The steps had once led to the home of nineteenth-century writer Abigail Dodge.

REARED *in a* GREENHOUSE

Miss Dodge had been born in Hamilton and under the pen-name of Gail Hamilton she had written magazine articles, stories, and books. Today, the Hamilton Public Library has a Gail Hamilton Meeting Room.[12]

Some time earlier Dorothy had apparently settled on the date of her mother's birthday, July 17, to announce her wedding plans—with or without her father's permission. Freddy backed her wholeheartedly: "I suppose you will be back about June 15 and a month and three days from then I expect you to take the bit between the old teeth and make a compound declaration of independence and alliance. The lesser guns of the family will be and are behind you."

On July 1 she broke the news to her father: "Poor Father, I am sorry for him, terribly sorry—but for myself I am in heaven. Freddy an angel joins in my joy. Blessed am I in brothers and all." That same day she dispatched a joyful letter to Standish, saying that while her father had not exactly consented to their marriage, he had agreed that they might "renew their acquaintance" and then, if they found they hadn't changed, they could announce their engagement. This was opening enough for Dorothy: "Although I have not spoken of a wedding yet to Father, I am determined to marry the following month, if you are, too! … Now I can count in hours that coming of that supreme moment which was once years away."

What led her father to change his mind? Had Dorothy informed him earlier in the year that she would be telling the world on July 17 of her marriage plans, setting July 1 as the date for his final word on the subject? Or did she simply wait until that day, present her plans as a fait accompli, and ask one last time for his consent? Standish was as mystified then as we are today. In a long letter written to Dorothy the next day, he asked: "How did you ever bring your Father around? He was so set against this and being a man of very strong purposes anyway, I thought only a miracle would do the trick. But you are a miracle to me, so that explains it." And maybe it does.

With her father's consent, the floodgates of happiness opened. Into her July 1 letter to Standish, Dorothy had slipped a little ditty playfully picturing her state of mind: "Whatever I try to do/ Write, read or play/There is always an image/That gets in my way." She echoed the thought in her diary: "I am happy, cannot sit still or apply my mind. I am in heaven, heaven." Standish was just as distracted, writing Dorothy, "I feel as if I had been living all day in one of those wonderful daydreams that I never expect to come true.… It has put me in an awful daze today. I haven't known whether I was coming or going."

They both looked back on the long wait philosophically. "It has been well worth waiting for," wrote Standish, "for as you say in your wonderful letter … they have been profitable years, and our joy is the greater now because of what we have endured."

With her father's consent Dorothy and Standish, at long last, were at liberty to see each other. They didn't lose any time. Standish arrived that Friday evening, July 3, for a weekend in Hamilton, and Dorothy's diary for that date has an entry in Standish's handwriting: "To my darling, on the happiest day of my life."

Saturday and Sunday they made the rounds, telling neighbors and friends the good news. The following weeks were a whirl of activity. Dorothy chose a ring, wrote letters, told more people, made lists, had wedding dress fittings, attended teas, lunches, went swimming, played tennis. All the while, she retained her concern for those closest to her, especially brother Fred who was having trouble settling in professionally: "Poor Fred. I wish he could find congenial work. He is not happy." The engagement dinner took place as planned, on July 17: "Engagement dinner on my Mother's birthday. All our benefactors and benefactresses come! I am sorry for Father."

Two weeks later, on July 31, 1931, Dorothy's diary came to an abrupt end. There would be some sporadic notations about her new life in the months to come, and she would dutifully record the teeth and words, pains and sittings-up of her first-born, me. But with my brother Stanna's (Standish, Jr.'s) christening on April 22, 1934, she gave up entirely her lifelong habit of penning her daily thoughts, impressions, and doings. Perhaps married life offered her new outlets that lessened the need to confide her thoughts on paper. Certainly, as the years went by, the responsibilities of marriage would leave little time for diary writing. Whatever the cause, the final entries showed she remained the same Dorothy who had suffered untold teenage pangs of unworthiness: "My hubby is an angel and spoils me. I must reform and be less selfish." And the same Dorothy who had tended faithfully to the memory of her mother. These words are the final entry: "He [Stanna, at his christening] wore the same dress as little D. and my mother."

— • —

Their families and friends rejoiced over the news of Dorothy and Standish's engagement. Nearly one hundred fifty letters poured in. "Fine" was the term that cropped up most often about Standish. "Lovely girl," wrote Standish's male friends to him, and "great girl" and "grand girl and great addition to the ranks of the sisters '24"—this last signed, "Yours in PC," as the Porcellian Club "brothers" referred to their club.

Only a few letters alluded—delicately—to the long and troubled prelude to the marriage. A friend who knew them both wrote Standish about his difficult role: "You have been placed in a hard position these past years and you have conducted yourself in a manner that has been a tremendous credit to yourself." Uncle Beek wrote Dorothy to praise her for her forbearance: "You must always remember that the sacrifice you made was the right thing to do and ensured the continuance of that wonderful affection and admiration your father has for you. It probably prevented a disaster that you and he would never have ceased to regret."

Many who had been close to Grandma Amory wrote Dorothy of the happiness this engagement would have brought to her. "I wish Grandma could be here to see your happiness," wrote Aunt May, "but perhaps she knows all about it."

In congratulating her, Dorothy's four uncles each exhibited his own distinctive personality. Uncle Beek's letter, though sincere in commending her for her patience, was filled with mock gravity. "I am afraid this means that we shall have no further irresponsible trips abroad together—and that much needed efforts to improve the mind, manners, and morals of my little school girl niece will have to be curtailed. However, you have had the wonderful advantage of one trip with your uncle, and have learned, I trust, that it is not nice to seize another's coffee, to demand the best rooms, and to use vulgar language to express your emotions."

Uncle Gren's letter was characteristically more serious: "Your startling and interesting letter came in this morning's mail. You have my sincere wishes for every happiness. I hope the young man whom I do not know is worthy of you—I am afraid, however, that I am hoping too much, for I firmly believe that no one is worthy of you. You are unique—at least I think so—always kind and considerate and good from the foundation up.... My hands are outstretched above your head in the act of blessing. Affectionately, G. L. W."

The two Amory brothers also wrote true to form. Gentle Uncle Billy looked forward to bringing Standish to Wareham "where we can feed him to the mosquitoes and see how he bears up under real hardship." Reprobate Uncle George, who had once turned to his dinner partner and said with a straight face about my abstemious mother, "I'm worried about Dorothy. You know, she drinks like a fish," couldn't think of anything but his next cocktail:

> DEAREST DOROTHY:
>
> You know how I love you. I feel that you and Standish will be so high-toned that you will not have anything to drink when I call. So I suggest
>
> | 10 cases of gin | $450 |
> | 2   "   of whiskey | $100 |
> | | $550 |
>
> Hope to see a lot of you. As ever G. G. A. p.s. Do as you see fit, anything suits me.

Some of the most touching notes came from the servants Dorothy loved and who in turn loved her: from Sarah McGlame, married and living in Roxbury, "I cut out your picture in the Paper. You look very much like your Dear Sweet Mother," and from Annie in West Roxbury, "I feel so happy ... for Mr. Bradford to win the love of the daughter of my dear Dorothy. She was a lovely girl and made a beautiful Bride and you are like her Sweet and gentle."

— • —

Mr. and Mrs. Frederic Winthrop request the pleasure of your company at the marriage reception of his daughter Dorothy and Mr. Standish Bradford on Saturday the twenty-ninth of August at one-thirty o'clock Groton House Hamilton Massachusetts

The favor of a reply is requested

The day finally arrives.

Dorothy and Standish on their wedding day, with the Groton House view of the Ipswich River below

The press made much of a match that linked two families whose histories were so entwined with that of Massachusetts. "It was a new page in the history of famous American families when Dorothy Winthrop and Standish Bradford were married" began the caption under a photograph of the newlyweds as they stood on the steps of Christ Church in Hamilton, "for the bride is a lineal descendant of Governor Winthrop of the Puritan Massachusetts Bay Colony and the bridegroom is a descendant in the eleventh generation of William Bradford, Pilgrim governor of Plymouth."[13] Wrote *Town Topics* of the match, "Perhaps you can conjure up something more redolent of New England than the conjunction of the names of Dorothy Winthrop and Standish Bradford—I can't."

Not all the press treated the event with dignity. New York columnist Cholly Knickerbocker, for example, had greeted the engagement with a reference to the unusually short period of time between the date of the official engagement announcement and the wedding itself, six weeks later, on August 29. In a piece dated July 20 in the *New York American*, he wrote, "Society, especially the inner circle in which the Winthrops and the Bradfords are such polished figures, will be duly

REARED *in a* GREENHOUSE

impressed with the news that Dorothy and Standish will allow little grass to grow beneath their pedal extremities before they are made as one." The *Boston American* elevated old family to royal family: "Concealed behind a palm tree was the little Princess Dorothy of the Winthrop family, whose troth to the Prince of Bradford was recently announced, attired in a summery black and white silk, most becoming." The *Boston Advertiser* got its old families mixed, identifying the "bride" as a descendant of "Myles Standish." Everyone, however, had the good taste not to mention the fate of the country's first Dorothy Bradford: Governor William Bradford's wife Dorothy had mysteriously fallen overboard and drowned while the *Mayflower* rested quietly at anchor and William was off exploring.[14]

The wedding party was rather lopsided. On the distaff side there were two attendants—sister Katharine Winthrop and cousin Jean Sears. On the male side, the usher "squad," as one paper put it, numbered thirteen, including best man (and brother) Thomas Bradford, Chandler Bigelow, P. Shaw Sprague, Sidney Graves, Harrison Gardner, and John Monks (son of Standish's father's best man George H. Monks), all of Boston, also William A. Coolidge of Manchester, Walter Amory of Providence, Richard Storey of Hamilton, Robert Winthrop and Barclay Henry, both of New York, Frederic Winthrop, Jr., of Hamilton, and Richard J. Norris of Brookline. Two ministers presided—Reverend William F. A. Stride, rector of Christ Church, assisted by Reverend Endicott Peabody, founder and rector for fifty-six years of Groton School.

Dorothy wore a gown of white satin cut on princess lines and a veil of old family lace. She carried no bouquet. It was all, wrote *Town Topics*, "in keeping with the family traditions of quietness and restraint." For her old friend Goaty, Nancy Murray Spencer, however, it brought a rush of emotion:

Dorothy Winthrop Bradford with her father at her wedding

> Darling, Just a week ago at this time you and Standish were kneeling at the altar and over your heads two moths were dancing and pirouetting in a most lovely and beautiful way. Dearest Dimples, I don't know when I've been so moved as I was on Saturday. I don't know whether it was your loveliness, for you were very beautiful on that day, there was a light from within that shone from your eyes as though your soul were in them, and that seemed to glow in your cheeks which were delicately tinged; or whether it was the simplicity of the service with everything real and true, or what it was but I couldn't look at you either as you went up the aisle or came down for fear of disgracing myself further.

Everyone was thrilled over the match—everyone, that is, but poor unreconciled Fred Winthrop. In a letter dated September 16, hardly two weeks after the ceremony, while Dorothy was still honeymooning in Chester, Nova Scotia, in her new in-laws' modest summer cottage, he wrote her:

I was very glad to get your letter of the 11th and to learn that you were well and happy. We have been having very hot weather for some days but to-day is much cooler. Mama and I are alone here.... I sat up with Fred last Thursday evening, I think it was, and when I left in the morning he had not got up. When I returned to luncheon, I asked for him; and Nat said he had taken his car and gone to Long Island. He had said nothing about going to me and I have heard nothing from him since he left. Bachrach got permission to give a photograph [wedding portrait] to several papers. The photographers are really extraordinarily good. It will be difficult to choose which one or ones to have printed. There are many letters and several packages waiting for you. Your loving father, F. W.

Dorothy and Standish honeymooned in September 1931 in Nova Scotia at his family's summer cottage.

A New Generation

chapter SEVENTEEN

*With motherhood, my mother would become fulfilled, stepping into
the roles of the mother she had longed for and the grandmother she
had loved.* From top left, clockwise: *with me, her first-born;
with Stanna; with Katharine; with her last-born, Libby*

She $kept$ $them$ in an envelope labeled "Sorrow and Joy," the letters containing the double message, one consoling her on her father's death and the other congratulating her on my birth, her first child. For the death on May 5, 1932, was followed within two weeks by the birth on May 18, the first locking fast the doors of her past and the second opening wide the windows on the new. More even than her marriage the previous August, these events marked the turning point in Dorothy Bradford's life.

It must have been three or four months after the wedding that her father's cancer was discovered. Sister Katharine remembered that he had appeared in good health at Christmas; the following spring she came home from Foxcroft for one last visit. It was colon cancer, which would take the life of his son Fred forty-eight years later, in February 1979. In those days, the prospects of survival for cancer victims were much grimmer than now.

They operated, and as he lay in pain at Phillips House in Boston Dorothy would trek into the city weekly to visit him. It wasn't easy to get away, for she was busy settling into a cold, drafty house—hiring and training a staff that included a Salvation Army couple with children and various field hands—and adjusting to marriage and the prospect of a new baby. Between visits she wrote her father short letters with diverting news. She'd learned from friends of Herman van Roijen's that "the Kaiser's step-daughter wears white cotton stockings and black patten leather slippers and is very stupid!!" She wrote that "the census-taker came while I was out and the

REARED *in a* GREENHOUSE

cook quite forgot to mention the children living with us, but said he had two dozen chickens!!" Their trips together to Europe had cemented their relationship, and in her notes she reminisced, knowing that this would cheer him: "We are going to a fancy dress dinner and I shall be a Dutch girl with wooden shoes. It makes me quite homesick for Holland of three years ago." And always she sounded a note of hope, though she must have known the truth. The last letter, dated April 9, 1932, begins, "I have been feeling so happy ever since seeing you so much better yesterday. Please keep it up! I have great faith that all will straighten out in time, though it takes long, and that faith makes me happier than anything on earth."

It wasn't long after this that the hospital could do no more and they brought Frederic home to 299 Berkeley Street. On May 5 he died, aged sixty-three. Obituaries appeared in several papers. Perhaps he would have favored the *Transcript*'s, which listed not only his many historical society affiliations but all his Winthrop antecedents—Governor John Winthrop, John, Jr., Wait Still, John, John Still, Francis Bayard, Thomas Charles, and Robert.[1]

Portrait of Fred Winthrop, painted by Herman Hanatscheck, 1925

They took the body for burial in the Winthrop crypt at Green-Wood Cemetery in Brooklyn. "I hope you won't go to Greenwood," Aunt Kitty Kean cautioned. Such a trip would have been hard to bear—the tomb with all its long-dead Winthrops and the mother she'd barely known would only have deepened the gloom that had descended over Dorothy with her father's death. And then there was the baby to think of, due almost any day. Harriet Saltonstall Gratwick, her friend from the cross-country trek to the West and Alaska, understood how she felt, writing:

> I can imagine what an emotional turmoil you must be in.... I am so thankful that you … have Standish there to give you strength (though I doubt if your own supply would *ever* give out); you would have been in such a difficult, depressing situation otherwise. I have never told you how much I admired your unselfish devotion to your father, and after seeing you both in Oxford and London, I've always had a sneaking feeling that in his own peculiar way he must have been very devoted to you. Your relationship must have been strong and subtle and most intricate, and I can imagine the mingled feelings its severance will arouse in a heart as faithful and honest as yours.

I arrived sooner than expected, probably, my mother thought, hastened by the shock of her father's death. My own father remembered the lilacs in bloom. My mother recalled that, too, but remembered as well the rattling, bumpy car ride over pre–Route 128 roads to the Boston Lying-In Hospital. She told me that after my birth the gloom that had clouded so much of her youth, and returned with such force at her father's death, disappeared forever. It's not a remark I take personally. Rather, I see my arrival as the moment when my mother at last would have a chance to play the part of the mother she had missed so deeply—and to model herself after the grandmother she had so adored.

Perhaps if her father had lived, the birth of his daughter's first child might have softened his heart. Dorothy's stepmother believed so, and, freshly mourning her husband's death, found words to bring some joy to Dorothy: "How perfectly grand! I am thrilled that it is all safely over.... I am glad it is a girl because Father would be so pleased to have a little Dorothy." Deborah Cronin, one of the servants in Dorothy's mother's household, linked the death of the first Dorothy to the birth of the third Dorothy with these few words sent from Ireland:

> Please accept my heartfelt sympathy in the death of Your Dear Father.... It brought back to my mind Your Father's words when he had to part with Mrs. Winthrop Your precious Mother. He said Debra, how can we live here any more? So it is only a short time when they have met again.... And only a short time when Your Sorrow has been turned into Joy. Congratulations to you and Mr. Bradford on the birth of your daughter.

— • —

After the death of her father, my mother, barely twenty-seven, had become a member of the "older generation," an adult, the final authority. She was at the helm, deep in the country with a new husband and a new baby. Beyond Hamilton, the country was in the depths of the Great Depression, homeless were sheltering in boxcars, and many were postponing their children for fear of the future. "We are living in a fools' Paradise," my mother said, years later. What prompted this I don't remember, but she could well have been thinking of her own and her family's good fortune during those dark years. Their wealth had not been wiped out, she and her brothers had come into inheritances from their father, and labor was cheap and plentiful. In 1932 Robert built a beautiful big house in Old Westbury for himself and Theo, on prop-

The farm house on Black Brook Farm in January 1935. My parents lived here until they had it torn down in 1936.

REARED *in a* GREENHOUSE

erty provided by Uncle Beek on his three-hundred-acre estate. In 1935 Freddy and Angela purchased Groton House from the family,[2] and Angela would quickly brighten it up, adding cheerful draperies and upholstery and changing the flow of the rooms. Sally Winthrop, at fifty, chose to move away, to a new life in Manchester on a spectacular rocky promontory above Singing Beach, a crescent contour of sand that squeaked magically when you scuffed along it, with a spellbinding view of the ocean beyond. There, she built for herself and Katharine (Nat had married in 1935) a magnificent Georgian-style house that dominated the view from the beach below.[3]

My parents needed a proper house, too. By 1936 there were already two children, me and Stanna, and more were planned. The old house on Black Brook Farm was sinking so deep that the front door wouldn't open and squirrels had been found in my bedroom. My mother carefully discussed her plans with Robert, and he advised her that she could just afford a house of the proportions she had in mind. And so, late in 1936 as the old house began to come down to make way for a new one, the Bradford family began a year's diaspora, moving to Boston, to Groton House, and to Coolidge Point while their new house was being built.

— • —

In November 1936, as my parents were closing the door on their first house, the doors were opening to another establishment, this one at 395 Essex Street in nearby Salem—the North Shore Mothers' Health Office. Its purpose was to provide birth control information to married women whose health would be endangered if they bore another child but who could not afford a private physician to prescribe a contraceptive. Its executive committee chairman was Dorothy W. Bradford.

The birth control movement was still young and, particularly in Massachusetts, highly inflammatory. In 1929 birth control pioneer Margaret Sanger had been banned from speaking at a forum in Boston's Ford Hall—only to appear anyway, a band of tape plastered across her mouth. In 1936 Mrs. Sanger's American Birth Control League was barely fifteen years old but already it had some 375 clinics operating nationwide. Only one of these was in Massachusetts—established in 1932 in

Brookline by the Massachusetts Birth Control League. It was operating illegally, for Massachusetts was one of only two states that still banned birth control.[4] The law that pertained was the arcane Comstock Act of 1873 (and a companion 1879 Massachusetts statute), which was still on the books and which listed distribution of contraceptives as an offense "against Decency."[5] The validity of applying the yardstick of decency became more questionable than ever in 1936, when the American Medical Association held that birth control devices could be legitimately dispensed by doctors. The decision was long overdue, as most members of the AMA were already helping their patients by providing contraceptives. But with the official stamp of approval from the association, the Massachusetts Birth Control League decided to open additional clinics in the state. The North Shore Mothers' Health Office was one of them.

Busy having a new house built and raising two babies, my mother certainly did not need to get involved in this controversial field. An article in the *Salem Evening News*, dated March 11, 1987, made this point some fifty years later when, during the last year of her life, my mother was honored by HealthQuarters, Inc., of Beverly for her life's work in reproductive health: "Dorothy Bradford could easily have led a life of quiet comfort.... [She could have been] a typical wealthy suburban matron.... Instead, she became a [champion of women's reproductive health rights, stepping] over the line from the very private world into the glare of the public eye, subjecting herself to criticism and even arrest for a cause in which she believed."[6]

— • —

REARED *in a* GREENHOUSE

For at least a decade, forces had been building that would steer my mother into the limelight. In 1925 she'd written an impassioned letter to her friend Nancy Murray:

> The inferior people breed like guinea pigs and rabbits, whereas the best people of the land have very small families or none at all. They are overrun by inferior fellows.... Men are *not* born equal any more than other animals, and much greater attention is given to the breeding of dogs, horses, cattle etc. than to the breeding of humans.

It sounds chilling today. But hers was a time when "PC" still stood for Porcellian Club, and Dorothy's was hardly a voice in the wilderness. In 1927 Oliver Wendell Holmes would thunder from the Supreme Court bench, "Three generations of imbeciles are enough." Society, he wrote, would do better "to prevent those who are manifestly unfit from continuing their kind" than "to execute degenerate offspring for crime or to let them starve for their imbecility."[7,8] The eugenicists and sterilization advocates were trumpeting that "defective germplasm" bred "inferior stock" and that nearly everything from "phlegmatic temperament" to "moral turpitude" was inherited.[9] In some states, women could be sterilized if they were "feebleminded," insane, or had physical disabilities like blindness or deafness.[10] Even the more moderate Margaret Sanger believed that there should be "more children from the fit, less from the unfit."[11]

Over the next ten years my mother gradually modified her position. Her first exposure to mistreated children had come through the Society for the Prevention of Cruelty to Children, and in describing them she had lumped the terms "feebleminded" and "morally deficient" indiscriminately with "maltreated" and "unfortunate." But even then, she understood that you couldn't just wipe people out or even simply prevent births: "Birth control first, then guidance and education and improved environment and discipline." By the mid-1930s my mother was sounding more measured and humane. "Conditions were distressing," she would write, explaining her involvement with the North Shore Mothers' Health Office. "Mothers did not want any more children—and children of twelve did not want the babies that somehow they were having."[12]

She developed her position on birth control methodically, studying all sides of the question and filing information she gathered under topics ranging from "population" to "crime," from "patients" to "R. C." (Roman Catholic). Though she was a member of the American Eugenics Society (perhaps it was her sly way of getting their mail!), my mother realized this group was extreme. A news story in her files warned that their rhetoric could all "too easily ... be made a cloak for class snobbery, ancestor worship and race prejudice." The mainstream public, moreover, was gradually turning its attention to the related and alarming problem of population growth. My mother's files are brimming with talk of it—the exploding birth and survival rates that had brought the world population from one to two billion between 1800 and 1938. If this trend continued, cautioned one article, two-thirds of the next generation of children would be born into families least equipped to rear them.

A NEW GENERATION

Perhaps more important, my mother had had two children and better understood the time, effort, and stress that went into childrearing. In her files is a longhand account of a thirty-six-year-old woman who had had nine pregnancies and six living children. They were "all undernourished, skinny, pale little things. The father was on WPA. The mother had a venereal disease … [was] generally debilitated and … weighed 90 pounds." The local doctor refused to waste his time on the case. The mother feared she might have a mental breakdown, thought she could "bear no more." But she wanted to live for the sake of her children. Birth control proved to be her salvation. Within two years, my mother wrote, she had become "a different person. She has put on 30 pounds; has lost her fear of going insane or dying. She even has the energy to bake bread for the neighbors and so make a few extra pennies. The family have moved to another house and for the first time in their lives, the children now have a bathtub and inside plumbing."

More than anything, it was the children who drew my mother to women's reproductive health. She loved children. Over the years, her letters were filled with anecdotes about them. In December 1952 she wrote me about little Grant Winthrop, who was so frightened by a slightly tipsy Christmas-party Santa Claus that, when he got home, he said, " 'I do not want Santa Claus coming into my room tonight. Please lock the doors and windows and and take my stocking right out of here.' " Another time, she wrote me about "little David Forbes [who] knelt by his bed to say his prayers. But first he turned to his mother and solemnly said, 'Gee, the devil hates to see me do this!!' "

My mother at the 1937 birth control clinic trial (Boston Herald, *mid-July 1937*)

AT SALEM BIRTH CONTROL TRIAL

(Boston Herald-Associated Press Photo)
Prominent at Salem birth control hearing. Left to right: Mrs. Dorothy Winthrop Bradford, descendant of first Massachusetts Governor and executive chairman of the raided North Shore Mothers Health Office, and Dr. Lucile Lord-Heinstein of Dorchester, clinic physician.

Salem Birth Control Clinic Faces Closing as Court Drafts Decision

She welcomed the town children onto our place. In December 1960 she wrote me, "All the little boys in Hamilton have taken to skating, the refined ones on our back pond and the hoodlums from Harrigan's Field on our front pond." In May 1957 a little girl got lost in our woods. The mother was frantic, and the police were all out hunting. My mother was asked if she would come out of her garden and help look.

So off I started and hardly had I reached the bridge over our brook than I heard a cry, ever so faint.… But I started to RUN and this time I mean run, and soon the cry came again and again, still very feeble, but more and more surely a child's cry. Near the old MacIntosh apple orchard in among the pines I finally found her flat on her tummy under a fallen tree. No, it had not fallen on her. She had just crawled under it for safe keeping. So, I sat her on my lap and dried her tears which stopped as soon as I promised to take her home to Mummy.… The police found us, but [they] had been driving around in a cruiser and how they had expected to hear any crying over the noise of the motor or why they expected to find the child within sight of a road or bridle path is beyond me. I gently suggested this to them and they were not pleased! … When I returned to my weeds, Leonard [the old-timer who worked on the place] came along and said, "Funny thing the way children get lost these days. It never happened in my day!!"

REARED *in a* GREENHOUSE

When she was being interviewed for her HealthQuarters award, it was the children my mother spoke of. She explained that "after observing women losing their patience and beating up their children in public, I knew something was very wrong … these women … had too much to cope with. And I said, 'Let's do something about it.' "[13]

— • —

The North Shore Mothers' Health Office was a modest operation—just a few rooms on Essex Street in Salem's residential section. It was open only on Friday afternoons, from 1:30 to 4:00. On Friday, June 3, 1937, four women were on duty at the clinic with some fifteen clients. In charge was Dr. Lucille Lord-Heinstein, a doctor from Dorchester. One of the patients, a Mrs. Rose Bertoletti, was examined and found to have extremely high blood pressure. She told Dr. Lord-Heinstein that she already had several children and neither wanted nor could afford any more. Properly referred by a nurse from the WPA, she qualified as a legitimate candidate for birth control. Dr. Lord-Heinstein gave her a diaphragm.

At that moment, several uniformed police burst in. Mrs. Bertoletti—a trap—met them at the door. The *Salem Press* thought the raid was outrageous. These "dumb clucks of cops," it groused, "finally let their self-importance get the best of their judgment and started putting the pin into the wrong people. The birth control group have plenty of what it takes to chase a gang of mentally muscle bound bulls up an alley."

We children always liked to imagine our mother, primly attired in a white, button-down dress with the obligatory broad-brimmed hat, being hauled off to jail. Alas, that didn't happen. She wasn't even at the clinic when the police burst in, seized confidential medical records and birth control "paraphernalia," and lodged complaints against the attending doctor, nurse, and social workers. She did, however, attend all the court sessions, and as the test case wended its way through the Massachusetts judicial system she issued increasingly strong public statements. She defended the work of the clinic, pointed up the irony that legitimate medical duties should be considered immoral and illegal, and vowed to carry the fight on at higher levels.

Salem District Judge George B. Sears oversaw a boisterous courtroom on Monday, July 12, 1937. "DRS. DEFY LAW AT BIRTH TRIAL," blazoned the front page headline in the next day's Boston *Daily Record*. "OVATION AT TRIAL" … "SOCIETY FOLK BACK BIRTH CONTROL!" Beneath these banners, the story described "a courtroom packed with some 200 spectators, many socially prominent, [who] applauded vigorously, cheered, and stamped their feet in approval." The cheers had erupted when Dr. Peer Johnson of the Beverly Hospital, a locally revered physician, had said that "regardless of the law" he would do his duty as a physician and prescribe contraceptives as a health safeguard for women with "mental disease, over-active thyroid, venereal disease, cancer, malnutrition, tuberculosis, or comparable conditions."

Our house, in 1937 and 1987. At left, the courtyard and the front of the house, still under construction in May 1937; *at right,* the house where my mother lived for 50 years, from the terrace side in 1987, photographed by granddaughter Dodi Wexler. The place was sold in 1994.

If a doctor defying the law was front page news, the Lady Bountiful angle was a nice added touch. Dubbing her variously as a descendant of Governor John Winthrop (*Boston Herald*, July 12, 1937), "Hamilton social registerite" (Boston *Daily Record*, June 23, 1937), and wife of a "Boston society lawyer" (Boston *Daily Record*, July 14, 1937), the reports reveled in the role of Mrs. Bradford, who testified that the clinic was nonprofit and set up to help the underprivileged.

The alliance of doctors and blue bloods was fated to lose its case. In his decision the judge said he felt obliged to find the defendants guilty, since the law was unequivocal about the illegality of birth control. The sentence, however, was minimal because, in his view, the defendants sincerely believed they were were acting in the interests of humanity. The *Salem Press* weighed in during the week of July 17 with a blistering editorial, opining that the trial had been conducted as a "mumbo-jumbo of legislative word-splitting," and that the government had become "a paradise of … horse traders in human values."

The heat intensified as police raids spread to Boston. The Salem case did no better under Essex County Superior Criminal Court Judge Wilford D. Gray, who in October imposed the minimum $100 fine for each defendant. He opened a small window of hope, however, begrudgingly admitting that public opinion might have "changed considerably since the statute was passed in 1879." This statement, my mother felt, was the very impetus the birth control crusaders needed to take the issue to the state legislature. This was where the battle would be won—but not for another thirty years.

— • —

In 1937, a year after its brave beginnings, the Salem clinic appeared conclusively closed. An excellent moment, my mother decided, to open the doors of her new house for a luncheon to honor the three defendants at the Salem trial. It was early November when a band of clergymen and lawyers, socialites and social workers—more than a hundred in all—drove down the Bradfords' long dirt drive, through

REARED *in a* GREENHOUSE

stands of tall pines and a meadow with a long rolling hill that shut off the world to their left, and arrived at the large Georgian brick house, its two wings embracing a spacious pebbled courtyard.

The finishing touches were still being made.[14] The electricity had been installed, the plumbing hooked up. The water from the three new wells had been tested, the barn shingled and the two new coal-burning Aga ranges (the latest thing in stoves) were in place. The guests were directed right, down two halls, past the sun room on their left, to the "big" room—a perfect size for just such community gatherings and a room that would hold many more over the next fifty years.

In 1940, as advocates sought to pass a referendum legalizing birth control in Massachusetts, my mother produced her fourth and last child and received a note of congratulations from her sister Katharine addressed to "Mrs. Standish Bradford (pillar of B. control - tut tut)." Shown here, Stanna, 6, Libby, a few months, Katharine, 1½, and myself, 8.

No doubt some members of the North Shore Mothers' Health Office and the Massachusetts Birth Control League gawked at this house in progress, with its seven family bedrooms upstairs and another five in the maids' wing. But when the Reverend Milo E. Pearson of Salem rose to speak, his conviction of the rightness of their actions must soon have drawn the full attention of the group. A reporter from the *Salem Evening News* was present and quoted him liberally in the November 9 issue. Addressing the three defendants, Dr. Pearson expressed his regret for "any inconvenience or embarrassment" which their affiliation with the clinic's work may have caused them and pointed out that any "praise or … blame" should be shared by all. "Every one of us engaged in this enterprise," he said, was acting "in good faith" and in the belief that we were within the law. No matter what the legal outcome, he stated, "humanly … and morally speaking, we are on absolutely solid ground."

Four months later, in February of 1938, the Massachusetts Supreme Court instituted the state's final ban on birth control. All six Massachusetts birth control clinics were closed. My mother reacted with an indignant statement picked up by the papers in Ipswich, Beverly, Salem, and Boston. Other parts of the country, she asserted, were aghast, saying

> that witchcraft days have returned to Massachusetts! Common sense is outraged by a decision so out of touch with the realities of the world today. It means that a law is construed to interfere with a medical practice approved by the American Medical Association. It means that a safeguard to the health of women and children is considered illegal. It means the continued prevalence of abortion, an evil which has been reduced to a minimum in communities with medically directed birth control clinics. It means that by the suppression of medically directed birth control an impetus will be given to the underground bootleg trade in contraceptives.

It was a pretty professional pronouncement to have come from a North Shore "society matron," and attorney Robert Dodge, who had lost the case, wrote to commend her.

A NEW GENERATION

The U.S. Supreme Court that October refused to hear the case. So the birth control supporters decided to try a different tack—a statewide referendum. In 1940 Margaret Sanger came to Massachusetts, where she and local leaders went barnstorming for signatures to get the measure on the ballot. My mother, more of a homebody now that she had four children under ten, nevertheless put pen to paper to aid in the referendum effort. The volunteers at the Birth Control Federation of America must really have hustled when they got her letter requesting rebuttals to eight tough charges of the birth control opponents, for they sent her a four-page typewritten answer in less than a week—and apologized for not answering sooner!

The letter requested "*facts* and *figures*" to aid her in answering "certain charges against birth control," for example,

"Birth control is un-American."
To refute this, I should like to know

1. total no. of clinics and in which states
2. number in hospitals
3.   "   run by public funds
4. names of states having B. C. as part of public health program and the statistical results.

The letter went on in this vein, also requesting the source for each fact cited. My mother wanted to be scrupulously accurate because she intended to take her battery of arguments to her state legislators.

In 1966, fifty years after Margaret Sanger had been arrested for opening the first birth control clinic in the country, Massachusetts finally came around. On May 10, Governor John Volpe signed into law a measure ending the eighty-seven-year ban on birth control. A broader bill was passed soon after, lifting virtually all restrictions on getting or giving birth control devices or information.

In 1980 Emily Lodge sent my mother a poem of her own composition celebrating the long-awaited triumph.

Here's to enchanting Dorothy
The lady of the Pill
She fought, she won,
She helped instill
The people far and near
With hearts and guts and
Stubborn wills
To persevere until the final finish and
The glorious victory of
The Pill.

World War II

chapter EIGHTEEN

*Standish Bradford, in his army uniform, coming down the stairs
of the Somerset Club on a snowy winter day during the war*

In the summer of 1939, with Europe on the brink of war, Angela and Fred Winthrop thought nothing of taking a trip abroad to show off their children to various members of her enormous family—her parents and her ten brothers and sisters. They now had three little ones in tow—Iris, four, Ann, nearly three, and Adam, not quite a year old. Nanny was there, as she always would be—the young Scotswoman, Euphemia Chisholm, whom Angela had fortuitously hired even before Iris's birth to share the sport of raising seven boisterous children. On the fateful day of September 3, when Great Britain and France declared war on Germany, the family was in France winding up its stay at Les Essarts, the Forbes family home at St. Briac on the rugged coast of Brittany.[1]

Stranded at Les Essarts, with all telephone communications cut, mail irregular and English newspapers almost impossible to come by, Angela wrote my mother that she hoped that her American extended family hadn't "been worrying on account of our being over here." When she sat down to write this letter of reassurance on September 3, she determined to avoid war talk. But there was no stopping the words. The resulting six-page letter not only reflected her customary spunk, but also foreshadowed the grit and grace with which the British nation would endure the terrible years to come.

> Naturally, we still had the firm hope, almost conviction, that war could be averted, not by another Munich, but simply by Hitler's finally realizing that England and France would stand behind Poland—and that to invade Poland would mean a war whose

REARED *in a* GREENHOUSE

outcome could only be the defeat of Germany and the thorough destruction of National Socialism. However, the die is cast and the butchering is about to begin, and all because of one madman at the head of a people who are too pitifully blind to see where he is leading them. It's so terrible it simply doesn't bear thinking about. Our only consolation is knowing that what we are fighting for is not only the rights of a brave country, Poland, but for the cause of democracy in its best sense, freedom of thought and word and action for every man. I say *we*, because I can't see how the United States—as the best and largest democracy in the world—can possibly stay out of the struggle, for long.

Perhaps the United States could toy momentarily with the idea of staying out of the war. For Angela's own family, however, there was no such option. As she went on in her letter, one sister, Griselda, was a volunteer nurse in a London hospital. Another, Rosemary, was in the Red Cross in Paris and "would probably be sent to some base hospital near the front." Brother Jock was a policeman in London, directing people to shelters during air raids. Brother Ian was in the Civil Air Guard. "In fact," she wrote, "everyone of any reasonable age is doing something—which after all is the only way to live through a time like this without losing one's mind." Of her siblings, only her two youngest sisters would be exempt; they would move to Pau in the south of France, which—because of Spain's "firm" declaration of neutrality—was expected to remain "perfectly safe."[2]

The old Les Essarts, the Forbes home on the coast of Brittany, before World War II. It was destroyed during the war and then rebuilt. (Courtesy Angela Winthrop, photo rephotographed by Philip Reeser)

Next to such prospects, Angela's description makes her family's enforced delay at Les Essarts sound like a lark, one that could have continued indefinitely:

> Since general mobilization, there is a great dearth of manpower on the farms around—just when the wheat of which there is a huge crop this year is ready for threshing. So those of us who are here have been keeping somewhat busy helping the women, old men and children. It's wonderful exercise and they are very grateful and ply us with cider.
>
> Meanwhile, here we are, children flourishing and mercifully unperturbed by these unpleasant events—and here we stay until it is possible for us to leave on some Dutch or American boat. No doubt we shall be able to do so before very long, and until then we are perfectly safe here. In fact, if we were obliged to stay here for the whole war … there would be nothing to worry about—unless Germany won—and I don't see how they can. The sea full of fish and cabbages in the garden and a cow in the yard—starving would be an impossibility!

She signed off with a flourish: "Lots of love to you from us all, to Hell with Hitler, long life, liberty, and the pursuit of happiness."

In late November the family were finally able to book space on the S.S. *Manhattan*. So a two-car caravan set off for Bordeaux—Fred and various menfolk in one and Angela, children, and nursemaids (Nanny had an assistant called Dulcie) in the other. Although she and the children spent the rest of the war safe in the United States, Angela did more to bring home the reality of the European carnage to the small Hamilton tribe of Winthrops and Bradfords than did any of those scratchy CBS radio broadcasts from the war zone. Everyone knew the story, for example, of how sisters Rosemary and Eileen had taken their bikes and fled Paris for the south of France when the German army marched in on June 14, 1940. It was a story that my mother would recount again, in 1982, when being interviewed by some Hamilton school children who wanted a first-person recollection of the war from someone ancient enough to remember it.

> The people who went in automobiles were stuck by the side of the road when their gas ran out. The German airplanes would swoop over them and shoot at them. Of course, they tried to dive into the ditches but there wasn't always a place to hide. My sister-in-law's two sisters could leave their bikes by the side of the road and rush into the fields—or go by little farm roads where no one would find them and nobody would shoot at them. They stopped at all the farms and helped themselves to milk and eggs because all of the farmers had fled. When they finally got to the south of France, it was already occupied by the Germans, but they knew people so they were safe.
>
> One day, the two girls had somehow collected … a whole group of children who had been lost, abandoned by the roadside. They were taking care of these children when a young German soldier came over and said to them, "Oh, it looks so nice over here. You seem to be doing so well with those children and they seem to be so happy. I wish you would let me just come and talk to you." They answered, "Certainly not, we are at war with you," and the soldier replied, "Yes, but you started the war." That was the German point of view.

Even more vivid proof of the war, however, came with the arrival at Groton House of British refugee children, sent stateside to escape the blitzkrieg from families known to Angela's mother. Eventually, at the Fred Winthrops', there would be twenty-one people at table each day. The children's parents stayed behind, some with pistols under their pillows, to do what they could to help defeat the Axis. To us young people in Hamilton it seemed almost unimaginable—youngsters our age separated from their parents for no one knew how long. The fighting itself seemed incomprehensibly distant. But its consequences were there among us: children who might lose their parents, who might not have a home to return to.

— • —

Angela, of course, was right. The United States could not stay out of the struggle. But she was wrong about the timing. It took more than two years and a greater threat than watching Europe being swallowed up by the Germans to galvanize "the best and largest democracy in the world." Meanwhile, the passion to become involved gathered speed across the nation. Since the mid-1930s Americans had listened to Hitler raving over shortwave radio, watched as the Axis formed and gathered terrifying force. My mother, like so many Americans, had friends and family in the war zones. There were not only Angela's family, but her own cousins, the van Roijens, in Holland; her step-cousin and school chum, Jean Patten Pellegrini-Quarentotti, in Italy; and her dear friends, the Guillenchmidts, in Paris. Whatever would become of them? How long could America sit on the sidelines and watch?

My father would always remember December 7, 1941, the evening of Pearl Harbor. As he wrote my mother on V-E Day (the end of the war against Germany), "It was a dark wintry night and I drove over to Essex to try to start the organization there of the home guard." Though forty-one when the war broke out, he attempted to enlist right away. But it would take months to process his application. My parents were in Wareham having Sunday lunch at Uncle Billy Amory's on September 3, 1942, when a telegram arrived informing him that he had been accepted.

Official picture of Standish Bradford in uniform, undated

My father decided to serve in the army. Finding it full of Southerners, he concluded that most of the men from the Northeast preferred the navy, where life was reputed to be less grubby and dangerous. Two of my mother's brothers joined the navy, Robert and Nat (Robert not by choice; he had been turned down by the army as too old), as did close family friend Harrison Gardner. Fred Winthrop was in the army, as were others my family knew well—Cabot Lodge, Chandler Bigelow, Archibald Alexander (Jean Sears' husband), and lifelong pal and neighbor Forrester A. "Tim" Clark.

To a man, most Americans in uniform hoped to see the glory of action, so it rankled my father when he found himself assigned stateside. Fred Winthrop, assigned to Honolulu as the chief of information and education, Central Pacific Command, looked wryly at the cushy life that the military had dealt him. He described it in an August 1944 letter to my mother: "My office is very fine. I sit in solitary splendor in a single room with no one but myself. [It is in the] corner of the building with the trade wind blowing my papers constantly all over the floor."

Robert Winthrop, who had been dispatched to run the post office in Trinidad,[3] understood my father's disgruntlement. But his advice was to stay put. Should Standish be reassigned, Robert wrote my mother in a May 1943 letter, he would probably "be stuck in some out-of-the-way place, doing a considerably less important job than he has now. I wish all the men at home that are bellyaching because they are still in the country and doing nothing because of it, could spend a while in a place

MAJ. F. WINTHROP JR.

Right: Robert Winthrop served his country during World War II in Trinidad, running the post office.

Far right: Frederic Winthrop spent most of World War II in Hawaii.

Nat Winthrop in his navy uniform, with sons, from left, Beek, Matthew, and John

like [Trinidad].… Of course," Robert ended his letter wistfully, "to lead the invading armies into Germany would be something else again, but I doubt whether that is in the cards for many of us."

Robert was mistaken about the cards that would be dealt to his brother-in-law. Within a year my father was in England, where final plans were being secretly shaped for what would be, in Winston Churchill's words, "the greatest amphibious operation in history"—the invasion of Normandy.[4] On D-Day, June 6, 1944, the first waves of American troops landed on Utah and Omaha beaches and were battling to establish a foothold for the march eastward across France to their final destination, Berlin.

Lieutenant Colonel Bradford arrived in Normandy barely a month after D-Day, on an LST, riding "ashore … in a black sedan and [being] saluted by unsuspecting members of the military who thought it must be a General." His letter, written to Freddy on October 15, continued that the American operation was "still in a narrow stretch along the beaches, and at night our artillery operated from behind us." The closeness to battle was just what he had hoped for. As Fred had written his sister in August: "Brad wanted to get near enough to smell gunpowder."

Bad weather had kept the Allied troops bogged down on that slender beachhead in Normandy, but, shortly after my father's arrival, the Americans succeeded in breaking out. By the end of the first week in August, General George S. Patton's newly formed Third Army had closed off any line of resistance to the west, from Brittany.

REARED *in a* GREENHOUSE

Thousands of German troops had been garrisoned there, taking over homes and villas. Les Essarts, where Angela had imagined she could safely wait out the war, was lived in by German soldiers and fortified bunkers had been built on the cliffs above the channel—part of the incredible 3,750-mile Atlantic Wall from the Netherlands to the Spanish border that the Germans installed to repulse any attack.[5] When the Americans landed, the Germans blew it up. The local people tried to help save it, but the Germans held them off with machine guns. When the Forbeses returned after the war, they found nothing but a charred shell where their house had stood.[6] General Patton's assignment was to strand the German troops along the coast, penning them in and leaving them to wither.[7] Once this job was completed, Paris was reclaimed. American, British, and Canadian forces pressed on swiftly. By September 11, however, enemy resistance had stiffened, advances were harder won, and supplies were stretched to the limit.

In mid-August my father was made commanding officer of the 71st Replacement Battalion, Third Army. It was a glorious assignment. Their work was critical, for resistance was fierce and casualties high. Reinforcements were needed continually, fresh troops who could step in where others had been mowed down. The Allies seemed to have almost unlimited reserve manpower. The Germans had virtually exhausted theirs. His assignment placed my father hard by some of the heaviest fighting in France. The Third Army was leading advances along the American forces' southern flank, racing from St. Malo to Le Mans, to Chartres, and on to Nancy. My father's own unit spent their days "bivouacking at a great rate" and working to replace the wounded to keep the front line strong. Their achievements were highly regarded. As my father himself would write my mother on August 12, 1945, he thought this was an "outstanding" operation: the 71st Replacement Battalion was thought by many to be "the best forward battalion" and the 10th, to which he would be assigned next, would do an equally exemplary job, training four thousand men in a month from service to infantry troops.

Another plus: General Patton was a hometown hero, a career army man and native Californian who had married one of the Ayers—Beatrice Banning Ayer—an aunt of Theo's (Robert's now ex-wife).[8] Even though she and George spent only summers at Green Meadows, the farm she had bought in 1927 smack in the heart of Myopia Hunt Club territory, Hamilton claimed Patton as its own. Tough, hot-tempered, and in love with war, he had outraged the press and offended many in 1943 by his highly publicized slapping of an American soldier. But by war's end it was these very traits that, as my father wrote my mother on July 4, 1945, made him "the most popular of all the four Army generals."

General George S. Patton, conquering hero of World War II and sometime Hamilton resident (courtesy Library of Congress)

My father wrote my mother as often as he could that summer of 1944, giving her a flavor of his work. On August 11:

> The job of closing an old camp and opening a new one, coordinating the move, operating in both camps at one time while the move is in progress, seeing that the men don't miss any hot meals, and all the other details, is a full-time job for all daylight hours.... Being a forward battalion, we operate alone and all the planning is done by us. It is really great fun and gives us all a feeling we are doing our part in the war.

By mid-August they had moved eight times in considerably fewer weeks. On clear nights they slept out under the stars; on rainy ones, in their pup tents. My father wrote with relish about the sites they chose. Once he set up his tent at the edge of a field, behind the stump of an old chestnut tree. There was a hedgerow nearby, one of those high stands of ancient trees with roots a thousand years old that crisscrossed the French countryside, some with cows behind, others, with the enemy.[9] Another time they camped in a virgin forest of great white oaks, a wondrous but dark setting made more chilling by constant rain. Once they were in an American-owned chateau with a park stocked with deer, pheasants, and trout and a little river where the troops enjoyed bathing in the fresh water.

If the countryside was tranquil, its inhabitants were seldom so. A baron and baroness whose chateau had survived the occupation with its gilded furnishings intact had lost their only child to starvation in a German prison camp. Heightening the tragic irony, the Germans had allowed the parents to visit the boy just before his death, publicizing this as a good-will gesture to the French. My father wrote my mother about this couple, and about another family, husband and wife and seven children, who had spent the war crowded into the back of the house while the Germans occupied the main sections. Another chateau had been left "like a pigpen" after the Germans carried away "all but a few pieces of valueless furniture." But overall, the country people looked pretty well nourished. "The farmyards are well stocked with cows, sheep, and poultry," he wrote. Perhaps Angela had been right. Perhaps with cabbages, and fish, and a cow in the yard, starving would have been impossible.

The Allied sweep through France was bringing not food, but freedom, to the conquered French people. Wrote my father to my mother on August 26, 1944: "You cannot imagine the expressions of joy on the people's faces as we pass through the towns. As far as I can see, most [of them] spend the entire day by the side of the roads waving, making V's, saying '*Vive l'Amérique*,' and the children hold signs in English saying Good Luck."

All letters written by and to U.S. service personnel were scrutinized by the censors for any information that might unwittingly help the enemy. My father always wrote home guardedly, accepting the need for caution. Just how important it was became plain to him one day on meeting a mother in a small town where his battalion was stopping. As he wrote my mother on August 22, the woman came up to him accompanied by a little boy, with tears in her eyes and her lower jaw trembling— obviously agitated by the appearance of a contingent of American soldiers. Just a week earlier, she told my father, her older son had been killed by a bomb. If the Germans discovered the presence of Americans, she feared they would surely come back.

Within security limits, my parents played a game: he dropped obscure hints as to where he was and she tried to unravel them. My mother knew exactly what he was referring to when he wrote that "keeping up with our friend from Topsfield Road" (General Patton) left him almost no free time. This next clue, from a letter of October 1, 1944, took more time to figure out: "Strange as it may seem, I am reminded quite a lot of Mrs. Ted Spencer these days, especially her sunny side." Mrs. Ted Spencer was my mother's old friend Nancy Murray Spencer; on September 16 the Third Army had won a bridgehead at the Moselle River in the city of Nancy and had become heavily engaged on the Metz-Nancy line. It was my mother who ran into trouble. The Red Cross, she wrote my father, would not accept a note in which she had used the nickname Nat instead of Nathaniel.

Without knowing his exact location, my mother had a pretty good idea in the fall of 1944 that her husband was in the thick of things. As September gave way to October, the fun of summer camping was being displaced by the discomfort of constant rain. On October 4, my father wrote he was sitting in front of a fire and looking forward to his first hot bath since June. With worse days ahead, he asked my mother to help him order an army arctic sleeping bag. "Dampness gets into all bed clothes and one can't get it out," he wrote.

My mother's hopes that my father would be home by Christmas soon evaporated. The November rains were the worst in Europe for many years, flooding rivers and streams and making quagmires through which the infantry had to struggle. By mid-December the Third Army had ground to a halt at the Siegfried Line, and to the north, on December 16, the Fifth and Sixth Panzer armies began a savage counter-attack that would drive a sixty-mile wedge into the heart of the Allied forces. This famous struggle, the Battle of the Bulge, was—as Winston Churchill put it—to be Germany's "final massed attack of the war."[10] It was a cause for no little worry to the Allied Command. The home front, too, was jolted. Two days later my mother wrote my father that a "cloud seems to hang over me." On December 21, with Christmas only four days away, she wrote another troubled letter to my father:

> The news from the front is ... very disturbing. Those Germans are amazing people. I don't see how they do it and I wish we could put a stop to them and their evil ways forever....
>
> I thought you would be home by now and the waste of war would be over. It seems like a long, long time, but we are in the hands of God or Fate and we can but accept it and do the best we can.

My mother didn't know it then, but at the start of the Battle of the Bulge my father had been given a new command, farther away from the front. He felt torn by his luck. "I should have loved to have been" with them, he wrote my mother later, "but for you and the children." In a letter to my mother dated January 3, 1945, friend

Harrison Gardner, identifying his address as "completely at sea," put a different twist on my father's role in the Battle of the Bulge:

> I almost forgot to tell you. Last week I had tea and strumpets [*sic*] with General MacArthur who told me that Standish was personally, alone, responsible for stopping the Germans in France in the recent unpleasantness. Mac told me that with complete disregard for his own safety, Standish stood up in his jeep and coolly shouted "*Ils ne passeront pas.*" [They shall not pass.] But his French was so bad that the Germans thought he said, "Hitler has married Eleanor Roosevelt" so that was too much and they all quit, every damn one of the them.

——— • ———

My mother told me years later that she would sometimes lie awake at night worrying what would happen should our father be killed. She wrote him of friends who had lost their lives, of others who had been wounded, and of the waste of it all. The dark side of the war, however, was seldom the focus of her letters to my father, and over the years it would recede from the portrait she would paint of her life during those days. Instead, she reminisced about how the war allowed her to relive the simpler days of her youth, when horses were used for transportation and everyone lived off the land. My father had written her that he looked at the war as a "great adventure" in which everyone in the family would play a part. My mother surely agreed. She entered into the war effort with relish, rigging up the pony cart instead of revving up the car, harrowing the fields and spreading manure, creating a vegetable garden and freezing the produce, spotting planes and working at the hospital. She remembered fondly the slower pace of life:

The pony cart was a lovely, slow way to get around during World War II. In our courtyard, July 1941, with Indiana in the shafts and me at the reins

REARED *in a* GREENHOUSE

We mostly walked and bicycled and drove the pony.... We actually had a lot of fun bicycling. You went along so slowly and saw everything. There are lots of things you miss whizzing by in an automobile. And it really was a very pleasant life ... though it wasn't very nice that we should get pleasure out of awful things like that, like a war.

Everyone was planting "victory gardens." My mother's involved a meticulous battle plan that began in January with the marshaling of seeds, continued in February with the careful drawing up of plans for the order of planting, moved on to March with the preparation of the soil, and went into high gear in April and May with the planting of seeds. By summer, enemies were out in full force—the corn-borers and the slugs, the Japanese beetles and the potato bugs, the raccoons and the woodchucks. Rather than guns, my mother became an expert in the natural weapon systems of organic gardening, and her troops flourished. "I am so grateful for every mouth-full of corn, limas, asparagus, raspberries, etc. etc.," she wrote my father at the end of the first summer. "You can't imagine how good they taste, nor how well fed the children look." Not all the Hamilton ladies agreed that growing vegetables was a pleasure. One of them, a golfing, bridge-playing, hard-drinking member of the Myopia Hunt Club set, growled in disgust at her own hard-won peas: "I planted 'em, I grew 'em, I weeded 'em, I picked 'em, I shelled 'em, I cooked 'em, and I say 'To hell with 'em!' "

My mother loved the whole process, not just the growing. There was also the revolutionary technology of freezing. She studied the manuals, popped the vegetables into boiling water, plunged them into icy water, packed, sealed, and labeled waxy cartons, and arranged the bulging boxes neatly in her enormous, spanking new deep-freeze in the basement. Nothing was haphazard about such operations. It was important to do them right—and it was hard.

Just how hard is clear from instructions she kept on how to prepare milk to churn into butter. First, it had to be set in a separator and held at 50 degrees for 12 to 24 hours. (How did one do that in the changeable climate of New England?) Then the cream that was supposed to have risen was to be heated to 145 to 150 degrees for 30 minutes. (What if one had a temperamental stove?) Or the fresh cream could be "adjusted" to 65 to 70 degrees for 12 to 16 hours. After all that, one could expect to get a modest 4¼ pounds of butter from the cream obtained from 100 pounds of milk.

Despite the work, the rationing of meat and butter made my mother grateful for the cows and other livestock on the place.

Chickens we had, and cows, and then we got some pigs. Think how lucky we were. Because we had all the butter we wanted, all the meat we wanted, we became very popular. We churned our [cream] into butter. And we gave butter away for Christmas presents.

But then ... we had to feed the cows and horses. We had a lot of hay, but we could scarcely get any grain. As a matter of fact, that was rather good for the horses. They had less pep. They were more manageable. We had trouble getting any grain for the chickens, so we used to feed them table scraps. And we used to feed them scraps from the fish store, old fins and heads and tails and things like that, which the fish man didn't want. The chickens kept on eating these fish scraps, and pretty soon the eggs started tasting like fish. We would kill a dozen chickens at a time and put them in the deep freeze. You know it's no fun plucking a chicken, and when I had finished plucking a chicken, I decided I would never eat another.

Chickens you had plucked yourself were bad enough. Squirrels were worse still. But my mother had to be supportive when my brother Stanna offered to supplement the meat supply by shooting these scurrying, long-tailed rodents. The cook even entered in, preparing the game he had shot and serving it up covered with gravy. "Can you imagine anything worse or more unappetizing?" she asked later. "It would come in on a plate [looking] like a squirrel."

At the time my mother thought little of all that work. But years later, as she looked back upon her wartime world, she marveled at the lack of men to help.

There were no men anywhere. All the husbands and fathers were in the Army.... There were no doctors.... They ... and the nurses had gone overseas. There was one doctor from Marblehead who was willing to come and do what he could. He died of a heart attack when he was only 38 ... just worked himself to death.... And the plumbers had gone overseas. My husband was overseas. All of our neighbors were overseas. On the place, all we had were two old men, Leonard and Clarence, who had always worked there. They were getting on in years, but never mind, they were full of strength and energy. But the best workers we had were ... little boys 12 years old. They were particularly wonderful. I think they enjoyed the challenge, and they felt pretty big, too.

By today's standards, my mother was no feminist. She and the other women carried on with no thought that their work might be leading to some kind of "empowerment." They just did what they had to do. My mother had seen other women in her family coping alone. When her husband Jeffie had died, Aunt Clara Coolidge had just turned forty—the same age as my mother during the war—and she had forged ahead, raising her sons and running substantial establishments on both Coolidge Point and in town. My mother's sister Katharine was another example. Unmarried until the age of thirty-three, "she has made a life for herself by herself," wrote my mother admiringly in a July 8, 1944, letter to my father.

My mother had assumed a traditionally male role when she chose to oversee the design and construction of the family's new house. It was not a matter of gender. The new house on Black Brook Farm would be paid for with her money, she had firm convictions about comfort and practicality, so it was she who worked most closely with architect J. Hampden Robb. My father was well pleased with the house and, when he left for England, he was confident that he was leaving the place itself under "very intelligent direction." It had occurred to him that he should have gathered everyone—the children, the servants, and the two farmhands—and made it clear to them that Mrs. Bradford would be in charge. As he wrote my mother on March 7, 1944:

REARED *in a* GREENHOUSE

In any operation, whether it is a business, the army, a farm or a household, there has to be a head who makes all the decisions, and those decisions are final, and should be accepted without question or delay. The job of everyone else is to make it easy for [the head] by willing compliance with whatever [decision is made]. This is so fundamental that it doesn't really need saying but it might have been a good idea merely to get the whole outfit working as a group.

It wasn't long, however, before my father discovered that my mother was not only making the decisions for everyone at home, but that she didn't necessarily even welcome his input. Soon after his arrival in England, she apparently wrote admonishing him not to tell her how to run things, for he wrote her back on June 1, "You [said] you didn't want any advice unless you asked for it." Though he couldn't remember what he had written to provoke this comment, he apologized, adding "if I get too paternalistic again, let me know."

My father accepted her warning and thereafter limited himself largely to observations about European agriculture. He wrote of the French practice of conserving and using liquid manure, how soil with limestone might affect the bone structure of cattle, of the potential for artificial insemination, of the effects of the plentiful European rainfall on tree size, and of hot frames and cold frames and greenhouses. My mother took up those of his ideas that she found practicable. Concerning liquid manure, for example, she wrote on November 23, 1944:

I have just located an old-fashioned watering can, such as used to keep the dust down on city streets, and it will soon be spreading manure all over our hay fields! It is the funniest looking thing and takes me back to my earliest memories.... The liquid manure has no objectionable odor, whereas when Leonard and I investigated the cesspool, it was overpowering.

After the war, my mother and father agreed to divide responsibility for the farm: the cattle would be his realm, gardening hers. My father had discovered that in England this wasn't an odd arrangement. The owner of one of England's finest herds, for example, knew each of his cows individually, "which his wife can't understand," my father wrote on June 30, 1944, "as she says they all look alike." As for gardening, my father dared intrude on his wife's sacred territory only insofar as to suggest how she might handle a predatory deer. "Shoot him!" he wrote her on May 1, 1944, "but first get permission from the Gloucester game warden." His instructions were precise on how to carry out the execution: "You will find some shells near my shotgun on the chest of drawers in my bathroom closet. I would lie in the arbor vitae before dawn as about the best chance to get a shot and if you do, aim for just behind the forequarter about halfway down from the shoulder."

New England has never been known for its congenial weather, but 1944 and 1945 were rougher than usual. The summer of 1944 brought a severe drought. "We have only about half a potato crop this year," my mother lamented in September, "and the plain is in bad shape." The fall brought a hurricane and the threat of an extended

power outage. "I am glad you were so ingenious about the deep freeze," my father wrote her on December 30, 1944, on being informed that she had insulated it with every blanket in the house. "It would be a terrible blow to lose all the good things you have stored away." The winter brought unprecedented cold and snow, and with the spring and early summer of 1945 came rains that threatened the crops. My father understood the pressures. "You at home have the problems and the worries," he wrote my mother on February 17, 1945. "We over here all agree that it is much harder on you than on us." More than sympathetic, he was filled with pride about how well she was managing. "It seems you are handling everything perfectly," he wrote her July 18, 1944, "and you have so many things on the fire at once." He missed being out in the fields himself, writing on June 30, 1944, "How I would like to change places with you or rather be with you when you … and the children had been haying till 8:15 and 8:30 two days in a row. It must have been exciting the night you got the load in just before the thunderstorm." He worried about her overdoing. "You told me about working till your back and arms were gone, spreading manure," he wrote her two days later. "It is tough work and I wish you would try my idea about supervising more and working less."

— • —

Engrossing as she found it, farming took only a portion of my mother's time and energies. One thing after another got jotted down on lists, reflecting the unrelenting tug of a million numbing chores. "Hose for dogwood," began one, penciled on the back of a letter from my father, "measure trunk, gas into tank, auto tax, cats before 9 a.m., Kitty's tomatoes, spray garden, return cellar key, ranges, glue." Sometimes emergencies crowded out the daily tasks: Stanna unintentionally slammed the door on his sister Katharine's finger, several Clark children moved in when their mother became ill, a terrible fire broke out in Harvard Forest.

Rationing took a toll on her ingenuity as well as her time. She had to keep track of not only the five family ration books but also those of the four household staff—baby nurse Jerry, waitress Hazel, chambermaid Mary, and cook Anne.[11] Born and raised to be frugal, my mother seemed to enjoy the game of making do with less. Take the shoe shortage, for example: "You had to have coupons for shoes. And that was all very well if you were fully grown and your feet were stabilized. But it was terribly hard to keep your children in shoes because their feet grew so fast. You could only buy them shoes twice a year." My mother used her shoe coupons to buy shoes that fit her. Then she turned them over to Stanna and me, since our feet were about the same size as hers. To conserve precious gas, after driving us to the school bus each morning, she would park and then walk the mile home across the fields. In the afternoon, she would walk back to the car and drive us home. This was one of her wartime secrets.

The shortages were not only on the home front. Messages came from my father requesting not only the extra-warm sleeping bag, but such things as woollen socks and pajamas, cigars, and Baker's chocolate. In my father's opinion, by late summer 1945 food appeared scarcer for people in the United States than for the troops abroad.

My mother took the shortages in stride, but she did cast a quizzical eye on some of the home front activities that had been dreamt up in the name of war preparedness.

> In the beginning we had soldiers stationed in Hamilton and they lived in the Town Hall. I don't know exactly what they did. I suppose they drilled and trained and were prepared in case of anything....
>
> We had civil defense.... A regular Army officer came down and drilled us. I can't imagine why we needed to be drilled. We were divided up into different groups ... groups which were supposed to understand how to drive trucks, how to repair trucks when they were broken down. And then there were those of us who were supposed to cook for all of the refugees who were going to stream out of Beverly when the bombs dropped. Of course they never did drop.

She took up new patriotic tasks while continuing to carry out her civilian duties such as holding office in the Episcopal Christ Church Guild. "Congratulations," wrote my father on May 12, 1944, "on your re-election to secretaryship of the Guild for the eighth consecutive year." He worried, though, that she was taking on too much. "Don't let Sybil Wolcott suck you into any more work in the hospital or anywhere," he wrote in the same letter.

My mother, of course, went right on volunteering at the hospital and everywhere else they were looking for help—although she may have questioned the use of it all.

> A lot of us volunteered [at the Beverly Hospital]. We would work in the wards and we would work in the kitchen. [One] day I was in the emergency and [a man] drove up in a great hurry in a taxi cab and he rushed into the hospital and he showed that he had lost a finger. It got cut off somehow. So, of course they yelled at me to go and get the finger out of the taxi cab. But the taxi cab had gone and no one had taken the ... number. I couldn't find the cab. And the poor man never got his finger.

— • —

The four of us, not long before my father joined the army, c. 1942: Libby, 2, Katharine 3, Stanna, 9, and me, 10

World War II liberated America's women as surely as it did the conquered countries of Europe and Asia. With millions tasting the freedom and income from work in factories and the armed forces, the clock could never be turned back to the days when women would live solely in the shadow of men. Even though my mother and her lady friends in Hamilton did not take paying jobs, they surely felt a sense of accomplishment at coping alone, a feeling that they were as competent as any man.

Perish the thought, however, that one would breathe such an idea to one's husband. My mother's letters reflected her continued reliance on my father. Reading them now, and thinking how independent she was to become, I wonder whether there wasn't a dollop of diplomacy in her words.

She found social life as a single woman a particular trial. "It has given me a very great inferiority complex," she wrote my father July 8, 1944.

> I have issued many futile invitations or do I mean "many invitations in vain." And I asked well ahead! In my youth I wished I could ask people freely to my house and I liked them and felt they would like to come, but, of course, home conditions made it almost impossible to have them. Now I can ask them as freely as I want, but why should they want to come to see me? They only want to come if they can see you, too! I need your reflected glory in which to shine. Alone I am nothing.

Raising four young ones alone was hard, too. I was not quite thirteen when my father left for the war, exactly my mother's age when her own father had gone overseas in World War I. Stanna was eleven, Katharine five, and Libby four. For Stanna particularly, she wrote in the fall, she felt my father's being away made a great difference. "A boy resents a woman bossing him. He respects his father more." After a particularly mischievous prank that Stanna and I perpetrated, she wrote on September 4, 1944, "I am very much troubled today and feel inadequate in bringing up the children." Preparing the hay fields, she felt, also needed a man. Next year, she wrote that same month, it would be carried out "under *your* leadership."

Though only a small number of her letters to my father survive,[12] my mother must have written to him constantly. He would get four or five in a bunch, and he would read them again and again, sometimes by flashlight in his pup tent at night. "Your letters are the best part of my life," he wrote her February 9, 1945. When she protested (perhaps too much) that the life she described in them was "drab," he disagreed. Perhaps those years of chatting with her cheery grandmother had trained her. Perhaps she had inherited from her mother the ability to see the drollery in every

REARED *in a* GREENHOUSE

humdrum tale. Wherever she got the talent, by the time World War II came along, my mother knew how to write an entertaining letter.

The children, of course, were the apple of her writerly eye. On July 8, 1944, she wrote my father about taking Katharine to the hospital with an infected foot.

> Dr. Johnson put her to sleep a few minutes and cut it open. She was awfully good; you can't imagine how good, but after she came out of the anesthesia she had a jag on such as I've never seen. She was so funny and animated and used such long sophisticated words and never stopped talking. She was sitting bolt upright with rosy cheeks talking away, so I asked her what she would like for supper. "Nothing," she answered cheerfully. "I feel much too sick."

On August 16 she described Libby learning to swim.

> Libby had her first diving lesson today and landed flat on her tummy! She practices her strokes all over the floor and even in bed.… [She] is so small and sometimes she seems to be exhausted and about to sink beneath the waves and many a kind lady has given her a helping hand, only to be looked at reproachfully because Libby wanted to swim "all by her own self."

On December 18, even as premonitions of the calamitous Bulge offensive weighed her down, she couldn't repress her amusement about the children. Katharine and Libby were coloring Christmas decorations, she wrote, and Libby "chose the gloomiest colors, greys and muddy greens, etc." As she dusted the bronze statue of Apollo, naked but for a detachable fig leaf, the girls asked her, "Who is that? Is he a minister?"

And she told him how the children missed him. "Today," she wrote in August, "Libby got up from her rest and *tidied up her bed* because she said her Daddy was coming to see her at 3 o'clock!" And in the fall, she wrote that Stanna "is awfully sweet about you and says, 'I have so many things to talk over with Daddy. Gee, I wish I could see him.' "

A refreshing change during the summers my father was away was the move to Coolidge Point, at the invitation of Aunt Clara, to enjoy the sea breezes, ocean swimming, and some relief from the constant pressure of farm life (although my mother still drove home dutifully twice a week for full days of gardening and freezing vegetables). She wrote my father of the new sights and happenings in Magnolia. The evening of August 15, 1944, was typical: "The children have been swimming the last two evenings and so have several other people, including numberless sandpipers. I am so glad to be here.… How we shall miss it all when we go home again!" Aunt Clara had whispered to her that "the Point is full of romance." "How could it fail to be," my mother wrote my father,

My sisters, Libby, 5, and Katharine, 6, at the Magnolia Beach Club in August 1945

"it is so beautiful!!" The evidence was everywhere. There was even a "funny skinny little" about-to-be "Grottie" age fourteen who had fallen "desperately in love with … a great big heavy awkward girl of 15!!" The lass kept the little lad out till after eleven each night, wrote my mother, and "he is so slight … the Point is worried at his lack of sleep."

On Thanksgiving Day 1944, she wrote my father about an unaccustomedly grand social outing in Hamilton.

> On Wed. I put on my best long evening dress, my gold shoes, my carriage boots (as it was storming) and your army raincoat!! Then in state and comfort I drove the Buick to Mabel's to a real dinner party of gentile [*sic*] speech and manners.… [Dick Storey, the host, related that] one day he met "an old man named Eustis" from Virginia who said he had been to school in Mass. Dick said "Are you related to Morton Eustis?" to which the man replied "I am Morton."[13] Dick said "Morton was an old man and I am an old man. I forget how old we all are because in the army I associate with youngsters." Nat has said the same thing and Nat is only 32!

—— • ——

The Battle of the Bulge gave the Allies their last scare. After this, victory was certain. By March 29, 1945, the American army was in Frankfurt, the Ruhr and its 325,000 defenders were encircled, and Germany's western front had collapsed. Even the sudden death on April 12 of President Roosevelt, whose unflinching war leadership had won the unabashed admiration and even the 1944 vote of rock-ribbed Republican Standish Bradford, could not dampen the mood of confidence.

On May 7, at 2:41 a.m., U. S. general Bedell Smith and German general Alfred Jodl signed the treaty agreeing to Germany's unconditional surrender. All hostilities ceased at midnight on May 8. My father went to Paris the day after V-E Day. The celebration was still at fever pitch. It "was a mad house," he wrote my mother, "dancing on the sidewalks and thousands of people … walking arm-in-arm on the streets and singing and laughing."

This was Paris's second mass celebration in fewer than nine months. The previous August, when Allied troops entered the city, there had been a "rapturous demonstration, German prisoners were spat at, collaborators dragged through the streets, and the liberating troops feted."[14] My father had visited frequently since that time, almost always looking up my mother's Russian refugee friends the Guillenchmidts, whose daughter Natasha he had met some sixteen years earlier while she was in Boston studying stenography. On one such trip, he also succeeded in tracking down Angela's sisters Griselda and Eileen. He learned that their mother had come to visit and had left taking with her all the toilet paper in the apartment. "That damage," he reported to my mother on March 4, 1945, "had not been repaired." Later still he had lunch with Bill and Susan Mary Patten—he, the Billy Patten of Hell Hall memory, and she, after Bill's death, to become Mrs. Joseph Alsop and a personality of some note in Washington, D.C.

REARED *in a* GREENHOUSE

My father would have another seven months in Europe before he finally came home—bringing a European theater ribbon with four stars, a Bronze Star, and a promotion to full colonel to attest to a job well done. But by mid-April army life had already changed for the better. He found lodging with a lovely French family, the Lepissiers. Each morning, he wrote my mother, Madame Lepissier put fresh lilacs in his room and "there is a sweet smelling vase of them on this table as I write. I face the French doors leading onto my balcony and they stand wide open and the evening breeze is just a whisper."

For a while he was stationed in Barbizon, whose name he didn't mention, instead hinting to my mother that he was in "a place where artists have gathered in the past and famous pictures you have known well were painted." Later he moved to Versailles, where his office was "quite de luxe with two big French windows on the second floor." One evening in late June, he wrote that he was

> sitting in the garden of the house in which I live listening to a 16-piece orchestra playing at the tennis club a little ways away.... You would be interested in the garden. Almost every inch is cultivated with flowers and vegetables interspersed. Roses, lilies and four other flowers are in bloom and there are many others. Around the inside of the wall are espaliered fruit trees, lilacs, and birch with their tops cut off so the branches fall like willows and a blue spruce very much out of place.

Throughout the summer he played tennis nearly every evening, four or five sets at a time, giving rise to an "extraordinarily tough" equipment problem—not enough tennis balls, shirts, and shorts—which he asked my mother to remedy.

Assigned to the occupying armies, my father ended up in Berlin in the "fascinating" position, as he described it in a July 23, 1945 letter to his mother, of director of the U.S. Legal Division of Control in occupied Germany under General Lucius Clay, responsible for all legislation and general law questions for the German transitional government. In Berlin he went to the opera and the symphony, and even, one afternoon, to an American-style football game. The height of luxury, just before his forty-fifth birthday, September 23, 1945, was an evening with two Englishmen, both brigadier generals, at their accommodations, a lovely house overlooking a lake. "We had a five-course dinner," he wrote, "served by a German butler and followed by liqueurs and coffee in the best style."

To the victors were going the spoils. No one on the Allied side thought for a minute that the rewards were not well deserved, for the very names of the German leaders—Hitler, Goebbels, Goering—had an enduring ring of evil. In a letter dated June 2-3, my father wrote my mother that he had met with one lieutenant colonel who was stationed in Berchtesgaden: "He is living in Herman Goering's lodge. It is most sumptuous with thick rugs, silver plate and paintings." The officer had told him about Hitler's dwellings:

> His main place was pretty well demolished by the British air raids, but the "Eagles Nest" was still intact. To reach it you enter through great metal doors in the side of a mountain and then take an elevator several hundred feet up. The building itself

extends to the edge of the precipice and the plate glass windows are vertically above the drop. The place is furnished with rolling couches, a big gaming table, and elaborate kitchens and utensils. They found so much wine that the colonel is tired of drinking it.

My father himself went into a cellar of the Reich Chancery where he met with a Soviet captain whose troops had taken it originally. The captain showed my father "where they found Goebbels and his wife and four children, the latter five poisoned."

The most graphic images of war in my father's letters from Germany, however, were of the citizenry, the Germans whose lives had been devastated by war. On August 10 he wrote:

> They were everywhere. Mostly just standing around in shabby clothes but many pushing their little carts or carrying baskets or bundles somewhere. All looked pretty down at the heel and actually most of them have nothing.… The children look awfully nice. Most are blonds and all are healthy with good expressions and a complete absence of any perceptible after-effect from the bombing. Those that escaped death appear unaffected. The tragedy of the whole thing grows on you. 28,000 to 60,000 people were killed in less than half an hour in one town bombed by the British, and there are several towns where the total number of people killed in a single raid far exceeded that figure.
>
> Here in Berlin, they say the destruction is worse than elsewhere.… Most of the buildings are standing but I would estimate more than 90 percent were damaged.… There are many Germans about but how they live and what most of them have to live for in Berlin is a mystery. A few are employed by the UN and a few run food shops but otherwise there is no business or trade. I think they will move to the country and Berlin will become depopulated. Overall is the pall of dirt and now weeds.
>
> On the way to the office are several streets where fine houses are completely gutted. One still gives out an ugly odor. Yesterday I saw a girl standing crying as she looked through a fence into a bombed out house. The Germans have a word for "the future has no hope" and they are using it.

Perhaps my mother felt ambivalent about these pathetic pictures. There was the admiration she had expressed for Germans on her trips to Europe, the appalling fact that these hard-working people had fallen for the leadership of a madman and entered willingly into a war that resulted in the deaths of millions of innocent people, and her mixed feelings about Fräulein. Fräulein was to spend World War II in Germany, and when it ended letter after pitiful letter arrived in Hamilton, pleading for help. My mother wrote back and tried to send her packages of food and clothing, but it seemed that nothing got through. One letter from Fräulein, dated August 4, 1946, begins:

> I have written to you so many letters and I did not get a word from you if you did receive one of them. How are you all. I have been thinking of you all, all this terrible time we did pass through. Munich lies in [illegible] and ashes. I have been very ill for one whole year and still so weak and miserable unable to walk.… I would need something that I may get strength. Milk in boxes, *real coffee*, salted butter, rice, lard and flour so I could get bread baked. Dorothy do help me, I know you will. Also, if you could spare

old boots and a few aprons with long sleeves. Have got no underwear cannot get any stockings also. I am as thin you would not recognize me. My Dear Dotty, it is so hard for me to ask you all these things.

My father, too, felt torn about the enemy. He wrote that he and his fellow officers spent many hours dissecting the German character. "I do not want them to suffer unreasonably," he commented, "but I don't trust them at all and I do not want them to have another chance."

On Sunday June 24, 1945, about halfway between V-E Day and V-J Day (August 15), the town of Hamilton had held its own victory celebration. Everyone in town turned out to welcome its adopted son, General George S. Patton, whose Third Army had swept the Germans before it and whose brusque and brilliant leadership had made him so popular. A few days earlier more than a million persons had cheered him en route a mile-long trip from Bedford Airport to Boston. In Hamilton, there was music by the 102nd Regimental Band from Lynn and the Hamilton High School girls' glee club. Patton made a brief speech, reported in the June 25 issue of the *Salem Evening News*. "It is difficult for you to stand here this afternoon and real- ize what your sons, brothers, and husbands have kept from you. Your railroads are running, your bridges are still up, and your homes are still standing." Thousands of well-wishers were out that afternoon, and he invited them all to come onto the plat- form to shake hands after his talk. "But remember," he warned them, "there'll be no damned squeezing."

The celebration in June, wrote my father, must have "caused great excitement." "How very, very right you were about him when all the others were blaming him," his July 8, 1945, letter continued, referring to Patton's famous slapping incident. My mother had defended General Patton against those who had lost faith in him, and my father liked her pluckiness. More, he valued her opinion: "I have great respect for the soundness of your judgment and am always interested to have your opinions in matters of public interest. [In conversations about current affairs], I have often quoted your opinion."

This was General Patton's last visit to Hamilton. He had planned to be back for Christmas, after finishing out his wartime duties in Europe. On December 9, 1945, just one day before his flight home, however, he was in an automobile accident that resulted in his death. Not even his body was returned home, for General Eisenhower had ordered that all American soldiers who died in Europe were to be buried where they had died.[15] My father was luckier. On December 10, the day after General Patton's accident, he arrived home in Hamilton.

— • —

Whether or not my mother felt some sympathy for the Germans, her first allegiance was naturally to her own family and friends who had suffered at their hands. Most precarious was the situation of Jan Herman and Anne van Roijen and their three little children, Tina, Jan Herman, Jr., and Digna, all under five when Holland was overrun in May 1940. My mother marveled at the stories of their dangerous life in The Hague during the German occupation. In 1939 Jan Herman had been reassigned from Tokyo, where he had served as secretary to the Netherlands legation, to the Netherlands Ministry of Foreign Affairs, where he had been appointed chief of the political division. The German occupation soon put an end to his government service, and Jan Herman spent most of the war either as a high-level operative in the Dutch underground or as a prisoner of the Germans. The family had almost nothing to eat during the war years, somehow surviving on sugar beets and tulip bulbs. The children were reluctant to eat the tulips unless they had been reassured that the flowers would be orange—Holland's national color.[16]

One of the activities in which Jan Herman was involved was clandestinely tuning in to the BBC. My mother described how dangerous it must have been.

> You were not allowed by the German soldiers to keep a radio. But Cousin Anne and Cousin Herman took their radio and they put it in Cousin Anne's closet where she kept her dresses. They put in a false floor. Every afternoon at 5, it was arranged that somebody would listen to the BBC. She went into her dress closet and she got down on the floor and she would put her ear to the floorboards. And Cousin Herman would wander around outside, keeping watch.

Anne van Roijen's brother was in the Dutch army. The Germans were killing all the Dutch military personnel, so the van Roijens hid him, my mother remembered, "up in the attic, where there was a sort of vent. Just as soon as the Germans came, which they often did to investigate the house, he would scramble up into the vent. They never found him."

Three times Jan Herman was imprisoned by the Germans: "They had put him in solitary confinement for 40 days, where he lost a lot of weight and got very thin. He was questioned by the Gestapo and he said his inquisitors were so stupid that he could answer their questions with no trouble at all."

Another time he was sent by the leaders of the Resistance to iron out some misunderstandings with the government in exile. The first challenge was to get to London, where the government was operating. He carried false papers and walked though fields from farm house to farm house. No one challenged him and he made it to the British lines. If he hadn't known one of the British officers, however, he might have been imprisoned. As it was, he was escorted to London. The suspense for the family was terrible, my mother remembered. They had a plan by which he would notify them if he arrived safely: "At 5 every afternoon, Anne would tune into the BBC. The code for his safe arrival would be 'Oh, I have found just the governess for the children.' She listened each day for several days, and finally she heard the strange message and she knew all was well."

In April 1945 Jan Herman represented the Dutch government in San Francisco for the founding of the United Nations. The war was still on, and he traveled incognito under the name of Mr. de Groot. His arrival in New York triggered a mysterious phone message to Mrs. Standish Bradford in Hamilton that she should travel right away to New York to meet with a Mr. de Groot. She took the midnight train, was ushered in to meet Mr. de Groot, and on entering the room, found—as she had suspected—her cousin Herman van Roijen.

My mother's high regard for her Dutch cousins was returned in full measure. As Jan Herman was returning from the San Francisco conference to Holland, he sent her a telegram with this important request: "Anne wrote saying son name Willem Joris John Winthrop van Roijen born and Anne joins me in asking you to be godmother."

In Italy, Sally Winthrop's niece Jean Patten Pellegrini-Quarentotti and her family were living almost as precariously as the van Roijens. They took in refugees, filling every building on the place, including the chicken coop. They existed entirely on produce grown on their farm, and Jean carefully preserved it and hid it away in the cellar. When the Americans invaded, soldiers occupied their place and helped themselves to all the food she had carefully stored away. She and her children were left destitute and new refugees were turned away. That wasn't the last of Jean's problems. One day, as she was riding her bike, she was accosted, beaten cruelly, and left lying on the road. "She kind of crept home. And naturally she recovered—but it was a terrible thing," recalled my mother. Jean suspected it might have been one of the spurned refugees.

Lotti and Clarigi della Gherardesca, the Taylor cousins whom my mother had met in Florence in 1923, were suspected of being Fascists. By coincidence Sandro Cagiati, a suitor of my mother's sister Katharine and a bit of a wag, was working in the U.S. intelligence service and shortly after the war was assigned to investigate the middle-aged sisters. My mother recalled that "Sandro expected to come back and tell me the worst." But according to everybody to whom he spoke, the suspects "were good and saintly women."

Neither of my parents ever returned to Europe after World War II. But sister-in-law Angela and her close friend and neighbor Joan Appleton, both of whom had been raised in England and had family there, left for Europe before the dust began to settle. Joan went first, when the war was still on, transported by bus, eyes bandaged (to keep her destination a secret even from her), helmet on, to an unknown U.S. embarkation port where she was packed onto a crowded military vessel. Her convoy, attacked by submarines, was secretly ordered to change course in mid-Atlantic, from Great Britain to France. On landing, she boarded a bitterly cold train for Paris, where she expected to work with prisoners of war but ended up working with the U.S. WACs. Joan was in the streets of Paris for V-E Day, nearly crushed underfoot and losing all the buttons off her uniform jacket in the melee.

Angela followed her abroad directly after the war, stopping first in England to see those of her family who had toughed it out there, then on to France where she found the rest of her brothers and sisters. Shortly after her departure, a hometown newspaper featured a jaunty photo of her with the news that Mrs. Frederic Winthrop of Groton House, Ipswich, had recently left by air for her duties as acting director of programs and operations in France for the Save the Children Federation.

Angela had written my mother from Brittany when the war first broke out. Now, at war's end, she wrote her again to report on the devastation the war had left in its wake.

> We have absolutely no idea in the U. S. A. what war means to a civilian population, whose homes and acres are the battlefield through no fault of their own. It would be a good lesson in humility to many of us to see how these people are living. And must live for perhaps years to come. In Normandy, in Alsace, in Lorraine, in so many places. It is heartbreaking to see so much terrible destruction—and yet I suppose in another twenty-five years, we shall have forgotten how terrible it was—even the victims will hardly remember! It's a funny life. Maybe the atom bomb is the best way out![17]

After the war family haying became more a photo op than a race against time and the elements, c. 1946.

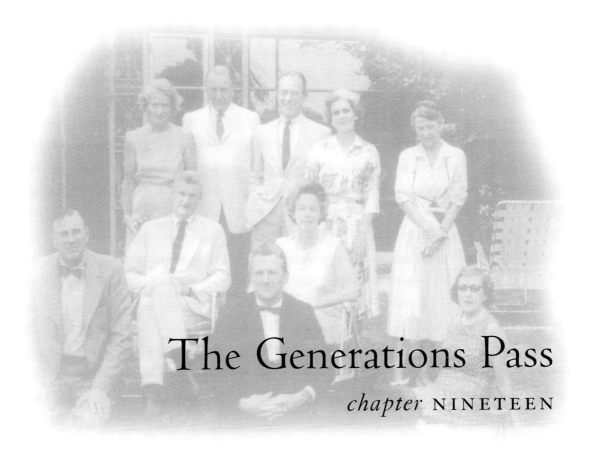

The Generations Pass

chapter NINETEEN

"The inlaws and the outlaws," as my mother's generation of Winthrops referred to themselves and their spouses. Taken at our house, early 1950s. From left, back row: Katharine and Shaw McKean, Fred and Angela Winthrop, Dorothy Bradford (weighed down by the responsibilities of entertaining?); front row: Robert Winthrop, Standish Bradford, Nat and Eleanor Winthrop, Meg Winthrop.

With World War II my mother's extended Winthrop family shifted generational gears, as the old generation finally gave way to the new. Changes were taking place in her own generation as well, as Robert and Nat divorced and remarried and Katharine—the last to marry—found a mate. By 1950 the five couples were configured the way we knew them as we grew up. Meanwhile, my generation (Winthrops, Keans, and van Roijens), which had been launched in 1921, continued to proliferate. Thirty-three children had arrived by the war's end, and sixteen more would be born thereafter, the last arriving in 1958. Today, as the millennium approaches, it is happening again: Most of us are somewhere in the broad rainbow of middle age and all too few of my mother's generation are still with us. The clan has come a long way since Kate and Robert Winthrop settled down to have a family nearly a century and a half ago.

I suspect my mother in her youth might have viewed her Winthrop uncles and aunts as virtually indestructable, just as we did her generation. From the time she was seven until she turned twenty-three, the nine stood firmly in place: her father, her two Winthrop uncles (Gren and Beek), her two Winthrop aunts (Kitty and Tina), and their respective mates. In my case, I remember being impressed when I viewed my ten Winthrop elders at our house in the early 1950s, convening for their annual meeting of the Sarah T. Winthrop Memorial Fund.[1] I too thought of them as a permanent fixture, a handsome tribe—our parents, Uncle Fred and Aunt Angela,

Aunt Katharine and Uncle Shaw McKean, Uncle Bob and Aunt Meg, and Uncle Nat and Aunt Eleanor.

No doubt my mother had a more realistic sense of mortality than we did, owing to the deaths early on not only of her mother but of Uncle Gren's wife, Mary, and Uncle Dudley. The full unraveling of the elder generation, however, didn't begin until 1928, with the death of Aunt Melza. Three more died in the early 1930s: my mother's father in 1932, her uncle Herman van Roijen in 1933 and aunt Tina van Roijen in 1934. Four years later, on August 5, 1938, the youngest of the group—my mother's stepmother, Sally Winthrop—met a shocking and untimely death. I was six at the time and remember going to Singing Beach in Manchester and seeing my Aunt Katharine sitting alone and apart. My mother explained to me that she was sad because her mother had just died, and I wondered how anyone as old as my aunt (she was then twenty-four) could possibly have had a mother. I knew nothing of the facts. That this was only Sally Winthrop's second summer in the beautiful house on the cliff above the beach. That she had been killed on a trip to New Hampshire, sitting in the back seat with her chauffeur at the wheel. That a truck had crashed into their car, killing her but not the chauffeur. That at the time of her death, she was only fifty-three.

Beekman Winthrop, portrait by Hermann Hanatschek (courtesy Harvard University Portrait Collection, gift of Robert Winthrop, 1986)

By 1940 only three Winthrops of the older generation remained—Uncle Gren, seventy-six; Aunt Kitty Kean, seventy-four; and Uncle Beek, sixty-six. The youngest—and to my mother the closest—died first. She called him B. O. B. (Best of Beekmans, though he wrote her that B. O. U., Best of Uncles, or B. O. W., Best of Winthrops, would have done just as well). He, too, had many pet names for her: Miss Winthrop, ex-president, Señorita Dorothy Winthrop, Princess Dorothéa Winthrop, Miss Dotty of Danvers,[2] and "Dearest B. N. [Best Niece] and then some!" He worried about her weight: "Seriously, you are altogether too thin; you should get some good doctor to prescribe for you."

For Uncle Beek my mother must have represented the daughter he had never had. "He was full of fun and he loved children," my mother would say. I can remember him still, for when I was quite young he came to visit us. He sat in our library, a roguish old man, and pulled handkerchief after white handkerchief out of his vest pocket in a seemingly interminable stream that amused and amazed us.

Sometime toward the end of his life he wrote my mother a poem entitled "A Search for a Substitute B. N.," explaining how she had won top rank in his affections out of a possible field of eight nieces or nieces-in-law:[3]

One is still blissful in honeymoon's heaven
[Hildie van Roijen who married Bobby van Roijen in 1938],
A fact which reduces the number to seven
One has six children—enough of a "fix"
[Elizabeth Styvesant Kean who married Robert Winthrop Kean in 1920],
Leaving the number to select from as six.
One is completely unaware I'm alive [?]
Hurriedly, therefore, I turn to the five.

One lives in Holland—next to Germany's door
[Anne Van Roijen who married Jan Herman van Roijen in 1934]
In view of this fact, one can count only four
The next cares for horses much more than for me
[quite possibly Theo Winthrop, Robert's wife],
Reducing the number, really, to three.
One is a "dear," but has too much to do [could be Fred's wife Angela]
The available ones amount only to two.
The two that are left are considerate and kind
[most likely Katharine and certainly Dorothy]
Their language to me is much more refined
In consumption of liquor they don't overdo
Alas! and alack! That applies not to you[4]
And still when I think of the times that we've had,
Besotted—and gay—good, indifferent or bad,
In Paris, or Spain, on the Steamer at Sea,
In camp on Lake Squam, at Estill, S. C.
At home, which was best—in Mass. or N. Y.
Or out at my place on Long Island, nearby,
In spite of your faults, you're like an old shoe,
—a Joy and a Comfort—so I still cling to you.

He bought her presents. Late in 1938 he wrote describing a shopping expedition he had taken for his "B. N.":

You know I am not well—old and feeble ... but I thought to myself "This may be my last Christmas and I must not disappoint my aging niece" so I sallied forth ... on foot and by bus and made my way to the emporium of Mark T. Cross. There I encountered a teeming mass of humanity—or inhumanity. The mart was filled with a surging crowd of females who jostled me, tossed me hither and yon, and finally left me disheveled and weak, clothes awry, hair tousled, pale and with dented hat near a magnificent floor walker. Looking at me disdainfully, he remarked "What do you want?" Almost out of breath, I replied with voice gasping, "I want a lunch basket." "No lunch baskets are given out here," he said. "Go to the Charity Organization Society, where Christmas baskets are given to the down and outs."

My mother with Stanna and me, c. 1935. "You are altogether too thin," Uncle Beek wrote my mother about the time this picture was taken.

The picnic basket was found and the shopper survived, but with continued intimations of his own mortality. In 1939, at sixty-five, he resigned from the family firm, writing only partly in jest: "Did you know I have been bounced from Robert Winthrop and Co? So no longer am I a banker—no longer either am I a farmer. I am giving up my cows!" Despite his age he remained sharp. "What a memory!" wrote Herman van Roijen to my mother after visiting Uncle Beek in Old Westbury in the summer of 1939. He and his uncle had been kidding about Herman's having once loaned Dorothy " 'immoral' books." Herman had joked that these were probably something innocent like Walter Lippmann's *Preface to Morals*—to which Uncle Beek had responded, " 'Not at all, I remember quite well. It was a book called *Simon, Called Peter.*' "

On January 7, 1940, Uncle Beek wrote the letter to my mother that used the term "the holy society" to describe the remnants of the Winthrop family who gathered for Saturday evening dinner—by then only he and Uncle Gren were be able to attend. His final letter to her, dated May 21, 1940, congratulated her on her thirty-fifth birthday. His handwriting was strong and graceful. Though it might have been a breach of etiquette to comment on the birthday "of a lady after she has left youth behind and is hurtling toward forty," he chose this day to write, "if only to reiterate that I have always considered the 21st of May a very fortunate one for our family."

The last person to sign the guest book that Beekman Winthrop had kept since he was governor of Puerto Rico was Dorothy W. Bradford. She included the date of her arrival, October 13, 1940, and a brief message: "England invaded October 13, 1066." Less than a month later, November 10, 1940, Uncle Beek died. His brother Grenville would live a little over two years more, until January 19, 1943. The last letter that my mother received from the group came from an ailing Aunt Kitty Kean, written February 2, 1943, two weeks after Grenville's death. Her own husband, Hamilton Fish Kean, had died two days after Christmas in 1941. But her letter to my mother was filled with her worries about what would happen to her brothers' possessions.

> I wish I could decide what to do with Uncle Beek's house. I wish you wanted it, or Robert, Fred, or Nat! I wish Robert could be here, working for Uncle Gren, instead of for the country. I think of all the beautiful things in his collection and wonder just what will be done with them all....
>
> I don't think any girl or woman ever had such brothers as mine. All four, so different, and so adorable, and each one so wonderful to me. I have had great happiness and I *try* to think of this instead of the lonely present, without so many of "dearest and my best."
>
> It is dreadful to be the last of one's generation.

She would not remain alone for long. On August 21, 1943, six months after this last letter, Kitty Winthrop Kean died.

In New York City the Winthrop imprint vanished fast. Grandma Winthrop's grand house at the corner of Park Avenue and 37th Street had already disappeared, torn down and replaced in 1931 by the far more imposing Union League Club, with its marble-paved entrance, grand staircase, and mahogany-paneled libraries. That Kate Winthrop ever resided at the club's address is today long forgotten; as far as the club is concerned, the place was purchased from J. P. Morgan, Jr., who had been buying up all the property on his block during the 1920s, including, presumably, Kate Winthrop's house.[5] Aunt Kitty's worries about what to do with Uncle Beek's townhouse in New York at 117 East 69th Street were well founded. The family didn't sell it until 1951, when the N. Y. Pharmaceutical Association finally purchased it. In 1977 Henson Associates, of Muppets fame, bought it and it remains in their hands to this day.[6] As for Uncle Gren's house at 15 East 81st Street, after a few years housing nuns connected with a nearby church, it was purchased in 1984 by the Angiolina Company, an outfit headquartered in the Netherlands Antilles. The company did a major two-year renovation, keeping the original woodwork paneling but installing a great new marble staircase and purchasing $20 million in artwork. Today a very private Kuwaiti lives there, surrounded by art that might well appeal to Uncle Gren were he to return for a viewing.[7]

— • —

While the bricks and mortar of their lives proved ephemeral, the Winthrop reputation began to harden over time. I think especially of my grandfather, Frederic Winthrop, who—with his money and Yankee thrift—would become an object of caricature. In Joseph Alsop's memoirs, for example, Fred Winthrop appears as the stereotypical old-line, upper-crust WASP.[8] Alsop wrote of "a rather nice man" with

REARED *in a* GREENHOUSE

a "well-known *Mayflower* name," Standish Bradford, who was wooing Fred Winthrop's daughter Dorothy. "The enormously rich" Winthrop "was heard to grumble that he didn't want his daughter to marry into 'that Mayflower lot' because they were 'a pack of thieves and poor debtors.' "

Alsop relished the tale of Mr. Winthrop's going to Boston to buy melons, a trip he made, he told a friend, because "the Italian in Faneuil Hall market has the cheapest melons in Boston." A few days later Fred Winthrop was back on the train with the same melons in hand, explaining to the same friend that he was returning the melons because they were "overripe" and he wanted to get his money back. "This is a true story," wrote Alsop, "and it still makes me laugh every time I think of it. Here was a man with $40 million, the equivalent of $400 million nowadays, and he was going to great trouble to save no more than a few dimes." The arch tone was part of the Alsop trademark (Robert Winthrop remembered Alsop from Harvard as a terrible snob), but the remark about Winthrop's millions couldn't have been accurate, for Alsop had no way of telling what the Winthrops were worth. Robert, the family financial guru, thought $40 million "possible" in the twenties but certainly not after the stock market crash.

Joe Alsop wasn't the only one taking wild guesses about the Winthrop wealth. The family also turned up in Ferdinand Lundberg's notorious *America's Sixty Families*,[9] ranked twenty-second among the country's sixty richest families. Lundberg based the order of wealth on income tax returns filed in 1924 and published in the *New York Times* in September 1925. (The year 1924 marked the debut of the income tax, and the *Times* published a listing of everyone who paid taxes of $500 or over!) Lundberg's analysis shows six Winthrops, with "miscellaneous sources of wealth," paying an aggregate tax of $651,188 on a net aggregate income of $1,735,000 and a net aggregate fortune of $34 million. If one examines the *Times* itself, however, one sees the whole thing as highly suspect. To be sure, the paper lists six Winthrops, but their taxes total only $161,708, putting them below even the lowest ranking of the Lundberg list—S. S. Kresge, with taxes of $188,608. Equally curious, many rich Winthrops, including Fred Winthrop himself, are missing from the *Times* listing.[10] Finally, the Lundberg and Alsop numbers do not jibe: the $40 million fortune Joe Alsop attributed to Fred Winthrop would have been larger than the $34 million Lundberg credited to all his six Winthrops combined.

But facts be damned. In Boston today, a story is still being swapped about the rich and parsimonious Fred Winthrop. I was stunned when I heard it not long ago, for it couldn't possibly have been true. The tale goes that when the Winthrops were living at 299 Berkeley Street, the most expensive house in Boston, they would call down the dumbwaiter each morning with their breakfast order: two eggs, toast, orange juice, coffee, for example. One morning, Mr. Winthrop was said to have called down, "Only one egg this morning. Mrs. Winthrop died in the night." When I confronted the raconteur with the facts of the case (Fred Winthrop's heart-brokenness over Dorothy's death and the fact that Sally had outlived him), he asked in surprise, "But isn't it true? I've heard the story for years."

Another Fred Winthrop legacy hangs today in downtown Hamilton at the corner of Union and Linden Streets—a small plaque, hidden behind a weed tree on a school gate, with an inscription nearly obliterated by rust:

These school grounds
were given
to
The Town of Hamilton
by Frederic Winthrop
in memory of his wife
Dorothy Amory Winthrop
1878–1907

On January 21, 1920, on the seventeenth anniversary of his wedding day, Frederic Winthrop had given to the town of Hamilton a four-acre lot to be used "for a playground or school house or park." He wrote his mother-in-law, Libby Amory, the next day that it was his intention—and had been so voted by the Hamilton selectmen—that the lot should "be kept by the town *forever* as a memorial to Dorothy Winthrop ... and ... *forever* known as the Dorothy Winthrop Memorial [italics mine]." In 1930, two years before his death, the town voted to construct a new high school on the land and to name the site and the land around it the Dorothy Winthrop Memorial Playground. Fred Winthrop offered to donate gates and hedges. By 1977 Fred Winthrop had been dead for nearly fifty years and the "forever" seemed a forlorn hope. "Where is the Dorothy Winthrop Memorial Park?" queried the Hamilton Historical Society in a newsletter that year. The answer was supplied by my mother. "If you look closely at the gate to the school grounds," another Hamilton old-timer added, "—if the sun is just right—you can make out the ... inscription."

If not distorted like the grotesqueries of the gossips, my mother's descriptions of her father had something of the shadowy qualities of that faded sign. When she spoke of his activities and interests, he came across more as a pastiche than a person. We could see that he had a touch of each of his brothers in him. He enjoyed travel, adventure, and the outdoors like Uncle Dudley; he was interested in public affairs like Uncle Beek; and his keen pursuit of history was as intense as Uncle Gren's pursuit of art. But the descriptions seemed lifeless. The other brothers had their colorful obsessions and my mother spoke of those freely. But she rarely spoke of my grandfather's obsession—the loss of his first wife—so we didn't realize how thoroughly this had consumed him. Yet as my mother's diaries show, this was the core theme of his life and of her childhood as well.

Even had Dorothy lived, however, Frederic Winthrop would doubtless strike our generation as a stiff, remote character. I always imagined him as a little scary, like the father in Longfellow's "The Children's Hour" who loved his children dearly but who received them in his study only during that brief time "between the dark and the daylight/ When the night is beginning to lower." His values and standards were certainly those of an earlier era, summed up by his neighbor Anne Rice who wrote my mother after his death of the fine upbringing he had given her and her brothers: "to love truth—treat every man justly—and have respect for parents." My mother acknowledged that he often seemed unapproachable, but chalked this up to his discernment about people, suggesting that beneath the reserve lay a warmly loving heart. As she wrote me November 2, 1957,

> My father claimed that he was not interested in people, and yet he had a greater depth of love than anyone I ever knew. He loved his family, he had a few really good friends, and to these he was gentle and kind and considerate. But he did not care to see anyone else. He did wonderful things for his employees if he considered them worthy, but there were not too many of these as my father's standards were very high. He was a stern disciplinarian, but somehow we never questioned this and felt that he always acted with our interests at heart.

Nothing, neither his continuing gloomy obsession with her mother nor his obstinate refusal to accept my father, shook my mother's loyalty. She forgave Fred Winthrop everything. To her, what counted was that he was "very fair, just as fair as he could be … and … very strong." She and her brothers were all "devoted to him," she said, for "when he was around everything was all right."

— • —

I confess to some bias, but I think Frederic Winthrop, despite his failings, didn't do such a bad job in bringing up his children. His fairness and his concern with their interests must have overridden the negatives—the tensions in the Winthrop household, the cleft between his two sets of children, the void for the older set that Sally Winthrop could never fill. Somehow none of this resulted in "dysfunctional" adults; all five of his offspring grew up to be decent citizens, each with individual charm and humor.

Robert Winthrop, senior partner, Wood, Struthers and Winthrop, late 1960s (from a brief history of the firm published at that time)

My mother's older brother Robert stood always at the head of the family, at a far remove from us on Wall Street, where he had succeeded Uncle Beek in 1939 at the helm of Robert Winthrop and Company. As children we understood nothing about the market, had little comprehension of the Great Depression, no inkling of how the company had reshaped itself during the 1930s, weathered the war, or was riding into the 1950s. Yet his career was a mini-history of the cataclysmic changes that had rocked Wall Street over the two decades. After surviving the crash, the firm had increased its emphasis on buying and selling stocks on commission, previously only a small part of the business. At the same time, it gradually sold off the railroad bonds dating back to the Moses Taylor era that represented a substantial portion of most of

BY DEGREES PENSIVE, the recipients of honoraries lend an ear to Commencement oratory during the Morning Exercises: Washington Post Company Chair Katharine Graham, experimental chemist E. Bright Wilson, financier Robert Winthrop, art historian Meyer Schapiro, theoretical physicist Victor Weisskopf, and author-diplomat Carlos Fuentes. (Photo: Joe Wrinn)

Scientists, Publisher Among Honorary Degree Recipients

Robert Winthrop, third from left, among 1983 honorary degree recipients at Harvard. The others are from left: Washington Post Company Chair Katharine Graham, experimental chemist F. Bright Wilson, art historian Meyer Schapiro, theoretical physicist Victor Weisskopf, and author-diplomat Carlos Fuentes.

the family's accounts, and moved instead into municipal bonds, whose tax-free status made them more attractive. During the war, while my uncle was in the navy, the company had to be turned over to non-Winthrops, just as it had been during the latter years of Uncle Dudley's tenure. But when the war was over Robert was back, presiding as managing partner over what would be the explosive growth of the stock market during the 1950s.[11]

In addition to his immediate professional responsibilities, over time Robert served on boards of banks and investment and insurance companies. He also has had wide philanthropic concerns, Harvard first among them. The seventeen Winthrop family portraits were but a hint of his beneficence toward his alma mater. He provided scholarship funds for students with leadership ability, served on the Overseers Visiting Committee of Harvard Medical School, chaired the Visiting Committee on Athletics, and, together with brother Fred, endowed a Winthrop Chair of History and of Medicine. In June 1983, he was awarded an honorary degree, which carried this message: "A grateful university pays honor to a devoted and generous son whose vision and conviction have enlarged the scope of Harvard's usefulness to the world of scholarship." In New York, he gravitated to hospital-related philanthropy, serving for ten years as president and then, with Meg, as long-time trustee of Nassau Hospital in Mineola (later renamed Winthrop University Hospital) and generously supporting the New York and the Columbia-Presbyterian Hospitals. His sports life was legend—shooting in South Carolina and Scotland, salmon fishing in Canada, golfing wherever. He served as president of the North American Wildlife Foundation and as commissioner of the Long Island State Park Commission. We, as his country nieces and nephew, found him courtly and shy and admired him from afar.

Though until my mother's generation divorce was unknown in the Winthrop family, when Robert remarried in 1942 to Margaret Stone Mann, my mother decided that, in some cases, divorce was a very good thing. Robert was happy, and that was all that counted. Aunt Meg, Uncle Bob's new wife, was ultra-elegant, with perfect taste and a fashionable lifestyle. From our standpoint her most astounding contribution was bringing the plantation into the twentieth century. In the early 1950s, my mother wrote me a letter describing, with some skepticism, her new house, set apart from the more rustic cabins and soon known as "2 Park Avenue": "I wish you could see Uncle Bob and Aunt Meg's house. The decor is the last word out of 'Home Beautiful.' It is very attractive, but not appropriate for Groton Plantation and Aunt Meg wears beautiful dinner gowns for dinner at 8 p.m. All I brought was a clean skirt and shirts."

My mother's younger brother Freddy, Uncle Fred, lived out his father's fears, abandoning business and becoming a gentleman farmer like himself, but Fred Winthrop, Sr., needn't have worried. Fred Winthrop, Jr., died a well-loved figure in the community, acclaimed in his obituary for his "many and varied interests," and for giving "generously of his time, energy and means to civic and charitable causes." As my mother wrote me in 1961, "and then there is Uncle Fred, unknown to the world, doing much good locally in his quiet way and beloved by many." He held many town offices,

Fred Winthrop, Jr., 60, everyone's favorite photo

including a membership on the school board, and founded the Winthrop Foundation for the Deaf at the Massachusetts Eye and Ear Infirmary. The world of offices and regular hours, however, never appealed to him. Interested in zoology, he tried working for the Agassiz Museum for a couple of years after quitting the Boston office of his stockbrokerage firm but that too didn't suit. Instead he decided to establish a commercial dairy operation on the place, and this soon became a going concern on the North Shore. A great hunter and marksman like Robert, he believed that habitat must be preserved and worked all his life for conservation and land and wildlife management. I remember how he would pull up to our house in his sleek green Mercedes convertible with the FW plates, smile and joke, and spend hours amiably chatting with our parents.

The Fred Winthrops, 1971. From left, back row: Jonathan, Grant, Robbie, Freddy, Adam; front row, Iris (Freeman), Fred Winthrop, Angela, and Ann (Getchell).

My mother often spoke of what a wonderful father he was, how he loved each of his seven children—Iris, Ann, Adam, Freddy, Jr., Grant, Robbie, and Jonathan—and supported them all as they found their different ways. On January 17, 1979, Fred wrote a letter to my mother: "Dearest Dotty Dimples, It has been a blessing to have you as a sister, confidante and wise friend all these years. You are never failing in wisdom, kindness, fortitude and a charming sense of humor. There should be more people like you; but that is impossible. God bless you and much love, Freddy." He died of colon cancer, as

had his father, almost a month later, on February 16, 1979. On the envelope my mother wrote, "Delivered to me by Freddy, Jr., a few days after Freddy died."

My mother's youngest brother Nat, Uncle Nat, had always been out of step with the family. The Winthrop children were taught how to ride as a matter of course. But Nat, my mother remembered, "never really took to riding. I don't know what he thought a horse was … sort of an automobile or a machine of some sort." As an adult he remained offbeat, wearing red socks on the posh River Club's tennis court and perilously navigating a bicycle through the streets of New York City. Traveling was so in his blood that, though he had a law degree and practiced with the New York law firm of Shearman and Sterling, he vowed not to become a partner with any firm, choosing instead to take periodic sabbaticals in exotic spots around the world. One year it was Lebanon, another, it was sub-Saharan Africa. His fascination with the unfamiliar also drew him to support causes that might lead to better international understanding, prime among them the Experiment in International Living.

Nat may have marched to a different drummer because of his father's favoritism toward the older three. As one of the less favored Nat struck out on his own, always "open to new ideas, new philosophies, new people" (to quote one of his sons at his memorial service). This quest led him far from family orthodoxies, creating an ardent Democrat and an equally unenthusiastic shot (the only bullets he liked were aces on the tennis court). Nat was just turning twenty when his father died, perhaps just in time, for he said that had his father lived longer the two of them would not have agreed on anything. Nat was a chip off the old block in other ways, however. He was, said his son at the service, "extraordinarily fair"—the very same words my mother used in describing her father.

Nat's marriage to Serita Bartlett in 1935 lasted twelve years, a year less than Robert's, but enough time to produce four children: John, Matthew, Beekman, and Serita. Different as "chalk and cheese," as son John put it, they divorced under the strain and separation of the war years. Nat remarried in 1950 to Eleanor Beane. My mother had met Eleanor in 1940 through the Wellesley College vocational office when she was searching for a summer tutor for me and my brother. Miss Beane, as we would call her, recalled the interview: she said she found Mrs. Bradford "enchanting," screwed up her courage to ask if there was laundry service in the Bradford household, and when my mother answered in the affirmative, instantly accepted the job. On her arrival at 484 Main Street, she found the house perfectly beautiful and fully staffed and the children looking cherubic—though they were far from angels.

My mother wrote her later telling her that on the day of her departure, Stanna, about six, had been discovered hiding behind a wing chair in the big liv-

Eleanor and Nat Winthrop on their wedding day, June 17, 1950 (to their left, Nat's son Beek and daughter Serita)

REARED *in a* GREENHOUSE

Far left: *"Miss Beane" brushes my hair, summer of 1940.*

Left: *The Nat Winthrops, Christmas 1959.* From left, back row, *Eleanor, Stephen, Nat, Sr.;* middle row, *John, Matthew, Serita, Beek;* front row, *Nina, Kate, Nat, Jr.*

ing room (where children were not allowed), tears in his eyes. He put his hand over his heart and said, sobbing, "It hurts right here." A few years later Stanna sent a Valentine to Eleanor:

> DEAR ELAENOR,
>
> Thank's a lot for the airplane book. I'm awful glad because I have ten airplane books now and I like yours second best. It was just about the best book I got for Christmas.
>
> ~~Love, Sincerley~~
> *Your truly* ~~*Yours*~~
> Stanna

Eleanor and Nat had another four children—Nat, Jr., Kate, Nina, and Stephen—and lived a full, fascinating, and frenetic life that suited them both. My mother wrote of a fleeting glimpse of them in October 1960, about ten years after they were married.

> On Saturday, Eleanor and Uncle Nat dropped in on a flying trip, just long enough to make 6 telephone calls and dash off to see several other people. "And where shall we have dinner?" asked Eleanor. "If we are at someone's house at dinner time, they will be sure to feed us," said Uncle Nat. He would welcome anyone at any time to eat with him, so everyone will surely welcome him.

Summing him up, my mother thought of Nat, the pest of her youth, as the one who ended up holding the larger family together.

THE GENERATIONS PASS

Katharine Winthrop at Wimbledon, 1942. She was, my mother told us, the first woman to play tennis in shorts at Wimbledon in front of the Royal Family.

There he lived in New York City … the center of everything, and he kept in touch with all the members of the family, all sides of the family, the most distant cousins you can imagine, cousins that came from Italy, the Dutch cousins, he took them in when they came to New York, he was wonderful that way, wonderful. And he and I could on the whole see eye to eye on most things. We'd finished fighting.

He died in June 1980, of a heart attack, while running for a train. My mother didn't go to the memorial service (she'd given up traveling because of her own and my father's health) but a friend wrote her about it. "Robert," she wrote, "looked terribly sad. I suppose he feels very alone, now, with … Freddy and Nat … both gone. I know Nat was a pillar of strength in the family."

While Nat was suffering by comparison with his brothers, Aunt Katharine—as a girl and as the youngest—had somehow escaped the family strains. For her, everything came easily. As she grew from a teenager to a woman in her early thirties, she moved on from four junior national tennis titles to five national women's titles (indoor in both singles and doubles) and thirteen national rankings in women's singles, including twice in ninth place (1936 and 1939). In 1936 she played on Centre Court at Wimbledon where her partner was the great Alice Marble and her costume, according to my mother, was shorts—making her the first woman to play before the queen so clad. Just before the start of the war, she made a tour of South and Central America with Sarah Palfrey and Jack Kramer.[12]

On turning thirty, however, Kay—as most people called her—still wasn't married, and my mother was wondering why. She wrote my father in Europe, "She is very attractive, a good sport, does everything well, is an extrovert full of fun and sought after by everyone, especially the older married men." Three years later, in 1947, just such a gentleman engineered a seat next to her at a dinner party. He was fifty-six-year-old Quincy Adams Shaw McKean, who bore the triple first names of his distinguished grandfather[13] and who had spotted her at cocktails and switched the place cards! Kay entranced Shaw, as they called him, with her ready laugh and

Katharine Winthrop, pictured left and right, *bests Dorrance Chase,* center, *in acrobatic win. (Clipping from* Boston Herald, *March 21, 1935)*

REARED *in a* GREENHOUSE

her interest in dogs, horses, and foxhunting. Shaw's marriage to Margarett McKean, whom my mother had met almost twenty years earlier and whose "fascinating house and children" she'd noted in her diary, had by then disintegrated. He wanted a simple life, loved his children, dogs, gardens, and sporting; Margarett was an artist, emotionally unstable and increasingly discontent with the Boston life Shaw represented. By the summer Shaw had gone to Reno and Katharine had written my mother, "I want you and Standish to know that I am going to marry Shaw McKean. I don't believe it will be a great surprise to you as gossip has had it so." They were married in October, less than a year after they met. And unlike Shaw's first go-round, for both Kay and him this would be both the right marriage and the right life.[14]

Katharine and Shaw McKean with sons David, Robbie, Tommy, and John in 1958 (courtesy John W. McKean)

On the occasion of the birth of Aunt Katharine's fourth son, nine-pound David, in 1956, my mother wrote me that "a fortune-teller once predicted she [my aunt] would be a 'mother of men.' "[15] The boys had come in quick succession, over eight years, and my mother thought them bewitching, writing me in October 1957 that "four adorable little McKean boys came to call a few days ago bringing an armful of chrysanthemums from Poppa's garden…. John is quite serious and grown-up, but very sweet. Tommy is a fascinating imp, Robin is enchanting, so bright and such a mischief! David is fat and placid so far."

Even before her birthing was behind her Katharine was back on the courts, winning four senior national titles and ranking between first and ninth in senior doubles almost every year between 1955 and 1970, when she finally retired at the age of fifty-six. She kept on playing into her seventies, however, eventually stooping to join even such as me. But her standards remained high, and I remember her scolding us for saying "Good shot" when a point had been won as the result of an unforced error. She was admitted into the New England Tennis Hall of Fame in 1990. But it was more than her tennis that won her this honor. As was said at the induction ceremony, "Kay was a solid hitter from the back court and an effective volleyer from the fore…. Kay is a gracious lady … it is easy to tell which 'big' players are 'big' people." Reflecting on the differences between her sister and herself, my mother wrote me in March 1959, "She had the poise and led the gay life, but our lives are equally happy in their different ways. Chacun à son goût."

Aunt Katharine died February 12, 1997. Fate dealt her a cruel hand in her final years, with Alzheimer's disease extinguishing her physical vigor and her ability to engage in the conversational thrust and parry she had so enjoyed. Her smile remained to the end, however. That's how I think of her—the "Winthrop" smile crinkling her eyes and deepening her "Winthrop" wrinkles, a heart-tugging reminder not only of her own healthier days but also of my mother and the rest of her generation.

— • —

The front page of Ellery Kirke Taylor's genealogical rendering of the Winthrop family (courtesy New England Historic Genealogical Society)

As a historian, my mother's father was, of course, no scholar. Despite all those years shepherding the Winthrop family history at the Massachusetts Historical Society, a contemporary would eulogize him merely as a "faithful attendant" at monthly meetings—one who, by mingling with members new and old, "did much to hold the Society together and make all who came look forward to the next meeting with pleasure."[16] Nonetheless, his bequests to the society, together with those of his siblings, have made publication of Winthropiana something of a cottage industry there. Six volumes of *Winthrop Papers: Series I* have come out, bringing publication of family correspondence up to 1654,[17] and plans for future volumes will update the series to the time of the American Revolution. In addition, a second track of publications is being planned, *Winthrop Papers: Series II*, for related Winthrop writings. The most recent is the 1997 edition of *The Journal of John Winthrop*, edited by University of Pennsylvania colonial historian Richard Dunn and published by Harvard University Press. Others in the works are seventeenth-century Winthrop *Religious Writing; Legal Papers*, providing texts of the first John's religious manuscripts based on his sermon notebooks, and edited by Francis Bremer and *The Medical Notebooks of John Winthrop, Jr.*, edited by Charles Anderson.[18]

Whether today's Winthrops all have an equal interest in these ancient jottings is a good question. The volumes of *The Winthrop Papers* my mother owned had a virginal quality, with many pages still uncut. But then, she was a woman, so whether she read them or not perhaps didn't count. Fred Winthrop passed on to his three sons a more active concern, and between them they made possible both a history of the Winthrop family from its beginnings in America till the 1940s and a biography of Moses Taylor, Grandma Winthrop's father and stoker of the Winthrop family coffers.

At the time of Fred Winthrop's death the name Winthrop still had a romantic ring, or—as Philadelphia genealogist Ellery Kirke Taylor put it sometime in the late 1930s—"Now there is something in the family name of WINTHROP that fires the enthusiasm of anyone gunning for forebears." Suspecting some remote link with his wife's family, Taylor himself took off after his prey, only to discover with great surprise "practically nothing printed on this [the Winthrop] clan." Undaunted, he unearthed as many Winthrop connections as he could, including Uncle Beek, to help him piece together a complete Winthrop genealogy. The result was *The Lion and the Hare, Being the Graphic Pedigree of over One Thousand Descendants of John Winthrop 1588–1649*, the first comprehensive tracing of family connections ever compiled.

REARED *in a* GREENHOUSE

His work couldn't have pleased Uncle Beek—or indeed any living Winthrops—for it was far from reverential. Not only that, it tracked women who had lost their Winthrophood through marriage all over the United States and into Canada and found many remote Winthrops in England. It made short work of the colonial Winthrops, focusing on their drinking and womanizing.[19] The sections on twentieth-century Winthrops had disrespectful titles like the "Fox Hunting Squires" near Boston; "Back Bay Quiet," with Frederic Winthrop identified as the tribe "sachem"; and the "Long Island Sound Smart Set," where Beekman Winthrop, Esq., of Westbury, Long Island, was to be found. Taylor even listed the names of eighty Winthrop descendants who owned yachts—among them Hugh D. Auchincloss, Percy Chubb, 2nd, and Charles Francis Adams—but, perhaps to the relief of the conservative Robert Winthrop sons, none were Real Winthrops, that is, men who bore the last name of Winthrop.

Though an extraordinary piece of genealogy, *The Lion and the Hare* was hardly a serious historical study, and only 125 copies were made.[20] Beekman Winthrop's real interest was to have someone write a work that would tell the life stories of the various male Winthrops in the Winthrop family portraits. In 1939, the year that *The Lion and the Hare* came out, he began to investigate the possibility of a more Winthrop-friendly book. He died before he could complete the project, but Robert and Fred, who'd been brought up by their father on the importance of being Winthrop, would pick up the reins. They decided the scope should be expanded to include the nearly eighty Winthrop males who had lived in America from 1630 through their father's generation. They selected their father's old stomping ground, the Massachusetts Historical Society, to undertake the project, and they funded a society member, one-time Harvard professor Lawrence Shaw Mayo, to research and write the book.

It took four years of work. In 1948 *The Winthrop Family in America* was published. This was far more comprehensive than a standard genealogical work. Typically, genealogists either create charts, as Taylor did, or they focus on a family's historical high points, describing the lives of a few prominent ancestors and omitting the rest.[21] Mayo combined both approaches, giving a wide-ranging view not only of the well-known handful of Winthrops but of dozens of long-forgotten ancestors as well. To some present-day Winthrops, Mayo's mind-numbing recital of the doings of one "Mr. Winthrop" after another may appear more hagiography than history. But behind the mannerly academic prose lies a huge mound of information, warts and all.[22] For Winthrops of today and tomorrow, the book is a factual foundation for pondering the question on which my mother was raised—the importance of being Winthrop—and perhaps to wonder whether being a Winthrop has any importance at all.

My mother's brother Nat spearheaded a second effort to document family history, a biography of Moses Taylor. As Nat wrote family members on December 18, 1970, Taylor was "the gentleman from whom most of us trace whatever affluence we may have." One hundred years after his death, Moses Taylor's story had become as

Uncle Billy Amory as I remember him

dim as the Winthrops'. "When the great cases of papers of Moses Taylor in the New York Public Library are opened for research," wrote one historian, "there will be a chance for an illuminating study in the early stages of economic imperialism."[23] Unfortunately, the book commissioned by Nat and other family members was far from illuminating. Businessman and historian Daniel Hodas's *The Business Career of Moses Taylor* is a dull recital of business dealings, without shape or spirit. Nonetheless, for the family it filled a gap. As my mother wrote on the title page of one of her copies: "Moses Taylor was the father of Katharine Winthrop, my paternal grandma. *Jacob* Taylor was the father of said Moses Taylor. So *Jacob* Wexler, my grandson [then six], has the same name as his great^1, great^2, great^3, great^4 grandfather. We never knew it until long after he was named!!!! Dorothy W. Bradford."

——— • ———

What of the other side of the family, the Amorys and the Gardners? Why did they never achieve the mythic proportions in my mother's family stories that the Winthrop aunts and uncles were to assume? Part of it was that we knew the few there were pretty well, so my mother didn't have to tell stories about them. We would visit Uncle Billy and his wife Aunt May in Wareham, in the clapboard house lovingly christened Mosquito Hut a half century earlier by Grandma Amory. They were simple, quiet people, Aunt May with her amazing shell collection housed in a hut of its own and Uncle Billy with the glass eye that he would place in the middle of his forehead at breakfast to amuse his great-nieces and -nephews. At some point they would quietly die, leaving no children and barely a trace in our young lives.[24] Aunt Clara was something else, domiciled in the grand manner in the Marble Palace, the summer retreat that she and her husband had built before the turn of the century in Magnolia. I would be invited to join my mother and other adults for lunch parties there, where I remember my aunt, pristine in a yellow linen dress decked with pearls, gossiping about her sons Jeffie (highly commendable), Billy (equally satisfactory), and Bunny as they called Amory (always up to something inappropriate). Sometime around 1950 she had a stroke, then lingered on for years, increasingly unaware of her surroundings. My mother would faithfully go and visit her, and when Aunt Clara died, age eighty-five, on August 4, 1957, she wrote me of her passing:

> The funeral was in her patio, that great big sort of outdoor room in one wing, of the Manchester house. Everywhere were beautiful flowers with the blue sea beyond and a perfect summer's day. Twice during the funeral a little humming bird flew into the patio, visited each flower, and then flew out again. [My mother pasted in a picture of a red hummingbird sipping a yellow flower.] It was just the sort of day and sort of scene

that Aunt Clara loved. The room was overflowing onto the lawn with all the people she had loved in her life and most of them were my age or younger, for all her own contemporaries have long since died. I remember her now, not as she was during her illness, but gay and strong and warm-hearted as she used to be. I have never been to an older person's funeral before to which so many younger ones came. Quite a tribute to her.

The other relative on the Gardner side was Cousin Mary Curtis, the unfortunate daughter of my mother's Great-Aunt Helen who had traveled to Egypt with my mother's mother in 1900. It was as hard to imagine that Cousin Mary and Aunt Clara were first cousins as it must have been earlier to imagine that her mother, Helen Curtis, and Grandma Amory were sisters. She lived near us in Hamilton, in the house she had bought in the early 1920s, located next to the town cemetery and known in town as the Old Maid's Paradise. My mother did have stories about her, mostly poking fun at her increasing bewilderment at the twentieth century. But she included her in family events, for which Cousin Mary was most appreciative, writing her once: "There is no one who is nearer my heart, both by inheritance and for your own sweet self." She rode horseback and took walks till she was in her eighties, introduced herself to new people as "Miss Mary Curtis and unlikely to change," and

Aunt Clara (Mrs. T. Jefferson Coolidge) as I remember her. Here she is with her first grandson, T. Jefferson Coolidge IV, born October 6, 1932 (courtesy Dr. Catherine Lastavica)

when she died at ninety-six one of my mother's friends wrote to say they would miss having her at town meetings, where you could count on her "to speak out for the horses."

Winthrops also had the advantage of numbers. We had nearly two dozen Winthrop first cousins and an equal number of second cousins but only three Amory–Gardner second cousins. Grandma Amory had always been acutely aware of the possibility of families (or at least family names) vanishing. In her genealogical jottings she had noted that her ancestors, the Russells and their British forebears, starting with Nicholas Pitt of Dorsetshire, had both become "extinct." Her own branch of the Gardner family had died out with the early death of her brother, and she and her sisters (and their children) metamorphosed into Curtises, Brookses, and Amorys. Also gone was the Amory name in her husband's branch of the family since neither of his sons, Billy or George, had children. (Refer to Charts 8 and 9.) During the early years of the twentieth century Grandma Amory watched in trepidation, fearing that even her extended Gardner family name would also die out. "All our hopes depend on this young man, being the only one to carry on the name," she wrote under a clipping about George Peabody

Gardner, Jr., her Uncle John's great-grandson. "Now he has two *girls*. 1915," she wrote in a disconsolate postscript. Below that was a relieved "Now a son. 1917."[25] (Refer to Chart 10.)

Our second cousins on Grandma Amory's side were Aunt Clara Coolidge's three grandchildren, the children of her son Jeff—Kitty Lastavica, Jeffie and Lindsay Coolidge. But none has had children, and the prospect is that this branch, too, is headed for extinction.[26] Thus, just as the great nineteenth-century surge of Winthrop males has narrowed in the twentieth to focus on the grandsons of Frederic Winthrop, Sr., so too has Grandma Amory's entire legacy been funneled into the grandchildren of the same Fred Winthrop whom her fourth child—daughter Dorothy—married. In other words, of all the descendants of Elizabeth Gardner Amory now alive, none are named Gardner or Amory, but a good number are named Winthrop.

What would have been the reaction of Fred Winthrop, Sr. — who said of his sisters, "They were only girls. You can't carry on a family that way!" — if he could have seen this array of great-grandchildren he and Dorothy would have had? Only two out of 21 would be males with the surname Winthrop — Robbie, far right, and Frederic, third male from right — both the sons of Freddy and Susie Winthrop. The photo shows the 16 grandchildren of Fred and Angela Winthrop (13 of them girls); it was taken at the wedding of Freddy and Susie's daughter Rebecca to Ron Monahan in June 1996. (Courtesy Freddy and Susie Winthrop)

REARED *in a* GREENHOUSE

A Habit of Happiness

chapter TWENTY

My mother, photographed by granddaughter Dodi Wexler
during the last summer of her life

*S*he held his hand as he lay there, in the hospital bed in the library. "Take a breath for Dodi," she urged him, "Take a breath for Jacob," and so on, a breath for Sarah, for Tanya, for Gavin, for Amanda, for Standish, for Frederic. And that was how, at eighty-two, my father quietly breathed his last, with his hand in my mother's, as the hay ripened outside and the late afternoon sun poured through the windows of the wood-paneled den he loved so well. Three generations of Dorothys were with him, my mother, myself, and my daughter, Dodi, as was my son, Jacob. We were there because we always summered in Hamilton. The rest of the family wasn't because, though he had had a series of strokes and been barely conscious during the final days, there was no way to predict when the end would come. So it was only in name that the other grandchildren—my brother Stanna's Tanya, Amanda, and Standish Bradford, and my sister Libby's Sarah, Gavin, and Frederic Borden—were present for my father's last moments on June 19, 1983.

The eight, four girls and four boys born over a span of nine years, were accustomed to seeing their grandparents placed quite differently from the way they were that day. Grandpa, to be sure, would usually be sequestered in the den, his private lair. But Grandma would be in the dining room, the grandchildren's main thoroughfare through the house, and there, from her dappled green chair, she would wave and smile as they raced noisily back and forth. The grandchildren also noticed that their grandparents slept in separate bedrooms, that Grandpa had the airy master bedroom with the graceful twin beds, the dressing table and chaise longue, and that Grandma had retreated to a narrow bedroom a little down the hall, with her desk on one side and her bed on the other, and on a small table next to it, an ancient black and white TV with a knob to change the stations. Sarah Borden, my sister Libby's daughter, remembered spending the night in the room next door and hearing the TV's "busy, normal, cheerful, comical tones" late into the night. "I am sure she never missed Grandpa in the next room," Sarah wrote. "I am sure that her sleep was free and dreamless and that she had earned this—the right to fall asleep gradually with the TV on and the sound turned low, in the shifting, shallow light of the 70s sitcoms."

The grandchildren all thought of Grandpa as big and strong and scary. They thought of Grandma as small and delicate and sweet. They were "an odd couple," said Amanda, Stanna's younger daughter.

—— • ——

I never realized just how far apart my parents had grown until I read their courtship correspondence in researching this book. What astonishing ardor! Where had it gone? What had happened to dash the hopes and dreams of the summer of 1931?

Reflecting in a January 1959 letter to me on why she'd been attracted to my father, my mother made it sound as if the two had been lost souls who found one another.

Standish Bradford in the den he loved so well

> No "acceptable" boy ever cared for me, no matter how many my brothers brought home and no matter how many danced with me at parties.... Daddy was quite different from the other boys—very quiet, no smoothness, no polish, no savoir faire, so to me he was full of charm. He was in many ways, as you express it, "screwed-up" but so was I. Perhaps we were both in revolt against the superficial and artificial aspects of life.

Marriage turned out to be hard work, she found—not that this was bad. She held the view, now gone with the wind, that the main burden of a successful marriage falls upon the woman, writing me in June 1956, "Above all, a man wants to feel important and needed and looked up to. This is the secret of success … it is up to the girl or wife to set the pattern." The next year she conceded it was a two-way street: "No matter who you marry, the adjustment is difficult! Husband and wife both have to work hard and sacrifice themselves to make marriage a success. But this builds character. NOTHING is more rewarding than a happy marriage. Affection grows with the years."

She seemed fully satisfied with her choice, writing me again in 1959, "At all events, as I look back over the years and see what all those 'acceptable' boys have done with their lives, I thank God I did not have to share it with them! Those 'all-round normal

Right: *My father always adored my mother. Here they are, during the summer of 1979, married almost 50 years.*

Far right: *My mother, the reluctant party-goer, clings to my father as they chat with an unidentified gentleman, sometime in the 1950s or 60s.*

great guys' don't always make the best husbands or provide the most worthwhile lives." Being happily married didn't depend on romantic love, she commented in a letter the following year: "Happy marriages are based on so many humdrum qualities that are still there after the period of 'being in love' has passed. Friendship, understanding, respect, admiration, humor, kindness to mention a few."

As for my father, he always adored my mother. "To begin with," he wrote in his fiftieth reunion Harvard class report, "I think it is correct to say that my life has been principally governed by a wonderful person whom I was lucky enough to marry back in 1931."[1] He was unabashedly proud of her, praising her to me in a November 1958 letter as "on the ball—physically and mentally." The loving way he would look at her, his assurance when he said that "everyone loves your mother," was convincing proof that he did, too.

Much of what divided my parents could be chalked up to good old-fashioned gaps between "his" and "hers." His cows, her vegetable garden. His Myopia golf, her Christ Church services and service. His conservative Republican candidates, her League of Women Voters. He voted for Nixon, she for Kennedy. He looked back on World War II as glory days; she looked back with horror on the death and destruction and worked for civil defense and peace. He loved to play bridge and sip high-balls; she preferred reading and afternoon tea. He would revel in parties and she would sit in the corner with a friend or go home early. When once she took him to a high-minded discussion group, he was the one who left early, and when she hosted a Parish Life Conference at the house, he "hid in the den and shut the door tight." She took it all in good humor, calling herself a "party poop" and writing me in July

REARED *in a* GREENHOUSE

1951 of a "Stradivarius quartet and 3 harps" that they were planning to attend: "Of course, he may walk out in the middle, which will be exciting, or he may enjoy it, which would be thrilling." Though each usually accepted the other's world in the spirit of *vive la différence*, the reality was that they had little in common, and after a while, it meant that they had little to converse about.

The widest divide came over us children. My mother never got over my father's reaction to my arrival. "Isn't she just the most wonderful thing you've ever seen?" my mother had gushed. "No," was my father's candid reply, perhaps disappointed that the woman he had dreamed of so long would be exclusively his but a short nine months. They headed down different child-rearing paths. The destination they had in mind was the same; they both set high standards for us. But to prod us along the path my mother was approachable, forgiving, fun; my father, offputting, unbending, and grave. Eleanor Winthrop remembered my mother spending hours painstakingly gluing together a vase my brother had broken, overcompensating, some might say, for any guilt he might feel. My father was never a soft touch; he would force us to dive, or to gallop our horses downhill, or play baseball in the sweltering sun, sturdy physical conditioning that I for one hated and feared. Or he'd deliver one of his well-meaning lectures, which felt to me like a finger scraping across a blackboard. As a judge, which he was to become, he was said to bend over backward in favor of the defendant, but I never felt he made any allowances for us. Understandably perhaps, we children tended to line up on my mother's side. All eyes at table would be turned toward her, while my father would glare silent and unapproachable at the other end.

My mother suffered, though in silence, when she thought he was bearing down too hard. She also tried to understand his behavior. Aunt Clara had warned her that husbands are likely to be jealous, even of the children, and that could explain a lot. My father's sister Barbara thought he was taking out on his children the insecurities he felt as a boy, and that figured, too. Many of his own family, cousin G. Gardner Monks suggested in his memoir, *Beginnings*, were condescending about my father's hard-won accomplishments:

"Isn't she wonderful?" my mother gushed, as she held me in her arms in the early summer of 1932. "No," my father answered, as he looked suspiciously at his new-born daughter.

> He was a very diligent worker, and what he achieved he got the hard way. He had a consuming ambition to go to Groton, though wagging tongues said he was setting his sights too high. But he got into Groton, did creditably, and was I think, Captain of the football team his final year. He wanted to go to Harvard, and again tongues wagged, but similarly he not only proved them wrong again, but compiled an excellent record in sports, and an adequate one in the class room. Then Harvard Law School, and once again the pattern was repeated, and once again he proved his detractors wrong, and went on to graduate.[2]

A HABIT OF HAPPINESS

Right: *Uncle Tom Bradford, playing with Stanna and me while our mother watches, 1935*

Far right: *Grandma Bradford in chair behind my mother, Libby, and me, in 1942*

When Frederic Winthrop, Sr., joined his company of detractors, it must have been a bitter pill for him to swallow. Then, after marriage, the academic abilities that were "adequate" for Groton and Harvard didn't pass muster at Ropes and Gray, for he never made partner. Nowadays, of course, no one stays on at a law firm in the position of an associate-for-life. Surely, for him, remaining at Ropes and Gray in the second rank must have been a source of gnawing humiliation.

In our eyes, his family were little brown wrens compared to the more richly plumed Winthrops. We all liked our sweet Bradford grandmother (our Bradford grandfather died in 1935). My father was a good son, particularly admiring her spirit, "a point of view in life," he wrote her October 14, 1945, "which is so healthy and free from fear." Her reaction to the end of the war—"It's been a grand fight"—had prompted his comment. It had been her attitude, he pointed out, when he had played football and it was "what I hope to inherit from you." His younger brother Tom, dear as he was, was severely dyslexic and considered dumb by everyone.[3] He moved to Cleveland and then Alabama, struggled to make a living for his wife and four girls, and died young.

Equally kind and thoughtful, his sister Barbara became part of a running family joke when at the age of fifty she finally married, to a bizarre gentleman named George Coffin. Uncle George, whose livelihood seemed to come from writing books on mushrooms and bridge,[4] was a long-ago suitor of my aunt's whom her father had forbidden to visit the very weekend he had planned to ask for her hand in marriage. Thirty years later he was a widower, and this time he was able to propose. She turned to my parents for advice, announcing carefully to them, "I am *thinking* of getting married." My father's reaction, my mother wrote me on July 14, 1956, was simply to say "That is great" and to rush off to the golf links. Everyone else applauded, "so there she was all engaged without meaning to be!"

REARED *in a* GREENHOUSE

Their wedding took place on our lawn, and the comedy as recounted in my mother's letter continued:

> Aunt Barbie and Uncle George had spent the night with us so as to be sure that both
> would remember to be present for the wedding.... Aunt Barbie and I went down-
> town to buy all the last-minute things she had forgotten such as a bra and peds for her
> feet. At eleven, everyone went upstairs to get dressed and at eleven thirty, the guests,
> none of whom knew each other, began to arrive.... We were about to start proceed-
> ings when we realized there was no minister! ... Rev. Stride was out in his garden and
> had completely forgotten to come!!!! For one hour we waited.... Just before the bride
> appeared, our truck drove over the lawn with Leonard [who worked on the place] at
> the wheel, much to the amusement of the guests, who by now must have had their
> doubts about us anyway.

Uncle George and my aunt turned out to be a devoted couple. Sometimes we wondered why. He would arrive for Christmas dinner in an orange hunting cap and hand out his latest tracts on mushrooms and bridge to even the tiniest child. Then after a copious intake of ice cream, he would lie on his back on the floor and pro-claim that he was "a little bug." My mother couldn't suppress her mirth describing a reluctant visit she and my father made one Easter to the Coffins':

> Daddy sat there on the point of dozing off while Uncle George read us from a great
> sheaf of papers, his original doggerels!! He was proud of them and they were so poor.
> Daddy nodded and nodded, his eyes growing more and more glazed, while Grandma
> smiled sweetly from her wing backed chair and Aunt Barbie and I listened attentive-
> ly and laughed appreciatively. Just as Daddy was about to fall off his chair or burst
> into a snore, we decided to go home and so saved the day!

My father may have harbored disappointments about his work and have thought we children didn't always live up to his expectations, but he found plenty of com-pensations in the world outside. My mother wrote his mother on October 19, 1943, shortly before he expected to be sent overseas, "As always, he has thrown himself wholeheartedly and with enthusiasm into what he undertakes." So he would continue. He served as Hamilton town counsel for twenty years; was treasurer and advisor on the campaigns of local Republican congressman Bill Bates; was head of the St. Timothy School board of trustees; and was for seven years a judge of the Third Essex District Court, retiring only at the legally imposed age limit of seventy-two. He was just as tenacious about improving our place, always out chopping wood, shoveling manure, and pitching hay. When first married, he started a local soft-ball team called the Bradford Tigers, and in his fifties he took up golf, setting up a driving range in the basement so as not to waste a precious moment in the snows of winter. Even as he became older and weaker he took it upon himself—perversely, I thought—to build a stone wall, stone by heavy stone.

My father, captain of the eponymous Bradford Tigers, the Hamilton softball team he established

My parents on their fiftieth wedding anniversary, August 29, 1981

He went about his activities so quietly that many who read his obituary in the June 21, 1983 *Boston Globe* wrote my mother of their surprise to learn how many things he had accomplished. Wrote Bess Karrick, widow of my mother's long-ago suitor David Karrick who himself had become a commissioner of the District of Columbia, dying shortly after his appointment by President Eisenhower as ambassador to Ecuador: "Standish had certainly served his country and community so much more than most." There were similar refrains in the scores of letters that came to my mother after my father's death. Many remembered how he went out of his way to be kind and helpful. Others commented on how they had turned to him for wise counsel. In a touch of irony, the word gentleman—the very term Frederic Winthrop, Sr., had used in 1904 to describe his occupation—turned up more than once: as one friend put it, he was the "epitome of the New England gentleman."

But no man, they say, is a hero to his valet or, in my case, to his child. The crux of the problem was that I—perhaps more than my siblings—simply couldn't communicate with my father. My mother, with her self-deprecating humor, was much more comfortable to be around. In his letter Freddy Winthrop, Jr., mentioned the "mischievous sparkle in his eye." But I, for one, couldn't kid my father, no matter what cockamamie thing he was up to—digging a mucky old ditch where we were supposed to swim; refusing treatment, in time-honored Christian Scientist fashion, until a thorn prick turned into life-threatening blood poisoning; swimming in dangerous tidal waters that had swept others out to sea; leading the charge to keep girls out of Groton. He always seemed adamant that what he did was right and wise. He also voiced a sense of entitlement that I found alien beside my mother's "the meek shall inherit the earth" attitude. "I truly believe you and I have far more than our share of the blessings and the good things of human life," he wrote her in September 1944. "However, I also believe we are entitled to them for we both have sacrificed many things and have exercised self-discipline to have obtained what we have now."

What really struck a false note for me was something he used to say to my brother: that you could tell "if a man is telling the truth by the way he walks." All too often he did not even seem honest with himself. I remember how he denied any wrongdoing, when he took up what my mother delicately described as "chain drinking." This began when he was in his midseventies and his last job, as counsel for a friend's business, was coming to an end. For this man who had driven himself relentlessly all his life, having nothing to do all day meant that cocktail hour began earlier and earlier. His alcoholism and his failure to admit there was a problem eventually led to an unbridgeable gulf between my parents. My mother, I think, coped with her feelings of repugnance and helplessness by heeding some advice from Al-Anon. Her attitude was that if you can't save the alcoholic, save yourself. If you can't still love the alcoholic, it is not your fault. You are not responsible. You cannot control their drinking. Be detached.

Sometimes, blurry minded, my father would try to make an effort with his grandchildren. I remember how he would sit with my children, bourbon glass by his side, playing poker. And I remember him in the Hamilton cemetery in 1979 at my husband's burial, a tall, bent figure, the only one of our stoic little group who had tears streaming down his cheeks. But he remained apart. His friends stayed away. He spent most of his time alone in his den. After he died, there was no church service, just a family burial. His drinking, I think, had severed the last remaining ties between my parents. Long before his physical death my mother had become resigned that the man she had loved and married had vanished, and by the time he actually died her mourning was already over and done with.

— • —

"When I think of Grandma," my daughter Dodi recently reminisced,

the first word that pops into my head is giving. I don't mean in the financial sense, although … she would take us to Pattie Anne's [the North Shore *ne plus ultra* of children's clothing stores] … and I would buy lots of Izod products.… Our happiness made her happy. When the ramshackle shed looked like an interesting project, she supported my endeavors in fixing it up into a real cousins' clubhouse that we were proud of and enjoyed—a place of our own. At Christmas, when I was in first grade, I asked for Super Heroes. Instead of giving me just one, she gave me five. I was thrilled at the extravagance. To counteract the male, she also gave me a large-bosomed Barbie. I still have a picture of her sitting on the ground, mortified, trying, with little success, to reclothe her strange shape. Maybe the Super Heroes weren't so bad.

I worried that she was indulging the children. But then I remembered that she had done the same for us, giving us the furniture right out of her house, until the big living room had nothing left but the vast, ink-stained Persian rug with a sprinkling

BEING A GRAND-
MOTHER, MY
MOTHER THOUGHT,
WAS THE "CROWNING
JOY OF LIFE."
From left: *"gardening" with
Sarah Borden, about 5, in
1976; with Dodi Wexler, 3, in
Hamilton, summer of 1972;
with Jacob Wexler, 2, summer
of 1973; with Tanya Bradford,
about 1, in 1972.*

of tilting tables, a chipped highboy, and frayed chairs and sofas. Told us to help ourselves to all the jewelry she'd inherited—but by no means to tell the IRS. Only once,
in the 1930s, had she splurged in a major shopping spree, buying the most exquisite
furnishings, the most elegant sconces, the most graceful chandelier, for the new
house. It was a work of art, her first and last, and after the finishing touches she lost
interest. The furniture was not re-covered until her interior decorator sister-in-law
Barbara needed the work. The walls stayed untouched for decades and were repaint-
ed only because it was a way to let the student-in-residence work off his rent. My
mother treated her person no better than the house. Always a fresh button-down
shirt, a wrap-around denim skirt, and someone's cast-off running shoes. Only when
Mrs. Hale, a widowed friend, had a dress business did my mother indulge, though
the many outfits she bought thereafter simply languished unworn in her closet.[5]

When she was seven, Tanya, my brother's older daughter, would sit with
Grandma cleaning the oil painting that hung over the fireplace in the den. It was of
wild boars in gray-snowy woods on an overcast eve. A proper restorer would have
cringed watching the two of them with Ajax, sponges, and water, diligently scour-
ing the surface. But as new boars appeared, and the snow's whiteness emerged, and
the sunset came out in its purple-pink glow, they didn't care a whit if their work was
also dimming the value of the painting itself.

Whether my mother really cared nothing for worldly possessions, it's hard to say.
I always took her hair-shirtedness at face value. She had, after all, been born and
raised with the virtues of Yankee thrift and shabby gentility. I assumed she meant it
when something was lost or broken and she would reassure us, "Don't worry, it's
only a thing." But the truth may be that she was still affected by the self-doubt of her
teenage years, that—just as, when at sixteen she had sat on a log in the woods with
wet cold feet watching her father chopping down a tree and scolded herself for being
"too fond of solid comfort"—she still felt that she deserved nothing, no crumb of lux-

REARED *in a* GREENHOUSE

ury or comfort. Whatever the case, she saw no point in inflicting her scruples (or hang-ups) on her grandchildren. As Dodi said, "she loved her grandchildren and she wanted for us to enjoy the spoils of life. I think she understood children and that they have the weakness of wanting."

My mother—perhaps thinking of two-year-old Standish, my brother's son, running naked through the dining room (she called him Lord Godiva)—laughingly said that children are "all little savages." But making them feel guilty about their childish ways was no solution, she was sure. She had herself known what it was to be young and to feel distressed, and angry, and mean—and ashamed of herself for such feelings. Understanding and reassurance, she had learned from those painful years, were the keys that unlocked children's better natures. As she wrote me in February 1958, "praise and encouragement have produced far greater results in this world than fault-finding and belittlement—especially with tender flowers who have been reared in greenhouses like me."

My mother had a knack for entering a child's make-believe world. Dodi again:

One day I wanted to go find Unga's, my imaginary friend's, house. I was convinced that she lived in the woods by the driveway somewhere. Grandma, just as sure as I, accompanied me on my quest. I remember being pretty tired by the end of the drive and leaving my tricycle. Grandma put me on her back and carried me to the big rock in the Gaffney Lot where we sat and recuperated. I remember finding all these old tools with Grandma, and we had a secret place where we would go. We would play Mr. Bradford and the Boys. When we were finished, we would hide the tools in a rotten stump until the next time.

My mother would often reflect on the importance of understanding. " 'To understand all is to forgive all,' " she wrote me once, quoting the familiar saying: "Understanding is something worth working for, both between individuals and between nations." She lived by these words. When one grandchild stole, when another ran away, she didn't scold or get angry. She asked why, what drove them to it. There would be a reason, and when the reason was addressed a solution was at hand.

Their grandmother was more than her grandchildren's playmate, more than their confessor. She was their booster, the one who always made them feel they were important. Among Tanya's most vivid memories was Grandma welcoming her when her family came for Sunday lunch: "She was so cute, sitting in her chair with her feet together in those Nike sneakers and that wrap-around skirt, and she'd asked you how you were, and when you answered, she'd lean forward and look at you so intently to hear what you were saying. She'd clasp her hands together, in front of her, and she'd look so happy, so genuinely excited."

My mother, about 80, on the terrace in Hamilton

— • —

"Being a grandmother," my mother once told my sister Libby, "is the crowning joy of life." She had had to wait until she was almost sixty-four for that day to arrive. But the interim years had been filled with so many other projects and interests that I am almost surprised that grandmothering outweighed them. During her forties and fifties, as her nest emptied, her life filled as never before. "Like a whirling dervish spinning," she'd written me the year she turned fifty, "between Guild, church bldg. program, Children's Friend Society, Civil Defense, and Libby's party and of course Christmas shopping!" In addition to community work she gorged on lectures, much as she had done as a young girl in her father or grandmother's tow. Just before turning fifty-five, she wrote me, "Really stepped out last week; first to hear Columbus Iselin, the fair-haired boy of my youth, and now an eminent, grayhaired professor at Harvard and MIT, speak on Oceanography.… Next we dined at the World Trade Center to hear all about the importance of Free World Trade.… Next week I shall … go … to hear Nehru (not THE Nehru) speak on India's population problems and then to Cambridge to hear Tillich." She also devoured worthy books, just as she had in her early twenties: "Have been having an orgy of reading lately. The last book was about Albert Schweitzer's philosophy of life, his religion etc."

She was no longer cowed and bowed by the "sad, sinful world" she found out there. The more she threw herself into public causes, the greater her optimism that something could be done to change things. In February 1960 she wrote me quoting

REARED *in a* GREENHOUSE

Emily Lodge: "If we do not blow ourselves up, it is the most exciting age of all history." She viewed the wayward world, I think, the way she did the wayward child: seeing not what it was at that moment, but what it could become. Ahead of her time in the 1930s in her involvement with family planning, and in the 1940s with organic gardening, she kept on pioneering over the years that followed. Locally, she was a founder of the League of Women Voters in Hamilton-Wenham; she helped organize local open-space planning and recycling efforts; she experimented with solar energy and prefabricated house construction: she was a founder of the Christ Church Guild and the Christ Church Thrift Shop; and though she was never confirmed in the Episcopal Church, she was the first woman to be elected to the vestry. She went to meetings of the Bahá'ís, a fringe cult that had infiltrated Hamilton and horrified old-timers like Cousin Mary Curtis, who warned my mother that they were only after her money. She was a spirited supporter of international causes that were also considered pretty knee-jerk by some of her ilk. As she wrote me in 1960,

IT'S HERE: Showing the new "Know Your Town" booklet to Supt. of Schools Hammond A. Young is Mrs. Standish Bradford. chairman of the League committee in charge of publication. Two hundred copies were presented to the schools.

My mother in the September 17, 1969, Hamilton-Wenham Chronicle

> World Trade, Disarmament, International Law and an International Police Force, and Population Control, and a shift in emphasis from hate and fear toward understanding and love (in its broad sense)—that is the millennium toward which we work under the leadership of
>
> > The Quakers
> > The UN and the UWF [United World Federalists]
> > Religion
> > Psychologists
> > League of Women Voters
> > etc. etc. etc.

Her obituary in the *Hamilton-Wenham Chronicle* of December 2, 1987, had it right, I think, when it chose far-sightedness as the theme of her life. Mrs. Bradford would be remembered, it said, "as forward-looking, as one who thought about the world around her, as a person who identified problems before they became universally acknowledged and then sought practical ways to help."

Hamilton today has become so homogenized, the social divisions of her father's day so nearly obliterated, that it is hard to grasp just how difficult a struggle it was for my mother to find her place in the town's shifting demographic landscape. The life she chose was drastically out of step with what had been expected of her. She never forgot her father's dismay that she had chosen to marry, paraphrasing his views in a letter to me, "a person of no social or economic position, a complete unknown!" She often reflected on how she felt caught between those with whom she supposedly belonged and those with whom she felt comfortable. For years, she wrote, she had been haunted by the "spectre of a Proper Bostonian." Finally, though, she had concluded that "they are a narrow-minded, eminently successful and complaisant group who never let down the bars to anyone not cast in their own mold!! … a small group growing ever smaller." She also came to realize that "most of the people I loved were neither members of the fashionable set nor Society leaders." At this point, "it was a great relief to be able to let them (the 'Right People') go from my consciousness." She was free at last to devote herself without compunction to the life of the town.

—— • ——

Countrified to the core—a friend told me of meeting her in the woods and hearing her tell of how she loved the trees, and the place, and the land[6]—my mother was forever reporting on the doings of that old rascal, the weather. In February 1960 she wrote me a glowing description of winter: "Monday a light snow all day and the world all covered by a soft white mantle. But what happened in the night? We awoke to a world of glittering ice, everything was encased and one could have skated on the lawn and every tree was mirrored. And today, snow again! Never have I seen the country more beautiful." Even dreary November could fill her soul, as it did later that year: "The woods are so beautiful and to me there is no music like the wind in the pine trees." Or it could tickle her, as it had four years earlier: "Yesterday was 40 degrees colder than the previous day and finished every growing thing. Only the geese do not seem to mind. That must be why they are called geese."

She was less enraptured by the "kine," as she called the Devon cattle that my father imported from England. Never mind that my father would be honored in 1978 with an award of merit from the Devon Cattle Society for contributing to development of the breed. My mother couldn't take his hobby seriously. Again, from her letters: [February 1953] "Yes, we just had another calf. The cellar of the barn is

Scenes from Blackbrook Farm in winter

REARED *in a* GREENHOUSE

rapidly filling up and I guess we are Kulaks by now. We have *long* since outgrown the cow barn.... [October 1960] We now no longer refer to our bull as Johnny, but we address him properly as Count Cistern (sp.???). Several of the Countesses and little Counts and Countesses are also going to the show.... [July 1961] All goes well on the farm excepting that Kathy Kow should have calved a month ago but is being very stubborn about it.... [November 1961] Daddy is sending eight animals to the cattle show in Timonium (near Baltimore) but one small heifer died of a broken heart at the thought of such a separation. The symptoms were bloat.

My father with two of his Devon cattle, c. early 1960s

Daddy may go to the show himself, but once was enough for me!! That was two years ago, the cows looked so bored, the spectators cold and belligerent, Daddy distressed, Senator [Wayne] Morse [another Devon cattle devotee] cocky (but still quite charming) and I vowed never again!!!"

Most of all, I remember the fun my mother had gardening. The North Shore Garden Club once requested her resignation "as I work so much in my garden I have no time for their tea meetings!!!" Her hands, Dodi thought, gave her away: "I remember the feel of her solid, used hands. They were gnarly, dark, strong, nails always short—the sign of a real person." At eighty, she was still ordering and planting seeds so her progeny could reap the benefits all summer. Her plans were always more exuberant than our appetites. Even during the last summer of her life the raspberries flourished, the lettuce and corn were plentiful, the beans and tomatoes sublime.

Advertisement for Tisted Count, head of imported Devon herd

She christened the rows of corn after the grandchildren—and I think she approached raising vegetables the way she did rearing children. You had to start out planting straight rows, keeping down the weeds, and setting clear limits. But then you let nature flourish, gave them their heads. "Try to keep pace with the growth of the children," she wrote me once, "and see them more as they are rather than as the dream children of long ago.... Let the children grow up even though every gain tugs at your heart strings. *By letting them go you keep them*." So it was with her methodically planned garden. In the end, it was delightfully ordered chaos: heavily laden raspberry vines that had escaped their own site and lined themselves up along the front fence; the odd sunflower, bent down from the weight of its bloom; the random pitchfork; the ancient handplow; the Have-a-Hart trap waiting to be set for its evening quarry; the potato plants gray with fireplace ashes to ward off potato bugs; the odd

A HABIT OF HAPPINESS

Right: *My mother collected "sayings," even in her garden. This one was in "Darwin's garden," a kind of antechamber to her real garden where she let nature take its course just to see what would happen.*

Far right: *My mother in her garden, 1950s*

dish of beer to drown the slugs; and most tangled of all, "Darwin's garden," a sort of antechamber to the main garden that my mother had left to seed itself, "just to see what would happen."

— • —

Sometimes during those summers in Hamilton my father would wander into the dining room where my mother and I sat chattering, and smilingly wonder, "Haven't you girls run out of things to talk about yet?" We never did, because I found my mother's talk an unending source of amusement, information, and wisdom. How did she squirrel it all away, I wondered, that eclectic mix of psychology and genetics, gossip and gospel, history and heredity that filled the hours? Today her letters, full of arcane non sequiturs, of comical gems like those with which Grandma Amory used to season her correspondence, bring back memories of our chats. "He is a great man, I think," my mother wrote me in April 1961 of Winston Churchill, "though certain Guild ladies violently disagree with me, because rumor says that Churchill once walked down the upstairs hall stark naked smoking a cigar." "Polo grows more and more popular [in Hamilton]," she wrote later that year. "Recently in Nigeria, they put a stop to certain tribal raids and ritual murders by substituting polo!" And this in 1960: "But how we are progressing! We have had dial telephones for a whole week now, which is just 19 years later than the smallest hamlet in Spain installed a dial system."

Family stories were just part of the conversational stew at my mother's house. "They made me become sort of a romantic," said granddaughter Amanda. "I always wanted to know the stories of growing up in the olden days." Amanda loved exploring the house, all those old trunks in the attic with their old clothes and exotic stamps from long-ago travels. And she loved it when my mother would go through all the old family jewelry and, like Grandma Amory, tell stories about the people it had

REARED *in a* GREENHOUSE

My mother christened her rows of corn after her eight grand-children. Here they are in the summer of 1980, standing, from left: *Tanya Bradford, Sarah Borden, Amanda Bradford;* seated, from left: *Gavin Borden, Standish Bradford, Jacob Wexler, Frederic Borden, Dodi Wexler.*

My mother, 82, in her chair in the corner of the dining room where she told her family sto-ries. (Courtesy, Salem Evening News)

belonged to. "She really embodied the old-fashioned world to me," said Amanda. Tanya confessed that often the events her grandmother recounted were, as many a grandchild thinks, "really bland." But she found the stories entertaining anyway: it was the delivery, she thought, her grandmother's soft, compelling voice, the animation and life in her face.

It almost cast a spell, the soothing effect my mother's words had on people. I'm thinking particularly of the last night of Kitty Moynihan's life, which my mother described to me in a letter written April 13, 1961. Kitty dated way back, having been hired as a chambermaid by my grandfather shortly after his first wife's death. My mother would have been about three at the time, too young to remember anyone in the house. She therefore had no idea who it was when a little lady with an even tinier boy came to be standing next her at the Hamilton horse show some thirty years later. But when my mother smilingly offered to hoist the little boy on her shoulders so he could see better, the woman thought she recognized my mother. "Are you Dorothy Winthrop?" she asked. "I recognize your smile." Kitty was soon working for us, and would tell my sister Libby all about those sad days in the Winthrop household after our grandmother had died. She said the servants

A HABIT OF HAPPINESS

would gather in their quarters every day at five to say their rosaries and weep over the death of their beloved mistress. They did this, she claimed, every day for a year.

I remember Kitty as a dear, roly-poly, grandmotherly type, who'd invite my brother and me to Sunday breakfast at her house in downtown Hamilton and serve us unorthodox and sinfully delicious baked beans and apple pie. Her job at our house was to pinch-hit for whichever maid was off that day. She regularly outcooked, out-nannied, outcleaned, and outwaitressed the regulars. She was essentially alone in the world, for her husband was an alcoholic and the little son grew up to be a ne'er-do-well who would spend his life in and out of jail. When, after the war, Kitty had a near-fatal heart attack, it deprived her of her only source of livelihood—her ability to work.

Kitty was one of the first people after the Guillenchmidts who gave my mother a chance to do something small and private for an individual. In one of her flights into the future, she ordered Hamilton's first prefabricated house, a little square dwelling with only one story, so that Kitty could follow doctor's orders and not climb any more stairs. The neighbors on Union Street had never seen anything like it: great chunks of siding trucked in and fitted together to make a complete house in a matter of weeks. Kitty enjoyed her new home, but in time her heart troubles got worse and my mother moved her to a nursing home. She visited Kitty there regularly, undoubtedly one of the few people who came by. One day Kitty asked my mother if she would do something for her. "Of course," my mother had answered. It was a martini she wanted, so from then on, my mother arrived at the nursing home with a brown paper bag containing a martini in a mayonnaise jar. I have often reread the story my mother wrote me of Kitty's death, for I'm touched at the image of my mother's calming presence at her side.

> Poor Kitty died 4 a.m. on Tuesday morning. Do you know the line in Gray's "Elegy"—"on some fond breast the Parting Soul relies"?[7] How true this is. It is one thing to die surrounded by those one loves—but quite another to die alone in a nursing home. The nurses are kind and sweet, but they are strangers. They called me Monday evening to say Kitty had had another heart attack and was sinking fast. When I arrived she was in great mental distress and seemed to be fighting every inch of the way. Poor Kitty, she called for her "baby boy." What could one answer? Anyway, I talked to her about you all, whom I feel she loved next best to her own. When I told her of your last letter, she said "May all her dreams come true." As I talked about news of you and Katharine and of Stanna's and Libby's visits home, she grew quieter and quieter, relaxed and peaceful. It was the most wonderful thing I have ever seen. She lived a few hours after that, but remained peaceful the whole time.

— • —

"It is sad work, growing old," Grandma Amory, then in her midseventies, had once written my mother. "Everyone ought to be knocked on the head at sixty-five." My mother thoroughly agreed, in principle. But just as Grandma Amory had made fun of her own old-age feebleness, my mother laughed off her various ailments as "sliding down the slippery slope." She had glaucoma, a weak heart, searing headaches

My mother with two of her favorite people, brother Freddy (left) and Forrester A. "Tim" Clark, c. the 1950s. Tim and she grew up as neighbors in Boston and the Clarks were our friends and neighbors in Hamilton. In the summer of 1987 widower Tim Clark proposed to, and was immediately accepted by, a widowed Emily Lodge — a turn of events that my mother found quite breathtaking. Emily and Tim's marriage lasted a happy five years, until her death in 1992.

brought on by polymyalgia (a painful, debilitating disease of the muscles and nerves). But she took them in stride, and as her nurse Marion Dempsey put it, "She just went about her day as if nothing was wrong."

My mother had long since made the necessary preparations for an orderly departure from this world. In 1976 the family acquired a nice, neighborly plot in the Hamilton cemetery, across from the McKeans and next to our long-time friends, the Tim Clarks. "How senseless!" she'd written me in 1947 of the notion of being buried in some family plot far away. The comment was apropos of a Bradford burial ground in Providence, Rhode Island, but Green-Wood Cemetery could not have been far from her thoughts. For her part, she wrote, "I would rather be buried where I lived."[8]

My mother in her seventies

Keeping where she lived as beautiful as it had been during her lifetime became another of her last goals. In 1974 she started "scheming" to ensure that Black Brook Farm would remain open for public recreation after her death. Riders, hikers, young people on bikes and children with skates, skis, and sleds—everyone but snowmobilers!—had felt free to come and go as they pleased during her lifetime, down the driveway, up the hill, onto the ponds. But the town had tripled in size since the war and development pressures were growing. It would be "dismal," she thought, "if in the days to come some developer were to destroy all this quiet enjoyment of a beautiful place." The solution, eight years in the making, was yielding all development rights on half of the land to the Essex County Greenbelt Association.[9]

A HABIT OF HAPPINESS

She might have given the whole place away to the town except that those "world-ly considerations" that had given her pause when her father had threatened disinheritance remained paramount in her mind. She still wanted "the best" for us children, and this too she arranged carefully before she died. The most imaginative part of her bequests was a series of little houses she bought in Hamilton when real estate was considered a brilliant investment. They were to go to us at her death, but in the meantime she used them to promote her own charitable ends. At 71 Union Street (Kitty's old house) and then at 175 Linden Street, the occupant was the church organist and the rent was paid to Christ Church; at 60 Howard Street lived the assistant minister, rent again payable to Christ Church; at 69 Union Street lived the widow of Leonard Davidson (workman on Black Brook Farm until his death), no rent.

My mother's final preparations were for her own funeral. She would sometimes wave offhandedly at the papers hanging by clothespins from the string across her closet ceiling and tell us that among them we'd find the one we needed, after she had died. And of course, we did. There it was, diffidently labeled, "Funeral wishes DWB, suggestions only!"

During those last years, she had to admit that her "get-up-and-go had got up and went." But, as she had for years, she still kept scrupulously to her weekly schedule. If she was at the Christ Church Bible class, it was Tuesday; if she was at the hairdresser it was Wednesday; if she was lunching with "Auntie" Joan Appleton it would be Thursday; and if she was at the Christ Church Thrift Shop it was Friday— replaced by the Lunch Club during her last years.

Apropos of Tuesday, my mother remained as consumed by religion at the end as she had been late in her teens. But over the years she'd become even more ecumenical, increasingly sure that Christianity had its points but no monopoly on truth. Judaism and the Bahá'í religion interested her more. She stuck with the Bible class because she thought the Bible—without the theological trappings—had more truth than what was preached from the pulpit. Even here, however, according to her

Joan Appleton and my mother, about 80, lunching at the Myopia Hunt Club

teacher Eleanor Vandevort, or Van as they called her, she didn't accept everything at face value and often made "unusual" points. In fact, my mother had virtually given up on the church by the end, though the local clergy never gave up on her. One of her Bible class friends told me of the time near the end of her life when a minister—hoping still to convince her to get confirmed—came by "for a talk" one day. Knowing something was up, my mother changed the subject every time he mentioned religion. When her friend asked my mother later what they had talked about, my mother answered, "Well, we talked about the weather, we talked about polo, we talked about the Thrift Shop." "You really outwitted him," her friend had laughed. And my mother laughed, too, for she knew she had.

REARED *in a* GREENHOUSE

Her Wednesday outing to the hairdresser suggested to what lengths my mother would go to help people without embarrassing them. Traveling to Magnolia, where The Perfect Setting was situated, was quite a trek for a hairdo, especially for one who'd worn her hair the same way for more than half a century and who, as Eleanor Winthrop put it, always looked "deliciously the same." But a weekly hair appointment was an imaginatively painless way to enable Barbara, the hairdresser with a hard luck story of alcoholism and no bank credit, to repay my mother for the new beauty parlor roof that she had financed. Perhaps my mother also enjoyed revisiting Magnolia, the lovely seaside spot where she had spent so many happy hours with her mother's sister, Aunt Clara, and where she had kept vigil over her Grandma Amory during her dying days.

The Auntie Joan lunches on Thursdays carried on the Winthrop-Appleton friendship that dated back to sixteenth-century England and had been renewed when my grandfather moved to Hamilton at the turn of the century. Auntie Joan was in the somewhat sad position of presiding over the final years of Appleton Farms as the oldest single-family-owned working farm in America, for with her husband Frank's death, the line had run out. She continued the farming, however, and she and my mother talked endlessly of cattle and cats, birds and seeds, current events, religion and books. When the two of them lunched together, it was often at Woolworth's and, Auntie Joan told me, someone once took them for school teachers, they looked so plain and talked so much.

The Thrift Shop, where my mother would sort donations or run the cash register Friday mornings, was a small, musty place filled with old clothes, toys, and appliances. Back in the 1950s she had supplied men to build shelves and paint the old horse stall where the shop had started. Soon it moved downtown near the railroad depot. My mother was thrilled when, in December 1960, the landed gentry began "emptying their attic right into our shop and the customers come in droves." But when she tried to empty the Bradford closets into the shop, a problem arose. One of her Thrift Shop co-workers told me that some of my father's clothes were so old and out of style, "they looked as though they belonged to Abraham Lincoln." And when my mother was discussing with one of her nurses which of her old coats she should give to the shop, the nurse was reminded of President Kennedy's famous line: "Ask not what you can do for your Thrift Shop. Ask what your Thrift Shop can do for you."

The Lunch Club that eventually replaced the Thrift Shop on Fridays consisted of four octogenarians, all of whom had known each other their entire lives: Emily Lodge, her oldest friend and cousin; Mabel Thayer Storey, her step-cousin; and Billy Coolidge, her only remaining first cousin on her mother's side. She was lucky, and she knew it, to end her days among her oldest friends and relatives, particularly in a world of retirement communities and nursing homes. My mother savored the stability and continuity in her life. But though she was perpetually nourished by the past, she never retreated into it.

— • —

In November 1987 her calendar was ever the same: "Bible" on Tuesday, "hair" on Wednesday, "JEA" on Thursday, and "lunch with Emily" on Friday. On Thanksgiving, November 26, the notation was "6 Bs, 4 Bordens, NY, 3 Wexlers." She seemed more subdued than usual during that family gathering but just as cheerful as ever. By Saturday morning everyone had gone their separate ways save my son Jacob and me. My mother and Joan Appleton chatted on the phone that day about the family visit. "She was laughing and expressing how much she loved having you all capering round the house," Auntie Joan wrote me later.

Her first heart attack struck late Saturday afternoon and she was rushed by ambulance to the Beverly Hospital. When they brought in the oxygen canister (a dead-ringer for a fire extinguisher), she quipped, "Where is the fire?" She smiled bravely and radiantly as we left her for the night. But on Sunday morning there was another heart attack. It was all over. Emily Lodge had spoken to her only a day or two before her death. "Your mother," she wrote us, "was ready and at peace."

When the minister who was to officiate at my mother's memorial service came to the house, he asked us to give him some insights into her thoughts (he was a new man who didn't know her well). Perhaps he found it peculiar, but we decided to take him to my mother's bathroom and the closet that adjoined, where we would later find her diaries. In these two rooms she kept her clippings, the inspirational sayings she loved to collect. She had them everywhere, pinned to her bathroom walls, stuck in her mirror, neatly arranged in photo albums, placed in folders, hanging on clothespins, clippings old and yellowing, new and crisp. The practice was more popular in her grandmothers' day and both of them kept sayings. We used to tease her about it. But she internalized the messages and the minister grasped this right away. In preparing our remarks for my mother's memorial service, we four children came quite independently to the same word to describe our mother—"saint." The notion was, I suppose, corny. Certainly unfashionable. Probably even implausible. But it seemed to fit her nonetheless. She had a special light which my sister Katharine described at the service, quoting a perfect stranger who had once caught a glimpse of our mother and remarked, "She has the sweetest expression I have ever seen."

My mother would surely have demurred, but I hope she might also have been pleased by the characterization. Her life's goal, I think, was to follow in Grandma Amory's footsteps. "She has devoted her whole life to others and they love her" was how, as a teenager, she had described her grandmother. While working on this book I have often been struck, not only by how near she came to living up to this ideal, but how closely the circumstances of her life at the last mirrored those of her grandmother. Like her grandmother's, my mother's role as grandmother loomed ever larger while she was in her seventies, even as her powers to cope were diminishing. She too had a widowed daughter, an ailing husband, and grandchildren who would look to her as to no one else for comfort, love, and support. Like Grandma Amory, my mother faced these late-life tests with joy and optimism. "Grandma was human— and divine," she'd written when Grandma Amory died. That pretty much summed up how we felt about my mother after her death.

One of the "deep thoughts" my mother saved was on a card from Christ Church, signed by Reverend William F. A. Stride:

Why were the Saints, saints? Because they were cheerful when it was difficult to be cheerful, patient when it was difficult to be patient; and because they pushed on when they wanted to stand still, and kept silent when they wanted to talk, and were agreeable when they wanted to be disagreeable. That was all. It was quite simple and always will be.

Another clipping suggested that saintliness was easy, that saints were simply "happy, radiant people who love." My mother, I think, belonged to the school of sainthood that believed happiness was a struggle. In the notebook of philosophical musings she kept in her twenties, she had written, "Happiness is an attitude of mind and can to a great degree be cultivated." From then on, I think, she went about acquiring the art. One of her techniques was to count her blessings, a strategy of Grandma Amory's. Like her grandmother, she also fought the temptation to fuss, writing me in January 1959, "As for the New England belief that it is weak to complain—with that I agree." It was better to laugh, she believed, as Grandma Amory always did, even though she feared at times, as she wrote me in the summer of 1956, that her own sense of humor had "perhaps dried up the milk of human kindness." True happiness, to quote another of her sayings, was to be found in living for others: "The happy people are the selfless people. The ones who forget themselves in others. They do not wonder what other people are thinking of them. Some may be born this way. Others must practice a selfless attitude until it is a habit."

In time, happiness became a habit for her, too. When young, she struggled to be cheerful, patient, agreeable. By the end this very struggle had transformed her, had made her one of those "happy, radiant people who love."

A final photo, taken by granddaughter Dodi Wexler
during the last summer of her grandmother's life

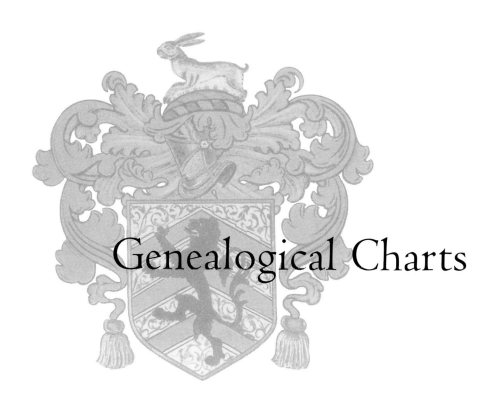

Genealogical Charts

List of Charts

—— • ——

Sources:

On the Winthrop side, the principal source was Elizabeth Bradford Borden and John Winthrop's *The Winthrop Family in America, A Genealogical Updating 1833-1988*, supplemented for earlier generations by Mayo's *The Winthrop Family in America* and Taylor's *The Lion and the Hare*. Charles Getchell, Ham Kean, and David van Roijen filled in gaps. On the Gardner-Amory side, I relied on Gardner's *Gardner Memorial: A Biographical and Genealogical Record of the Descendants of Thomas Gardner, Planter* together with genealogies created by Libby Amory. Supplementary input came from George Herrick, Dr. Catherine Lastavica, and Harry Lodge. The Bradford genealogical information was based on Monks' *Beginnings,* and the Moses Taylor family tree was based on Hodas' *The Business Career of Moses Taylor: Merchant, Finance Capitalist, and Industrialist.*

· CHART 1 ·

The Seven "Important" Winthrops

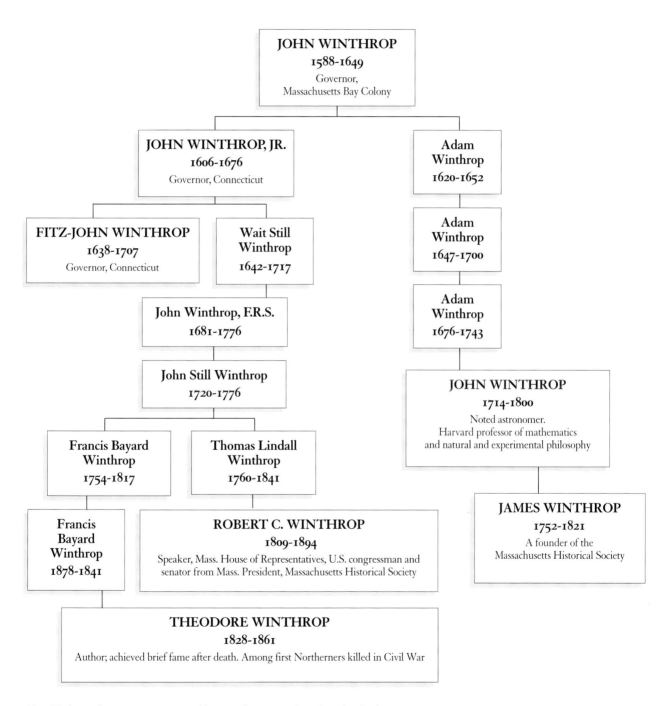

JOHN WINTHROP
1588-1649
Governor,
Massachusetts Bay Colony

JOHN WINTHROP, JR.
1606-1676
Governor, Connecticut

Adam
Winthrop
1620-1652

FITZ-JOHN WINTHROP
1638-1707
Governor, Connecticut

Wait Still
Winthrop
1642-1717

Adam
Winthrop
1647-1700

John Winthrop, F.R.S.
1681-1776

Adam
Winthrop
1676-1743

John Still Winthrop
1720-1776

Francis Bayard
Winthrop
1754-1817

Thomas Lindall
Winthrop
1760-1841

JOHN WINTHROP
1714-1800
Noted astronomer.
Harvard professor of mathematics
and natural and experimental philosophy

Francis
Bayard
Winthrop
1878-1841

ROBERT C. WINTHROP
1809-1894
Speaker, Mass. House of Representatives, U.S. congressman and
senator from Mass. President, Massachusetts Historical Society

JAMES WINTHROP
1752-1821
A founder of the
Massachusetts Historical Society

THEODORE WINTHROP
1828-1861
Author; achieved brief fame after death. Among first Northerners killed in Civil War

Note: Winthrops whose names appear in capital letters are the "important" Winthrops listed in the *Dictionary of American Biography*

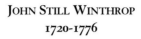

· CHART 2 ·

In the Nineteenth Century,
An Abundance of Winthrops

JOHN STILL WINTHROP

1720-1776

Recouped genealogical fortunes of Winthrop family.

12 ISSUE:

7 sons, 4 with sons

FRANCIS BAYARD WINTHROP

1754-1817

Founded "older" New York branch of Winthrop family.
Only male line surviving today

JOHN STILL WINTHROP

1785-1855

FRANCIS BAYARD WINTHROP

1787-1841

Moved to New Haven

WILLIAM HENRY WINTHROP

1791-1860

Returned to New London, home of paternal grandfather

THOMAS CHARLES WINTHROP

1797-1873

My mother's paternal great-grandfather

HENRY ROGERS WINTHROP

1811-1896

Son Buchanan and grandson Henry Rogers prominent in Fred Winthrop's day. Male line ended with death in 1958 of Henry Rogers

---

JOHN STILL WINTHROP

1813-1860

Founded Florida branch; male line most likely now extinct

CHARLES EDWARD WINTHROP

1816-1888

Established Illinois branch of family. Family still extant in 1940s

---

WILLIAM HENRY WINTHROP

1819-1895

Sold Fisher's Island in 1863. His great-grandson John most likely end of male line

---

ROBERT WINTHROP

1833-1892

All 12th generation male Winthrops descended from him

GRENVILLE WINTHROP

1837-1869

His great-grandson Grenville Bayard III most likely end of male line

---

— · CHART 2 · —
~ *continued* ~

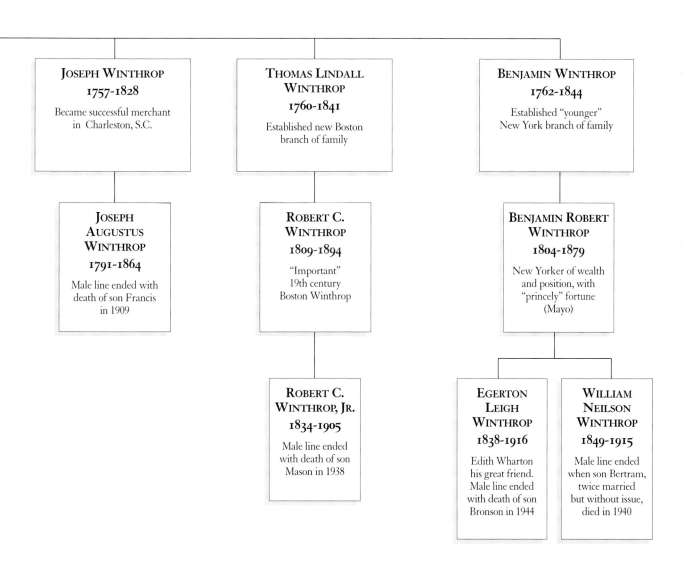

JOSEPH WINTHROP 1757-1828	THOMAS LINDALL WINTHROP 1760-1841	BENJAMIN WINTHROP 1762-1844
Became successful merchant in Charleston, S.C.	Established new Boston branch of family	Established "younger" New York branch of family

JOSEPH AUGUSTUS WINTHROP
1791-1864

Male line ended with death of son Francis in 1909

ROBERT C. WINTHROP
1809-1894

"Important" 19th century Boston Winthrop

BENJAMIN ROBERT WINTHROP
1804-1879

New Yorker of wealth and position, with "princely" fortune (Mayo)

ROBERT C. WINTHROP, JR.
1834-1905

Male line ended with death of son Mason in 1938

EGERTON LEIGH WINTHROP
1838-1916

Edith Wharton his great friend. Male line ended with death of son Bronson in 1944

WILLIAM NEILSON WINTHROP
1849-1915

Male line ended when son Bertram, twice married but without issue, died in 1940

CHART 3 ·

Descendants of Thomas Charles Winthrop: Carrying on the Family Name

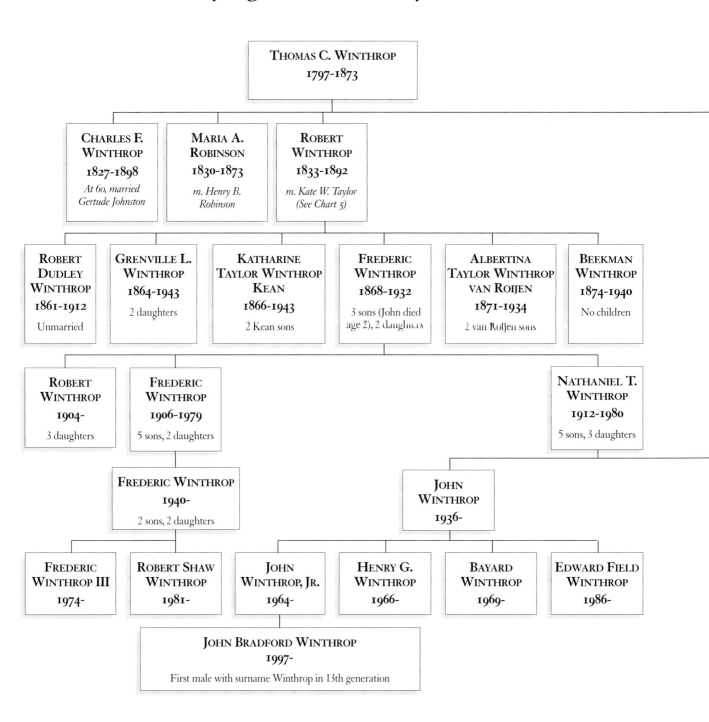

THOMAS C. WINTHROP
1797-1873

CHARLES F. WINTHROP
1827-1898
At 60, married Gertude Johnston

MARIA A. ROBINSON
1830-1873
m. Henry B. Robinson

ROBERT WINTHROP
1833-1892
m. Kate W. Taylor (See Chart 5)

ROBERT DUDLEY WINTHROP
1861-1912
Unmarried

GRENVILLE L. WINTHROP
1864-1943
2 daughters

KATHARINE TAYLOR WINTHROP KEAN
1866-1943
2 Kean sons

FREDERIC WINTHROP
1868-1932
3 sons (John died age 2), 2 daughters

ALBERTINA TAYLOR WINTHROP VAN ROIJEN
1871-1934
2 van Roijen sons

BEEKMAN WINTHROP
1874-1940
No children

ROBERT WINTHROP
1904-
3 daughters

FREDERIC WINTHROP
1906-1979
5 sons, 2 daughters

NATHANIEL T. WINTHROP
1912-1980
5 sons, 3 daughters

FREDERIC WINTHROP
1940-
2 sons, 2 daughters

JOHN WINTHROP
1936-

FREDERIC WINTHROP III
1974-

ROBERT SHAW WINTHROP
1981-

JOHN WINTHROP, JR.
1964-

HENRY G. WINTHROP
1966-

BAYARD WINTHROP
1969-

EDWARD FIELD WINTHROP
1986-

JOHN BRADFORD WINTHROP
1997-
First male with surname Winthrop in 13th generation

REARED *in a* GREENHOUSE

· CHART 3 ·

~ *continued* ~

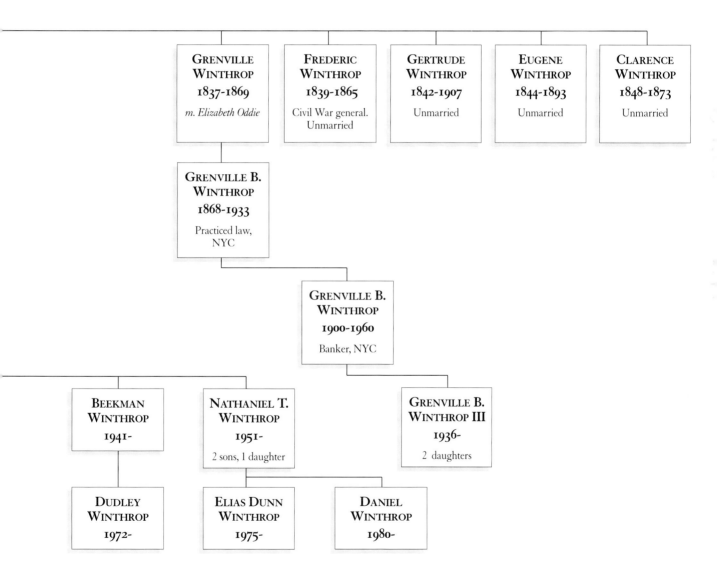

GRENVILLE WINTHROP
1837-1869

m. Elizabeth Oddie

FREDERIC WINTHROP
1839-1865

Civil War general.
Unmarried

GERTRUDE WINTHROP
1842-1907

Unmarried

EUGENE WINTHROP
1844-1893

Unmarried

CLARENCE WINTHROP
1848-1873

Unmarried

GRENVILLE B. WINTHROP
1868-1933

Practiced law,
NYC

GRENVILLE B. WINTHROP
1900-1960

Banker, NYC

BEEKMAN WINTHROP
1941-

NATHANIEL T. WINTHROP
1951-

2 sons, 1 daughter

GRENVILLE B. WINTHROP III
1936-

2 daughters

DUDLEY WINTHROP
1972-

ELIAS DUNN WINTHROP
1975-

DANIEL WINTHROP
1980-

Note: Four other male Winthrop lines extant during Thomas Charles' day have become extinct: the Charleston branch (1909); the Boston branch (1938); the younger NYC branch (1944); and the older NYC branch (1958).

· CHART 4 ·

Descendants of Moses and Catherine Taylor

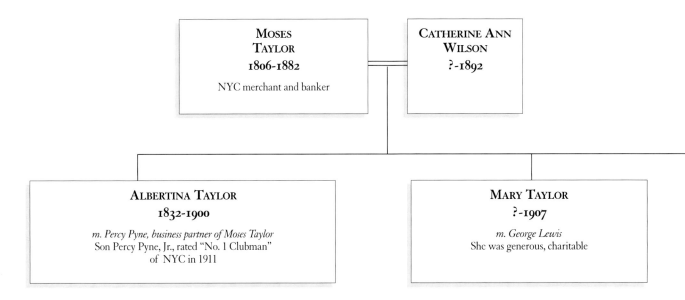

MOSES TAYLOR 1806-1882 NYC merchant and banker	**CATHERINE ANN WILSON** ?-1892

ALBERTINA TAYLOR 1832-1900 *m. Percy Pyne, business partner of Moses Taylor* Son Percy Pyne, Jr., rated "No. 1 Clubman" of NYC in 1911	**MARY TAYLOR** ?-1907 *m. George Lewis* She was generous, charitable

—— · CHART 4 · ——

~ continued ~

GEORGE TAYLOR

dates unknown

Unmarried.
Held diplomatic posts
in N. Africa/Near East

KATE WILSON TAYLOR
1839-1925

"Grandma Winthrop"

HENRY A. C. TAYLOR

m. Lottie Fearing;
Josephine Johnson,
wealthy Newport widow.

Daughter Harriet
m. Count Giuseppe
della Gherardesca (1903).

Son Moses
m. Edith Bishop (1896)
after Gertrude Vanderbilt
chose Harry Payne

· CHART 5 ·

Descendants of Robert and Kate Winthrop

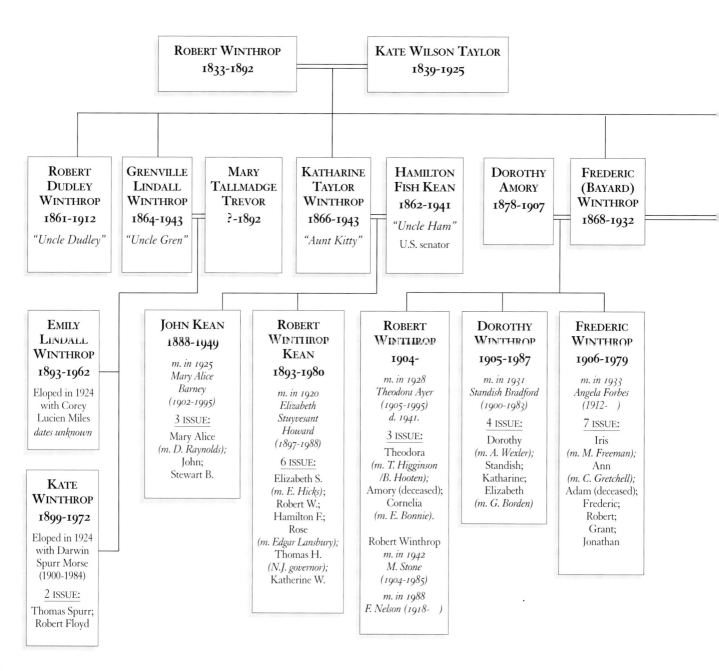

ROBERT WINTHROP
1833-1892

KATE WILSON TAYLOR
1839-1925

ROBERT
DUDLEY
WINTHROP
1861-1912
"Uncle Dudley"

GRENVILLE
LINDALL
WINTHROP
1864-1943
"Uncle Gren"

MARY
TALLMADGE
TREVOR
?-1892

KATHARINE
TAYLOR
WINTHROP
1866-1943
"Aunt Kitty"

HAMILTON
FISH KEAN
1862-1941
"Uncle Ham"
U.S. senator

DOROTHY
AMORY
1878-1907

FREDERIC
(BAYARD)
WINTHROP
1868-1932

EMILY
LINDALL
WINTHROP
1893-1962

Eloped in 1924
with Corey
Lucien Miles
dates unknown

KATE
WINTHROP
1899-1972

Eloped in 1924
with Darwin
Spurr Morse
(1900-1984)

2 ISSUE:

Thomas Spurr;
Robert Floyd

JOHN KEAN
1888-1949

*m. in 1925
Mary Alice
Barney
(1902-1995)*

3 ISSUE:

Mary Alice
(m. D. Raynolds);
John;
Stewart B.

ROBERT
WINTHROP
KEAN
1893-1980

*m. in 1920
Elizabeth
Stuyvesant
Howard
(1897-1988)*

6 ISSUE:

Elizabeth S.
(m. E. Hicks);
Robert W.;
Hamilton F.;
Rose
(m. Edgar Lansbury);
Thomas H.
(N.J. governor);
Katherine W.

ROBERT
WINTHROP
1904-

*m. in 1928
Theodora Ayer
(1905-1995)
d. 1941.*

3 ISSUE:

Theodora
*(m. T. Higginson
/B. Hooten)*;
Amory (deceased);
Cornelia
(m. E. Bonnie).

Robert Winthrop
*m. in 1942
M. Stone
(1904-1985)*

*m. in 1988
F. Nelson (1918-)*

DOROTHY
WINTHROP
1905-1987

*m. in 1931
Standish Bradford
(1900-1983)*

4 ISSUE:

Dorothy
(m. A. Wexler);
Standish;
Katharine;
Elizabeth
(m. G. Borden)

FREDERIC
WINTHROP
1906-1979

*m. in 1933
Angela Forbes
(1912-)*

7 ISSUE:

Iris
(m. M. Freeman);
Ann
(m. C. Gretchell);
Adam (deceased);
Frederic;
Robert;
Grant;
Jonathan

· CHART 5 ·
~ continued ~

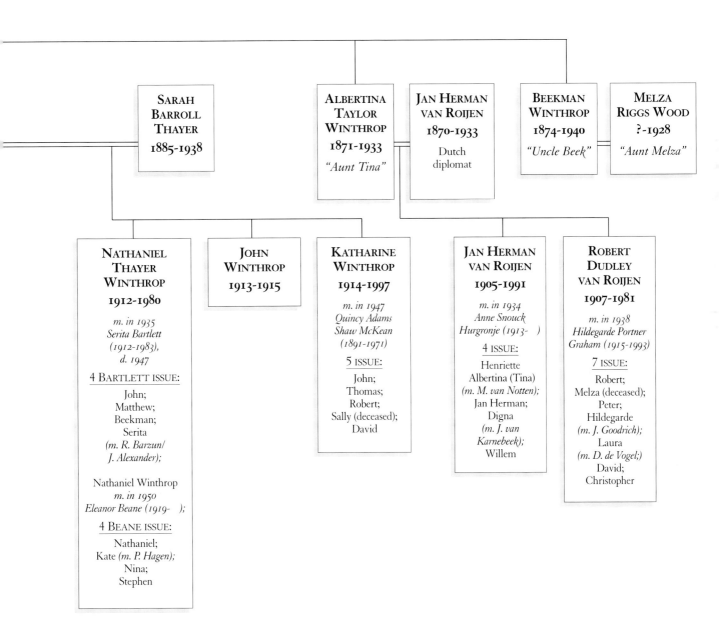

**SARAH
BARROLL
THAYER**
1885-1938

**ALBERTINA
TAYLOR
WINTHROP**
1871-1933
"Aunt Tina"

**JAN HERMAN
VAN ROIJEN**
1870-1933
Dutch
diplomat

**BEEKMAN
WINTHROP**
1874-1940
"Uncle Beek"

**MELZA
RIGGS WOOD**
?-1928
"Aunt Melza"

**NATHANIEL
THAYER
WINTHROP**
1912-1980

*m. in 1935
Serita Bartlett
(1912-1983),
d. 1947*

4 BARTLETT ISSUE:

John;
Matthew;
Beekman;
Serita
*(m. R. Barzun/
J. Alexander);*

Nathaniel Winthrop
*m. in 1950
Eleanor Beane (1919-);*

4 BEANE ISSUE:

Nathaniel;
Kate *(m. P. Hagen);*
Nina;
Stephen

**JOHN
WINTHROP**
1913-1915

**KATHARINE
WINTHROP**
1914-1997

*m. in 1947
Quincy Adams
Shaw McKean
(1891-1971)*

5 ISSUE:

John;
Thomas;
Robert;
Sally (deceased);
David

**JAN HERMAN
VAN ROIJEN**
1905-1991

*m. in 1934
Anne Snouck
Hurgronje (1913-)*

4 ISSUE:

Henriette
Albertina (Tina)
(m. M. van Notten);
Jan Herman;
Digna
*(m. J. van
Karnebeek);*
Willem

**ROBERT
DUDLEY
VAN ROIJEN**
1907-1981

*m. in 1938
Hildegarde Portner
Graham (1915-1993)*

7 ISSUE:

Robert;
Melza (deceased);
Peter;
Hildegarde
(m. J. Goodrich);
Laura
(m. D. de Vogel;)
David;
Christopher

· Chart 6 ·
Ancestors of Charles Walter Amory

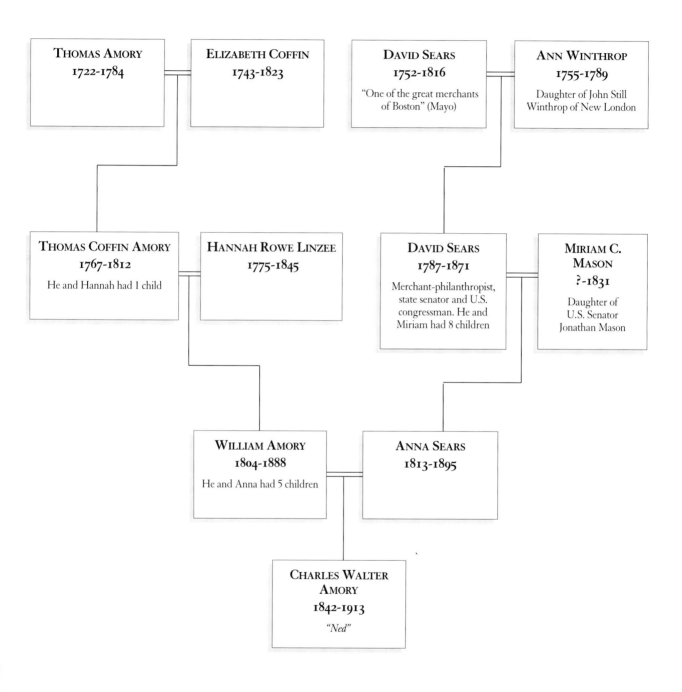

THOMAS AMORY
1722-1784

ELIZABETH COFFIN
1743-1823

DAVID SEARS
1752-1816

"One of the great merchants
of Boston" (Mayo)

ANN WINTHROP
1755-1789

Daughter of John Still
Winthrop of New London

THOMAS COFFIN AMORY
1767-1812

He and Hannah had 1 child

HANNAH ROWE LINZEE
1775-1845

DAVID SEARS
1787-1871

Merchant-philanthropist,
state senator and U.S.
congressman. He and
Miriam had 8 children

MIRIAM C. MASON
?-1831

Daughter of
U.S. Senator
Jonathan Mason

WILLIAM AMORY
1804-1888

He and Anna had 5 children

ANNA SEARS
1813-1895

CHARLES WALTER AMORY
1842-1913

"Ned"

· CHART 7 ·

Ancestors of Elizabeth Gardner Amory

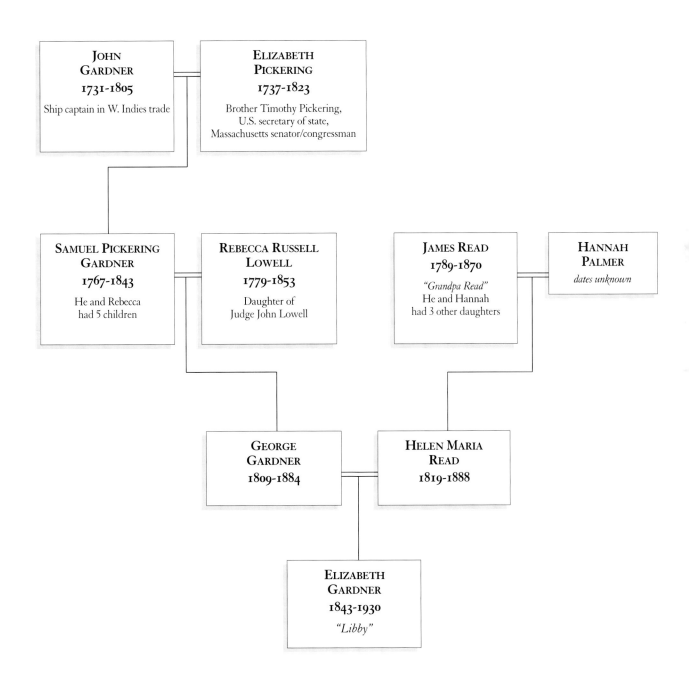

JOHN GARDNER
1731-1805

Ship captain in W. Indies trade

ELIZABETH PICKERING
1737-1823

Brother Timothy Pickering,
U.S. secretary of state,
Massachusetts senator/congressman

SAMUEL PICKERING GARDNER
1767-1843

He and Rebecca
had 5 children

REBECCA RUSSELL LOWELL
1779-1853

Daughter of
Judge John Lowell

JAMES READ
1789-1870

"Grandpa Read"
He and Hannah
had 3 other daughters

HANNAH PALMER

dates unknown

GEORGE GARDNER
1809-1884

HELEN MARIA READ
1819-1888

ELIZABETH GARDNER
1843-1930

"Libby"

GENEALOGICAL CHARTS

· CHART 8 ·

Descendants of George and Helen Gardner

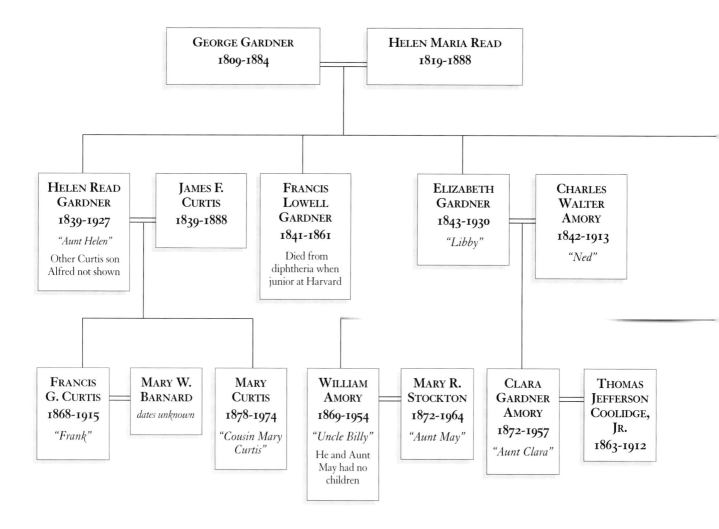

GEORGE GARDNER
1809-1884

HELEN MARIA READ
1819-1888

HELEN READ GARDNER
1839-1927
"Aunt Helen"
Other Curtis son Alfred not shown

JAMES F. CURTIS
1839-1888

FRANCIS LOWELL GARDNER
1841-1861
Died from diphtheria when junior at Harvard

ELIZABETH GARDNER
1843-1930
"Libby"

CHARLES WALTER AMORY
1842-1913
"Ned"

FRANCIS G. CURTIS
1868-1915
"Frank"

MARY W. BARNARD
dates unknown

MARY CURTIS
1878-1974
"Cousin Mary Curtis"

WILLIAM AMORY
1869-1954
"Uncle Billy"
He and Aunt May had no children

MARY R. STOCKTON
1872-1964
"Aunt May"

CLARA GARDNER AMORY
1872-1957
"Aunt Clara"

THOMAS JEFFERSON COOLIDGE, JR.
1863-1912

· CHART 8 ·

~ continued ~

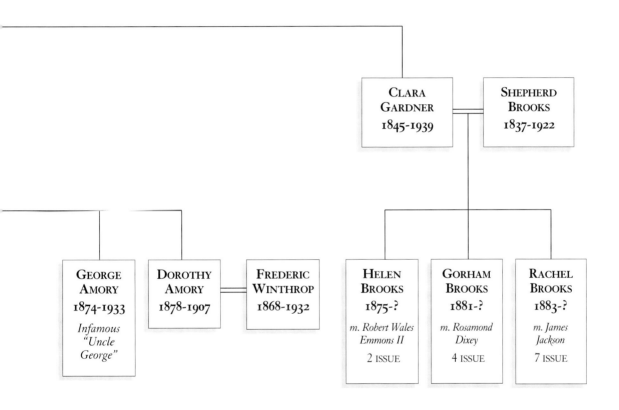

GENEALOGICAL CHARTS

Chart 9
Descendants of Libby and Ned Amory

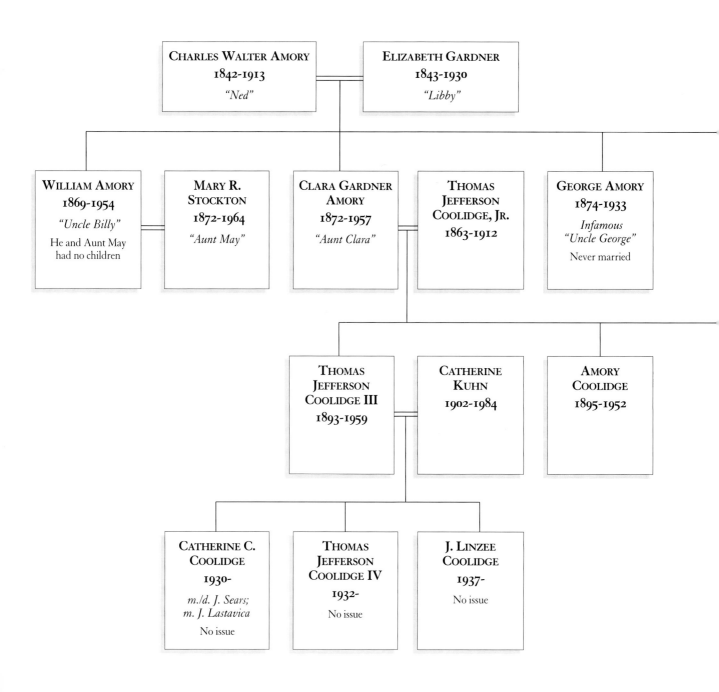

Charles Walter Amory
1842-1913
"Ned"

= **Elizabeth Gardner**
1843-1930
"Libby"

Children:

- **William Amory**
  1869-1954
  "Uncle Billy"
  He and Aunt May had no children

  = **Mary R. Stockton**
  1872-1964
  "Aunt May"

- **Clara Gardner Amory**
  1872-1957
  "Aunt Clara"

  = **Thomas Jefferson Coolidge, Jr.**
  1863-1912

  Children:

  - **Thomas Jefferson Coolidge III**
    1893-1959

    = **Catherine Kuhn**
    1902-1984

    Children:

    - **Catherine C. Coolidge**
      1930-
      m./d. J. Sears;
      m. J. Lastavica
      No issue
    - **Thomas Jefferson Coolidge IV**
      1932-
      No issue
    - **J. Linzee Coolidge**
      1937-
      No issue

  - **Amory Coolidge**
    1895-1952

- **George Amory**
  1874-1933
  Infamous
  "Uncle George"
  Never married

· CHART 9 ·
~ continued ~

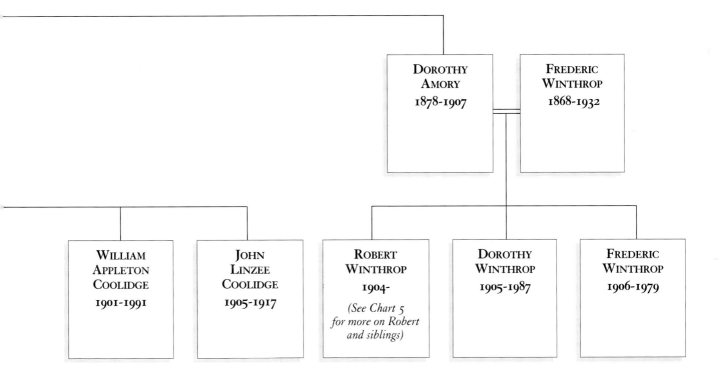

DOROTHY
AMORY
1878-1907

FREDERIC
WINTHROP
1868-1932

WILLIAM
APPLETON
COOLIDGE
1901-1991

JOHN
LINZEE
COOLIDGE
1905-1917

ROBERT
WINTHROP
1904-

*(See Chart 5
for more on Robert
and siblings)*

DOROTHY
WINTHROP
1905-1987

FREDERIC
WINTHROP
1906-1979

— CHART 10 ·

Descendants of John Lowell Gardner: Carrying on the Family Name

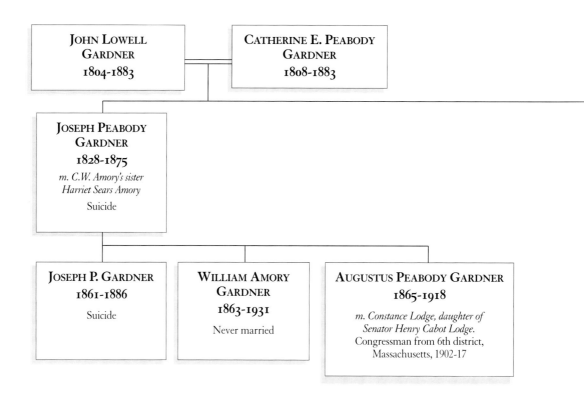

| JOHN LOWELL GARDNER 1804-1883 | CATHERINE E. PEABODY GARDNER 1808-1883 |

JOSEPH PEABODY GARDNER
1828-1875

m. C.W. Amory's sister Harriet Sears Amory

Suicide

JOSEPH P. GARDNER
1861-1886

Suicide

WILLIAM AMORY GARDNER
1863-1931

Never married

AUGUSTUS PEABODY GARDNER
1865-1918

m. Constance Lodge, daughter of Senator Henry Cabot Lodge.
Congressman from 6th district,
Massachusetts, 1902-17

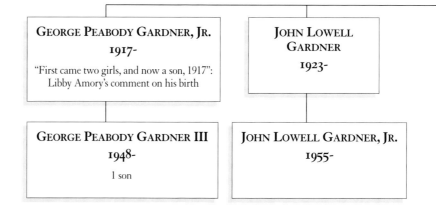

GEORGE PEABODY GARDNER, JR.
1917-

"First came two girls, and now a son, 1917":
Libby Amory's comment on his birth

JOHN LOWELL GARDNER
1923-

GEORGE PEABODY GARDNER III
1948-

1 son

JOHN LOWELL GARDNER, JR.
1955-

Note: Women are identified by married names.

REARED *in a* GREENHOUSE

— · CHART 10 · —

~ continued ~

GEORGE AUGUSTUS GARDNER
1829-1916

m. Eliza Endicott Peabody

Ancestor of all descendants
of John Lowell Gardner
alive today

JOHN LOWELL GARDNER, JR.
1837-1898

m. Isabella Stewart Gardner

Their only son John Lowell Gardner died, age 2.

He and Isabella adopted 3 sons of Joseph Peabody
and Harriet Gardner

JULIA GARDNER COOLIDGE
1841-1921

m. Joseph Randolph Coolidge, T. J. Coolidge, Sr.'s brother (see Charts 8 and 9)

ELIZA BLANCHARD GARDNER SKINNER
1846-1898

m. Francis Skinner

GEORGE PEABODY GARDNER
1855-1939

m. Esther Burnett
First of four generations of
George Peabody Gardners

OLGA ELIZA GARDNER MONKS
1869-1944

"Aunt" Olga Monks

m. George Howard Monks (see Chart 15)

GEORGE PEABODY GARDNER
1888-1976

m. Rose Phinney Grosvenor.
"This is the only one to carry on the name": notation in Libby Amory's genealogy

ROBERT GROSVENOR GARDNER
1925-

STEWART A. GARDNER
1951-

1 son

LUKE G. GARDNER
1957-

2 sons

CALEB P. GARDNER
1984-

NOAH G. GARDNER
1987-

· CHART 11 ·

Why Robert C. Winthrop Was Libby Gardner's "Uncle Winthrope"

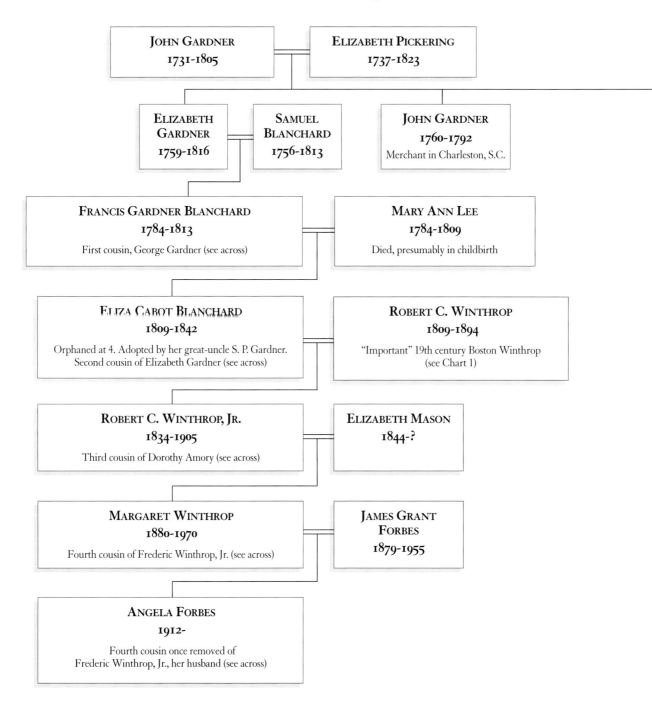

JOHN GARDNER
1731-1805

ELIZABETH PICKERING
1737-1823

ELIZABETH
GARDNER
1759-1816

SAMUEL
BLANCHARD
1756-1813

JOHN GARDNER
1760-1792
Merchant in Charleston, S.C.

FRANCIS GARDNER BLANCHARD
1784-1813
First cousin, George Gardner (see across)

MARY ANN LEE
1784-1809
Died, presumably in childbirth

ELIZA CABOT BLANCHARD
1809-1842
Orphaned at 4. Adopted by her great-uncle S. P. Gardner.
Second cousin of Elizabeth Gardner (see across)

ROBERT C. WINTHROP
1809-1894
"Important" 19th century Boston Winthrop
(see Chart 1)

ROBERT C. WINTHROP, JR.
1834-1905
Third cousin of Dorothy Amory (see across)

ELIZABETH MASON
1844-?

MARGARET WINTHROP
1880-1970
Fourth cousin of Frederic Winthrop, Jr. (see across)

JAMES GRANT
FORBES
1879-1955

ANGELA FORBES
1912-
Fourth cousin once removed of
Frederic Winthrop, Jr., her husband (see across)

REARED *in a* GREENHOUSE

· CHART 11 ·
~ continued ~

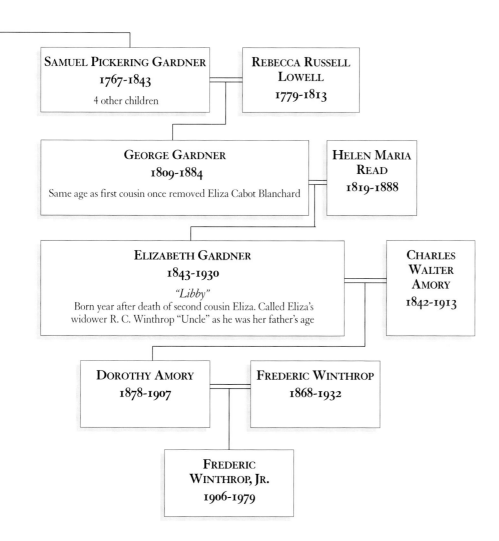

SAMUEL PICKERING GARDNER
1767-1843

4 other children

REBECCA RUSSELL LOWELL
1779-1813

GEORGE GARDNER
1809-1884

Same age as first cousin once removed Eliza Cabot Blanchard

HELEN MARIA READ
1819-1888

ELIZABETH GARDNER
1843-1930

"Libby"
Born year after death of second cousin Eliza. Called Eliza's widower R. C. Winthrop "Uncle" as he was her father's age

CHARLES WALTER AMORY
1842-1913

DOROTHY AMORY
1878-1907

FREDERIC WINTHROP
1868-1932

FREDERIC WINTHROP, JR.
1906-1979

Note: This chart also shows why Angela and Frederic Winthrop, Jr., were fourth cousins once removed on the Gardner side.

·CHART 12·

Why Frederic Winthrop and Dorothy Amory
Were Third Cousins Once Removed

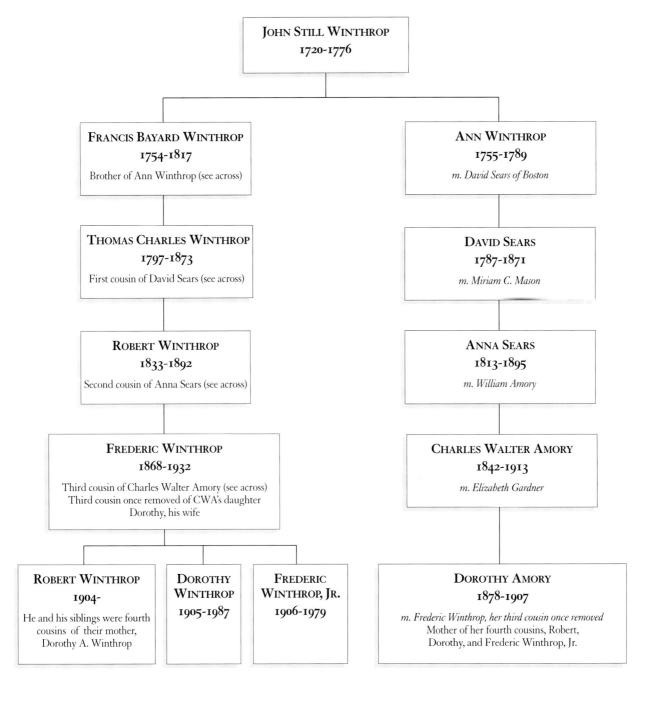

JOHN STILL WINTHROP
1720-1776

FRANCIS BAYARD WINTHROP
1754-1817

Brother of Ann Winthrop (see across)

ANN WINTHROP
1755-1789

m. David Sears of Boston

THOMAS CHARLES WINTHROP
1797-1873

First cousin of David Sears (see across)

DAVID SEARS
1787-1871

m. Miriam C. Mason

ROBERT WINTHROP
1833-1892

Second cousin of Anna Sears (see across)

ANNA SEARS
1813-1895

m. William Amory

FREDERIC WINTHROP
1868-1932

Third cousin of Charles Walter Amory (see across)
Third cousin once removed of CWA's daughter
Dorothy, his wife

CHARLES WALTER AMORY
1842-1913

m. Elizabeth Gardner

ROBERT WINTHROP
1904-

He and his siblings were fourth
cousins of their mother,
Dorothy A. Winthrop

DOROTHY
WINTHROP
1905-1987

FREDERIC
WINTHROP, JR.
1906-1979

DOROTHY AMORY
1878-1907

m. Frederic Winthrop, her third cousin once removed
Mother of her fourth cousins, Robert,
Dorothy, and Frederic Winthrop, Jr.

· CHART 13 ·

Why Dorothy Winthrop Bradford
and Emily Sears Lodge Were Cousins

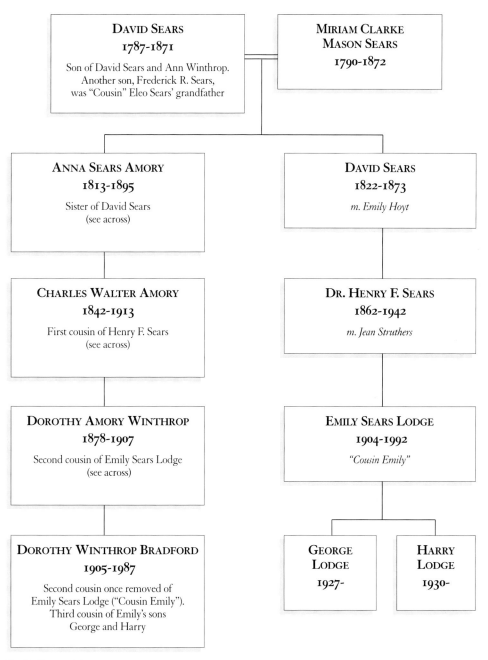

DAVID SEARS
1787-1871

Son of David Sears and Ann Winthrop.
Another son, Frederick R. Sears,
was "Cousin" Eleo Sears' grandfather

MIRIAM CLARKE
MASON SEARS
1790-1872

ANNA SEARS AMORY
1813-1895

Sister of David Sears
(see across)

DAVID SEARS
1822-1873

m. Emily Hoyt

CHARLES WALTER AMORY
1842-1913

First cousin of Henry F. Sears
(see across)

DR. HENRY F. SEARS
1862-1942

m. Jean Struthers

DOROTHY AMORY WINTHROP
1878-1907

Second cousin of Emily Sears Lodge
(see across)

EMILY SEARS LODGE
1904-1992

"Cousin Emily"

DOROTHY WINTHROP BRADFORD
1905-1987

Second cousin once removed of
Emily Sears Lodge ("Cousin Emily").
Third cousin of Emily's sons
George and Harry

GEORGE
LODGE
1927-

HARRY
LODGE
1930-

Note: Women are identified by married names.

· Chart 14 ·
Why Angela Forbes and Frederic Winthrop, Jr., Were Fourth Cousins on the Winthrop Side

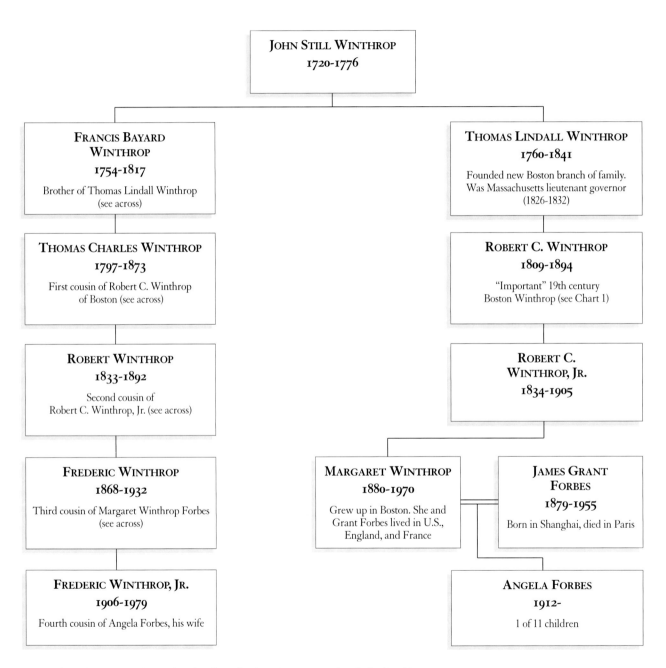

JOHN STILL WINTHROP
1720-1776

FRANCIS BAYARD WINTHROP
1754-1817

Brother of Thomas Lindall Winthrop
(see across)

THOMAS LINDALL WINTHROP
1760-1841

Founded new Boston branch of family.
Was Massachusetts lieutenant governor
(1826-1832)

THOMAS CHARLES WINTHROP
1797-1873

First cousin of Robert C. Winthrop
of Boston (see across)

ROBERT C. WINTHROP
1809-1894

"Important" 19th century
Boston Winthrop (see Chart 1)

ROBERT WINTHROP
1833-1892

Second cousin of
Robert C. Winthrop, Jr. (see across)

ROBERT C.
WINTHROP, JR.
1834-1905

FREDERIC WINTHROP
1868-1932

Third cousin of Margaret Winthrop Forbes
(see across)

MARGARET WINTHROP
1880-1970

Grew up in Boston. She and
Grant Forbes lived in U.S.,
England, and France

JAMES GRANT
FORBES
1879-1955

Born in Shanghai, died in Paris

FREDERIC WINTHROP, JR.
1906-1979

Fourth cousin of Angela Forbes, his wife

ANGELA FORBES
1912-

1 of 11 children

Note: Refer to Chart 11 to see why Angela and Fred were fourth cousins once removed on the Gardner side.

REARED *in a* GREENHOUSE

· CHART 15 ·

How "Aunt" Olga Monks Was Related to Dorothy Winthrop and Standish Bradford

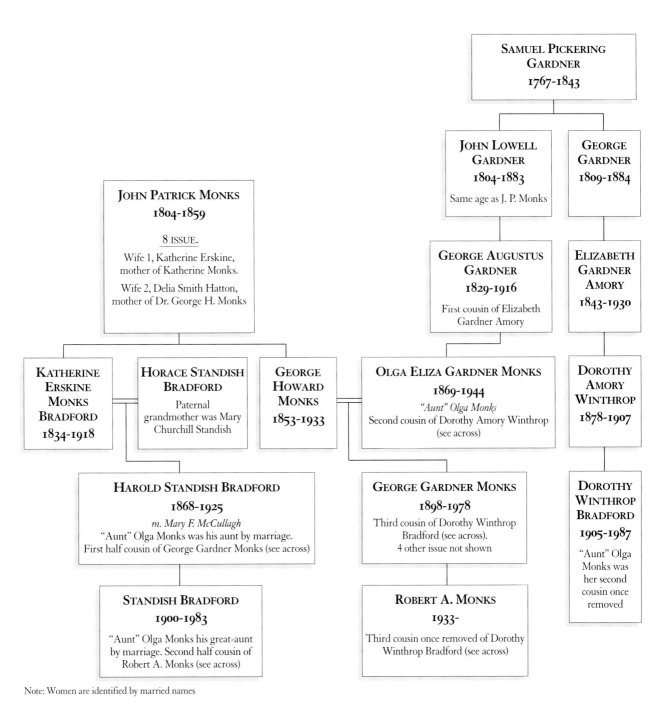

SAMUEL PICKERING GARDNER
1767-1843

JOHN LOWELL GARDNER
1804-1883
Same age as J. P. Monks

GEORGE GARDNER
1809-1884

JOHN PATRICK MONKS
1804-1859

8 ISSUE.

Wife 1, Katherine Erskine, mother of Katherine Monks.

Wife 2, Delia Smith Hatton, mother of Dr. George H. Monks

GEORGE AUGUSTUS GARDNER
1829-1916
First cousin of Elizabeth Gardner Amory

ELIZABETH GARDNER AMORY
1843-1930

KATHERINE ERSKINE MONKS BRADFORD
1834-1918

HORACE STANDISH BRADFORD
Paternal grandmother was Mary Churchill Standish

GEORGE HOWARD MONKS
1853-1933

OLGA ELIZA GARDNER MONKS
1869-1944
"Aunt" Olga Monks
Second cousin of Dorothy Amory Winthrop
(see across)

DOROTHY AMORY WINTHROP
1878-1907

HAROLD STANDISH BRADFORD
1868-1925
m. Mary F. McCullagh
"Aunt" Olga Monks was his aunt by marriage.
First half cousin of George Gardner Monks (see across)

GEORGE GARDNER MONKS
1898-1978
Third cousin of Dorothy Winthrop Bradford (see across).
4 other issue not shown

DOROTHY WINTHROP BRADFORD
1905-1987
"Aunt" Olga Monks was her second cousin once removed

STANDISH BRADFORD
1900-1983
"Aunt" Olga Monks his great-aunt by marriage. Second half cousin of Robert A. Monks (see across)

ROBERT A. MONKS
1933-
Third cousin once removed of Dorothy Winthrop Bradford (see across)

Note: Women are identified by married names

Notes

preface

1. This is based on the invaluable genealogy *The Winthrop Family in America, A Genealogical Updating: 1833–1988,* compiled by John Winthrop and my sister Libby Borden. I have used 1985 as the cutoff date, since that is when my mother began recounting her memoirs. Of course, the family has continued to grow since them.

chapter ONE

1. E. Digby Baltzell. *Puritan Boston and Quaker Philadelphia.* The Free Press. A Division of Macmillan Publishing Co. New York. 1979. P. 48. A second historian expanded on this theory: "As they gathered together in their pure churches, placing the mark of holiness on their own foreheads and of damnation on most of their neighbors, the experience could not fail to induce … intellectual arrogance." (Edmund S. Morgan. *The Puritan Dilemma: The Story of John Winthrop.* Little, Brown and Company. Boston. 1958. Pp. 79–80.)
2. This was said of a Captain Dudley Saltonstall, whose mother was a Winthrop. (Samuel E. Morison. *John Paul Jones.* Little, Brown and Company. Boston. 1959. P. 43.)
3. Grandma Amory's "mini-history" was a small typewritten volume she called *The Gardner Family of Salem and Boston,* based on papers she had gathered from her grandfather Samuel Pickering Gardner. She also used a study of the Gardner family written by a member of the Essex Institute, Frank Augustus Gardner, M.D., entitled *Thomas Gardner, Planter, and Some of His Descendants.* In time, Dr. Gardner's account would be expanded into the *Gardner Memorial: A Biographical and Genealogical Record of the Descendants of Thomas Gardner, Planter,* privately printed by Newcomb & Gauss Co. Salem, Massachusetts. 1933. This is a standard, unpretentious genealogy that provides a useful guide to the history of the Gardners in America.

    The official Gardner position as set forth in the *Gardner Memorial* (p. 12) was fully in accord with Grandma Amory: Thomas Gardner had indeed been slighted by history. In 1616, after the situation had proved impossibly rough at Cape Ann, the Dorchester Company in England had dispatched Roger Conant from nearby Nantasket to help. It was he who had written that those who moved on to Salem stayed "to the hazard of their lives." Frank Augustus Gardner added: "and it is a matter of shame and deepest regret that many an historical writer of old Massachusetts has failed to give due credit for the laying of the foundation of this grand old Commonwealth."

4. Robert C. Black III. *The Younger John Winthrop*. Columbia University Press. New York. 1966.

5. Fred Winthrop was a direct descendant of only two—the first two governors John. Moreover, no New York Winthrops appear; all notable Winthrops represent New England branches of the family.

6. Undated clipping from the *Boston Evening Transcript*, under the byline of James Grant Wilson. Found among Fred Winthrop's papers. According to Donald Yacovone of the Massachusetts Historical Society, who is overseeing the collection of Robert C. Winthrop's papers described in the following note, this was probably true. Robert C. Winthrop did indeed "know everybody."

7. Above all, the Massachusetts Historical Society believes that Robert C. Winthrop remains "understudied," an "important, fascinating" man about whom, a century after his death, no biography has yet been written ("M.H.S. Miscellany," Number 61, Spring 1995, a periodic publication of the Massachusetts Historical Society). In an effort to rectify this gap, the MHS is currently engaged in a project to make Winthrop's enormous body of papers (5,400 relevant manuscripts at the MSH plus thousands more at other libraries) available to scholars.

8. *The Generations Joined: Winthrops in America*. A Massachusetts Historical Society Picture Book. Massachusetts Historical Society. Boston. 1977. Though "handsome in its way," Robert C. Winthrop, Jr., wrote petulantly, the new location was so "remote" from his own home that he found going there had become "of the nature of a special expedition"—one he eschewed, "preferring to work in my own home."

9. Note written by Grandma Amory on an obituary notice about John Winthrop by the president of the Lenox Club.

10. The distinction comes from Baltzell, p. 33. Baltzell was not referring specifically to Fred Winthrop.

11. The fate of the third journal gives some hint as to the wonder that family papers survive at all, considering their years of haphazard storage in stuffy attics and dank cellars. This one (the second chronologically) was found in a church tower in 1816, turned over to the Society with great fanfare in 1825, loaned to historian James Savage for copying and footnoting, and while in his custody destroyed in a fire that broke out in his library.

12. In 1817 they had been divided between Frederic's grandfather Thomas Charles Winthrop and three of his brothers.

13. Lawrence Shaw Mayo. *The Winthrop Family in America*. The Massachusetts Historical Society. Boston, Massachusetts. 1948. P. 3.

14. The list appears at the end of Cleveland Amory's *Who Killed Society?* A letter to me from Henry Beckwith, secretary of the New England Historic Genealogical Society's Committee on Heraldry, dated June 27, 1994, confirms that Fred Winthrop asked for confirmation, stating: "This committee registered the Winthrop arms in 1916, the person submitting the application being one Frederic Winthrop, Esq., then of 299 Berkeley Street, Boston." The first ten names registered were Washington, 1; Appleton, 2; Bowen, 3; Bulkeley, 4; Dumaresq, 5; Gore, 6; Winthrop, 7; Pynchon, 8; Helmershausen, 9; and Coggeshall, 10.

15. Mayo, p. 134. It was sold by the profligate John F. R. S. (Fellow of the Royal Society) to James Bowdoin, who had held a mortgage on the property since 1717.

16. The full quotation is cited in Richard D. Brown. *Massachusetts, A Bicentennial History*. W. W. Norton & Company, Inc. New York. 1978. Pp. 27 and 28. It reads: "Wee shall find that the God of Israel is among us, when tenn of us shall be able to resist a thousand of our enemies, when hee shall make us a prayse and glory, that men shall say of succeed-

ing plantacions: the lord make it like that of New England: for we must Consider that wee shall be as a Citty upon a Hill, the eies of all the people are upon us .... [The community would be required to] entertaine each other in brotherly Affeccion ... abridge our selves of our superfluities ... delight in eache other ... rejoyce together, mourne together, labour, and suffer together, allwayse having before our eyes our Commission and Community in the worke."

17. Richard S. Dunn. *Puritans and Yankees: The Winthrop Dynasty of New England. 1630-1717*. Princeton University Press. Princeton, New Jersey. 1962. P. 59 (on Ipswich see pp. 64–65; on Saybrook, 66–69; and on New London, pp. 72–74).

18. Mayo, pp. 72 and 145–46.

19. Moses Yale Beach. *The Wealthiest Citizens of New York*. 1844. From entry on Henry R. Winthrop.

20. *Winthrop Family Portraits at Harvard*. John Winthrop House. Harvard University. April 1956.

21. Robert Winthrop gave the fourteen portraits—plus a fifteenth of his father Frederic Winthrop—outright to Harvard in 1964, making permanent what had begun in December 1955 as a twenty-five-year loan. In 1986, he also gave the university his portraits of his uncles Grenville and Beekman Winthrop. Though his seventeen-portrait gift was far and away the largest, Winthrops have been giving family portraits to Harvard for more than a century starting with Thomas Lindall Winthrop's gift of a portrait of Governor John Winthrop (Massachusetts Bay Colony) in 1835 (source: Sandra Grindlay, Curator of the Harvard University Portrait Collection).

22. It could also have been Charlotte, Egerton's daughter, but her advanced age (she was then twenty-seven) and impending marriage (she married Henry Spencer Cram in September later that year) would have reduced her eligibility (see Mayo, p. 410).

23. Mayo, p. 350, quoting literary friends of Egerton.

24. Edith Wharton, in *A Backward Glance,* devotes several pages to Egerton Winthrop (see *Edith Wharton. Novellas and Other Writings*. The Library of America. New York. 1990. Pp. 854–57). She wrote that she despaired of understanding how "an intelligence so distinguished and a character so admirable [could have] been combined with interests for the most part so trivial." It seemed strange to her that "the most stimulating of talkers in a congenial group" would take "far more trouble about the finish and perfection of his dinners than about the choice of his guests." She revered him for the intellectual worlds he had opened for her—those of the great French novelists, French historians and literary critics of the day, and of nineteenth-century Darwinian and evolutionary science. When he died, she greatly missed his sure counsel: "Even now that I am old," she wrote, "and he has been so many years dead, it still happens to me, when faced by a difficulty, to ask myself: 'What would Egerton have done?' " But she despaired of his tendency, and that of others like him, to have "made so little use of their abilities."

25. *Winthrop, Stimson, Putnam & Roberts: History of a Law Firm*. 1980.

26. For example, Fred's father, Robert Winthrop, was identified as a cousin of his brother Charles Francis Winthrop, in the latter's obituary. And Fred himself was identified as the brother of his first cousin Grenville Bayard Winthrop when serving as his best man; moreover, his name was spelled Frederick and the groom's name was spelled Greenville. Even R. W. B. Lewis, in his compendium of Edith Wharton's letters, would refer to Fred's mother, Mrs. Robert Winthrop, as "Mrs. Grenville Winthrop" although at that time, Mrs. Grenville Winthrop (her daughter-in-law) had been dead for twenty-five years.

27. Marjorie B. Cohn. "Turner•Ruskin•Norton•Winthrop." *Harvard University Art Museums Bulletin*. Fall 1993. P. 62, footnote.

28. Quoted in Cohn, p. 54, from Martin Birnbaum. *The Last Romantic*. Twayne. New York. 1960. P. 180. The phrase is also used in Ellery Kirke Taylor's *The Lion and the Hare*. P. 15.

29. In the *Dictionary of American Biography*, Winthrops were listed first in a short list of seven families that had exercised "first family leadership" in Boston for over two hundred years. Baltzell, p. 470.

30. In New York, they were Fred Winthrop's third cousins Bronson and Egerton, his second cousin Buchanan, his first cousin Grenville Bayard, and his three brothers, and in Boston, one fourth cousin Robert Mason. Only three of these had sons, Buchanan, Grenville Bayard, and himself. Fred seems to not to have tracked the other branches—in New London, Charleston, South Carolina, and Illinois.

31. Robert Winthrop Kean in *Fourscore Years: My First Twenty-four* (Privately printed. 1974. P. 62) makes this point, and the term has been perpetuated further in *The Winthrop Family in America, A Genealogical Updating 1833–1988*, in the dedication to Dorothy Winthrop Bradford, "who, more than any of us, generated warmth and affection among the scattered members of 'The Holy Family.'"

32. With Beekman's death ten months later, and those of his sister Kitty and brother Grenville three years later, the curtain would ring down on the lives of the "holy family," or "holy society," or at least on their branch of the ninth generation of the Winthrop family in America.

33. These families did have hardy, patriarchal roots. Grandma Amory's great-uncle Timothy Pickering was secretary of state under Presidents George Washington and John Adams, then senator and congressman from Massachusetts. The first great Lowell was Grandma Amory's great-grandfather (the first of three Judge John Lowells) appointed by President George Washington as judge of the U.S. Circuit Court of Massachusetts and then by President Adams as chief justice of the U.S. Circuit Court (including Maine, New Hampshire, and Rhode Island). Her great-uncle Francis Cabot Lowell introduced the power loom.

34. Cleveland Amory. *The Proper Bostonians*. Parnassus Imprints. Orleans, Massachusetts. 1947. P. 14.

35. From a postscript to the Gardner history that Grandma Amory typed and secured with a straight pin in one of the copies.

36. The Richard Russell family arrived in Charlestown, New England, in 1639; Percival Lowle came to New England in 1639, age sixty-eight; Thomas Amory arrived in Boston in 1720, although his father had landed in Charleston, South Carolina, in the seventeenth century. The Amory genealogy had been prepared in conjunction with a book entitled *The Descendants of Hugh Amory, 1605–1805* (Gertrude Euphemia Meredith. London. Privately printed at the Chiswick Press. 1901).

37. The genealogy I have is annotated in my mother's hand, but there is no doubt that it is her Grandmother Amory's markings that she has transcribed.

38. Meredith. The tale my mother told us—that one of our ancestors drowned in a vat of liquor—is verified (type of liquor unclear) on page 101 of *The Descendants of Hugh Amory, 1605–1805*, in which Thomas' wife Rebecca writes: "Mr. Thomas Amory died June 20, 1728, at five o'clock in the morning, by a very sad accident. Going into the still-house to look after some necessary affair fell into a cistern of returns. There being nobody therein there [died] as was the sovereign will of God."

39. She supposed that said crest had been brought to America by quite another "Gardner"—Lion Gardiner (no known relative)—and that her grandfather had "probably adopted [it] … on account of the name."

40. At the convention that wrote the Massachusetts Constitution, Judge Lowell came up with the clause: "All men are born free and equal and have certain natural, essential, and inalienable rights, among which may be reckoned the right of enjoying and defending their lives and liberties."

41. The town of Wenham seems a fitting resting place for the outfit, for it was in Wenham that the first of the Gardners in my mother's stories, John Gardner, settled after retiring from his seagoing days. As my mother wrote in notes pertaining to her donation, he and his wife Elizabeth Pickering Gardner had "very wisely" moved to Wenham and "promptly *purchased* a pew in the Wenham church" and a large farm. Today, Elizabeth Pickering Gardner lies buried in the Wenham Burying Grounds, the town next to Hamilton where their great-great-great granddaughter, my mother, would be born more than a century later (*Gardner Memorial*, p. 10).

42. Actually, a couple of women made their way into the Winthrop family portraits: Mary Winthrop, daughter of Fitz-John, and Phebe Taylor Winthrop, wife of Francis Bayard Winthrop.

43. She copied these words from something historian Francis Parkman had written on "a loose sheet shut in his notebook."

chapter TWO

1. Gardner. *Gardner Memorial*. Pp. 162–63. Libby Amory's grandfather, James Read, lived at 68 Beacon Street for ten years, next door to Libby and Ned Amory, according to Libby's handwritten note above a picture of the house at 67 Beacon.

2. Robert Shackleton. *The Book of Boston*. The Penn Publishing Company. Philadelphia. 1916. P. 8. Cows were freely pastured on the Common until about 1830. Around the time of the Revolution, according to Shackleton, John Hancock, he of the "mighty signature," had been entertaining French officers and learning that his own cows had not given enough milk for his guests, sent his servants out onto the Common to milk every cow there, regardless of ownership.

3. Elizabeth Gardner Amory's memoirs. Private collection in my possession.

4. From a clipping in a collection of Sears letters, left to her children by Mrs. Amory (presumably Mrs. William Amory).

5. *"Our First Men," or a Catalogue of the Richest Men of Massachusetts*. Fetridge and Company. Boston, Massachusetts. 1851.

6. This was the time that the Sears sisters played a game of musical houses, with Anna and William Amory moving from 43 to 41 Beacon, another Sears sister Grace moving into 43 Beacon, and Harriet and George Crowninshield moving to Brookline. The three Beacon Street locations remained Sears land until the elder Searses died in 1871 and the Somerset Club bought numbers 42 and 43. The club added 41 when Ned's mother died in 1895. The house changes are described in a handwritten caption beneath a drawing of 42 Beacon Street, 1820, in Grandma Amory's hand and included in a volume of Sears letters.

7. From a sketch of William Amory, found in the scrapbook containing Sears letters left by Mrs. Amory to her children. The sketch was written by an unnamed friend of his son Francis.

8. *"Our First Men," or a Catalogue of the Richest Men of Massachusetts*.

9. James Read Chadwick. *A Brief Sketch of the Life of James Read*. A paper read before the Hyde Park Historical Society. The Merrymount Press. Boston. 1905. P. 7. The ad appeared in the July 5, 1824, edition of the *Boston Courier*.

10. From Libby Amory's "few words of description" of people she knew.

11. Chadwick, p. 8.

12. From a letter in the possession of Dr. Catherine Lastavica.

13. James Read's obituary (a press clipping in Libby Amory's scrapbook—no date or newspaper) noted that "His course in the panic of 1837 is familiar to most of us, and is almost without a parallel. When he was obliged with many others to succumb to the pressure, he gave his word to his creditors that his obligations would be fulfilled. He more than kept his promise, for he paid every dollar of his debts with every cent of the interest due." The obituary also mentioned his "sweet and calm" life, pointing out that "his step was as elastic, his smile as kindly, and his whole bearing as manly and noble the day he died as it was fifty years ago."

14. George Gardner's letter sets the amount at $755,000, adding that, though Read also had $1.1 million in assets, much of this was in bad notes.

15. Chadwick, pp. 11 and 12.

16. Chadwick, p. 2.

17. While daughter Helen's marriage to George Gardner progressed satisfactorily, much in the lives of Hannah Read's other three daughters warranted maternal hand-wringing. There was Lucy Tappan, Libby Amory wrote, "unhappy [after separating] from her husband after their two sons and only children died of scarlet fever." There was Louisa Chadwick, who was "happy enough till Chadwick went crazy and from the asylum committed suicide by drowning." And there was Sarah, who "never married for she said she saw her sisters were not very happy in the married state and she thought she would not try it."

18. From Libby Amory's "few words of description" of people she knew.

19. Gardner, *Gardner Memorial*, pp. 100–101.

20. In 1851, John Lowell Gardner was listed in the *Catalogue of the Richest Men of Massachusetts* as worth $500,000. Cleveland Amory, *The Proper Bostonians*, p. 48, provides the $5 million figure. The *Gardner Memorial* simply says he left a large estate (p. 155).

21. Cleveland Amory, *The Proper Bostonians*, p. 48.

22. Gardner, *Gardner Memorial*, pp. 149–151 and 162.

23. A handwritten note written by Libby Amory on her Gardner genealogy beneath the date of her grandparents' marriage, October 18, 1838.

24. Gardner, *Gardner Memorial*, pp. 163–4.

25. Isabella Stewart Gardner is the only "Gardner" listed in the *Dictionary of American Biography*.

26. Louise Hall Tharp. *Mrs. Jack: A Biography of Isabella Stewart Gardner*. Peter Weed Books. New York. 1965. P. 14.

27. What Libby Gardner thought of all this can be surmised from a note she affixed years later to the frontispiece of a copy of the "advice" that her aunt, Mrs. Horace Gray, her father's sister Sarah, had borrowed and returned expurgated. This note said that the pages that had been cut out contained warnings "not to be dissipated; and giving pictures of the horrible old age and disease of roués—she thought such subjects should never be mentioned!" (This copy of "Advice to My Sons" is among the papers of George Gardner, now in the possession of Dr. Catherine Lastavica.)

28. From 1838 to 1848, George was officially a member of John L. Gardner & Co. at 47 India Street (*Gardner Memorial*, p. 162) but correspondence between the two brothers dating back to 1831 and now in the possession of Dr. Catherine Lastavica indicates that they were working together well before that date. George Gardner appears to have left his brother's firm in 1848 and to have gone into business with one George J. Furness. In

1859, he took on John Gardner's son Joseph P. Gardner as his partner (*Gardner Memorial*, p. 162).

29. George's comment in a letter to John was a wry "The furniture is very handsome. The bill, the handsomest part of the concern, has not made its appearance yet."

30. From a letter from George Gardner to a friend who wanted information for a classbook. Boston, November 29, 1878. Letter in the possession of Dr. Catherine Lastavica.

31. Letter from George Gardner to John Gardner, from the collection of Dr. Catherine Lastavica.

32. From an October 1833 letter to his brother John, in the collection of Dr. Catherine Lastavica.

33. From his summary of his life, in the possession of Dr. Catherine Lastavica.

34. From a letter from one of his friends, in a collection of letters concerning his death, in the possession of Dr. Catherine Lastavica.

35. From a bound book of letters relating to the death of Francis L. Gardner found among the papers of his father George Gardner, now in the possession of Dr. Catherine Lastavica. The letter describing the circumstances of his death was from his father to one of Frank's friends (Otto Harlan) in Germany.

36. Elizabeth Gardner Amory. *The Gardner Family of Salem and Boston*. Pp. 60–61.

37. Chadwick, p. 9.

38. From Libby Amory's "few words of description" of people she knew.

39. From a letter Libby Amory wrote my mother in June 1923.

40. Mayo, p. 396.

41. J. C. Warren. *Class of 1863 of Harvard College. Memoir of Charles Walter Amory*. The University Press. Cambridge. 1914. Pp. 2 and 3.

42. From a letter written by Libby Amory to my mother in June 1923.

43. *Harvard Memorial Biographies*. Volume II, Appendix I. Sever and Francis. Cambridge, Massachusetts. 1866. Of the 938 Harvard graduates, nongraduates and professional school scholars who fought in the Civil War, 117 died.

44. Geoffrey C. Ward with Ric Burns and Ken Burns. *The Civil War: An Illustrated History*. Alfred A. Knopf. New York. 1990. P. 289.

45. Dr. Catherine Lastavica thinks he probably had amoebic dysentery.

46. James M. McPherson. *Battle Cry of Freedom: The Civil War Era*. Oxford University Press. New York. 1988. Pp. 737–38.

47. The Northern side of the story was in a paper written by Reverend Charles A. Humphreys, chaplain, Second Massachusetts Cavalry. The rebel account came from John F. Munson, an active member of Mosby's partisan rangers. Both are among papers kept by Libby Amory.

48. William Best Hesseltine. *Civil War Prisons: A Study in War Psychology*. F. Ungar. New York. 1964, c. 1930. Over the next two generations, at least 250 firsthand accounts would pour forth, kindling and rekindling the outrage over what was viewed as the inhumanity of the jailers toward the jailed.

49. William Amory even sent a letter of introduction from Robert C. Winthrop to his cousin Dr. Henry Winthrop of Charleston. Had he been in a position to look up Dr. Winthrop, Ned Amory wouldn't have found him for he was away at the time (from a letter dated October 18, 1864 from Henry Winthrop to Robert C. Winthrop, quoted in Mayo, p. 281).

50. J. C. Warren, p. 5.

51. McPherson, p. 858.

52. Libby Amory kept all Ned Amory's letters and my mother had them retyped in a collection for each of her children.

53. Shelby Foote. *The Civil War: A Narrative*. Random House. New York. 1958. P. 806.
54. Ned mistakenly thought his own commanding general was at the meeting. In fact, Sheridan was crossing the James River with his mounted troops to get into position for the final assault.

chapter THREE

1. After her marriage, Kate would drop the Taylor and become Kate Wilson Winthrop.
2. Daniel Hodas. *The Business Career of Moses Taylor: Merchant, Finance Capitalist, and Industrialist*. New York University Press. New York. 1975. P. 130.
3. The existence of these infants is not generally known by the family. Neither was recorded in Mayo or included in any family genealogy. Kate T. Winthrop's birth and death was verified by Green-Wood Cemetery, which provided a copy of the record of her interment there on April 11, 1894, showing that she died on June 3, 1860, age "2 hours." We can only guess about the second child, Grenville M. Winthrop. The family vault at Green-Wood includes a catacomb inscription that reads: Grenville M. Winthrop, 1863. The New York City Department of Records and Information Services, Municipal Archives, however, could produce no record of either the birth or death of a Grenville Winthrop for the year 1863.
4. Company brochure entitled "Wood, Struthers & Winthrop." 1968. P. 1.
5. "Read" could also be "Reed." The former spelling was used in a small notice about Robert Winthrop's joining the firm, pasted in Kate Winthrop's "inspirational" scrapbook, which is in the possession of Hamilton Fish Kean II. The latter was in Robert Winthrop's obituary, found in Fred Winthrop's scrapbook.
6. Another notice pasted in Kate Winthrop's notebooks.
7. Clifford Browder. *The Money Game in Old New York: Daniel Drew and His Times*. University Press of Kentucky. Lexington, Kentucky. 1986. Pp. 57 and 125. In December 1865, the Stock Exchange moved to a new location at 10 and 12 Broad Street. P. 125.
8. Henry Clews. *Fifty Years on Wall Street*. Irving Publishing Company. New York. 1908. P. 676. Clews includes Moses Taylor in a chapter entitled "Men of Mark" along with such names as Russell Sage, Cyrus W. Field, Chauncey M. Depew, Levi P. Morton, John A. Stewart, and Philip D. Armour.
9. Kean, p. 43.
10. Hodas, p. 2.
11. Hodas, p. 5.
12. Hodas, p. 6.
13. Moses Yale Beach. *The Wealthiest Citizens of New York*. Arno Press. New York. 1973. This is from the listing of 1844. In the listing of 1854, the importance of Astor's "gold" is once again cited.
14. Harold van B. Cleveland, Thomas F. Huertas, with Rachel Strauber et al. *Citibank. 1812–1970*. Harvard University Press. Cambridge, Massachusetts. 1985. P. 22.
15. Hodas, pp. 188–89. Hodas doesn't provide a direct explanation of Taylor's rejection, simply quoting a letter from an old friend, Boston sugar merchant Philo Shelton, who wrote him, "Like you I want to be free from all political careers."
16. Hodas, p. 160.
17. Hodas, p. 5.
18. Ward McAllister. *Society as I Have Found It*. Cassell Publishing Company. New York. 1890. P. 129.
19. Bruce Bliven. *New York: A Bicentennial History*. W. W. Norton and Co. New York. 1981. P. 81.

20. William Thompson Bonner. *New York, The World's Metropolis*. Commemorative Edition. R. L. Polk and Co. New York. 1924. P. 355.

21. Arthur Quinn. *A New World. An Epic of Colonial America from the Founding of Jamestown to the Fall of Quebec*. Berkley Books. New York. 1994. P. 136.

22. Dunn, p. 55.

23. Dunn, p. 284.

24. Mayo, p. 126.

25. John, Jr., knew this singularly beautiful island from his frequent trips along the Connecticut coast and wanted it for himself. The Massachusetts General Court granted it to him in 1640 (Mayo, p. 46).

26. John, Jr., received the rights to the mine in 1644. In his section on fifth-generation John Still Winthrop, Mayo describes it as "one of the most doubtful assets of this almost land-poor branch of the Winthrop family" (p. 155).

27. Legacy of John Winthrop, Jr.'s brother Deane Winthrop in 1655 (Mayo, p. 72).

28. Mayo, p. 162.

29. Lila Parrish Lyman. "The New London Homestead (1754–1892) of the Winthrop Family." Published for the New London County Historical Society. Pequot Press. Stonington, Connecticut. 1957.

30. Mayo, p. 163.

31. Understandably, perhaps, for his mother, Elizabeth Shirreff, John Still's second wife, was British and her brother was among the British forces stationed in New York (Mayo, p. 220).

32. John Still's other sons may not have fought in the war, but neither did they flee the country after the war, as most Loyalists were forced to do. Moreover, their Winthrop cousins in Boston were fiery opponents of the British.

33. Mayo, p. 265.

34. Joseph Alfred Scoville. *The Old Merchants of New York*. Volume III (by Walter Barrett). Greenwood Press. New York. 1968.

35. The signing was an informal affair, just a pact among the city's merchants who used to gather under the buttonwood tree at 60 Wall Street and who decided one day in 1792 to adjourn inside the Tontine Coffee House across the street and pledge to sell stock among themselves. They would continue to meet in secret until 1817, when they wrote a constitution and created the Exchange Board, which by the 1830s would enable New York to edge out its rivals, Boston and Philadelphia, and become the foremost money center in the country (Bonner, p. 419, and Browder, p. 57).

36. Bonner, p. 404. The bank's charter was not renewed at the time of the War of 1812.

37. Mayo, p. 202.

38. Mayo, pp. 262–79.

39. Assembled by Moses Yale Beach, publisher of the *New York Sun*.

40. Since Henry Rogers was no laggard—he was top of his class at Yale and had a highly successful law practice specializing in the management of large estates—over time he would amply prove his position among the wealthy (Mayo, p. 362).

41. A glorious marriage, indeed, not only linking direct descendants of two colonial governors—Governor Peter Stuyvesant, governor of New York, and John Winthrop, governor of Massachusetts Bay Colony—but also bringing into the Winthrop family prospects of inheriting proceeds from the lovely sprawling eighty-acre Stuyvesant farm that belonged to Judith's father, Petrus. Located near Bowery Village between Third Avenue, the East River, 6th and 23rd Streets, once tilled by fifty Negro slaves, the farm would appreciate in value and become, sadly to those who had loved it, the Bowery in years to come (*Historic Families in America*. Vol. 3, p. 136, and Mayo, p. 221).

42. Mayo, p. 278.

43. Mayo, p. 278.
44. *New York Times*. April 3, 1865, p. 1, and April 4, pp. 1 and 8.
45. *New York Times*. April 3, 1865, p. 1.
46. Bonner, p. 104, states that over 100,000 New Yorkers were in uniform by the end of the Civil War. The population of the city in 1860 was 813,669 (cited in John L. Andriot. *Population Abstract of the United States*. Andriot Associates. McLean, Virginia. 1980. P. 565).
47. This fact was much ridiculed by social critics like Cleveland Amory and Dixon Wector, who conveniently overlook that three of the wives died. Cleveland Amory writes in *The Proper Bostonians* that "the Winthrops, unable to keep up with the fast marital pace set by their original Governor John—who was married four times, and all to women of wealth—finally went into banking" (p. 41) and Dixon Wector (in *The Saga of American Society: A Record of Social Aspiration, 1607–1937*. Charles Scribner's Sons. New York. 1937. P. 39) points out that John, disapproving of tobacco, drinking toasts, and shooting wildfowl ("being a poor marksman"), "allowed himself only the indulgence of marriages."
48. The letter continues: "I trust that Christian prayer, and severe battling with myself, may overcome this prejudice of mine in time, but at present my knowledge of the motives which govern man in their relations towards women is so limited that I cannot but attribute his *extreme haste* for *more loves* to a mastery of buttocks over brain—or in other words, *matter* over mind."
49. In another letter, Frederic joked about cashing his paycheck before the month was out: "The *risk* is great, I admit, but my pecuniary wants are greater—and I shall try my best not to get killed during the month."
50. Repeated on April 6 in the Philadelphia *Public Ledger*.
51. Since the mid-1860s, six male Winthrop branches in New England and New York have died out, or appear on the verge of doing so. In New York, two of the branches directly descended from sixth-generation Francis Bayard have ended: the Egerton Leigh Winthrop branch (the younger branch), which disappeared when Bronson died in 1944 (his brother Egerton had died in 1926, leaving only a daughter) and the elder Buchanan branch, when Henry Rogers died in 1958, leaving no sons. A third line, also directly descended from Francis Bayard, the descendants of his son Francis Bayard in New Haven, came to an end in 1899 with the death of William Woolsey Winthrop. In Boston, the last male of the line descended from sixth-generation Thomas Lindall was Robert Mason Winthrop who died in 1938. Still living today in addition to Robert Winthrop's descendants are two males with the surname Winthrop. One is John Winthrop, who lives in Florida and is descended from the New London branch. As the father of daughters, his line is fated to disappear with his death. The other is Grenville Bayard Winthrop III ("Pete"), great-grandson of Robert Winthrop's brother Grenville. Born in 1936, he lives in New Hampshire. But with his death, his line too will die out because he had only daughters. In addition, there was in Illinois a branch of Winthrops which was extant in 1944 and another one in Florida (not the John Winthrop of the New London line mentioned above) which appears to have been headed for extinction. But no one in the family knows what has become of either of these branches, and I hope I will be forgiven for this parochial view of the prospects for the Winthrop family name. (Mayo was the prime source here, updated by my phone calls to John Winthrop of the New London branch and Pete Winthrop of New Hampshire, both of whom verified that, without sons, they will most probably be the last of their lines.)
52. Robert Winthrop. Draft history of Robert Winthrop & Co. 1973. Property of Wood, Struthers and Winthrop Management Company in New York City.

53. Kean, p. 43.

54. Vincent P. Carosso. *The Morgans: Private International Bankers. 1854–1913*. Harvard University Press. Cambridge, Massachusetts. 1987. P. 138.

55. Baltzell, p. 233.

56. Ron Chernow. *The House of Morgan: An American Banking Dynasty and the Rise of Modern Finance*. Simon & Schuster. New York. 1990. Pp. xi and 33–34.

57. Bonner, pp. 250 and 425.

58. Hodas, p. 265.

59. David McCullough. *Mornings on Horseback*. Simon and Schuster. New York. 1981. P. 127.

60. *Town Topics*, a magazine that became fabled, and feared, for its witty and irreverent accounts of the doings of society.

61. As quoted in Bonner, p. 148.

62. Cleveland Amory. *Who Killed Society?* P. 119.

63. Kean, p. 43.

64. Kean, p. 46.

65. Eleanor Dwight. *Edith Wharton: An Extraordinary Life*. Harry N. Abrams, Inc. New York. 1994. P. 64, quoting Wharton contemporary Maud Howe Elliot.

66. Blanche Wiesen Cook. *Eleanor Roosevelt*. Vol. I: 1884-1933. Penguin Books. New York. 1992. P. 144.

67. Kean, p. 46.

68. The story (perhaps apocryphal) is from John Winthrop, my mother's brother Nat's oldest son.

69. Chernow, pp. 46–47.

70. Chernow, p. 116.

71. Hamilton Fish Kean has Kate Winthrop's records on her luncheons and dinners for the years 1898–1900 and 1921.

chapter FOUR

1. My mother said it was the Japanese who found Fred Winthrop exotic: "They had never seen anyone like my father, so tall and light-skinned. When he took a bath they poked holes in the wall of a bathhouse so they could see him better."

2. The picture, as was often true, did not do justice to its subject.

3. Samuel Worcester Rowse is listed in Mantle Fielding's *Dictionary of American Painters, Sculptors and Engravers*. Compiled by James F. Carr. J. F. Carr. New York. 1965. P. 311.

4. A newspaper clipping in Libby Amory's scrapbook.

5. A clipping in Libby Amory's scrapbook.

6. This comes from a handwritten addendum by Libby Amory to a letter written by Anna Sears Amory to her son Ned, dated November 8, 1867, in her collection labeled Sears Letters, Volume II.

7. From a four-page description (no author identified) of William Amory, found in a collection kept by Libby Amory labeled "Sears letters, left by Mrs. [Anna Sears] Amory to her children."

8. From Libby Amory's scrapbook.

9. This hideous place was sold after George Gardner's death, in 1905 becoming the property of Frederick Ayer of Newton.

10. Warren, pp. 1 and 2.

11. T. Jefferson Coolidge. *The Autobiography of T. Jefferson Coolidge 1831–1920*. Houghton Mifflin Company. Boston. 1923. P. 105. In his autobiography, Coolidge also notes that he had gone to Harvard with George Gardner's nephews, John Lowell Gardner's sons; that he went into partnership early on with J. L.'s son Joseph Peabody Gardner; and that he and George Augustus Gardner went to Cuba together in 1861.

12. Coolidge, p. 8.

13. This paragraph is based on Francis Lowell Coolidge. "Thomas Jefferson and Mehitable Sullivan Appleton Coolidge." *Collected Papers of the Monticello Association*. Volume II. Chapter XXII. Editor, George Green Shackelford. Monticello Association. Charlottesville, Virginia. 1984. Pp. 140–150.

14. Shackleton, p. 191.

15. All this from items in an envelope labeled by my mother: "Trip to Europe 1892. Grandma, Grandpa, Mother, Cousin Helen Brooks."

16. Marian Lawrence Peabody. *To Be Young Was Very Heaven*. Houghton Mifflin Company. Boston. 1967. Pp. 164–65.

17. The word she used to describe Fred in a letter to Billy.

18. Those who knew him later said they remembered no stutter or stammer—indeed, my mother's recollection was that "he could speak very well."

19. Wharton, p. 855.

20. *Winthrop, Stimson, Putnam & Roberts: A History of a Law Firm*, p. 12.

21. Kean, p. 50.

22. Eleanor Winthrop.

23. At one point in their relationship, Fred Winthrop decided to burn all the diaries; in fact, he destroyed only those between 1895 and 1897.

24. Cleveland Amory notes in *The Proper Bostonians* (p. 19) that one way to measure the "dynastic proportions" of Boston's First Families is by successive generations whose names have appeared on the Harvard class lists. It was comforting to consult Mayo and discover that Winthrops can stand as tall as any Saltonstall, for example, in the continuity of their presence in the Harvard annals.

25. In the nineteenth century, Winthrops at Harvard were mostly sons or later descendants of Thomas Lindall Winthrop.

26. David McCullough in *Mornings on Horseback* (pp. 195–217) writes of the effect on young Teddy Roosevelt, class of 1880, of being a Harvard undergraduate (he would have overlapped Dudley by a year).

27. Cleveland Amory in *The Proper Bostonians* (p. 302) gleefully reports that this graciously named club began in 1791 simply as the Pig Club, an appellation selected to celebrate the taste for roast pork of its two (old Boston) founding members, Francis Cabot Lowell and Robert Treat Paine.

28. From a story in the *N.Y. Sun*, 1905, in Fred Winthrop's scrapbook.

29. The article is in French and is dated November 12, 1895. It applauds the old class of cultivated Americans, stating that they "*sourient de pitié et haussent les épaules devant l'ostentation des parvenus*" (smile with pity and shrug their shoulders before the ostentation of the parvenus). For four centuries, it continues, Winthrop men and women "*ont jeté de l'éclat sur l'histoire de cette famille tant en Amérique qu'en Angleterre*" (have brought as great credit to this family in America as in England).

30. The clipping in Fred's scrapbook goes on to explain that the "floral breakage" was soon corrected by "men with brooms and stepladders," who perhaps also succeeded in dispelling any thought that the accident presaged evil for the young couple.

31. Fred seldom identified the paper he had cut his clippings from, though he often wrote in the date.

REARED *in a* GREENHOUSE

32. Mayo, p. 430.
33. As recounted by my mother in her tape-recorded memories.
34. Letter from Fred to Dorothy, dated March 19, 1902.
35. Kean, p. 134. Robert Winthrop Kean was born in Elberon (1893). During his early years, the large cottage next door that had belonged to his great-grandfather Moses Taylor was rented.
36. Mayo, p. 421.
37. James Kilgo. *Pipe Creek to Matthew's Bluff: A Short History of Groton Plantation.* Vanguard Press. Burlington, Vermont. c.1989. P. 100.
38. McCullough, pp. 333–341.
39. Kean, p. 50.
40. Kean, p. 50.
41. Robert Winthrop. Draft history of Robert Winthrop and Company.
42. Clews, pp. 437 and 444.
43. Mayo, p. 382. Mayo provides no source for this story.
44. Kate W. Winthrop. Last Will and Testament. Fourth and fifth clauses. April 19, 1917. Furnished me by Wood, Struthers and Winthrop Management Corporation.
45. John Dennis Brown. *101 Years on Wall Street. An Investor's Almanac.* Prentice-Hall. Englewood Cliffs, New Jersey. 1991. Pp. 226–27. According to this study, the Dow-Jones industrial average rose from 40.45 in 1896 to 156.66 in 1925.
46. Mayo, p. 428.
47. According to Libby Amory's Gardner Genealogy, Frank died fourteen years later, in 1914, at only forty-six, in an insane asylum, a year after marrying Minnie Barnard. (The year of his death is more likely to have been 1915. The *Gardner Memorial*, p. 165, states that he was appointed in 1915 to the job he had held for one year as associate curator of the Chinese and Japanese department of the Boston Museum of Fine Arts but it also states that his will was proved on December 9, 1915.)
48. In her 1924 diary, my mother revealed the identity of Miss Hedley (she spelled the name Headley). Her first name was Mitty and she was "a very attractive" English girl on the same boat as her father and Billy Amory on their trip up the Nile. It was Billy who was quite taken with Mitty. The diary continues that her father, however, "stayed with her in England on his way home and shortly after his returning to the USA, he wrote to her and announced his engagement—to which she had replied 'That explains many things.' " In 1924, Mitty Hedley had become an English doctor's wife.
49. In addition to Fred's diaries, much of the chronology of this chapter was drawn from a short history of his long efforts to win Dorothy's heart that he wrote, years later, for his children. It was on lined yellow paper, and begins and ends as follows: "To my children: If I should die before you grow up, I think it would be of interest to you to know about how I met and loved your mother. . . . In all the years that I knew your Mother, I never found a single trait or characteristic that was not perfect. She was the best, kindest, sweetest, most unselfish most considerate and perfect person that I can imagine. Nothing that she ever did or said could jar on me. We never had a disagreement or a sharp word. She was an angel, if there ever was one, the best of wives, the best of mothers, the best of daughters."

chapter FIVE

1. From a letter Libby Amory wrote Dorothy a few months after the wedding.
2. The New York "clientele" included the three Winthrop brothers, the two Winthrop sisters, and two other New York-based ushers, J. A. Burden and F. N. Watriss. The New

York ushers were outnumbered by Frederic's Boston friends from his Harvard days: the bride's brothers William Amory 2nd and George Amory, plus T. Nelson Perkins, Hugh Whitney, Ingersoll Amory, Francis R. Bangs, and Rodolphe L. Agassiz.

3. It had been built by Hamilton resident Robert Dodge.

4. Janice P. Pulsifer. *Changing Town: Hamilton, Massachusetts 1850–1910*. 1976. Reprinted in 1985 by the Hamilton Historical Society. Pp. 36–44. Quoting Robert Grant in *The North Shore of Massachusetts*. P. 35.

5. From the Hamilton town voting lists.

6. Pulsifer, pp. 36–44.

7. Pulsifer, pp. 24–30.

8. Pulsifer, p. 33.

9. *Growing Up in Boston's Gilded Age: The Journal of Alice Stone Blackwell, 1872–1874*. Ed. Marlene Deahl Merrill. Yale University Press. New Haven. 1990.

10. Reverend Robert F. Ippolito, M. S. *A Short History of the Rice Estate 1890–1945. Ipswich, Massachusetts*. Ipswich. 1976. The place was sold in 1945, becoming the National Shrine and Seminary of Our Lady of La Salette.

11. James S. Geiger. *Appleton Farms 1638–1988: A Brief Agricultural History*. Privately published.

12. Gordon Abbott, Jr. *Saving Special Places: A Centennial History of the Trustees of Reservations. Pioneer of the Land Trust Movement*. The Ipswich Press. Ipswich, Massachusetts. 1993. P. 120.

13. Robert C. Black III *The Younger John Winthrop*. Columbia University Press. New York. 1966. Pp. 67–76.

14. Dunn, pp. 64–65 and 73.

15. Geiger, pp. 6 and 7.

16. Abbott, p. 120, quoting from a 1938 article in the *Ipswich News-Chronicle*. As of August 31, 1998, the ownership of the farm will pass from the Appleton family to the Trustees of Reservations.

17. This was Nancy's own version of the story. See Christopher Sykes. *Nancy: The Life of Lady Astor*. Panther Books. Granada Publishing. London. 1979. P. 60.

18. Sykes, pp. 60–66.

19. The entire story, written in my mother's hand on a loose piece of paper and tucked in her 1920 diary, went as follows:

GROTON HOUSE

Mr. Shaw gave his son and daughter-in-law a house in Hamilton as the young Mr. Shaw liked the country there. Mr. Shaw bought the land and Mr. Bob and his wife lived in the cottage which Grandma lived in before it burned down, until Groton House should be built. Only the first floor had been completed when young Mr. Shaw and his wife quarrelled and divorced, so old Mr. Shaw sold the place to Father after finishing the house as cheaply as possible. The third floor was just a large attic, which Father built over later.

Father liked Hamilton, as he often stayed there, and Mother had stayed with the young Shaws in Grandma's cottage and liked it also. Mr. Appleton was very fond of Mrs. Shaw and named Nancy's Corner just outside our entrance after her.

She went abroad to England and married Lord Astor. Mr. Shaw married again and named his second son the same as his first. Lady Astor is a friend of Cousin Jean's [Sears]. It seems strange that Lady Astor's eldest son [Bobbie III] has not seen his father since the divorce and most likely doesn't even remember him. . . .

20. From a small clipping in Libby Amory's scrapbook.
21. Abbott, pp. 129–130. Charles Atherton, secretary, U. S. Fine Arts Commission, said that the house is well known to architects on his staff.
22. From Libby Amory's annual listings in her "Stardrifts Birthday Book." Curiously, she puts what appears to be a rental fee of "$3,000" beside "Clara's White Cottage," where she began to stay in 1918. Could the very rich widow of T. J. Coolidge have charged her aged mother rent?
23. Libby Amory's "Stardrifts Birthday Book."
24. Dorothy A. Winthrop datebook for 1904.
25. Pulsifer, p. 120, quoting a passage from *Divine Guidance* by nineteenth-century Hamilton author Gail Hamilton.
26. This was reported by a Mrs. Hume. She was a friend of Libby Amory's who had known Dorothy's mother at Wareham and Miss Folsom's School for Girls.
27. Occupation Fred Winthrop listed when registering Dorothy's birth in 1905. Hamilton town records.
28. Amory, *Who Killed Society?*, p. 197.
29. From Dorothy Winthrop's 1921 diaries, quoting Mrs. Hume.
30. Their signatures are in Beekman Winthrop's guest book, which he kept from his assignment in Puerto Rico until his death.
31. Stanley Karnow. *In Our Image: America's Empire in the Philippines*. Ballantine Books. New York. 1989. P. 112.
32. This is from a long profile by Frederick T. Birchall, preserved, like many other press clippings cited here, in a scrapbook kept by Frederic Winthrop. The Birchall story begins:

> At Harvard, young Beekman Winthrop was neither a bookworm nor an idler. He was not physically built for athletics like his elder brother Frederic, noted as the strongest man in the University in his day, so he didn't seek fame either on the football field or the river. After graduating, he went to the Harvard Law School for three years more. Then he looked about for a career.
>
> The Spanish War was just over. It had left the Philippines and other large stretches of territory on Uncle Sam's hands. Young Winthrop thought he saw his chance in the new possessions. The Taft commission was about to set out for the Philippines to install a civil government there in place of military rule. Young Winthrop asked for a job, got a one-thousand-dollar clerkship under the commission, and set out for the islands across the world.

33. Peabody, pp. 337–38.

chapter SIX

1. Dr. Porter was the father of Peggy (Mrs. Chandler) Bigelow, who would be one of my mother's great friends throughout her life.
2. From the doctor's description of what they expected to accomplish by surgery, Libby Amory's horror seems well placed: "He said it would improve, and if the pleurisy was only *water* on her lungs she could easily have it removed, but if *blood* it would be serious, but he thought it was all right."
3. Dr. Crockett said this to Jeff Coolidge.

4. Emily Sears Lodge said that Fred Winthrop used to tease her and her sister Jean about their "flapper-length" dresses, which came just above the knee and which he pretended to find scandalous.

5. The letter concludes: "I loved dear Dorothy so dearly myself that I say little to comfort him for I feel as if a great comfort and light had gone out of my life—I will write you often dear Mrs. Amory—I am so happy you have the children, this our dear child would have wished. Thank-you many times for writing me—Most affectionately, K. T. Winthrop."

6. These words were found in my mother's "Good Luck Diary," in which she recorded key events in her life (mostly relating to her mother's death). This description was in the entry space for August 26, 1920. Perhaps her Grandmother Amory had described her father's condition to her.

7. The barn burned down around 1930.

8. Nathaniel Thayer, Sr., had business dealings with Frederic Winthrop's grandfather, Moses Taylor, in 1865, attempting to interest Taylor in investing in the Hannibal and St. Joseph Railroad. In 1870, both Nathaniel Thayer and Robert Winthrop were board members of the Manhattan Coal Company, a company with which Moses Taylor was closely affiliated. Other railroad negotiations took place in 1875, these with regard to the Michigan Central railway system (from Hodas).

9. Eleanor Winthrop.

10. Eleanor Winthrop.

11. Eleanor Winthrop.

12. Eleanor Winthrop.

13. Angela Winthrop.

14. According to this account, the land had been valued at $84,200 and the house at $80,800.

15. Katharine Winthrop McKean said looks were misleading and that it was actually a very pleasant house.

16. From the memento that Libby Amory wrote about Ned Amory after his death.

17. Libby Amory's "Stardrifts Birthday Book."

chapter SEVEN

1. Robert "Robbie" Winthrop (hereafter referred to as Robbie).

2. The rest of that sentence has been inked out, in the first instance of self-censoring to occur in Dorothy's diaries. Over the next few years, more black swatches would obscure the written lines and also large sections of pages would be cut out.

3. History would repeat itself in the next generation, when Nathaniel's son Matthew, at exactly the same age, was stricken with what appeared to be the same kind of epileptic seizures. This time, however, medical science was more advanced and his life was saved.

4. The scene of the little dog at the door became family lore, remembered by Dr. Catherine Lastavica, who would have been Linzee's niece.

5. Dr. Catherine Lastavica.

6. My mother wondered whether this was a genetic trait, similar to that in the Sears family which had afflicted Anna Sears Amory, her great-grandmother, and which showed up in subsequent generations of Searses. In the 1930s, Fred agreed to try on one ear a new operation being pioneered by a New York doctor. The operation was successful, the procedure was gradually accepted by the medical community at large, and later Fred had the operation done on his other ear. My mother remembered his elation afterwards: "I can hear the birds sing," he told her.

7. In ink, on a postcard, dated November 14, 1916.

8. From Libby Amory's listing of summer residences in her "Stardrifts Birthday Book."

9. My mother especially liked the story about the Lodges' trip accompanying Soviet leader Nikita Khrushchev across the U. S. in 1959. He and Emily were about to leave, but the senior Mrs. Lodge, his mother, was lying gravely and inconveniently ill in their house in Beverly, where she had been moved owing to the imminence of her demise. Of course, they had no choice but to set off, but before they departed, Cabot took the doctor aside and sternly ordered him, "Whatever you do, don't let her die before I get back."

10. These stories are courtesy of Harry Lodge, Emily's younger son. Emily related the identical tale about Libby Amory's trying to get Dorothy to wear lipstick, but her version omitted her own role in the affair.

11. Henry Adams. "Frederic Winthrop: A Memoir." From the Proceedings of the Massachusetts Historical Society, Volume 65.

12. In German: Meiner Lieben Dorothy/Dein Leben sei fröhlich u. heiter/Kein Leiden betreibe dein Herz/Das Glück sei stets dein Geleiter/Nie treffe dich kummern Schmerz./Gewidmet von deinem dich immerliebenden Fräulein Wilhelmine Hofmeister.

13. Hixie got his comeuppance a few months later. To escape the fighting, he had enrolled in the Naval Academy at Annapolis. On November 11, 1918, the day the war ended, Robert wrote Dorothy with glee: "Now the war is over, he will have to slave away at Annapolis for s-e-v-e-n long years, Ha! Ha!"

14. About ten years later, during the presidency of Calvin Coolidge, Grandma Amory would remember the excitement of that presidential visit and comment in a letter to her friend Fanny Blake: "The Coolidge family meet every ten or twenty years and they have asked Clara to let them meet at her house this year, so she expects eight hundred on Saturday. The President is not coming. Neither am I. How do you like Hoover? Very nice I think. His grandmother was an Indian, the daughter of White Plume." My mother must have been amused by the newly found link between the Boston Coolidges and President Calvin Coolidge, writing me on September 8, 1957: "The Boston Coolidges were no relation of Calvin Coolidge until he became President. Then a sudden close relationship arose!"

chapter EIGHT

1. Elsewhere in her diary, Dorothy wrote, "Dr. Thayer said Fred was the most popular boy in Saint Mark's. Not only with boys, but with teachers."

2. U.S. Census, 1920.

3. Prohibition had begun the year before. Fred Winthrop, notwithstanding, had some of the forbidden brew on him, stashed away in a hip-pocket flask.

4. Grandma Amory's doctor couldn't explain how she broke the rib; he thought it might have happened when she fell off a chair when she first became ill. Curiously, when she was in her seventies, the same thing happened to my mother. She began experiencing terrible pain in her chest, and after a number of consultations, her doctor finally "discovered" that she had broken several ribs—whether from coughing or falling in her garden, he never knew.

5. Mademoiselle Cossini, whose real name was Germaine Brisson, was a leading contralto on the opera stage in Paris. Ten years Emily and Jean's senior, Mademoiselle Cossini had become a Sears intimate during World War I, which she had spent in America giving erudite lectures in the living rooms of Boston's well-heeled literati.

6. Kilgo, p. 100.
7. Kean, p. 51.
8. Eleanor Winthrop.
9. Harvard College. Class of 1896. *Twenty-fifth Anniversary Report: 1896–1921*. Privately printed for the class. Before becoming "unoccupied," George G. Gardner wrote that he had "spent one year in the Law School.... Was a stock broker for fifteen years. During the war I worked in the Red Cross in Boston."
10. Dr. Catherine Lastavica.
11. When she was old, my mother would ask for "soothing cereal" for lunch.
12. There is a twenty-one-year gap in Grandma Winthrop's entertainment logs, extending from December 24, 1899, to January 6, 1921.

chapter TEN

1. "The May School Class Book: Class of Nineteen Twenty-three." The Andover Press. Andover, Massachusetts.

chapter ELEVEN

1. From a letter from Dorothy Winthrop to Standish Bradford written in 1927.
2. It's a little unclear who these twenty-one could have been, as there appeared to be only fifteen family members in residence: seven Winthrops, five Pattens, two Moltkes, and Grandma Thayer. Maybe the rest were included under the "everyone she could think of" category.
3. This is how Eleanor Winthrop described her husband Nat's aunt. Aunt Nina had come to live with her nephew at 770 Park Avenue after his divorce, where she helped oversee his children and acted as his hostess.
4. Eleanor Winthrop remembered this choice detail about Billy Patten.
5. Again, the source is Eleanor Winthrop, who furnished the additional detail that Arthur's Aunt Nina would suggest that he do his needlepoint in the other room. Since he was only eight that summer, the needlepoint work would have gone on later, perhaps even when he was working as a night watchman and telling people he was in the securities business.
6. Bobby was Carl Adam's nickname.
7. Eleanor Winthrop says that Hill Hall is now a women's prison.
8. My mother recalled the biting incident on the staircase whereas Eleanor Winthrop said it happened in the nursery.
9. Katharine Winthrop McKean swore this was true.
10. According to my mother's brother Robert, Arthur Patten was behind their sudden departure. Arthur had spat at Freddy, Jr., as he was going upstairs and Freddy gave him a good spanking in return. Unfortunately, the scene was witnessed by Grandma Thayer and Robert's stepmother and "all hell broke loose," with the blame directed at Freddy. At this Fred Winthrop, Sr., said he'd had enough, he was taking his older sons to Paris. They left the following morning.
11. Researchers are even today trying to sort out one Groton from another. Frank Bremer, professor at Millersville University who is making a study of the early history of the

Winthrops in England, described the confusion in the Massachusetts Historical Society's "Groton Gazette" (Number 2, Winter 1997). One of the knotty questions that has been bedeviling Bremer is where Groton Manor actually stood. It now turns out, Bremer reports, that the "manor house" was called Groton Hall and was leased to someone else when Adam Winthrop purchased the estate from Henry VIII in 1544. Winthrop enlarged the church rectory and called it his "mansion house," and this became known as "Groton Place." Some years later, when John Winthrop (the future governor) had become "lord of the manor," he occupied "Groton Place" while his mother and father lived in "Groton Hall" (by then vacated by the lessors). Until recently, everyone thought that only Groton Hall, the original manor house where John Winthrop didn't live, still stood. Bremer's sleuthing, however, has found that John Winthrop's actual house, Groton Place, still also stands, but that the addition of a Georgian facade has long disguised its true identity.

12. Dunn, pp. 313–14. "My great Grandfather … lyes there," Fitz-John wrote a cousin. "He had one son that was my grandfather that went into New England."

13. Mayo, pp. 135–36.

14. From a newspaper clipping in Fred Winthrop's scrapbook.

15. From an anonymous diary of a young man who was traveling in Europe with Bronson Winthrop in 1909, found at the New-York Historical Society.

16. His colleague Martin Birnbaum described how carefully he did this: "With infinite patience he drew plans of his grounds to scale and never tired of planting trees, laying out attractive paths, constructing fountains on his spacious lawns" (Cohn, p. 52).

17. There would eventually be eleven.

18. Cousin Eleo, as she was known in the family, was my mother's second cousin once removed, on the Amory side. Her father, Frederick R. Sears, Jr., of Boston, according to my mother, was "the queerest man who ever lived." (Refer to Chart 13.)

19. The Boston Forbes clan had three branches—the so-called long-tail Forbeses, the so-called short-tail Forbeses, and Angela Forbes' line—all associated with the nineteenth-century China trade and all descended from the Reverend John Forbes. This common progenitor was chaplain of the British forces that took over from the Spaniards in St. Augustine, Florida, in 1763; Reverend Forbes moved to Milton, Massachusetts, with his Milton-born wife, the former Dorothy Murray, after the Revolution. Fame and fortune came to the branches of his family descended from his two grandsons, John Murray Forbes and his brother, Robert Bennett Forbes. John Murray Forbes, of the "long-tail" line, went to China when he was barely twenty and accumulated a fortune by the time he was thirty. Back in Boston and Milton, he invested in development of the West and pyramided a second fortune as a railway magnate. His son William Hathaway Forbes organized, for Alexander Graham Bell, a company that eventually became AT&T. Brother Robert Bennett Forbes, of the "short-tail" branch, became a legendary sea captain who also accumulated a fortune in the China trade. The "tail" designations related to the length at which these two branches cut their horses' tails: Robert Bennett Forbes clipped his horses' tails short so they would make a smart appearance as carriage horses; brother John Murray Forbes left his horse's tails uncut as it was considered more kindhearted to let them remain natural. The third branch of the family was descended from Reverend John Forbes' eldest son, James Grant Forbes, and it too became part of the China trade, though with less lucrative results. It was James Grant Forbes' great-grandson, also James Grant Forbes, who married Margaret Winthrop of Boston.

20. The Forbeses had found the Depression inconvenient financially, and so the story goes that they bought a large villa on the Brittany coast where they lived long enough each year to allow them to avoid English taxes, and briefly enough to avoid the French.

chapter TWELVE

1. Emily Sears was involved in the Harvard French Club, which periodically put on French plays for their own, and perhaps their friends', amusement.
2. Cabot had moved to New York after he met Emily, having been hired as a reporter on the *Evening Transcript*. He came up weekends to see her, but Emily was a popular girl and attracted others. She told me of a particular young man with whom she'd sit of a summer evening on the brick wall outside her house. One evening they were making quite a commotion. The old nurse, who was always around, peered out the window and warned, "Be a lady Emily, be a lady." The racket, it transpired, had nothing to do with romance: Emily and the young man had been passing the evening tossing bits of the porch furniture at one another.
3. Years later, the esteemed *New York Times* columnist James Reston would echo this thought. When asked what he thought of Henry Cabot Lodge, he answered, "Well, he got that wonderful woman to marry him." (David Halberstam. "A Writer Ahead of His Times. James Reston Led, and Many Followed." *The Washington Post*. December 8, 1995. Style Section. P. 1.)
4. Dorothy overheard her father say this one evening during a discussion he was having with some friends. Their position had been that work was the foundation of the Mormon religion and that it is "essential for happiness." Dorothy's diary entry continues with the following comment in German (translated here): "He said he himself loved to write, but he couldn't do it. He couldn't express himself well. My poor dear father, I wish he'd known how to write well or had had some other interest, because then he would have been happier. But he would have been even happier if only our dear mother were here." Her use of German suggests she may have considered this so delicate a subject that, even in her diary, she felt obliged to hide her views behind the use of a foreign language.
5. The high proportion of college-bound girls was unprecedented; less than half the class had gone on to college the year before, only three girls had gone in 1921, and just a third of the class in 1920. Predictably, Miss May's graduates went to the Seven Sisters colleges: in Dorothy's year, Vassar claimed four, Smith and Radcliffe three each, and Bryn Mawr two.
6. This story was found on a loose sheet of paper tucked into my mother's philosophical journal. Dorothy commented that she thought the minister's wife might have been behind this response.
7. From a letter to Dorothy Winthrop from Standish Bradford dated October 1926.
8. Robbie Winthrop's summary of Robert Winthrop's life. September 22, 1995.
9. His father, F. Murray Forbes, Sr., and James Grant Forbes were brothers.
10. Joseph E. Garland. *Boston's Gold Coast*. Little, Brown and Company. Boston. 1981. Pp. 207–208.

chapter THIRTEEN

1. Cohn, p. 33.
2. Cohn, p. 49. The quotes are Winthrop's notes, based on Norton's lectures.
3. Stephen Birmingham. *"Our Crowd": The Great Jewish Families of New York*. Harper & Row. New York. 1967. Pp. 259–60.
4. Dwight, p. 88.

5. Carole Owens. *The Berkshire Cottages: A Vanishing Era*. Cottage Press, Inc. Englewood Cliffs, New Jersey. 1984. Pp. 160–65, 180–83, and 193–94.

6. Kean, pp. 144–45. Mayo, p. 423.

7. Kean, p. 144.

8. Cohn, p. 37.

9. Owens, p. 39.

10. Owens, p. 121. Henry White married Emily Thorn Vanderbilt after her first husband, William Sloane, died (Owens, p. 25).

11. Carole Owens' book provides detailed descriptions of thirty-seven of the "cottages," presumably those she considered most noteworthy. Groton Place is not among them.

12. These were some of the features emphasized in an undated three-page flyer prepared by real estate brokers Wheeler and Taylor, Inc., and found in the Lenox Library.

13. Owens, p. 197.

14. Anecdote from Patty Foley, in charge of the Boston University Tanglewood Institute, summer 1994.

15. Cohn, p. 54.

16. The list was compiled using Amory, *Who Killed Society?*, and Owens, pp. 232–34, which lists about seventy of the cottages. In addition to the Sloanes and the Stokeses, other Four Hundred members were the Newbold Morrises, among the oldest of New York's English manorial families, and members of the Freylinghausen, Lanier, Bishop, Bend, and Appleton clans.

17. Margaret Terry Chanler. *Roman Spring: Memoirs*. Little, Brown and Company. Boston. 1934. P. 238.

18. Interview with Marjorie B. Cohn, summer 1994. Her research indicates that his last major trip was to Europe in 1911.

19. Cohn, p. 52, quoting Martin Birnbaum. *The Last Romantic*. Twayne. New York. 1960. The New York house, which he built in 1919, was more a museum than a home. Pictures were hung everywhere, one above another; there was an Italian room, a pre-Raphaelite room, an Ingres room, a Blake room, and a Gill-Beardsley room.

20. Cohn, p. 36.

21. Cohn, p. 36.

22. Interview with Joan Appleton, summer 1994.

23. For the last two years of his life (1917–19), Carnegie summered in Lenox.

24. Cohn interview. Cohn speculates that whereas Winthrop was honest, others may have been cheating on their taxes.

25. In the two photographs of Robert Winthrop that my mother had, he is old, with a pince-nez, thinning white hair, and bushy white beard and mustache. His portrait at Wood, Struthers and Winthrop looks almost identical, though the angle is just different enough to suggest it was painted from life and not from either of the photographs.

26. Only four letters from Kate Winthrop were found among Dorothy's papers: November 25, 1916; April 12, 1920; September 22, 1921; and May 24, 1925. In each case, her grandmother provided only the date and the month and Dorothy conscientiously added the year.

27. Edith Wharton. *The Letters of Edith Wharton*. Ed. R. W. B. Lewis and Nancy Lewis. New York. Charles Scribner's Sons. 1988. Pp. 259 and 485. Excerpts from letters to Mary Cadwalader Jones written in 1911 and 1925.

28. Kate W. Winthrop. Last Will and Testament. April 19, 1917. P. 4.

29. Kate W. Winthrop. Last Will and Testament. Codicil dated October 8, 1924, Third Clause reads in part, "I revoke the appointment ... made to the issue of my son Grenville

Lindall Winthrop.... In the event [that he die before me] I do hereby appoint, give, devise and bequeath [his] share of the funds held in trust for me under the will of Moses Taylor ... to my remaining children ... and [their] issue."

30. Conjecture by Eleanor Winthrop.

31. A clipping in one of my mother's scrapbooks entitled "Memorial Exhibition Emily Winthrop Miles (1893–1962) September 12–September 27."

32. Clipping cited in note 31 above.

33. Grenville Winthrop. Last Will and Testament, dated July 11, 1940, and supplied to me by Wood, Struthers and Winthrop.

34. Letter from Thomas S. Morse to me, dated May 12, 1996.

35. Grenville Winthrop. Last Will and Testament. The twelfth clause refers to Dudley's money, which was to go outright to Robert, Frederic, and Nathaniel Winthrop; the thirteenth refers to the income from Kate Winthrop's money, which was to go to Robert Winthrop during his lifetime, with the principal upon his death to be transferred to "the descendants of ... Kate W. Winthrop" in "proportions" to be designated by Robert Winthrop in his will (Robert renounced the power of appointment in an addendum to the will dated April 6, 1943, stating that accepting it "would subject my estate and the property subject to such power to heavy estate taxes at the time of my death"); and the first codicil, dated December 6, 1940 (Beekman had died November 10, 1940), stated that the income from the funds that he had inherited from Beekman should be for the use of his nephew Robert and that upon his death the principal should be divided among the sons of his brother Frederic and after their deaths, among their sons "bearing the surname 'Winthrop.' "

36. Interview with Angela Winthrop, 1994.

37. Harvard University Art Museums Archives. Paul J. Sachs files. Letter from Grenville L. Winthrop to Paul J. Sachs. July 12, 1941.

38. Harvard University Art Museums Archives. Grenville L. Winthrop's diary of visitors.

39. Eleanor Winthrop.

40. Owens, p. 129.

41. Cohn interview.

42. My mother gave the portrait to John Winthrop, her brother Nat's oldest son. She used to tell us this story, but it also appears in Agnes Mongan's preface to the catalogue for the Fogg Winthrop exhibition of 1969, *Grenville L. Winthrop: Retrospective for a Collector*. Fogg Museum of Art. Cambridge, Massachusetts. January 23–March 31, 1969.

chapter FOURTEEN

1. Tea, it seemed, was the only social occasion on which two young unmarrieds might be alone together. As Dorothy explained to Standish in a letter dated March 7, 1929: "I don't think we better lunch together ... but we might go there to tea afterwards.... I don't see much difference between tea and lunch, only one is 'done' and the other isn't."

2. The collection of hundreds of white cards carrying invitations to "Mr. Bradford" would stand more than two feet tall before he finally left the bachelor ranks. Among them, my favorite came from one Edwin N. Ohl: "Dear Bradford, You will make no engagements for the evening of Saturday October the twenty-eighth. Yours sincerely."

3. Isabella Stewart Gardner left Olga Monks her trademark pearls and two huge diamonds, the "Rajah" and the "Light of India" (Tharp, p. 316).

4. G. Gardner Monks. *Beginnings*. Printed by Colonial Offset Printing, Inc. Portland, Maine. Undated. Pp. 3 and 4.

5. His brief obituary in the *Boston Herald* described him as a "retired art dealer."

6. Katharine McKean.

7. Monks, p. 27.

8. Zabdiah, son of Zabdiah, was a Baptist pastor and his son Horace Standish, baptized in the Providence River, was valedictorian of his 1860 Brown University class, and spent the bulk of his career as a mining engineer, traveling throughout North America. (From typewritten sheets belonging to Standish with brief sketches of Rev. Zabdiah Bradford, Horace Standish Bradford, and Harold Standish Bradford.)

9. Dunn, p. 11.

10. Malcolm Freiberg. "The Winthrops and Their Papers." *Proceedings of the Massachusetts Historical Society*. Volume LXXX. 1968. P. 55. (Paper read at the May 1968 meeting.)

11. Standish Bradford. "Notable Descendants of Governor William Bradford." My brother discovered this twenty-page typed manuscript among my father's possessions. This paragraph and the one above quotes or paraphrases my father's words.

12. Bradford Smith. *Bradford of Plymouth*. J. B. Lippincott Company. Philadelphia. 1951. Pp. 11 and 12.

13. Description quoting a letter from Standish to Dorothy while she was en route to Europe in April 1929, recalling their climb up Turner Hill three years earlier.

14. Dorothy wrote to Standish, in April 1929, that when he proposed to her two years earlier, it was "before I loved you."

15. Never one for alcohol herself, Dorothy nevertheless thought it "ridiculous … [when] the Prohibitionists … issued a bible in which all reference to wine, drunkenness, vineyards, or grapes has been omitted!"

16. In 1934 Herman would marry a brilliant Dutch girl, Anne Snouck Hurgronje, as his career headed toward the pinnacle of the Dutch Foreign Service. In 1938 Bobby would marry a beautiful, big-hearted, and artistic American girl, Hildegarde Porter Graham, and settle in Washington, D.C., with a magnificent estate in nearby Warrenton, Virginia.

17. Quoting one Major L. E. Vining, in a book entitled *Held by the Bolsheviks* that Dorothy read in London in 1927.

18. Natasha's trip cost a total of $175. Dorothy wrote one check for $145 for her passage on the *Cleveland* and a second for $30, which included $20 for a cabin on the upper deck, $8 for an alien head tax, and a $2 French port tax.

chapter FIFTEEN

1. Scott C. Stewart. *The Sarsaparilla Kings: A Biography of Dr. James Cook Ayer and Frederick Ayer with a Record of Their Family*. Privately printed. Cambridge, Massachusetts. 1993. The story of the Ayer family fortune is in fact remarkable, a true rags-to-riches nineteenth-century saga filled with grit, brains, and hard work. Theo's grandfather Frederick and his brother James Cook were born in a roadside cottage at Ayer's Mills, Connecticut, and the boys lost their father early. (Frederick Ayer, Sr., died at thirty-three of anemia and exhaustion from overwork.) So impoverished were his widow and children that James went to work at the age of eleven at his grandfather's carding mill, Frederick was set to farm chores at the age of four, and the children were farmed out to various relatives. James, the more ambitious and intellectually curious of the brothers, moved to Lowell, where he had a prosperous uncle, James Cook. Here, as an apothecary's apprentice and, by twenty-two, owner of the pharmacy, he would spend evenings in the back room working with various ingredients to develop a medicine called Cherry

Pectoral, with a secret ingredient of one-sixth of a grain of heroin in each bottle—a boon to harassed mothers and harassed coughers. Sales boomed, thanks to Cook's brilliant use of the new medium of advertising. In 1855, Frederick left his successful dry goods business in Syracuse to become a partner in J. C. Ayer & Company, by then—outside the cotton mills—Lowell's largest employer. With Frederick's arrival, new patent medicines appeared: Extract of Sarsaparilla, Ague Cure, Hair Vigor, and later, Hall's Hair Renewer (a competitor they bought up). James and Frederick joined the ranks of the richest people in Lowell. The company continued to grow, petering out only at the end of World War II, when the patent medicine business was supplanted by penicillin and modern medicines.

Frederick Ayer moved to Boston in 1899 and built an Art Deco townhouse at 395 Commonwealth Avenue, which was considered "very brash by the old money" in Boston. In 1905, he bought a place in Pride's Crossing and built an enormous Italian Renaissance mansion overlooking the Atlantic. His lavish entertainments perhaps intimidated proper Bostonians; the Loring sisters in the estate next door heartily disapproved. Katherine Ayer Merrill, however, said that Frederick never made any pretense of being a proper Bostonian, "a group that tended to be cold, unadventurous, and restricted to one another's society." Theo's father Chilly continued to generate gossip when, after World War II, he married his secretary, was dropped from the *Social Register*, and arranged for his wife's mother to move in with them and cook.

With Theo Ayer's marriage to Robert Winthrop, according to the *Boston Sunday Post* (April 15, 1928), the Ayers had reached "the highest pinnacle of Hub society." The tables had turned, however, by the time of Theo's death in 1995. Her *New York Times* (June 15, 1995) obituary, commenting on her marriages (first to Robert Winthrop and then to blue-blooded Virginian Dr. Archibald Cary Randolph) wrote, "Married well twice and was born better."

2. Dorothy's comments in letters she wrote Standish dated respectively February 14 and January 25, 1928.

3. In fact, they became engaged three years and four months after this meeting.

4. In a letter of April 3, 1929, Dorothy referred to "last spring [1928] when again you asked me and I did love you" (he first proposed in the spring of 1927). There is no other record of Standish's having proposed a second time during the spring of 1928 or indeed, that Dorothy had grown to love him at that time. All she could manage to him in April was that she was "very fond" of him. In her heart of hearts, however, she may have felt more—but was unable, because of her loyalty to her father together with her "state of upheaval," to admit this to herself, let alone to Standish.

5. From Dorothy's large diary, in an entry dated September 14, 1928.

6. In a letter dated October 4, 1928, Dorothy said she never meant that she *wouldn't* do housework but that "I think it foolish to get tired out if one does not have to and lose one's health."

7. From a letter Dorothy wrote, March 7, 1929.

8. Many years later (February 1945), while stationed in Europe during World War II, Standish wrote Dorothy about what that meeting had meant to his mother. She had just written her son about that day, saying: "I recognized something in her straightforward honest eyes that gave me a sense of security and dependableness—that has always remained." Standish then wrote that he remembered his mother's look when she returned that afternoon from the art museum: "Her face shone with happiness in the kind of girl you were."

9. Grandma Amory's great-granddaughter Dr. Catherine Lastavica gave me a tour of the old house before it was torn down.

10. This is confirmed in a July 27, 1930, letter from Uncle Beek which states, "As I understand, your Father said he would give his consent on January 1, 1932 if you still feel the same."

chapter SIXTEEN

1. The joke has a history, for Dorothy had already written to Standish about how she and her cousin Jean had spent their days together in South Carolina over Christmas. "Jean is giving me French diction and singing lessons!! And I am trying to teach her how to eat and put on a few pounds." A futile exercise all round, one imagines, for Dorothy was much too gaunt and abstemious a soul ever to teach anyone else to eat. As for learning to sing—there never was a less melodious instrument than the voice of Dorothy Winthrop Bradford.

2. One family member has voiced the suspicion that—because of his stingy ways—Fred Winthrop might have taken only one cabin aboard ship for the two of them. The only notation about sleeping arrangements in Dorothy's travel journal refers to their staying in a romantic old hostelry in Normandy, where Dorothy writes that "Father is already snoring comfortably on the other side of the wall." The more compelling question, to my mind, is why Sally Winthrop did not, or was not chosen to, accompany her husband on his travels.

3. This is an undated entry in Dorothy's large diary. It could have been written in September of the previous year, when she spoke to her father about Standish, but since it appears that that understanding lasted only a few days, this might have been written later.

4. George Whitman. *The Beekman Winthrop House*. 1983. This is an academic thesis of some sort, written when the house made its way into a listing of the New York City Landmarks Preservation Commission in 1981. It was found in the New-York Historical Society.

5. Robbie Winthrop. Summary of Robert Winthrop's life. September 22, 1995.

6. Robert Winthrop. Draft history of Robert Winthrop & Co. dated July 13, 1973.

7. Article by David Ignatius, in the *Wall Street Journal*, 1985. Found among my mother's papers.

8. Nelly O'Brien hung over the fireplace in our living room for many years, remaining there unperturbed even after someone shot a BB gun into her arm, leaving a small hole. My mother repeatedly offered to give her to any Fred Winthrop offspring who might want her but they all politely declined. It ended up in the hands of my sister Katharine, but she learned to her distress that too many years of smoky fires and too accurate a BB gun aim had eroded Nelly's value to almost nothing.

9. This diary entry appears to have been written around February 7, 1931, although, because it spills over onto the top and sides of pages, it is impossible to be entirely certain of the year. It is a safe guess that Dorothy wouldn't have written with such commitment a year earlier.

10. Pulsifer, p. 32.

11. Quote from Hamilton resident Carroll Daley in Pulsifer, p. 58. The rest of the paragraph reads: "Trees and landscaping were Mr. Matthews's hobby. [On the property was] ... Cilley's Hill, all grass with no trees, and high enough to give a view over all of Hamilton and beyond, even to the ocean on clear days.... There was a swamp filled with cat-o-nine-tails, and bobolinks in season. Once, when it was fully flooded, I remember boys going

out in the area on rafts. Just behind were the Myopia polo fields and tracks of the active Essex branch of the Boston and Maine Railroad."

12. Hamilton Historical Society Bulletin. Number 68. October 1980.

13. A clipping in the scrapbook my mother kept of the articles about her wedding. Atypically, she didn't note the newspaper from which this one was taken.

14. Smith, pp. 19 and 143. The author points out that the mystery of Dorothy Bradford's death has never been solved: it seems odd that no one tried to save her, but most likely the difficulties of the journey and the new life had unhinged her mind.

chapter SEVENTEEN

1. The text (in part) was as follows:

> Funeral services for Frederic Winthrop, former Harvard athlete and in his early life identified with Boston banking, will be tomorrow in Emmanuel Church at 2:30 p.m. He died yesterday after a long illness in his home, 299 Berkeley street.
>
> Mr. Winthrop had estates at Hamilton and Allendale county, South Carolina. As a banker he had been a member of the firm of Robert Winthrop & Co. He retired from active business many years ago.... At Harvard, he excelled in sports, being heavyweight boxing champion as well as a member of the crew.
>
> He was a member of the Massachusetts Historical Society, the New York Historical Society, the American Antiquarian Society, Colonial Society of Massachusetts, Military History Society, Boston Society, and Society of Colonial Wars.

2. Whether he bought it from the estate or from his brothers is a fact that has been lost in the mists of time.

3. Elsie P. Youngman. *Summer Echoes from the Nineteenth Century: Manchester by the Sea*. Don Russell. Rockport, Massachusetts. 1981. P. 111.

4. Connecticut was the other.

5. The federal Comstock Act of 1873, named after Anthony Comstock, president of the New York Society for the Suppression of Vice, was designed to "suppress ... obscene literature and articles of immoral use" among which was included literature or articles for "the prevention of conception, or for causing unlawful abortion." Massachusetts passed a parallel statute in 1879.

6. HealthQuarters was founded in 1970 as the North Shore Regional Family Planning Council to carry on the work begun by the North Shore Mothers' Health Office. Dorothy Bradford was one of its original incorporators. In February 1987, she was honored as the first recipient of the Dorothy W. Bradford Award, established by HealthQuarters to "recognize dedication and excellence in the advancement of women's health care on the North Shore."

7. His rationale was that, since the state had the power to call upon its "best citizens" to give up "their lives" in case of war, it should also be able to call on those "who already sap the strength of the state for these lesser sacrifices ... in order to prevent our being swamped by incompetence."

8. "Sterilization: A Factor in Population Quality Control." Birthright, Inc. Princeton, New Jersey. 1949.

9. Marion S. Norton. "Heredity and Twelve Social Problems." A pamphlet produced as part of a four-part series entitled *A Study of Social Problems with a Solution*. Published through the Princeton League of Women Voters. Princeton, New Jersey. 1935. Pp. 8 and 18.

10. Between 1907 and 1936, a total of 23,166 "eugenic" sterilizations had been performed in the twenty-nine states where the procedure was legal. Nearly 11,000 of these were done in California, which was considered "highly selective" in choosing to sterilize people sent to state institutions. Though half the "feeble-minded" who were paroled had been sterilized, only one-sixth of those placed in institutions for the insane were sterilized before being released. In every case, the sterilization was undertaken after careful study by medical specialists and the written consent of the nearest relative (Human Betterment Foundation. "Human Sterilization Today." Pasadena, California. Undated pamphlet [mid-1930s]. Pp. 5 and 8). By 1950 the total had risen to 50,000, or an average of only 1,200 a year, and the procedure was legal in twenty-seven states (Birthright, Inc. "Sterilization for Human Betterment: A Presentation." Pamphlet published in Princeton, New Jersey. 1950. P. 4).

11. Michael K. Flaherty. "A White Lie." *The American Spectator*. August 1992. Flaherty writes that Sanger defined the "unfit" as "all non-aryan people" and that she estimated that these people—the "dysgenic races"—comprised 70 percent of the American population.

12. From "A Tiny History of Family Planning in Essex County," a short history Dorothy Bradford typed on a single sheet of paper and tucked away among her files.

13. *Salem Evening News*. March 11, 1987.

14. Contractor W. A. Wentworth would not receive the final installment on his contract until December 28, 1937.

chapter EIGHTEEN

1. On August 23, 1939, German foreign minister Joachim von Ribbentrop flew to Moscow to sign a nonaggression pact with the Soviet Union, a surprise union that cleared the way for Germany to invade Poland at dawn a week later, on September 1.

2. All the Forbes children survived the war and, miraculously, all lived on for almost another forty years until the death of James, eighty-five, in the summer of 1993.

3. According to Robbie Winthrop, letter to me dated September 22, 1995.

4. Winston S. Churchill. *Triumph and Tragedy*. Houghton Mifflin Company. Boston. 1953. P. 3.

5. Stephen Ambrose. "The Battlescape of Normandy." *New York Times*. April 17, 1994. Travel Section, p. 15.

6. Angela Winthrop. The house was rebuilt and is now run as an inn, where family and friends visit each summer.

7. Churchill, p. 32.

8. Bea Patton was the fourth of five Ayers who would buy big estates in Beverly Farms, Pride's Crossing, or Hamilton.

9. Ambrose.

10. Churchill, p. 276.

11. Sometimes the government seemed overgenerous in its allotments. In 1944, our family would have been permitted 160 pounds of sugar for canning and preserving; with half that amount, we put up three hundred quarts of finished canned fruit plus all the jams and jellies we could eat. The next year, with only forty pounds, we put up four hundred quarts of canned fruit.

12. Those written during the summer of 1944 and a few written around Thanksgiving and Christmas of that year.

13. The same Morton Eustis who would be killed later in the war.

14. Churchill, p. 36.

15. Robert H. Patton. *The Pattons: A Personal History of an American Family*. Crown Publishers, Inc. New York. 1994. P. 282.
16. Tina van Notten-van Roijen added this detail.
17. Even in her most serious moments, Angela couldn't repress her sense of humor. She ended her letter, "and give my love to all the local gentry you may be seeing.... I think of them often in between visits to the dressmaker, hatshop, hairdresser, beautician, movies, theatre, opera, Montmartre and so on."

chapter NINETEEN

1. The Sarah T. Winthrop Memorial Fund was established by Nat in memory of his mother. Meetings were held annually and the money was given to various mutually agreed upon causes. In time, the foundation was dissolved (except for activities in South Carolina) because of changes in the tax laws.
2. Danvers was a town near Hamilton but in those days, when one referred to "Danvers," one meant its most famous landmark, the insane asylum (as we then called it), which was located there.
3. By my count, Beek would have had four nieces—Fred's daughters Dorothy and Katharine, and Grenville's Kate and Emily—and six nieces-in-law—John and Robert Winthrop Kean's wives; Jan Herman and Robert van Roijen's wives; and Dorothy's brother's Robert and Fred's wives. Be that as it may, I've identified the obvious choices in his poem and put question marks by the rest.
4. It was a running family joke that my mother—a near teetotaler—drank heavily.
5. Rodger Friedman. "The Union League Club Art Collections." The Union League Club. New York. 1995. I also spoke with David Wright at the Morgan Library, who had never heard of Kate Winthrop.
6. Whitman.
7. Jeff Brown of Green Drake Corporation, an overseas offshore company that manages the property, gave me this information.
8. Joseph W. Alsop with Adam Platt. *"I've Seen the Best of It."* W. W. Norton. New York. 1992. Pp. 24–25.
9. The Vanguard Press. New York. 1937. In his *Puritan Boston and Quaker Philadelphia*, Digby Baltzell characterizes the Lundberg book as "notorious."
10. The *Times* listing included H. R. Winthrop [Henry Rogers] at 11 Wall Street with $112,321; Benjamin R. Winthrop at 82 Liberty with $4,489; Neilson Winthrop at 32 Liberty with $2,149; G. L. Winthrop (Grenville) at 40 Wall Street (the address of Robert Winthrop and Company) with $35,807; M. R. (Melza Riggs, Beekman's wife) Winthrop, also at 40 Wall Street, with $4,193; and Sarah T. Winthrop, also at 40 Wall Street, with $2,749. It does not list five other rich Winthrops: Grandma Winthrop and her sons Frederic Winthrop and Beekman and their two cousins Bronson Winthrop, a very successful lawyer in New York, and his brother Egerton Leigh Winthrop, also a prominent New York lawyer.
11. Robert Winthrop. Draft history of Robert Winthrop and Company. 1973.
12. From information supplied me by John McKean, her oldest son.
13. He was the son of Quincy Adams Shaw's daughter, Marian, who married Henry P. McKean of New York. This made him the nephew of Bobbie Shaw, who had been briefly married to the future Lady Astor and briefly owned the property that became Groton House Farms.

14. The description of Shaw and Katharine's courtship and his marriage is based on Honor Moore's *The White Blackbird: A Life of the Painter Margarett Sargent by Her Granddaughter*. Viking Penguin. New York. 1996. See pp. 149–150 and 288–89. Honor Moore wrote of Shaw McKean's first marriage that for him, it had been the wrong marriage but for Margarett, it had been the wrong life.

15. A fifth, a daughter Sally, was born with a tragic birth defect—an underdeveloped brain—and spent her nineteen-year life being cared for in an institution.

16. Adams, p. 7.

17. The first two volumes came out in Fred Winthrop's lifetime. Volume III was published in 1943, IV in 1944, V in 1947, and VI in 1992.

18. The Massachusetts Historical Society. "Groton Gazette, the Newsletters of the Winthrop Papers Projects." Volume 1, Number 1, Winter 1995–1996.

19. Of the arrival in the New World of Governor Winthrop and his company, for example, he writes that the "emigrants … were tired of ship's stores which included 20,000 biscuits and 10,000 gallons of beer. The family have never cared for that beverage since then." Of John, Jr.'s, interest in medicine, he wrote that "Winthrop had a wide practice but not holding an M. D. he sent no bills." Of Fitz-John he writes that he was the "most war-like," seeming to "delight in daring any danger," but that he was "shy in the light that lies in ladies' eyes."

20. The book contains eighteen charts—complex, spidery tangles—which offer a comprehensive picture of families in the U. S., West Indies, England, and elsewhere, who can trace their ancestry back to John Winthrop.

21. Interview with Donald Yacovone of the Massachusetts Historical Society.

22. Behind a liberal dusting of politesse, Mayo introduces us to Wait Still, judging the Salem Witch Trials; John, F. R. S., deserting his family; Robert C. Winthrop, Sr., maligning President Lincoln; and his son, Robert C., Jr., peevishly reclusive.

23. Robert Greenhalgh Albion. *The Rise of New York Port (1815–1860)*. Charles Scribner's Sons. New York. 1970. P. 182.

24. William Amory died on January 16, 1954, age eighty-four, of cancer, and May Amory 10 years later, on August 25, 1964, age ninety-two.

25. The son was George Peabody Gardner. Two more sons followed, John Lowell Gardner in 1923 and Robert Grosvenor Gardner in 1925, and now there are six male Gardners in the next generation (refer to Chart 10).

26. Clara Coolidge had four sons, but only one, Thomas Jefferson Coolidge, had sons. Today, these sons are in their fifties and sixties and neither has yet had a son.

chapter TWENTY

1. From my father's entry in *Harvard College Class of 1924: Fiftieth Anniversary Report*. Cambridge, Massachusetts. 1974.

2. Monks, p. 27.

3. Monks, p. 28.

4. This, at any rate, is what my brother Stanna thinks. No one else seems to know.

5. According to Eleanor Winthrop, my mother was known as the Aunt Kitty Kean of her generation. Aunt Kitty, as a congressman's wife, was constantly entertaining by way of mammoth tea parties. One day a friend noticed that she had her dress on inside out and told her so. Aunt Kitty looked down. "So I do," she said, and went on preparing to greet her guests.

6. The chance meeting was with Pansy Prince Haley, granddaughter of my mother's father's friend Dolph Agassiz.

7. Thomas Gray. "Elegy in a Country Churchyard." My mother knew the whole, long poem by heart and would recite it to herself when she couldn't sleep at night.

8. My mother was not alone in her generation in not wanting to be carted off to Green-Wood. When Nat died, Robert called his widow, Eleanor, to ask whether he had wanted to be buried with the ancestors. The answer was "No." Nat's ashes were scattered partly at the plantation and partly at Groton House Farm. Fred chose to be buried in the woods on Groton House Farm.

9. The Spring 1983 issue of the Association newsletter carried the announcement: "Conservation restriction, Hamilton. From Mrs. Standish Bradford, 37 acres now restricted permanently for conservation purposes. This means that the land will remain open, not to be developed. The rolling grassland extends a corridor of open space from Patton Park through the Myopia schooling field to Cilley's Hill."

Bibliography

books

Abbott, Gordon, Jr. *Saving Special Places: A Centennial History of the Trustees of Reservations: Pioneer of the Land Trust Movement*. The Ipswich Press. Ipswich, Mass. 1993.

Alsop, Joseph W. with Adam Platt. *"I've Seen the Best of It."* W. W. Norton. New York. 1992.

Amory, Cleveland. *The Proper Bostonians*. Parnassus Imprints. Orleans, Mass. 1947.

————. *Who Killed Society?* Harper and Brothers. New York. 1960.

Andriot, John L. *Population Abstract of the United States*. Andriot Associates. McLean, Va. 1980.

Auchincloss, Louis. *The Winthrop Covenant*. Houghton Mifflin. Boston. 1976.

Baltzell, E. Digby. *Puritan Boston and Quaker Philadelphia*. The Free Press. New York. 1979.

Beach, Moses Yale. *The Wealthiest Citizens of New York*. Arno Press. New York. 1973.

Birmingham, Stephen. *"Our Crowd": The Great Jewish Families of New York*. Harper & Row. New York. 1967.

Black, Robert C., III. *The Younger John Winthrop*. Columbia University Press. New York. 1966.

Bliven, Bruce. *New York: A Bicentennial History*. W. W. Norton. New York. 1981.

Bonner, William Thompson. *New York, the World's Metropolis*. Commemorative Edition. R. L. Polk and Co. New York. 1924.

Browder, Clifford. *The Money Game in Old New York: Daniel Drew and His Times*. University Press of Kentucky. Lexington. 1986.

Brown, John Dennis. *101 Years on Wall Street. An Investor's Almanac*. Prentice Hall. Englewood Cliffs, N. J. 1991.

Brown, Richard D. *Massachusetts, A Bicentennial History*. W. W. Norton. New York. 1978.

Carosso, Vincent P. *The Morgans: Private International Bankers. 1854–1913*. Harvard University Press. Cambridge. 1987.

Chanler, Margaret Terry. *Roman Spring: Memoirs*. Little, Brown. Boston. 1934.

Chernow, Ron C. *The House of Morgan: An American Banking Dynasty and the Rise of Modern Finance*. Simon & Schuster. New York. 1990.

Cleveland, Harold van B., and Thomas F. Huertas, with Rachel Strauber et al. *Citibank, 1812–1970*. Harvard University Press. Cambridge. 1985.

Clews, Henry. *Fifty Years on Wall Street*. Irving Publishing Company. New York. 1908.

Cohn, Marjorie B. "Turner • Ruskin • Norton • Winthrop." *Harvard University Art Museums Bulletin*. Fall 1993.

Cook, Blanche Wiesen. *Eleanor Roosevelt*. Vol. I: 1884–1933. Penguin Books. New York. 1992.

Coolidge, T. Jefferson. *The Autobiography of T. Jefferson Coolidge 1831–1920*. Houghton Mifflin. Boston. 1923.

Dictionary of American Biography. Published under the auspices of the American Council of Learned Societies. Scribner. New York. 1981.

Dunn, Richard S. *Puritans and Yankees: The Winthrop Dynasty of New England 1630–1717*. Princeton University Press. Princeton, N. J. 1962.

Dwight, Eleanor. *Edith Wharton: An Extraordinary Life*. Harry N. Abrams, Inc. New York. 1994.

Fielding, Mantle F. *Dictionary of American Painters, Sculptors and Engravers*. Compiled by James F. Carr. J. F. Carr. New York. 1965.

Flaherty, Michael K. "A White Lie." *The American Spectator*. August 1992.

Fogg Museum of Art. *Grenville L. Winthrop: Retrospective for a Collector*. Cambridge. January 23–March 31, 1969.

Foote, Shelby. *The Civil War: A Narrative*. Random House. New York. 1958.

Freiberg, Malcolm. "The Winthrops and Their Papers." *Proceedings of the Massachusetts Historical Society*. Volume LXXX. 1968.

Gardner, Dr. Frank Augustus. *Gardner Memorial: A Biographical and Genealogical Record of the Descendants of Thomas Gardner, Planter*. Privately printed by Newcomb & Gauss Co. Salem, Mass. 1933.

Garland, Joseph E. *Boston's Gold Coast*. Little, Brown. Boston, Toronto. 1981.

Growing Up in Boston's Gilded Age: The Journal of Alice Stone Blackwell, 1872–1874. Ed. Marlene Deahl Merrill. Yale University Press. New Haven. 1990.

Harvard College. Class of 1896. *Twenty-fifth Anniversary Report: 1896–1921*. Privately printed for the class.

Harvard Memorial Biographies. Volume II, Appendix I. Sever and Francis. Cambridge. 1866.

Harvard University. *Winthrop Family Portraits at Harvard*. John Winthrop House. April 1956.

Hesseltine, William Best. *Civil War Prisons: A Study in War Psychology*. F. Ungar. New York. 1964.

Hodas, Daniel. *The Business Career of Moses Taylor: Merchant, Finance Capitalist, and Industrialist*. New York University Press. New York. 1975.

Karnow, Stanley. *In Our Image: America's Empire in the Philippines*. Ballantine Books. New York. 1989.

Kilgo, James. *Pipe Creek to Matthew's Bluff: A Short History of Groton Plantation*. Vanguard Press. Burlington, Vt. c.1989.

Mayo, Lawrence Shaw. *The Winthrop Family in America*. The Massachusetts Historical Society. Boston. 1948.

McAllister, Ward. *Society as I Have Found It*. Cassell Publishing Company. New York. 1890.

McCullough, David. *Mornings on Horseback*. Simon & Schuster, Inc. New York. 1981.

McPherson, James M. *Battle Cry of Freedom: The Civil War Era*. Oxford University Press. New York. 1988.

Monticello Association. *Collected Papers of the Monticello Association*. Volume II, Chapter XXII. Ed. George Green Shackelford. Charlottesville, Va. 1984.

Morgan, Edmund S. *The Puritan Dilemma: The Story of John Winthrop*. Little, Brown. Boston. 1958.

Morison, Samuel E. *John Paul Jones*. Little, Brown. Boston. 1959.

Owens, Carole. *The Berkshire Cottages: A Vanishing Era*. Cottage Press, Inc. Englewood Cliffs, N. J. 1984.

Peabody, Marian Lawrence. *To Be Young Was Very Heaven*. Houghton Mifflin. Boston. 1967.

Pulsifer, Janice P. *Changing Town: Hamilton, Massachusetts 1850–1910*. 1976. Reprinted in 1985 by the Hamilton Historical Society.

Quinn, Arthur. *A New World: An Epic of Colonial America from the Founding of Jamestown to the Fall of Quebec*. Berkley Books. New York. 1994.

Scoville, Joseph Alfred. *The Old Merchants of New York*. Volume III (by Walter Barrett). Greenwood Press. New York. 1968.

Shackleton, Robert. *The Book of Boston*. Penn Publishing Company. Philadelphia. 1916.

Smith, Bradford. *Bradford of Plymouth*. J. B. Lippincott. Philadelphia. 1951.

Sykes, Christopher. *Nancy: The Life of Lady Astor*. Panther Books. Granada Publishing. London. 1979.

Tharp, Louise Hall. *Mrs. Jack: A Biography of Isabella Stewart Gardner*. Peter Weed Books. New York. 1965.

United States Census. 1920.

Ward, Geoffrey C., with Ric Burns and Ken Burns. *The Civil War: An Illustrated History*. Alfred A. Knopf. New York. 1990.

Wector, Dixon. *The Saga of American Society: A Record of Social Aspiration, 1607–1937*. Scribner. New York. 1937.

Wharton, Edith. *The Letters of Edith Wharton*. Ed. R. W. B. Lewis and Nancy Lewis. New York. Scribner. 1988.

Edith Wharton. Novellas and Other Writings. The Library of America. New York. 1990.

Winthrop, Kate W. Last Will and Testament. April 19, 1917.

Winthrop, Grenville. Last Will and Testament. July 11, 1940.

Winthrop, Robert C. *Life and Letters of John Winthrop Governor of the Massachusetts Bay Company at Their Emigration to New England, 1630*. Ticknor and Fields. Boston. 1864.

Youngman, Elsie P. *Summer Echoes from the Nineteenth Century: Manchester by the Sea*. Don Russell. Rockport, Massachusetts. 1981.

pamphlets, periodicals, etc.

Adams, Henry. "Frederic Winthrop: A Memoir." From the *Proceedings of the Massachusetts Historical Society*. Volume 65.

Anonymous diary of a young man who was traveling in Europe with Bronson Winthrop in 1901, found at the New-York Historical Society.

Birthright, Inc. "Sterilization: A Factor in Population Quality Control." Princeton, New Jersey. 1949.

———. "Sterilization for Human Betterment: A Presentation." Pamphlet published in Princeton, New Jersey. 1950.

Geiger, James S. *Appleton Farms 1638–1988: A Brief Agricultural History*. Privately published.

Hamilton Historical Society Bulletin. Number 68. October 1980.

Human Betterment Foundation. "Human Sterilization Today." Pasadena, California. Undated pamphlet (mid-1930s?).

Ippolito, Reverend Robert F., M. S. *A Short History of the Rice Estate 1980–1945. Ipswich, Massachusetts*. Ipswich. 1976.

Lyman, Lila Parrish. "The New London Homestead (1754–1892) of the Winthrop Family." Published for the New London County Historical Society. Pequot Press. Stonington, Conn. 1957.

The Massachusetts Historical Society. *The Generations Joined: Winthrops in America*. A Massachusetts Historical Society Picture Book. Boston. 1977.

The Massachusetts Historical Society. "M. H. S. Miscellany." Number 61. Spring 1995.

The Massachusetts Historical Society. "Groton Gazette." Ed. Francis Bremer and Donald Yacovone. Number 2. Winter 1997.

The May School. "The May School Class Book: Class of Nineteen Twenty-Three." Andover Press. Andover, Mass.

Norton, Marion S. "Heredity and Twelve Social Problems." A pamphlet produced as part of a four-part series entitled *A Study of Social Problems with a Solution*. Princeton League of Women Voters. Princeton. 1935.

"Our First Men," or a Catalogue of the Richest Men of Massachusetts. Fetridge and Company. Boston. 1851.

Taylor, Ellery Kirke. *The Lion and the Hare*. Copy at the New England Historic Genealogical Society.

Wheeler and Taylor, Inc. Mid-1940s flyer on Groton Place. Found in the Lenox Library.

Whitman, George. *The Beekman Winthrop House*. 1983. Found at the New-York Historical Society.

Winthrop, Stimson, Putnam & Roberts: History of a Law Firm. 1980.

Winthrop, Robert. Draft history of Robert Winthrop & Co. 1973. Property of Wood, Struthers and Winthrop Management Company, New York City.

"Wood, Struthers & Winthrop." Company brochure. 1968.

family documents, published and unpublished

Amory, Elizabeth Gardner, compiler, using papers from her grandfather Samuel Pickering Gardner. *The Gardner Family of Salem and Boston*.

Borden, Elizabeth Bradford, and John Winthrop. *The Winthrop Family in America, A Genealogical Updating: 1833–1988*. 1988.

Bradford, Standish. "Notable Descendants of Governor William Bradford."

Chadwick, James Read. *A Brief Sketch of the Life of James Read*. A paper read before the Hyde Park Historical Society. Privately published. Merrymount Press. Boston. 1905.

Monks, G. Gardner. *Beginnings*. Printed by Colonial Offset Printing. Portland, Me. Undated.

Humphreys, Reverend Charles A. "Account of C. W. Amory's Captivity." From Humphreys' account of the history of the Second Massachusetts Cavalry. Read as a paper before the Loyal Legion in 1864.

Kean, Robert Winthrop. *Fourscore Years: My First Twenty-four*. Privately printed. 1974.

Meredith, Gertrude Euphemia. *The Descendants of Hugh Amory 1605–1805*. London. Privately printed at the Chiswick Press. 1901.

Stewart, Scott C. *The Sarsaparilla Kings: A Biography of Dr. James Cook Ayer and Frederick Ayer with a Record of Their Family*. Privately printed. Cambridge, Mass. 1993.

Warren, J. C. *Class of 1863 of Harvard College. Memoir of Charles Walter Amory*. The University Press. Cambridge. 1914.

Winthrop, Robert ("Robbie"). Summary of Robert Winthrop's life. September 22, 1995.

newspapers

Most of the quotes from newspapers are taken from family scrapbooks. Where these have been annotated with source and date in the scrapbook, I have included this information. Other quotations from newspapers have been sourced in notes or in the text.

Acknowledgments

S*o many of the extended* family have helped me put this book together that I hardly know where to begin. I mention first Robert Winthrop, my uncle, and Eleanor Winthrop, my aunt, for their extraordinarily generous help, which helped make possible, as Eleanor put it, this memorial "to your dear mother who meant so much to me." Others of my mother's generation, including Emily Lodge Clark and my aunts Katharine McKean and Angela Winthrop, also shared their memories of my mother's life.

In my generation, I've reached out to every branch of the extended family and thank them all for patiently answering what has been, in some cases, an endless stream of questions and requests. First, the first cousins: among the Robert Winthrops, Amory Winthrop (whose death early in 1998 was a sad blow to us all) slogged cheerfully and enthusiastically through early drafts and Dola provided me with photo help. Among the Fred Winthrops, Freddy, Jr., introduced me to the box of materials left by the Civil War General Frederic Winthrop; peripheral though he was to the story, these papers gave me the hook to create two parallel Civil War chapters. He and his brother Robbie also filled in several critical gaps. Among the Nat Winthrops, I thank John for his continuing responsiveness and encouragement, Serita for her positive response to part of the manuscript, and Nat for his astute critique of the entire, very rough first draft. John McKean has been great all along, answering queries on the McKean side of the family.

Moving on to the second cousins: Ham Kean has been ever cooperative on the Kean side, particularly letting me read Grandma Winthrop's commonplace books, guest lists, and menus. I have three generations to thank for information on the van Roijen branch: Anne van Roijen, widow of Jan Herman van Roijen, Jr.; her daughter Tina van Roijen van Notten; and Tina's daughter Henriette Houben-van Notten. I couldn't have written the chapter on Grenville Winthrop without the insights and cooperation of his grandson Tom Morse. Kitty Lastavica has been an endless font of intelligence on all things Gardner, Amory, and Coolidge, in particular sharing with me the papers of George Gardner, our common great-great-grandfather, and Linzee Coolidge's boyhood diary.

On to the third cousins (once removed!), Harry Lodge has been ever helpful with information and pictures relating to his wonderful mother, Emily Lodge. Further afield yet, my appreciation extends to more distant relatives and relatives-through-marriage, including Chuck Getchell for tracking down Fred Winthrop facts, John Sears for helping me on Longwood, George Herrick for updating me on Gardners and his sister Nina for giving me Marian Lawrence Peabody's book, Bobby Monks for permission to use Bradford pictures, and Richard Kerry for providing background on the Forbes side of the family.

In Hamilton, several of my mother's friends shared their memories of my mother with me—Joan Appleton, Marion Dempsey, Bea Edmondson, and Eleanor Vandevort—and Marcie Homer helped me track down materials at Harvard. In Washington, V V Harrison participated in the initial exploration of my mother's papers and helped convince me that here was a story worth telling and Richard Krimm steered me toward some excellent source material.

A number of busy people in outside organizations have been most responsive. I particularly cite Jim Cloonan at Wood, Struthers and Winthrop, who has helped me through many a murky moment, ever-helpful Donald Yacovone of the Massachusetts Historical Society, and enthusiastic Abbie Smith and Marjorie Cohn at the Fogg Art Museum. In addition, I appreciate the assistance of David Lambert at the New England Historic Genealogical Society, Scott Marshall at Edith Wharton Restoration, Inc., Dennis Lesieur at the Lenox Library, Margize Howell at Donaldson, Lufkin & Jenrette, Arthur Crosbie at the Hamilton Historical Society, Francis Bremer at Millersville University, and many others.

From a technical standpoint, I am greatly beholden to my brilliant first editor, Connie Buchanan. She exercised a sure eye for balanced structure and apposite language together with a stern pencil for the extraneous, the redundant, the clumsy, the inconsistent, and the just plain erroneous. It is thanks to her that the best of the story has emerged and that it moves along at a good clip. Thanks also to editor Natalie Bowen for providing a second, highly professional inspection of the text. Finally, Marianne Lown, a former colleague and a good friend, not only read the manuscript along the way but also generously volunteered her superior editing talents for a final critical read-through at the end. I'm grateful as well to Chrome and Dodge Color, the photographic studios in the Washington area that so carefully and skillfully developed the fragile old negatives and copied the dozens of irreplaceable pictures I gave them. My thanks also go to the staff at Vertigo Design for their artistry and ingenuity in weaving the many illustrations into the text.

Last, but hardly least, I am beholden to my immediate family. The grandchildren wrote short pieces and described to me how they remembered their grandmother, bringing the last chapter alive. My siblings have embraced the project, spurring me on year after year. In addition, my sister Libby Borden ensured that the company established by her late husband Gavin Borden, Garland Publishing, now a member of the Taylor and Francis Group, help arrange for design, printing, marketing and publication of the book. My sister Katharine is helping with distribution. My brother Stanna has been a major help with pictures and outside sources. As for my long-suffering children Dodi and Jacob, I shall be forever grateful to them for keeping after me, urging me time and again, "Go for it, Mom."

REARED *in a* GREENHOUSE

Index

A

C

D

H

I

J

K

L

M

N

Nahant, Massachusetts, 55
New London, Connecticut, 7, 39
New York City, 37-40, 43-48, 64-65, 155-156, 271, 324
Newport, Rhode Island, 37, 218
Nitze, Paul, 206-208, 273-274, 275
Norris, Richard J., 281
North Shore Mothers' Health Office, 287-288, 291, 293
Norton, Charles Eliot, 218, 222
Norton, Sally, 222

O

O'Brien, Nelly, portrait of, 274

P

Palfrey, Sarah, 332
Palmer, Hannah, 19
Papanti, Lorenzo, 24
Paterson, Robert Warden, 222
Patten, Anna Thayer, 109, 183-184, 275-276
Patten, Arthur, 184-185
Patten, Jean. *See* Pellegrini-Quarentotti, Jean Patten
Patten, Nancy. *See* DeVeau, Nancy Patten
Patten, William, 184, 312
Patten family, 175, 194, 244-245
Patton, George S., 300-301, 303, 315
Peabody, Catherine E.. *See* Gardner, Catherine Peabody
Peabody, Endicott, 281
Peabody, Marian Lawrence, 60, 95
Peabody family, 11
Pearson, Milo E., 293
Pellegrini-Quarentotti, Jean Patten, 183-184, 275-276, 317
Perkins, Elliot, 197
Pertzoff family, 246-247

Pilgrims, 236, 237, 280
Pollard, Priscilla, 198
Porcellian Club (at Harvard University), 63, 195, 201, 235, 274, 278, 289
Porter, Dr., 101, 104
Potter, Hamilton, 195
Prendergast, Mamie, 224
Prescott, W. Amory, 11
President Wilson (ship), 176-178
Prince, Anna Agassiz, 197
Prince, Frederick H., 82, 83, 197
Prince, Gordon, 197
Puerto Rico, 93-97
Puritans, 5, 186, 237, 280
Puritans and Yankees. The Winthrop Dynasty of New England, 1630-1717 (Dunn), 186
Pyne, Albertina Taylor, 45

R

Randolph, Theodora Ayer (Winthrop), 234, 250-251, 266, 272-273
Rantoul, Harriet, 147
Rantoul sisters, 127
Read, Hannah Palmer, 19
Read, Helen Maria. *See* Gardner, Helen (Read)
Read, James, 19, 24
Religious Writing; Legal Papers (Bremer, ed.), 334
Rice, Anne Proctor, 83, 190, 327
Rice, Charles Goodnough, 83
Robb, J. Hampden, 306
Robert Winthrop and Company, 44-45, 64, 65, 68, 89, 153, 273, 323, 327-328
Rockefeller, John D., 231
Roosevelt, Sara Delano, 46
Roosevelt, Theodore, xii, 63, 67, 93-95, 200
Ropes and Gray (law firm), 242, 344
Rowse, Samuel Worcester, 51, 58
Russell family, 11-12, 337

REARED *in a* GREENHOUSE

REARED *in a* GREENHOUSE